SPSS® Statistics
for Data Analysis
and Visualization

SPSS® Statistics for Data Analysis and Visualization

Keith McCormick
Jesus Salcedo

with

Jon Peck and Andrew Wheeler

WILEY

SPSS® Statistics for Data Analysis and Visualization

Published by
John Wiley & Sons, Inc.
10475 Crosspoint Boulevard
Indianapolis, IN 46256
www.wiley.com

Copyright © 2017 by John Wiley & Sons, Inc., Indianapolis, Indiana
Published simultaneously in Canada

ISBN: 978-1-119-00355-7
ISBN: 978-1-119-00557-5 (ebk)
ISBN: 978-1-119-00366-3 (ebk)

Manufactured in the United States of America

10 9 8 7 6 5 4 3 2 1

Library of Congress Control Number: 2017936609

We would like to dedicate this book to Jon Peck, who retired from more than 30 years with SPSS and IBM while this book was in its final stages. We wish him the best of retirements even though he probably won't be able to resist staying in the SPSS community in some form.

About the Authors

Keith McCormick is a data mining consultant, trainer, and speaker. A passionate user of SPSS for 25 years, he has trained thousands on how to effectively use SPSS Statistics and SPSS Modeler. He blogs at `keithmccormick.com`.

Jesus Salcedo is an independent statistical consultant. He is a former SPSS Curriculum Team Lead and Senior Education Specialist, who has written numerous SPSS training courses and trained thousands of users.

Jon Peck, recently retired from IBM and SPSS, was instrumental in developing and introducing the R and Python connections to the SPSS community. This expertise made him uniquely qualified to produce Chapter 18. He is the author of all the extension commands discussed in that chapter and has a patent pending on the algorithm in SPSSINC TURF procedure discussed there. He can be reached at `jkpeck@gmail.com`.

Andrew Wheeler is a professor of criminology at the University of Texas at Dallas and a former crime analyst. The application of geospatial techniques in his research created the opportunity for a powerful real world example in Chapter 8. He has used SPSS for over 10 years, and often blogs SPSS tutorials at `andrewpwheeler.wordpress.com`.

About the Technical Editors

Jon Peck, now retired from IBM, was a senior engineer, statistician, and product strategy person for SPSS and IBM for 32 years. He earned a Ph.D in economics from Yale University, and taught econometrics and statistics there for 13 years before joining SPSS. He designed and contributed to many features of SPSS Statistics and has consulted with and trained many users. He remains active on social media and in consulting.

Terry Taerum has fifteen years' experience as a statistician at the University of Alberta, fifteen years as a data analyst at SPSS Inc., and five years as a predictive analyst and consultant with IBM Inc.

Credits

Project Editor
Tom Dinse

Technical Editors
Jon Peck
Terry Taerum

Production Editor
Dassi Zeidel

Copy Editor
Kim Cofer

Production Manager
Katie Wisor

**Manager of Content Development
& Assembly**
Mary Beth Wakefield

Marketing Manager
Christie Hilbrich

**Professional Technology &
Strategy Director**
Barry Pruett

Business Manager
Amy Knies

Executive Editor
Jim Minatel

Project Coordinator, Cover
Brent Savage

Proofreader
Nancy Carrasco

Indexer
Johnna VanHoose Dinse

Cover Designer
Wiley

Cover Image
iStock.com/agsandrew

Acknowledgments

Keith and Jesus are especially proud to have worked with Bob Elliot before he retired. Our good friend Dean Abbott recommended Keith to Bob when Bob was seeking out a follow up to Dean's excellent Applied Predictive Analytics, but specifically in SPSS Statistics. Without both of them, this book would not have been created.

Terry's and Jon's contribution extended well beyond technical reviewing. We consider both of them mentors and friends. Jon took over technical reviewing when Terry took on a new role with a return to IBM. Jon, in particular, was an interlocutor and trusted advisor, and we produced a better book as a result.

Tom, our project editor, had to be patient with us. Deadlines slipped, contributors became unavailable, and Bob retired before the book was complete. Whenever it seemed that something wasn't quite as it should be, it was often Tom that ultimately made it right. He deserves credit for multiple roles, and we thank him.

We would also like to thank all of the many SPSSers that we turn to when we have a question even if they haven't heard from us in a while. We love the sense of community that we have all managed to maintain even when so many have moved on to other roles. And we thank Jason for capturing that sense of community in his foreword.

Contents at a Glance

Contents

Foreword

In my various roles at SPSS and IBM I met Keith and Jesus many years ago. They both have over 20 years of statistical consulting experience, and they both have been training people on statistics and how to use SPSS for many years. Each has in fact trained thousands of students. They are uniquely qualified to bring the message and content of this book to you, and they have done so with rigor and grace. SPSS has so many techniques and procedures to perform both simple and complex analysis, and Keith and Jesus will introduce you to this rich tapestry so that it pays dividends in benefiting your endeavors in driving societal change based on data and analytics for years to come. This book goes beyond the elementary treatments found in most of the other books on SPSS Statistics but is written for users who do not necessarily have an advanced statistical background. It can make the reader a better analyst by expanding their toolkit to include powerful techniques that he or she might not otherwise consider but that can have a big payoff in increased insight.

Keith and Jesus' outstanding new book on SPSS Statistics has brought back so many thoughts about this great product and the influence it has had on so many people that I thought I would briefly reminisce.

I first became involved with this software when I went to work for SPSS in 1995 as Director of Quality Assurance. A year earlier, SPSS had released its first Microsoft Windows product—which, while solid, did not really take advantage of the amazing possibilities a true graphical interface could provide. This was a huge and important time for the company as the SPSS team was hard at work revolutionizing both the front-end user interface and the output to create a standard that is still in place and considered best of breed today. These innovations enabled sophisticated pivot table output as well as much more customized graphical output than had ever been attempted before. Indeed, in the years to come it was that spirit of always getting ahead of every technological trend that would keep this software right in the heart of what the data analysis community demanded.

When I say the heart of the data analysis community I am not in any way exaggerating. This software has been used by hundreds of thousands of students in college and graduate school and by similar numbers in government and commercial environments worldwide. Over the years I have literally had hundreds, if not thousands of people say to me "I used SPSS in college" when I introduced myself. And of course, I can't leave out the bootleg copies I have seen in innumerable places during my travels and personally purchased on the streets of Santiago and Beijing.

Impressive? Absolutely. But of course the real question is … WHY is SPSS so heavily used and so well loved? WHY has its community of users stayed vibrant and loyal even eight years after the company itself was acquired by IBM?

The answer is the combination of power and simplicity combined with elegance. This is a big statement. To back this up—and apropos of the subject matter—I'll contribute a data point as my best evidence. A few years ago, when I was still with IBM (which acquired SPSS in 2009), we hired a summer intern who had used our software for a semester in college. After about a month on the job, we debriefed her on the progress of her user interface design assignment. She discussed at length the challenges she was having coming up with a design that was up to the standard of the rest of the product in terms of simplicity, backed by immense power. This led to a discussion of the first time she used the product as a student. Of course, opening a "statistics" product for the first time filled this iPhone-using millennial with much trepidation; however, as she described to us within just a few minutes she was loading and manipulating data, building predictive models, and producing output for her class. In just a short time beyond that she was digging into the depths of some of the power the product provided. Even a user nearly born and bred with the beautiful user designs of the smartphone consumer era was right at home using SPSS. What an amazing statement in and of itself. Think about it! This is made even more extraordinary because this same student had interactions with professors and researchers on her campus who were using—in fact, relying on—that very same product to do their cutting-edge work. As I said, the answer is the combination of power and simplicity combined with elegance.

This amazing simplicity does not come at the expense of power. As Keith and Jesus make clear in this book, SPSS Statistics is an incredibly powerful tool for data analysis and visualization. Even today there is no tool that works with its users of any level (novice, intermediate, or expert) to uncover meanings and relationships in data as powerfully as SPSS does. Further, once the data has been prepared, the models built, and the analysis done, there is no software available that is better at explaining the results to non-data analysts who have to act on it. This increases the value of the tool immeasurably—since it creates the understanding and confidence to deploy its insights into the real world to create real value. Having seen this done so many times, by so many people, in so many domains, I can say to those starting with this product for the first time that I truly envy you—you are about to start on a journey of learning and getting results that will amaze you—and the people you work with.

Let's put this all in perspective. This product is now in its sixth decade of existence. That's right—it first came out in the late 1960s. How many products can you name that have survived and prospered for that long? Not many. The Leica M camera and the Porsche 911 car with their classic timeless designs come to mind, but not much else. How many COMPUTER products? Even less; perhaps only the venerable IBM mainframe, in fact. But here we have IBM SPSS Statistics—not only surviving but still as relevant and vital as ever—right in the midst of the new age of big data and machine learning, heavily used by experts who dig deep into data and model building, but usable by novices in the iPhone era as well.

Now, let us switch our focus from celebrating the vibrancy and staying power of the SPSS journey and into the heart of what Keith and Jesus have addressed in this book. This is first and foremost a book for data analysis practitioners at intermediate and advanced levels. The question this begs is how this product can help that audience create the most value in the modern era.

Unlike the world of the late 1960s when SPSS was created, we now live in an age where there are many tools to do quick and fast analysis of datasets. For example, Tableau is a fine tool for more business-oriented users with less data analysis training to get immediate and useful visual insights from their data. So what then is the need for IBM SPSS Statistics in this new world?

To answer that question, let me take you back several years to a conference called "MinneAnalytics," sponsored by a Minnesota-based organization of analytic professionals, where I delivered a presentation on Advanced Analytics called "What's Your World View?" In that presentation, I envisioned a rapidly approaching new age where "big data" would meet advanced analytic techniques running in real time and that combination would drive every decision-making aspect of how our society would work. I compared the importance of this movement to previous huge steps that changed the very foundation of society—including the invention of the automobile and the invention of assembly-line production for manufacturing many different types of goods.

Well, a mere three years later that "future" society is here already—right now. It is happening all around us. Analytics on big data is driving decision making and processes everywhere you look. Hospitals apply real-time analytics to data feeds from patient-monitoring instruments in intensive care units to message doctors automatically that their patient in the ICU will shortly take a turn for the worse. Firms managing trucking use analytics to intervene proactively when the system tells them one of their drivers is predicted to have an accident. Airplanes and cars apply real-time analytics to engine sensors to predict failure and inform the pilots and drivers to take action before such failure occurs. Indeed, big data analytics has become one of the most disruptive forces in business history and is unleashing new value creation quite literally wherever you look. All of these examples clearly show a fundamental point—quick visual understanding is one thing—but deep insight yielding confidence in a predictive model that is deployed in real time at critical decision points at vast scale is quite another. It is in this realm of confirmation and confidence that SPSS Statistics shines like no other.

Mass deployment of advanced analytics will create benefits for society that are for all intents and purposes unimaginable. Assuming, of course, that the deployed analytics are in fact correct (and with the right tweaking and trade-offs between accuracy and stability) and deployed properly. It is the almost unique benefit of SPSS that no matter what language in which those analytics are built (SPSS, R, Python, supervised or unsupervised, standard or machine learning, executed programmatically or through visual interfaces, or any other variant you can think of) the product can be used to confirm confidence that the desired results will be achieved, and in understanding the risks involved. It can also be used to explain the results to others in the enterprise, aligning those who need to be in the know on exactly and precisely how analytics drive their new business models. There is no better "hub" for data scientists to practice their craft and contribute their value to the creation of a new world—a new world of staggering rates of change guided or driven by data and analytics.

IBM SPSS Statistics is the perfect tool for this new world when used by well-trained analysts who can put all the data and all the insights together without mistakes to create the most value. People who can take the output of machine learning, add traditional data and then other new forms of data (like sensors and social media for example), to get insights well beyond those quick insights from Tableau and other surface-level tools. People who know how to use the advanced capabilities of the tool, such as the ability to do mixed model analysis of data at different levels (for example, within a hierarchy to find even deeper insights). Such a tool, in the hands of such people—well-trained data scientists— can drive us into this new remarkable world with both confidence and safety. To become one of those who drive this societal transformation using SPSS you can benefit from having this book as your guide.

Enjoy the book…and enjoy the next 50 years of IBM SPSS Statistics as well!
— Jason Verlen

Jason Verlen is currently Senior Vice President of Product Management and Marketing at CCC Information Services, based in Chicago. Before moving to CCC he spent 20 years at SPSS and then IBM (after its acquisition of SPSS) in various roles ending with being named Vice President of Big Data Analytics at IBM.

Introduction

This book is a collaboration between me (Keith) and several other career-long "SPSSers," and the editorial decisions about what to cover, and how to cover it, are greatly affected by that fact. My own career took a turn down a road that led to a life of learning, teaching, and consulting about SPSS almost 20 years ago. I was contemplating a PhD in Psychometrics at the University of North Carolina, Chapel Hill. My plans didn't get much further than auditing some prerequisites and establishing residency. So, on paper, I hadn't made much progress, but moving 1000 miles (from Massachusetts) to relocate and purchasing a house represented a milestone in my life and career. I'm still in that same house (more than 22 years now), and I'm still using SPSS almost daily. Like many things in life, it seems almost accidental. I was doing contract statistics work using SPSS, working from home while I planned for a life in graduate school, and I drove up to Arlington, VA to take advantage of what SPSS training then called the training "subscription."

The concept was to take as many classes as you can manage in a year. It was remarkably cost effective. I was able to convince my primary contract client to pay for the subscription under the condition that I covered all other expenses, and didn't let it affect my deadlines. I already had several years of daily SPSS use under my belt, so I was hardly a rookie, but it was too good to pass up. I found a summer sublet in Washington, DC, took advantage of the training classes almost daily for a couple of months, learned all the latest features, learned about modules that I had never tried, made some good new friends, and worked late into the evening trying to keep my contract research work on schedule. Then suddenly I was asked if I wanted to relocate and take on teaching the basic classes in that same office. I declined the full-time position (the grad school idea was still alive), but I did start making occasional trips. Within a year they were frequent trips, and it became effectively full time, including training trips all over the United States and Canada.

A bit of nostalgia, perhaps, but there is a good reason to reflect on that time period in SPSS Inc.'s history. As Jason Verlen notes in his foreword to this book, the mid to late '90s was a pivotal time in the development of SPSS. With Windows 95 came a whole new world, and SPSS Inc. leaped into the fray. Also, in the late '90s, SPSS Inc. bought ISL, and with it, Clementine. The revolutionary software package then became SPSS Clementine, and is now called IBM SPSS Modeler. While this book is dedicated to SPSS Statistics and not SPSS Modeler, my career certainly was never quite the same since. Although that was the acquisition that most influenced my career, it was certainly not the only one. There were numerous acquisitions during that period, growing the SPSS family to include products like AMOS, SPSS Data Collection, and Showcase.

It was also a bit of a golden age in SPSS training. Almost 20 of us offered SPSS training frequently. On any given day, there were at least a couple of SPSS training events being held in one of several cities that had permanent full-time SPSS training facilities. Traveling to public training was common then—online training hadn't yet arrived. It simply was how training was done. In light of this very active, live, corporate-managed, instructor-led training economy more than 30 distinct classes were offered that represented 50–60+ days of training content. It took me three years before I found myself teaching 80% of them, and even longer before I taught all of them. Classroom training was seen as a key way to support the user community, so even classes that were infrequent, and therefore not very profitable, were still scheduled to support the product. Everything changes over time, and certainly traveling cross-country to a corporate training center for 5 continuous days of training, with a stack of huge books, along with 16 strangers from other companies seems quaint now.

For all of us who experienced it as trainers and participants, however, we are forever changed. One of the things that always struck me, and that still knocks me off my feet, was that the 32 books we used were not enough! SPSS had so many great new features coming out with each new version that it was hard to keep up, even though we were in the classroom three-quarters of the time. The Arlington office frequently had another trainer teaching in a room next door, so we would have lunch together, and admit to each other that we had left ourselves with a few too many pages for day three. Day three! And that was just the Regression class! We'd sometimes lament that someone had shown up for a class, but had skipped one or more of the three prerequisites. Can you imagine? Seven days of prerequisites to take a training class! It just wouldn't work to require that many days now, but we worked hard, and covered a lot of ground, and we went through all the software output, step by step. Then we would make a change to the model, or respond to an audience question, and go through the entire output again, step by step. Go ahead and admit it—if you are like us it probably sounds great. And it was.

My friend and coauthor Jesus Salcedo had a similar experience, and in those same classrooms. He also had an interest in psychometrics, except that he actually acted on his interest and earned his PhD. We met in the very busy New York City SPSS Training office when I was sent there as a contractor during his tenure. He was the full-time trainer in that office. We'd often chat about our favorite course guides (and least favorite) and became friends over an occasional shared meal in that Empire State Building office, or nearby in New York's Koreatown neighborhood. So, the perspective that we both start with is that SPSS is a big topic, a worthy topic, and frankly, a sometimes intimidating topic. We still feel this way today. There is so much to learn that we struggle to keep up with everything new. At a consultancy where we worked for a time as a team, we put together a series of monthly seminars that proved to us again that there was always something new to learn. Each and every month, we discovered new features when we were preparing for a new topic. So tens of thousands of training hours later, we still learn something new all the time.

Of course, we aren't asked to really show what we can do as often as we used to be. The reason, of course, is that training these days is rushed. We are often asked to cover two days' worth of information in just one, or five days' in just two, or ten days' in just four. It happens all the time. We are pros, and we do as we are asked, but we know, we really know, that to do a proper job it takes more time. The book market is flooded with rookie SPSS books. The more advanced books tend to be more advanced in the theory, but not at all advanced in the practice of using SPSS, its efficient use, or the sophisticated use of its features. A major motivation in writing this book is the loss of organizational memory that has occurred since in-depth specialized SPSS training courses have started to disappear over the last ten years.

So, with this book, we get to call the shots, and what we are trying to offer all of you is a chance to learn some intermediate to advanced topics thoroughly enough that you will be tempted to use them yourself, very possibly for the first time. We don't try to cover every topic—barely two dozen out of a hundred that we could have chosen, in fact. This is not at all encyclopedic. It certainly is also not a book-length treatment on a single subject. It gives you a taste of what attending one of our classes 15 years ago might have been like—a couple hours' worth on each of several interesting, powerful topics that you might not even know existed.

The Audience for This Book

We think that this book fills an important niche. Books on the fundamentals of using SPSS Statistics are not in short supply. There are certainly dozens of them. Some are better than others. Naturally, we are proud of our own contribution: *IBM SPSS Statistics For Dummies, 3rd Edition* (Wiley, 2011). However, this book is certainly not a book about the fundamentals of settings up SPSS properly, or running routine statistics like T-tests or Chi-Square. Nor is this book a good choice for reviewing Statistics 101. Knowledge of topics like Ordinary Least Squares regression and ANOVA is assumed.

Since beginning the quest to contribute something we felt was new and needed for the SPSS Statistics community, Jesus Salcedo and I have consistently thought of the same audience. We have imagined the intermediate-level practitioner, perhaps relatively new or perhaps even a long-time user of SPSS, who is stuck in a rut. We imagine ourselves in a sense. If it wasn't for our training careers, forcing us to learn the new features as soon as they come out, we probably wouldn't be familiar with all of the techniques in this book. We use the shortcuts because we are active in the corporate community of SPSS, yet we meet veteran users all the time who don't even know they exist. We have our own personal favorite techniques, tips, and tricks, but we know many users who know their theory very well, yet haven't discovered a key feature that could make their analysis more effective, even though it's been in the last 10 versions. I mention this specifically because it is a constant, even humorous, but telling exchange:

"Wow, that is amazing. I'm so glad that they added that feature. It must be brand new."

"Actually, we've had that since version X. It's been around for about 8 years."

So the phrase "spread their wings a bit" has been used between us since the early days of this book. We've been writing for the kind of SPSS user that we've met in class over many years: the kind who might know more about SPSS than their colleagues or their boss; the kind who knows all the logistics of SPSS pretty well; the kind who knows the logistics of SPSS pretty darn well, but sometimes gets frustrated knowing that there is another way to tackle a problem, but there is no time to research that right now; and the kind who wants to know that there are a few interesting professional development opportunities out there, but isn't quite sure which ones to explore, and there never seems to be much of a training budget to pursue them.

We are exploring this "expand your knowledge" theme rather broadly, including topics like Hierarchical Linear Modeling, but also techniques like Graphics Production Language. This is firmly a software book. We assume that you use SPSS, and you are interested in all aspects of it. In short, we assume that you use it fairly often, and you want to slowly and surely work toward being a "power user" even if you don't describe yourself that way today.

How This Book Is Organized

The book is organized into 18 chapters in 4 major parts. In addition to this organizational overview, there is a short introduction at the start of each part that discusses the specific techniques covered in each chapter, and whether the techniques are in SPSS Base or require one of the modules. We aren't shy about showing you a feature in one of the modules when appropriate, and there is a thorough discussion of bundles and modules near the end of this introduction.

Each of this book's four parts has a collection of techniques that fits a particular theme, and each part begins with an introduction that summarizes how the pieces fit together. It will always be helpful to take a quick look at these introductions before diving into a chapter within a part of the book because they will clarify why the chapters are sequenced the way they are, and anything that you should know about prerequisites. Cross referencing within parts will be more common than between parts, but you'll find advice will be given about chapters found in other parts as well.

The four major parts are as follows:

- **Part I: Advanced Statistics:** In this section, we focus on statistical techniques that you can turn to either when more traditional or more common techniques might pose problems, or when you face situations where there is a more sophisticated option awaiting you if you are willing to try it. So we tackle options like Structural Equations modeling, but also options like Bootstrapping.

- **Part II: Data Visualization:** We have not restricted ourselves to how to make bar charts and pie charts in this section. Frankly, those topics would not deserve a major section of this length, wouldn't be all that interesting to experienced users, and would belong in a different kind of book. In this section, we bring the full power of SPSS to bear on data. We believe that Data Visualization includes properly analyzing and prepping the data to facilitate visualization so techniques like Correspondence Analysis are fair game. Also, we cover advanced features that you may not be familiar with, and brand new features in the most recent versions like GeoSpatial Association Rules.

- **Part III: Predictive Analytics:** Predictive analytics and data mining are more associated with SPSS Modeler than SPSS Statistics. Can SPSS Statistics be an effective option? We answer in the affirmative, walk through the differences between statistics and data mining, and introduce some algorithms available in SPSS Statistics.

- **Part IV: Syntax, Data Management, and Programmability:** Thirty years ago, an SPSS user could not escape learning SPSS Syntax, but now you can. Why tackle SPSS Syntax? What features have been added both to the language and the menus to add in the logistics of SPSS? What is programmability, and how can you take advantage of its features without having to become a serious programmer? These are the questions we answer in this final part of the book.

You may be curious about the authors' various contributions. Jesus' presence was felt in each and every chapter, but he was lead author on Chapters 3, 4, 7, 10, 12, and 17. Jesus collaborated extensively with Keith on Chapters 2 and 5. Andrew contributed Chapter 8, and Jon contributed Chapter 18. Jon's contribution goes far beyond a single chapter in that his knowledge and role of technical reviewer had a positive impact on the entire book. In addition to the chapters on which he was lead, Keith wrote the front matter and the book and part introductions. Keith will serve as primary contact for the authors and can be reached at `keithmccormick.com`.

How to Use This Book

All of the examples in this book come with practice datasets, and when necessary, supporting SPSS Syntax. This is a hands-on book. You can read it on a plane or during a commute, but at some point you will want to sit down at the computer and try these techniques. All of the chapters are hands-on in this way, and chapters are rarely a prerequisite for other chapters.

All practice datasets and supporting SPSS Syntax are available on this book's webpage on `Wiley.com`. Go to `http://www.wiley.com/WileyCDA/` and search for "SPSS Statistics." On the page of results that opens, select this book, then, on the book's main webpage, locate the "Downloads" section and click the "Click to Download" link.

There are a couple of notable exceptions. You will always want to read the short introduction of each of the four major parts of the book before reading chapters in that part. Chapters 5 and 6 are a pair and are best read together, and in order. The opening chapter of Part III, "Predictive Analytics," Chapter 11, should be read before the others in Part III, especially if you are new to data mining. The opening chapter of Part IV should be read before the others if you are new to Syntax.

If you don't have a module, but the chapter looks interesting, think about taking advantage of the software trial. Trial versions always have the complete complement of modules. AMOS is a little different. It is standalone sibling software that belongs to the SPSS family, but is not part of SPSS Statistics, per se. You can get a trial of it as well. You may want to read a number of chapters in anticipation of using the trial to make the best use of the time period. A popular way to learn SPSS, and get more time to have access to it, is to take a class. Many classes, both online and local to you, probably would allow you to use a student version. The combination of this technique and the trials should allow you to try everything that you read about in the book.

The Themes of the Book

Alternate strategies when statistical assumptions are not met and the ongoing debates surrounding p values

The debates between the frequentists and the Bayesians, traditionalists and data miners, proponents of p values and proponents of effect sizes, can be fascinating, but can also be frustrating. If you have mastered one approach, but have not mastered the alternative, it can be frustrating. If you are exploring other options, but your colleagues are not encouraging, that can also be frustrating. This book is not about these debates, but it is about options. The discussions about options will sometimes make it seem that we are entering the fray. Mostly, however, we want to show you that SPSS may offer alternatives that you have not yet mastered. Specifically, when we think that the traditional approach may fail you because you don't meet the assumptions there are at least three other options to explore:

- Use a technique with different assumptions.
- Use a technique that doesn't have classical assumptions.
- Use additional or alternate reporting criteria.

We won't review the traditional approaches all that much, and we largely assume them (Chapter 1 may be a bit of an exception, so please do read that chapter first). We do try to open up completely new avenues. For example, while we don't discuss Bayesian approaches, we do try to open the door to new approaches by introducing Bootstrapping and Monte Carlo Simulation. Also, in a very real sense the section on Predictive Analytics will force you to reexamine to a degree what we are doing when we do hypothesis testing. There is a whole literature around these debates and we will occasionally mention books in the text to further pursue these topics.

Expanding the toolkit for data visualization in SPSS Statistics, broadening the notion of what effective visualization is

SPSS users are somewhat notorious for performing "analysis" in SPSS, but then reporting and charting elsewhere, usually in Excel. Those of us who use SPSS every day are frankly somewhat bemused by this. SPSS gets better and better with each release, and we gave up this kind of patchwork approach in the '90s. However, we are also trainers. We see lots of end users, and we understand why it seems like a good idea—and more rarely we see situations where something within SPSS truly isn't working out for a client. It is not displaced loyalty on our part to encourage a more comprehensive use of SPSS. We've seen the horror of wasted effort of constantly moving back and forth, often by cutting and pasting.

This was a major motivation for dedicating such a large portion of the book to visualization. SPSS has tremendous power that many have not yet discovered. Also, we strongly believe that visualization is not just about colors and shapes. Data has to be prepared to support visualization, and that often requires distilling the patterns down to their essence so that they can be visualized. That is why we believe that Chapters 8, 9, and 10—which are all powerful examples of analysis in support of visualization—belong in this book, and specifically in the visualization section. Correspondence Analysis, Multi-Dimensional Scaling, Spatio-Temporal Prediction, and Generalized Spatial Association Rules (all addressed in these three chapters) produce compelling visualizations but they do so by crunching the input data in powerful ways.

Exploring predictive analytics and performing predictive analytics tasks in SPSS Statistics

Data mining, as a phrase, seems a bit out of fashion these days, but the collection of techniques the phrase represents is on the rise. "Data mining," however, probably is the phrase that makes most salient the potential contrast between itself and the techniques of traditional statistics. The similarities are fairly obvious, and to some, the differences can cause concern. What are we "proving" with data mining? they might ask. It is not a small question. We dedicated the entire "Predictive Analytics" section of five chapters to this theme. Also, the section introduction is very much a part of the discussion. Taken together, these chapters come the closest to forming a book within a book.

Increasing sophistication with the mechanics of SPSS Statistics

Power users of SPSS all use SPSS Syntax, at least occasionally. Back in the '90s when the lead authors were really getting started in SPSS there was a bit of tension between those who used Syntax and those who used only the GUI. As Jason Verlen points out in his foreword to this book, 1995 was a critical and exciting time of transition for SPSS. The GUI was becoming more feature rich than ever before. However, those who already had a great deal of experience recognized that the GUI was only catching up, it sometimes seemed to them more trouble than it was worth, and it briefly seemed like the SPSS community was going to become two communities. This never happened. Everyone uses the GUI, and rightly so. It is powerful and elegant. It is hard to imagine not using it. So what about Syntax? Well, SPSS doesn't force competence in this area as much anymore. But to the expert user, there are absolutely times when it is the best choice.

Experiencing some newer or under-appreciated techniques of SPSS

The module (and bundle) system of features has tended to create a large collection of third-party SPSS training guides that focus solely on SPSS Base. The fear, we speculate, is that the authors of those books don't want to cover anything that some readers might not have access to. They are truly numerous, and scores of books cover the basics. As career-long members of the SPSS community and as SPSS trainers, we've seen the resources on more advanced techniques dwindle, and related courses are rarely offered. These are truly powerful techniques, and they deserve a wider audience. We feel that more advanced users need a support system, too.

We want to reverse that trend to the small degree that one book can accomplish. The bundle system makes many of these modules more readily available. So much so, that we frequently meet clients that have modules that they don't know they have. Five of the chapters include material that requires nothing more than SPSS Base. Most do, however. The alignment of the chapters, modules, bundles, and techniques is outlined in the next section. So while the reader should be cautioned to investigate what they have access to at home and office, we urge a wider audience of users to be familiar with the full spectrum of what SPSS can do.

Understanding the SPSS Bundles and the SPSS Modules

For decades within the SPSS community, add-on modules have allowed the price of SPSS Base to be a lower entry level than the full package. IBM has introduced bundles of modules, and as a result, you might hear less and less about the individual modules. This could cause confusion if one person who is used to the old system is discussing functionality with someone who has just bought a bundle. There are numerous places on the IBM website to get further clarification, including this URL: `http://www-01.ibm.com/software/analytics/spss/products/statistics/edition-comparison.html`.

The following chart shows the relevance of the modules to the topics and chapters in this book.

IBM SPSS EDITIONS	IBM SPSS MODULES	STANDALONE INTERFACE AND INSTALL?	CHAPTER	TECHNIQUES COVERED
Standard	Advanced Statistics		4	HLM
	Custom Tables			
	Regression			
Professional	Categories		3	Ordinal and Categorical Regression
			9	Correspondence Analysis
			10	Multidimensional Scaling
	Data Preparation		12	
	Decision Trees		14	CHAID & CRT
	Forecasting			
	Missing Values			
Premium	Bootstrapping		2	
	Complex Samples			
	Conjoint			
	Direct Marketing			
	Exact Tests			
	Neural Networks		13	
	Amos	Yes	1	

The New SPSS Subscription Bundles

As this book goes to press in early 2017, IBM has announced an SPSS Statistics subscription offering. Paid monthly, among its features is that it is easy to update and it is easy to add features like those discussed in this book. The numbered versions do not go away and the bundles described in the previous table do not go away. This is just a new option. Noteworthy to readers of this book is that two modules, Data Preparation and Bootstrapping, which each get a dedicated chapter, are included as part of "Base."

The following chart shows where in this book the subscription and add-ons are discussed.

	MODULES INCLUDED	CHAPTER
Subscription "Base"	Data Preparation	12
	Bootstrapping	2
Custom Tables & Advanced Statistics Add-On	Custom Tables	
	Regression	
	Advanced Statistics	4
Complex Sampling & Testing Add-On	Complex Samples	
	Exact Test	
	Conjoint	
	Categories	3 (Categorical Regression)
		9 (Correspondence Analysis)
		10 (Multidimensional Scaling)
	Missing Values	
Forecasting & Decision Trees Add-On	Forecasting	
	Decision Trees	14
	Neural Networks	13
	Direct Marketing	

What's New in SPSS 23 and 24?

SPSS Statistics has a new release just about every year. As of the final stages of writing this book, version 24 has been available for several months. The following themes represent some of the key features and capabilities that have been added in versions 23 and 24.

Temporal Casual Modeling (TCM), *Spatio-Temporal Prediction* (STP), and *Generalized Spatial Association Rule* (GSAR) are all quite new, and were a major theme of the version 23 release. They all involve using space and time data to make predictions. The Geospatial Analytics material covered in Chapter 8 addresses some of these new features. *Categorical Principle Components Analysis* (CATPCA) also was enhanced in version 23.

Reporting features have been enhanced in recent versions. Web reporting has been completely redesigned for 23, and the Custom Tables module got a major upgrade with the release of 24. The table displayed in Figure I-1 illustrates the increased access to inferential statistics and greater flexibility of combing a variety of descriptive statistics in a table. Significance test results in the traditional style can now be shown in the main table. The pivot table TableLooks and graph templates offer new options, and a cleaner, more modern look. The figure features the new pivot table default template in version 24. The new ChartLooks can be downloaded at `https://developer.ibm.com/predictiveanalytics/wp-content/uploads/sites/48/2016/04/Chartlooks.zip`.

					Employment Category					
			Clerical			Custodial			Manager		
			(A)			(B)			(C)		
			Mean	95.0% Lower CL for Mean	95.0% Upper CL for Mean	Mean	95.0% Lower CL for Mean	95.0% Upper CL for Mean	Mean	95.0% Lower CL for Mean	95.0% Upper CL for Mean
Current Salary	Educational Level (years)	8	$22,316	$20,992	$23,641	$30,808 A	$29,940	$31,675	.	.	.
		12	$25,276	$24,548	$26,004	$31,581 A	$30,452	$32,710	$59,400[1]	.	.
		14	$31,625	$25,548	$37,702	.	.	.	.	.	.
		15	$31,176	$29,704	$32,648	$24,300[1]	.	.	$47,662 A	$32,349	$62,976
		16	$36,281	$32,805	$39,757	.	.	.	$56,417 A	$50,441	$62,393
		17	$32,100	$14,480	$49,720	.	.	.	$69,813 A	$61,377	$78,248
		18	$55,412	-$90,232	$201,057	.	.	.	$67,904	$56,301	$79,506
		19	$36,000[1]	.	.	.	.	.	$73,925	$66,129	$81,721
		20	.	.	.	.	.	.	$64,312	$1,576	$127,049
		21	.	.	.	.	.	.	$65,000[1]	.	.

Results are based on two-sided tests assuming equal variances. For each significant pair, the key of the smaller category appears in the category with the larger mean.
Significance level for upper case letters (A, B, C): .01
Significance level for lower case letters (a, b, c): .05[2,3]

1. This category is not used in comparisons because the sum of case weights is less than two.

2. Tests are adjusted for all pairwise comparisons within a row of each innermost subtable using the Bonferroni correction.

3. Pairwise comparisons are not performed for some subtables because of numerical problems.

Figure I-1: Example of version 24 custom table

There has also been a focus on accessing a diversity of data sources. Version 23 added bulk data loading which improves performance. Version 24 included substantive changes and improvements to the process of bringing in data including new interfaces and options. The improvements focus on excel data and .CSV files, and improve both importing and exporting. Smarter importing algorithms result in faster, more accurate importing of data.

An ongoing theme over the last several years that continues with the recent versions is programmability. R and Python have been part of the SPSS Statistics toolkit for many years now, but with version 24 it is substantially easier to get started. The Custom Dialog Builder has received major enhancements. The SPSS team and the SPSS community have made "extensions" readily available on the Internet, and with version 24 you can access these materials from the menus, as shown in Figure I-2. Chapter 18 provides a great introduction to the whole topic of programmability.

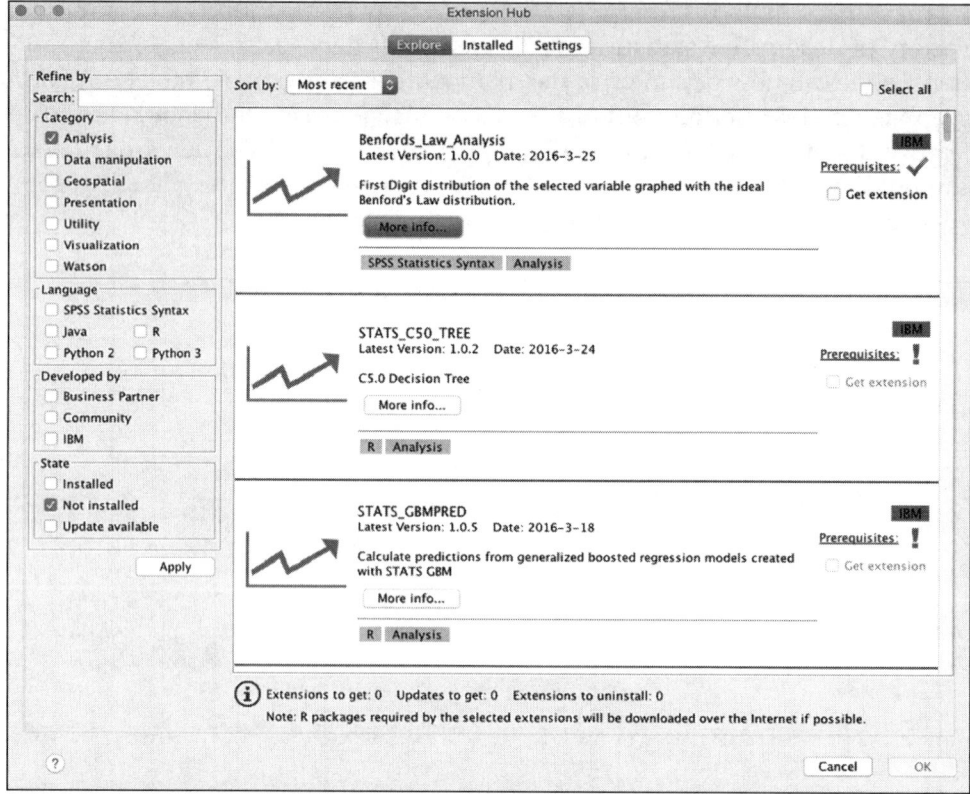

Figure I-2: The Exension Hub

Advanced Statistics

The theme of Part I is advanced statistical techniques. How advanced? Obviously, this is a matter of perspective and is highly individual, but we've collected four techniques that we feel deserve detailed attention. We are not seeking out obscure techniques. Quite the opposite. We have selected techniques that we think deserve attention because they apply in myriad situations, yet, somehow, they have not found as wide an audience as they deserve. For instance, who among us does not routinely fail to meet statistical assumptions, particularly distributional assumptions? It happens so often that the temptation among some seems to be not to worry about it. In my experience (Keith), this doesn't truly take the form of stopping to worry about assumptions. Rather, we grow tired of explaining technical assumptions checking to our colleagues. We surreptitiously check them, but fear that if we use a technique that is perceived as advanced that our audience won't be ready for it.

This part of the book can be seen as an alternate way forward. We truly believe that if a more appropriate technique, instead of the standard technique when assumptions have not been met, is used it actually makes the narrative that we tell about our data easier to analyze, easier to write up, and easier for our colleagues to understand. Chapters 2 and 3, in particular, pick up on this theme, although it is an important theme of the entire book. Bootstrapping, discussed in Chapter 2, is a wonderful way of dealing with data that does not meet our normality assumptions. Modern computers do it easily—certainly more easily than the computers of just a decade or two in the past. Also, if we as analysts become familiar with it, it is not that difficult at all to incorporate it into our analyses.

Another assumption that is frequently broken concerns the level of measurement of variables used in linear regression. Linear regression will probably always be among the most popular and widely used techniques—and for good reason. However, its popularity and the fact that our colleagues are generally familiar with it often tempts us to bend the rules. Many simply bring ordinal variables into standard regression, yet it is not difficult to take a more appropriate approach, one specifically suited for variables that are not scale. Chapter 3 introduces some of these regression approaches.

Hierarchical Linear Models have been quite popular for many years. In this case, perhaps our goal is less to raise awareness and more to provide a gentle introduction to a topic where many find they need a bit of coaching. It is potentially a big topic with plenty of dedicated texts, but Chapter 4 will be quite helpful if the subject has been on your to-do list for some time and you want to get started.

Chapter 1 is a bit different than most of the chapters in the book. The emphasis on the point-and-click aspect of the methods discussed is reduced. The reason is that several methods are included in the chapter and they are compared and contrasted with one another. If each of them were discussed in detail, along with all menu and output options, the chapter could easily grow very lengthy. The goal is to both review some of the multivariate analysis options in SPSS Statistics as well as introduce Structural Equation Modeling (SEM) and SPSS AMOS. The narrative is built around a single dataset and the many ways of testing some hypotheses about the dataset. Previous knowledge of AMOS is not required, and the chapter will be insufficient to act as a thorough AMOS primer. The focus is on the AMOS output and comparing it to the SPSS Statistics output. However, you will leave the chapter with a good introduction to SEM and what it brings to the table. If you could use a bit of a review in techniques like ANCOVA, MANOVA, and MANCOVA, then you are strongly encouraged to read Chapter 1 first.

In This Part

Comparing and Contrasting IBM SPSS AMOS with Other Multivariate Techniques

Structural Equation Modeling (SEM) truly is a family of techniques, and the literature offers many dedicated texts, both introductory and advanced. IBM SPSS AMOS, the tool we discuss in this chapter, is both a standalone tool and integrated with SPSS Statistics (in that they share .sav data files) with a long history as part of the SPSS family. Since IBM acquired SPSS in 2009, it has marketed it in a variety of ways, sometimes bundling with add-on modules causing potential confusion that it is an add-on module itself. It has its own unique graphical user interface (GUI). The chapter spends a substantial amount of time analyzing a single case study dataset using several approaches before turning our attention to AMOS, so it is a good review of multivariate techniques in SPSS Statistics. It should prove valuable on this level as well as an introduction to SEM, even if you never acquire AMOS. Certainly, you should consider downloading an AMOS trial to explore the case study results and to get a richer introduction to AMOS, but the chapter should be clear even if you don't attempt using the AMOS interface.

Although AMOS is unique in the book in that it has its own GUI, this chapter doesn't discuss the GUI in detail. The focus is on interpretation of results and what makes the AMOS approach special. The standard approach in this book is to spend considerable time performing steps in the SPSS Statistics GUI. In this chapter, the first two-thirds clarify where various multivariate techniques are found in the SPSS GUI. The final third discusses parallel techniques available in AMOS. If you opt to give AMOS a try, and I encourage you to, the AMOS User's

Guide does a wonderful job at explaining the GUI. It is one of the best guides of its kind that I've encountered. Something that the AMOS guide does not do is compare and contrast AMOS's output with SPSS output. That is really the whole point of this chapter—by answering the questions What does SEM and AMOS add to one's statistical toolkit, and When is one tool preferable to another?

The motivation in attempting SEM via AMOS instead of ANOVA or Regression is not as simple as those methods failing to meet assumptions. It is more subtle than that. The case study presented in this chapter shows that it is more about telling a richer, more complete story than you could with other techniques. We begin by exploring the data with standard techniques, but no single analysis will do the job. SEM, in this case, becomes the best way to test our full theory with a single model. Don't let the new interface scare you away. AMOS is powerful, and is SPSS dataset friendly, even though the interface is very different. You won't need to create AMOS Graphics diagrams because completed diagrams (in the form of .amw files) are provided. These will allow you to explore the completed solution. The focus will be on interpreting results and not the point-and-click steps required to build the diagrams.

A NOTE ON WHY WE CHOSE TO PLACE THIS CHAPTER FIRST

The choice to place this chapter first—a chapter that requires AMOS—may be surprising. If you do not have AMOS yet, there may even be a temptation to jump ahead to a chapter discussing a technique that you have at the ready, but this chapter also serves as a good review of material for a number of chapters that follow, especially Chapters 2, 3, and 4. For that reason to place it first is to place it in its natural location. Conceivably, you could read just the first half of the chapter in preparation for the rest of the book via reviewing of the standard techniques, but once you've seen the data analyzed in these ways, seeing how it all can be examined through a different lens should prove interesting even if you are not immediately clicking along.

The chapter unfolds in a way that you might find surprising at first. We begin the case study in SPSS Statistics, and we will be using a single .sav data file throughout. You can find AMOS PSAT data.sav on the book's website along with the .amw files. We will attempt a number of different techniques on the data before we try AMOS, including a section about each of the following:

- T-test
- Analysis of Covariance (ANCOVA)
- Multivariate Analysis of Variance (MANOVA)
- Multivariate Analysis of Covariance (MANCOVA)

Basic familiarity with the family of ANOVA techniques is assumed, and we move briskly into the case study exploring the strengths and weaknesses of different possible analyses before we get to AMOS. Because you see several iterations before getting to the AMOS version, the chapter is able to compare and contrast multivariate techniques in SPSS Statistics and SEM in AMOS. Table 1-1 at the end of the "Factor Analysis and Unobserved Variables in SPSS" section—where SPSS approaches end and AMOS approaches begin—summarizes the multivariate tests made to that point in the chapter. You might want to occasionally jump ahead to that table to help "keep score" on our progress. There is a similar table, Table 1-3, at the end of the "AMOS" section.

We don't focus on learning all that AMOS can do (it is feature rich) nor on the full theory or complexity behind SEM. We simply use a single case study to show that we can analyze the data in SPSS Statistics, but the analysis doesn't fully reflect the theory behind the case study until we reach the final model in AMOS. No prior knowledge of AMOS or SEM is assumed. The case study is interesting enough, I think, to make the chapter enjoyable even if you know a bit about either (or both) topics, but these two topics are too broad to offer much more than a taste in this chapter. One aspect of the case study that warrants attention, but won't be discussed thoroughly until the AMOS section, is the direction of causality. As we are frequently warned in Stats 101, establishing a correlation between A and B does not establish that A is causing B, nor that B is causing A. In fact, we are cautioned, it might even be neither of those. We will stick with the hypothesized relationships that inspired the data collection in the first half of the chapter, but in the final section we will spend some time specifically on the direction of causality and how AMOS can shed light on it.

The case study dataset `AMOS PSAT data.sav` contains the PSAT test results for 222 sophomores in five high schools in the same greater metropolitan area. The Preliminary SAT/National Merit Scholarship Qualifying Test (PSAT/NMSQT) is the test that students take that helps them qualify for the National Merit Scholarships as juniors in high school, but many students also take it as practice for the SAT. This group was part of a study and was explicitly encouraged to take it a year early, so no particular assumptions about their college intentions can be made. They are likely fairly close to the general population, and not necessarily college bound. The data was collected in the mid-1990s. The Myers-Briggs Type Indicator (MBTI) was also administered to the same students during the study, which was used as a learning style indicator.

The purpose of the unpublished research was to determine if one learning style might have an advantage over others. Uncovering the mechanism of the advantage was a different challenge. One explanation proposed by the researchers was one group was better at guessing at questions that were a bit beyond their classroom training. The mechanism won't be explored in detail here. We will focus on trying to quantify the possible gap given control variables. The "A Bit about Learning Styles" sidebar elaborates on the thought behind the working hypothesis.

Classes were examined in the school transcript and categorized as *honors* or *non-honors* in each of four categories: English, math, science, and social studies. An overall level variable was created using these four variables by calculating the percentage of honors. Possible additional control variables in the dataset include sex and class rank.

We hypothesize that honors will outperform non-honors on both subscales, and an additional advantage will go to those with an intuitive learning style. Obviously, other hypotheses are completely plausible. Notably, the causality could flow in the opposite direction. Especially bright students might be invited to take honors classes and might naturally get higher scores, but not because of their course selection. Some schools require evidence of high scores on similar tests to earn the right to take honors classes. Excellent grades (reflected in class rank) might be driving the taking of honors classes. For now, we will adopt the study's hypotheses as our own, but in the final section will explore the direction of causality in AMOS and see if we can't shed some light on some of these alternative theories.

A BIT ABOUT LEARNING STYLES

The two styles were the sensing (S) learning style and the intuitive (N) learning style. The differences between the two were described originally by Jung, but not explicitly as learning styles, and in a rather different context. Some relevant differences are that sensors (S) prefer using established methods of problem solving that they have rehearsed. They like extrapolating from past experience. intuitives (N) are sometimes bored by repetition so their problem solving can involve creatively exploring new methods and finding new relationships. They like extrapolating from theory and testing their new hypotheses.

The hypothesis of the researchers (who included Keith), and which will act as our working hypothesis in this chapter, is that honors classes are taught in such a way that they better prepare students to perform well under conditions of uncertainty and will produce higher test scores. Honors classes, more than non-honors classes, require and reward going a bit beyond one's training. Naturally, honors students might find also fewer questions that are beyond their training than non-honors students. Comfort in the intuitive style is hypothesized to come in handy when particular PSAT questions (particularly as a sophomore) are beyond one's training. Finally, intuitives (N) might be hypothesized to be somewhat more comfortable when struggling with a question they haven't encountered before and have to guess.

At the risk of stating the obvious, some learning and academic tasks simply align better with either using established methods or finding new patterns. Students will be expected (and most would agree should be expected) to flex and use both approaches. What theory would predict is at times of stress (long hours of work, learning something for the first time, pressure to perform, and so on) working in the opposite style becomes especially difficult.

T-Test

First, we will establish that there is a difference between the two learning style groups, and then explore a number of ways that we can do a formal test of the hypothesis. This chapter is essentially an exploration of how to measure this gap while handling these potential control variables in a way that is accurate, defensible, persuasive, clear, and hopefully even elegant. Generally, the more you pile on control variables and interaction terms, the more you might persuade certain members of your audience, but it complicates the narrative, endangering clarity. Worse, to a critical eye, too many variables along with too many hypothesis tests and coefficients puts persuasion at risk for another reason—because parsimony is valued in analysis.

So let's begin with the most basic statement of the hypothesis. Students who prefer two learning styles, intuition (N) and sensing (S), get different overall scores. Phrased that way, a straightforward T-test seems to be in order. PSAT scores in this dataset range from 40 (low) to 160 (high). Throughout the chapter we will use the AMOS PSAT data.sav dataset and our dependent variable (Test Variable) will be PSAT, which is the combined test score. Our independent variable (Grouping Variable) will be SN as shown in Figure 1-1. Note that SPSS requires you to declare the two groups, which are S and N. When defining using the Define Groups subdialog (not shown) remember that it is case sensitive.

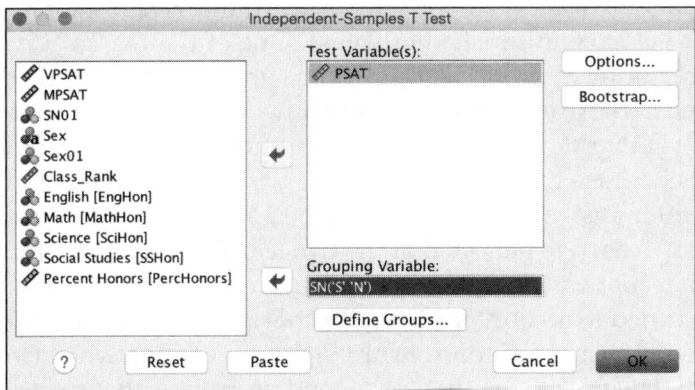

Figure 1-1: T-test dialog

The results, shown in Figure 1-2, confirm our hypothesis, in a sense. It is significant. We know this because we've passed the Levene's Test (it is above 0.5 at .866) if we accept the normality assumption, and we can use the standard significance test in the top row of the Independent Samples Test. It is well below .05 with a value of .000. Of course, p values like this are not exactly zero, and SPSS will allow you to show many more decimal places if you choose. No need to do that in this case. In Chapter 2 we will explore bootstrapping which would be an option if we actually had difficulty with the normality assumption.

More importantly at present, there is about a 10-point difference between the two groups. The S mean is 79.70 and the N mean is 90.53. (Note that if you are more familiar with SAT scores, the equivalent would be 100 points. You can simply multiply any PSAT score by 10.) This is not a trivial difference, and reflects a Cohen's d of .58, which would be considered "moderate." SPSS Statistics does not support Cohen's d in the T-test menu, but there is a way to request it in SPSS, which is discussed in Chapter 18.

T–Test

Group Statistics

	SN	N	Mean	Std. Deviation	Std. Error Mean
PSAT	S	125	79.70	18.308	1.638
	N	97	90.53	19.031	1.932

Independent Samples Test

		Levene's Test for Equality of Variances		t–test for Equality of Means					95% Confidence Interval of the Difference	
		F	Sig.	t	df	Sig. (2–tailed)	Mean Difference	Std. Error Difference	Lower	Upper
PSAT	Equal variances assumed	.029	.866	-4.297	220	.000	-10.830	2.520	-15.797	-5.863
	Equal variances not assumed			-4.276	202.531	.000	-10.830	2.533	-15.824	-5.836

Figure 1-2: T-test results

I don't think that many researchers or readers of research would be completely satisfied by our T-test. It is consistent with our hypothesis, and we have established a difference, but we have unfinished business. One of the two groups could be college bound, taking appropriate courses to support that; the other group might not be. One of the groups could have parents that help them with their homework, and the other does not. (Note that we can't randomly assign them to the two groups because they aren't treatment groups. They belong to the groups because of their answers on a paper and pencil questionnaire.) Of course, we don't have any reason to believe that the two learning styles are tied to these effects, but each reader will have his or her favorite explanation and will wonder why we haven't tried to account for them. In short, we have no control variables. We will address the issue of control variables soon enough when we attempt an ANCOVA in the very next section. A second problem is that we are using combined scores and not verbal and math separately. I will explain why this is an issue, and make in attempt to address it when we try MANOVA.

ANCOVA

Analysis of Covariance (ANCOVA) will let us deal with the first of our issues. We will add a variable measuring the percentage of honors of the classes that they are taking. One could have all kinds of debates about the direction of the causality and the nature of relationship between this variable and test performance. In particular, in the "The Direction of Causality" section later in this chapter, we will revisit this issue using AMOS. For now, the working hypothesis is that one would expect honors students to go into a PSAT testing situation with a preparation that is more suited to the test than a non-honors student both in terms of the amount of material that will be familiar and even the style of teaching found in honors classes. Then we proceed to compare Ns and Ss, but with that expected advantage taken into account. If we succeed we will claim that we have established a difference between the two groups even after having controlled for the influence of another variable, level of class difficulty.

Before we can proceed we have to deal with an assumption of this approach—the homogeneity of slopes assumption. While we won't be going into a lot of technical detail, checking this assumption visually will also allow us to get a nice look at what we are trying to do. We will be using a colored scatter plot in Chart Builder. (If you are new to Chart Builder, it is discussed in Chapters 5 and 6.) As shown in Figure 1-3, we will use PSAT as the y-axis, Percent Honors as the x-axis, and SN as the color.

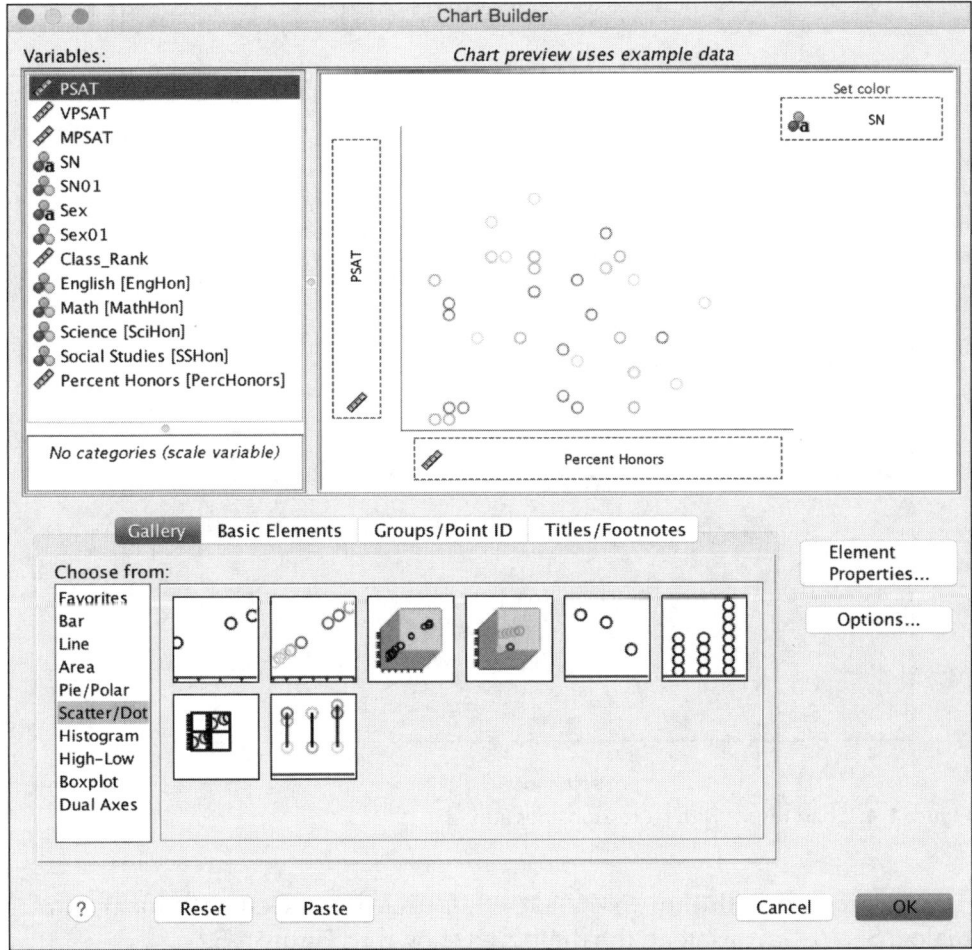

Figure 1-3: Chart Builder dialog

I've edited the results a bit, shown in Figure 1-4, to make the pattern clearer. I've added "fit lines" for the two subgroups. The two parallel lines represent the performance of Ns and Ss. The higher of the two lines represents Ns. Moving from left to right, as Percent Honors gets larger, associated with lower difficulty, the PSAT scores tend to go down. The gap between the performance of Ns and Ss seems quite uniform. SPSS has added two regression equations, and R2 results, along with our fit lines. Note that the slope of the two lines is very similar, but the Y intercepts show a more than 4-point gap. Consistent with those equations, the lines appear nearly parallel. That is the meaning of the homogeneity of slopes assumption, which we appear to have met. Put that another way, SN and Percent Honors do not interact. Interactions will be discussed again, especially in Chapter 13. Figure 13-4 shows a similar graphic but using a dataset where an interaction is present.

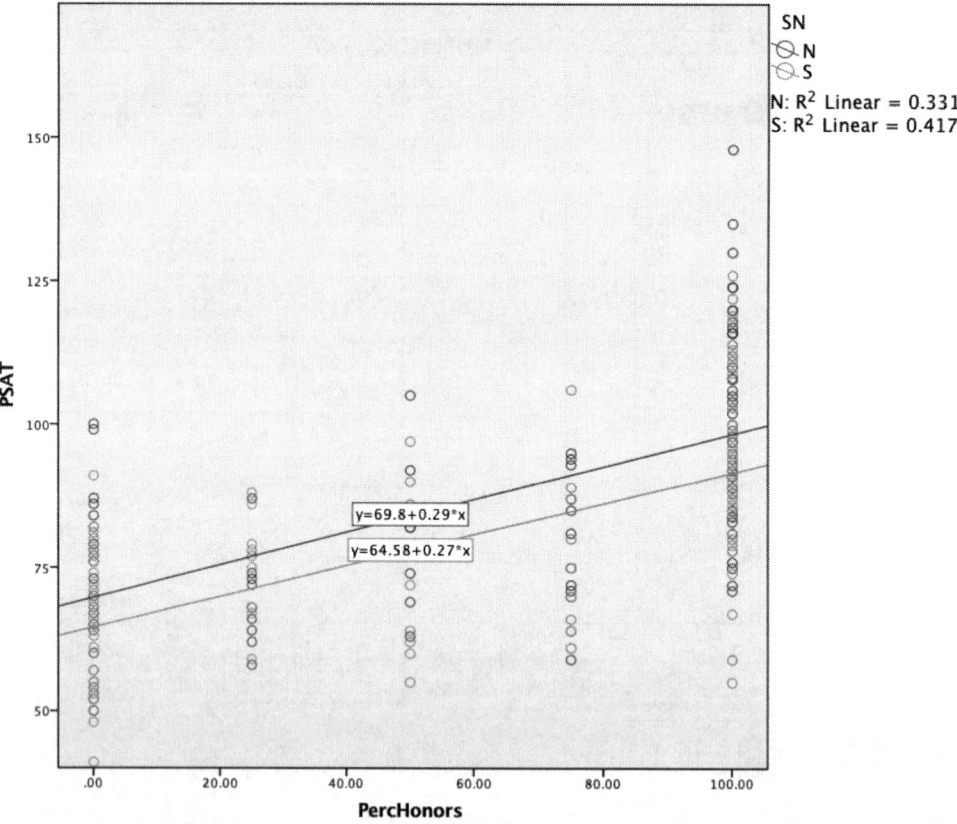

Figure 1-4: Chart results with regression lines added

Let's proceed with the ANOVA itself, found in the General Linear Model dialog. Select Univariate in the dialog, as shown in Figure 1-5.

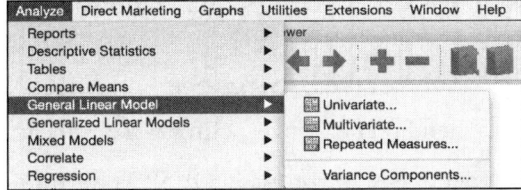

Figure 1-5: General Linear Model menu options

PSAT will be our Dependent Variable, SN will be a Fixed Factor, and PercHonors will be a Covariate, as in Figure 1-6. We will request Parameter Estimates in the Options submenu, but make no additional changes, as in Figure 1-7.

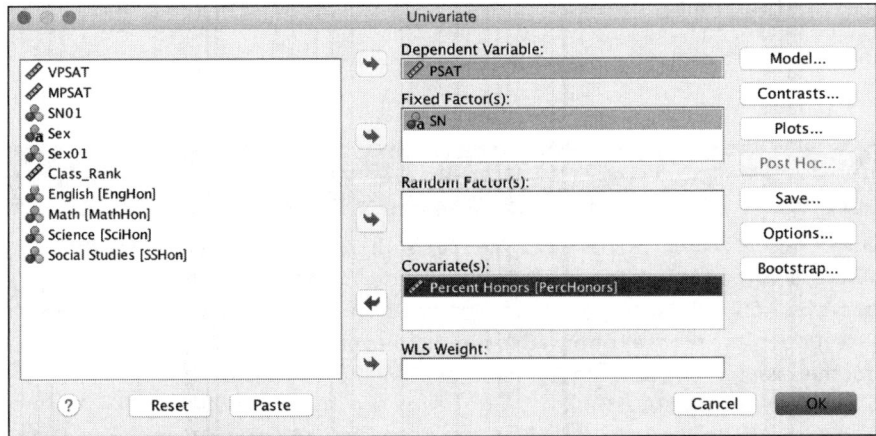

Figure 1-6: Univariate dialog

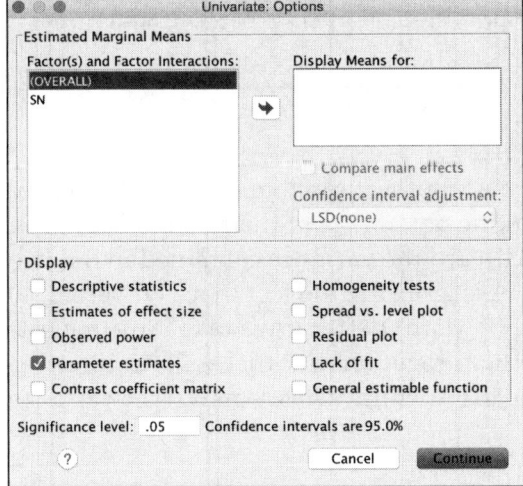

Figure 1-7: Univariate options subdialog

The results, shown in Figure 1-8, are consistent with the visualization and so far our hypotheses have been correct:

- Percent Honors is significant (Sig. column of the Between-Subjects Effects).
- SN continues to be significant even when PercHonors is acting as a covariate.

But what is the magnitude of the impact of SN in the ANCOVA? That question is better answered with the Parameter Estimates table that we requested, also shown in Figure 1-8. The impact of SN is somewhat smaller with the addition of the covariate, at 6.317 points, but it is not trivial in size. Remember in the more familiar scale of the SAT this would be 63 points. The magnitude of the effect of honors/non-honors levels, however, is quite large. The difference between a student with all honors versus no honors would be estimated to be a gap of almost 28 points on the PSAT scale, which would be 280 points on the SAT scale.

TACKLING ORDINAL DATA: THE ORIGINAL FORM OF THE TRANSCRIPT VARIABLES

When the transcripts were originally analyzed for both sophomores and juniors, the classes were described in four categories not two: Advanced Placement (1), honors (2), non-honors (3), non-college prep (4). The fourth category would include examples like taking accounting as a math as opposed to non-honors pre-calculus. It was dichotomized for this example because the sophomores didn't have AP options, and only a handful of classes were labeled four.

It doesn't have a direct bearing on the chapter, but it is interesting to reflect on how to handle a four-category ordinal variable like this. One option would be categorical regression, which we will cover in Chapter 2. Another option would be Latent Class analysis. SPSS does not offer it in the menus but it is available as an "extension." While Latent Class is not one of the examples shown, the book offers a chapter-length introduction to extensions in Chapter 18.

As we've already mentioned, there is another problem. We have two subscores: math and verbal. We aren't taking advantage of them. We would have greater statistical power if we didn't discard the variance contained in the two subscores. In other words, the ANOVA is ignoring the fact that a 60 Verbal/40 Math is not the same as a 40 Verbal/60 Math. Better if we take advantage of two subscores, and not simply add them together, but that will require two dependent variables. So now it is time to try Multivariate Analysis of Variance (MANOVA).

Univariate Analysis of Variance

Between–Subjects Factors

		Value Label	N
SN	N	Intuition	97
	S	Sensing	125

Tests of Between–Subjects Effects

Dependent Variable: PSAT

Source	Type III Sum of Squares	df	Mean Square	F	Sig.
Corrected Model	35217.733[a]	2	17608.866	81.154	.000
Intercept	293095.26	1	293095.26	1350.794	.000
PercHonors	28812.019	1	28812.019	132.787	.000
SN	2040.034	1	2040.034	9.402	.002
Error	47518.614	219	216.980		
Total	1665169.0	222			
Corrected Total	82736.347	221			

a. R Squared = .426 (Adjusted R Squared = .420)

Parameter Estimates

Dependent Variable: PSAT

Parameter	B	Std. Error	t	Sig.	95% Confidence Interval Lower Bound	95% Confidence Interval Upper Bound
Intercept	64.263	1.879	34.206	.000	60.560	67.966
PercHonors	.276	.024	11.523	.000	.228	.323
[SN=N]	6.233	2.033	3.066	.002	2.227	10.239
[SN=S]	0[a]	.	.	.	.	.

a. This parameter is set to zero because it is redundant.

Figure 1-8: ANCOVA results

MANOVA

Multivariate Analysis of Variance (MANOVA) allows us to have two (or more) dependent variables. There is a lot of confusion around MANOVA, and even folks that are really quite sophisticated statistically can fall prey to the confusion. In a very real sense, MANOVA has only one dependent variable but a dependent variable that requires more than one variable to measure it effectively. For this reason the dependent variables should be related conceptually. For instance, a concept like anxiety might be measured by a variety of "manifest" variables like sleeplessness, change in appetite, and so on. Even though the manifest variables would be dropped into the MANOVA dialog and there would be no anxiety variable physically present in the dataset, the anxiety concept is a critical part of the story. If a pair (or group) of dependent variables in a MANOVA were completely unrelated it would beg the question of why they were part of the same test. One can think of the dependent variable as a latent variable (from the Latin for "lie hidden"). The latent variable is not directly observed or measured. AMOS makes this more explicit than MANOVA as we will see when we discuss AMOS. Another way of referring to such variables is to call them unobserved variables.

In our example, we use VPSAT and MPSAT together, as dependent variables, to measure readiness for college, each picking up on different aspects of the readiness concept. Years ago, these tests were referred to as "aptitude" tests. More recently the terms "reasoning" or "assessment" have been used. We won't debate that here, but since the goal is to predict the readiness for college, we will simply refer to the unobserved variable as "readiness." There will be test results that will attempt to measure differences between that readiness and the SN variable, which will be a Fixed Factor. MANOVA is also found in the General Linear Model menu, but this time we will access the necessary dialog using the Multivariate submenu (not shown). The Multivariate dialog, set up with our variables, is shown in Figure 1-9. Just as we did with ANCOVA we will request Parameter Estimates in the Options subdialog (not shown).

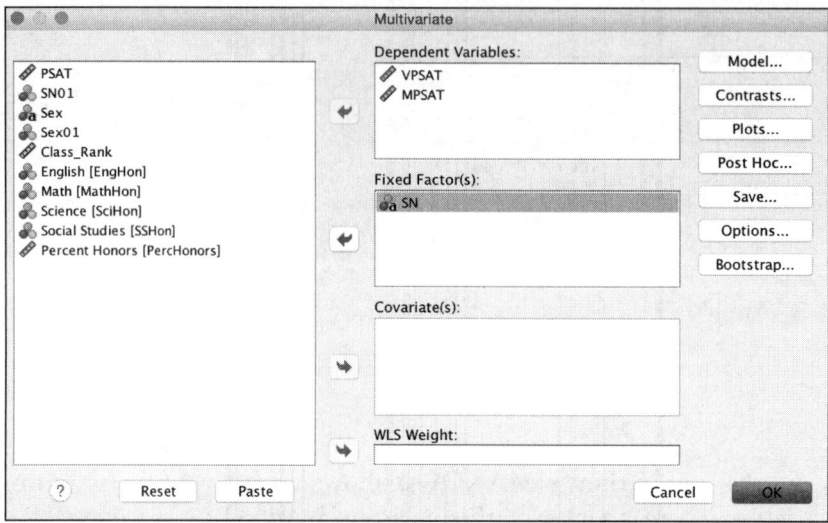

Figure 1-9: Multivariate dialog

We will also be interested in the verbal and math variables as individual variables, but they now share the spotlight with the latent, unobserved dependent variable. Combined score, however, is not used, because our subscales, working as a pair, give us a better way of measuring an overall difference.

This produces an intimidating amount of output (Figures 1-10, 1-11, and 1-12), but it reveals much that we have not seen thus far. The four Multivariate Tests, despite their varying ranges of being conservative and liberal, and with their varying assumptions, all agree that the combination of subscales, when analyzed as a pair, show a significant difference between our learning style dichotomy categories (Figure 1-10).

SPSS provides four multivariate tests in part because they differ in various ways, and are favored by different groups of researchers and under different circumstances. One could dedicate a substantial discussion to the four tests, but since they all agree in this case, we will focus on the fact that S and N have now been established to have a different mean on the unobserved variable "readiness" as measured by our pair of dependent variables.

General Linear Model

Between-Subjects Factors

		Value Label	N
SN	N	Intuition	97
	S	Sensing	125

Multivariate Tests[a]

Effect		Value	F	Hypothesis df	Error df	Sig.
Intercept	Pillai's Trace	.954	2288.230[b]	2.000	219.000	.000
	Wilks' Lambda	.046	2288.230[b]	2.000	219.000	.000
	Hotelling's Trace	20.897	2288.230[b]	2.000	219.000	.000
	Roy's Largest Root	20.897	2288.230[b]	2.000	219.000	.000
SN	Pillai's Trace	.079	9.396[b]	2.000	219.000	.000
	Wilks' Lambda	.921	9.396[b]	2.000	219.000	.000
	Hotelling's Trace	.086	9.396[b]	2.000	219.000	.000
	Roy's Largest Root	.086	9.396[b]	2.000	219.000	.000

a. Design: Intercept + SN
b. Exact statistic

Figure 1-10: MANOVA Multivariate Tests

The next portion of the output is shown in Figure 1-11. The most important part of the Tests of Between-Subjects Effects is the significance of the SN difference on the two subscales. On both, SPSS reports a p value of .000. Once we have established a significant difference, the magnitude of the difference is what is more interesting. The Parameter Estimates show that the SN gap is 6.1 points on the verbal subscale and 4.7 points on the math subscale.

Tests of Between-Subjects Effects

Source	Dependent Variable	Type III Sum of Squares	df	Mean Square	F	Sig.
Corrected Model	VPSAT	2044.163[a]	1	2044.163	17.680	.000
	MPSAT	1212.661[b]	1	1212.661	12.875	.000
Intercept	VPSAT	412767.82	1	412767.82	3570.041	.000
	MPSAT	378872.99	1	378872.99	4022.466	.000
SN	VPSAT	2044.163	1	2044.163	17.680	.000
	MPSAT	1212.661	1	1212.661	12.875	.000
Error	VPSAT	25436.378	220	115.620		
	MPSAT	20721.632	220	94.189		
Total	VPSAT	439508.00	222			
	MPSAT	401457.00	222			
Corrected Total	VPSAT	27480.541	221			
	MPSAT	21934.293	221			

a. R Squared = .074 (Adjusted R Squared = .070)
b. R Squared = .055 (Adjusted R Squared = .051)

Parameter Estimates

Dependent Variable	Parameter	B	Std. Error	t	Sig.	95% Confidence Interval Lower Bound	Upper Bound
VPSAT	Intercept	40.408	.962	42.015	.000	38.513	42.303
	[SN=N]	6.118	1.455	4.205	.000	3.250	8.985
	[SN=S]	0[a]	.	.	.	.	.
MPSAT	Intercept	39.288	.868	45.260	.000	37.577	40.999
	[SN=N]	4.712	1.313	3.588	.000	2.124	7.300
	[SN=S]	0[a]	.	.	.	.	.

a. This parameter is set to zero because it is redundant.

Figure 1-11: Additional MANOVA results

So, what do we conclude?

- S and N differ on "readiness."
- S and N also differ on both subscales.
- The S/N difference is a bit larger on verbal than math, but both differences are significant and substantial in size.

What is missing from our analysis? With our ANCOVA we had a control variable, but it is lacking from this most recent attempt. It is time to add a covariate back, which we will do in the next section by attempting Multivariate Analytics of Covariance (MANCOVA).

MANCOVA with a Single Covariate

Having done the analysis step by step it won't be difficult to describe what we are attempting to do with our Multivariate Analysis of Covariance (MANCOVA). We will continue to assess differences between S and N on readiness, but with a covariate. We will use the same covariate we used in our ANCOVA example, PercHonors. We will set up our dialog just like Figure 1-9 except that we are adding in our covariate (Figure 1-12).

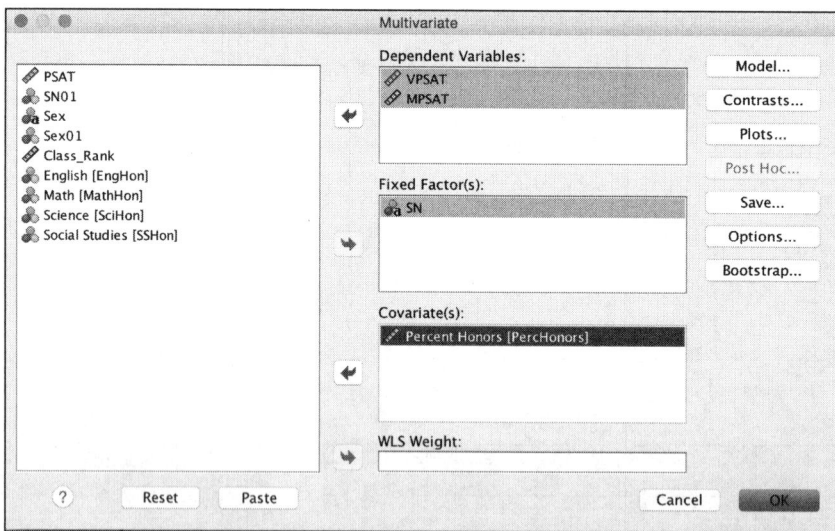

Figure 1-12: T-test dialog

Everything else will remain the same including our request for parameter estimates in the Options dialog (not shown).

I've edited the results to simplify the Multivariate Tests for two reasons: All four of the tests agree (even producing the same p values) and because Pillai's Trace is generally favored. The edited results appear in Figure 1-13. (For the curious, the pivoting trays feature was used to do the editing.) The addition of the covariate has changed the significance of the SN gap very slightly. It is now reported to be .008, but is still well below .05.

General Linear Model

Between–Subjects Factors

		Value Label	N
SN	N	Intuition	97
	S	Sensing	125

Multivariate Tests[a]

Pillai's Trace

Effect	Value	F	Hypothesis df	Error df	Sig.
Intercept	.862	679.159[b]	2.000	218.000	.000
PercHonors	.378	66.305[b]	2.000	218.000	.000
SN	.043	4.887[b]	2.000	218.000	.008

a. Design: Intercept + PercHonors + SN
b. Exact statistic

Figure 1-13: MANCOVA Multivariate Tests results

When analyzed individually, the VPSAT and MPSAT subscales show a significant difference between our learning style dichotomy categories (Figure 1-14). The key results among the tests are the significance of .003 for SN difference on the verbal subscale, and .024 for the SN difference on the math subscale.

Tests of Between–Subjects Effects

Source	Dependent Variable	Type III Sum of Squares	df	Mean Square	F	Sig.
Corrected Model	VPSAT	9855.934[a]	2	4927.967	61.234	.000
	MPSAT	7831.592[b]	2	3915.796	60.808	.000
Intercept	VPSAT	75661.018	1	75661.018	940.149	.000
	MPSAT	70924.879	1	70924.879	1101.388	.000
PercHonors	VPSAT	7811.771	1	7811.771	97.068	.000
	MPSAT	6618.931	1	6618.931	102.785	.000
SN	VPSAT	728.316	1	728.316	9.050	.003
	MPSAT	330.491	1	330.491	5.132	.024
Error	VPSAT	17624.606	219	80.478		
	MPSAT	14102.701	219	64.396		
Total	VPSAT	420502.00	222			
	MPSAT	401457.00	222			
Corrected Total	VPSAT	27480.541	221			
	MPSAT	21934.293	221			

a. R Squared = .359 (Adjusted R Squared = .353)
b. R Squared = .357 (Adjusted R Squared = .351)

Figure 1-14: MANCOVA Tests of Between–Subjects Effects results

The effect is shown in the Parameter Estimates (Figure 1-15)—an advantage for Ns of 3.7 points on the verbal, and 2.5 points on the math. Of course, we've consistently seen a difference. Now with the addition of the covariate, the differences are a bit smaller, but the differences are non-trivial. Combined and translated into the SAT scale, that would represent 62 points.

Parameter Estimates

Dependent Variable	Parameter	B	Std. Error	t	Sig.	95% Confidence Interval	
						Lower Bound	Upper Bound
VPSAT	Intercept	32.372	1.144	28.293	.000	30.117	34.627
	PercHonors	.144	.015	9.852	.000	.115	.172
	[SN=N]	3.724	1.238	3.008	.003	1.284	6.164
	[SN=S]	0ª	.	.	.	.	.
MPSAT	Intercept	31.891	1.023	31.159	.000	29.874	33.908
	PercHonors	.132	.013	10.138	.000	.106	.158
	[SN=N]	2.509	1.107	2.265	.024	.326	4.691
	[SN=S]	0ª	.	.	.	.	.

a. This parameter is set to zero because it is redundant.

Figure 1-15: MANCOVA Parameter Estimates

MANCOVA with Four Covariates

We've managed to perform a test that is pretty close to our original hypotheses and also fairly close to what we will attempt in AMOS. There is a temptation to quit while we are ahead, but to get a full appreciation of the difference between our multivariate menu options and AMOS we should allow our model to get a little bit more complex. We certainly don't want to just throw variables into our model, but we are using PercHonors as if it is a direct measurement of the difficulty of classes taken. It is just a summary calculation of four different levels of difficulty. Should we be using the original variables and measuring the impact of each one? We will try exactly this kind of thing in AMOS, but for the first time there is nothing that is quite analogous to it in SPSS Statistics. There is an option that may seem a stronger analogy than it is. We can drop all four level variables into the covariates area in the MANCOVA dialog as shown in Figure 1-16. We're going to attempt MANCOVA using all four level variables, coded 0 for non-honors or 1 for honors, as covariates: English Honors (EngHon), Math Honors (MathHon), Science Honors (SciHon), and Social Studies Honors (SSHon). (Figure 1-16). It will serve our purpose for now, but there will be no sense in which the four covariates are components of an unobserved variable. As we will see later in the chapter, when we get to AMOS we will also have an unobserved variable "level."

The Multivariate Tests produce a similar result as the previous MANCOVA. It has again been edited to show only Pillai's Trace. The other three tests showed the same pattern. Pillai's Trace now has a p value of .006 indicating that "readiness" has an SN gap even when controlling for all four level variables (Figure 1-17). Some fascinating additional information is now available. We can now see that math honors and science honors are significant at .000 and .001, but English honors and social studies honors are not significant. Notably, they aren't particularly close.

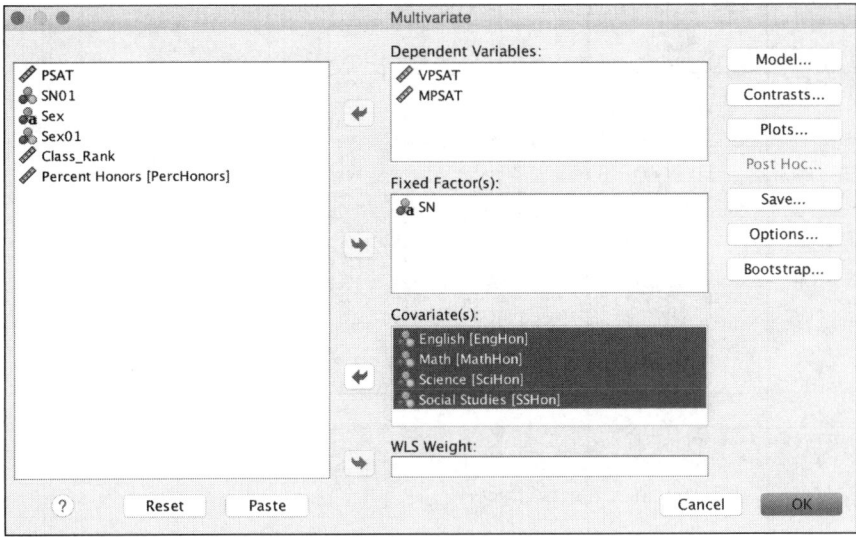

Figure 1-16: MANCOVA dialog with four covariates

General Linear Model

Between–Subjects Factors

		Value Label	N
SN	N	Intuition	97
	S	Sensing	125

Multivariate Tests[a]

Pillai's Trace

Effect	Value	F	Hypothesis df	Error df	Sig.
Intercept	.869	710.461[b]	2.000	215.000	.000
EngHon	.002	.265[b]	2.000	215.000	.768
MathHon	.095	11.295[b]	2.000	215.000	.000
SciHon	.066	7.563[b]	2.000	215.000	.001
SSHon	.007	.798[b]	2.000	215.000	.452
SN	.047	5.258[b]	2.000	215.000	.006

a. Design: Intercept + EngHon + MathHon + SciHon + SSHon + SN

b. Exact statistic

Figure 1-17: Pillai's Trace results

Also noteworthy is that the same findings apply to both subscales (Figure 1-18). The SN gap has a p value of .002 on verbal, and .016 on math. The finding of significant differences for math honors and science honors, but not for English honors and social studies honors is quite consistent on both math and verbal. We don't want to overanalyze the slightly lower p value on verbal. The Parameter Estimates will be a better way to look at the magnitude of the difference.

Tests of Between–Subjects Effects

Source	Dependent Variable	Type III Sum of Squares	df	Mean Square	F	Sig.
Corrected Model	VPSAT	10245.097[a]	5	2049.019	25.679	.000
	MPSAT	8753.075[b]	5	1750.615	28.687	.000
Intercept	VPSAT	75108.821	1	75108.821	941.287	.000
	MPSAT	71284.416	1	71284.416	1168.134	.000
EngHon	VPSAT	36.880	1	36.880	.462	.497
	MPSAT	19.254	1	19.254	.316	.575
MathHon	VPSAT	763.236	1	763.236	9.565	.002
	MPSAT	1330.646	1	1330.646	21.805	.000
SciHon	VPSAT	811.529	1	811.529	10.170	.002
	MPSAT	751.237	1	751.237	12.310	.001
SSHon	VPSAT	11.580	1	11.580	.145	.704
	MPSAT	46.212	1	46.212	.757	.385
SN	VPSAT	751.154	1	751.154	9.414	.002
	MPSAT	359.730	1	359.730	5.895	.016
Error	VPSAT	17235.444	216	79.794		
	MPSAT	13181.218	216	61.024		
Total	VPSAT	439508.00	222			
	MPSAT	401457.00	222			
Corrected Total	VPSAT	27480.541	221			
	MPSAT	21934.293	221			

a. R Squared = .373 (Adjusted R Squared = .358)
b. R Squared = .399 (Adjusted R Squared = .385)

Figure 1-18: MANCOVA Between-Subjects Effects

Let's briefly ponder the lack of significance for English and social studies. One criticism of the PSAT in the '90s (the controversy prompted a revision) was that the verbal questions weren't particularly like classroom work in English. Question types like analogies struck some critics as being more like logic than English class. We won't explore that argument here, but it is worth mentioning it if the result seems strange. The reading comprehension passages in the verbal section are often science passages. So comfort with that style of reading is helpful, and on occasion familiarity with the actual content of the passage can be helpful. This explanation would raise another question however: Why doesn't social studies help when there are also reading comprehension passages that use that subject matter? Since our hypothesis is primarily focused around establishing an SN gap even when covariates are applied, the evidence continues to support our primary claim while producing a couple of mysteries yet unexplained.

The Parameter Estimates are interesting (Figure 1-19). All four of the honors coefficients for verbal show an advantage for taking honors. The significance values and the confidence interval, of course, reveal that we can't be certain that these coefficients are positive for English and social studies as the confidence intervals include zero. The safest conclusion is simply that there is no evidence that they help. The SN gap for verbal is almost 4 points (it would be nearly 40 points on the SAT scale).

Math is a little different. There is even a suggestion that taking social studies honors might hurt. It is not significant, so perhaps we should not speculate, but the negative coefficient does get one's attention. Since it sometimes hard to resist the temptation to wonder, perhaps students that focus on science and math by taking honors in those classes, but take non-honors in social studies actually have the ideal profile. Perhaps there is only so much time in the day to study, and that combination is ideal for the kind of aptitude that the PSAT is measuring?

Parameter Estimates

Dependent Variable	Parameter	B	Std. Error	t	Sig.	95% Confidence Interval	
						Lower Bound	Upper Bound
VPSAT	Intercept	32.549	1.148	28.353	.000	30.286	34.812
	EngHon	1.477	2.173	.680	.497	-2.806	5.760
	MathHon	5.584	1.805	3.093	.002	2.025	9.142
	SciHon	6.487	2.034	3.189	.002	2.478	10.497
	SSHon	.773	2.030	.381	.704	-3.227	4.774
	[SN=N]	3.784	1.233	3.068	.002	1.353	6.214
	[SN=S]	0[a]	.	.	.	.	.
MPSAT	Intercept	32.243	1.004	32.117	.000	30.265	34.222
	EngHon	1.067	1.900	.562	.575	-2.678	4.813
	MathHon	7.373	1.579	4.670	.000	4.261	10.485
	SciHon	6.242	1.779	3.509	.001	2.735	9.748
	SSHon	-1.545	1.775	-.870	.385	-5.043	1.954
	[SN=N]	2.618	1.078	2.428	.016	.493	4.744
	[SN=S]	0[a]	.	.	.	.	.

a. This parameter is set to zero because it is redundant.

Figure 1-19: MANCOVA Parameter Estimates

Let's take stock. The 2nd MANCOVA is fairly close to proving our hypothesis. There are two shortcomings. The four level variables are not being treated as a set of variables—they are simply being used as an unrelated set of covariates. It would be better if they were collectively representing a latent variable. We're nearing the end of the options we will pursue in SPSS Statistics, but we will be able to revisit that in AMOS. The second shortcoming is that the output is getting rather complex. Depending on our audience, we might have some work to do walking them through the logic. Before we move on to AMOS we have two loose ends:

- ■ We have covariates that we haven't tried, specifically sex and class rank.

- ■ We want to try to pursue this notion of unobserved variable further in SPSS.

A LITTLE HISTORY

The SAT was developed in the early 20th century to give working class male students (female university students were rare) a chance to go to university. It was felt that the Greek and Latin exams that were used one hundred years ago for college admission favored the very wealthy who could afford elite prep schools. In fact, each Ivy League school was essentially paired with a prep school. One can imagine that the profile and styles of the students who did the best on those exams might be quite different. Maybe there is something about what they were trying to accomplish—tapping into "native ability" and not highly structured formal training—that causes these patterns to arise.

Other Factors and Covariates

Before we summarize our progress thus far, let's take a quick look at an alternate MANCOVA shown in Figure 1-20. It is best to satisfy our curiosity about sex and class rank since we won't be able to try every combination in AMOS. The results shown in Figure 1-20 show that SN, Class_Rank, and Sex are all significant, below .05. We continue to see a similar pattern with our set of level variables. Once again, the table has been edited to show only Pillai's Trace.

Multivariate Tests[a]

Pillai's Trace

Effect	Value	F	Hypothesis df	Error df	Sig.
Intercept	.722	275.937[b]	2.000	213.000	.000
SN	.044	4.902[b]	2.000	213.000	.008
Sex	.036	3.926[b]	2.000	213.000	.021
Class_Rank	.072	8.268[b]	2.000	213.000	.000
EngHon	.002	.168[b]	2.000	213.000	.846
MathHon	.047	5.268[b]	2.000	213.000	.006
SciHon	.061	6.871[b]	2.000	213.000	.001
SSHon	.014	1.512[b]	2.000	213.000	.223

a. Design: Intercept + SN + Sex + Class_Rank + EngHon + MathHon + SciHon + SSHon

b. Exact statistic

Figure 1-20: Alternate MANCOVA Multivariate Tests

The overall SN effect is still significant. This is important because it doesn't appear that the SN gap was really some kind of grade effect in disguise. The model is getting more complex yet the p value for SN has remained fairly constant. So our working hypothesis is still intact, but where do we go from here? Is it best that we keep all of these variables in? What additional light do they shed on our model except to further reinforce that none of them has made the SN variable non-significant?

The Parameter Estimates (Figure 1-21) provide additional detail. The SN gaps are smaller than when we started, but even with all of these control variables they are non-trivial: 3.7 points on the verbal and 2.3 points on the math, which would be about 60 points combined on the SAT scale. There are a couple of surprises. There is a gender gap favoring men, slightly larger than the SN gap, on math, but there is no significant gender gap on verbal. Social studies, although non-significant, looks like it might have a gap of about the same magnitude as sex and SN on the math but in the opposite direction. The confidence interval ranges from a 6-point penalty to a 1-point advantage. It could very well be a fluke, but it makes one wonder if the pattern would clear up (in either direction) with a larger dataset.

Parameter Estimates

Dependent Variable	Parameter	B	Std. Error	t	Sig.	95% Confidence Interval Lower Bound	Upper Bound
VPSAT	Intercept	37.738	2.285	16.513	.000	33.233	42.242
	[SN=N]	3.676	1.223	3.007	.003	1.266	6.086
	[SN=S]	0[a]	.	.	.	.	.
	[Sex=F]	-.173	1.229	-.141	.888	-2.594	2.249
	[Sex=M]	0[a]	.	.	.	.	.
	Class_Rank	-.035	.013	-2.738	.007	-.060	-.010
	EngHon	.777	2.203	.353	.725	-3.565	5.119
	MathHon	3.896	1.889	2.062	.040	.172	7.620
	SciHon	6.000	2.017	2.974	.003	2.023	9.976
	SSHon	.248	2.022	.123	.903	-3.737	4.232
MPSAT	Intercept	39.717	1.941	20.463	.000	35.892	43.543
	[SN=N]	2.286	1.038	2.201	.029	.239	4.333
	[SN=S]	0[a]	.	.	.	.	.
	[Sex=F]	-2.656	1.043	-2.545	.012	-4.713	-.599
	[Sex=M]	0[a]	.	.	.	.	.
	Class_Rank	-.043	.011	-3.949	.000	-.064	-.021
	EngHon	1.071	1.871	.572	.568	-2.617	4.759
	MathHon	5.116	1.605	3.189	.002	1.954	8.279
	SciHon	5.757	1.713	3.360	.001	2.379	9.134
	SSHon	-2.540	1.717	-1.480	.140	-5.925	.844

a. This parameter is set to zero because it is redundant.

Figure 1-21: Alternate MANCOVA Parameter Estimates

The only possible theory, and it is not terribly convincing, would be the "only so much time in the day" type speculation that we made earlier. We could easily assemble a half dozen significant MANCOVA variants. How would we best choose among them? Certainly we could try to make the choice within SPSS itself, but this is truly where we turn our attention to AMOS. We will have ways that will bring a more satisfying sense of closure to which model is the best marriage of theory and data. As I mentioned at the end of the last section, we have one remaining item of unfinished business. We are going to generate some factor analysis results in SPSS in order to be able to compare those results to our very first AMOS example.

Factor Analysis and Unobserved Variables in SPSS

This section will be an unsatisfying introduction to factor analysis if you are new to the topic. I have a very modest goal, and it is based on the assumption that many readers of this book will be more familiar with the factor analysis menus in SPSS than they are with AMOS. The goal is simply to generate some values in SPSS that will exactly match the values that we will generate in AMOS in our first AMOS example. For those readers with some familiarity with the factor analysis output, this may help you make the leap to AMOS. If you are not familiar with factor analysis, this short section will have less value, but you can certainly continue on with the AMOS example. It will simply be that matching the numbers won't be as revealing for you.

Our example is straightforward enough. We take the four level variables and force them onto one factor and very briefly examine the results. We want to see if all four variables contribute to the factor, and how well the factor incorporates their variance. Factor Analysis is found in the Analyze menu (Figure 1-22). We will choose all four level variables as shown in Figure 1-23.

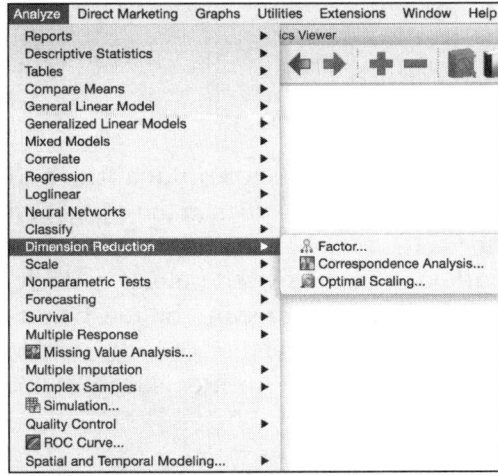

Figure 1-22: Factor Analysis menu

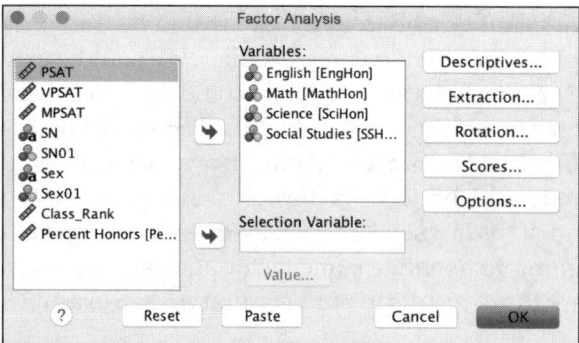

Figure 1-23: Factor Analysis dialog

In order to get results that match both the output in this section and what we find in the AMOS output, you have to change the default extraction method. In the extraction subdialog (Figure 1-24) choose Maximum likelihood and choose a fixed number of factors. We want and hypothesize a single factor. Notably, the default setting, "Based on Eigenvalue" (shown), also produces a single factor.

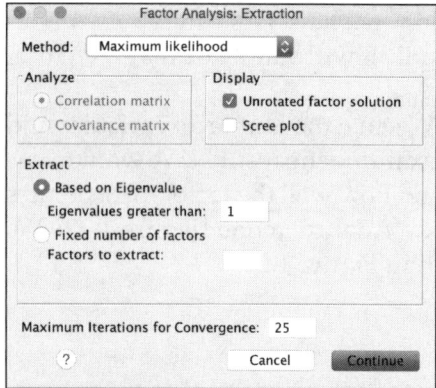

Figure 1-24: Extraction subdialog

The factor analysis results (Figure 1-25) show both the communalities and the factor loadings. The communalities, specifically the values in the extraction column tell us the fraction of the variance in the variables explained in the factor. Once we are in AMOS that factor will be our unobserved (latent) variable. If one of the variables was not contributing to our factor we might question its inclusion. The column in the factor matrix shows the correlation of each variable with the factor. We will see these same values in AMOS in Revisiting Factor Analysis and general orientation to AMOS.

Factor Analysis

Communalities

	Initial	Extraction
English	.662	.765
Math	.549	.615
Science	.618	.703
Social Studies	.614	.695

Extraction Method: Maximum Likelihood.

Factor Matrix[a]

	Factor
	1
English	.875
Math	.784
Science	.838
Social Studies	.834

Extraction Method: Maximum Likelihood.

Figure 1-25: Factor Analysis results

Table 1-1 summarizes multivariate tests performed in this chapter.

Table 1-1: A Summary of the Multivariate Tests Performed in SPSS

	QUESTION	CONCLUSION	LEFT UNRESOLVED
T-Test	Do S and N scores differ on the PSAT combined score?	There is a significant difference between S and N scores.	No control variables
"ANCOVA Graphic"	Do we meet the homogeneity of slopes assumption?	Yes. The lines are parallel.	
ANCOVA with SN and Percent Honors	Do S and N scores differ even when level is a control variable?	Both SN and Level are significant.	PercHonors is not the ideal covariate.
Formal check of ANCOVA assumption	Do we meet the homogeneity of slopes assumption?	The interaction term is not significant, but now SN is not significant.	Fitting non-significant coefficients reduces our statistical power.
MANOVA	Do S and N scores differ on "readiness" using the math and verbal subscores?	SN scores differ overall as well as on verbal and math individually.	We are back to having no control variables.
MANCOVA with Percent Honors	Do S and N scores differ on the PSAT even when controlling for average level of difficulty?	SN scores differ even when adding the control variable.	We are still using an average of our set of variables.

Continues

Table 1-1 (*continued*)

	QUESTION	CONCLUSION	LEFT UNRESOLVED
MANCOVA with four level variables	Do S and N scores differ on the PSAT even when controlling for level of difficulty in four categories?	SN scores differ even when adding the set of four control variables.	We are fairly close to addressing our real research question, but the output is getting quite complex.
Alternate MANCOVA with more variables	Are the other variables significant?	SN is still significant when combined with Sex, Level, and Rank.	The issue of which variables to keep and/or drop to finalize our model is getting more complex.
Factor Analysis of the level variables	Can the four honors/non-honors variables be used to estimate an unobserved variable "level"?	All four variables contribute to the variance of the unobserved variable.	Can this unobserved variable be used to predict another one (readiness)?

AMOS

At the risk of ruining the suspense, an AMOS model is shown in Figure 1-26 that is not unlike the 2nd MANOVA (the one in the "MANCOVA with Four Covariates section and with the Parameter Estimates as shown in Figure 1-19). We spend the balance of this chapter discussing this model and other AMOS models using our case study dataset. We will have a lot to say about interpretation, but much less to say about the mechanics of drawing the diagram. Unlike Figure 1-26, statistical results are shown in most AMOS diagrams, which will be discussed in some detail later in the chapter. The one sentence description of this diagram is: The unobserved variable Level and the observed variable SN01 predicts the unobserved variable Readiness.

Revisiting Factor Analysis and a General Orientation to AMOS

In all of our AMOS examples, the AMOS Graphics diagrams will already be built and available on this book's website on `Wiley.com`. AMOS Graphics diagrams end in the file extension `.amw`. Our first diagram is named `Chapter 1 amos level only.amw`. Launch AMOS Graphics and open the file. Once opened your screen should look like Figure 1-27.

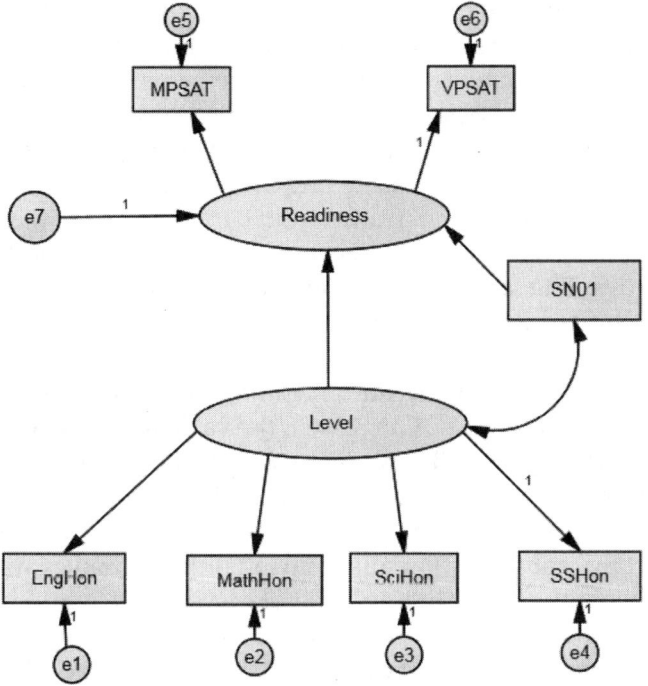

Figure 1-26: An AMOS model similar to our MANCOVA

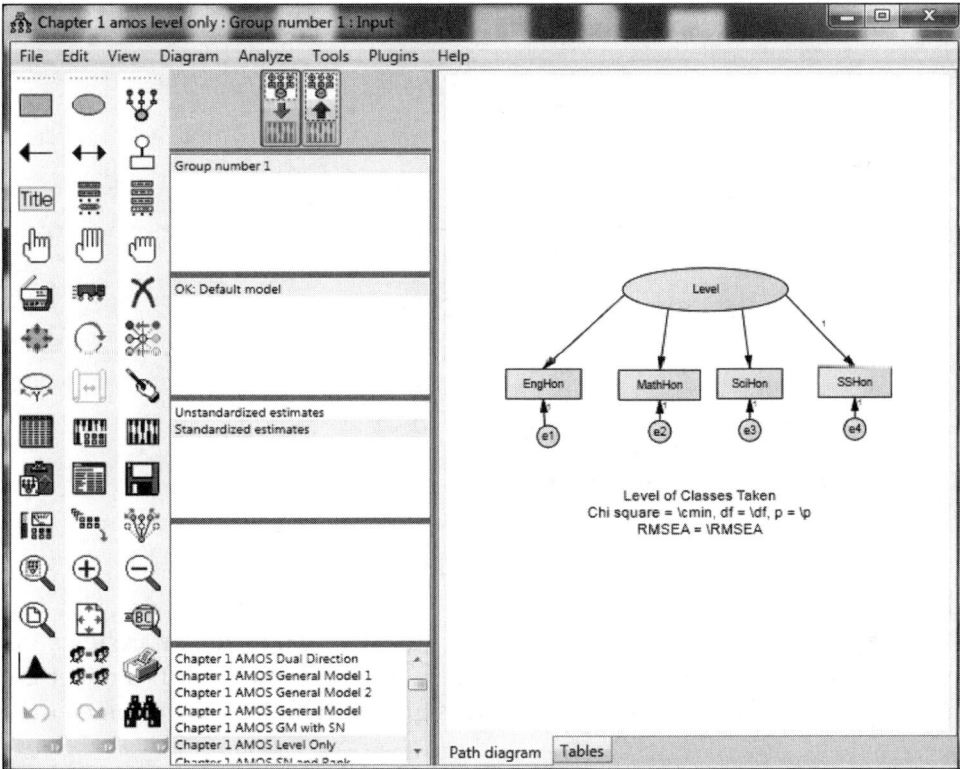

Figure 1-27: The AMOS interface

Notice the large collection of icons on the left including trucks, magic wands, and binoculars. AMOS has a very different interface than SPSS Statistics. The basic idea is if we can successfully draw a diagram that represents our model, AMOS will take care of most of the details. You can probably guess the use of the tools, for example that the truck involves moving and the copier involves copying. We will be extremely light on details regarding the mechanics of drawing. We will focus instead on revisiting our narrative from earlier in the chapter interpreting increasingly sophisticated models and comparing them to the models we build in SPSS Statistics. The idea is that if you become intrigued—and I hope you do—you will seek out ways to learn to draw diagrams including using the AMOS User's Guide.

Let's take a closer look at the diagram and add in some of the calculations performed by AMOS as shown in Figure 1-28. In AMOS the variables shown as rectangles are observed variables. You will recognize our four level variables. Ovals (or circles) are unobserved variables. Level is our unobserved, or latent, variable as measured by four observed variables. Notice that the arrows are drawn pointing away from the unobserved variable. The four other variables are error terms. The values at the upper right-hand corner of our four rectangular observed variables are our communalities that we saw in the factor analysis output in Figure 1-25. The values adjacent to the arrows are the factor loadings, also in Figure 1-25, which were the correlations of the four variables with the factor. In this case, just as before, the factor is our latent variable Level.

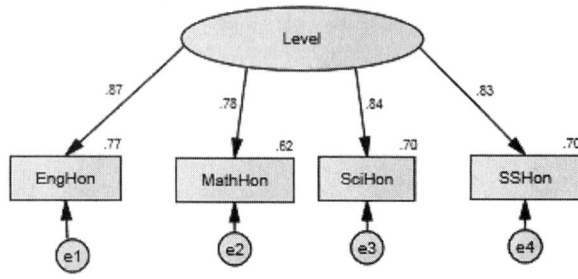

Level of Classes Taken
Chi square = 2.296, df = 2, p = .317
RMSEA = .026

Figure 1-28: An AMOS version of our factor analysis

Goodness of fit statistics is an important topic in AMOS. The text below the diagram includes two of these statistics, which we will discuss now; later in this chapter you see more goodness of fit statistics. The Chi square tests the null hypothesis that the model fits the data, so we do not want to reject the null hypothesis. The fact that the p value is greater than 0.05 is welcome news.

The Chi square is one of the most widely reported tests even though it has issues. The most important concern is that when one has a few hundred cases or more, virtually all models will fall below 0.05. Our sample size of 222 is about right to avoid this particular problem, so the result is meaningful.

The RMSEA (Root Mean Square Error of Approximation) is among the more widely reported measures of fit. Experts differ on acceptable values, but most consider values below 0.05 to represent good to excellent fit. We are well below that threshold. As we will see later we can build confidence intervals around RMSEA and further extend our use of this test. This aspect of RMSEA will be discussed, along with other measures of fit, in the "Adding S/N to the General Model and Revisiting Fit" section later in this chapter.

In all of these examples, the AMOS graphics .amw files are provided. You will not have to draw the diagrams. Table 1-3 at the end of the chapter recaps all of the AMOS diagrams and the .amw file names. In order to navigate the .amw files, you will need to know about three key features of the interface: switching between input and output diagrams, recalculating estimates, and viewing text. All three are shown in Table 1-2.

Table 1-2: Some important icons

ICON	NAME	FUNCTION
	View input/output path diagram	Toggles between drawing mode and results. Choose the icon on the right of the pair to see the results. Below these two icons in the center of the screen you can choose standardized or unstandardized estimates.
	The "abacus": Calculate Estimates	If any changes are made to the input diagram, results will have to be recalculated.
	View Text	The measures of fit are found in the text output.

The General Model

Now let's move closer to the research hypothesis. Recall that for now we will follow the lead of the researchers who collected the data. Our hypothesis is that both "level" and S/N predict "readiness" as measured by the PSAT. At the beginning of this chapter, we started with S/N and a simple T-test. With AMOS, it makes more sense to show an example of the "general model" before adding S/N. The general model is essentially like a regression, but with latent variables as both the dependent and the independent. Consider Figure 1-29. Shown is Chapter 1 amos general model 1.amw.

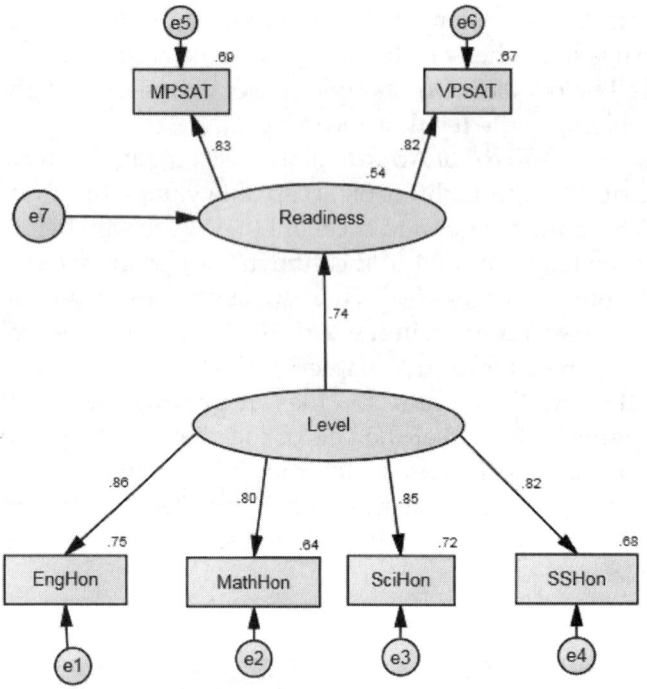

Level of Classes Taken
Chi square = 20.028, df = 8, p = .010
RMSEA = .082

Figure 1-29: Our "General Model"

Below the menu options Tools and Plugins (Figure 1-27) are two rectangular buttons (see also Table 1-2). The one on the left is the "input path diagram" and the one on the right is the "output path diagram." For the remainder of the chapter we will be looking only at the output. In the output mode, one can choose either unstandardized or standardized estimates. The standardized estimates are shown in Figure 1-29, which is otherwise similar in many ways to Figure 1-26.

The idea is that "Level" (as predicted by our four observed honors variables) is predictive of "Readiness" (as predicted by our two observed PSAT subscales). The goodness of fit tests are mediocre at best. The Chi square is significant at 0.01, which means the model doesn't fit well. The RMSEA would be considered mediocre or borderline. We won't worry too much about this since our hypothesis includes S/N. Also, the 0.54 shown above Readiness is the R Squared of Level predicting Readiness.

Before moving on to a model with S/N, let's tie up a couple of loose ends. Chapter 1 amos general model 2.amw (not shown) is provided with the book's downloads for your reference. It has the directionality in the opposite direction compared to our model in Figure 1-29. Note that the goodness of fit statistics are the same. A better way to test the directionality will be to build a model with both directions, and we will do just that in the "The Direction of Causality" section later in this chapter.

Second, let's briefly discuss the magnitude of the coefficient. To see that, we would request the unstandardized estimates (not shown), which reveals that the coefficient of Level on Readiness is 17.17. This means that the presence of honors is worth about 17 points on the PSAT scale (or 170 on the SAT scale). If one isn't careful, it is easy to get a bit mixed up. Because we are predicting a latent trait composed of two subscales, the coefficient is in the metric of a single subscale, not the combined score. So, the impact on combined score would be about twice that. Consider two figures showing regression results in SPSS Statistics to clarify this.

I've modified the PercHonors variable by dividing by 100 to give it a range of 0 to 1 instead of 0 to 100. This is consistent with how the data in AMOS is being handled because it is using the four observed variables (which are coded 0/1). Note that the weight for VPSAT is 15.210 (Figure 1-30), and the weight for PSAT is 28.998 (Figure 1-31).

Coefficients^a

Model		Unstandardized Coefficients		Standardized Coefficients		
		B	Std. Error	Beta	t	Sig.
1	(Constant)	33.455	1.106		30.256	.000
	PercHonors_1	15.210	1.454	.576	10.460	.000
a. Dependent Variable: VPSAT						

Figure 1-30: Estimating a verbal effect using regression

Coefficients^a

Model		Unstandardized Coefficients		Standardized Coefficients		
		B	Std. Error	Beta	t	Sig.
1	(Constant)	66.075	1.817		36.365	.000
	PercHonors_1	28.998	2.389	.633	12.136	.000
a. Dependent Variable: PSAT						

Figure 1-31: Estimating a combined score effect using regression

Adding S/N to the General Model and Revisiting Fit

We have a few more experiments to make using AMOS, but we've reached an important milestone. We are about to add S/N to the general model, which will test the original hypothesis. In a sense we've come full circle since the results we explored in Figure 1-19. The results with S/N added are shown in Figure 1-32. I've chosen the unstandardized estimates this time so that we can compare the impact of our two predictors, Level and S/N. Remember that we have to double the coefficients to get a rough idea of the impact on combined score, and multiply that by 10 to translate into the SAT scale. In short, while

16.5 is much larger than 3.03, the impact of S/N is non-trivial. If we switch to standardized (not shown) we discovered the R2 has climbed only a little to .57. It is a small but non-trivial increase. The goodness of fit tests are better, but not great. The Chi square is borderline, but on the wrong side of 0.05. The RMSEA is low enough to be a borderline fit.

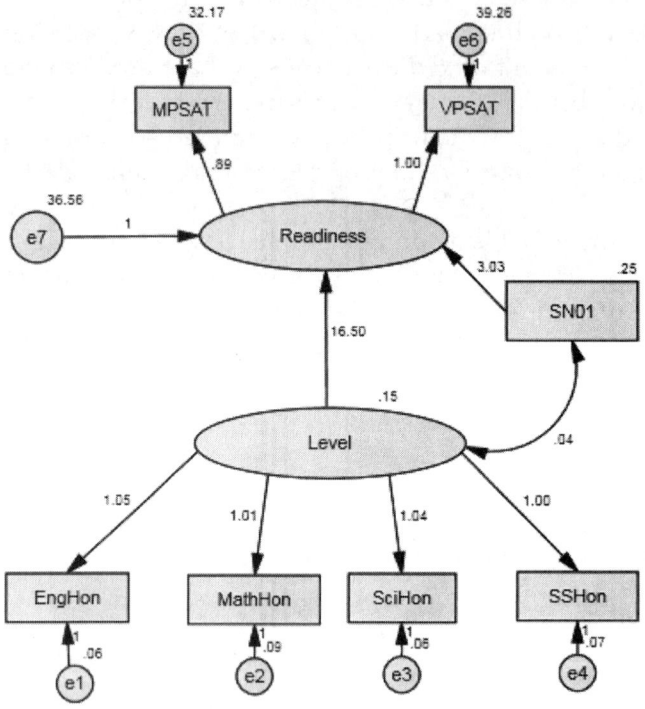

Level of Classes Taken
Chi square = 21.598, df = 12, p = .042
RMSEA = .060

Figure 1-32: General Model with S/N

This model represents our original hypothesis: Honors classes help prepare students for the kinds of "tricky" questions (that force skills to be applied in unexpected ways) that they will encounter on the PSAT and that the intuitive learning style offers an added advantage on those kinds of questions. This is a good time to dig deeper and examine more measures of fit. The subject could easily fill a chapter, and a large chapter at that. The sheer wealth of options can make this one of the more intimidating topics to those new to SEM and AMOS. We will limit ourselves to just a few more options, and in

Table 1-4, at the very end of the chapter, there will be a summary of some of the fit measures for the more important AMOS models that are explored in this chapter. In order to see more fit measures we will switch to the Text Output as shown in Figure 1-33.

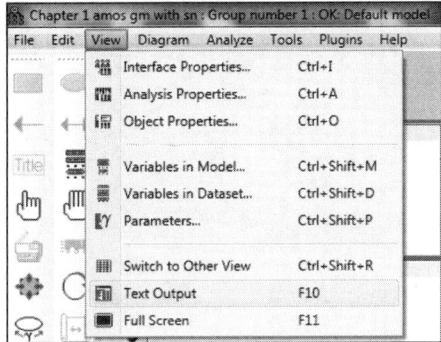

Figure 1-33: The View menu

Once in the text output, expand the Model Fit section as shown in Figure 1-34.

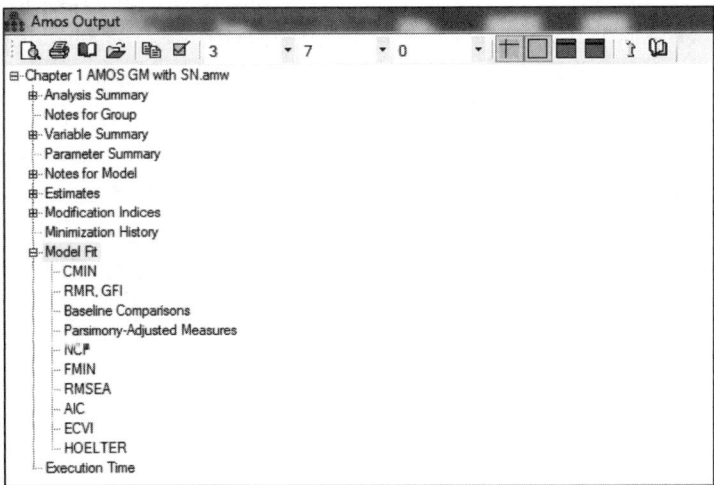

Figure 1-34: Outline pane of the AMOS Text Output

The options are extensive, sometimes to the point of being intimidating. Figure 1-35 shows only the top portion including the CMIN measures that we will discuss, and the TLI (Tucker Lewis Index), which is found under Baseline Comparisons.

Model Fit Summary

CMIN

Model	NPAR	CMIN	DF	P	CMIN/DF
Default model	16	21.598	12	.042	1.800
Saturated model	28	.000	0		
Independence model	7	828.445	21	.000	39.450

RMR, GFI

Model	RMR	GFI	AGFI	PGFI
Default model	.132	.973	.937	.417
Saturated model	.000	1.000		
Independence model	14.255	.381	.175	.286

Baseline Comparisons

Model	NFI Delta1	RFI rho1	IFI Delta2	TLI rho2	CFI
Default model	.974	.954	.988	.979	.988
Saturated model	1.000		1.000		1.000
Independence model	.000	.000	.000	.000	.000

Parsimony-Adjusted Measures

Model	PRATIO	PNFI	PCFI
Default model	.571	.557	.565
Saturated model	.000	.000	.000
Independence model	1.000	.000	.000

NCP

Figure 1-35: Top portion of Model Fit Summary

Further down are two pieces of output that we will include in our discussion. RMSEA, a particularly important one, is shown in Figure 1-36, and the Hoelter is shown in Figure 1-37.

RMSEA

Model	RMSEA	LO 90	HI 90	PCLOSE
Default model	.060	.011	.100	.303
Independence model	.417	.393	.442	.000

Figure 1-36: RMSEA results

HOELTER

Model	HOELTER .05	HOELTER .01
Default model	216	269
Independence model	9	11

Figure 1-37: Hoelter results

All of the fit statistics results for the measures of fit that we discuss are summarized for four of our AMOS models to prevent you from having to look up all of them with a scratch pad in hand. That information is shown in Table 1-4 at the very end of the chapter.

We've already discussed the significance of the Chi-square and its sensitivity to sample size. CMIN/DF, which is simply the Chi-square divided by the degrees of freedom, is among the oldest measures of fit in SEM. It is worth mentioning primarily because it is an ingredient in other more elaborate measures of fit. CMIN/DF ratios that approach 1 are desirable as that would assure a non-significant p-value. Our value of 1.8 is not too bad, but notice that it is not quite low enough to grant us a non-significant p-value. The Tucker Lewis Index (TLI) is one of several that include Chi-square and DF as ingredients, but with an adjustment favoring parsimony. A good TLI value will approach 1.0, but from the other direction. A score of .9 is considered acceptable, and a score above .95 is considered good. Our value of .979 is promising.

Let's revisit RMSEA. As a measure of error, smaller is better. A lower bound of the confidence interval (LO 90) would be nice because it would indicate that an error of zero is within the confidence interval. We don't quite achieve that, but it is rather low at .011. It would also be nice if the upper bound (HI 90) were low enough that it would be under our upper limit for RMSEA itself. Since we like RMSEA to be under a value more like .08, we don't quite achieve that either. However, over the years rules of thumb for RMSEA have sometimes allowed for an RMSEA as high as our value so it isn't too bad. Our p-value of .042 (which we've already discussed) is testing whether our error is significantly greater than zero. PCLOSE is an interesting test—it is testing whether or not our error is greater than .05. So rather than testing for perfect fit, it is testing for "close" fit. Our PCLOSE is non-significant so we don't have to reject the null hypothesis of a close fitting model. In short, this is good news.

There is certainly no shortage of creative fit measures in SEM. The Hoelter is an interesting test—it tells us what sample size would have been low enough to get a p value above 0.05 on our chi-square. We just barely fell below 0.05 on our p-value. We also know that a large enough sample size will guarantee this outcome, and a small enough sample size will guarantee that we are above 0.05. If it is a very low number (under 200 or so) we would conclude that our model wasn't capable of being saved by a smaller sample size. However, our value of 216 is just a few cases below our sample size of 222. This would be considered information in favor of our model. Note that it is only relevant when the p-value is significant, so it has been marked as N.A. (not applicable) for one of the models in Table 1-4 at the end of the chapter.

Revisiting the Other Covariates

Much earlier in the chapter, we considered sex and class rank as covariates. Let's see if adding those to our model will be helpful. Figure 1-38 adds sex to the model we just saw in Figure 1-32. The initial reaction, just from looking at the caption, is that is not a better fitting model. The p-value is much smaller, and the RMSEA is larger. These are unstandardized values as they were in Figure 1-32 so we can see that the parameter estimate for S/N has barely moved from 3.03 to 2.82. We don't have any hypothesis that sex and S/N are explaining the same variance, but it seems like our earlier model was better. If you are curious about some of the other fit measures they are listed in Table 1-4 at the end of the chapter. For instance, the TLI is above .95, an acceptable value, but the fit measures have all moved in the wrong direction.

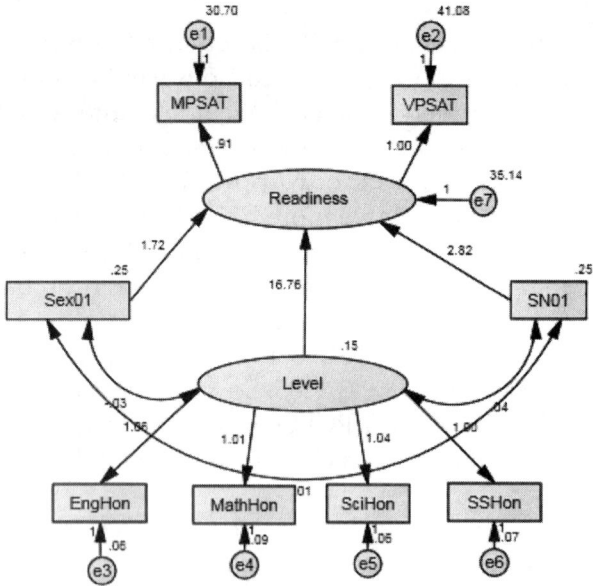

PSAT and Difficult Level of Classes Taken with both SN and Sex
Chi square = 33.563, df = 16, p = .006
RMSEA = .070

Figure 1-38: General Model with S/N and sex

An attempt with class rank instead of sex has performed a bit better as shown in Figure 1-39. The p-value is low, but the RMSEA is nearly as good as our hypothesized model in Figure 1-32. The model is not listed in Table 1-4, but it is a fairly good model. Note that the parameter estimate for S/N has not moved, now at 2.92, but it does not appear that rank and S/N are competing for the same variance. The most straightforward conclusion is to stick with our working hypothesis and leave sex and rank out.

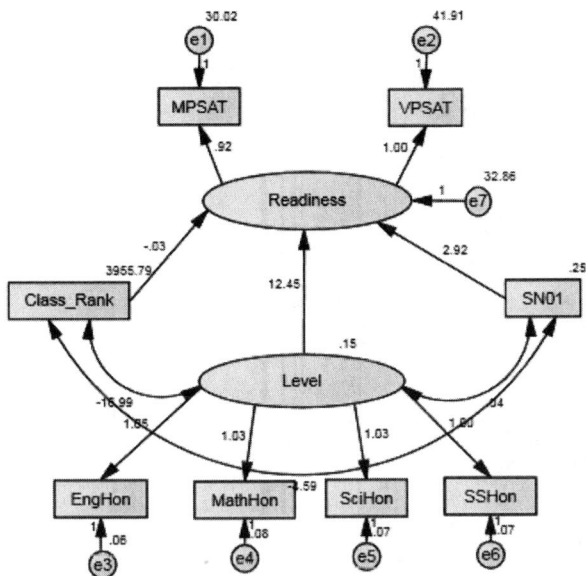

PSAT and Difficult Level of Classes Taken with both SN and Rank
Chi square = 29.303, df = 16, p = .022
RMSEA = .061

Figure 1-39: General Model with S/N and rank

The Direction of Causality

A fascinating option with SEM and AMOS is to explore directionality by considering both directions in the same model. Felson and Bohrnstedt did a famous study in 1979 using this technique that is always shown in the AMOS documentation (Felson, R.B. & Bohrnstedt, G.W. "'Are the good beautiful or the beautiful good?' The relationship between children's perceptions of ability and perceptions of physical attractiveness." *Social Psychology Quarterly*, 42, 386–392. 1979). They studied whether there was a two-way causation between academic ability and perceived attractiveness. We will use a similar approach (Figure 1 40) but our question will be whether readiness predicts level, or level predicts readiness or perhaps it is a two-way causation. The logic behind a "downward" causation would be that bright students take tougher classes and therefore also get better scores. The logic behind an "upward" causation would be the argument made by the researchers who collected the data that the nature of the preparation in honors classes was better preparation for the kinds of ambiguity found in some PSAT questions. The results are shown as standardized scores to aid in direct comparison.

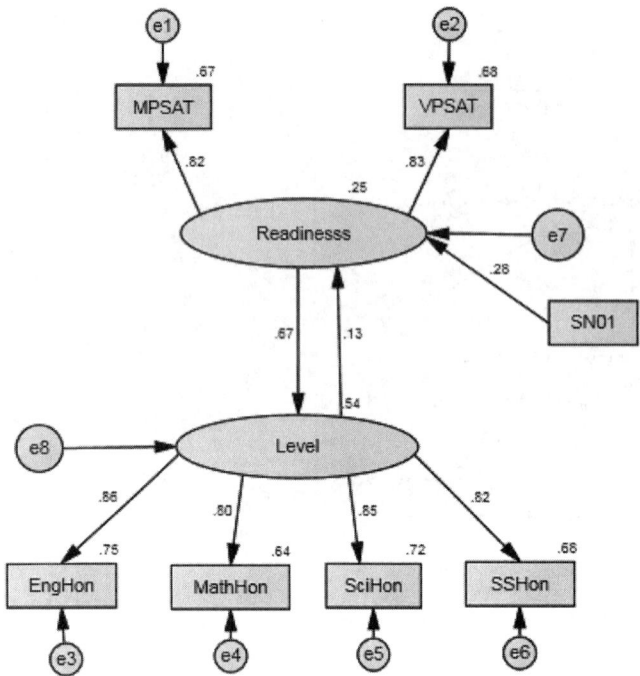

PSAT and Difficult Level of Classes Taken with SN
Chi square = 21.598, df = 12, p = .042
RMSEA = .060

Figure 1-40: Dual causality

The results are clear—the magnitude of one is much greater than the other. The evidence for readiness causing level is much stronger. The natural next experiment is to build the model with the causality in only one direction as shown in Figure 1-41. The result is quite strong. All of the fit measures are improved. It is not that dramatic a departure from the original hypothesis in an important respect. The nature of the study was to see if the S/N difference was significant, which it appears to be. Notice that the nature of this diagram is that S/N has a direct effect on readiness, and only an indirect effect on level.

The p-value is non-significant. The RMSEA is the best so far. The TLI (shown in Table 1-4) is the best so far at .983. And the LO 90 of the RMSEA is 0 (also in Table 1-4). So we've come full circle. We've established a significant effect of S/N on the PSAT after starting with a simple t-test and after much exploration and a modification to our hypothesis regarding the direction of causality. In the following two tables, we recap our AMOS models. Table 1-3 shows all of the models and their .amw file names. Table 1-4 recaps the measures of fit for four of the models.

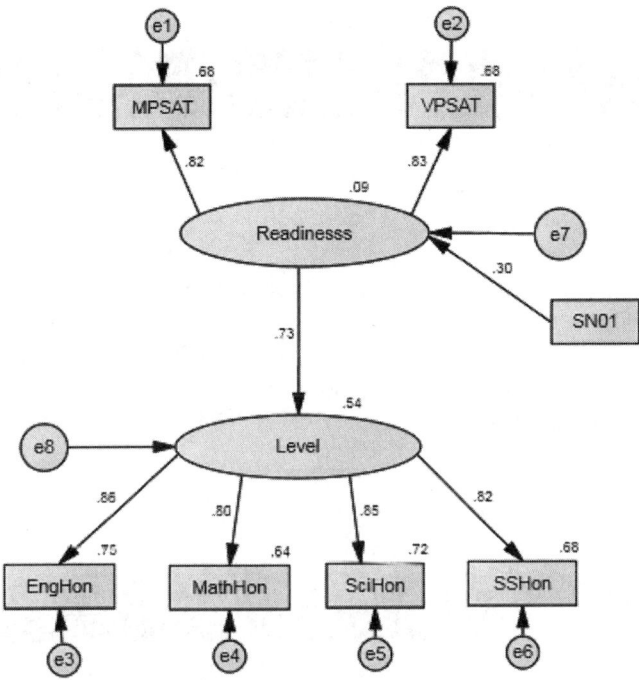

PSAT and Difficult Level of Classes Taken with SN
Chi square = 21.739, df = 13, p = .060
RMSEA = .055

Figure 1-41: Our best model

Table 1-3: A Summary of the AMOS Models

	QUESTION	FIGURE	AMOS GRAPHICS FILE
Level only	Can we establish an unobserved variable using the four level variables?	Figure 1-28	Chapter 1 AMOS level only.amw
General Model 1	Is our unobserved variable "level" predictive of another unobserved variable, "readiness"?	Figure 1-29	Chapter 1 AMOS general model 1.amw
General Model 2	Could the causality go in the opposite direction?	Not Shown	Chapter 1 AMOS general model 2.amw
GM with S/N added	Is SN an additional significant predictor of readiness?	Figure 1-32	Chapter 1 AMOS GM with SN 2.amw

Continues

Table 1-3 (*continued*)

	QUESTION	FIGURE	AMOS GRAPHICS FILE
GM with S/N and Sex added	Is Sex a significant predictor?	Figure 1-38	`Chapter 1 AMOS SN and sex.amw`
GM with S/N and Rank added	Is Rank a significant predictor?	Figure 1-39	`Chapter 1 AMOS SN and rank.amw`
Dual Direction Model	Which direction of causality best fits the data?	Figure 1-40	`Chapter 1 AMOS Dual Direction .amw`
"Best" Model	Does the dual direction model inspire a different option?	Figure 1-41	`Chapter 1 AMOS Best Model.amw`

Table 1-4: A Summary of the Fit Measures for Four of the Models

	GENERAL MODEL 1	GM WITH SN	GM WITH SN AND SEX	"BEST" MODEL
DF	8	12	16	13
P value	.010	.042	.006	.060
CMIN/DF	2.504	1.800	2.098	1.672
TLI	.972	.979	.963	.983
RMSEA	.082	.060	.070	.055
LO 90	.038	.011	.036	.000
HI 90	.129	.100	.104	.095
PCLOSE	.104	.303	.144	.375
Hoetler 0.05	172	216	174	N.A.
Figure	Figure 1-29	Figure 1-32	Figure 1-38	Figure 1-40

THE PROBLEM OF UNIDENTIFIED MODELS

This chapter has shown a collection of Amos models that can be estimated, but this is not true of all the models you might think of. Amos models estimate their parameters, which correspond to arrows in the diagrams, from the correlations or covariances of the observed variables in the model. Those correlations and covariances are determined, in theory, by the structure of the model and the parameter values. If that relationship is unique, i.e., there is only one possible representation in terms of the parameters, the model is said to be *identified*. If, however, there are multiple sets of parameter values that imply the same correlations or covariances, then the parameters cannot be uniquely determined, and the model is said to be *unidentified* or *underidentified*. We are not used to thinking about this in a simple regression model, which is actually a simple Amos model too, but such a model might be written as

$$Y = \alpha + \beta X + \delta\epsilon, \quad Var(\epsilon) = \sigma^2$$

where ϵ is the unobserved error term. We cannot estimate both δ and σ because only the combination matters, i.e., has an observable effect. In the regression model, therefore, we fix δ at 1 with no loss of generality.

In more complicated models such as those in this chapter, there are additional unobserved or *latent* variables. Since latent variables don't come with observable correlations, enough constraints such as setting $\delta = 1$ above or removing arrows in the model diagram need to be imposed to identify and estimate the model. At a minimum, there must be as many observable correlations or covariances as there are parameters. Amos will indicate in the text output if the model is probably unidentified, which parameters are unidentified, and how many additional constraints need to be imposed.

Monte Carlo Simulation and IBM SPSS Bootstrapping

In an ideal world, we would have the time and funds to obtain information from an entire population we're interested in, and then we could draw our conclusions; in the real world, this is rarely ever the case. Instead we have to rely on samples, and because of this, we want to ensure that our samples are representative of the population. In addition, because we are using samples rather than a whole population, the statistical techniques we use have assumptions that should be met so that these techniques are performing at their optimal level. However, there are occasions when traditional assumptions either do not hold or there is uncertainty in the sample values. To help alleviate these problems, IBM SPSS Statistics added two advanced statistical techniques that allow users to estimate statistics (like the mean, standard deviation, and so on): Bootstrapping, in version 18, and Monte Carlo Simulation, in version 21. SPSS Bootstrapping is a module, but Simulation is available to all users of SPSS Base.

The basic idea behind bootstrapping is that instead of obtaining additional samples from the population, we create additional samples by resampling data (with replacement) from the original sample. Each of the created samples will follow the same data distribution of the original sample, which in turn, follows the population. Bootstrapping also pertains to situations where the exact sampling distribution of the statistics is unknown or we have only asymptotic results. Monte Carlo simulation, on the other hand, starts by working with a particular distribution function (defined by specific model parameters), and we generate many samples so that we can compute the statistics of each sample and see how the statistics are distributed across the samples. The main difference is that with Simulation we are resampling input (independent variables) in order to generate distributions of the dependent variable. Simulation also lets us do what-if analysis. In the case of bootstrapping, we are using resampling to build a sampling distribution around a sample statistic to estimate the magnitude of uncertainty.

NOTE Bootstrapping is discussed again at the start of the second half of the chapter, which is dedicated to the topic.

Monte Carlo Simulation

Monte Carlo simulation is a computerized mathematical technique that allows researchers to account for risk in data analysis and decision making. This technique samples values at random from the input probability distributions. Each set of samples is called an iteration, and the resulting outcome from that sample is recorded. Monte Carlo simulation does this hundreds or thousands of times, and the result is a probability distribution of possible outcomes. In this way, Monte Carlo simulation provides a much more comprehensive view of what may happen. It tells you not only what could happen, but how likely it is to happen. That is, it estimates the entire distribution of the outcomes, not just, say, the conditional mean as regression would do.

There are two main uses for Monte Carlo simulation: generating simulated data and assisting in the development of predictive models. I mainly use Monte Carlo simulation to create new datasets. This way I can create variables, and specify their relationships, to show students different statistical techniques. The most common way to use Monte Carlo simulation, however, is to use it in conjunction with predictive models. For example, a model like linear regression requires that you have a set of known variables to predict an outcome. In many real-world situations, however, the predictor variables are not known with certainty, and users are interested in accounting for that uncertainty in their models.

Monte Carlo simulation models uncertain inputs with probability distributions and the simulated values for those inputs are generated by drawing from those distributions. The simulated values are then used in the predictive model to generate an outcome.

Monte Carlo Simulation in IBM SPSS Statistics

Before we access the data that we will use in this chapter, let's take a look at the initial available options for Monte Carlo simulation.

Select the Analyze menu, and then choose Simulation.

As shown in Figure 2-1, there are four options to perform Monte Carlo simulation. The options to Select SPSS Model File, Type in the Equations, and Create Simulated Data are collectively known as the Simulation Builder. This is an advanced interface for users who are designing and running simulations. It provides the full set of capabilities for designing a simulation, saving the specifications to a simulation, specifying output and running the simulation. The option to Open an Existing Simulation Plan is known as the Run Simulation dialog. This is designed for users who have a simulation plan and primarily want to run the simulation. It allows you to modify settings that enable you to run the simulation under different conditions, but does not provide the full capabilities of the Simulation Builder for designing simulations. In our case we will use the Select SPSS Model File option, because this is the most common way to use Monte Carlo simulation to assist with predictive modeling. Often in the real world, an expert designs the simulation model, and a business analyst uses that model with variations in the assumptions.

NOTE An IBM SPSS model file is an XML file that contains model PMML (predictive model markup language) created from IBM SPSS Statistics.

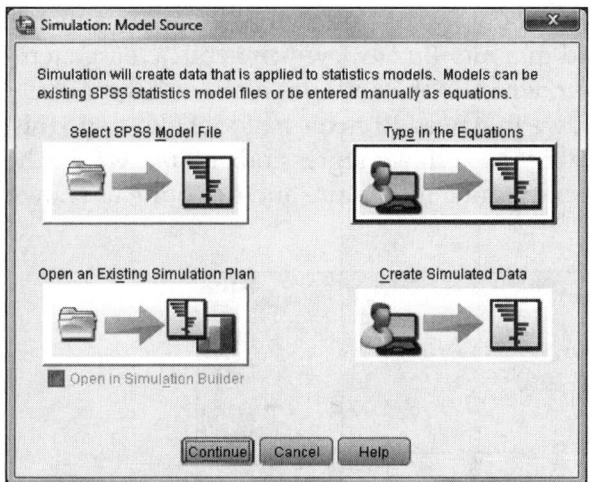

Figure 2-1: Simulation: Model Source dialog

Creating an SPSS Model File

In this example, we address the following research question: A business owner has historical data for portable fan purchases in his store. He also has information on the average temperatures for his store's location. Based on previous research, he knows that temperature is related to fan purchases. Unfortunately, he lives in an area where there is a lot of uncertainty in temperature, because temperature varies greatly. How many portable fans does he need in inventory so that at any moment he can provide fans to at least 75% of his customers? To access this data, open the dataset `Fans.sav` (see Figure 2-2).

	units	temp	discount
1	2700	90	.42
2	1875	96	.32
3	1200	72	.48
4	1320	48	.44
5	2100	90	.41
6	1350	90	.36
7	1875	90	.40
8	975	72	.07
9	1275	90	.40
10	1350	72	.45
11	1650	96	.42
12	1200	48	.30

Figure 2-2: Fans dataset

Notice that the data file in Figure 2-2 only has three variables: *units*, which is the number of portable fans sold in a month; *temp*, which is the average temperature in a month; and *discount*, which is the discount offered that month.

Before we create a simulation, we first need to create a model file. To do this, we will use linear regression. We are using linear regression because we will be predicting the number of units sold from temperature and discount, as shown in Figure 2-3.

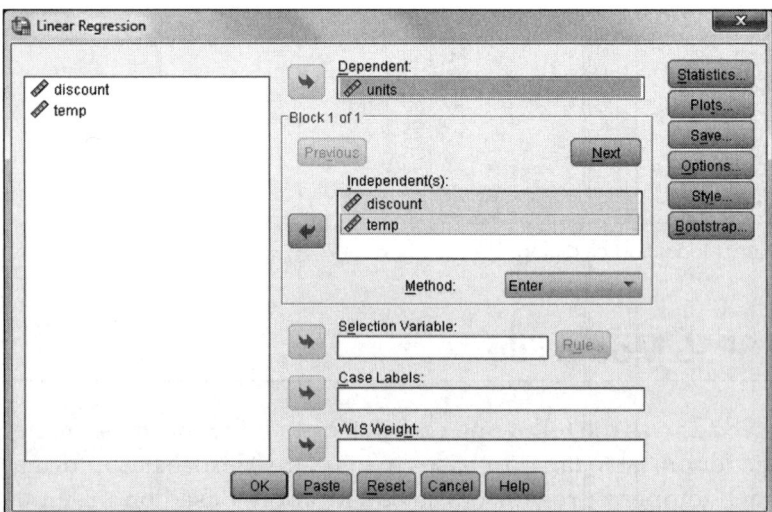

Figure 2-3: Completed Linear Regression dialog

1. Click the Analyze menu, and choose Regression ➪ Linear.
2. Within the Linear Regression dialog:
    ■ Place the variable Units into the Dependent box.
    ■ Place the variables Temp and Discount into the Independent(s) box.
3. Click Save.

   The Save dialog allows users to create and save a model file, which can then be used by the simulation dialog.
4. Click Browse.
5. Name the file Simulation, as shown in Figure 2-4.

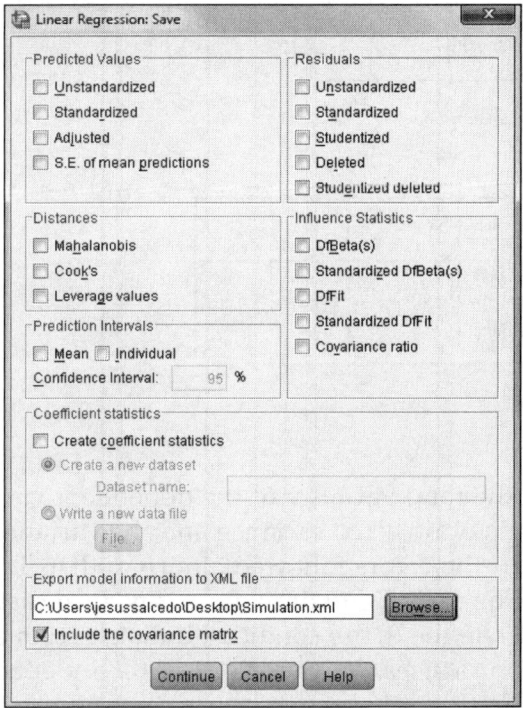

Figure 2-4: Completed Linear Regression: Save dialog

NOTE   Not every statistical technique produces PMML model files. The following are all the models supported by the simulation procedure: Linear Regression, Generalized Linear Model, General Linear Model, Binary Logistic Regression, Multinomial Logistic Regression, Ordinal Multinomial Regression, Cox Regression, Tree, Discriminant, Two-step Cluster, K-Means Cluster, and Neural Net.

6. Click Continue.
7. Click OK.

Figure 2-5 shows the linear regression results. We can see that we have a statistically significant model that accounts for about 43% of the variation in the number of portable fans sold. We can further see that both predictors are statistically significant.

Model Summary

Model	R	R Square	Adjusted R Square	Std. Error of the Estimate
1	.655[a]	.429	.426	600.820

a. Predictors: (Constant), temp Average Monthly Temp, discount Monthly Discount

ANOVA[a]

Model		Sum of Squares	df	Mean Square	F	Sig.
1	Regression	126782031.7	2	63391015.84	175.606	.000[b]
	Residual	168940995.3	468	360985.033		
	Total	295723026.9	470			

a. Dependent Variable: units Number of Fan Units sold

b. Predictors: (Constant), temp Average Monthly Temp, discount Monthly Discount

Coefficients[a]

Model		Unstandardized Coefficients		Standardized Coefficients	t	Sig.
		B	Std. Error	Beta		
1	(Constant)	-1221.608	165.398		-7.386	.000
	discount Monthly Discount	1736.355	271.075	.224	6.405	.000
	temp Average Monthly Temp	28.783	1.601	.629	17.975	.000

a. Dependent Variable: units Number of Fan Units sold

Figure 2-5: Linear regression results

It is important to note that the total variance of the dependent variance comes from two sources: the equation error variance and the variance due to the independent variables. If the errors followed a normal distribution, we could use the estimated error variance to draw from a normal distribution with that variance to generate the entire conditional distribution of the dependent variable. Simulation focuses the variations of the independent variables in the equation.

A model like this is certainly useful, because we can now estimate the number of portable fans we would sell in a month. However, this model does not answer the original question that we had, which is: How many portable fans do we need in inventory so that at any moment we can provide fans to at least 75% of the customers? To answer this question, we will use Monte Carlo simulation:

1. Click the Analyze menu, and choose Simulation.

2. Click Select SPSS Model File (since we now have a model file).

3. Click Continue.

4. Navigate to the Simulation model file that we just created.

5. Click Open.

To run a simulation, each input in the predictive model must be specified as either fixed or simulated. Fixed inputs are those whose values are known and remain constant for each case generated in the simulation. Simulated inputs are those whose values are uncertain and will be generated by drawing from a specified probability distribution.

If historical data is available for the inputs to be simulated, the distributions that most closely fit the data can be automatically determined, along with any correlations between those inputs. To do this, verify that each of the model inputs (Input column) is matched up with the correct field (Fit to column) in the active dataset.

6. Click Fit All.

The closest fitting distribution and its associated parameters are displayed in the Distribution column along with a plot of the distribution superimposed on the historical data. As shown in Figure 2-6, a triangular distribution was chosen for each field.

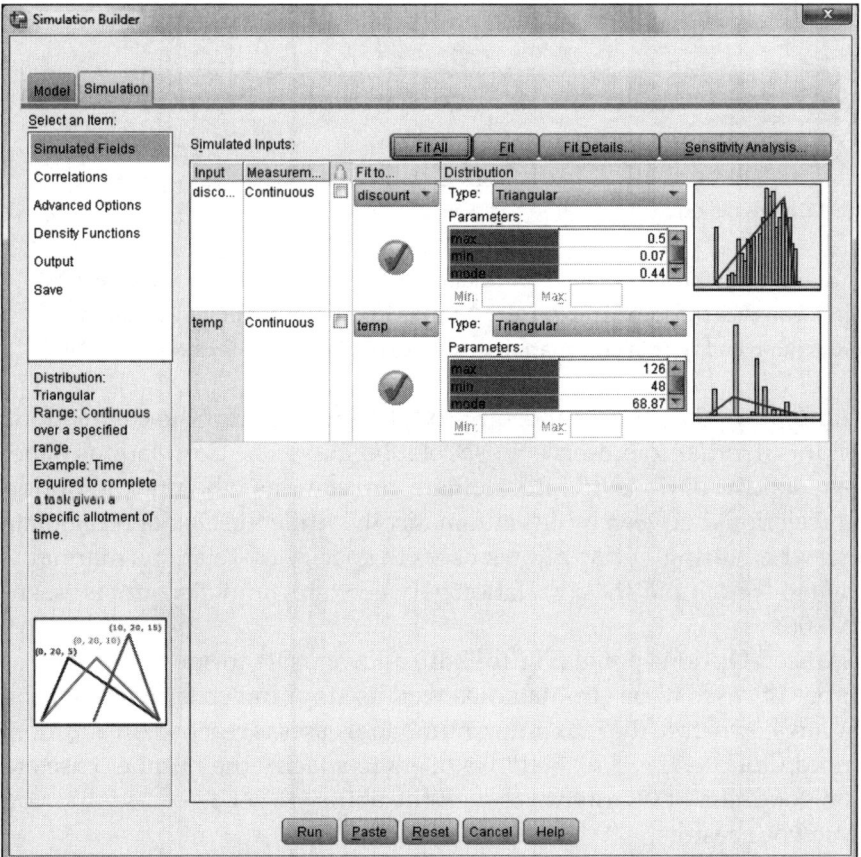

Figure 2-6: Simulated Fields panel

NOTE You can also manually specify distributions or correlations if historical data is not available or if you require specific distributions or correlations.

The Fit Details dialog displays the results of automatic distribution fitting for a particular input. Distributions are ordered by goodness of fit, with the best fitting distribution listed first. As shown in Figure 2-7, the Triangular distribution had the best fit for the input Temp.

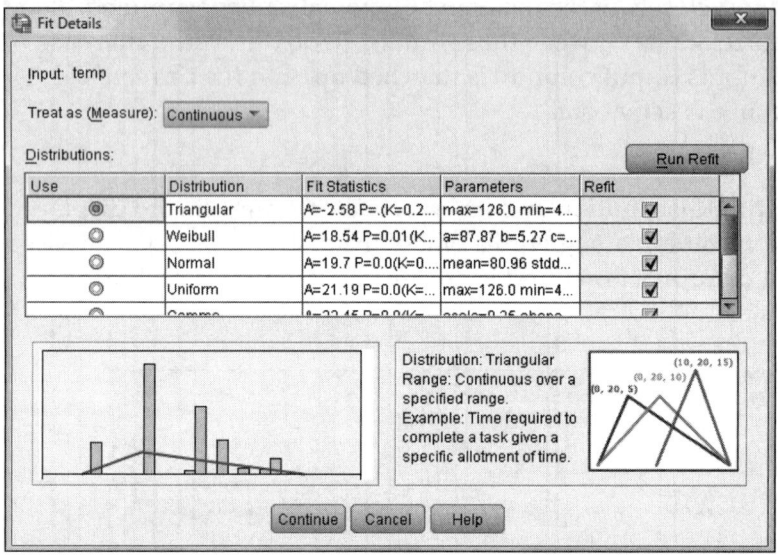

Figure 2-7: Fit Details dialog

NOTE Although in the initial simulation dialog we chose the option to select an SPSS model file, if you click the Model tab (Figure 2-8), notice that at this point you can still change your mind and type in an equation or create simulated data without a model.

When simulating data, it is important to take into account the correlations between inputs in order to preserve those relationships. The Correlations panel (Figure 2-9) has two options: the Recalculate correlations when fitting option specifies correlations between inputs automatically, while the Do not recalculate correlations when fitting option allows users to specify correlations manually. Notice that in our example, the correlation between temp and discount is essentially zero (-.06).

The Advanced Options panel (Figure 2-10) allows users to specify the maximum number of cases to be simulated as well as stopping criteria so that the simulation can stop before the maximum number of cases is reached. In addition, the Advanced Options panel also allows users to specify the number cases to use and the goodness of fit criteria, as well the ability to set a seed so that you can replicate your results.

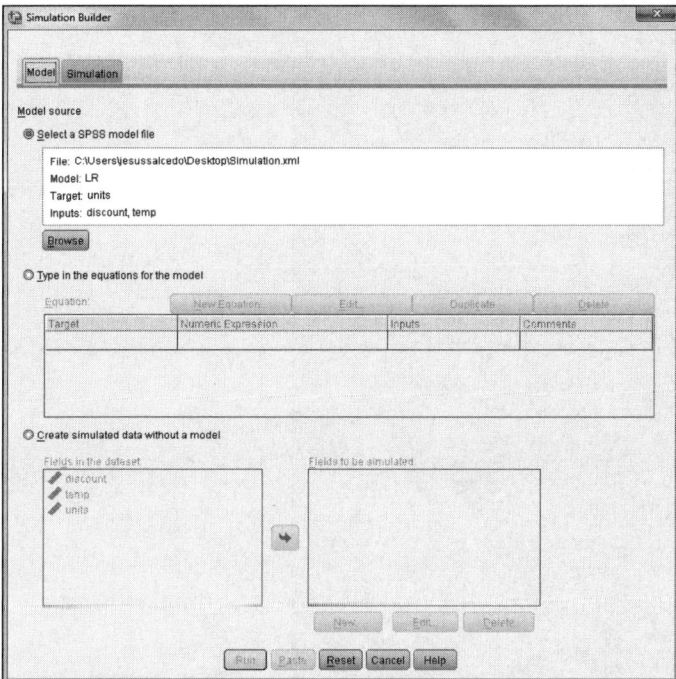

Figure 2-8: Model tab

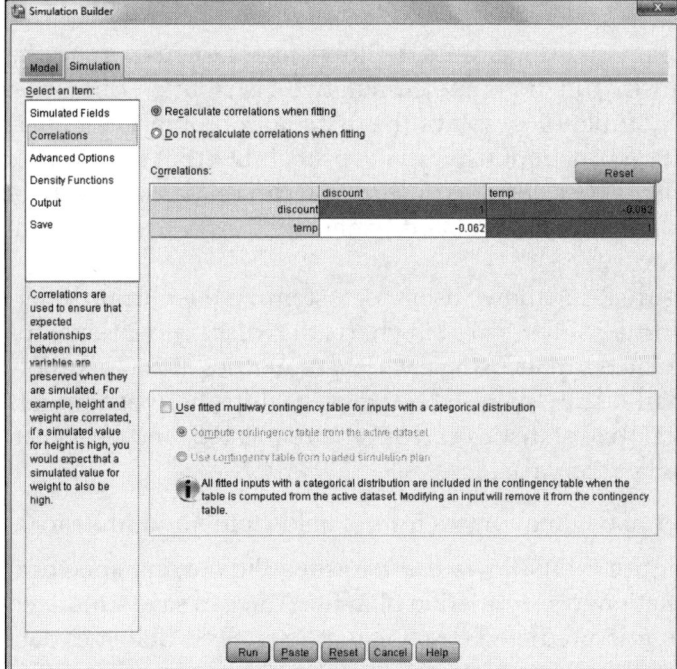

Figure 2-9: Correlations panel

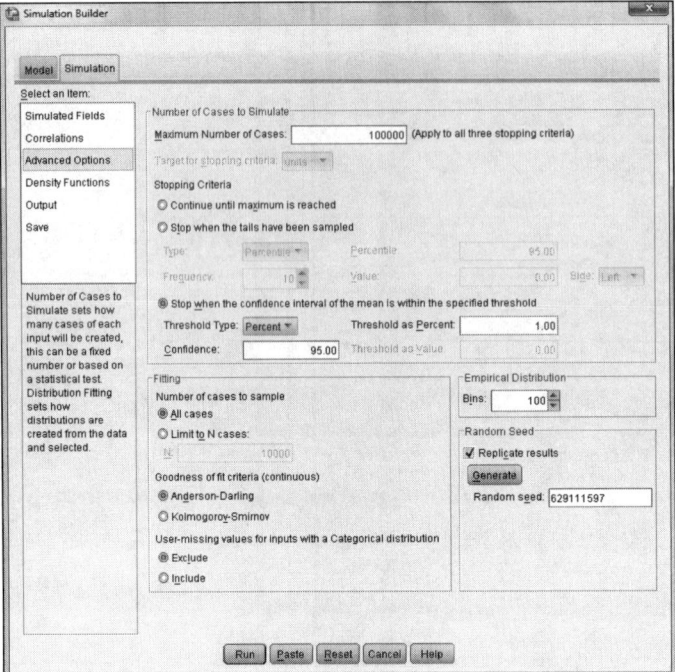

Figure 2-10: Advanced Options panel

The Density Functions panel (Figure 2-11) allows users to customize the output for probability density functions and cumulative distribution functions.

The probability density function displays the distribution of target values. The cumulative distribution function displays the probability that the value of the target is less than or equal to a specified value. You can request a variety of vertical reference lines to be added to probability density functions and cumulative distribution functions.

The Output panel (Figure 2-12) allows users to customize the output generated by the simulation. Tornado charts are bar charts that display relationships between targets and simulated inputs using a variety of metrics. Box plots allow users to view outliers, while scatterplots show relationships between targets and inputs. Various descriptive statistics can also be requested, and users can change the display format of the variables.

1. Change the number of decimal places for the fields temp and units to 0.

    The Save panel (Figure 2-13) allows users to save the current specifications for your simulation to a simulation plan file. You can save simulated inputs, fixed inputs, and predicted target values to an SPSS Statistics data file, a new dataset in the current session, or an Excel file. Note that this is generally not recommended as these files can be very large.

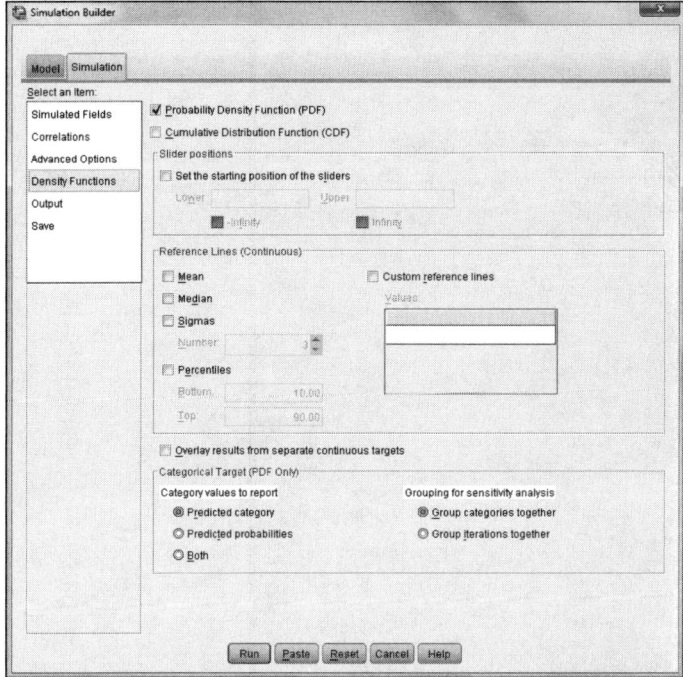

Figure 2-11: Density Functions panel

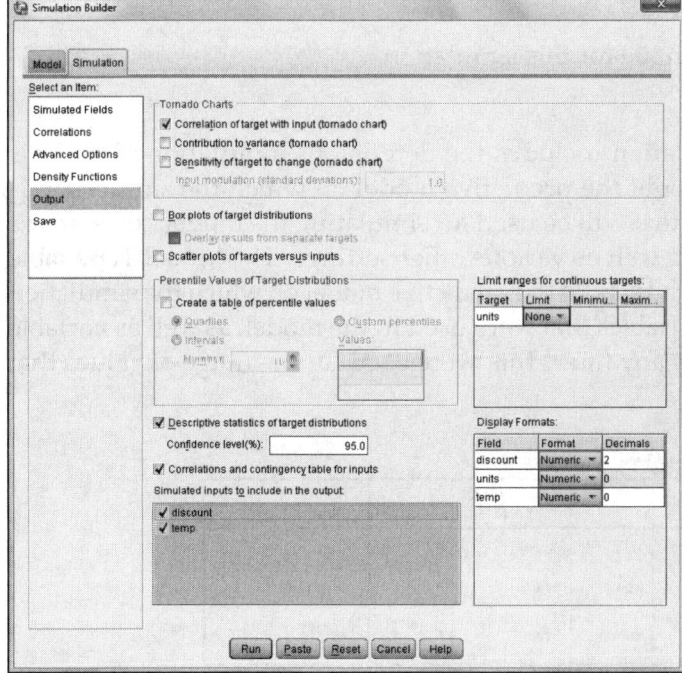

Figure 2-12: Output panel

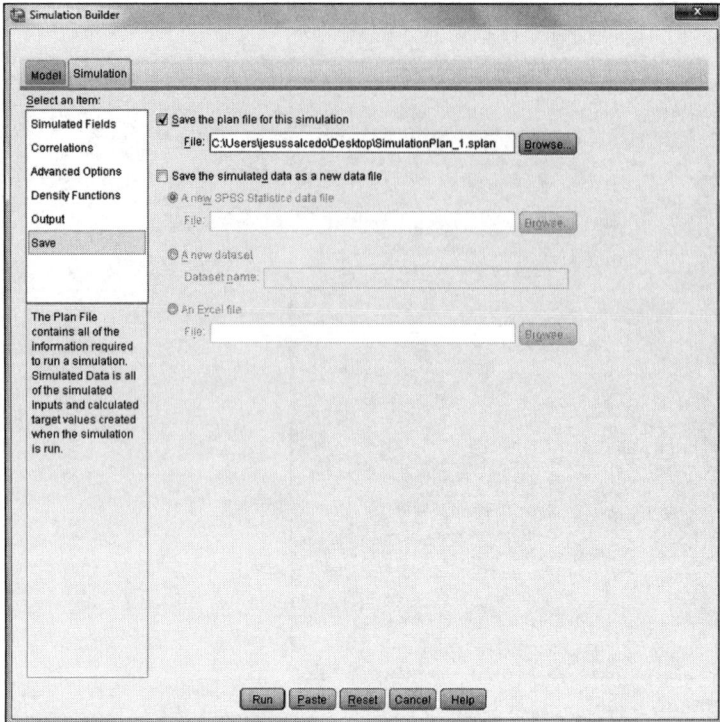

Figure 2-13: Save panel

2. Click Save the plan file for this simulation.

3. Click Run.

Output from a simulation includes the details of a simulation plan. This includes information about the predictive model on which the simulation is based, the distributions that will be used for simulating the inputs, correlations between those inputs, as well as various other settings. The Model Type table (Figure 2-14) displays details about the predictive model on which the simulation is based. It shows the variables that were used in the model, as well as variable properties. It also shows any filters that were used for the range of values that were simulated.

Model Type: Linear Regression

	Label	Simulation Role	Type	Measurement Level	Format	Filters Min	Max
discount	Monthly Discount	Input	Numeric	Scale	F,2	.	.
temp	Average Monthly Temp	Input	Numeric	Scale	F	.	
units	Number of Fan Units sold	Target	Numeric	Scale	F	.	

Figure 2-14: Model Type table

The Inputs Distributions table (Figure 2-15) displays the distribution associated with each input along with the parameters of the distribution. In our example, a triangular distribution was used and parameters shown are those required by a triangular distribution. The values shown here are values taken directly from our data.

Input Distributions

			Parameter Value
discount	Triangular	min	.07
		max	.50
		mode	.44
temp	Triangular	min	48
		max	126
		mode	69

Figure 2-15: Input Distributions table

The Correlations table (Figure 2-16) displays the correlations between the inputs that are to be simulated. In our example, there really is no correlation between the inputs temp and discount.

Correlations

	discount	temp
discount	1.000	-.062
temp	-.062	1.000

Figure 2-16: Correlations table

The Stopping Criteria table (Figure 2-17) displays the criteria that will be used for determining when to stop generating simulated cases. In our example, cases will be generated until the confidence interval of the mean of the target is within 1% of the mean value, when using a 95% confidence interval. In addition, we are also specifying that the maximum number of cases to be generated is 100,000.

Stopping Criteria

Maximum cases		100000
Mean within specified precision	Target	units
	Threshold	1.0%
	Confidence level	95.0%

Figure 2-17: Stopping Criteria table

The rest of the output displays the results of the actual simulation run. The Simulation Summary table (Figure 2-18) displays the maximum allowable number of cases, the number of cases that were actually generated, and whether any specified stopping criteria was achieved. In our example, we did achieve the stopping criteria and only 3262 cases were simulated.

Simulation Summary

Maximum cases	100000
Total simulated cases	3262
Stopping criteria achieved	Yes

Simulation Plan File: C:
\Users\jesussalcedo\Desktop\Simula
tionPlan_1.splan
Cases may be filtered because of
either targets or inputs that are
outside of the specified ranges.
Filtered cases are not included in the
simulated cases count.

Figure 2-18: Simulation Summary table

The Descriptive Statistics of Scale Targets (Figure 2-19) and Descriptive Statistics of Scale Inputs (Figure 2-20) tables display summary information about the distribution of the values of the simulated target and inputs. Notice that we obtain descriptive statistics like the mean, standard deviation, minimums, and maximums.

Descriptive Statistics of Scale Targets

	Mean	Std. Deviation	Median	Minimum	Maximum	95% Confidence Interval for Mean		Percentiles	
						Lower	Upper	5.0%	95.0%
units	1693.682	493.506	1648.664	429	3218	1676.746	1710.618	952.576	2554.687

Figure 2-19: Descriptive Statistics of Scale Targets table

Descriptive Statistics of Scale Inputs

	Mean	Std. Deviation	Minimum	Maximum
discount	.334	.096	.07	.50
temp	81.128	16.353	49	125

Figure 2-20: Descriptive Statistics of Scale Inputs table

It is always a good idea to make sure that your simulated values cover the entire range associated with your distribution. In our case it seems as though the range of simulated values are very similar to the range of the actual values.

The Correlations table (Figure 2-21) displays the correlations between the simulated inputs. As with the actual data, there really is no correlation between the inputs temp and discount.

Correlations

	discount	temp
discount	1.000	-.036
temp	-.036	1.000

Correlations between simulated
inputs may differ from
correlations specified for those
inputs in the simulation plan.

Figure 2-21: Correlations table

Probability Density charts (Figure 2-22) display the distribution of the target. This way you can see the range of values for the target, and you can see what the probability is of a particular outcome occurring. As a default, reference lines are placed at the 5% and 95% points of the distribution. The table displays the probability in the three regions bounded by the reference lines. If you recall, the purpose of this analysis is have enough portable fans in inventory so that at any moment we can provide fans to at least 75% of the customers. To figure this out, we need to add in an additional reference line.

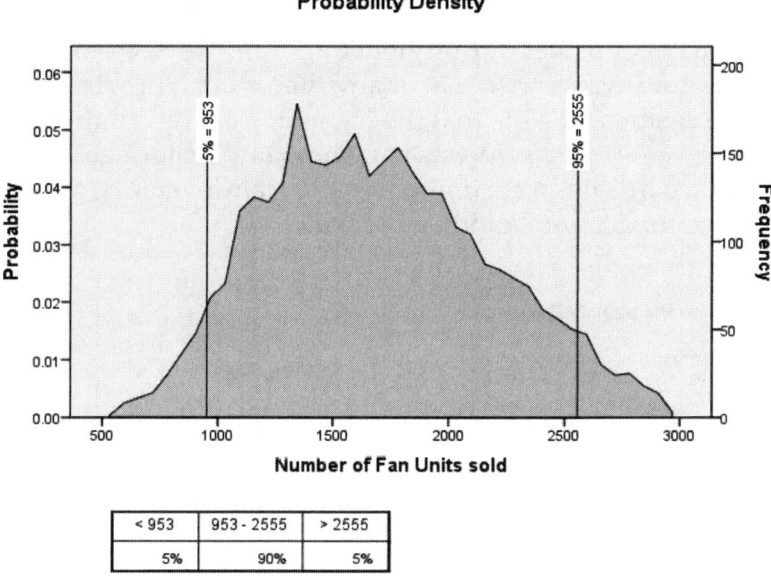

Figure 2-22: Probability Density chart

1. Double-click the Probability Density chart (to invoke the Graphboard editor).

2. Click Chart Options to open the dialog shown in Figure 2-23.

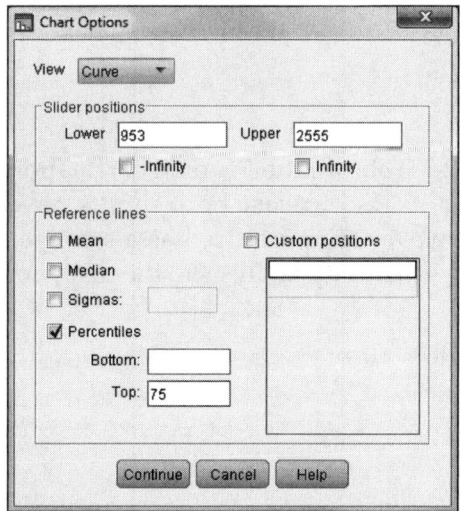

Figure 2-23: Chart Options dialog

3. Click Percentiles, and add the value **75** in the Top box.

4. Click Continue.

5. Close the Graphboard editor.

Notice that a new reference line has been added at the 75th percentile (Figure 2-24). We can now answer our original question: We need to have 2029 portable fans in our inventory so that at any time we can provide fans to at least 75% of the customers. Note that the regression analysis implicitly assumes that the number of units sold was not clipped by a shortage. If the data contained cases where sales were limited by available inventory, a technique that takes this into account would be needed.

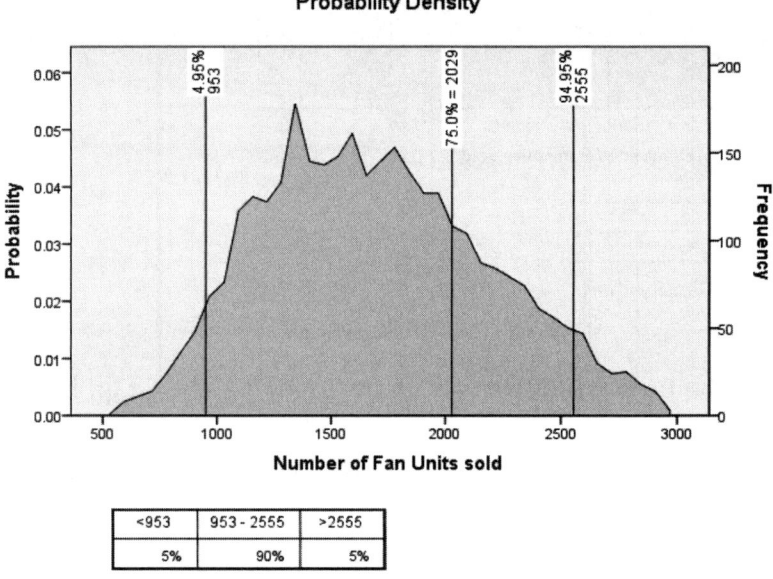

Figure 2-24: Edited Probability Density chart

The correlation tornado chart (Figure 2-25) shows the Pearson correlation between the target and its simulated inputs. In our case both inputs have a positive correlation with the target, however temperature has a stronger relationship than discount. You could do a sensitivity analysis to the discount as well.

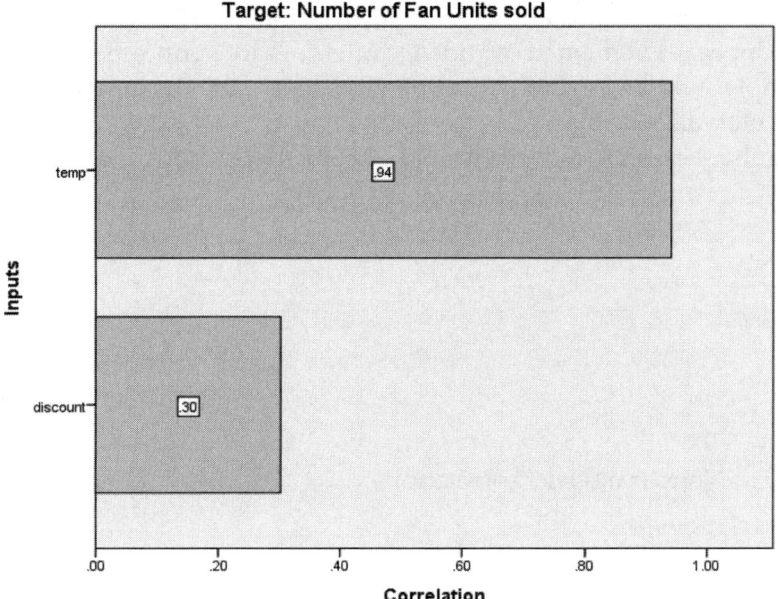

Figure 2-25: Tornado chart

IBM SPSS Bootstrapping

Resampling, as we have seen, is simply repeated sampling with replacement, drawing the resamples from your original dataset, thereby creating many and differing versions of that dataset. By default, IBM SPSS Statistics Bootstrapping creates 1,000 variant versions of a sample. Since you are resampling with replacement, a particular original case could appear once, not at all, or multiple times in any resample. With 1,000 resamples, you now have the raw material in the form of a sampling distribution, to calculate 1,000 different estimates of a statistic. It is then a simple matter to build a confidence interval and estimate sampling error around the statistics without making any distributional assumptions. No assumption of fitting the distribution to a Z, t, F, or any other known distribution is required. So, obviously this comes in handy when the assumptions are not met or the theoretical distribution of a statistic is not known or known only asymptotically. Another benefit is that this process can produce a confidence interval for virtually any statistic even if that particular statistic does not have a supported parametric confidence interval in SPSS. Unlike many other SPSS modules, the Bootstrapping module does not have a single set of menus, but rather appears as an extra option, in an extra sub dialog, in more than a dozen analysis menus. Confidence intervals around proportions, correlations, and many other statistics can be calculated, even if a confidence interval is not supported in the standard sub dialogs (if the Bootstrapping option is not available, the button does not appear). Even when confidence intervals are supported—as in the case of a simple standard mean—it is powerful to be able to compare the two confidence intervals side by side.

The following list shows procedures in IBM SPSS Statistics Base:

- Descriptives
- Frequencies
- Examine
- Means
- Crosstabs
- T-Tests
- Correlations/Nonparametric Correlations
- Partial Correlations
- One-Way
- Uni Anova
- Discriminant
- Binary Multi-Nomial Logistic Ordinal Regression

The next list shows procedures available if you have SPSS Bootstrap combined with the Regression or Advanced Statistics modules:

- **GLM:** IBM SPSS Advanced Statistics
- **Regression:** IBM SPSS Regression
- **Nominal Regression:** IBM SPSS Regression
- **Logistic Regression:** IBM SPSS Regression
- **GENLIN:** IBM SPSS Advanced Statistics
- **Linear Mixed Models:** IBM SPSS Advanced Statistics
- **Cox Regression:** IBM SPSS Advanced Statistics

The motivation behind bootstrapping to estimate uncertainty can be easily explained with a brief anecdote. I was once helping a water utility do reservoir-level forecasts. We were discussing how to handle a very unusual month. It was distorting the seasonal effect of that month of each year. The overwhelming temptation is to just drop the data point, and while that is sometimes a good move, it is not the only move. Also, in forecasting, dropping a data point is much less often an option than in some other techniques. I chimed in with the following notion. "A 50-year flood doesn't have to cause forecasting problems placed in the context of 50 years' worth of data, but a 50-year flood found in 36 months of data needs to be addressed in some way."

IMAGINARY REPETITIONS

When you are unaccustomed to resampling, it can seem a little unusual. We some-times forget that over many decades, the creation of sampling distributions through distributional assumptions has seemed odd to many influential statisticians. Sir Harold Jeffreys, a contemporary and intellectual sparring partner of R. A. Fisher, was among the most outspoken on this point. The following appears in *The Theory that Would not Die* by Sharon Bertsch McGrayne (Yale University Press, 2011). Note well that her book, and Jeffreys' point, is to critique the classical Fisherian approach (sometimes called frequentism) in favor of Bayesian analysis. Bootstrapping did not yet exist, but the quote still seems apropos given that we are considering sometimes using an alternative to the classical approach, the same classical approach that we are now so accustomed to that we rarely think of it in these terms.

Jeffreys thought it very strange that a frequentist considered possible outcomes that had not occurred. ... Why should possible outcomes that had not occurred make anyone reject a hypothesis? Few researchers repeated—or could repeat—an experiment at random many, many times. "Imaginary repetitions," a critic called them.

Bertsch McGrayne's discussion is based on Jeffreys' commentary in the early 1960s. Bootstrapping, as performed in the module, is attributed to Bradley Efron's *Bootstrap Methods: Another Look at the Jacknife* in 1979 (*The Annals of Statistics* vol.7 no.1: pp. 1–26).

Now, one doesn't use 50 years' worth of data to do forecasting, but the problem was that the unusual month represented 1/3 of the information on the month of October. The probability aspect of statistics is needed to determine how typical or atypical a sample data point is believed to be in the population. The data, without an analyst or local resident to interpret, would lead one to believe that such a flood would occur 1/3 of the time. A way to paraphrase my comment at the time is that more data would help. More data always helps puts outliers in a more accurate context. So how do you use more data when you don't have any more? Resampling, in a sense, is simply a way to generate more data. The name "bootstrapping," as in "pulling oneself up by one's bootstraps," makes explicit the seeming impossibility of making more data out of a single sample.

There are all kinds of reasons that our sample doesn't resemble the population perfectly. There are certainly numerous reasons why our samples don't resemble the distributions like the ones listed in statistical tables. But what if we had lots of samples? With multiple samples, we can build a distribution, and we wouldn't need the bell curve, or other distributions, to imitate the distribution by proxy. (Some have described what we do with known distributions as building sampling distributions through "imaginary repetitions" as discussed briefly in the sidebar.) The outliers, like the 50-year flood, might be found in some of the resamples, but the context provided by the other samples (resamples that did not contain the 50-year flood) dilutes the impact of the outlier. As analysts, we don't always have the benefit of personal experience (like being a local resident during a flood) to alert us to an outlier. Instead, we often struggle with the decision to keep it or drop it. Resampling, the core technique behind bootstrapping, puts outliers into a more proper context, removes the need to meet normality assumptions, and produces more robust statistics. It is not a panacea—biases and outliers will still affect us, and other assumptions remain required—but it is a great option when the standard options are problematic, and it is conceptually easy to explain the bootstrapping option to the audience of our analysis. Ultimately, it is just another way of determining what is typical, what is atypical, and how wide our confidence interval should be.

> **NOTE** The bootstrap is not a magic solution for a very small sample. In such samples it is not going to be all that accurate because there will not be much information about the distribution of the statistic available even with a large number of bootstrap replications. That is because the number of possible boostrap samples is too limited. The precision of the result is limited by the sample size regardless of the number of resamples. Also, if the boostrap results are very different from the results using classical methods, a hard look at the data may be beneficial.

Bootstrapping is also an interesting way to open the whole theme of this major section of the book. Why should we contemplate taking on an approach that is not the usual *Statistics 101* approach? One of the main motivations seems to be the avoidance of "breaking the rules," but we all know the normality assumptions are frequently not met. Why not avoid the assumptions altogether? In the case of bootstrapping, we might ponder an extreme solution. Why not always use bootstrapping and never have to worry about distributional assumptions again? The reluctance in years past would have certainly included the issue of computational intensity. Many analysts, who are mid-career now, grew up on home computers that were among the very first home computers. Our contemporary smart phones, and to a lesser degree even our microwaves and thermostats, would be serious competition for the oldest of them. I remember trying this kind of approach in SPSS during a seminar in the late '90s. A simple Crosstab calculation ran for a couple of hours and ultimately crashed. The same calculation now could easily run on my current laptop computer in just a few seconds. Imagine if one were trying to do it in the late '80s, or late '70s.

Of course, that is not the only concern. No one wants to have to complicate the narrative of their analysis write-up. But, in the case of bootstrapping, the approach is pretty straightforward. I've always thought, in fact, that understanding bootstrapping, and teaching the concept to our colleagues, really underscores what we are trying to do when we do meet distributional assumptions. It is impossible to understand and perform bootstrapping and not reflect on the magic number 1.96, and its role in determining the width of the 95% confidence interval around a simple mean. It makes normal distributions, and the tests that assume them, more tangible and less abstract. Some undergraduate textbooks have adopted this approach, notably *Mathematical Statistics with Resampling and R* by Laura M. Chihara and Tim C. Hesterberg (John Wiley & Sons, 2011), and the test presents the resampling method before the classical approach in the text. It may actually be easier to explain bootstrapping than classical Fisherian hypothesis testing to your colleagues in the workplace, especially if they are not already well grounded in the standard approach.

Proportions

At a bank with seven job categories, we are interested in looking at the distribution of those seven roles. A Frequencies table could certainly do the job, but it doesn't offer confidence intervals. If we wanted to know that the jobs were or were not related to other variables like gender or minority status we could also request a Chi-Square test of independence in the Crosstabs procedure, but again the confidence intervals would shed interesting light on the analysis. The Chi-Square would reveal whether the two variables (job role and gender, for instance) were not independent, but we might want to compare the confidence intervals of men and women on some of the roles. Bootstrapping allows us to add a confidence interval around dozens of tests that otherwise would not have them in SPSS Base. Note that CTABLES for version 24 does support some new confidence interval options that have not been available in CTABLES in past versions.

Let's first consider the simple distribution of the job roles in the Bank.sav dataset, found in the downloads for this chapter. (Note that the dataset referred to here is similar to, but not identical to a dataset that is used in some Help examples.) A simple Frequencies of the Employment Category variable (jobcat) with default settings reveals the data shown in Figure 2-26.

Employment category

		Frequency	Percent	Valid Percent	Cumulative Percent
Valid	Clerical	227	47.9	47.9	47.9
	Office trainee	136	28.7	28.7	76.6
	Security officer	27	5.7	5.7	82.3
	College trainee	41	8.6	8.6	90.9
	Exempt employee	32	6.8	6.8	97.7
	MBA trainee	5	1.1	1.1	98.7
	Technical	6	1.3	1.3	100.0
	Total	474	100.0	100.0	

Figure 2-26: Default frequencies report

In order to request the confidence intervals, we simply have to access the Bootstrap submenu within the Frequencies menu (see Figure 2-27). Keep in mind that the submenu will not appear without a license that includes the Bootstrap module. There are options within the submenu, but the most important is the check box that requests that bootstrapping be performed.

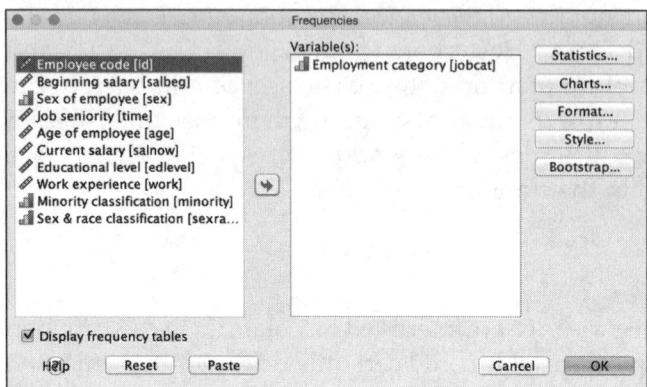

Figure 2-27: The Frequencies menu with the Bootstrap submenu

From within the submenu, request Perform bootstrapping as shown in Figure 2-28. The remaining settings can be left as the defaults.

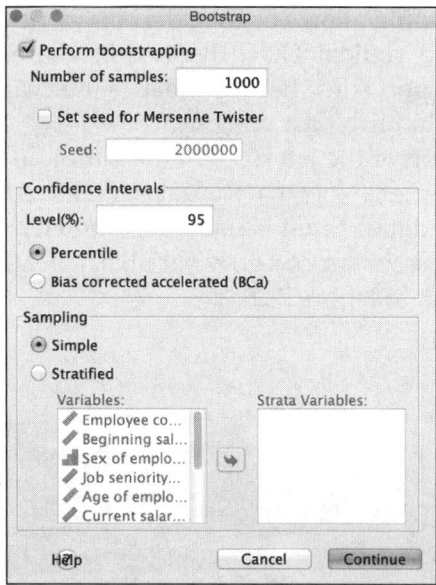

Figure 2-28: The Bootstrap submenu

The resulting output is rather straightforward. We have our Frequencies information, but with the addition of confidence intervals. In fact, four new columns have been appended, all related to the confidence interval. The bias indicates the magnitude of difference between the standard calculation and the bootstrap version. As shown in Figure 2-29, the Bias is near zero in every instance.

Employment category

		Frequency	Percent	Valid Percent	Cumulative Percent	Bootstrap for Percent[a]		95% Confidence Interval	
						Bias	Std. Error	Lower	Upper
Valid	Clerical	227	47.9	47.9	47.9	.1	2.3	43.2	52.3
	Office trainee	136	28.7	28.7	76.6	-.1	2.0	24.7	32.7
	Security officer	27	5.7	5.7	82.3	.0	1.1	3.8	7.8
	College trainee	41	8.6	8.6	90.9	.0	1.3	6.3	11.2
	Exempt employee	32	6.8	6.8	97.7	.0	1.2	4.4	9.1
	MBA trainee	5	1.1	1.1	98.7	.0	.5	.2	2.1
	Technical	6	1.3	1.3	100.0	.0	.5	.4	2.3
	Total	474	100.0	100.0		.0	.0	100.0	100.0

a. Unless otherwise noted, bootstrap results are based on 1000 bootstrap samples

Figure 2-29: Frequency table with bootstrap results

A common argument is made that we essentially have a census of current employees, obviating a confidence interval, but since this is a snapshot in time, there is a stronger argument that this is a sample drawn from a larger population of employees. This particular dataset reveals a difference in salary between men and women, and although we won't explore the salary issue at the moment, it raises the question of whether men and women at the bank are serving in similar or dissimilar roles. If so, is that a potential source of bias that could influence the salary distribution? Again, a Chi-Square could establish a lack of independence between the two variables, and in the case of this dataset, a Chi-Square would indeed show a lack of independence.

A more complete picture would include confidence intervals for both men and women so that we could compare them. A simple Frequencies will do the job. We simply have to Split on gender. The Data ⇨ Split File menu allows us to do just that. As shown in Figure 2-30, we will Compare groups based on Sex of employee (sex).

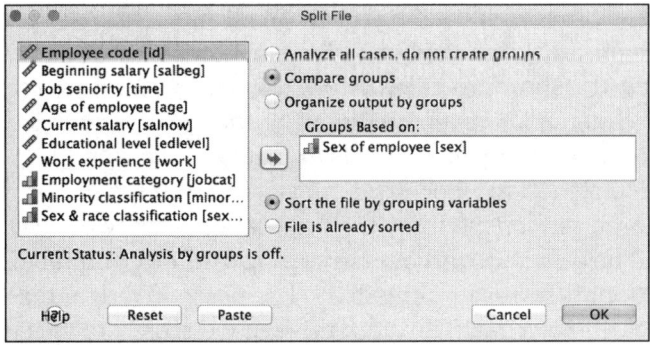

Figure 2-30: Split File menu

The results reveal more about the nature of the interplay between gender and job role (see Figure 2-31). In particular, it is interesting to identify the employment categories with overlapping confidence intervals and those that do not overlap. For instance, MBA Trainee clearly shows a larger number of men, but the small numbers make it hard to make an ironclad case that women are underrepresented as some of the bootstrap samples had just one male MBA Trainee (.4%), and some as many as three women (1.4%). Also noteworthy is that although the sheer number of Clerical is nearly the same (110 vs. 117), the proportions are quite different, and the confidence intervals built around the data for men and women just barely overlap. The confidence intervals for College Trainee and Office Trainee do not overlap, serving to draw more attention to them, especially College Trainee, which, lacking a large sample, might have been perceived as less interesting.

Employment category

Sex of employee			Frequency	Percent	Valid Percent	Cumulative Percent	Bootstrap for Percent[a]		95% Confidence Interval	
							Bias	Std. Error	Lower	Upper
Males	Valid	Clerical	110	42.6	42.6	42.6	−.1	3.1	36.8	48.8
		Office trainee	47	18.2	18.2	60.9	−.1	2.4	13.6	22.9
		Security officer	27	10.5	10.5	71.3	.1	1.9	7.0	14.3
		College trainee	34	13.2	13.2	84.5	.0	2.1	8.9	17.4
		Exempt employee	30	11.6	11.6	96.1	.0	2.0	7.8	15.5
		MBA trainee	4	1.6	1.6	97.7	.0	.8	.4	3.5
		Technical	6	2.3	2.3	100.0	.1	.9	.8	4.3
		Total	258	100.0	100.0		.0	.0	100.0	100.0
Females	Valid	Clerical	117	54.2	54.2	54.2	.1	3.3	48.1	61.1
		Office trainee	89	41.2	41.2	95.4	−.1	3.3	34.3	47.7
		College trainee	7	3.2	3.2	98.6	.0	1.2	.9	5.6
		Exempt employee	2	.9	.9	99.5	.0	.6	.0	2.3
		MBA trainee	1	.5	.5	100.0	.0	.5	.0	1.4
		Total	216	100.0	100.0		.0	.0	100.0	100.0

a. Unless otherwise noted, bootstrap results are based on 1000 bootstrap samples

Figure 2-31: Frequency table with bootstrap results and with a split applied

Bootstrap Mean

We've just seen an example of the Bootstrap allowing us to calculate a 95% confidence interval around a statistic that would simply not be available in frequencies otherwise. Now we will briefly consider the plain old mean. Obviously, we have numerous choices including the standard calculation, the trimmed mean, the M-estimators in the Explore menu, and even abandoning the mean for related statistics like the median. So why perform a bootstrap mean?

There are two sources of variation in a bootstrap mean. The first is sampling error, and if our sample is a biased lens to view the population, then we are in trouble. All techniques will be affected, and bootstrapping will offer no relief. The second source of variation is the resampling itself. The potential advantage of the bootstrap mean is that the data itself, through this second source of variation, is shedding light on the level of uncertainty concerning the mean, and this might be a superior approach to assuming that the data follows a particular theoretical distribution. In the standard approach, using standard error, we are simply using 1.96 as a multiplier to calculate the 95% confidence interval, and by doing so we are relying upon the truth of those distributional assumptions.

SPSS, in turn, relies upon us. While there are tests to check for distributional assumptions, they must be both requested and interpreted properly. SPSS will not warn us directly that we are relying upon assumptions that are not met. So, in short, the bootstrap mean cannot make our mean more accurate if our sample is biased, but it may give us a more accurate sense of our uncertainty around our mean. Figure 2-32 shows the Descriptives report from the Explore routine, but with the Bootstrap requested.

Descriptives

| | | Statistic | Std. Error | Bootstrap[a] | | 95% Confidence Interval | |
				Bias	Std. Error	Lower	Upper
solid waste (millions of tons)	Mean	.3801	.05715	.0036	.0564	.2829	.5035
	95% Confidence Interval for Mean — Lower Bound	.2645					
	95% Confidence Interval for Mean — Upper Bound	.4957					
	5% Trimmed Mean	.3323		.0086	.0502	.2555	.4532
	Median	.2865		.0042	.0482	.1929	.3679
	Variance	.131		.001	.062	.038	.270
	Std. Deviation	.36145		-.00927	.08640	.19457	.51914
	Minimum	.05					
	Maximum	1.97					
	Range	1.92					
	Interquartile Range	.27		.04	.10	.19	.53
	Skewness	2.616	.374	-.441	.750	.855	3.626
	Kurtosis	8.950	.733	-2.816	4.597	-.199	17.379

a. Unless otherwise noted, bootstrap results are based on 1000 bootstrap samples

Figure 2-32: Descriptives table with bootstrap results

The number of statistics capturing many aspects of the bootstrap sampling distribution that have confidence intervals around them is noteworthy. Normally, the standard error and the resulting confidence interval would only be calculated for three: Mean, Skewness, and Kurtosis.

Let's zero in on the mean itself in these results because it is the primary statistic that is calculated both ways. Note that the distance between the traditionally calculated lower bound is .1146 from the mean of .3801. As we would expect, the upper bound is exactly the same distance. This must be true because the lower bound and upper bound are not derived from the data directly—only the mean itself is. The bounds are merely a set distance from the mean as determined by our distributional assumptions. The resulting symmetry reveals nothing. It merely reflects back the nature of our method. The Bootstrap lower bound and upper bound are not symmetric, true to our skewed data. Fascinating, as well, is the presence of a confidence interval around the Trimmed Mean, and that it, as well, is not symmetric around the statistic. With skewed data such as this, the median is often the preferred choice. Isn't it nice to be able to report a confidence interval around the median?

Bootstrap and Linear Regression

We've seen in the previous section that bootstrapping cannot "fix" a biased sample. Rather, it sheds a different light on the level of uncertainty in our statistics, light that is truer to the nature of the data itself and unreliant on distributional assumptions. Now we have an opportunity to briefly investigate one of the most common and important techniques—Regression—through the lens of a highly problematic dataset–the `Waste.sav` dataset. It is small. It is highly skewed. Its issues with multicollinearity and suppression could serve as a case study in such problems, and that is precisely why it is an interesting example for our purposes. We will focus on just this one aspect: the difference in the assessment of uncertainty between the traditional approach and the bootstrapping approach. Let's begin with Figure 2-33 by orienting ourselves to the results using the traditional approach.

Coefficients[a]

Model		Unstandardized Coefficients		Standardized Coefficients	t	Sig.	95.0% Confidence Interval for B		Collinearity Statistics	
		B	Std. Error	Beta			Lower Bound	Upper Bound	Tolerance	VIF
1	(Constant)	121584.815	31680.944		3.838	.001	57201.391	185968.239		
	Industrial land (acres)	−52.486	17.913	−.232	−2.930	.006	−88.889	−16.082	.706	1.416
	fabricated metals (acres)	43.452	153.701	.045	.283	.779	−268.907	355.811	.178	5.626
	trucking and wholesale trade (acres)	250.324	88.553	.491	2.827	.008	70.363	430.285	.147	6.787
	retail trade (acres)	−859.706	376.371	−.439	−2.284	.029	−1624.584	−94.829	.120	8.311
	restaurants and hotels (acres)	13355.199	2281.798	1.083	5.853	.000	8718.028	17992.370	.130	7.712

a. Dependent Variable: waste_tons

Figure 2-33: Regression coefficients with standard confidence interval

The dependent variable is the amount of municipal waste as measured in tons. Each of the independent variables is the zoned use, in acres, of five different business types. Four out of five of the beta coefficients are significantly different than zero. The largest effect on the dependent variable is made by restaurants. Retail Trade, surprisingly, has a negative effect. Although we won't pursue it here, it doesn't take much detective work to reveal that something is amiss here. The correlation between Retail Trade and our dependent variable is actually positive. Either there is a powerful interaction or there is suppression (an insidious result of multicollinearity sometimes causing the sign of the coefficient to "flip"). Suppression, the culprit in this case, is a fascinating topic, but our concern at the moment is that the coefficient appears to be significant, and the very serious problems are appearing too subtly, especially to the untrained eye. While much smaller in effect, Industrial Land's negative coefficient draws attention to itself as well. The standardized coefficient for Restaurants and Hotels is above 1. The Collinearity Statistics are not extremely elevated, but they serve to increase concern. Alarm bells are sounding as to the trustworthiness of these coefficients, but more information is desirable, specifically an objective and accurate criterion around each coefficient that would allow us to quantify our concerns. Figure 2-34 shows the coefficients for the same regression model, but with bootstrap confidence intervals.

Bootstrap for Coefficients

Model		B	Bootstrap[a]				95% Confidence Interval	
			Bias	Std. Error	Sig. (2–tailed)		Lower	Upper
1	(Constant)	121584.815	10803.865	29171.764	.002		73649.418	188902.677
	Industrial land (acres)	-52.486	-7.961	95.675	.122		-268.636	141.718
	fabricated metals (acres)	43.452	165.378	320.146	.903		-583.829	728.734
	trucking and wholesale trade (acres)	250.324	34.185	210.849	.220		-120.838	677.298
	retail trade (acres)	-859.706	-383.783	791.696	.401		-2562.167	578.071
	restaurants and hotels (acres)	13355.199	220.244	3838.513	.001		4438.968	18256.165

a. Unless otherwise noted, bootstrap results are based on 1000 bootstrap samples

Figure 2-34: Regression coefficients with bootstrap confidence intervals

The bootstrap results seem to be just what we might desire. After all, what exactly becomes unstable when we do not meet distribution assumptions? The distributions themselves, the intervals and their widths, are the first to fail. The Bootstrap results actually show that only Restaurants and Hotels is consistently significant and positively correlated with the dependent variable. None of the variables are significant while negatively correlated with the dependent variable. The remarkable fact is that a single massive outlier (and there are plenty in this dataset) can cause a sign flip when the correlation is weak. You could explore these effects manually by deleting an observation, and observe the change in the regression results. This dataset, actually, can produce surprisingly varied results with the omission of a single case. Essentially, bootstrapping does this kind of experimentation systematically. Armed with this new evidence, our suspicions are confirmed, and we can proceed to look more carefully. All of the usual tricks come into play including the possible discarding of those outliers that are the most problematic, dropping independent variables, or transforming our independent variables. In short, while this second regression result is hardly the final word, and we would not be ready for publication, the bootstrap confidence intervals have proven their worth, providing a very different, and almost certainly more accurate sense of the level of certainty around these five coefficients.

Regression with Categorical Outcome Variables

Linear regression is one of the most widely used (and understood) statistical techniques. However, its typical use involves situations in which the outcome variable is continuous. Many situations in data analysis involve predicting the value of a nominal or an ordinal categorical outcome variable. For example, we may want to predict whether a student passes or fails a course, or we may want to predict a person's level of product satisfaction. In situations in which you have a nominal categorical outcome variable, researchers quite often use either binary or multinominal logistic regression.

In addition, regression is normally associated with the idea of having continuous predictor variables, so that we need to create dummy variables to represent categorical variables in a regression model. This, however, can become unmanageable when we have many categorical variables.

When researchers have an ordinal categorical outcome variable, they typically use either linear regression or logistic regression (in both cases ignoring the level of measurement of the variable). In these situations, it would be more effective to leave the variables in their original categories, yet still use them directly in regression, because with a categorical dependent variable, the linear regression assumptions are violated, and the results may be poor or, for nominal variables, meaningless.

Although logistic regression is certainly an extremely useful technique, the purpose of this chapter is to make you aware that other regression techniques are available, which in certain cases may be more appropriate than either linear or logistic regression. In particular, techniques have been developed to allow nominal and ordinal variables to be used directly in regression and to treat them not as interval-level variables, but at the appropriate scale on which they are measured.

Regression Approaches in SPSS

Generally, two approaches to regression have been taken:

- Treat the variables as nominal or ordinal and use various complicated functions to model the relationship between the outcome variable and the predictors (ordinal regression).

- Modify the values of the variables to create interval-level coding, then use these new values in standard linear regression (categorical regression).

The Regression submenu in SPSS Statistics contains various types of regression. However, in this chapter we focus on ordinal and categorical regression. Table 3-1 displays the different forms of regression that are available in SPSS Statistics (as built-in commands). Note that PLS is an extension command requiring the Python Essentials.

Table 3-1: Regression Techniques in SPSS Statistics

TECHNIQUE	GENERAL USE
Automated Linear Modeling	A version of linear regression that automatically prepares data to meet the assumptions of linear regression (transforms variables, trims outliers, creates dummy variables, and so on)
Linear	Used when you have a continuous outcome variable that is linearly related to one or more independent variables
Curve Estimation	Plots 11 different curve estimation regression models that allow for only one independent variable
Partial Least Square	Used when predictor variables are highly correlated or when the number of predictors exceeds the number of cases. It first extracts a set of latent factors that explain as much of the covariance as possible between the independent and dependent variables. Then a regression predicts values of the dependent variables using the independent variables.
Binary Logistic	Used in situations similar to a linear regression model, but the dependent variable is dichotomous
Multinomial Logistic	An extension of binary logistic regression where the dependent variable is not restricted to two categories
Ordinal	Used when you are predicting an ordinal-level dependent variable from several independent variables (these may be categorical or continuous)

TECHNIQUE	GENERAL USE
Probit	Used in situations where you have a dichotomous output that is influenced by levels of the independent variables. This procedure will allow you to estimate the strength of a stimulus required to induce a certain proportion of responses.
Nonlinear	Can create models with nonlinear relationships between independent and dependent variables, where you will need to define the equation that best captures the relationship
Weight Estimation	Linear regression assumes that variance is constant within the population under study. When this is violated and the differences in variability can be predicted from another variable, the Weight Estimation procedure can be used.
Two-Stage Least Squares	Linear regression assumes that errors in the dependent variable are uncorrelated with the independent variables. When this is violated, two-stage least-squares regression can be used.
Optimal Scaling (CATREG)	Quantifies categorical data by assigning numerical values to the categories, resulting in an optimal linear regression equation for the transformed variables

SPSS Statistics can perform both of the approaches mentioned in the introduction to this section. In the next few pages, we discuss both ordinal regression and categorical regression. However, before discussing the basics of ordinal regression, we first discuss the basics of logistic regression to provide a broader context.

Logistic Regression

Logistic regression is designed to use a mix of continuous and categorical predictor variables to predict a nominal categorical dependent variable. Logistic regression does not directly predict the values of the dependent variable. Instead, the logistic equation predicts the odds of the event of interest occurring. Specifically, the general equation for logistic regression is:

$$\ln(Odds) = \alpha + B_1 X_1 + B_2 X_2 + \cdots + B_k X_k$$

where the terms on the right are the standard terms for the independent variables and the intercept in a regression equation. On the left-hand side of the equation we have the natural log of the odds, and this quantity, ln(Odds), is called a logit. The logit function is actually one of a whole family of S-shaped functions, probit being the other well-known variant. As discussed in the following section, ordinal regression uses several link functions (for example, logit, probit) to relate the predictors to the outcome variable.

Ordinal Regression Theory

Ordinal regression (referred to as PLUM in syntax) is used when you are predicting an ordinal-level dependent variable from several independent variables (these may be categorical or continuous).

NOTE The ordinal regression procedure is part of the SPSS Statistics Base module.

When predicting ordinal-level responses, linear regression models do not work well because they assume the dependent variable is measured on an interval scale; therefore, linear regression models may not accurately reflect the relationships in the data. Some researchers apply linear regression to ordinal dependents, especially if the number of levels of the dependent is high (5 or 7). The underlying assumption of this practice, of course, is that the greater the number of levels, the more the variable approaches interval-level status. This assumption, however, may or may not be valid for given data.

Likewise, ordinal regression is preferable to multinomial logistic regression when predicting an ordinal-level variable because with this latter procedure, you lose the information contained in the ordering of the levels of the dependent variable, resulting in loss of statistical power.

Ordinal regression models are sometimes called cumulative logit models because ordinal regression typically uses the logit link function, though other link functions are available (as you see later in this section). When trying to predict cumulative probabilities for the categories, you fit a separate equation for each category of the ordinal dependent variable. Each equation gives a predicted probability of being in the corresponding category or any lower category.

For example, look at the distribution shown in Table 3-2. With no predictors in the model, predictions are based only on the overall probabilities of being in each category. The predicted cumulative probability for the first category, which equals the probability itself at this point, is 0.20. The prediction for the cumulative probability for the second category is 0.20 + 0.60 = 0.80. The prediction for the third is 0.20 + 0.60 + 0.20 = 1.00. The prediction for the cumulative probability for the last category is always 1, because all cases must be in either the last category or a lower category. Because of this, the prediction equation for the last category is not needed.

Table 3-2: Hypothetical Distribution of an Ordinal Dependent Variable

CATEGORY	PROBABILITY OF MEMBERSHIP	CUMULATIVE PROBABILITY
High Risk	0.20	0.20
Medium Risk	0.60	0.80
Low Risk	0.20	1.00

Ordinal regression is a special case of generalized linear modeling (GZLM) and identical parameter and model fit estimates can be obtained using the GZLM procedure, but the options vary somewhat between the ordinal regression procedure discussed here and GZLM (which can build many additional types of statistical models and therefore contains many options that do not apply, nor are necessary to ordinal regression).

Generalized linear models are a very powerful class of models, which can be used to answer a wide range of statistical analysis questions. The basic form of a generalized linear model is shown in the following equation:

$$\text{link}(\gamma_{ij}) = \theta_j - (\beta_1 x_{i1} + \beta_2 x_{i2} + \cdots + \beta_p x_{ip})$$

where:

Link( ) is the link function.

γ_{ij} is the cumulative probability of the jth category for the ith case.

θ_j is the threshold for the jth category.

p is the number of regression coefficients.

$x_{i1}\ldots x_{ip}$ are the values of the predictors for the ith case.

$\beta_1\ldots\beta_p$ are regression coefficients.

There are several important things to notice here.

First, the model is based on the notion that there is some latent continuous outcome variable, and that the ordinal outcome variable arises from discretizing the underlying continuum into ordered groups. The cutoff values that define the categories are estimated by the thresholds.

Second, the thresholds or constants (θ_j) in the model (corresponding to the intercept in linear regression models) depend only on which category's probability is being predicted. Values of the predictor (independent) variables do not affect this part of the model.

Third, the prediction part of the model ($\beta_1 x_{i1} + \beta_2 x_{i2} + \cdots + \beta_p x_{ip}$) depends only on the predictors and is independent of the outcome category. These first two properties imply that the results will be a set of parallel lines or hyperplanes—one for each category of the outcome variable.

Finally, rather than predicting the actual cumulative probabilities, the model predicts a function of those values. This function is called the link function, and the form of the link function can be chosen when the model is built. This allows users to choose a link function based on the problem under consideration to optimize results. Several link functions are available in the Ordinal Regression procedure.

As you can see, these are very powerful and general models. Of course, there is also a bit more to keep track of here than in a typical linear regression model. An ordinal regression model contains three major components:

▪ **Location Components:** The portion of the preceding equation that includes the coefficients and predictor variables is called the location component of the model ($\beta1xi1 + \beta2xi2 + \cdots + \beta pxip$). The location is the "meat" of the model. It uses the predictor variables to calculate predicted probabilities of membership in the categories for each case.

- **Scale Components:** The scale component is an optional modification to the basic model to account for differences in variability for different values of the predictor variables. For example, if men have more variability than women in their risk values (that is, the underlying continuous outcome variable), using a scale component to account for this may improve the model. A model with a scale component follows the form shown in this equation:

$$\text{link}(\gamma ij) = \theta j - (\beta1xi1 + \beta2xi2 + \cdots + \beta pxip)e\tau1zi1 + \cdots + \tau mzim$$

where

zi1...zim are scale component predictors (a subset of the x's).

τ1...τm are scale component coefficients.

Models with a scale component are known as unequal variance models, which indicate that the crossproducts of the regression coefficients with the predictor variables in the model need to be adjusted for unequal variances by using a scale variable.

When a scale component is used, the Parameter Estimates table will incorporate detection parameters (one per predictor) that measure the difference between the distribution of the levels of the dependent variable.

- **Available Link Functions:** The link function is a transformation of the cumulative probabilities that allows estimation of the model. They are used to relate the dependent variable's distribution to the predictors. The five link functions shown in Table 3-3 are available.

Table 3-3: Available Link Functions for Ordinal Regression

FUNCTION	FORM	TYPICAL APPLICATION
Logit	$f(y)=\ln(y / (1-y))$	Evenly distributed categories
Complementary log-log	$f(y)=\ln(-\ln(1-y))$	Higher categories more probable
Negative log-log	$f(y)=-\ln(-\ln(y))$	Lower categories more probable
Probit	$f(y)=\Phi-1(y)$, where $\Phi-1$ is the inverse standard normal cumulative distribution function.	Latent variable is normally distributed.
Cauchit (inverse Cauchy)	$f(y)=\tan(\pi(y-0.5))$	Latent variable has many extreme values.

Assumptions of Ordinal Regression Models

Ordinal regression models make fewer assumptions than linear regression models, but they do still make many of the same assumptions about the data. Ordinal regression models assume that:

- The dependent variable is an ordinal-level outcome variable.

- Independent variables can be categorical or continuous.

- Homogeneity of error variance for each level of the dependent variable is met (location-scale models can be used when violated).

- There is an adequate cell count (80% of cells should have a cell count of 5 or more, and no cells should have a count of zero). SPSS Statistics will print out a warning regarding the proportion of cells with a count of zero; however, if continuous variables are in the model, this warning is not a useful guide.

- Assumption of parallel lines. It is assumed that the b coefficients of the predictor for each level of the dependent variable should be the same. In other words, the "meat" of the equation ($\beta1xi1 + \beta2xi2 + \cdots + \beta pxip$) for each level of the dependent variable is the same; it is only the thresholds (θj) that differ among levels of the dependent variable.

Ordinal Regression Dialogs

In this example we use the file `Satisfaction.sav` (available on this book's website). This file contains customer satisfaction data from a large company:

1. To run ordinal regression, click Analyze ⇨ Regression ⇨ Ordinal.

   In the Ordinal Regression dialog you need to specify a dependent variable, as well as specify the model predictors. Note that the last category of the dependent variable will be the reference category. Continuous predictors need to be placed in the Covariate(s) box, while categorical predictors need to be placed in the Factor(s) box. As shown in Figure 3-1, we will be predicting the level of satisfaction from when the product was purchased and how important the product is to the customer's job (both predictors in this example are categorical variables).

2. Move satisfied into the Dependent box.

3. Move Important and When_Purchased into the Factor(s) box.

   Although the OK button is active, we want to specify some additional options, including the link function.

4. Click Options.

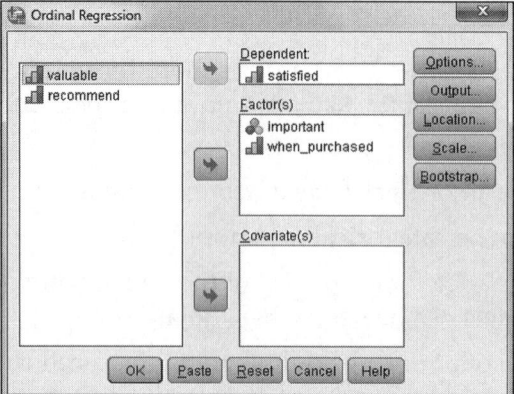

Figure 3-1: Ordinal Regression dialog

In the Options dialog (Figure 3-2), the Iterations section allows the researcher to fine tune the analysis to achieve convergence. Also, as a default, a 95% confidence interval is requested for parameters as well as a check for singularity (redundancy in predictors that leads to unstable parameter estimates). Also, no constant is added (Delta) to any cells with an observed frequency of zero.

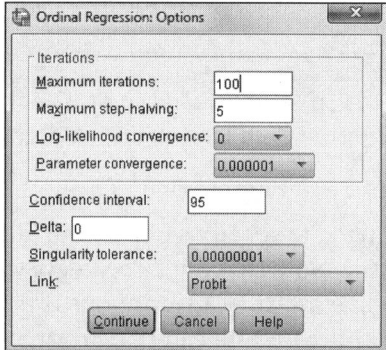

Figure 3-2: Options dialog

The link function specifies what transformation is applied to the dependent variable. As a default, the logit link function is used. You'll need to specify the appropriate link function based on the distribution of the dependent variable (refer to Table 3-2).

5. Click the drop-down list and select Probit.

The distribution of the dependent variable is displayed with a bar chart in Figure 3-3 (produced with the Chart Builder procedure). We are using the probit link function because the distribution of the variable satisfied seems to be somewhat normal, because most scores tend to be in the center portion of the distribution (the probit and logit links are usually very similar).

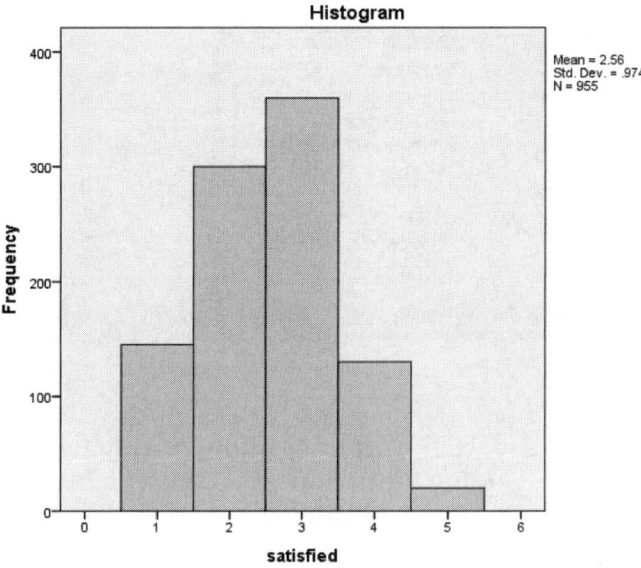

Histogram

Mean = 2.56
Std. Dev. = .974
N = 955

Figure 3-3: Distribution of the satisfied variable

6. Click Continue to return to the Ordinal Regression dialog (Figure 3-1).

7. Click Output.

The Display section of the Output dialog (Figure 3-4) provides users with the ability to assess the model. It is important to view the goodness of fit and summary statistics as well as parameter estimates (all of which are shown as a default) to assess model adequacy. It is also important to view the test of parallel lines because this is an important assumption for ordinal regression. The correlation or covariance parameter estimates, although not viewed often, can provide additional insight into variable relationships. Finally, the Cell information option provides frequency and residuals information (remember ordinal regression relies on the chi-square statistic). However, this information may not be useful when covariates are included in the model because many cells will have very small frequencies, and very large tables will be produced.

The Saved Variables section is used to save the predicted category (value) and probabilities associated with the predicted and actual categories that are output from the model. It also saves the estimated probabilities of classifying a factor/covariate pattern into response categories. Each of these options becomes another variable in the file that can be used in subsequent reports and analyses. The Predicted category option is especially useful to help build a classification table to determine the predictive accuracy of the model.

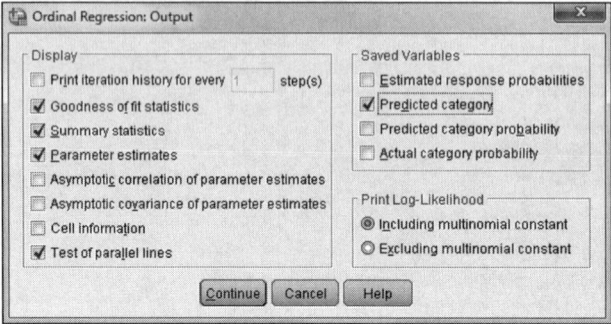

Figure 3-4: Output dialog

The Print Log-Likelihood section options allow researchers to select between including or excluding the multinomial constant. Including the constant gives the full value of the likelihood.

8. Select Test of parallel lines.

9. Select Predicted category.

10. Click Continue to return to the Ordinal Regression dialog (Figure 3-1).

11. Click Location.

In the Location dialog (Figure 3-5), the model predictors are specified. As a default, only the main effects will be included; however, the researcher may elect to include interactions as well (we will not do that here).

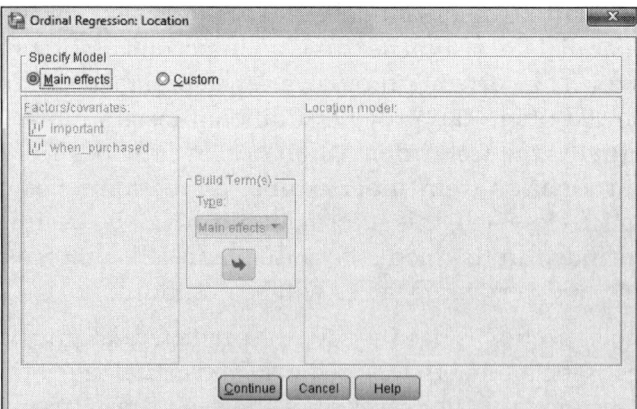

Figure 3-5: Location dialog

12. Click Continue to return to the Ordinal Regression dialog (Figure 3-1).

13. Click Scale to display the Scale dialog shown in Figure 3-6.

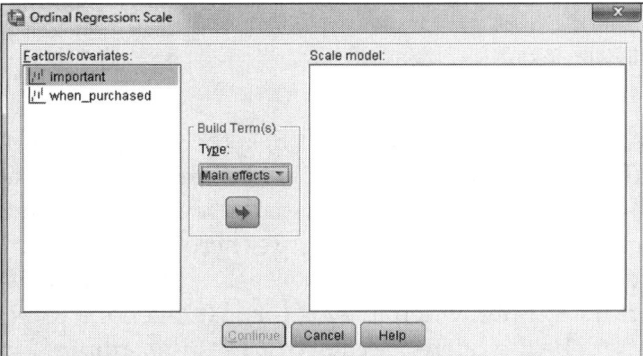

Figure 3-6: Scale dialog

Ordinal regression models assume that error variances are the same for all levels of the ordinal dependent variable. That is, the variability of the underlying continuous outcome variable does not differ across different values of the predictor variables. When this assumption is violated, parameter estimates are biased. The Scale option enables the estimation of separate variance models that eliminate the biased parameter estimates.

By default, researchers normally run ordinal regression models without a scale factor (that is, assuming an equal variance model). If goodness of fit statistics improve by adding a scale component, then the variability of the terms in the scale model is a significant contributor to explaining the variance of the dependent variable, and a location-scale model should be used.

14. Click Continue to return to the Ordinal Regression dialog (Figure 3-1).

15. Click OK to run the analysis.

Ordinal Regression Output

Figure 3-7 is the first piece of output, and it is a warning about cells with zero frequencies. This warning appears whenever any cell combinations have a frequency of zero. This is important information because certain fit statistics for the model depend on aggregating the data based on unique predictor and outcome value patterns. Whenever a continuous predictor is used, this results in a very large table with many empty cells, which makes it difficult to interpret some of the fit statistics. Researchers will have to be careful in evaluating these models, particularly when looking at chi-square–based fit statistics.

In our example we have an adequate cell count because 90% of cells have a cell count of 5 or more.

Warnings

There are 2 (10.0%) cells (i.e., dependent variable levels by observed combinations of predictor variable values) with zero frequencies.

Figure 3-7: Warning of cells with frequency of zero

The Case Processing Summary table (Figure 3-8) is the next piece of output. This table provides information on the number of valid cases and missing data for this model, as well as counts and percentages for the levels of the categorical variables in the model. It is important to make sure there are enough cases in each level or to think of ways in which to combine levels if there are not enough cases. It is also important to note which level is the last level of a categorical variable, because this will be the reference category. In this example "Strongly Disagree" will be the reference category for the dependent variable (level of satisfaction), "no" will be the reference category for the independent variable (how important the product is to the customer's job), and "recently" will be the reference category for the independent variable (when the product was purchased).

Case Processing Summary

		N	Marginal Percentage
satisfied	1 Strongly Agree	130	14.9%
	2 Agree	270	30.9%
	3 Neither Agree Nor Disagree	340	38.9%
	4 Disagree	120	13.7%
	5 Strongly Disagree	15	1.7%
important	1 yes	400	45.7%
	2 no	475	54.3%
when_purchased	1 a long time ago	515	58.9%
	2 recently	360	41.1%
Valid		875	100.0%
Missing		80	
Total		955	

Figure 3-8: Case Processing Summary table

The model fitting information (Figure 3-9) is a likelihood-ratio chi-square test of the current model versus the null (intercept only) model. Lower -2LL values indicate better fit. The significance value of less than 0.05 indicates that the current model outperforms the null model. (To see the full significance value, double-click on the value itself.) Recall that the null model is the model with only the threshold (Intercept only (θj)) and the Final model is including the threshold and the "meat" part of the model $(link(\gamma ij) = \theta j - [\beta 1xi1 + \beta 2xi2 + \ldots + \beta pxip])$. If this test is not significant, the remaining output is usually ignored because the model doesn't have explanatory power. In the example a statistically significant result was found, thus our model with two predictors is an improvement over no model.

Model Fitting Information

Model	-2 Log Likelihood	Chi-Square	df	Sig.
Intercept Only	380.895			
Final	71.556	309.339	2	.000

Link function: Probit.

Figure 3-9: Model Fitting Information table

The next table in the output is the Goodness-of-Fit table, shown in Figure 3-10. This table contains Pearson's chi-square statistic for the model and another chi-square statistic based on the deviance. These statistics are intended to test whether the observed data is inconsistent with the fitted model. When the data and the model predictions are similar, then you have a good model—this is indicated by obtaining non-significant results (as in our example).

Goodness-of-Fit

	Chi-Square	df	Sig.
Pearson	6.188	10	.799
Deviance	6.348	10	.785

Link function: Probit.

Figure 3-10: Goodness-of-Fit table

These statistics can be very useful for models with a small number of categorical predictors. Unfortunately, these statistics are both sensitive to empty cells. When estimating models with continuous covariates, there are often many empty cells. Therefore, you should not rely on either of these test statistics with such models. This is because with empty cells, you cannot be sure that these statistics will really follow the chi-square distribution, and therefore the significance values will not be accurate.

The Pseudo R-Square table (Figure 3-11) prints three measures of overall effect size. Nagelkerke's R-Square is the most commonly referenced, because it can attain the maximum value of 1, which the others do not. The table provides measures that are useful for comparing competing models. For a well-fitting model, Nagelkerke's R-Square should be close to 1. In this example, all of the measures are small to moderate, meaning that even though our model is statistically significant (as evidenced by the Model Information table), and the data is consistent with the model (as seen in the Goodness of Fit table), our model could still be improved considerably in terms of predictive ability (which is typically what you really care about). Note that pseudo-R squared is typically lower than what you might be used to with linear regression. Producing a confusion table may give a better idea of prediction power (see Figure 3-14).

Pseudo R-Square

Cox and Snell	.298
Nagelkerke	.319
McFadden	.130

Link function: Probit.

Figure 3-11: Pseudo R-Square table

The Parameter Estimates table contains the estimated coefficients for the thresholds (intercepts) and location parameters (slopes of the predictor variables). It summarizes the effect of each of the predictors, with an unstandardized coefficient, its standard error, a hypothesis test based on the Wald statistic, and a 95% confidence interval for the unstandardized coefficient.

In the output table (Parameter Estimates) shown in Figure 3-12, the "Threshold" rows contain information on the intercepts estimated for all but the highest level of the ordinal dependent variable. Threshold values are generally not important to interpretation of the results, but instead represent simple cutoff points. Most of the time, threshold values will be significant; however, it is possible that two thresholds will be non-significant. In that case, the levels of the dependent variable do not differ from each other, so those levels have the same equations and should be combined. In our example, the levels are significantly different from each other so levels should not be combined.

Parameter Estimates

		Estimate	Std. Error	Wald	df	Sig.	95% Confidence Interval	
							Lower Bound	Upper Bound
Threshold	[satisfied = 1]	-2.082	.093	500.770	1	.000	-2.265	-1.900
	[satisfied = 2]	-.909	.075	146.507	1	.000	-1.056	-.762
	[satisfied = 3]	.486	.072	45.508	1	.000	.345	.627
	[satisfied = 4]	1.727	.118	214.715	1	.000	1.496	1.958
Location	[important=1]	-1.368	.082	278.589	1	.000	-1.529	-1.208
	[important=2]	0ᵃ	.	.	0	.	.	.
	[when_purchased=1]	-.263	.074	12.474	1	.000	-.409	-.117
	[when_purchased=2]	0ᵃ	.	.	0	.	.	.

Link function: Probit.

a. This parameter is set to zero because it is redundant.

Figure 3-12: Parameter Estimates table

The "Location" rows summarize the effect of each predictor. While interpretation of the coefficients in this model is difficult due to the nature of the link function, the signs of the coefficients for the covariates and relative values of the coefficients for the factor levels can give important insights into the effects of the predictors in the model.

For example, both of the predictors, important and when_purchased, are statistically significant and they both have negative coefficients, which indicate that negative relationships exist between the predictors and the outcome.

For categorical variables, a factor level with a negative coefficient indicates a greater probability of being in one of the "lower" cumulative outcome categories. The sign of a coefficient for a factor level is dependent upon that factor level's effect relative to the reference category—in the example, the reference category is the last category or the "Strongly Disagree" group. In our case (for the variable important), the "Yes" group (important 1) is significantly different from the reference category, the "No" group (important 2), which means that customers that consider the software important to their job are more likely to endorse lower values on the satisfaction variable (lower values indicate more satisfaction) than the "No" group.

As another example, (for the variable when_purchased), the "Purchased a long time ago" group (when_purchased 1) is significantly different from the reference category, the "Recent" group (when_purchased 2), which means that customers that purchased the software a long time ago are more likely to endorse lower values on the satisfaction variable (lower values indicate more satisfaction) than the "Recent" group.

As in other forms of regressions, non-significant predictors could be dropped to improve the model.

The final piece of tabular output is the assessment of the parallel lines assumption. Recall that in ordinal regression there will be multiple regression equations, one for each level of the ordinal dependent variable (except for the last level). The parallel lines assumption means that the predictor coefficients are the same for each level of the dependent variable and that only the intercepts (thresholds) differ. Thus the regression lines are assumed to be parallel for each level of the dependent variable, indicating that the predictors have the same relationship to the different levels of the dependent variable. To assess this assumption, two models are compared to determine if the estimated model with one set of coefficients for all categories (Null Hypothesis) is similar to a model with a separate set of coefficients for each category (General). Well-fitting models result in a non-significant difference (as shown in Figure 3-13).

Test of Parallel Lines[a]

Model	-2 Log Likelihood	Chi-Square	df	Sig.
Null Hypothesis	71.556			
General	65.530	6.026	6	.420

The null hypothesis states that the location parameters (slope coefficients) are the same across response categories.

a. Link function: Probit.

Figure 3-13: Test of Parallel Lines table

If you see that the general model (with separate parameters for each category) gives a significant improvement in the model fit over the null hypothesis model (with one set of parameters for each level), then this assumption has been violated, and the parameter estimates may be seriously biased (that is, ordinal regression should not be used). To correct this, the researcher may try a different link function; collapse or reorder the categories of the dependent variable; eliminate non-essential predictors or collapse predictor categories; or as a final resort use multinominal logistic regression, because that procedure does not have this assumption, though it does result in the loss of statistical power.

As a final assessment of the model, a new variable indicating model predictions appears in the Data Editor.

Crosstabulating the dependent variable with the prediction (Analyze ➪ Descriptive Statistics ➪ Crosstabs) provides a classification table (Figure 3-14) used to assess the predictive accuracy of the model.

satisfied * Predicted Response Category Crosstabulation

			Predicted Response Category		
			2 Agree	3 Neither Agree Nor Disagree	Total
satisfied	1 Strongly Agree	Count	115	15	130
		% within satisfied	88.5%	11.5%	100.0%
	2 Agree	Count	180	90	270
		% within satisfied	66.7%	33.3%	100.0%
	3 Neither Agree Nor Disagree	Count	95	245	340
		% within satisfied	27.9%	72.1%	100.0%
	4 Disagree	Count	10	110	120
		% within satisfied	8.3%	91.7%	100.0%
	5 Strongly Disagree	Count	0	15	15
		% within satisfied	0.0%	100.0%	100.0%
Total		Count	400	475	875
		% within satisfied	45.7%	54.3%	100.0%

Figure 3-14: Crosstab between actual and predicted outcomes

The classification table shows there are no predictions for "Strongly Agree," "Disagree," or "Strongly Disagree," as all of these cases are misclassified. Almost 68% of the "Agree" category is correctly predicted and about 72% of the "Neither Agree nor Disagree" group are correctly classified. Overall, 49% of all cases ((0 + 180 + 245 + 0 + 0) / 875) were correct predictions. As was evidenced by the pseudo R-square statistics, the predictive accuracy of the current model is not great and can certainly be improved.

Categorical Regression Theory

Categorical regression with optimal scaling extends the regression model by quantifying categorical variables. Internally, interval scale values are assigned to each category of every variable so that these values are "optimal" with respect to the regression. Categorical regression maximizes the squared correlation between the transformed dependent variable and the linear combination of the transformed predictors. In other words, interval scale values are assigned so as to account for as much variance as possible in the dependent variable.

It is important to emphasize that whether a variable is nominal or ordinal, categorical regression will transform the scores so that the variable is measured in an interval scale (and thus could be used by linear regression). It does so by taking into account the scale on which the variable is measured and its relationship to other variables in the model.

In addition to the obvious benefit of using data of any scale, regression with optimal scaling can reduce multicollinearity among predictors, and it can model nonlinear relationships. This is because categorical predictors receive a different weight or score for each category, rather than one coefficient for the variable as a whole. Another benefit of categorical regression is that the output is similar to that produced by linear regression, so there is little added complexity when using this technique. Categorical regression is part of the categories module. Note that CATREG can be used with continuous dependent variables in order to take advantage of shrinkage estimators.

Assumptions of Categorical Regression Models

Categorical regression models make the same assumptions as linear regression models. In addition, categorical regression models assume that:

- There can be no negative numbers in the data and all the values must be integers (decimal digits are truncated).
- All nominal and ordinal variables should be coded so that their values are consecutive integers beginning with 1.

Categorical Regression Dialogs

In these analyses we will continue to use the file Satisfaction.sav. This file contains customer satisfaction data from a large company.

1. To run categorical regression, click Analyze ⇨ Regression ⇨ Optimal Scaling (CATREG).

   In the Categorical Regression dialog you need to specify a dependent variable, as well as specify the model predictors. As shown in Figure 3-15, we will be predicting recommendation from the variables: when the product was purchased, how important the product is to the customer's job, and level of satisfaction.

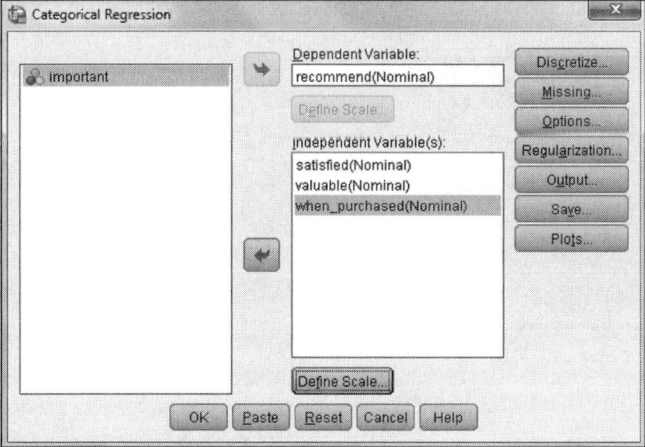

Figure 3-15: Categorical Regression dialog

2. Move the variable recommend into the Dependent Variable box.

3. Move the variables valuable, when_purchased, and satisfied into the Independent Variable(s) box.

A problem survey researchers often face is whether a "don't know" response is a true middle category between two extremes on a scale. If it is, the "don't know" response can be recoded to a middle value and used in the analysis.

In this example we will be predicting the recommend variable ("Would you recommend this product?"). The response categories are yes, no, and don't know. Many questions in surveys have a "don't know" category and we are often interested in using this category as valid data, along with the other responses because it may be of intrinsic interest. Because we want to include all three categories, we cannot use binary logistic regression for this situation.

The variables satisfied and valuable are coded on a one through five scale and could be treated as interval-level variables; however, categorical regression provides us with the opportunity to explore how closely they match interval scaling in their current coding (the variable when purchased is a nominal-level variable).

Before we proceed, we must tell SPSS Statistics on what scale each variable is measured:

1. Click the variable recommend, and then click the Define Scale button.

   The recommend variable is a nominal-level variable.

2. Click Nominal and then click Continue.

   Click each of the variables important, when_purchased, and satisfied, and then click the Define Scale button to display the dialog shown in Figure 3-16.

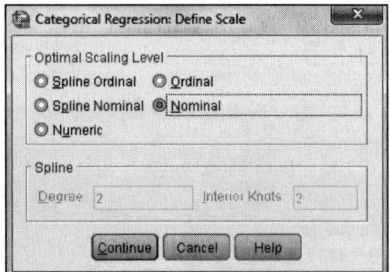

Figure 3-16: Define Scale dialog

3. Select Nominal and then click Continue.

All of the predictors could be defined as ordinal-level variables; however, doing this would restrict the procedure to create values for the variables that are ranked (this would keep the variables as ordinal). We recommend using the nominal level of measurement for categorical predictors so that the optimal coding quantifications are used (and this way we can see exactly how each level of a variable relates to the outcome variable).

4. Click Discretization.

The Discretization dialog (Figure 3-17) allows you to specify a method for recoding your variables. In our example this is not necessary because we do not have any string variables nor any variables with values less than or equal to zero.

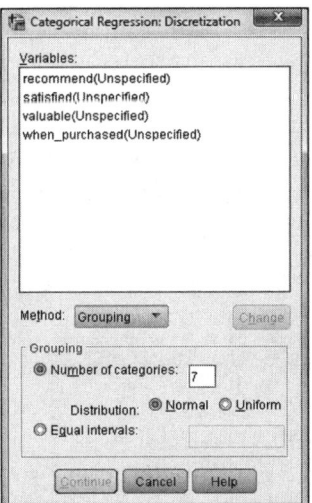

Figure 3-17: Discretization dialog

5. Click Cancel.

6. Click Missing Values.

The Missing Values dialog (Figure 3-18) allows you to choose how to handle missing values. Alternatively, we could have handled missing data before performing categorical regression. In our example we will use the default option, although we could decide to impute missing values with the mode or create an extra category for missing data.

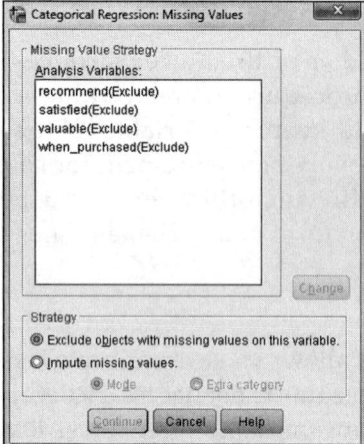

Figure 3-18: Missing Values dialog

7. Click Cancel.

8. Click Options.

The Options dialog (Figure 3-19) allows you to specify the initial configuration, iteration, and convergence criteria, supplementary objects, and the labeling of plots. Whenever at least one variable is coded as a nominal-level variable (as we did in the Define Scale dialog), the random initial configuration must be used.

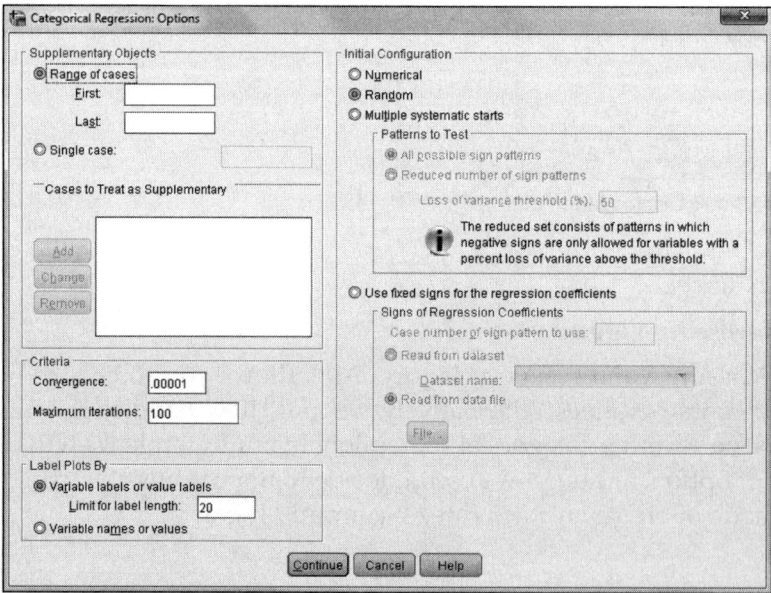

Figure 3-19: Options dialog

9. Click Random.

10. Click Continue.

11. Click Regularization.

The Regularization dialog (Figure 3-20) allows you to specify methods that can improve the predictive error of the model, by reducing the variability in the regression coefficients. We will not make any changes in this dialog at this time. Regularization is an important, although large, topic. It is a good reason to use CATREG when all the variables are scale level.

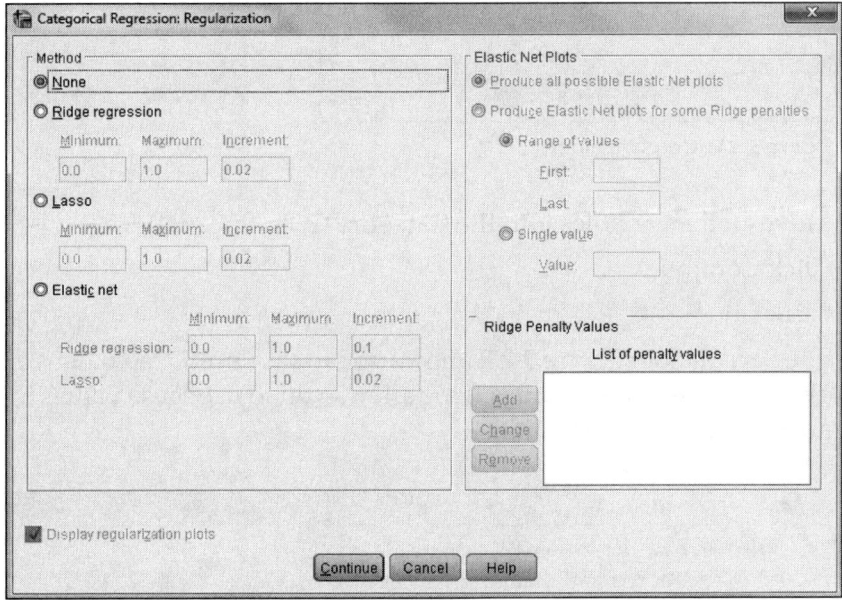

Figure 3-20: Regularization dialog

12. Click Cancel.

13. Click Output.

The Output dialog (Figure 3-21) allows you to specify the statistics you want to display as part of the output. The defaults are that you will see the multiple correlation coefficient, the ANOVA table, and the Coefficients table. In addition to these pieces of output, you typically want to ask to see a table of quantifications so that you can see the transformed values of the variables (the scores are standardized to have a mean of zero and a standard deviation of one). This will allow us to see the exact values that optimal scaling used to run the categorical regression.

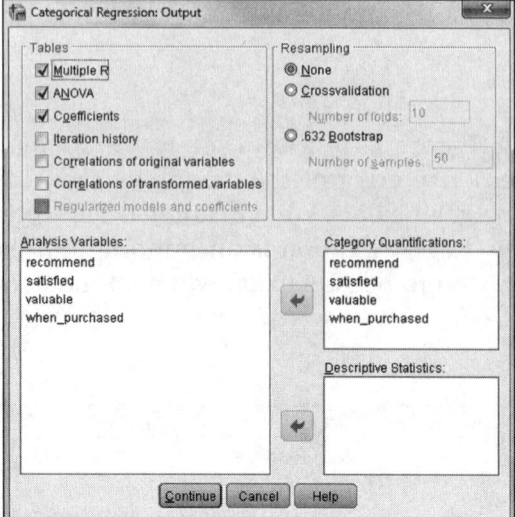

Figure 3-21: Output dialog

14. Move all the variables into the Category Quantifications box.

15. Click Continue.

16. Click Save.

    The Save dialog (Figure 3-22) allows you to save predicted values, residuals, and transformed values. This allows you to use these values in other analyses or procedures.

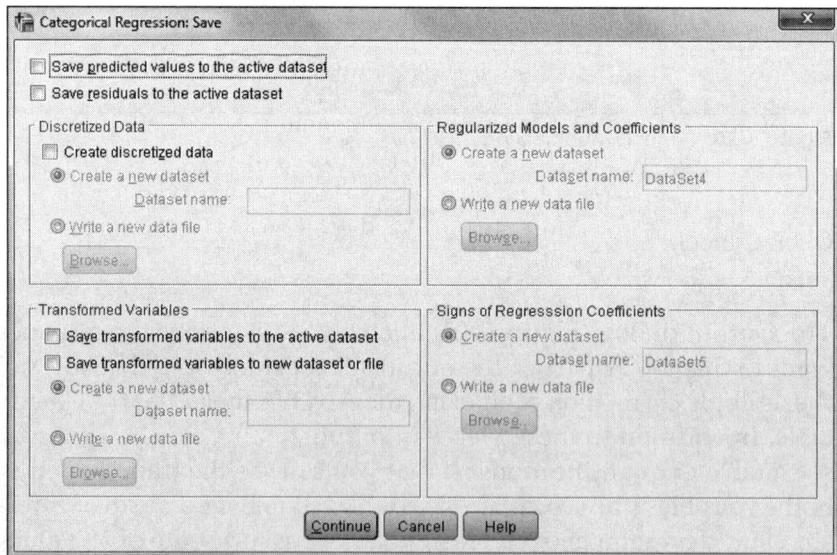

Figure 3-22: Save dialog

17. Click Cancel.
18. Click Plots.

The Plots dialog (Figure 3-23) allows you to create plots that show the relationship between the original variable values and the new transformed scores.

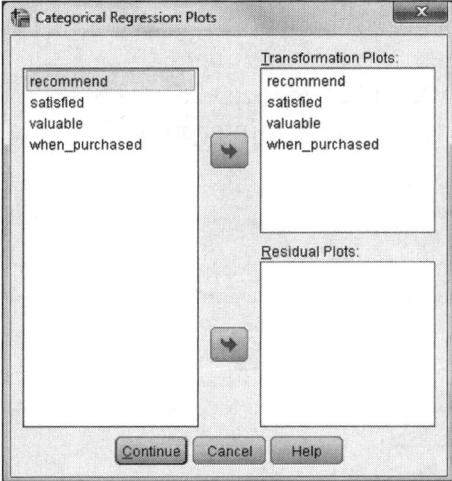

Figure 3-23: Plots dialog

19. Move all the variables into the Transformation Plots box.

We will now be able to see how the new transformed variables relate to the original variables.

20. Click Continue.
21. Click OK.

Categorical Regression Output

The Case Processing Summary table (Figure 3-24) displays the total number of cases in the data set, the number of cases in the analysis, as well as the number of cases that were excluded because of missing data. In our example about 10% of the cases were excluded due to missing data, which is not a huge amount. Of course we could have intervened to replace missing values either directly within the categorical regression procedure (refer to Figure 3-18 for options) or by using other methods within SPSS Statistics.

Case Processing Summary

Valid Active Cases	860
Active Cases with Missing Values[a]	95
Supplementary Cases	0
Total	955
Cases Used in Analysis	860

a. Excluded cases (first 30 are shown): 13 25 30 33 39 44 46 61 62 63 70 84 99 107 109 148 157 160 191 204 216 221 224 230 235 237 252 253 254 261.

Figure 3-24: Case Processing Summary table

The Model Summary and ANOVA tables (Figure3-25 and 3-26) are very similar to those produced by linear regression, and interpretation is the same.

Model Summary

Multiple R	R Square	Adjusted R Square	Apparent Prediction Error
.625	.390	.384	.610

Dependent Variable: recommend
Predictors: satisfied valuable when_purchased

Figure 3-25: Model Summary table

ANOVA

	Sum of Squares	df	Mean Square	F	Sig.
Regression	335.774	9	37.308	60.493	.000
Residual	524.226	850	.617		
Total	860.000	859			

Dependent Variable: recommend
Predictors: satisfied valuable when_purchased

Figure 3-26: ANOVA table

The Model Summary table provides several measures of how well the model fits the data. Multiple R, which can range from 0 to 1, is the multiple correlation coefficient between the dependent variable and the combination of the predictors; thus, the closer the multiple R is to 1, the better the fit. R Square, which can range from 0 to 1, is the correlation coefficient squared. It can be interpreted as the proportion of variance of the dependent variable that can be accounted for from the predictors. Adjusted R Square represents a technical improvement over R Square in that it explicitly adjusts for the number of predictor variables relative to the sample size.

Here the Multiple R correlation coefficient between the combination of predictors and the dependent variable is .625. If you square the multiple R, you get .390. Therefore, about 39% of the variance on the recommend variable can be predicted from the three independent variables.

Although the fit measures indicate how well you can expect to predict the dependent variable, they do not tell you whether there is a statistically significant relationship between the dependent and predictors. The analysis of variance table (ANOVA) presents technical summaries (sums of squares and mean square statistics) of the variation accounted for by the prediction equation. The main interest is in determining whether there is a statistically significant relationship between the dependent variable and the predictors. In our example, we can see that we have a statistically significant relationship between the predictors and the recommend variable.

Because significant results were found, we next turn to the Coefficients table (Figure 3-27) to view the regression coefficients. Note that the Coefficients table is a bit different than the typical coefficients table for linear regression. This is because categorical regression transforms and standardizes the values of the variables; therefore, only Beta coefficients are reported. In our example all three predictors are statistically significant, and the satisfied variable is the most important predictor (because it has the largest Beta coefficient). With regard to interpretation, we will hold off on that discussion until we view the transformation plots.

Coefficients

| | Standardized Coefficients | | | | |
	Beta	Bootstrap (1000) Estimate of Std. Error	df	F	Sig.
satisfied	.542	.038	4	200.578	.000
valuable	.121	.030	4	16.454	.000
when_purchased	.120	.028	1	18.893	.000

Dependent Variable: recommend

Figure 3-27: Coefficients table

To help you further understand the effect of the predictors, various types of correlations are shown in the Correlations and Tolerance table (Figure 3-28). Zero-Order correlations display the Pearson correlation between the transformed scores of each predictor and the transformed dependent variable. Note that the satisfied variable has the strongest correlation with the dependent variable. The partial correlation is the Pearson correlation between the transformed scores of each predictor and the transformed dependent variable after removing the effects of the other predictors from both the independent and dependent variables. The part correlation (semipartial correlation) is the Pearson correlation between the transformed scores of each predictor and the transformed dependent variable after removing the effects of the other predictors from just the independent variable.

Correlations and Tolerance

| | Correlations | | | | Tolerance | |
	Zero-Order	Partial	Part	Importance	After Transformation	Before Transformation
satisfied	.603	.534	.494	.837	.830	.546
valuable	.346	.141	.111	.108	.836	.548
when_purchased	.178	.151	.120	.055	.990	.984

Dependent Variable: recommend

Figure 3-28: Correlations and Tolerance table

Pratt's measure of relative importance is another way to determine predictor importance. The values of all the variables will sum to one, so therefore the satisfied variable accounts for 83.7% of the importance in the model. Because these values show relative importance that sum to one, they are additive, meaning that the satisfied variable and the valuable variable account for 94.5% of the importance in the model. It is important to remember, though, that here we are referring to relative importance; thus, we could have a model with very low explanatory power, yet have a variable with a high degree of importance to the model.

Finally, tolerance values are provided before and after the transformation of the data. Tolerance values range from 0 to 1, and higher values denote a higher proportion of uniqueness of the variable (less multicollinearity). Note that transforming the data improves tolerance, therefore this reduces multicollinearity (not that it was a problem with the original data in this example).

Figure3-29 through 3-32 display the transformed scores of the dependent and independent variables. Recall that we began this example by wondering whether the "Don't Know" response on the recommend variable should be coded as a middle category. The transformed scores on Figure 3-29 suggest that the "Don't Know" category should be coded as a middle category. It is these new values that are used in categorical regression (the Save dialog would have allowed us to place these values in the data editor, and then we could have run linear regression).

The transformed values take into account the relationship between the predictor and outcome variable. In addition, it is important to note that these values are only appropriate with this set of four variables because they have been based on the complete information for this set. That is, the quantifications are for the purpose of predicting the (transformed) dependent variable and do not necesarily indicate a tranformation that is appropriate for use in other contexts.

recommend[a]

Category	Frequency	Quantification
1 Yes	645	-.505
2 No	70	2.908
3 Don't Know	145	.845

a. Optimal Scaling Level: Nominal.

Figure 3-29: Quantifications table: recommend

Note that the satisfied variable is an ordinal-level variable.

satisfied[a]

Category	Frequency	Quantification
1 Strongly Agree	130	-.742
2 Agree	265	-.645
3 Neither Agree Nor Disagree	330	-.075
4 Disagree	120	1.962
5 Strongly Disagree	15	3.779

a. Optimal Scaling Level: Nominal.

Figure 3-30: Quantifications table: satisfied

However, the valuable variable is not an ordinal-level variable.

valuable[a]

Category	Frequency	Quantification
1 Strongly Agree	115	-.678
2 Agree	275	-1.117
3 Neither Agree Nor Disagree	280	1.001
4 Disagree	155	.166
5 Strongly Disagree	35	2.265

a. Optimal Scaling Level: Nominal.

Figure 3-31: Quantifications table: valuable

when_purchased[a]

Category	Frequency	Quantification
1 a long time ago	505	-.838
2 recently	355	1.193

a. Optimal Scaling Level: Nominal.

Figure 3-32: Quantifications table: when_purchased

Figure 3-33 through 3-36 display the transformation plots for each of our variables. These plots display the original category values on the x-axis and the transformed scores on the y-axis. In essence, the transformation plots are just visual representations of the values in the quantifications tables. Figure 3-33 shows the transformed values for the recommend variable. As mentioned previously, note that the 3 "Don't Know" category is in between the 1 "Yes" and the 2 "No" groups. Also note that lower values are associated with the "Yes" group.

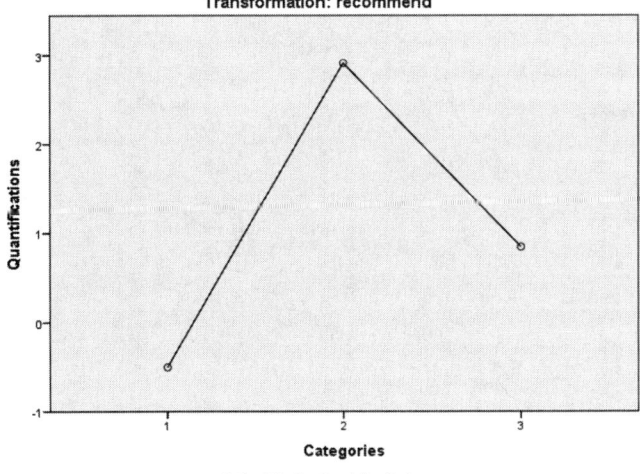

Optimal Scaling Level: Nominal.

Figure 3-33: Transformation plot: recommend

The satisfied variable (Figure 3-34) is a true ordinal-level variable (note the ranking of the values). However, because the categories are not equally spaced out, it is not an interval-level variable. Note that there is very little difference between 1 "Strongly Agree" and 2 "Agree," whereas the other groups are equally spaced out. Notice that the valuable variable (Figure 3-35) is really a nominal level variable, as satisfaction does not have a linear relationship with the categories of the valuable variable. Figure 3-36 shows the variable when_purchased only has two categories.

With regard to interpretation of the Beta coefficients, recall that all Beta coefficients were positive (refer to Figure 3-27). Notice that for the satisfied variable, lower values are associated with greater agreement, and as we saw in Figure 3-33, for the recommend variable, lower scores are associated with the "Yes" group. Therefore, lower values on the satisfied variable are associated with lower values on the recommend variable. In other words, higher satisfaction is associated with increased chances of recommending the product. This is why it is important to interpret the scores and Beta coefficients together.

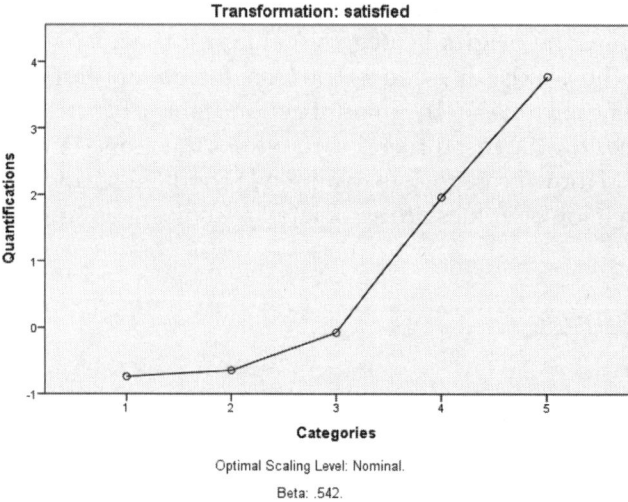

Figure 3-34: Transformation plot: satisfied

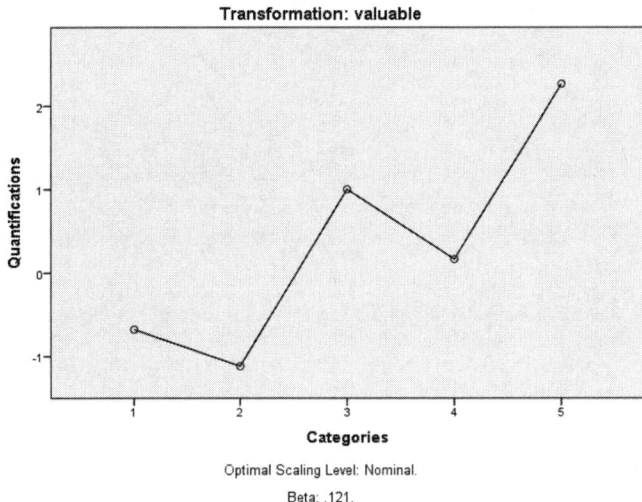

Figure 3-35: Transformation plot: valuable

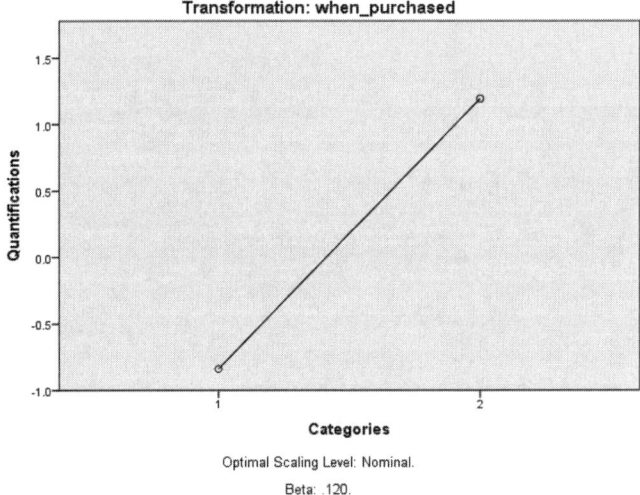

Figure 3-36: Transformation plot: when_purchased

Building Hierarchical Linear Models

Data often contain information that has a hierarchical (multilevel) structure. For example, a business may have many stores, and customer purchasing behavior at each store may be influenced not only by customer-level characteristics (for example, income, age, and so on), but also by characteristics of where the store is located (for example, a large urban center), as well as characteristics of the store itself (for example, store size, store condition, number of employees). In this case, we could develop a model using variables from all levels of this hierarchy (customer and store characteristics); however, if we just incorporate all these variables in a linear regression model, for example, this ignores the influences of store and location variables on customer-level variables, as well as the correlations that exist among the observations within levels (customers within a location). As another example, if we were investigating the effects of a new teaching method on math scores for a school district, we would need to take into account not only student characteristics (IQ, gender, and so on), but also the characteristics of the classrooms (for example, class size) and schools (for example SES).

In this chapter we discuss hierarchical linear mixed models. We start with an overview of the technique and then go through an example that illustrates where you can perform this technique within SPSS Statistics. We also discuss the options that are available within the hierarchical linear mixed models procedures, and we go over the interpretation of the output. Finally we discuss how you can compare models that have either different predictors or different structures. That is, one model might allow for two variables to have an interaction while another model might not allow for this.

Overview of Hierarchical Linear Mixed Models

Hierarchical linear mixed models (also known as multilevel models) are needed to take into account the hierarchical nature of the data. Linear mixed models adjust standard errors, which tend to be too small when using traditional models such as linear regression (because they do not take into account variation between predictors for different levels). The linear mixed models procedure, which we discuss in this chapter, can estimate a variety of complex models to predict a continuous outcome with both fixed and random effects at different levels.

Fixed effects are variables for which all levels of interest are included. For example, for the variable store condition, we might only have the values "old" and "new" and these are the only values we care about; therefore, the levels for the variable store condition are fixed. Random effects are variables for which not all possible values are included; the levels or values have been sampled from a larger population. For example, the store condition variable, in theory, could have had many values. However, if we did not have the time or funds to assess all of these values, we could have just randomly sampled some of the values, and therefore we would apply our findings not just to the actual values that were used in the analysis, but rather to the universe of potential values.

A Two-Level Hierarchical Linear Model Example

To introduce this topic let's consider a two-level hierarchical linear model where we are looking at customers that are nested within stores. (So the customer ID would be a random effect as actual customers are only a sample of the universe of potential customers.) In this two-level hierarchical linear model example, the dependent variable (purchase amount) can be expressed as a linear function of effects at two levels.

The Level 1 Model:

$$y_{ij} = B_{oj} + r_{ij}$$

where B_{oj} represents the mean purchase amount for store j and r_{ij} is the residual for customer i in store j (this represents the customer variation within stores).

The Level 2 Model:

$$B_{oj} = \gamma_{00} + \gamma_{01}X_j + v_{oj}$$

where γ_{00} is the average purchase amount across stores, γ_{01} is the coefficient associated with the effect of predictor X, and v_{oj} is the residual effect of store j (this represents the variation between stores after adjusting for predictor X).

If the two levels are combined into a single equation, we have:

$$Y_{ij} = \gamma_{00} + \gamma_{01}X_j + \nu_{0j} + r_{ij}$$

Here, the customer purchase amount is a function of two fixed effects (intercept and predictor X) and two random effects (store and customer within store). When this model is run using a linear mixed model, separate estimates of the customer-to-customer and store-to-store variation can be obtained, in addition to estimates for the fixed effects. The fact that we can determine how much variation is attributable to different random effects in the model is one of the advantages of using a linear mixed model. Following is a list of advantages of using linear mixed models:

- Improved estimates of coefficients for within level regression effects (because we can account for additional variation)
- Improved estimates of coefficient standard errors (because we can account for additional variation)
- Simultaneous estimation of effects at all levels
- Interactions across levels can be correctly modeled
- Unexplained variance from the model can be assigned to various levels

ASSUMPTIONS OF LINEAR MIXED MODELS

Linear mixed models have a lot of the same assumptions as linear regression, with a few differences. Most notably, linear mixed models do not assume homogeneity of variance and that the errors are independent. The following are assumptions for standard regression and for linear mixed models:

- There is a linear relationship between the independent and the dependent variables.
- All relevant variables and no irrelevant variables are included in the model.
- No multicollinearity.
- No outliers.
- Errors are normally distributed.

The following are only assumptions for linear mixed models:

- The covariance structure is properly specified.
- Higher-level variables are assumed to be a random sample (or complete sample) of all values at that level.

NOTE When developing a linear mixed model, you should have a good reason for including effects in the model, especially random effects and interactions between effects at different levels. The reasons can be theoretical, or based on previous work that you or others in your field have done.

Mixed Models...Linear

In this analysis we use the file `Merchandise sales.sav`, as shown in Figure 4-1. This file contains customer purchase data from a large company. The company wants to know if an experimental inventory method is effective at improving sales amount. This is the overall goal of the analyses: to investigate the effect of this inventory method on sales amount, while controlling for other influences.

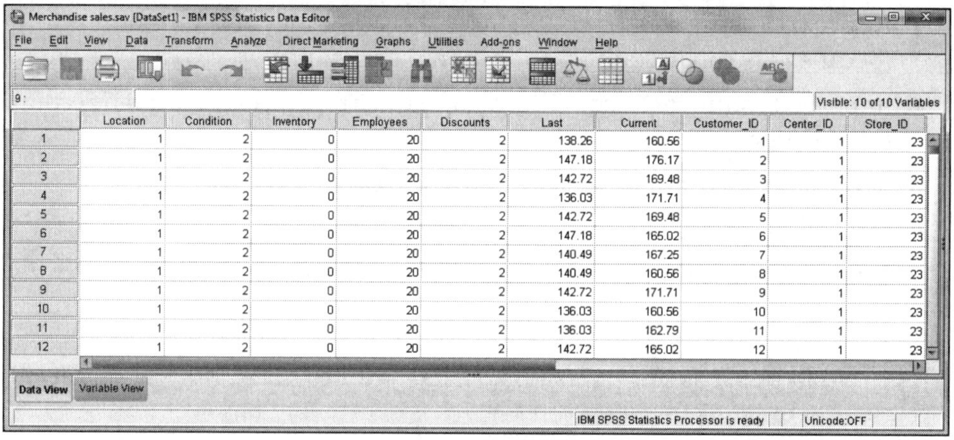

	Location	Condition	Inventory	Employees	Discounts	Last	Current	Customer_ID	Center_ID	Store_ID
1	1	2	0	20	2	138.26	160.56	1	1	23
2	1	2	0	20	2	147.18	176.17	2	1	23
3	1	2	0	20	2	142.72	169.48	3	1	23
4	1	2	0	20	2	136.03	171.71	4	1	23
5	1	2	0	20	2	142.72	169.48	5	1	23
6	1	2	0	20	2	147.18	165.02	6	1	23
7	1	2	0	20	2	140.49	167.25	7	1	23
8	1	2	0	20	2	140.49	160.56	8	1	23
9	1	2	0	20	2	142.72	171.71	9	1	23
10	1	2	0	20	2	136.03	160.56	10	1	23
11	1	2	0	20	2	136.03	162.79	11	1	23
12	1	2	0	20	2	142.72	165.02	12	1	23

Figure 4-1: Merchandise sales data

The data has a hierarchical three-level structure, with customers grouped within stores, and stores grouped within distribution centers. There are 23 distribution centers, 97 stores, and 2133 customers.

Now that we have data, follow these steps to create a hierarchical linear model:

1. Select the Analyze menu, and then choose Mixed Models.

   As shown in Figure 4-2, there are two options to create a hierarchical linear model: linear mixed models and generalized linear mixed models. This procedure expands the general linear model so that data are allowed to have correlated and nonconstant variability.

   Both of these options will create a hierarchical linear model; however, the generalized linear mixed models extend the linear model so that the outcome variable can have a non-normal distribution, linear relationships between the outcome variable and predictors are achieved via a specified link function, and observations can be correlated. For example, you might have data that follow a binomial distribution. In our case we could use either procedure to run the analysis; we will use both so we can point out some differences, but we will start by choosing Linear.

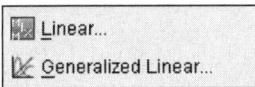

Figure 4-2: Analyze ⇨ Mixed Models menu options

2. Click Analyze ⇨ Mixed Models ⇨ Linear.

As shown in Figure 4-3, the first dialog that opens for the linear mixed models procedure is the Specify Subjects and Repeated dialog. When fitting a hierarchical linear model, you need to specify one or more subject variables to define the units for the study; if more than one variable is listed, the combinations of variable values define the units. In our example, we have customers that are sampled from stores, which are sampled from distribution centers, so there are different designations of the subject for effects at different levels in the model.

NOTE   This dataset has variable labels. In order to see the variables names, as shown in the following screen shots, go to Edit ⇨ Options ⇨ General and choose Display names.

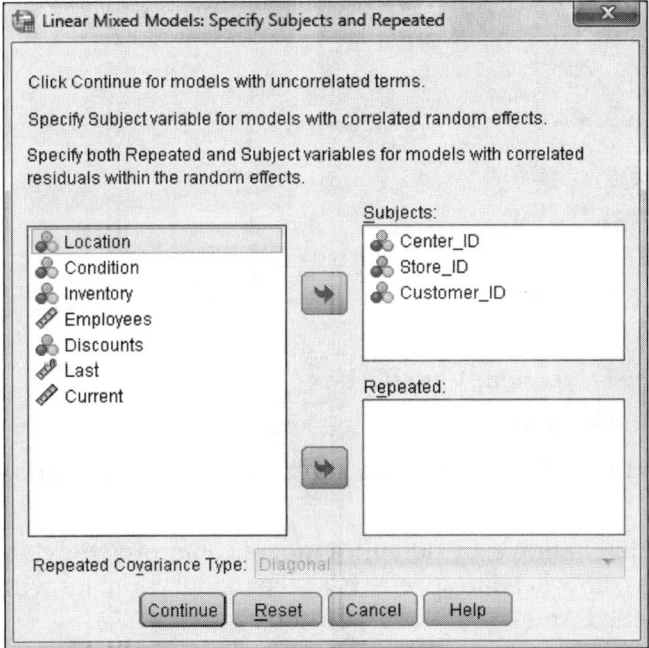

Figure 4-3: Specify Subjects and Repeated dialog

3. Move Center_ID, Store_ID, and Customer_ID into the Subjects box.

NOTE It is not necessary to add the variable Customer_ID in the Subjects box. Because each case is a customer, the linear mixed models procedure will treat customers as a source of random variation.

If you are conducting an analysis where subjects are assessed at multiple time points, you can specify any repeated measures variables and their covariance structure in the Repeated box.

4. Click Continue.

In the Linear Mixed Models dialog you need to specify a dependent variable, as well as specify the model predictors. Continuous predictors need to be placed in the Covariate(s) box, while categorical predictors need to be placed in the Factor(s) box. As shown in Figure 4-4, we will be predicting current sales from last month's sales, the number of store employees, store location, store condition, inventory, and whether the store accepts discounts.

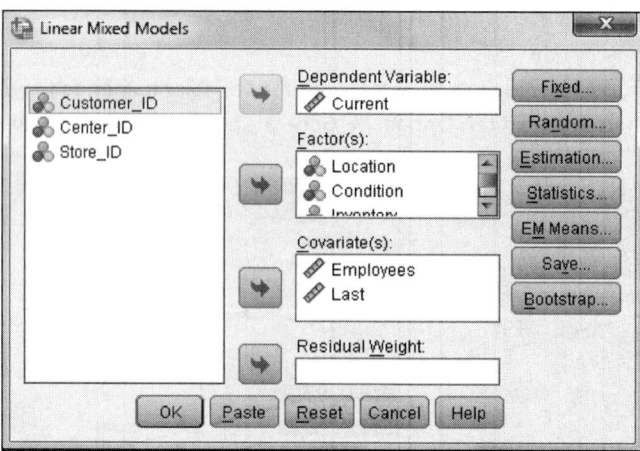

Figure 4-4: Linear Mixed Models dialog

5. Move Current into the Dependent Variable box.

6. Move Last and Employees into the Covariate(s) box.

7. Move Location, Condition, Discounts, and Inventory into the Factor(s) box.

Although the OK button is active, by default, a model containing only an intercept will be fit. We now need to specify how the model variables will be used by selecting the Fixed and Random buttons.

8. Click Fixed.

Main effects and interaction terms can be added to the model. When the Build terms option is selected in the Fixed Effects dialog you can use the drop-down menu to select the type of effect. Factorial is selected as a default, and this means that all main effect and interaction terms for factor variables selected in the Factors and Covariates list will be added to the model when the Add button is selected (be careful here because if all the variables are selected, this would create all the *n*-way interactions, not just two way interactions). Model terms for nested items can be constructed by clicking the Build nested terms option button, then using the By and Within buttons to construct model terms. As shown in Figure 4-5, here we will only use main effects as fixed effects.

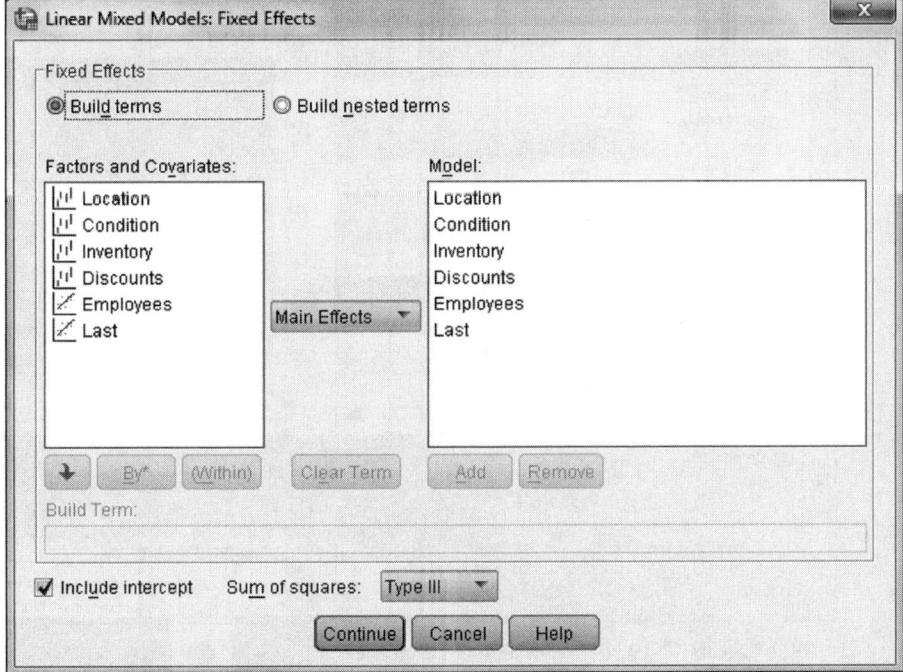

Figure 4-5: Fixed Effects dialog

9. Click the drop-down list and select Main Effects.

10. Select all the variables.

11. Click the Add button to move the variables to the Model box.

    Interactions could be added by clicking the drop-down list and specifying the variables to include. By default, an intercept is included.

12. Click Continue to return to the main Linear Mixed Models dialog shown in Figure 4-4.

13. Click Random.

The Random Effects dialog, shown in Figure 4-6, is used to specify the model terms for random effects. It is also used to specify subject groupings and the appropriate covariance structure. In our example, we already specified that all our predictors were fixed effects, so we will have no random effects. However, earlier we did indicate that Center_ID, Store_ID, and Customer_ID were Subjects variables, so we need to specify this information here.

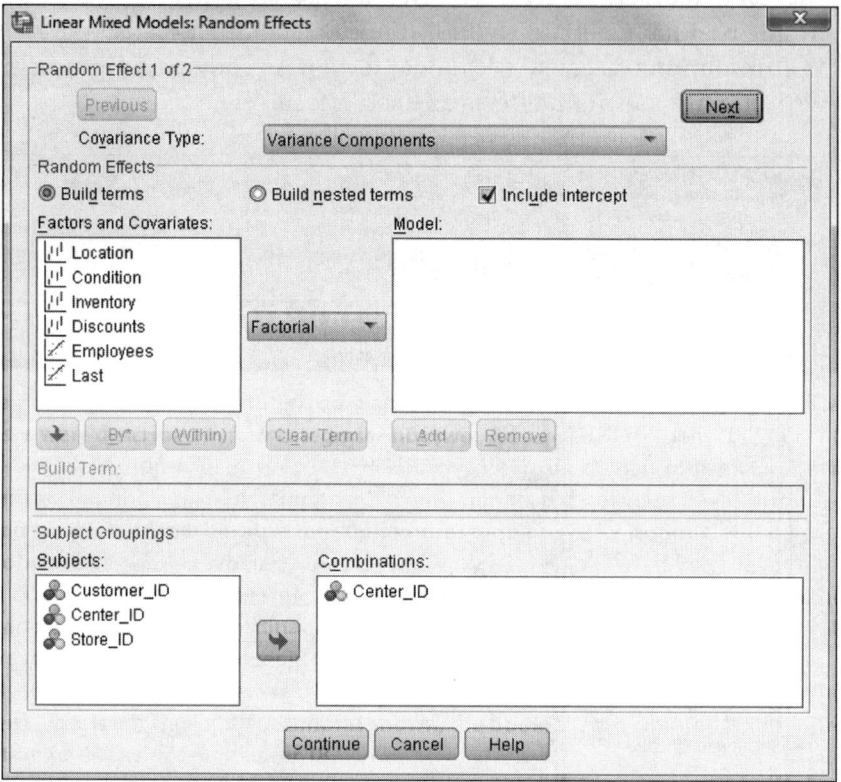

Figure 4-6: Random Effects dialog

The covariance type accounts for the relationships between the different hierarchical levels in the analysis. Variance Components is selected as the Covariance Type. This means that variance estimates will be made of the intercept based on the distribution center to distribution center variation. The Variance Components covariance type is often used for relatively simple models, but you should be aware that more complex covariance structures may be appropriate for certain types of models.

NOTE Specifying a covariance matrix to be estimated and variables for random effects is the core of a multilevel model and is what separates it from a standard general linear model.

14. Move Center_ID into the Combinations box.

15. Click Include intercept.

    As shown in Figure 4-6, Center_ID is placed in the Combinations list box because it determines the units used to calculate this variation (distribution center to distribution center variation).

NOTE How do you know which covariance type to use? As you will see in the output, the linear mixed models procedure provides information criterion measures that aid in evaluating and comparing models. These measures can guide the selection of a covariance model. These measures are not interpreted directly, but are used to compare alternative models applied to the same data, because lower values indicate better fit.

    Multiple random effects can be specified and each can have their own unique Covariance Type.

16. Click Next.

17. Move Store_ID into the Combinations box. The Combinations box will now have both Center_ID and Store_ID, as shown in Figure 4-7.

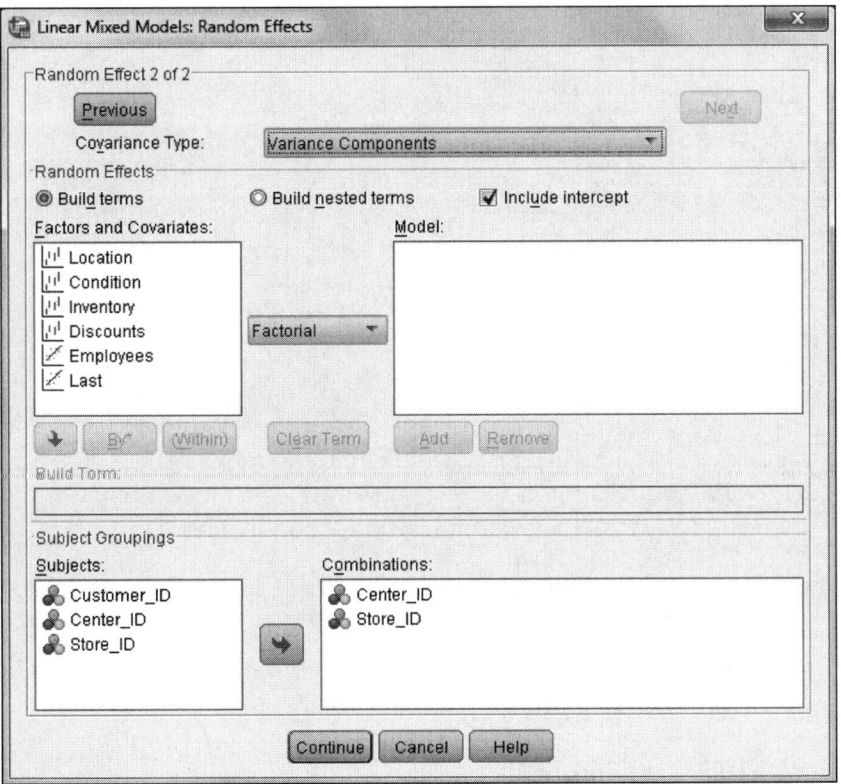

Figure 4-7: Random Effects dialog

18. Click Include intercept.

   As shown in Figure 4-7, by adding Center_ID and Store_ID into the Combinations box, we can now take into account distribution center to store variation.

19. Click Continue to return to the main Linear Mixed Models dialog shown in Figure 4-4.

20. Click Estimation.

   The Estimation dialog (see Figure 4-8) allows you to specify the estimation method and to adjust technical aspects of model estimation—we will not make any changes here. However, it is important to have a large sample; preferably at least 50 cases, at the higher levels.

> **NOTE**   The demands of maximum likelihood estimation mean that sometimes it will be difficult for the linear mixed models procedure to reach convergence. Pay careful attention to any warning you receive about problems estimating a model. You may need to try a different covariance structure, or specify the model differently. As a reference see http://stats.stackexchange.com/questions/116770/reml-or-ml-to-compare-two-mixed-effects-models-with-differing-fixed-effects.

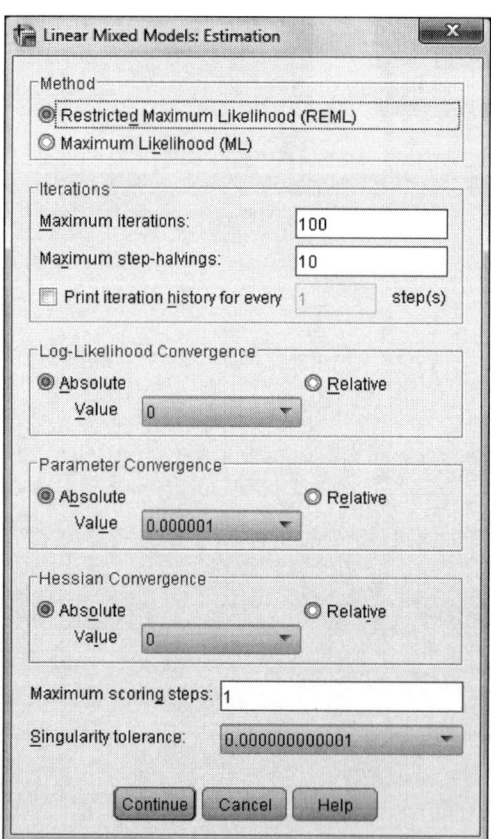

Figure 4-8: Estimation dialog

21. Click Continue to return to the main Linear Mixed Models dialog shown in Figure 4-4.

22. Click Statistics.

The Statistics button opens the dialog shown in Figure 4-9. This dialog provides options that control which statistical summaries are displayed in the output. It is common to choose the Parameter estimates, Tests for covariance parameters, and Covariances of random effects options.

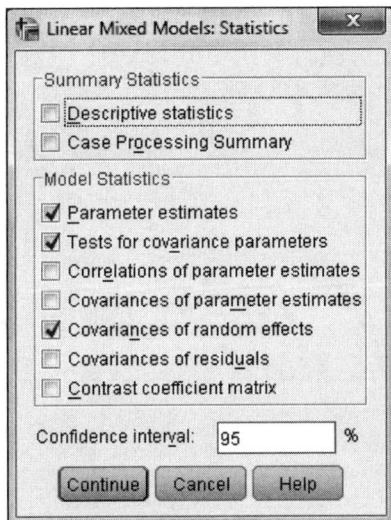

Figure 4-9: Statistics dialog

23. Check the Parameter estimates, Tests for covariance parameters, and Covariances of random effects check boxes.

24. Click Continue to return to the main Linear Mixed Models dialog shown in Figure 4-4.

25. Click EM Means.

Estimated marginal means for fixed effects can be displayed using the EM Means dialog (see Figure 4-10). You can also test for mean differences between categories to identify which factor levels differ from each other.

26. Click Continue to return to the main Linear Mixed Models dialog shown in Figure 4-4.

27. Click Save.

The Save dialog (see Figure 4-11) is used to save predicted values and residuals.

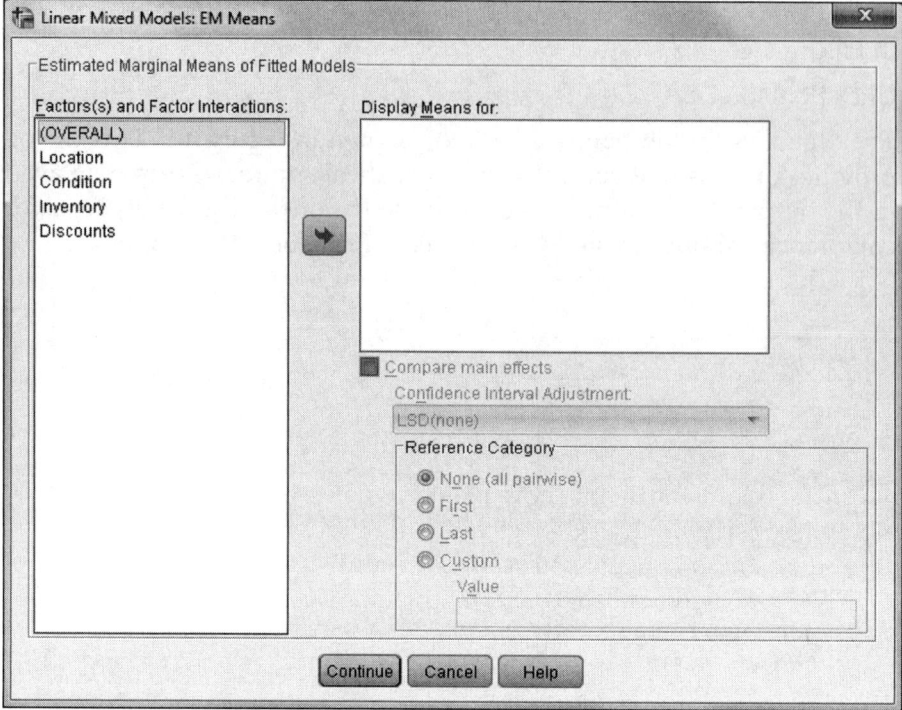

Figure 4-10: EM Means dialog

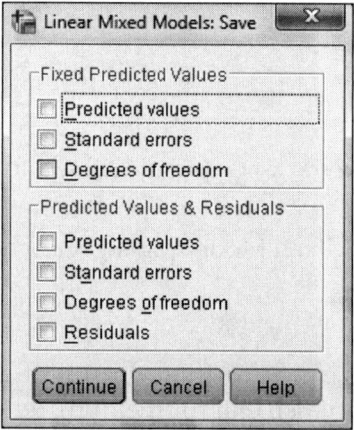

Figure 4-11: Save dialog

28. Click Continue to return to the main Linear Mixed Models dialog shown in Figure 4-4.

29. Click OK to run the analysis. You will see the tables described in the following section, Figures 4-12 to 4-17.

Mixed Models...Linear (Output)

The Model Dimension table (see Figure 4-12) identifies the model fit to the data and provides a valuable check to make sure that the model used is the one you intended. Effects are grouped by section pertaining to Fixed, Random, and Residual effects. Here we can see that all of our predictors are fixed effects, and the only random effects are based on the subject variables. The Number of Levels column is the number of categories for that predictor, while the Number of Parameters column lists the number of parameters needed to model each predictor. The covariance structure is the default of Variance Components (VC), which is adequate for many simple models. In particular, VC provides an estimate of the intercept variance.

Model Dimension[a]

		Number of Levels	Covariance Structure	Number of Parameters	Subject Variables
Fixed Effects	Intercept	1		1	
	Location	3		2	
	Condition	2		1	
	Inventory	2		1	
	Discounts	2		1	
	Last	1		1	
	Employees	1		1	
Random Effects	Intercept[b]	1	Variance Components	1	Center_ID
	Intercept[b]	1	Variance Components	1	Center_ID * Store_ID
Residual				1	
Total		14		11	

a. Dependent Variable: Current Current Sales.

b. As of version 11.5, the syntax rules for the RANDOM subcommand have changed. Your command syntax may yield results that differ from those produced by prior versions. If you are using version 11 syntax, please consult the current syntax reference guide for more information.

Figure 4-12: Model Dimension table

The measures in the Information Criteria table (see Figure 4-13) are used to compare different models applied to the same data; with lower values indicating a better fit to the data. We will use these measures when we run another model assuming different covariance structures (see Figure 4-31). For the moment, we will skip that table.

The Tests of Fixed Effects table (see Figure 4-14) allows us to determine which fixed effect predictors are statistically significant. In this example, all of the fixed effect predictors are statistically significant except number of employees.

Information Criteria[a]

-2 Restricted Log Likelihood	14201.783
Akaike's Information Criterion (AIC)	14207.783
Hurvich and Tsai's Criterion (AICC)	14207.795
Bozdogan's Criterion (CAIC)	14227.768
Schwarz's Bayesian Criterion (BIC)	14224.768

The information criteria are displayed in smaller-is-better form.

a. Dependent Variable: Current Current Sales.

Figure 4-13: Information Criteria table

Type III Tests of Fixed Effects[a]

Source	Numerator df	Denominator df	F	Sig.
Intercept	1	80.895	176.439	.000
Location	2	18.206	4.011	.036
Condition	1	21.161	4.414	.048
Inventory	1	57.446	87.417	.000
Discounts	1	2064.262	59.027	.000
Employees	1	60.454	.000	.990
Last	1	1612.532	685.469	.000

a. Dependent Variable: Current Current Sales.

Figure 4-14: Type III Tests of Fixed Effects table

Whereas the Tests of Fixed Effects table allows us to determine which fixed effect predictors are statistically significant, the Estimates of Fixed Effects table (see Figure 4-15) allows us to interpret the magnitude and direction of the effects.

Estimates of Fixed Effects[a]

Parameter	Estimate	Std. Error	df	t	Sig.	95% Confidence Interval	
						Lower Bound	Upper Bound
Intercept	104.278268	7.168531	57.228	14.547	.000	89.924771	118.631764
[Location=1]	-3.326007	5.261325	20.265	-.632	.534	-14.291760	7.639746
[Location=2]	10.455939	5.221442	16.764	2.003	.062	-.572158	21.484037
[Location=3]	0[b]	0	.	.	.	.	.
[Condition=1]	-9.742871	4.637587	21.161	-2.101	.048	-19.382806	-.102935
[Condition=2]	0[b]	0	.	.	.	.	.
[Inventory=0]	-13.791533	1.475074	57.446	-9.350	.000	-16.744820	-10.838245
[Inventory=1]	0[b]	0	.	.	.	.	.
[Discounts=1]	-3.766542	.490249	2064.262	-7.683	.000	-4.727976	-2.805108
[Discounts=2]	0[b]	0	.	.	.	.	.
Employees	.003913	.299409	60.454	.013	.990	-.594901	.602727
Last	.499280	.019070	1612.532	26.181	.000	.461875	.536684

a. Dependent Variable: Current Current Sales.

b. This parameter is set to zero because it is redundant.

Figure 4-15: Estimates of Fixed Effects table

Let's take a look at some of these predictors and their impact. For the variable discount, we see a statistically significant result and the parameter estimate is –3.77; this means that stores that do accept discounts earn about $3.77 less than stores that do not accept discounts (while controlling for all the other variables in the model). As another example, for the variable inventory (our main variable of interest), we see a statistically significant result and the parameter estimate is –13.79; this means that stores that have the standard inventory earn about $13.79 less than stores that have the experimental inventory (while controlling for all the other variables in the model). As another example, for the variable condition, we see a statistically significant result and the parameter estimate is –9.74; this means that stores that are older earn about $9.74 less than stores that are newer (while controlling for all the other variables in the model). Finally, the last month's sales parameter is 0.50, which indicates that a $1 increase in last month's sales is associated with a $0.50 increase in current sales (while controlling for all the other variables in the model). The Intercept is 104.28, which indicates the sales amount of a customer that has values of 0 on all the variables. Note that it is common to center continuous predictors (subtracting the mean from the variable), so that the intercept can be interpreted as the mean value of the continuous predictor rather than when the value is 0.

The last table reports the covariance parameters (see Figure 4-16). There is a residual covariance estimate of 39.10. There is an intercept covariance estimate of 83.63, when the subject is equal to distribution center. Finally there is an intercept covariance estimate of 37.73, when the subject is equal to distribution center and store. All of these covariance estimates are significant, which suggests that there is still significant variability to be explained within stores and between stores.

Estimates of Covariance Parameters[a]

Parameter		Estimate	Std. Error	Wald Z	Sig.	95% Confidence Interval	
						Lower Bound	Upper Bound
Residual		39.095704	1.235846	31.635	.000	36.747000	41.594526
Intercept [subject = Center_ID]	Variance	83.626062	32.791072	2.550	.011	38.776835	180.347835
Intercept [subject = Center_ID * Store_ID]	Variance	37.733515	7.526688	5.013	.000	25.523396	55.784824

a. Dependent Variable: Current Current Sales.

Figure 4-16: Estimates of Covariance Parameters table

Often, researchers will compare the results from the Estimates of Covariance Parameters table to a null model (a model that only includes the random effects). Such a model is shown in Figure 4-17. Compared to the null model, the addition of the two factor variables reduces the residual variability, from 50.32 to 39.10. This decrease of 11.22 suggests that the predictors account for about 22.30% (11.22/50.32) of the within-store variability in sales.

Estimates of Covariance Parameters[a]

						95% Confidence Interval	
Parameter		Estimate	Std. Error	Wald Z	Sig.	Lower Bound	Upper Bound
Residual		50.318063	1.577057	31.906	.000	47.320110	53.505950
Intercept [subject = Center_ID]	Variance	641.341649	205.005925	3.128	.002	342.768935	1199.989465
Intercept [subject = Center_ID * Store_ID]	Variance	162.402215	27.032628	6.008	.000	117.193998	225.049747

a. Dependent Variable: Last Last Month's Sales.

Figure 4-17: Estimates of Covariance Parameters table for a null model

Comparing our model (with predictors) to the null model (without predictors), the between-store variance in sales in the intercepts has dropped from 641.34 to 83.63. This suggests that within-store predictors account for about 86.96% (557.71/641.34) of the between-store variability in sales.

Comparing our model to the null model, the between-store variance in sales in the intercepts has dropped from 162.40 to 37.73. This suggests that within-store predictors account for about 76.77% (124.67/162.40) of the between-store variability in sales.

It seems that our model is an improvement over the null model. It also seems all of the variables were important predictors, except for the variable number of employees. Furthermore, there were differences between inventory methods, as the experimental method earned about $13.79 more than the standard method.

Mixed Models...Generalized Linear

As mentioned in the "Mixed Models...Linear" section earlier in this chapter, there are two options to create a hierarchical linear model: linear mixed models and generalized linear lixed models. Both of these options will create a hierarchical linear model; however, the generalized linear mixed models option extends the linear model to allow observations that are correlated, it allows for response variables from non-normal distributions, and it allows for response variables to come from distributions that are not linear. For example, you might have data that follow a binomial distribution. Earlier, we demonstrated the Linear Mixed Models option; now we will use the same data file and replicate our findings using the Generalized Linear Mixed Models option:

1. Click Analyze ➪ Mixed Models ➪ Generalized Linear.

   As shown in Figure 4-18, the first dialog that opens for the Generalized Linear Mixed Models procedure is the Data Structure dialog. Although the user interface looks very different, you are doing essentially the same thing as when using the first procedure. As in the previous example, when fitting a hierarchical linear model, you need to specify one or more subject variables to define the units for the study.

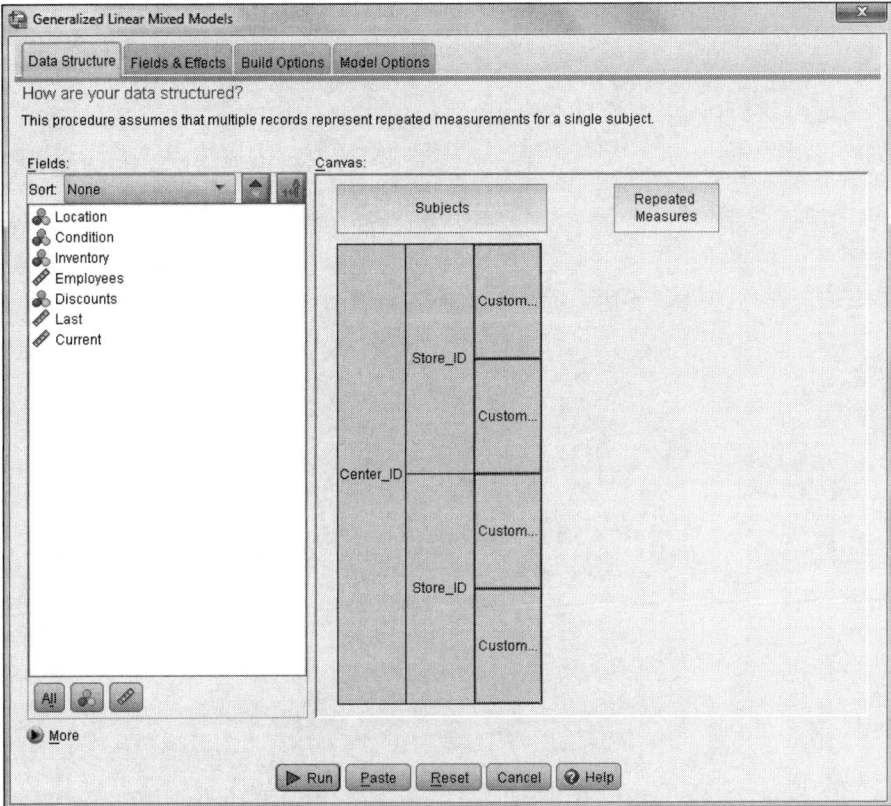

Figure 4-18: Data Structure dialog

2. Move Center_ID, Store_ID, and Customer_ID into the Subjects box.

   All of the variables specified in the Subjects list are used to define subjects for the residual covariance structure.

   If you are conducting an analysis where subjects are assessed at multiple time points, you can specify any repeated measures variables and their covariance structure in the Repeated Measures box.

3. Click the Fields & Effects tab.

   As shown in Figure 4-19, the Target item allows users to specify the target or dependent variable. You can also specify the Target's Distribution and the Target's Relationship (Link) to the predictors through the link function. The linear mixed model option assumed a normal distribution for the target and used an identity link function. Here, under the generalized linear mixed model option, you are not restricted to linear relationships. You can specify different distributions and link functions.

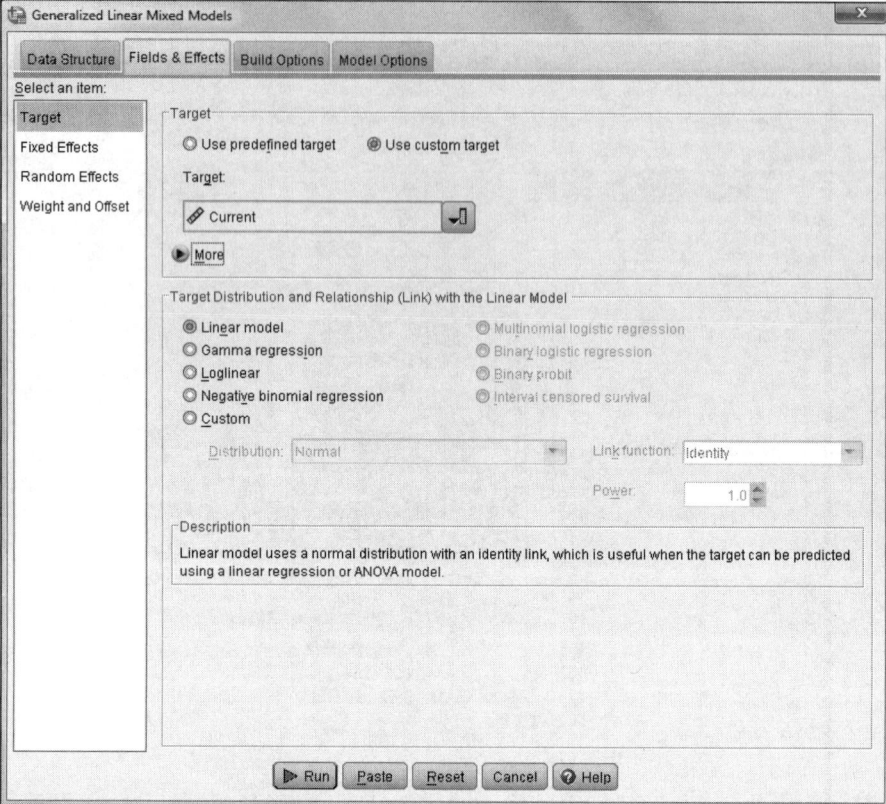

Figure 4-19: Fields & Effects: Target dialog

4. Click Use custom target.

5. Select the variable Current as the target.

6. Click the Fixed Effects item.

   The Fixed Effects item (see Figure 4-20) allows users to specify the fixed effects (predictor variables) in the model. Fixed effects factors are generally thought of as fields whose values of interest are all represented in the dataset. Categorical fields will be treated as factors and continuous fields will be treated as covariates.

7. Click Use custom inputs.

8. Select the variables Location, Condition, Inventory, Employees, Discounts, and Last and drag them to the Main drop zone to create main effects.

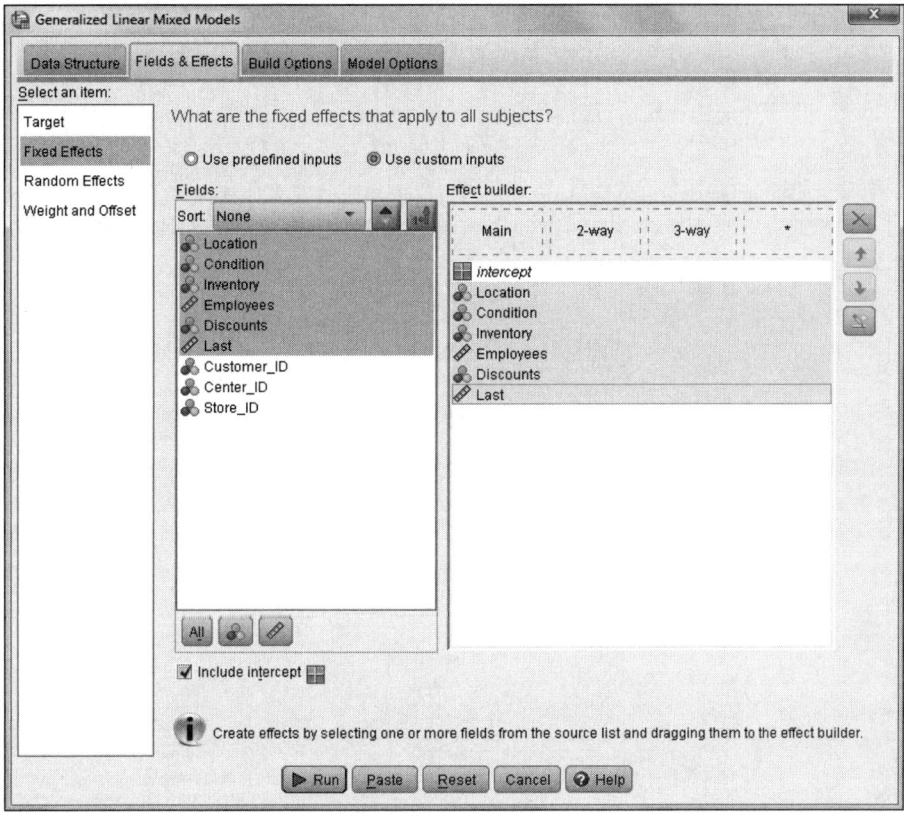

Figure 4-20: Fields & Effects: Fixed Effects dialog

9. Click the Random Effects item.

The Random Effects item (see Figure 4-21) allows users to specify the random effects in the model. Random effects factors are fields whose values in the data file can be considered a random sample from a larger population of values. They are useful for explaining excess variation in the target. The procedure automatically creates a Random Effect block for each subject beyond the innermost subject. Notice that two intercept-only random effect subject blocks were created for us, as opposed to the previous procedure where we had to create these; one block has Center_ID as the subject field and the other block has Center_ID*Store_ID as the subject field.

The first block should account for correlation between stores within the same distribution center. The second block should account for correlation between customers within the same store.

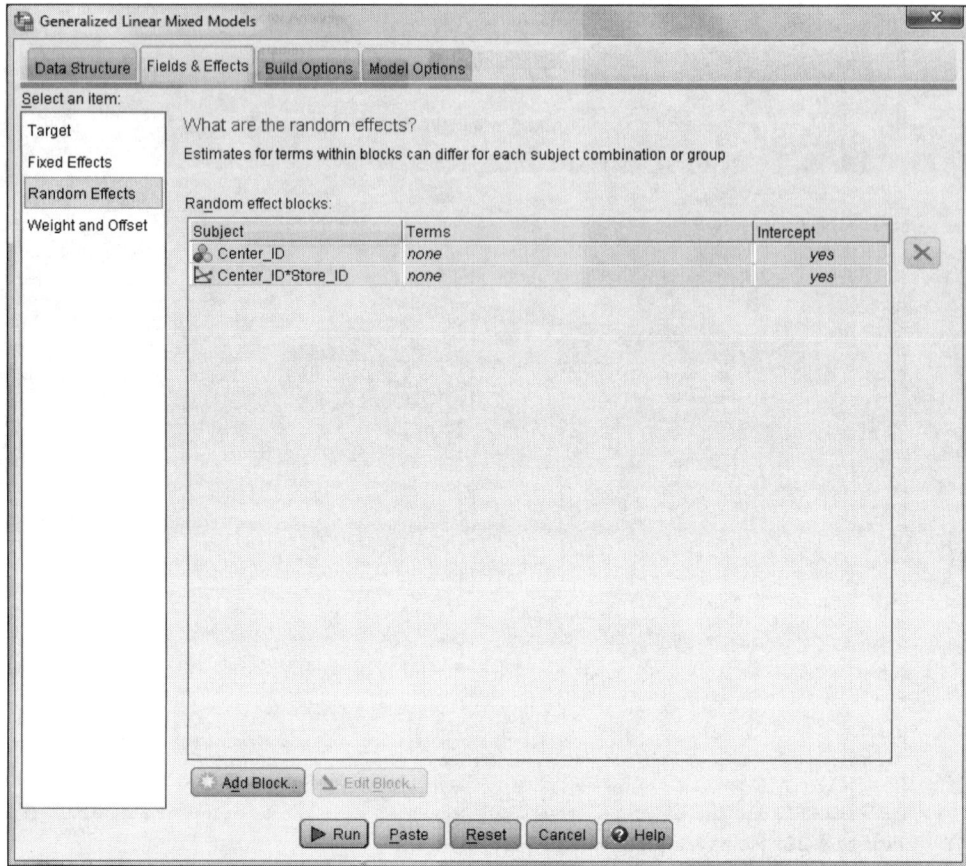

Figure 4-21: Fields & Effects: Random Effects dialog

10. Click Run.

11. Double-click the model object in the output viewer.

> **NOTE** Under Edit ⇨ Options ⇨ Output users have a choice of viewing the results
> from the generalized linear mixed models procedure as model viewer output (the
> default) or traditional tables. We show the results as model viewer output because
> it is the default. However, if you are estimating many models, activating and clicking
> through the panels gets frustrating; the pivot table view can be read more quickly.

Mixed Models…Generalized Linear (Output)

The Model Summary table (see Figure 4-22) confirms basic model selections like
the choices of target, probability distribution, link function, and model fit. The
Akaike corrected and Bayesian measures are used for selecting and comparing

models—smaller values indicate better models. Notice that these values are exactly the same as those obtained using the linear mixed models procedure.

Model Summary

Target: Current Sales

Target	Current Sales
Probability Distribution	Normal
Link Function	Identity
Information Criterion — **Akaike Corrected**	14,207.795
Bayesian	14,224.768

Information criteria are based on the -2 log likelihood (14,201.783) and are used to compare models. Models with smaller information criterion values fit better.

Figure 4-22: Model Summary

The Data Structure view (see Figure 4-23) shows the actual values for the first subject—this helps you to confirm your data structure.

Data Structure

Target: Current Sales

	Subjects		Target
	Distribution Center ID	**Store ID**	**Current Sales**
	1	23	160.56
	1	23	176.17
	1	23	169.48
	1	23	171.71
	1	23	169.48
Data For First Subject	1	23	165.02
	1	23	167.25
	1	23	160.56
	1	23	171.71
	1	23	160.56
Total Number of Levels	23	97	

Only the first 10 records are displayed.
One or more subject fields were specified but not actually used in the analysis.

Figure 4-23: Data Structure

The Predicted by Observed view (see Figure 4-24) shows the relationship between the actual values of the target variable and those predicted by the model. Ideally we would like to see that the points lie near the diagonal, which means that no records are fit badly by the model. In our example it seems the model is doing a good job.

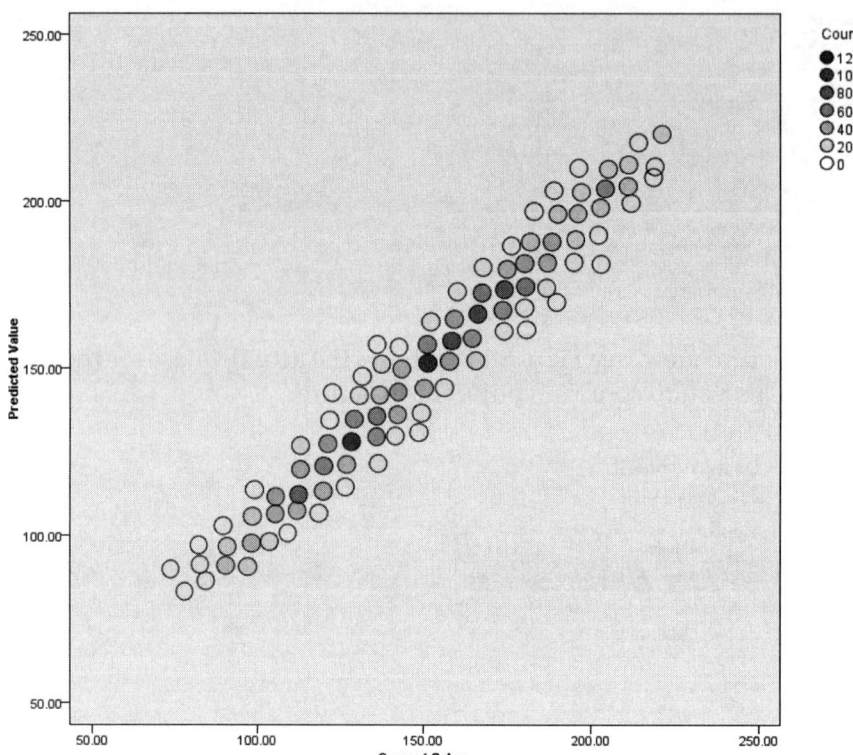

Figure 4-24: Predicted by Observed

The Fixed Effects view (see Figure 4-25) is a visualization of the traditional tests of the Fixed Effects table. The effects are ordered from top to bottom in the order in which they were specified on the Fixed Effects settings, and the thickness of each line is based on the statistical significance of the effect. In our example, the variables Inventory, Discounts, and Last have the thickest lines, while the variable Employees has the thinnest line.

1. Select Table in the style drop-down of the effects view.

    This is the traditional test of the Fixed Effects table (see Figure 4-26) for the overall model and individual predictors. The model is statistically significant, as are all the predictors except for the Employees variable. Notice that these values are similar to those obtained using the linear mixed models procedure.

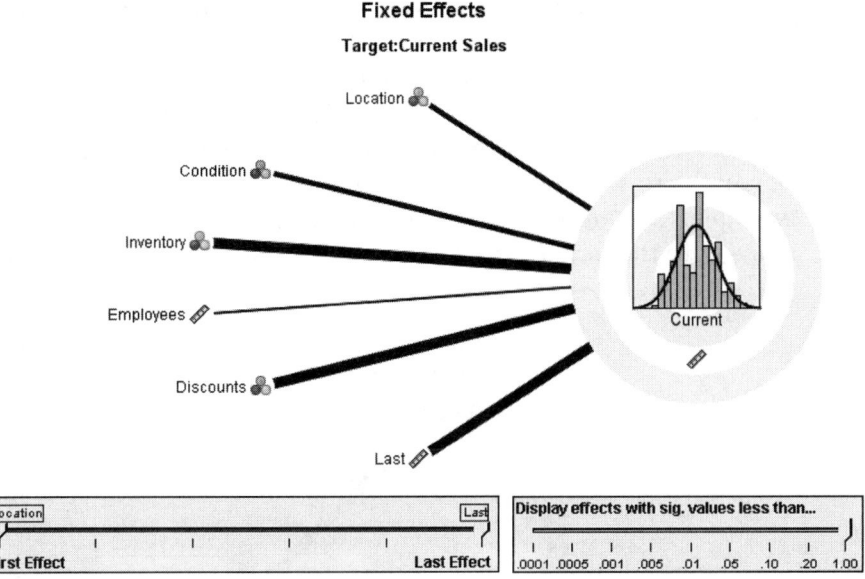

Figure 4-25: Fixed Effects (diagram)

Fixed Effects

Target:Current Sales

Source	F	df1	df2	Sig.
Corrected Model ▼	159.124	7	2,125	.000
Location	4.011	2	2,125	.018
Condition	4.414	1	2,125	.036
Inventory	87.417	1	2,125	.000
Employees	0.000	1	2,125	.990
Discounts	59.027	1	2,125	.000
Last	685.469	1	2,125	.000

Probability distribution:Normal
Link function:Identity

Location ———————————————————— Last
First Effect   Last Effect
Display effects with sig. values less than...

.0001 .0005 .001 .005 .01 .05 .10 .20 1.00

Figure 4-26: Fixed Effects (table)

The Fixed Coefficients view (see Figure 4-27) is a visualization of the traditional Parameter Estimates table. The coefficients are ordered from top to bottom in the order in which they were specified on the Fixed Effects settings, and the thickness of each line is based on the statistical significance of the effect. Also, the shading of the line indicates the direction of the relationship (blue is positive, while orange is negative). In our example, the variables Inventory and Discounts have negative relationships with the target, while the variable Last has a positive relationship with the target.

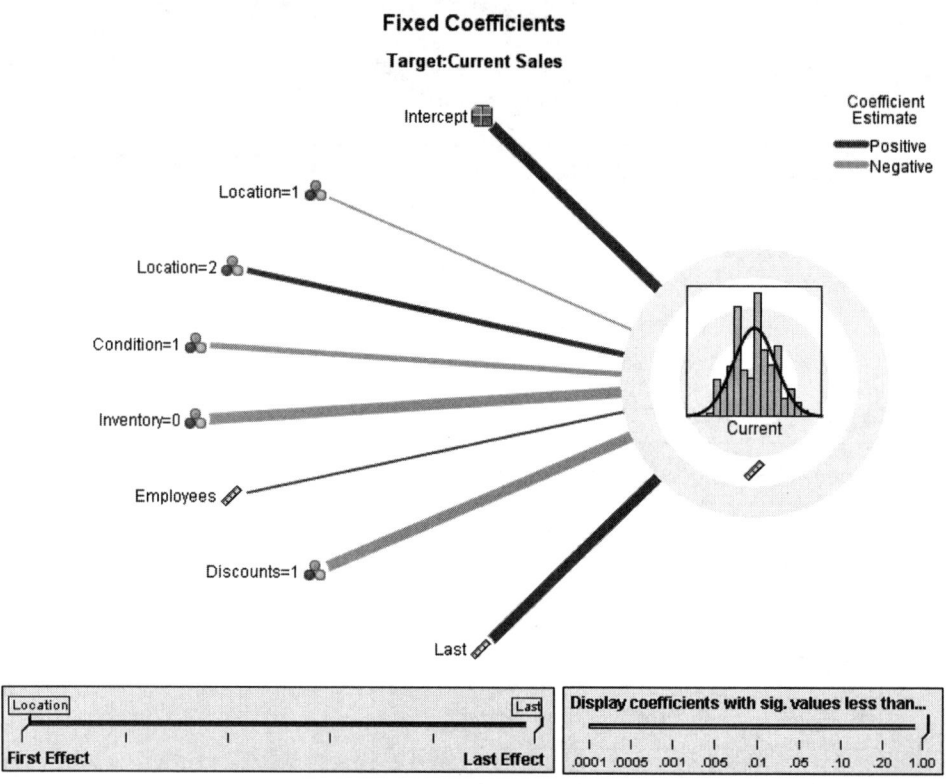

Figure 4-27: Fixed Coefficients (diagram)

2. Select Table in the style drop-down of the coefficients view.

   Similar to when we used the linear mixed models procedure, the Fixed Coefficients table (see Figure 4-28) allows us to interpret the magnitude and direction of the effects. Here we see the exact same result as when we ran the linear mixed model procedure.

Fixed Coefficients

Target:Current Sales

Model Term	Coefficient ▼	Std.Error	t	Sig.	95% Confidence Interval	
					Lower	Upper
Intercept	104.278	7.169	14.547	.000	90.220	118.336
Location=1	-3.326	5.261	-0.632	.527	-13.644	6.992
Location=2	10.456	5.221	2.003	.045	0.216	20.696
Location=3	0[a]					
Condition=1	-9.743	4.638	-2.101	.036	-18.838	-0.648
Condition=2	0[a]					
Inventory=0	-13.792	1.475	-9.350	.000	-16.684	-10.899
Inventory=1	0[a]					
Employees	0.004	0.299	0.013	.990	-0.583	0.591
Discounts=1	-3.767	0.490	-7.683	.000	-4.728	-2.805
Discounts=2	0[a]					
Last	0.499	0.019	26.181	.000	0.462	0.537

Probability distribution:Normal
Link function:Identity

[a]This coefficient is set to zero because it is redundant.

Figure 4-28: Fixed Coefficients (table)

The Covariance Parameters view (see Figure 4-29) displays the covariance parameter estimates and related statistics for residual and random effects. The residual covariance parameters are shown by default. Again, here we see the exact same result as when we ran the linear mixed model procedure.

Covariance Parameters

Target:Current Sales

Covariance Parameters	Residual Effect	1
	Random Effects	2
Design Matrix Columns	Fixed Effects	12
	Random Effects	7[a]
Common Subjects		23

Common subjects are based on the subject specifications for the residual and random effects and are used to chunk the data for better performance.

[a]This is the number of columns per common subject.

Residual Effect	Estimate	Std.Error	Z	Sig.	95% Confidence Interval	
					Lower	Upper
Variance	39.096	1.236	31.635	.000	36.747	41.595

Covariance Structure:Scaled Identity
Subject Specification:(None)

Figure 4-29: Covariance Parameters

Adjusting Model Structure

As an additional exercise, you can fit a linear regression model to this data; all you need to do is delete the two random effects blocks on the Random Effects item (see Figure 4-30).

1. Click Run.

2. Double-click the model object in the output viewer.

   As mentioned earlier, we could use information criterion values to compare models. Based on the information criteria (see Figure 4-31), the linear mixed model with two random intercepts is preferred over the linear regression model because it has smaller AICC (14207.795 vs. 14461.699) and BIC (14224.768 vs. 14467.329) values. In this way we can compare different models to determine which better fit the data.

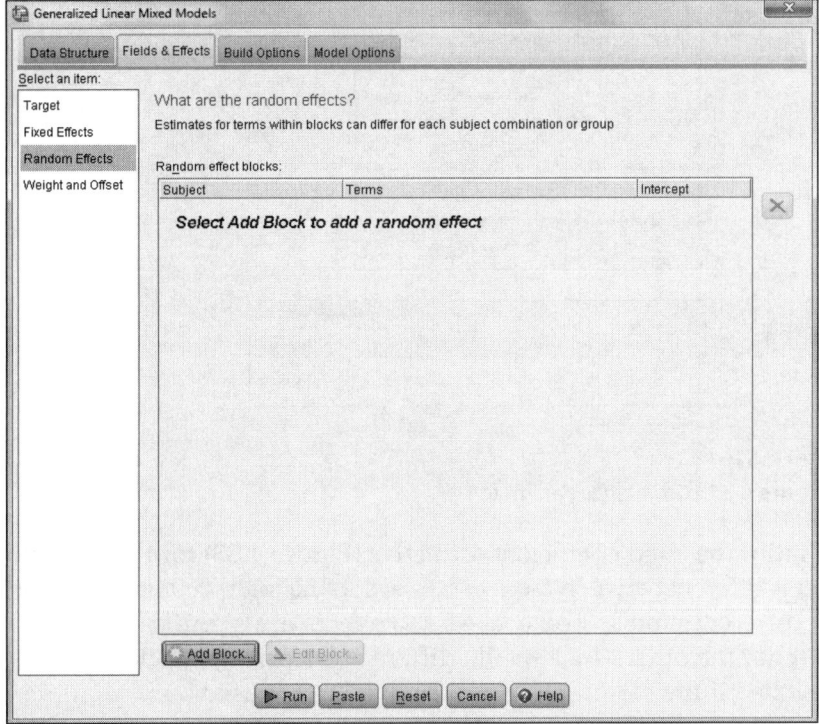

Figure 4-30: No random effects

Model Summary

Target: Current Sales

Target	Current Sales
Probability Distribution	Normal
Link Function	Identity
Information Criterion — Akaike Corrected	14,461.669
Information Criterion — Bayesian	14,467.329

Information criteria are based on the -2 log likelihood (14,459.667) and are used to compare models. Models with smaller information criterion values fit better.

Figure 4-31: Model Summary

In addition, the variance estimate for the residual effect is larger in the linear regression model than in the linear mixed model (Figure 4-32).

Covariance Parameters

Target:Current Sales

Covariance Parameters	Residual Effect	1
	Random Effects	0
Design Matrix Columns	Fixed Effects	12
	Random Effects	0

Residual Effect	Estimate	Std.Error	Z	Sig.	95% Confidence Interval	
					Lower	Upper
Variance[1]	51.316	1.574	32.596	.000	48.321	54.496

Covariance Structure:Scaled Identity

[1]This is the scale parameter.

Figure 4-32: Covariance Parameters

Finally, the fixed coefficient estimates (Figure 4-33) for the predictors are very different between the two models, so the interpretation of these effects is different (and in some cases the effects are significant in one model but not the other). As a result, different (incorrect) conclusions would be reached if the hierarchical linear model is not used.

Fixed Coefficients

Target:Current Sales

Model Term	Coefficient ▼	Std.Error	t	Sig.	95% Confidence Interval	
					Lower	Upper
Intercept	51.728	1.732	29.859	.000	48.331	55.126
Location=1	0.477	0.547	0.873	.383	-0.595	1.550
Location=2	1.724	0.490	3.517	.000	0.763	2.686
Location=3	0[a]					
Condition=1	-0.088	0.514	-0.171	.864	-1.095	0.919
Condition=2	0[a]					
Inventory=0	-13.450	0.331	-40.645	.000	-14.099	-12.801
Inventory=1	0[a]					
Employees	-0.213	0.065	-3.252	.001	-0.341	-0.084
Discounts=1	-2.001	0.428	-4.671	.000	-2.841	-1.161
Discounts=2	0[a]					
Last	0.910	0.008	109.038	.000	0.894	0.927

Probability distribution:Normal
Link function:Identity

[a]This coefficient is set to zero because it is redundant.

Figure 4-33: Fixed Coefficients

Data Visualization

The length of Part II, encompassing a wide variety of visualization topics in six chapters, is a perhaps a bit of surprise for some readers. When Jesus and I have spoken to clients about custom training engagements, trying to negotiate coverage and the amount of time to dedicate to each topic, the topic of visualization is often among the most difficult to navigate. Clients we have met seem to assume that they've got this topic covered, that it is the easiest to master on their own, or that maybe they don't need this material at all. In short, of all the topics in SPSS Statistics, it is the most commonly deemphasized in a client's wish list. Visualization is seen as an almost mechanical step—sometimes literally so—where the "results" are copied and pasted into a preexisting format that imitates earlier reports on older versions of the same data. Of course, not everyone is engaged in routine reports that are repeated on a monthly or quarterly basis, but the emphasis on visualization as business communication is common. We believe that visualization is powerful throughout the process of analysis and that one cannot separate the two.

Towards that end, Part II is lengthy and diverse. The first two chapters, numbered 5 and 6, can be thought of as a pair. In Chapter 5, the Graphboard Template Chooser is discussed, and the graphs are produced primarily using the menus. Of all the chapters in the book, it is, perhaps, the one focusing the most on fundamentals. It is important to include, however, because if you are new to graphing in SPSS, Chapter 6 will require some comfort in the graphing menus. Chapter 6 may prove a powerful experience if you dive in and try it. Graphing

Production Language (GPL) multiples the power of SPSS graphics by nearly an order of magnitude. It does require coding, so read Chapter 5 first, and consider reading Chapter 16 as well. Chapter 16 is a basic introduction to SPSS Statistics Syntax, so its importance as background for Chapter 6 is determined by your existing comfort with Syntax. Chapter 7 also utilizes Graphboard Template Chooser, but it is dedicated in its entirely to mapping. Since it spends time in some of the same menus, it is not a bad idea to read Chapter 5 before Chapter 7, but those interested in maps can probably start with Chapter 7 without much difficulty. Taken together, they are the most traditional of the chapters in Part II, but even veteran SPSS Statistics users should find a wealth of techniques that are new to them, and that make them both more comfortable and more ambitious in their use of SPSS Statistics graphics.

We are proud that we are able to add Chapter 8, dedicated to geospatial analytics. A major addition to SPSS features in version 23, we wanted a practical application using real world data. Predictive policing is fundamentally about having resources in the right place at the right time. Andrew Wheeler's expertise in this area was an ideal contribution to the understanding of this approach, and certainly added to our own sophistication with these techniques.

Chapter 9 combines topics from other chapters in a way that is somewhat unique in the book. The notion of perceptual mapping is to use the "data reduction" of rich datasets (with multiple dimensions) to make the data more easily visualized in a two dimensional graphic. Several techniques take advantage of this approach—correspondence analysis is just one of them. Since the focus of the chapter is on the creation and interpretation of the perceptual map itself, the theory behind the data reduction aspect is covered only in brief. The Multiple Correspondence Analysis technique is also used in Chapter 9 to create perceptual maps. Chapter 6 and Chapter 17 should be read first if you are new to the topics. Multidimensional Scaling also uses data reduction to produce perceptual maps. Chapter 10, therefore, continues our discussion, but with more emphasis on theory, and without a discussion of GPL or OMS. Therefore, one can actually read Chapter 10 without reading Chapter 9 first. We believe that the resulting graphics from both Chapters 9 and 10 are testament to one of the themes of Part II—that well executed graphics can be a powerful form of analysis, in and of themselves.

In This Part

Chapter 5: Take Your Data Visualizations to the Next Level
Chapter 6: The Code Behind SPSS Graphics: Graphics Production Language
Chapter 7: Mapping in IBM SPSS Statistics
Chapter 8: Geospatial Analytics
Chapter 9: Perceptual Mapping with Correspondence Analysis, GPL, and OMS
Chapter 10: Display Complex Relationships with Multidimensional Scaling

Take Your Data Visualizations to the Next Level

Many SPSS users miss out on the advanced data visualization capabilities in SPSS because they do their charting in Excel, or don't go beyond the basic capability of Chart Builder. However, data visualization is not just about sending a handful of data points to a charting menu. If it were, there would be little risk in doing your descriptive statistics in SPSS and your charting in Excel. The following are some reasons why it can be a less-than-efficient approach:

- Most users vastly underestimate what is possible with SPSS graphics.

- Moving data from SPSS to Excel is typically done manually with a copy-and-paste operation, which is risky and inefficient. For example, often a user wants a quick chart based on some of the contents of a pivot table. Little known is that you can activate the table, select rows or column, and choose Create Graph from the context menu to get a quick chart. This feature supports the most popular chart types, and the resulting chart can be edited in the Chart Editor.

- Graphical representation is best thought of as a single continuous process starting with data access, followed by data preparation and transformation, and ending with a visualization, preserving data integrity, and ensuring that the visualization is 100% consistent with the data.

At a minimum you should avoid the copy-and-paste maneuver by utilizing the Output Management System, which is discussed in detail in Chapter 17. In this chapter we survey the landscape of SPSS graphics. We will explore options, but the broader goal is to understand SPSS graphics using menus to pave the way for the discussion of Graphics Production Language (GPL) in Chapter 6. Candidly, SPSS graphics has grown confusing in recent versions because multiple, seemingly competing systems are vying for your attention (even though underneath they all use the same charting engine).

There are three graphing options in SPSS Statistics: Chart Builder, Graphboard Template Chooser, and the Legacy Dialogs. Each is discussed in this chapter. First, we explore the history behind the design of current graphics options in SPSS. We investigate an influential book, *The Grammar of Graphics* by Leland Wilkinson (Springer, 2005), because the author of that book played a role in the design of SPSS graphics. Also, the popular ggplot2 package in the R statistical programming language is named after that book. Many who are impressed with R graphics, and who might be a bit befuddled by SPSS graphics, probably don't realize that both are the intellectual heirs of the same author. We then discuss the graphing options in the menus, then the concepts behind them, and finally we walk through some examples.

Graphics Options in SPSS Statistics

The Graphs menu, shown in Figure 5-1, offers three fairly comprehensive submenus:

- Legacy Dialogs
- Chart Builder
- Graphboard Template Chooser

The three other menu items are extension commands (that generate GPL).

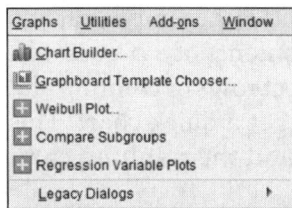

Figure 5-1: Graphs menu

Legacy Dialogs are the original graphing options in SPSS. The options here are the least interesting. For example, when you explore the Legacy Dialogs looking for Bar Charts, you are greeted with some pretty standard options, as shown in Figure 5-2.

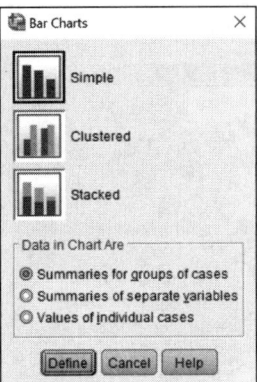

Figure 5-2: Legacy Bar Charts menu

In the next section we discuss this kind of design principle, but essentially it starts with a chart type followed by populating a fairly rigid structure with variables. Finally, there is usually pretty extensive editing involved. A quick look at the pasted syntax shows that there don't seem to be a lot of options, which would leave much of the work to the editing window:

```
GRAPH
  /BAR(SIMPLE)=COUNT BY degree.
```

NOTE If you are new to syntax, the opening chapter of Part IV, "Programming and Introduction to Data Manipulation," provides a good introduction to pasting syntax, and SPSS syntax in general.

This is one of the biggest problems with the legacy graphs. They have very simplified syntax, which seems like a good thing until you realize that everything is standardized. If you want to customize a graph, it has to be done after the fact (that is, the graph has to be manually edited). For those who use Excel, this may be the only approach to creating charts that you've tried. The heavy lifting is in the editing, and if you have been disappointed with SPSS, it is probably because you are frustrated with not being able to transform the resulting chart into what you want during the editing process. While the frustration is understandable, you can consider a completely different approach. That alternative approach, revolutionary in its thinking, is explored for the entire balance of the chapter.

The first menu option in Figure 5-1 is the SPSS Chart Builder. In this menu, more extensive options are available *before* you create the chart—that is before you get to the editing window—than are available in the Legacy Dialogs. Having these options available before you create the chart is important because the chart can be more easily automated, customized, and replicated. Most actions in the editing window, shown in Figure 5-3, are manual.

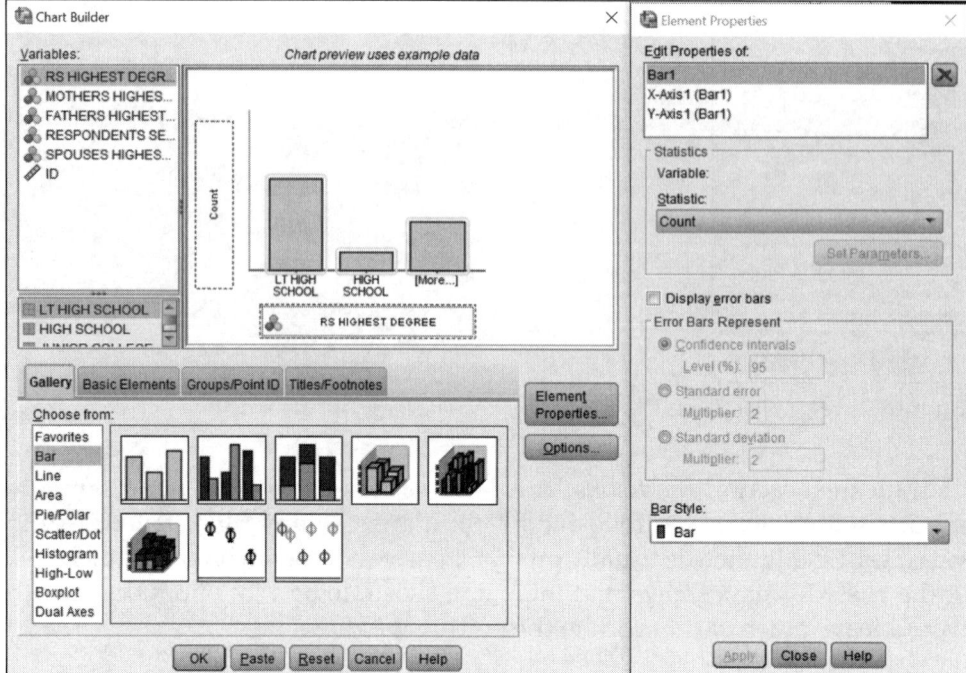

Figure 5-3: Chart Builder main menu

There is a clue that we have more options—the Basic Elements tab (see Figure 5-4), and the element properties. The revolutionary approach is to build up visualizations as a collection of elements, thoughtfully mixing and matching these elements, paving the way to many combinations that might be impossible if you were choosing only from the traditional choices in the gallery.

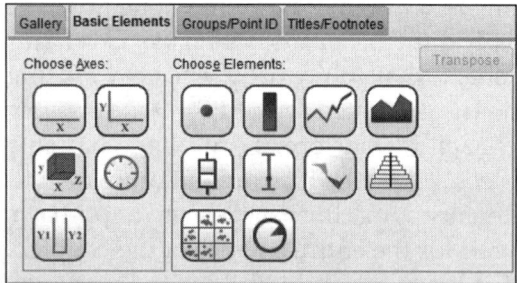

Figure 5-4: Basic Elements submenu

If we paste the SPSS syntax from this menu, the result provides further evidence that we are in new territory. The details don't matter now except to observe that, while clearly more complex, it is also richer in options: options that can be changed and options that can be saved for later, obviating spending all of our time in the editing window. This language, GPL, is the subject of Chapter 6. Learning GPL opens the doors to hundreds of options that you would not have via the menus. *The Chart Builder menus only allow you to do about 5 to 8 % of what is possible with the GPL language.*

```
* Chart Builder.
GGRAPH
  /GRAPHDATASET NAME="graphdataset" VARIABLES=degree
COUNT()[name="COUNT"] MISSING=LISTWISE
    REPORTMISSING=NO
  /GRAPHSPEC SOURCE=INLINE.
BEGIN GPL
  SOURCE: s=userSource(id("graphdataset"))
  DATA: degree=col(source(s), name("degree"), unit.category())
  DATA: COUNT=col(source(s), name("COUNT"))
  GUIDE: axis(dim(1), label("RS HIGHEST DEGREE"))
  GUIDE: axis(dim(2), label("Count"))
  SCALE: cat(dim(1), include("0", "1", "2", "3", "4"))
  SCALE: linear(dim(2), include(0))
  ELEMENT: interval(position(degree*COUNT),
shape.interior(shape.square))
END GPL.
```

The final Graphs menu choice is what we focus on in this chapter. The Graphboard Template Chooser (see Figure 5-5) allows users to select variables and then the appropriate charts are suggested based on the type of data. We can use a gallery approach, or an elements approach.

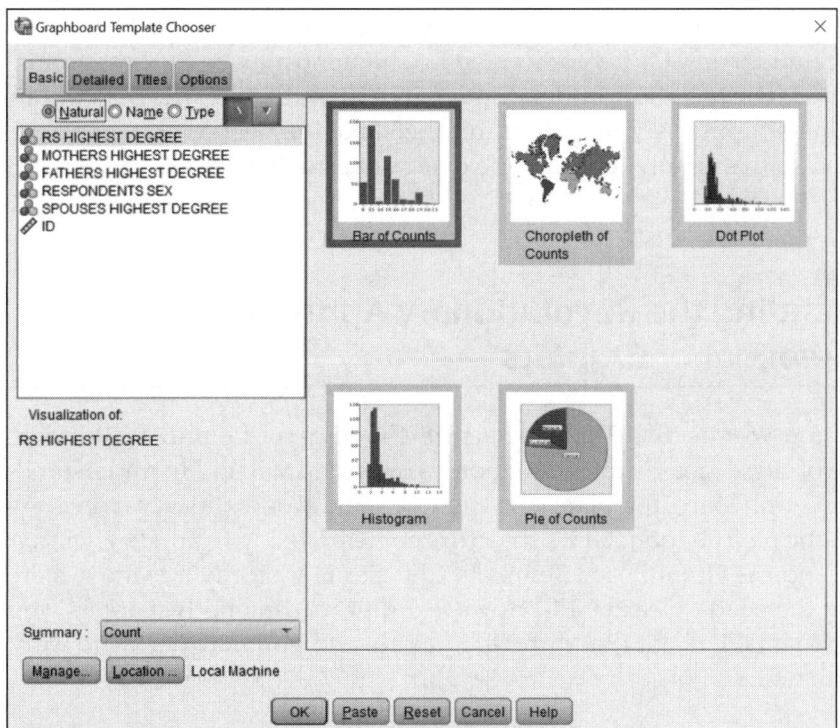

Figure 5-5: Graphboard Template Chooser main menu

In contrast to the Chart Builder, our syntax looks different. Note that both the Chart Builder and the Graphboard Template Chooser generate code using the GGRAPH command.

```
GGRAPH
  /GRAPHDATASET NAME="graphdataset"
    VARIABLES=degree[LEVEL=nominal]
    MISSING=LISTWISE REPORTMISSING=NO
  /GRAPHSPEC SOURCE=VIZTEMPLATE(NAME="Bar of Counts"[LOCATION=LOCAL]
    MAPPING( "categories"="degree"[DATASET="graphdataset"]
"Summary"="count"))
    VIZSTYLESHEET="Traditional"[LOCATION=LOCAL]
    LABEL='BAR OF COUNTS: degree'
    DEFAULTTEMPLATE=NO.
```

There is no denying that having three options gets confusing. Here is the bottom line for deciding which is right for you:

- If you don't have a long history with the Legacy Dialogs, then don't start now.

- If you like the convenience of menu-based help, and you want to create graphs based on suggestions after you have specified your variables, then the Graphboard Template Chooser is the way to go. You are in the right chapter for this option.

- If you want to create graphs from predefined galleries of chart types or build graphs from chart elements, or you are a programmer at heart, then Chart Builder and GPL as presented in Chapter 6 may be the best option. It is my favorite option, and the code is not difficult to learn. The options are almost limitless. But even if this feels like the best option, press on, and finish this chapter because the case studies will help you understand the next chapter.

Understanding the Revolutionary Approach in *The Grammar of Graphics*

In this section we discuss *The Grammar of Graphics* by Leland Wilkinson. Knowledge of these ideas is interesting on its own, and will aid in understanding why the Graphboard Template Chooser looks and works the way it does. As we show in the next chapter, GPL's structure comes directly from *The Grammar of Graphics*, and the Graphboard Template Chooser is basically a menu system to eliminate the need to learn GPL. However, after reading both chapters, you may decide that GPL is not that difficult after all, and you may decide to work directly with GPL.

Should you read *The Grammar of Graphics*? For most the answer is probably not, and to some it would seem a tortuous read and a strange book indeed, and for a few it would be a fascinating read. It is quite abstract, with lots of math notation, and is written for computer scientists and theoreticians. The practical nuts and bolts that are useful for the SPSS practitioner will be reviewed here.

A BIT OF *THE GRAMMAR OF GRAPHICS* PHILOSOPHY: SOME DEFINITIONS

Chart: Wilkinson views charts as *static* diagrams. The problem with this is that you are locked into a specific format. For instance, if you want SPSS or Excel to make a pie chart, you are asked to define what data the slices represent, and you are done. The basic form is predetermined by the software. Anything more requires editing, and your editing options might be limited. If we are not careful, or if our software is not careful, we might break the correspondence between the chart and the data during editing.

Graph: Wilkinson's use of this term may seem abstract at first, but the distinction with graphic is critical. A graph is a collection of points—technically a collection of "vertices" and "edges." He uses the same definition as students of graph theory, a branch of mathematics. For our purposes we can think of the "graph" as the data.

Graphic: A physical representation of a graph. In SPSS terms, a graphic is made up of elements. You might recall the Elements Properties in the menus. You may begin to see where this is headed—if you add aesthetics to the data in a graph, the graph can take on a particular form, a visual form. Each "element" (line, point, area, etc.) in an SPSS graphic has aesthetics.

For our purposes, what you need to know is that this approach is an alternative to having a chart typology. You can use a standard chart type as a starting off point, but this approach is different—it is all about *elements* and *aesthetics*.

- An *element* is a graphical feature like a line, a point, or an area.

- An *aesthetic* is what makes an element visible and distinct in the graphic. Examples include position, size, shape, color, transparency, and so on.

Each element and aesthetic can make a different aspect of your data visual. For instance, consider the bubble chart made famous by Hans Rosling `https://www.gapminder.org/world/`. Although he is using his own software in his well-received TED videos, it is easy to use his graphics as an example. A point element shows the location of the countries on two axes. This alone would be a standard scatter plot. By adding aesthetics he enriches the information content many fold. He uses color for *region of the world*, size for *population*, and even animation for *calendar year*. All of this is possible in the Graphboard Template Chooser, and we will do a case study like this.

Because the graphic elements and aesthetics are like words, and the grammar allows us to create "sentences," we can make countless visualizations. Rather than restricting ourselves to a dozen (or even several dozen) chart types, we have boundless options, including combinations of elements that the developers of the grammar possibly never envisioned themselves. If you can draft an example on a whiteboard, and the data is capable of showing the relationships, then there is a very good chance that you can create it in SPSS.

Sometimes we think we are helping our audience if we make charts very simple, and put only statistics on each slide. This actually forces us to use our memory to establish relationships. Rosling is showing a great deal of information all at once, but that is precisely what makes the relationships easy to see.

Bar Chart Case Study

For our first example, we will create a bar chart showing the relationship between how old people are when they have their first child and region of the country the live in. Then we will add a couple of variations like using color as an aesthetic to differentiate between men and women.

1. Open the dataset GSS2012 Bar Chart.sav.

2. To create a graph, go to the Graphs menu and choose Graphboard Template Chooser.

3. The default is the Basic tab. Notice that it seems like nothing is available, as seen in Figure 5-6.

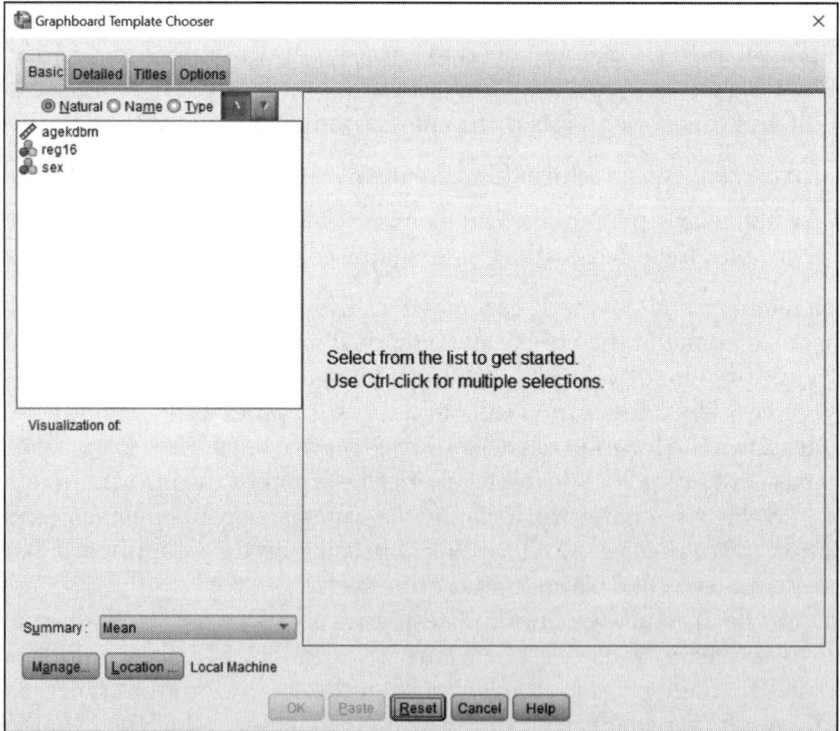

Figure 5-6: Graphboard Template Chooser Basic tab

4. Click on the variable reg16.

5. Hold the Control key down and also click on the variable agekdbrn. Notice that different visualizations become available as you specify which variables you want to display.

6. Specify Bar as the Visualization type, as shown in Figure 5-7.

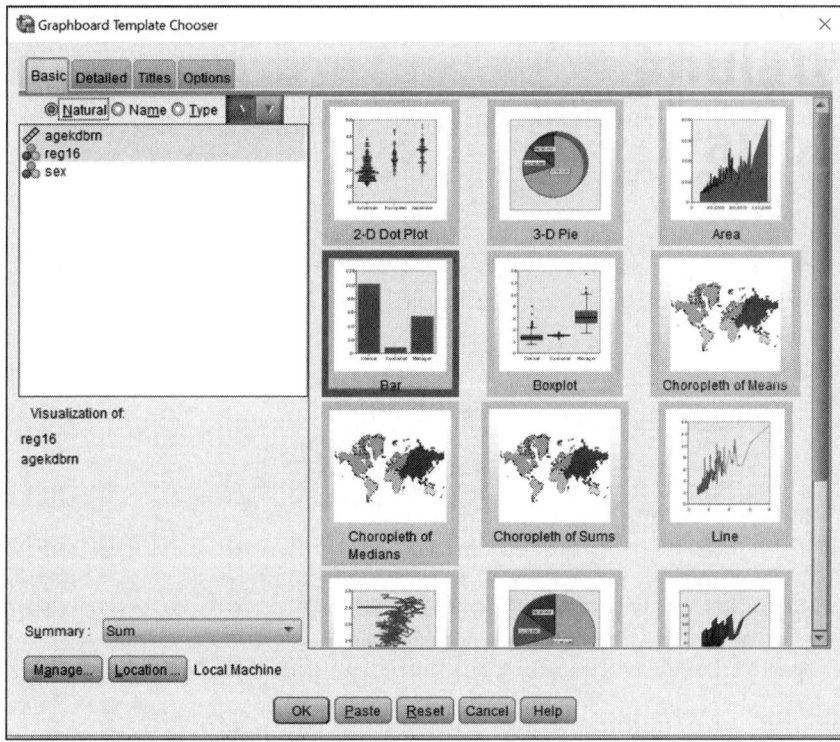

Figure 5-7: Graphboard Template Chooser fields specified

7. Choose Mean as the Summary. At this point we are ready to create a bar chart depicting the relationship between region of the country and age when first child is born.

8. Before we do this, click the Detailed tab.

9. The Detailed tab is another way to specify the same information as in the Basics tab, but with a little more control. (For example, if we had selected several categorical variables, the Detailed tab would allow you to better specify where you would like each variable to go.) Place the variable sex in the Color box, as shown in Figure 5-8.

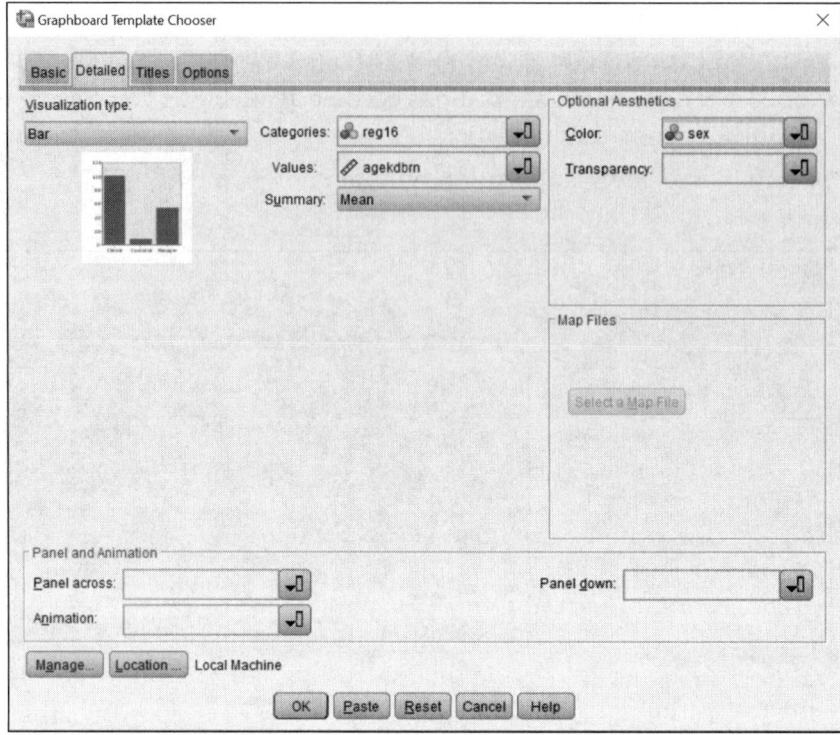

Figure 5-8: Detailed Tab

10. Click OK.

We have now created our graph, as shown in Figure 5-9.

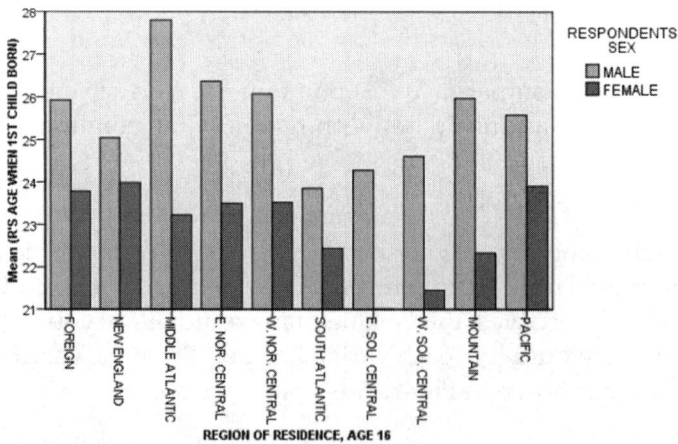

Figure 5-9: Bar chart

11. Once the graph has been created, double click on it to edit the graph, as shown in Figure 5-10.

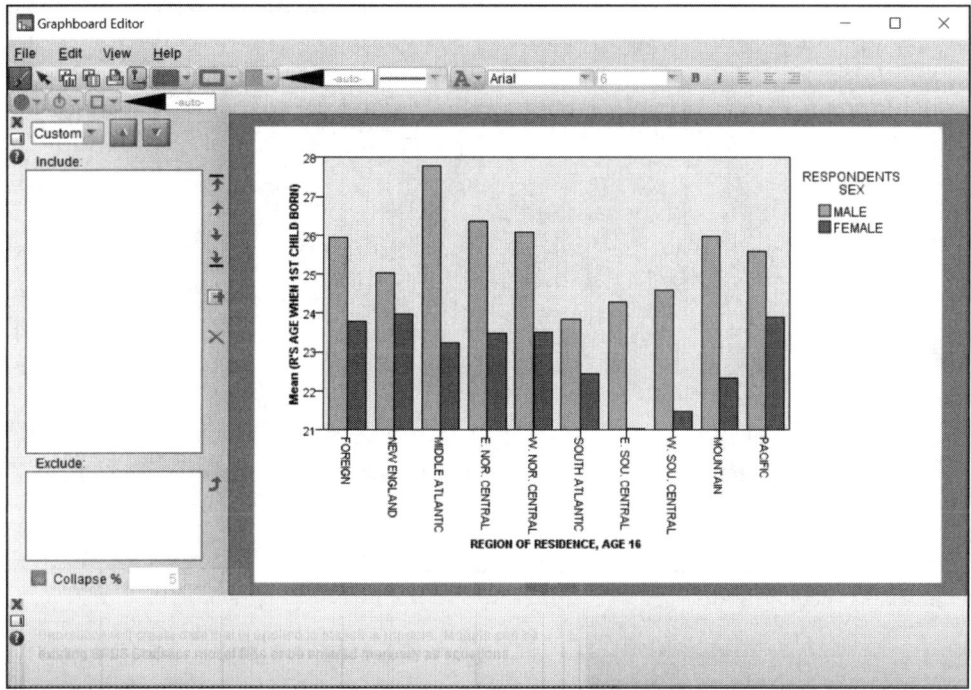

Figure 5-10: Graphboard Editor

12. Click on the View menu, go down to Palettes and select Properties and then select Categories. You can begin to see how the process is all about elements and aesthetics.

13. Let's sort the regions by statistic. To do this you will have to click Region of Residence, Age 16 at the bottom, which will then populate the window on the left with the available categories. You can move the categories around manually, but we will choose Statistics in the drop-down menu, (see Figure 5-11).

14. Now let's make this a range bar instead of a bar chart where the height is a mean. We will display the mean, but in a different way. Click the bars to activate them, and in the lower left choose Region: Range in the Summary box for our bars (see Figure 5-12).

At a glance we can see that the survey respondents in East South Central USA were the youngest on average when they had their first child. The bars are "range bars" showing minimums and maximums. Not surprisingly, in every region, the maximum age of the men was older.

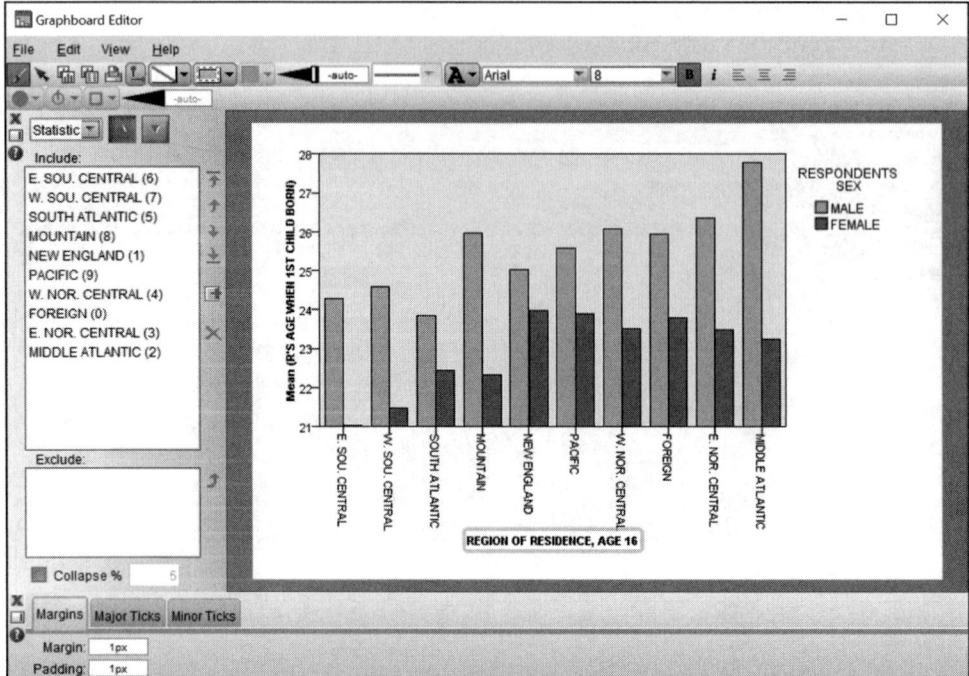

Figure 5-11: Regions sorted

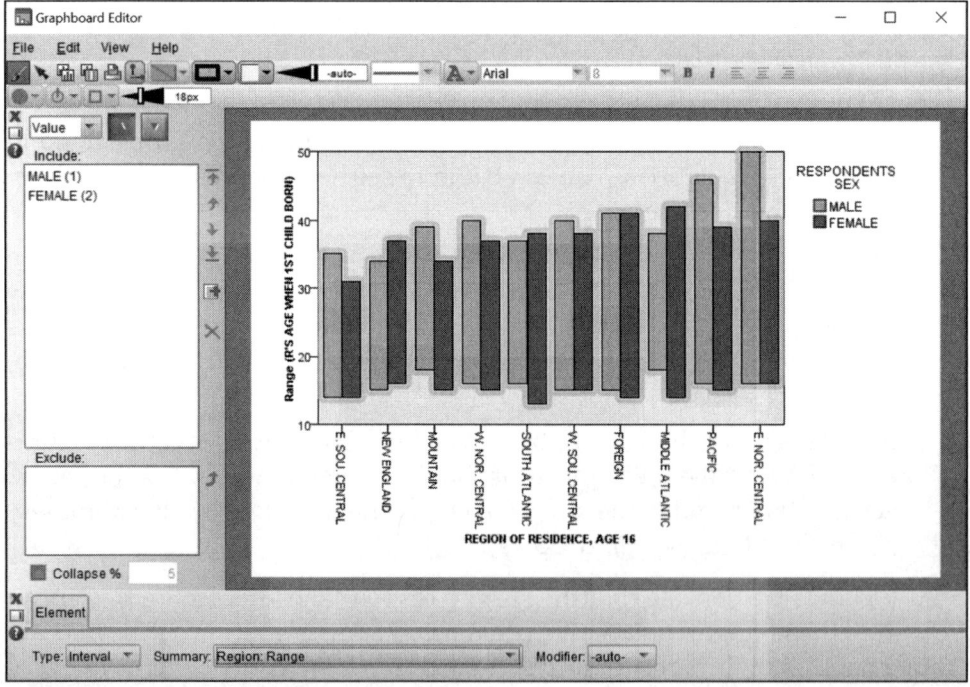

Figure 5-12: Region: Range as summary

At this point we could make many other changes. We could exclude categories, add captions, change font styles and sizes, etc.

Bubble Chart Case Study

In this case study, we are going to do a bubble chart, not unlike the ones made famous by Hans Rosling's TED videos. The advantages of this case study are:

- Bubble charts are popular.
- We will be doing this same chart as our first GPL example in the next chapter.

1. Open the State Ranks.sav file.
2. To a create a graph, go to the Graphs menu and choose Graphboard Template Chooser.
3. Because we will be using several variables, it will be easier to work with the Detailed tab. Click on the Detailed tab.
4. Select the Bubble Plot as out Visualization Type.
5. Place the variable Bachelors_Perc in the X-axis, Unemp in the Y-axis, Pop in the sizes variable, Zip1_Mod in the Color box, and State as the Data Label (see Figure 5-13). Zip1 is the first digit of the zip code, which can be a good basis for a region variable. Zip1_Mod is collapsed into fewer categories. State2 is a possible variant—it is the two-letter postal abbreviation.
6. Click OK.

As shown on Figure 5-14, the result on default settings shows the shape of our graphic. It already shows the pattern, but it could use some editing to be more readable.

Some possible edits for you to try are:

- Improve the labeling of the axes.
- Modify the point labeling.
- Remove the legends.
- Add gridlines.

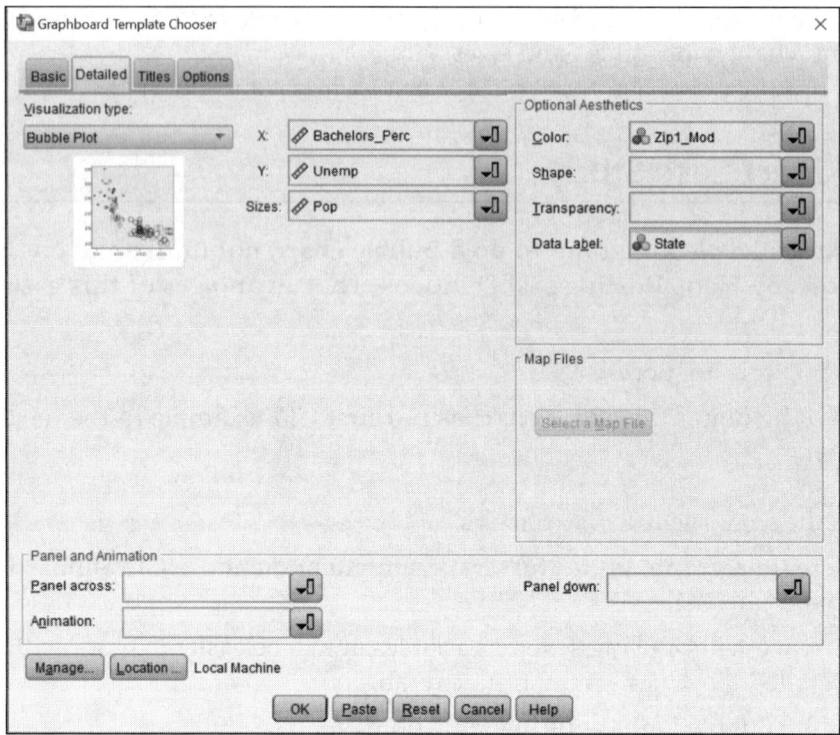

Figure 5-13: Bubble Chart Detailed tab

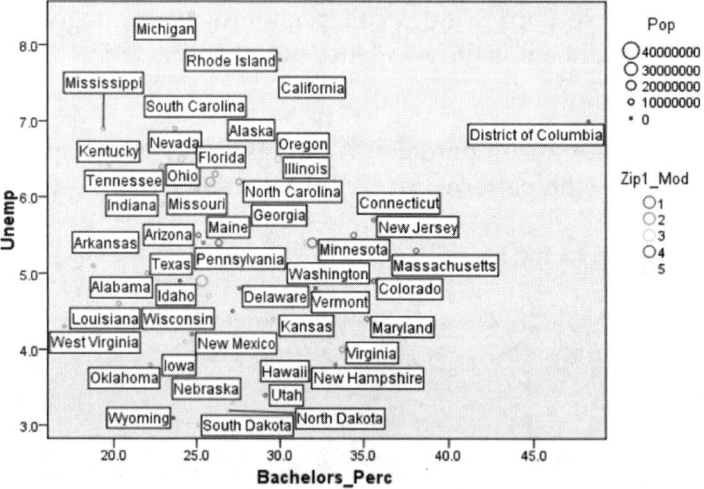

Figure 5-14: Bubble Chart

For now we will just modify the point labeling.

1. Double click on the graph to edit.

2. Click on any state name.

3. Use the toolbar to remove the white background behind the labels. Choose the option with the red line through the white background at the left of the top row of colors, which represents no background allowing you to see the gray background behind. I've also chosen no box or frame around the label, and chosen solid points with no border (see Figure 5-15).

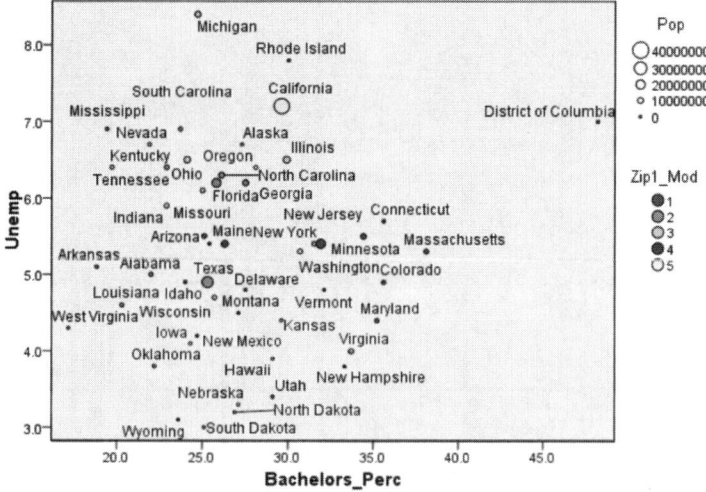

Figure 5-15: Edited Bubble Chart

In exploring the relationship between the percentage of adults (over 25 years old) who have earned a Bachelor's degree and the unemployment rate at the state level, we discover that the relationship is rather weak. What becomes interesting in this graphic are the outliers. West Virginia has lowest degree attainment, but does not have the lowest unemployment. Michigan is average on degree attainment, but is very high on unemployment. The District of Columbia is striking in that it occupies a completely different position on the graphic than any of the states. If we had done a traditional scatter plot without labeling, and without color, none of this would have been visible. Even though there is not a strong correlation here, we still learn a lot of these five variables: region, population, degree attainment, unemployment, and state.

The Graphboard Template Chooser was made available to the SPSS community as a way of avoiding having to learn GPL, although you've probably learned more about GPL than you realize. Take a little time to familiarize yourself with it. You may opt to circle back and apply the approach you've learned in this chapter, or you may decide to take what you've learned to the next level and build your graphics with a programming language approach.

The Code Behind SPSS Graphics: Graphics Production Language

In some ways this chapter is a continuation of the previous chapter. In Chapter 5 we used the Graphboard Template Chooser as a way to introduce Graphics Production Language (GPL). In this chapter the goal is to make GPL as painless as possible, but this time we will be using the Chart Builder. Our opening example will be the closing example from the previous chapter. Then we do a broader overview of GPL including GPL Help and advice on getting started. Finally, we return to the case study approach and have fun with the kinds of charts you can do in GPL. Don't forget to revisit the examples in Chapter 5. They can all be done in GPL as well.

Introducing GPL: Bubble Chart Case Study

In this example we will begin by recreating the bubble chart we created in Chapter 5; however, in this case we will be using the Chart Builder. We won't attempt to write the GPL from scratch in a blank window. Even if you had a complete understanding of the language, it would simply not be a good use of time. I never use this approach, and don't recommend it. This is in part because the GPL code begins with a batch of "boilerplate" code that defines the data to the graphics engine, and pasting from the Chart Builder generates that repetititve code for us. We will either paste SPSS syntax (including GPL commands) from the Chart Builder menu system, or begin with some earlier code that we know to work. In this case, we will copy and paste.

1. Open the dataset State Ranks.sav.

2. To create a graph, go to the Graphs menu and choose Chart Builder.

   The Gallery tab of the Chart Builder has many prefabricated graphs where we just need to specify the type of graph we would like to create, and then we supply the variables that belong in the graph.

3. Click Scatter/Dot and choose the Grouped Scatter choice as shown in Figure 6-1. This will get us 70 to 80% of what we need depending on how many features we want to add.

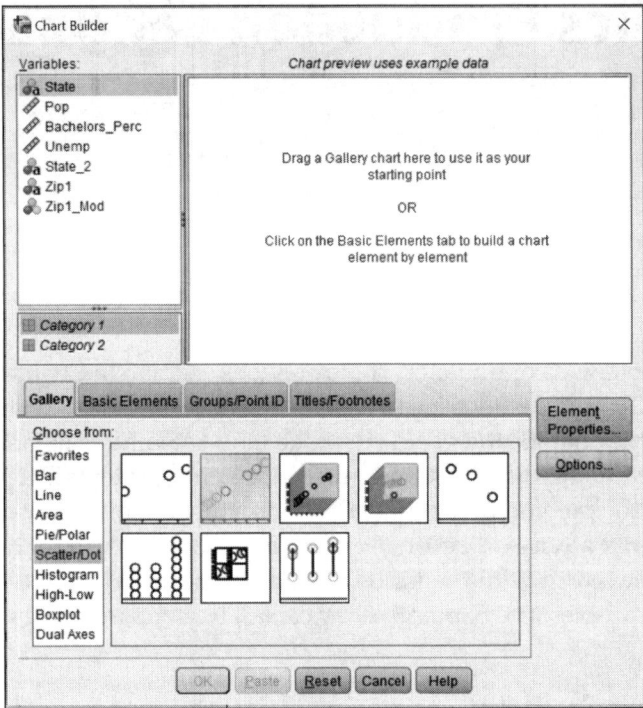

Figure 6-1: Chart Builder Gallery tab

4. Drag the Grouped Scatter Icon onto the Canvas. Notice that drop boxes appear that allow you to place variables onto the x and y axes as well as a set color box. Also notice that although a bubble chart always implies varying point size, the variable drag and drop areas do not include it. We will be adding that with code. Most of the other features are available, however.

5. Place the variable Unemp in the y axis.

6. Place the variable Bachelors_Perc in the x axis.
7. Place the variable Zip1_Mod in the set color box, as shown in Figure 6-2.

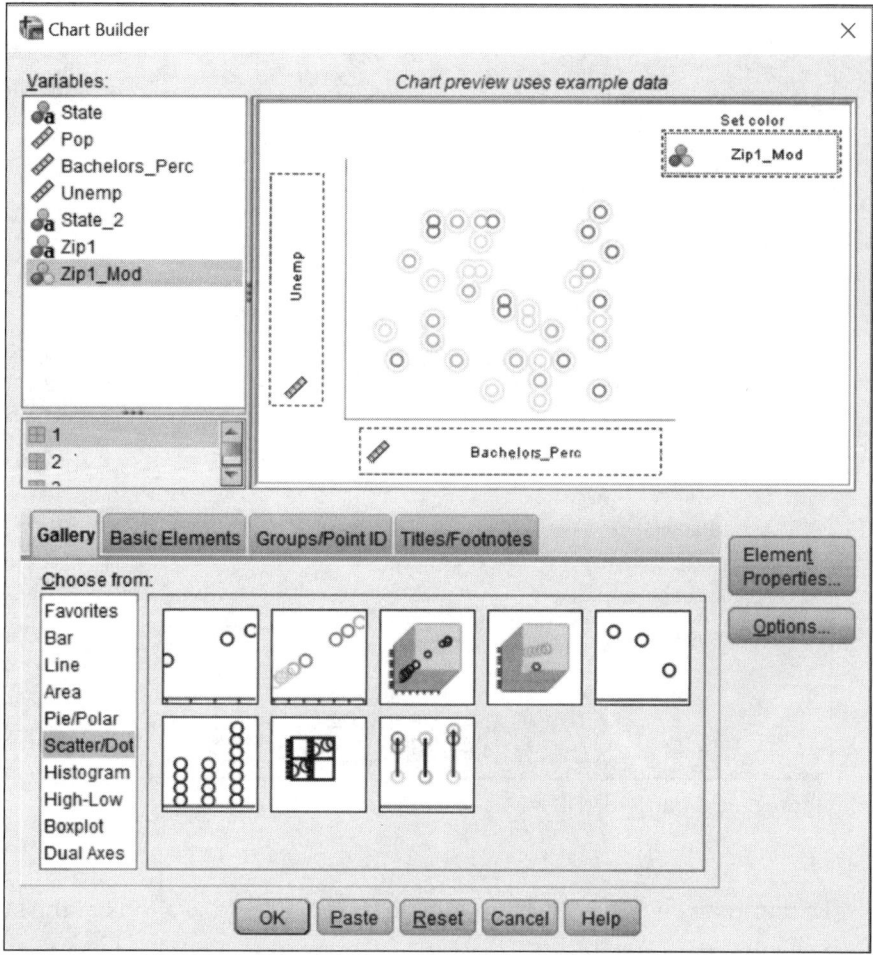

Figure 6-2: Preview of grouped scatterplot

The variable State will not have a home unless we request it.

8. Click on the Groups/Point ID tab.
9. Check Point ID Label.
10. Place the variable State in the Point ID box as shown in Figure 6-3.

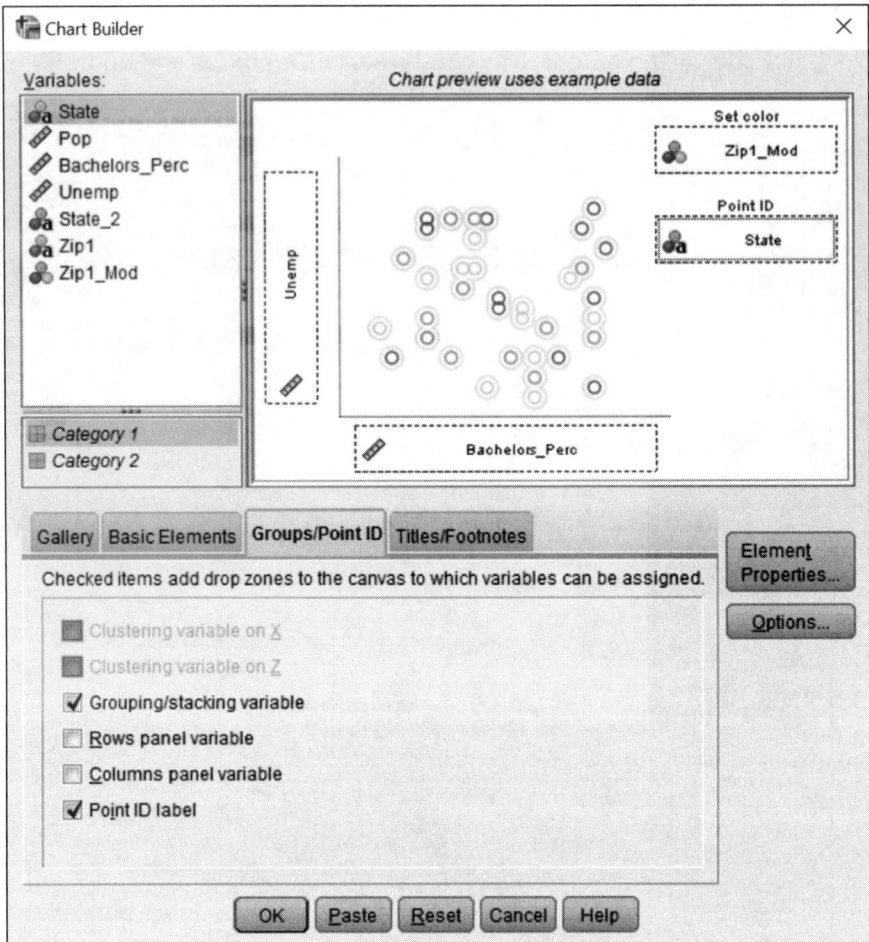

Figure 6-3: Groups/Point ID tab

Rather than clicking OK to create the graph, let's take a look at the syntax.

11. Click the Paste button.

A new window appears; this is the syntax window. The resulting SPSS syntax looks like this:

```
* Chart Builder.
GGRAPH
  /GRAPHDATASET NAME="graphdataset" VARIABLES=Bachelors_Perc Unemp
Zip1_Mod State MISSING=LISTWISE
    REPORTMISSING=NO
  /GRAPHSPEC SOURCE=INLINE.
BEGIN GPL
```

```
    SOURCE: s=userSource(id("graphdataset"))
    DATA: Bachelors_Perc=col(source(s), name("Bachelors_Perc"))
    DATA: Unemp=col(source(s), name("Unemp"))
    DATA: Zip1_Mod=col(source(s), name("Zip1_Mod"), unit.category())
    DATA: State=col(source(s), name("State"), unit.category())
    GUIDE: axis(dim(1), label("Bachelors_Perc"))
    GUIDE: axis(dim(2), label("Unemp"))
    GUIDE: legend(aesthetic(aesthetic.color.exterior), label("Zip1_Mod"))
    ELEMENT: point(position(Bachelors_Perc*Unemp),
color.exterior(Zip1_Mod), label(State))
    END GPL.
```

The first aspect of the structure to underscore is that this code has two distinct sections. The first, indicated with the opening GGRAPH command, also includes the GRAPHDATASET and GRAPHSPEC subcommands. This section of code terminating in a period is SPSS syntax. These keywords can be found in the Command Syntax Reference guide (found under the Help menu). Just as a reminder, the Command Syntax Reference guide contains every single syntax command in SPSS Statistics. The next section, indicated with the BEGIN GPL command, is a completely different matter—it is a different language.

> **NOTE** If you need a quick primer (or refresher) about SPSS syntax in general, Chapter 16 is dedicated to that topic.

The BEGIN GPL ... END GPL command itself is a syntax command, but its job is to indicate that the block of code within it is Graphics Production Language and not SPSS syntax. It has a different grammar and these commands are defined in a different document. The examples in the GPL Reference guide, discussed in the next section, can be confusing because they do not include the necessary GGRAPH subcommands. This chapter offers considerable assistance in that regard, but if you simply copy and paste the GPL examples without "wrapping" the necessary syntax around it, they will not work. The purpose of the /GRAPHDATASET subcommand is to inform the GPL parser as to what data, usually variables, from the dataset GPL has access to. Without this critical command, GPL does not have access to any data. The easiest method for including GPL code is the method that we will use—paste from the menus and then modify the GPL.

> **NOTE** GPL cannot be used with old style (batch) syntax, and macros should not be used in GPL code. Rather Python programmability is necessary in situations where you might be tempted to use a macro. Also, unlike the rest of SPSS Statistics, GPL syntax is case sensitive.

GPL has 10 statement commands (see the "GPL Help" section later in this chapter for a list of them). This example utilizes four of them: SOURCE, DATA, GUIDE, and ELEMENT. You won't master all of GPL in this chapter, but you are going to become much more familiar with the ELEMENT statement. Examples of elements, as we saw in Chapter 5, include points, lines, and intervals. This example currently has a point element with three aesthetics: position, color, and label. We will be modifying and adding to the aesthetics of this point element.

Let's start with a simple experiment involving a different statement.

1. Go to the Graphs menu and choose Chart Builder.

2. Click on the Options button.

3. Choose 150% for size.

4. Click OK.

5. Click Paste.

Now we discover a new statement:

```
PAGE: begin(scale(937px,750px))
```

The scale function has been populated with size parameters using px or points, the same system as font size. It's not the only option, however. You could use this instead:

```
PAGE: begin(scale(10in,6in))
```

You can choose cm for metric as well. Note well that there is also a required closing statement:

```
PAGE: end()
```

This is our first introduction to making little modifications, and I think that most would agree it was not so bad. A simple little setting like this could introduce a nice continuity into our presentations of data by making everything look uniform or to ensure that our graphics fit inside a Word document or PowerPoint presentation.

Now try returning to the menus to adjust the x and y axes.

1. Go to the Graphs menu and choose Chart Builder.

   Ensure that the Element Properties pop-up window is visible (if it is not, click on the Properties Elements button). Here we are just going to specify the minimum values for the x and y axes.

2. Select X-Axis1 (Point1).

3. Deselect Automatic for Minimum and choose 10.

4. Click Apply, as shown in Figure 6-4.

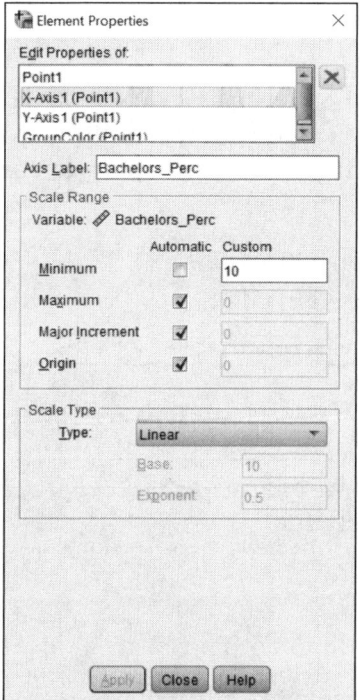

Figure 6-4: Element Properties

5. Select Y-Axis1 (Point1).

6. Deselect Automatic for Minimum and choose 2.

7. Click Apply.

8. Click Paste.

Here are the two new statements with the parameters we chose:

```
SCALE: linear(dim(1), min(10))
SCALE: linear(dim(2), min(2))
```

Now, let's try a third modification with an eye toward doing a bigger modification in the "Bubble Chart Case Study Part Two" section later in this chapter.

Be very careful with the parentheses, and type in this one. There is no way to paste it. This is our first constant using a word as a parameter. The Help file has a surprising number of options for modifying size including using the px, in, and cm indicators that we saw earlier.

```
ELEMENT: point(position(Bachelors_Perc*Unemp), color.exterior(Zip1_Mod),
label(State), size(size.small))
<Note that in GPL, the x axis variable always precedes the y axis
variable unlike what you might be used to>
```

Now onto our first major modification. It will require making changes in three areas, but the changes are not difficult. We are going to assign a variable size.

1. Specific that the variable Pop will be used in GGraph.

2. Specific that the variable Pop will be used in GPL.

3. Specific that the variable Pop will be the size variable.

```
* Chart Builder with Pop added for Size.
GGRAPH
   /GRAPHDATASET NAME="graphdataset" VARIABLES=Bachelors_Perc
Unemp Zip1_Mod State Pop MISSING=LISTWISE
     REPORTMISSING=NO
   /GRAPHSPEC SOURCE=INLINE.
BEGIN GPL
   PAGE: begin(scale(12in,6in))
   SOURCE: s=userSource(id("graphdataset"))
   DATA: Bachelors_Perc=col(source(s), name("Bachelors_Perc"))
   DATA: Unemp=col(source(s), name("Unemp"))
   DATA: Zip1_Mod=col(source(s), name("Zip1_Mod"), unit.category())
   DATA: State=col(source(s), name("State"), unit.category())
   DATA: Pop=col(source(s), name("Pop"))
   GUIDE: axis(dim(1), label("Bachelors_Perc"))
   GUIDE: axis(dim(2), label("Unemp"))
   GUIDE: legend(aesthetic(aesthetic.color.exterior), label("Zip1_Mod"))
   SCALE: linear(dim(1), min(10))
   SCALE: linear(dim(2), min(2))
   ELEMENT: point(position(Bachelors_Perc*Unemp),
color.exterior(Zip1_Mod), label(State), size(Pop))
   PAGE: end()
END GPL.
```

By specifying a varying point size using population, we have now created a bubble plot. (see Figure 6-5).

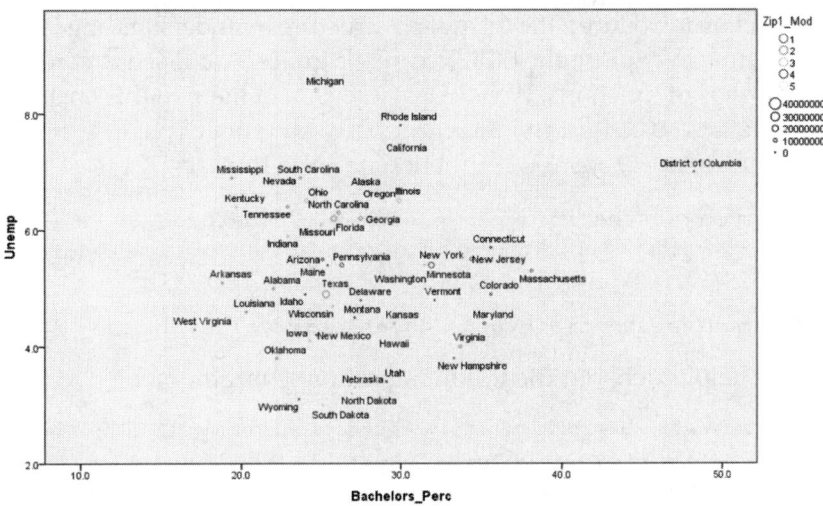

Figure 6-5: Bubble plot

GPL Help

Let's pause our case study to get more grounded in our options before we return to our bubble chart. We are going to explore the GPL Reference to learn what else we can do. First you will have to access the GPL Reference from the Help menu, as shown in Figure 6-6. To do this:

1. Click on the Help menu.

2. Select Topics.

3. Navigate down the left side of the window and expand the Reference dropdown.

4. Here you will find the GPL Reference guide.

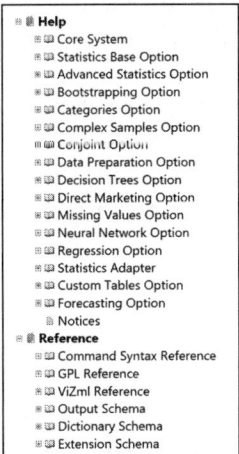

Figure 6-6: Help and Reference options

The previous section introduced the STATEMENT structure in understanding GPL. If you take the time to explore the GPL Reference guide, you'll see that there are dozens and dozens of functions. We will learn several of them in this chapter, including the `aestheticMaximum` and `aestheticMinimum` functions.

For example, the `aestheticMinimum` function has two formats:

```
aestheticMinimum(<aesthetic type>.<aesthetic constant>)
```

or

```
aestheticMinimum(<aesthetic type>."<aesthetic value>")
```

That might not help much, but the following example might:

```
SCALE: linear(aesthetic(aesthetic.size), aestheticMinimum(size."1px"),
              aestheticMaximum(size."5px"))
ELEMENT: point(position(x*y), size(z))
```

Applied to our example it will look like the following code snippet:

```
SCALE: linear(aesthetic(aesthetic.size), aestheticMinimum(size."5px"),
              aestheticMaximum(size."25px"))
```

TIP Often it is helpful to simply copy and paste the example into the Syntax window, make it a comment, so you are able to read it or copy it directly from that window.

Aside from functions, you can also use constants in GPL. For example, this is how a constant can be used in code:

```
SCALE: linear(aesthetic(aesthetic.size), aestheticMinimum(size.tiny),
              aestheticMaximum(size.large))
```

The Color Constants are a lot of fun, and there are a lot of colors to choose from. Just the As, Bs, and Cs include aliceblue, aqua, azure, bisque, black, blanched-almond, blue, blueviolet, brown, burlywood, cadetblue, chartreuse, chocolate, coral, cornflowerblue, cornsilk, crimson, and cyan.

Because we are in the middle of a case study involving point elements, you might want to review these first. Nonetheless, now that you've learned how to navigate the Help and put it to good use you can go in whichever direction your interests take you. The Example section of Help is also a great place to visit, now that you will be able to put it into context.

Bubble Chart Case Study Part Two

The starting point for this section is shown in Figure 6-5. We are going to make the following changes to the bubble chart we created in the "Introducing GPL:

Bubble Chart Case Study" section earlier in this chapter. The code to accomplish these changes is shown after the following list:

1. Make the points larger using `aestheticMinimum` and `aestheticMaximum`:

   ```
   SCALE: linear(aesthetic(aesthetic.size), aestheticMinimum(size."5px"),
           aestheticMaximum(size."25px"))
   ```

2. Add gridlines with the `gridlines()` function on the first two GUIDE statements.

   ```
   GUIDE: axis(dim(1), label("Bachelors_Perc"), gridlines())
   GUIDE: axis(dim(2), label("Unemp"), gridlines())
   ```

3. Make the points solid without a border by using both `color.interior` and `color.exterior`. Note that this affects two GUIDE statements as well as the ELEMENT statement.

   ```
   ELEMENT: point(position(Bachelors_Perc*Unemp), color.interior(Zip1_Mod),
   color.exterior(Zip1_Mod),
               label(State), size(Pop))
   ```

4. Remove the legend using the `null()` function on all three legend GUIDE statements.

   ```
   GUIDE: legend(aesthetic(aesthetic.color.interior), label("Zip1_Mod"),
   null())
     GUIDE: legend(aesthetic(aesthetic.color.exterior),
   label("Zip1_Mod"),
   null())
    GUIDE: legend(aesthetic(aesthetic.size), null())
   ```

The following is the complete syntax to create the bubble chart with the changes specified above.

```
* Chart Builder with Pop added for Size.
GGRAPH
  /GRAPHDATASET NAME="graphdataset" VARIABLES=Bachelors_Perc
Unemp Zip1_Mod State Pop MISSING=LISTWISE
    REPORTMISSING=NO
  /GRAPHSPEC SOURCE=INLINE.
BEGIN GPL
  PAGE: begin(scale(12in,7in)) SOURCE: s=userSource(id("graphdataset"))
  DATA: Bachelors_Perc=col(source(s), name("Bachelors_Perc"))
  DATA: Unemp=col(source(s), name("Unemp"))
  DATA: Zip1_Mod=col(source(s), name("Zip1_Mod"), unit.category())
  DATA: State=col(source(s), name("State"), unit.category())
  DATA: Pop=col(source(s), name("Pop"))
```

```
  GUIDE: axis(dim(1), label("Bachelors_Perc"), gridlines())
  GUIDE: axis(dim(2), label("Unemp"), gridlines())
  GUIDE: legend(aesthetic(aesthetic.color.interior),
label("Zip1_Mod"),
null())
  GUIDE: legend(aesthetic(aesthetic.color.exterior), label("Zip1_Mod"),
null())
  GUIDE: legend(aesthetic(aesthetic.size), null())
  SCALE: linear(dim(1), min(15))
  SCALE: linear(dim(2), min(2), max(9))
  SCALE: linear(aesthetic(aesthetic.size),
aestheticMinimum(size."5px"),
             aestheticMaximum(size."25px"))
  ELEMENT: point(position(Bachelors_Perc*Unemp),
color.interior(Zip1_Mod), color.exterior(Zip1_Mod),
             label(State), size(Pop))
  PAGE: end()
END GPL.
```

Figure 6-7 depicts the bubble plot with the first set of changes.

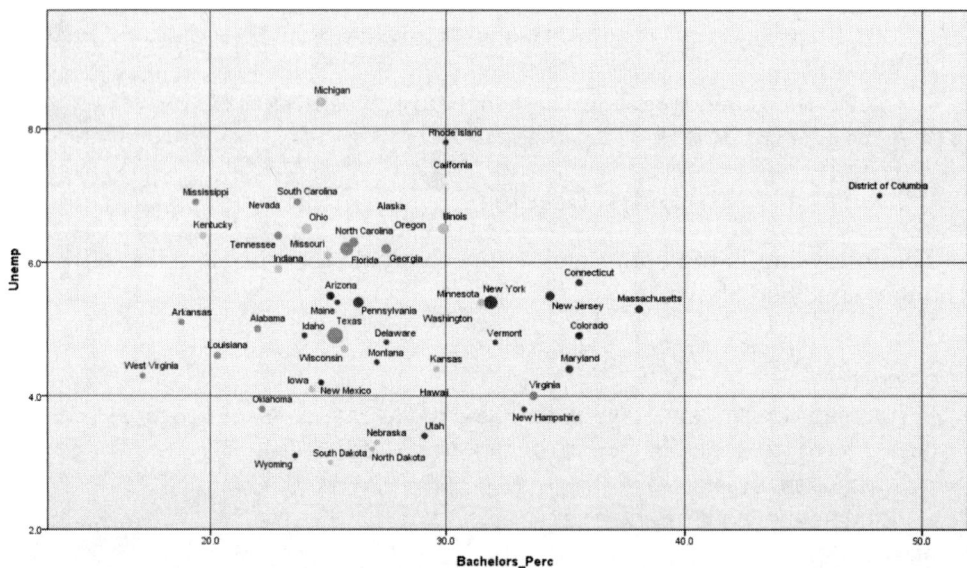

Figure 6-7: Bubble plot with changes

Color mapping is our next modification. Unfortunately to get the borderless effect, which I happen to like, you have to map color.interior and color.exterior, and it looks a bit verbose, but it is not that difficult. The following code allows us to control the exact colors that we use, which can be very powerful in ensuring that we have color consistency in our presentation. For example, using red and blue to color individual states on a political map of the United States means you probably don't even need a legend to identify what those colors symbolize (see Figure 6-8).

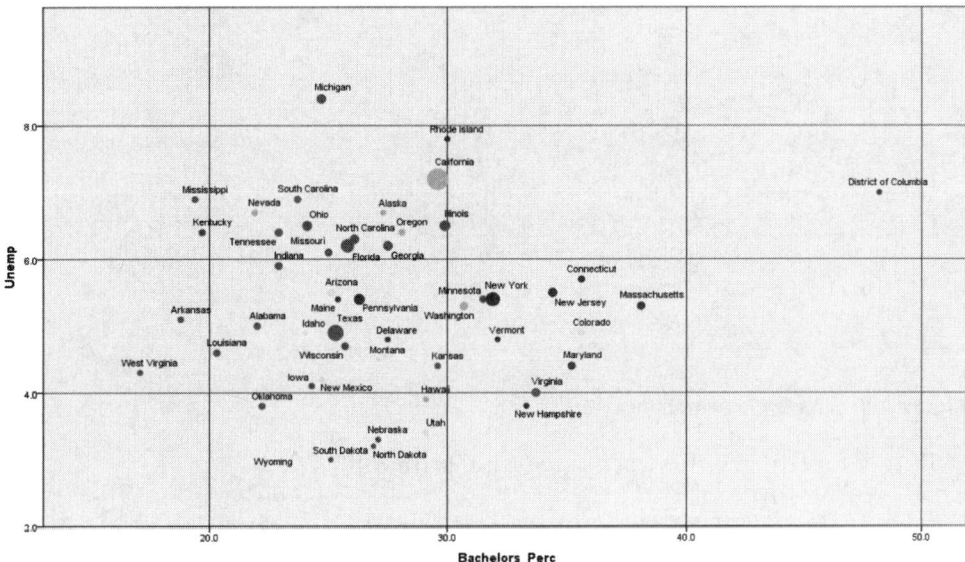

Figure 6-8: Bubble plot with red and blue states

```
SCALE: cat(aesthetic(aesthetic.color.interior), map(("1", color.blue),
("2", color.red), ("3", color.green), ("4", color.yellow),
("5", color.cyan)))

SCALE: cat(aesthetic(aesthetic.color.exterior), map(("1", color.blue),
("2", color.red), ("3", color.green), ("4", color.yellow),
("5", color.cyan)))
```

Finally, let's try an effect that can be quite powerful, but might be a bit too much for this example because there are five regions in Zip1_Mod, which can make the chart difficult to read. What if we were to draw a boundary around the points for those regions, much like slipping an elastic band around push pins where our point elements are located?

In the SPSS Statistics Help documentation we can find an example of bank salaries that emphasize how the female employees are in a narrow salary band, and don't experience many increases in their current salary above where they started at the bank. Let's try this on our example by inserting our variable names into the same line from the SPSS Statistics Help example:

```
ELEMENT: edge(position(link.hull(Bachelors_Perc*Unemp)),
color.interior(Zip1_Mod))
```

As shown in Figure 6-9, I think you will agree that it is a little too much distraction. However, I've found this function to be a useful one to have in the toolkit.

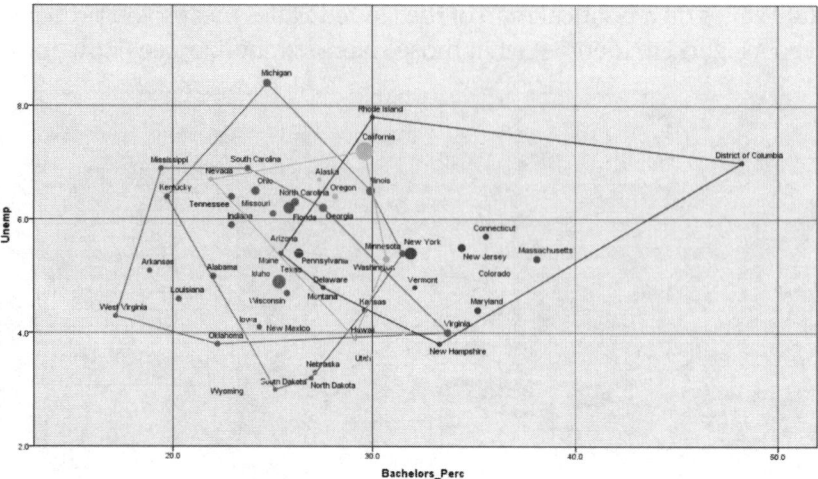

Figure 6-9: Bubble plot with bands

Purely for fun, try this variation (see Figure 6-10):

```
ELEMENT: polygon(position(link.hull(Bachelors_Perc*Unemp)),
color.interior(Zip1_Mod))
```

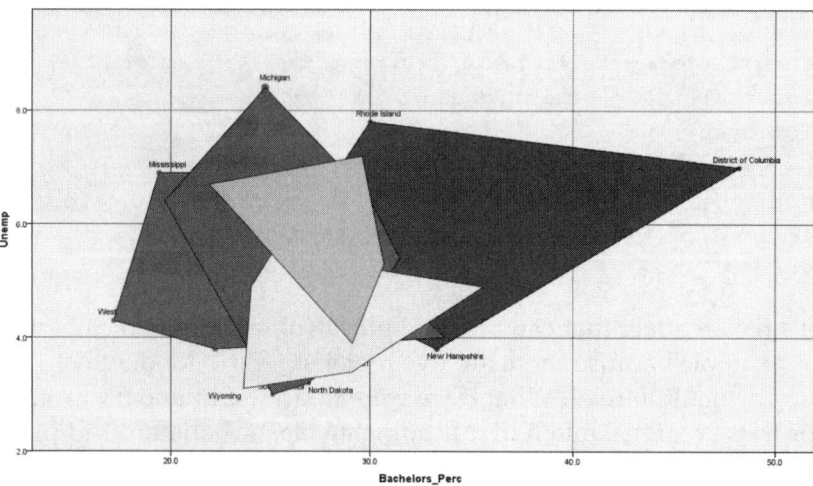

Figure 6-10: Bubble plot with polygon

Now that we have a good grounding we will work on a number of new case studies. Let's begin.

Double Regression Line Case Study

The next two examples use the data file `PainTreat.sav`. Three drug treatments for pain are being considered over two time periods. As shown in Figure 6-11, in each of the time periods we have a measurement for pain from 0 to 25, and we have the number of Physical Therapy hours that the patient received during that period.

	drug	pain1	pain2	pt1	pt2
1	1	14	8	3	3
2	1	4	1	3	11
3	1	6	3	13	7
4	1	9	4	2	0
5	1	7	1	10	6
6	1	13	10	4	0
7	1	12	10	9	10
8	1	7	1	6	4
9	1	11	7	7	9
10	1	9	6	3	10

Figure 6-11: PainTreat data file

We want to see the trend lines and regression lines for both time periods. Let's begin by pasting the GPL for a simple scatter plot.

1. Open the dataset `PainTreat.sav`.
2. To create the graph, go to the Graphs menu and choose Chart Builder.
3. Click Scatter/Dot and choose the Simple Scatter.
4. Drag the Simple Scatter Icon onto the Canvas.
5. Place the variable pain1 in the y axis.
6. Place the variable pt1 in the x axis, as shown in Figure 6-12.

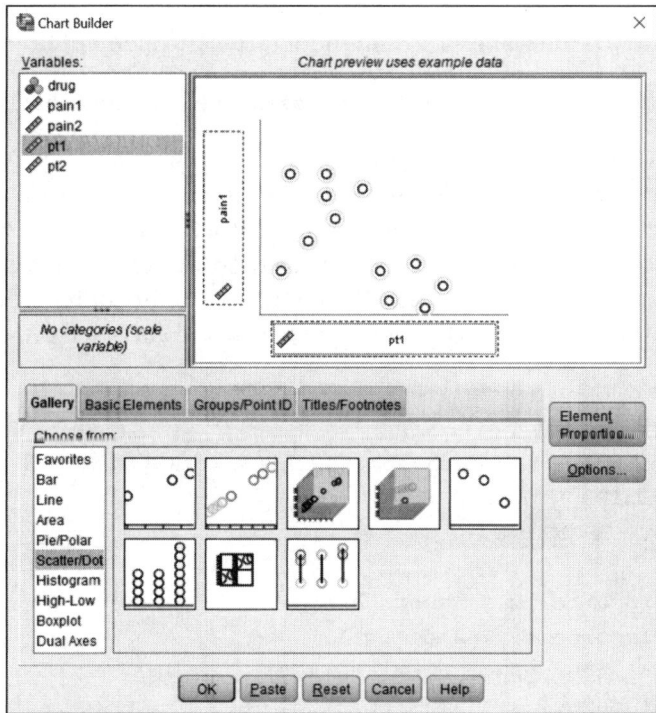

Figure 6-12: Scatterplot between pain and physical therapy during the first time period

7. Click Paste.

The scatterplot we are about to create shows the relationship between pain and physical therapy during the first time period. We could manually add a regression line with the Elements menu by choosing Add Fit Line at Total, but it is not at all clear how we are going to take the second period into account. It doesn't seem like this is an auspicious start, but we are actually half way there.

Here is the syntax we have so far:

```
GGRAPH
    /GRAPHDATASET NAME="graphdataset" VARIABLES=pt1 pain1
MISSING=LISTWISE
REPORTMISSING=NO
    /GRAPHSPEC SOURCE=INLINE.
BEGIN GPL
    SOURCE: s=userSource(id("graphdataset"))
    DATA: pt1=col(source(s), name("pt1"))
    DATA: pain1=col(source(s), name("pain1"))
    GUIDE: axis(dim(1), label("Hrs Physical Therapy - Period 1"))
    GUIDE: axis(dim(2), label("Pain - Period 1"))
    ELEMENT: point(position(pt1*pain1))
END GPL.
```

We can add a line with the following statement (after the element line):

```
ELEMENT: line(position(smooth.linear(pt1*pain1)), color(color.red) )
```

The pasted GPL is taking care of everything else. The points can stay (which is worth a try if you like), but they really will only detract when we add the other regression line. The final result is rather straightforward. We need to add the variables to the GGRAPH command as well as to their own DATA statements. We also add a footnote and a second line. We find a very uniform relationship between pain and physical therapy in the two time periods. Voila (see Figure 6-13)!

```
* Chart Builder.
GGRAPH
    /GRAPHDATASET NAME="graphdataset" VARIABLES=pt1 pain1 pt2 pain2
MISSING=LISTWISE REPORTMISSING=NO
    /GRAPHSPEC SOURCE=INLINE.
BEGIN GPL
    SOURCE: s=userSource(id("graphdataset"))
    DATA: pt1=col(source(s), name("pt1"))
    DATA: pain1=col(source(s), name("pain1"))
    DATA: pt2=col(source(s), name("pt2"))
    DATA: pain2=col(source(s), name("pain2"))
```

```
   GUIDE: axis(dim(1), label("Hrs Physical Therapy"))
   GUIDE: axis(dim(2), label("Pain"))
   GUIDE: text.footnote(label("Red: Time Period 1\nBlue: Time
Period 2"))
    ELEMENT: line(position(smooth.linear(pt1*pain1)), color(color.red) )
    ELEMENT: line(position(smooth.linear(pt2*pain2)), color(color.blue) )
   END GPL.
```

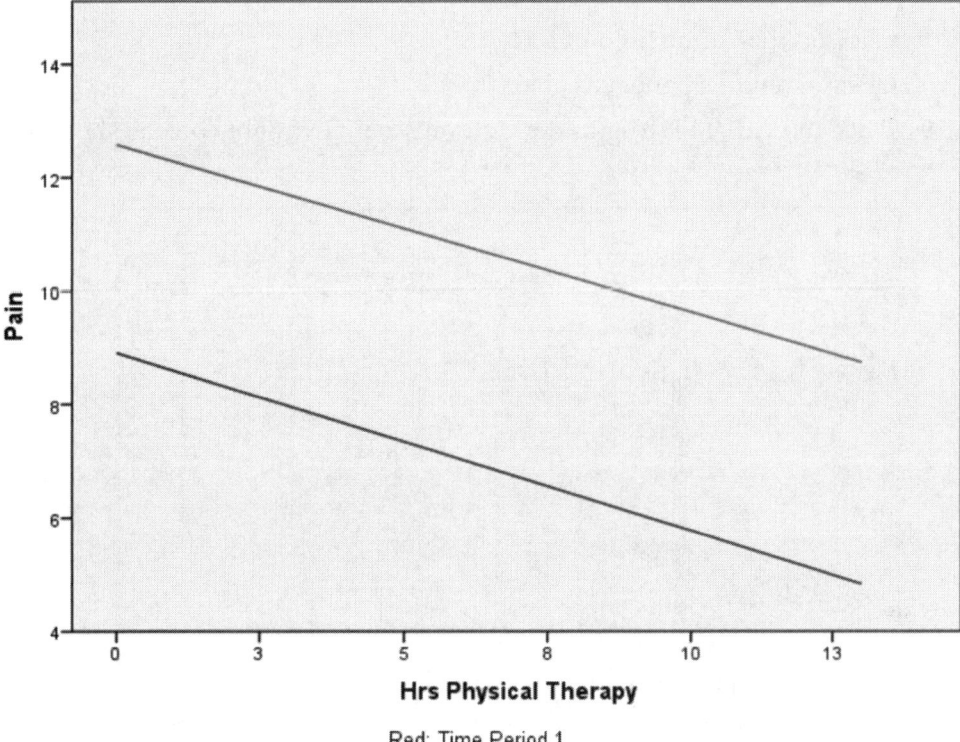

Red: Time Period 1
Blue: Time Period 2

Figure 6-13: Double regression line

Arrows Case Study

In this case study, we are going to attempt to display an entire study in one graphic. At first glance, our graphic, which we create in just a couple of manual steps after pasting, will seem a bit complex. A little complexity is worth it if it can reveal patterns in your data that you might otherwise miss. Our audience should tolerate two minutes to acclimate to our graphic if it reveals all of the major patterns in our data, especially when it reveals them through the lens of the complete dataset.

1. Open the dataset `PainTreat.sav`.

2. To create the graph, go to the Graphs menu and choose Chart Builder.

3. Click Scatter/Dot and choose the Simple Scatter.

4. Drag the Simple Scatter Icon onto the Canvas.

5. Place the variable pain1 in the y axis.

6. Place the variable pt1 in the x axis.

7. Click on the Groups/Point ID tab.

8. Check Columns panel variable.

9. Place the variable drug in the Columns panel variable box as shown in Figure 6-14.

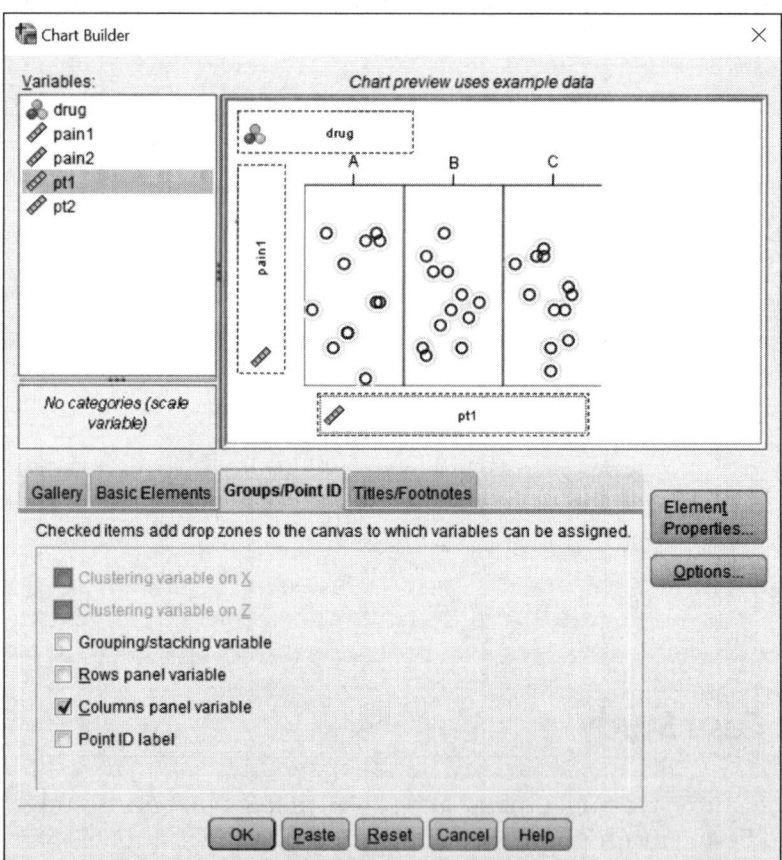

Figure 6-14: Preview of scatterplot with panel variable

10. Click OK.

Here is the pasted syntax:

```
* Chart Builder.
GGRAPH
  /GRAPHDATASET NAME="graphdataset" VARIABLES=pt1 pain1 drug
MISSING=LISTWISE REPORTMISSING=NO
  /GRAPHSPEC SOURCE=INLINE.
BEGIN GPL
  SOURCE: s=userSource(id("graphdataset"))
  DATA: pt1=col(source(s), name("pt1"))
  DATA: pain1=col(source(s), name("pain1"))
  DATA: drug=col(source(s), name("drug"), unit.category())
  GUIDE: axis(dim(1), label("Hrs Physical Therapy - Period 1"))
  GUIDE: axis(dim(2), label("Pain - Period 1"))
  GUIDE: axis(dim(3), label("Drug"), opposite())
  SCALE: cat(dim(3), include("1", "2", "3"))
  ELEMENT: point(position(pt1*pain1*drug))
END GPL.
```

Something new is the grammar of panels (also called facets). It is written almost as though it is a third dimension:

```
ELEMENT: point(position(pt1*pain1*drug))
```

NOTE A Row panel, as opposed to our Column panel, would have another dimension and would look like this:

```
ELEMENT: point(position(pt1*pain1*1*drug))
```

The 1 is just a placeholder, but there could be a variable there if you wanted a matrix.

We are going to take this graphic and make one major, rather tricky change. The + symbol won't be found in any pasted GPL, but this example is a simple, yet powerful, example of its use.

Replace the ELEMENT statement with this:

```
ELEMENT: edge(position(link.join(pt1*pain1*drug+ pt2*pain2*drug)),
shape(shape.arrow))
```

I've also made some cosmetic changes to the code. The scale of 14″ by 7″ that I've chosen looks good on my screen, but you might need to adjust. The Axis labels have been modified as well. The complete code is shown here, as well as the resulting graphic:

```
* Chart Builder.
GGRAPH
```

```
   /GRAPHDATASET NAME="graphdataset" VARIABLES=pt1 pain1 pt2 pain2 drug
MISSING=LISTWISE REPORTMISSING=NO
   /GRAPHSPEC SOURCE=INLINE.
BEGIN GPL
   PAGE: begin(scale(14in,7in))  SOURCE: s=userSource(id("graphda
taset"))
   DATA: pt1=col(source(s), name("pt1"))
   DATA: pain1=col(source(s), name("pain1"))
   DATA: pt2=col(source(s), name("pt2"))
   DATA: pain2=col(source(s), name("pain2"))
   DATA: drug=col(source(s), name("drug"), unit.category())
   GUIDE: axis(dim(1), label("Hrs Physical Therapy"))
   GUIDE: axis(dim(2), label("Pain"))
   GUIDE: text.footnote(label("Arrow indicates change
from Time 1 to Time 2"))
   ELEMENT: edge(position(link.join(pt1*pain1*drug+ pt2*pain2*drug)),
shape(shape.arrow))
   PAGE: end()
END GPL.
```

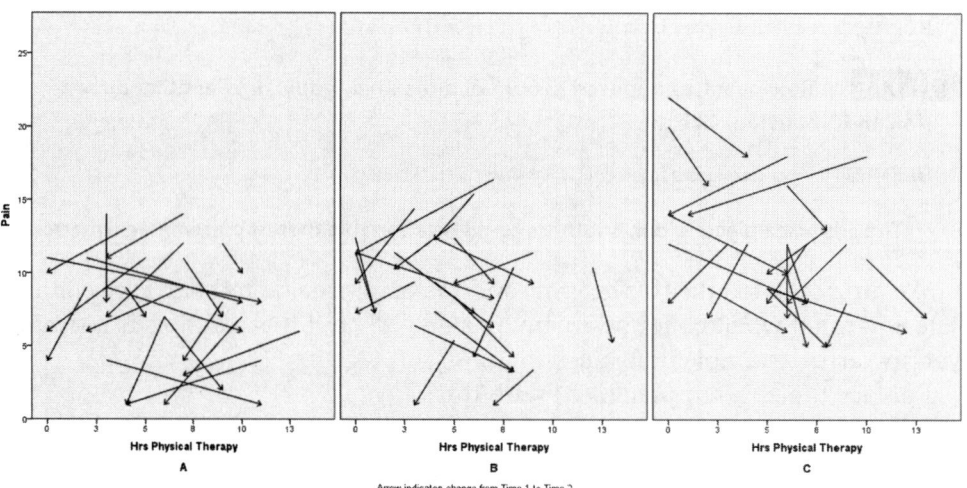

Arrow indicates change from Time 1 to Time 2

Figure 6-15: Change in pain by drug treatment

What do we learn about our data? Take a moment to acclimate and the feeling that you are looking at "pick-up sticks" will fade. Notice that all of the arrows are pointing down—all of them. That is incredibly striking. A mean or median would not inform us of that. The Drug C group has a striking pattern as well. They were in more pain at the beginning, and although the change in pain is similar to the other groups, they exit period 2 in more pain. Also noteworthy is the chaotic pattern of the arrows (change) some are straight, some titled to the left, and some titled to the right. The change in the amount of physical therapy from Period 1 to Period 2 is all over the place. That is exactly where my analysis would move next, and we might have missed it without this graphic.

MBTI Bubble Chart Case Study

This is a seemingly simple graphic (see Figure 6-16), but it is a wonderful example of how powerful GPL is. You might think that you could do this in Excel, but I doubt you can find an easy way (or any way) to do it. First, let's discuss what the graphic tells about the data. The bubbles (the size indicates group size) and the locations of the points are the group means. The regression trend line is, however, based on the entire dataset. This is terribly important, yet very difficult to do.

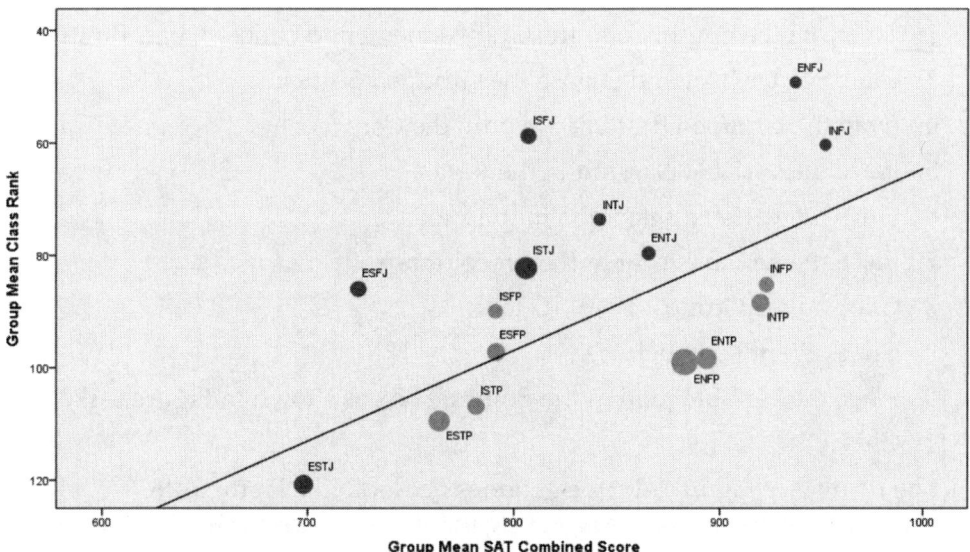

Point position is group mean. Point size indicates group sample size. Regression line N=050.

Figure 6-16: MBTI bubble chart

Let's discuss a bit about the study, because this is actual data. A large group of high school students were administered the Myers Briggs Type Indicator Instrument (MBTI). Shown are just the seniors who have taken the SAT. They were given group feedback sessions, and were given the opportunity for individual review of their results, but the data shown here was based on their paper and pencil results. It was not self-reported. Their class rank and SAT score was provided to the research team by the school district as part of the study so this was also not self-reported. One of the major findings is that the Js (Judging) tend to be above the regression line, and the Ps (Perceiving) tend to be below. ESTJ (Extraversion, Sensing, Thinking, Judging) is an exception, and is a bit below the line. ISFP (Introversion, Sensing, Feeling, Perceiving) is a bit above the line, and ESFP (Extraversion, Sensing, Feeling, Perceiving) is bit above, nearly resting on the line. We can conclude that Ps tend to be "underachievers" with scores that might imply stronger grades, and Js tend to be "overachievers" with grades that might cause one to expect higher scores. The terms overachiever and underachiever are stereotypes, but the consistency of the finding is intriguing. The graphic makes this finding clear, nearly at a glance, and the finding is quite striking.

So what's the big deal with this graphic? It isn't easy to do with most software. There are two choices, and neither is ideal. One option is that we could plot all the data, all 850 points. A second option is that we could build a chart on aggregated data. Let's consider a chart of all 850 points.

1. Open the dataset `sat_mbti_gpl_start.sav`.
2. To create the graph, go to the Graphs menu and choose Chart Builder.
3. Click Scatter/Dot and choose the Grouped Scatter.
4. Drag the Grouped Scatter Icon onto the Canvas.
5. Place the variable classran in the y axis.
6. Place the variable satcombo in the x axis.
7. Place the variable jpcat in the set color box.
8. Click on the Groups/Point ID tab.
9. Check Point ID Label.
10. Place the variable mbti in the Point ID box as shown in Figure 6-17.
11. Click OK.

The result (see Figure 6-18) we get does not look like Figure 6-16.

One could accuse me of exaggerating for effect, because using just the group averages seems like the more obvious way to go. Clearly, if we were working in Excel, we would find the 16 averages and *then* calculate the regression line. But that would be wrong. It would make our results look cleaner, distorting them in the process. GPL, with its origins in *The Grammar of Graphics*, makes it hard to lie with our data. Wherein lies the potential lie? Our trend line should be based on 850 cases. If we base it on N=16 then the correlations will be higher because we've washed out some of the noise.

This can be easily proven. In this case, if we run a correlation between the SAT scores and rank we get a Pearson correlation of –.435, and a Spearman correlation of –.431. This makes sense because as rank goes down, SAT score goes up. However, and this is critical, if we run the same analysis using the aggregated N=16 dataset (or a worksheet with just the average values) we get –.573 for the Pearson and –.582 for the Spearman. This is more than enough to make a visible difference and move the regression line. Our findings would be more consistent with theory, but we would be misleading our audience. An experiment will show that the change is not visually too dramatic for this dataset, but ESFP does move to the theoretical expected side of the line with an N=16 regression line. Our audience deserves the correct graphic.

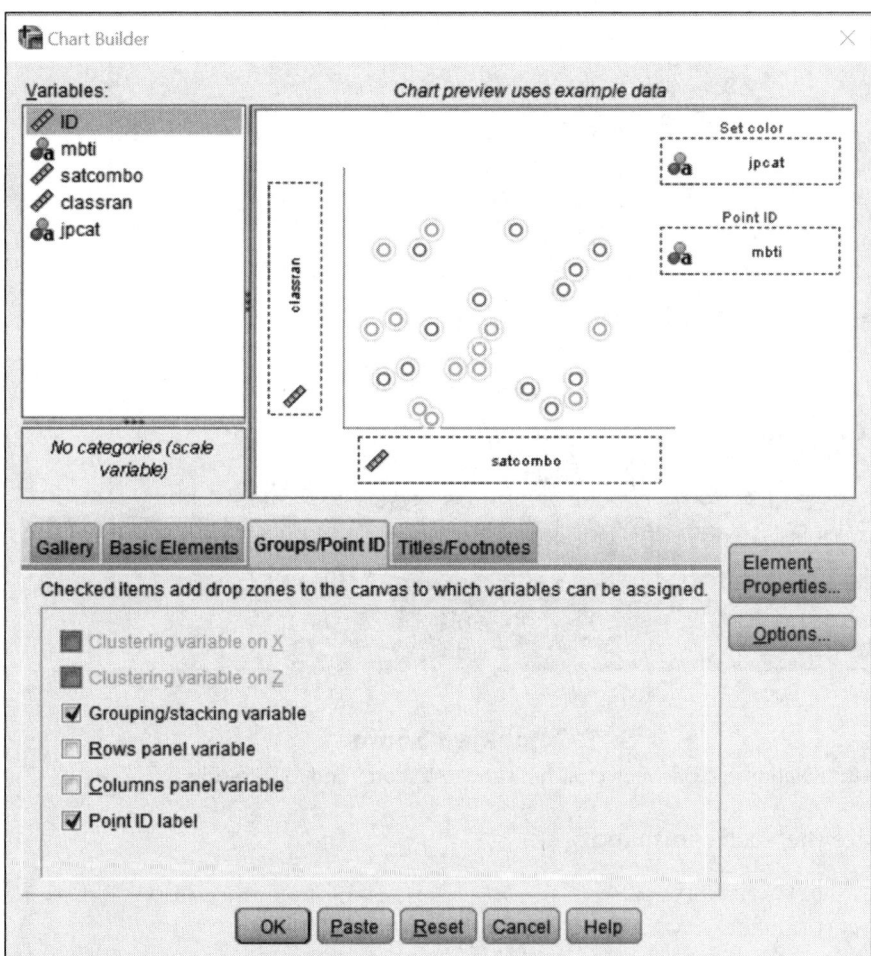

Figure 6-17: Preview of bubble plot

Here is the GPL code that does it. We will discuss the features that we haven't seen before in considerable detail, but will not review commands that we have already learned. Let's start with the GGRAPH command. We enter cool new territory. We have two GRAPHDATASET subcommands! We are going to start with a single dataset, then run an AGGREGATE command to create a second dataset, and then refer to both datasets in the GPL code. The line element will be based on an 850-row dataset, and the points will be based on the 16-row dataset.

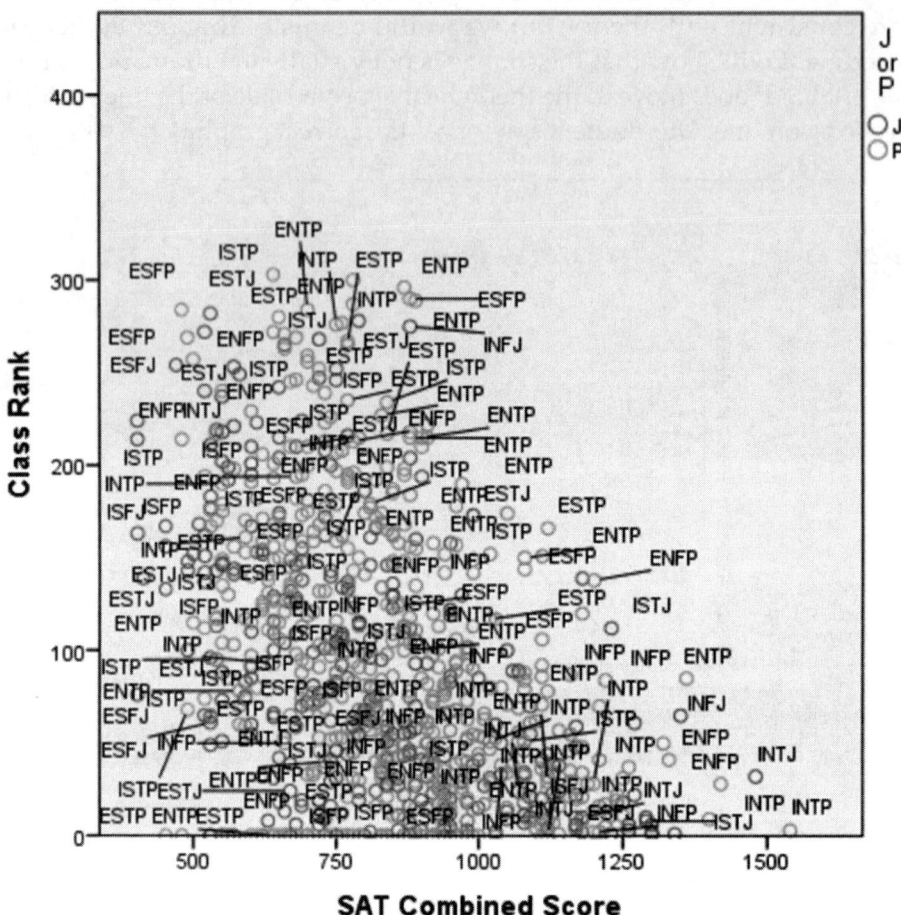

Figure 6-18: Relationship between class rank and SAT scores and MBTI results

Here are the AGGR commands:

```
DATASET ACTIVATE AllData.
DATASET DECLARE AGGR.
AGGREGATE
  /OUTFILE='AGGR'
  /BREAK=mbti jpcat
  /satcombo_mean 'Group Mean SAT Combined Score'=MEAN(satcombo)
  /classran_mean 'Group Mean Class Rank'=MEAN(classran)
  /N_BREAK=N.

DATASET ACTIVATE AGGR.
```

```
* Define Variable Properties.
FORMATS  satcombo_mean(F8.0).
FORMATS  classran_mean(F8.0).
```

An important detail is the use of the DATASET NAME command to choose the "window name" of AllData to refer to the original data, and AGGR to refer to our new 16-row dataset. The FORMATS command gets rid of decimal places to clean up our chart. It is much easier to do that now before we build the chart.

Note that as an example you could look at the GPL generated by Graphs ➪ Compare Subgroups, which uses two datasets—one with split files on and a separate one for the overall data:

```
GGRAPH
  /GRAPHDATASET NAME="graphdataset" DATASET = AllData
VARIABLES=ID
classran satcombo MISSING=LISTWISE
    REPORTMISSING=NO
  /GRAPHDATASET NAME="graphdataset2" DATASET = AGGR VARIABLES=N_BREAK
mbti classran_mean satcombo_mean jpcat MISSING=LISTWISE
    REPORTMISSING=NO
  /GRAPHSPEC SOURCE=INLINE.
```

Here is the GPL code:

```
BEGIN GPL
  PAGE: begin(scale(10in,6in))
  SOURCE: s=userSource(id("graphdataset"))
  SOURCE: s2=userSource(id("graphdataset2"))
  DATA: ID=col(source(s), name("ID"), unit.category())
  DATA: N_BREAK=col(source(s2), name("N_BREAK"))
  DATA: classran_mean=col(source(s2), name("classran_mean"))
  DATA: satcombo_mean=col(source(s2), name("satcombo_mean"))
  DATA: classran=col(source(s), name("classran"))
  DATA: satcombo=col(source(s), name("satcombo"))
  DATA: jpcat=col(source(s2), name("jpcat"), unit.category())
  DATA: mbti=col(source(s2), name("mbti"), unit.category())
  GUIDE: axis(dim(2), label("Group Mean Class Rank"))
  GUIDE: axis(dim(1), label("Group Mean SAT Combined Score"))
  GUIDE: legend(aesthetic(aesthetic.color.interior), null() )
  GUIDE: legend(aesthetic(aesthetic.color.exterior), null() )
  GUIDE: legend(aesthetic(aesthetic.size), null() )
  GUIDE: text.footnote(label("Point position is group mean. Point size
indicates group sample size. Regression line N=850."))
  SCALE: linear(dim(1), min(600), max(1000))
```

```
    SCALE: linear(dim(2), min(45), max(125), reverse())
    SCALE: linear(aesthetic(aesthetic.size), aestheticMinimum(size."8px"),
              aestheticMaximum(size."25px"))
    ELEMENT: point(position(satcombo_mean*classran_mean),
color.exterior(jpcat),
      color.interior(jpcat), label(mbti), size(N_BREAK))
    ELEMENT: line(position(smooth.linear(satcombo*classran))    )
    PAGE: end()
END GPL.
```

Here are some things to look for in the code:

- There are two SOURCE statements. Our original file is Source s, and our aggregated file is s2.

- The legends have been declared null() since we have a caption.

- The last GUIDE statement provides the caption.

- We've declared min and max dimensions and used the reverse() function.

- We've declared an aestheticMinimum and aestheticMaximum.

- The point element uses only variables from the second dataset, and the line element uses only variables from the first dataset. We are not allowed to mix and match within the same ELEMENT statement.

If you copy all the syntax code shown in this case study, you will be using the active dataset and the aggregated dataset created by the AGGREGATE command. Finally you will be using information from both datasets along with the aesthetics specified above to create Figure 6-16. This case study is a very simple example of the power of GPL.

Mapping in IBM SPSS Statistics

As researchers, it is very important that we are able to communicate our findings. Typically we hold meetings or write reports that allow others to understand what we have found. Graphs allow researchers to summarize data quickly and easily. Graphs also allow you to visualize data to better understand relationships among variables.

SPSS Statistics has several procedures that allow users to create graphs (for example, the Chart Builder, the Legacy Graphs, and the Graphboard Template Chooser). The standard graphs and charts in SPSS Statistics are complete entities, so that users need to know what they want to show in a graph before they create it. For example, I might want to create a scatterplot or a bar chart, so when using the Chart Builder or a Legacy Graph, I would choose a scatterplot or a bar chart type, and all the available elements of the graph would be chosen for me (of course the elements can be manipulated or removed using the Chart Editor).

The Graphboard Template Chooser, on the other hand, defines structure and elements of a graphic, not the entire graphic. For example, I may want to show the relationship between two categorical variables and one continuous variable, and I might want to display the mean for this combination of variables. With the Graphboard Template Chooser, users explore how best to visualize their data, or the Graphboard Template Chooser can recommend potential visualizations depending on the type(s) of data selected.

Creating Maps with the Graphboard Template Chooser

In these first examples, we will use the `Worldwidesales.sav` file. This file (see Figure 7-1) contains sales revenue broken down by product purchased and location.

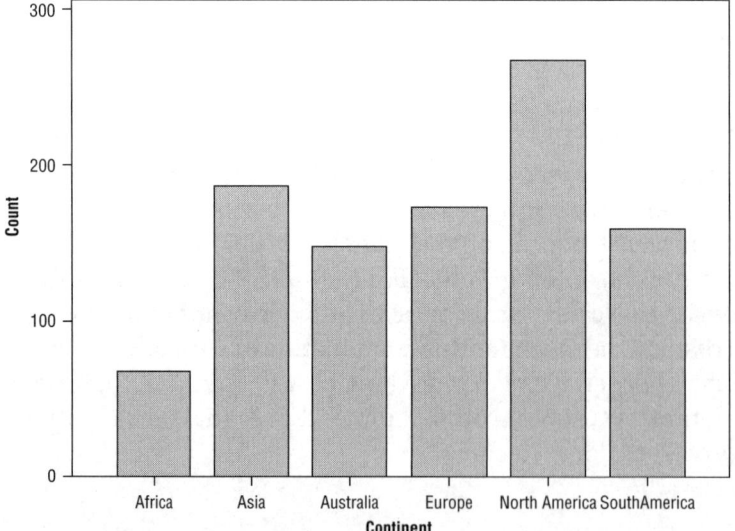

Figure 7-1: Worldwide sales data

Perhaps the simplest graph you can create using the Graphboard Template Chooser to show the distribution of customer locations is a bar chart. The bar chart shown in Figure 7-2 displays the number of customers in each continent, with each continent represented by a bar. The bars are arranged in alphabetical order. We can see that we have the fewest customers in Africa because it has the shortest bar, and North America is the continent where we have the most customers because it has the tallest bar.

Figure 7-2: Bar chart of customer location

However, when data has a geographical component, a better solution might be to use a map. Maps allow you to see patterns in the data that might not be evident in traditional charts, such as clusters or regions with a higher concentration of values. The map in Figure 7-3 shows the distribution customer locations. It shows the number of customers in each continent and each continent is represented by its geographical location. Furthermore, color saturation is used to represent values that correspond to the variables depicted on the map (here, darker values represent higher values). Maps give context that is meaningful.

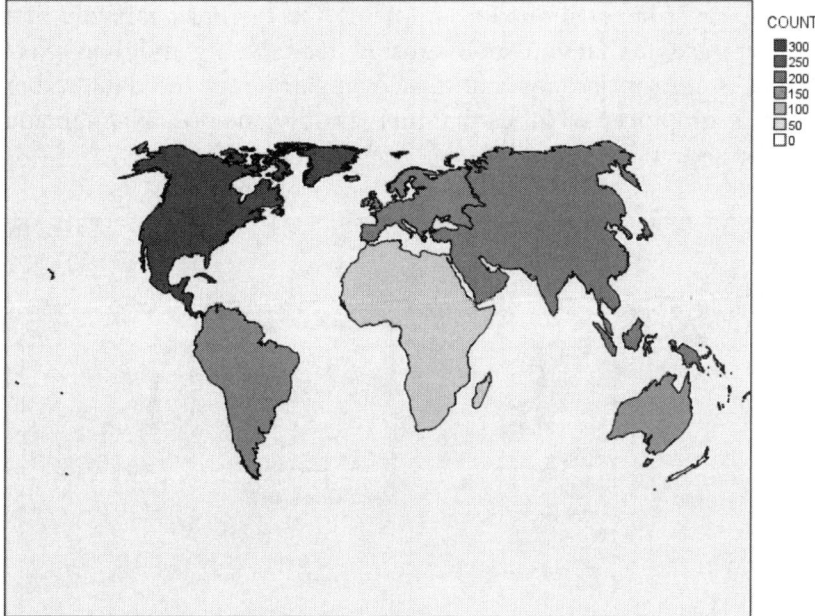

Figure 7-3: Map of customer locations

Maps can be used in a wide variety of settings to help answer many important questions. For example, organizations may want to know the location of certain client characteristics to determine where to send salespeople, where to hire additional employees, where to create new stores, which marketing campaigns to use, and so on.

Investigators can use maps to determine the locations of crimes, the spread of disease, fluctuations in temperature, population growth, distance traveled, where to send school buses, how to create new districts, and so on.

Creating a Choropleth of Counts Map

The Choropleth of Counts map is used when you have only one categorical variable to display, and the categorical variable is the data key. This is the simplest map you can create because it only requires one categorical variable.

This section walks you through the process of creating a Choropleth of Counts map:

1. To access the Graphboard Template Chooser, click Graphs ➪ Graphboard Template Chooser.

   Maps can be created from a single variable, or multiple variables. Maps can use categorical variables, continuous variables, and combinations of categorical and continuous variables.

2. Click the Continent variable.

   The Basic tab gives suggestions for templates. On the Basic tab, you first have to select the data that you are interested in analyzing and then select a graph that is appropriate for that data. You start from the data, rather than a specific graph type. Notice that there is only one possible map you can create (as shown in Figure 7-4).

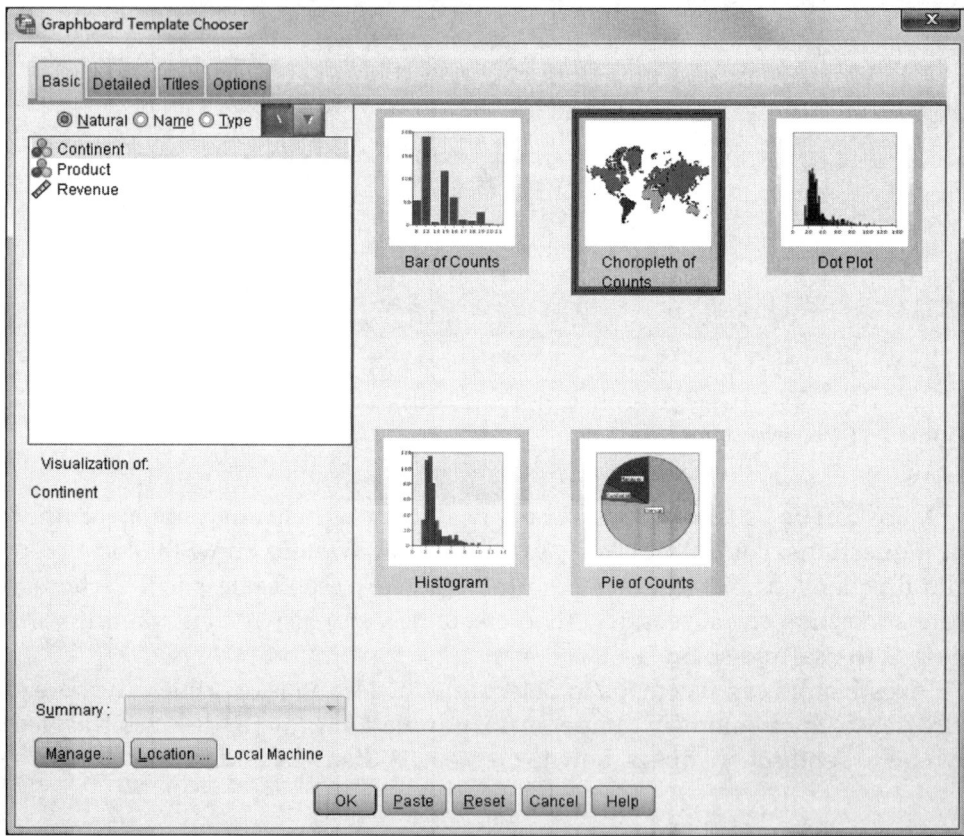

Figure 7-4: One variable selected

3. Click the Choropleth of Counts icon.

4. Click the Detailed tab.

   The Detailed tab is an alternative to the Basic tab where you can specify all required variables, summary statistics, and aesthetics. You select the graph type, specify the type of data, and then you can specify details that are not available on the Basic tab. The Detailed tab is optional for most visualizations; however, it is required when you are creating a map. You need to make sure that the right template and data key are selected. For example, if you have data for Africa, you need to make sure that the map template is also for Africa.

5. Click the Select a Map File button.

   The Select a Map dialog allows users to select the appropriate map and the template is specified next to the map box.

6. Click the Map drop-down list and select Continents.

   You then need to specify the map key. The map key contains the values that are represented on the map template. Then you need to specify the data key. The data key holds the values that you actually have in your dataset. A data key is a variable that contains the labels that correspond to the areas on a map. It is a way to tie the data to the map, so that the data can be displayed on the map correctly. It is important to make sure that the map and data key values match.

7. Click the Data key drop-down list and select Continent.

   You can click the Compare button after the appropriate map and data keys have been determined.

8. Click the Compare button.

   Now you can see which keys match between the map and data keys. Ideally you would like all the values to match. As shown in Figure 7-5, you want to make sure that all of the values for the data key match the values on the map. If your data does not have some of the values on the map key, that is okay. In our example Oceania appears on the map key but not in the data.

9. Click OK.

   Figure 7-6 shows the Detailed tab with the correct map file.

10. Click OK.

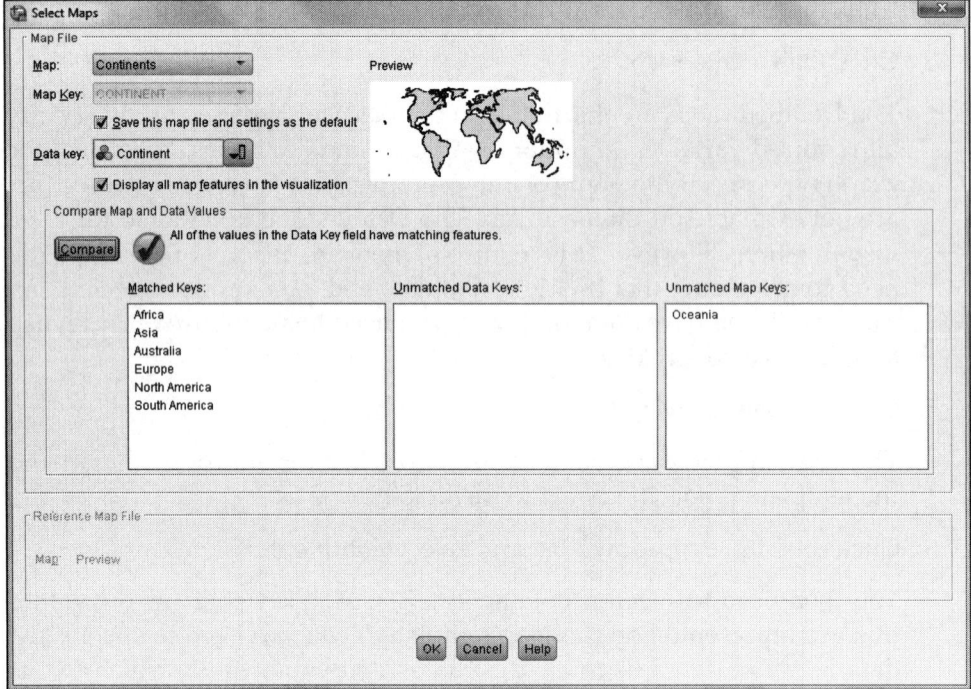

Figure 7-5: Select Maps dialog

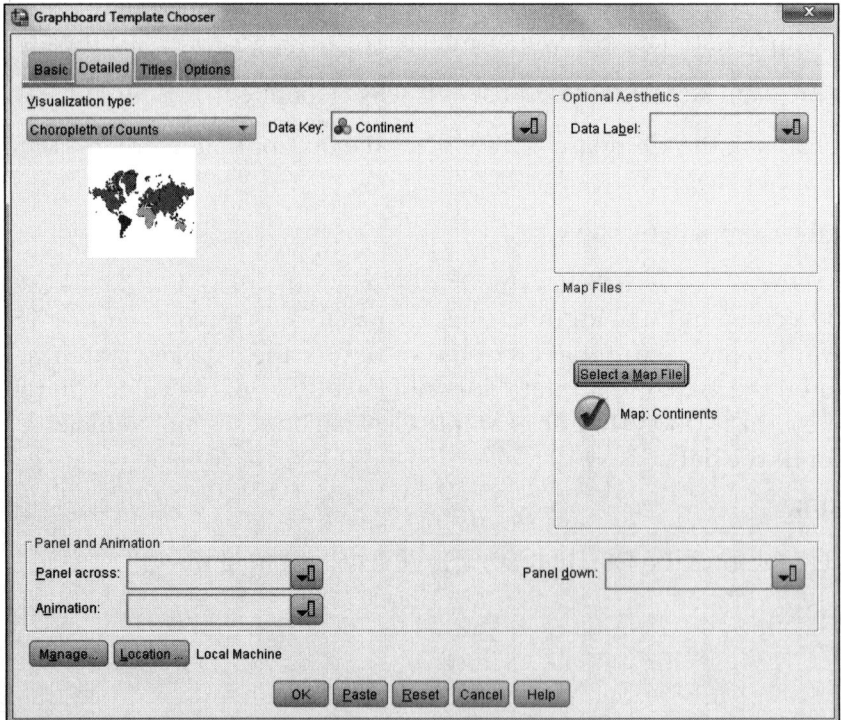

Figure 7-6: Completed Detailed tab

The Graphboard Template Chooser comes with several map files. You can view these map files by clicking the Manage button. Here you will be able to import or export map files. However, if you would like to create your own map files, you will need to use the map conversion utility. The map conversion utility is located under the Utility menu.

This type of map (Figure 7-7) is used when you want to see the frequency of different regions in your map or how often values for your data key occur. For example, it can be used when you want to look at number of sales or crimes in different regions. Color saturation is used to represent values that correspond to the variables depicted on the map (here, darker values represent higher values). We can see that we have the fewest customers in Africa because it has the lightest color, and North America is the continent where we have the most customers because it has the darkest color.

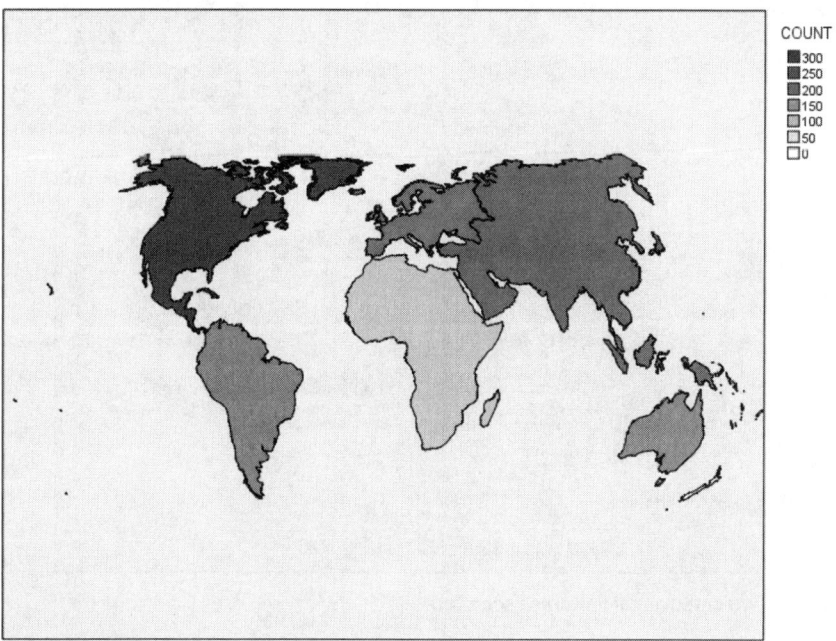

Figure 7-7: Choropleth of Counts

Creating Other Map Types

In this section you continue using the Graphboard Template Chooser to create additional map types.

Choropleth of Values

The Choropleth of Values map shows relationships between two categorical variables. Here the mode or most common value is what is depicted on the map as a different color.

Start by following these steps to create a Choropleth of Values map:

1. Click Graphs ➪ Graphboard Template Chooser.

2. Click the Continent variable.

3. Hold down the Ctrl key and click the Product variable.

   You have selected two categorical variables. Notice that six possible maps are available (as shown in Figure 7-8).

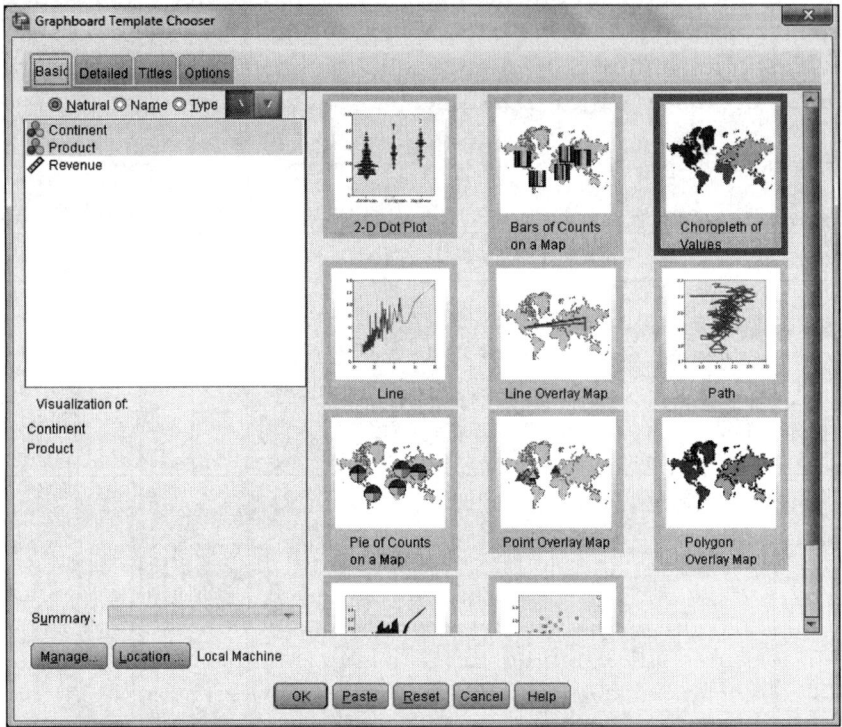

Figure 7-8: Two categorical variables selected

4. Click the Choropleth of Values icon.

   Make sure when using the Detailed tab that you are using the Continents map and that the Continent variable is the data key.

5. Click OK.

Figure 7-9 illustrates the relationship between the Continent and Product variables. The map shows that the continents of North America, Europe, and Australia prefer Product B, whereas Product A is the biggest seller in South America and Africa, and Asia has a preference for Product C.

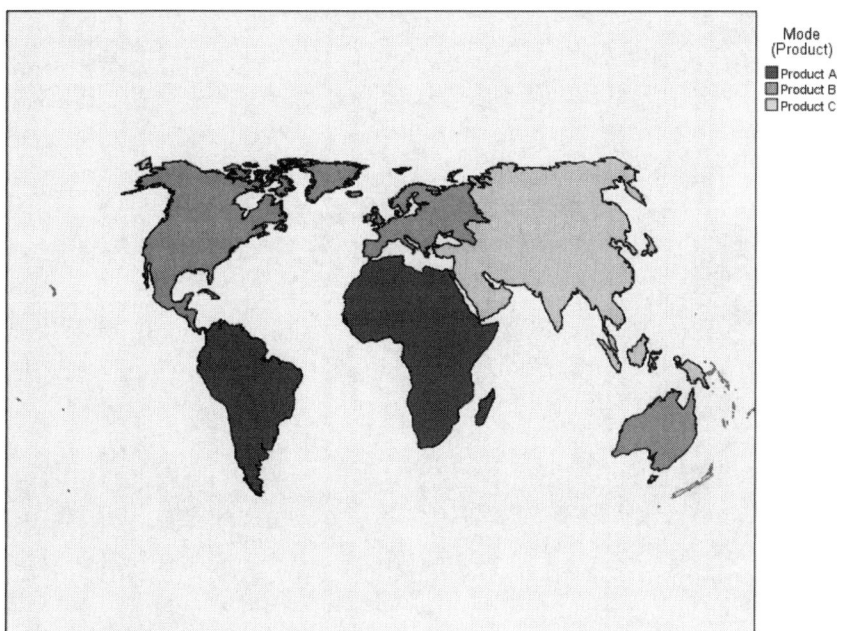

Figure 7-9: Choropleth of Values

Pie of Counts

The pie of counts on a map (or bar of counts on a map) shows relationships between two categorical variables. It displays the proportion of rows divided by cases for each category of a variable for each map feature (area) as pie (or bar) charts positioned in the center of each map feature.

Let's next create a Pie of Counts map for two categorical variables:

1. Click Graphs ⇨ Graphboard Template Chooser.

2. Click the Continent variable.

3. Hold down the Ctrl key and click the Product variable.

4. Click the Pie of Counts on a Map icon.

   Make sure that you are using the Continents map and that the Continent variable is the data key.

5. Click OK.

Figure 7-10 shows the relationship between the Continent and Product variables. The map shows the Product category breakdown within each Continent, so whereas the Choropleth of Values map showed only the modal response for each Continent, here we see the Product category breakdown within each Continent. Note that you can edit these charts.

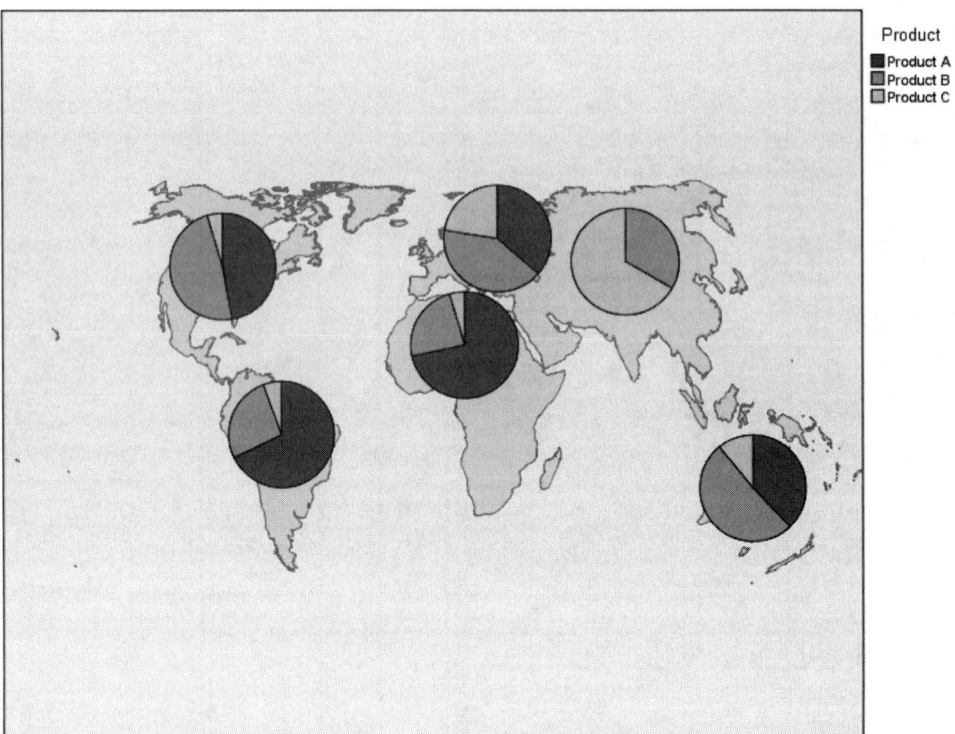

Figure 7-10: Pie of counts on a map

Choropleth of Sums

The Choropleth of Sums (means or medians) map shows relationships between a categorical and a continuous variable.

Now let's create a Choropleth of Sums map for one categorical variable and one continuous variable:

1. Click Graphs ⇨ Graphboard Template Chooser.

2. Click the Continent variable.

3. Hold down the Ctrl key and click the Revenue variable.

   You have selected one categorical and one continuous variable. Notice that you can create three possible maps (as shown in Figure 7-11).

4. Click the Choropleth of Sums icon.

   Make sure that you are using the Continents map and that the Continent variable is the data key.

5. Click OK to display the map shown in Figure 7-12.

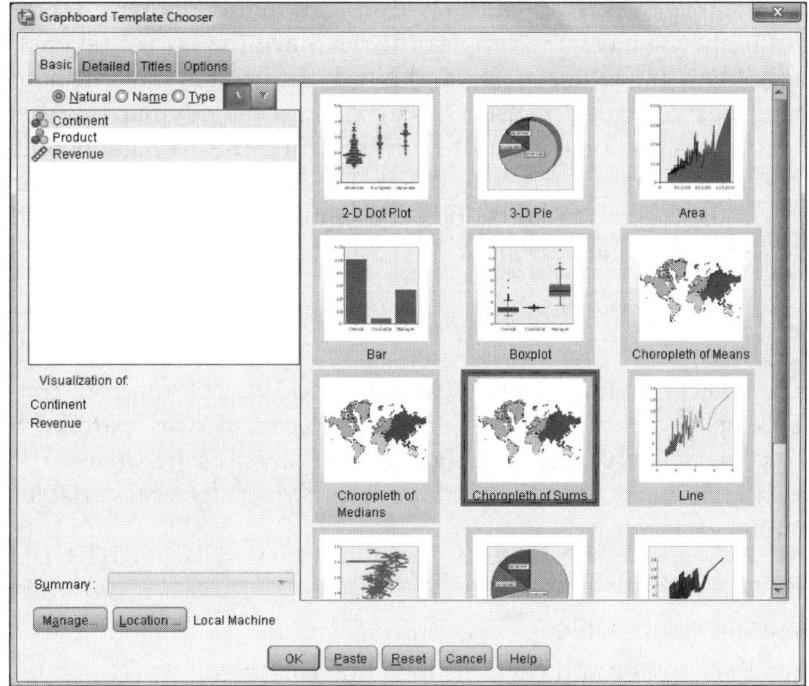

Figure 7-11: One categorical and one continuous variable selected

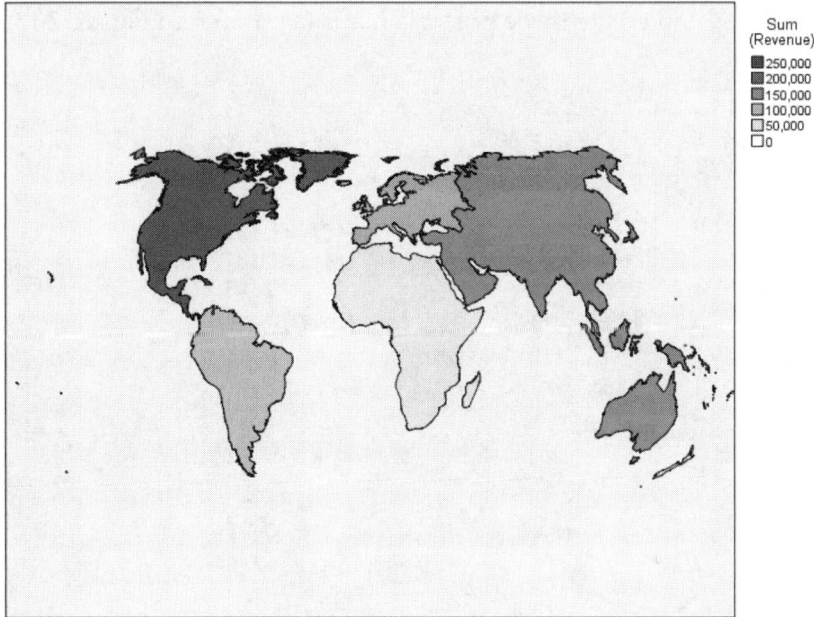

Figure 7-12: Choropleth of Sums

Color saturation shows the sum of values within each continent (here, darker values represent higher values). We can see that we have the lowest revenue in Africa because it has the lightest color, and North America is the continent where we have the most revenue because it has the darkest color. A map like this can be used in various situations, including investigating the average income per neighborhood or amount spent by country on health care. Note that in this dataset the mean is just the average revenue per country, while the user would probably want average revenue per capita.

Bars on a Map

The bars (pie or line chart) on a map requires two categorical variables and one continuous variable. It displays a summary statistic for each category of a variable for each map feature as bar (pie or line) charts positioned in the center of each map feature.

Now let's create one final map with this dataset for two categorical variables and one continuous variable:

1. Click Graphs ➪ Graphboard Template Chooser.
2. Click the Continent variable.
3. Hold down the Ctrl key and click the Revenue variable.
4. Hold down the Ctrl key and click the Product variable.
5. Select Sum in the Summary drop-down list.

   You have selected two categorical variables and one continuous variable. Notice that you can create three possible maps (as shown in Figure 7-13).

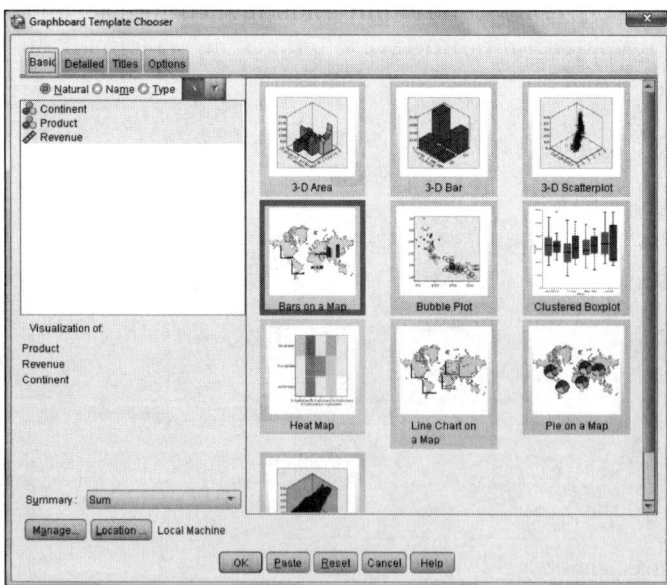

Figure 7-13: Two categorical and one continuous variable selected

6. Click the Bars on a Map icon.

Make sure that you are using the Continents map and that the Continent variable is the data key.

7. Click OK. You should see the map shown in Figure 7-14.

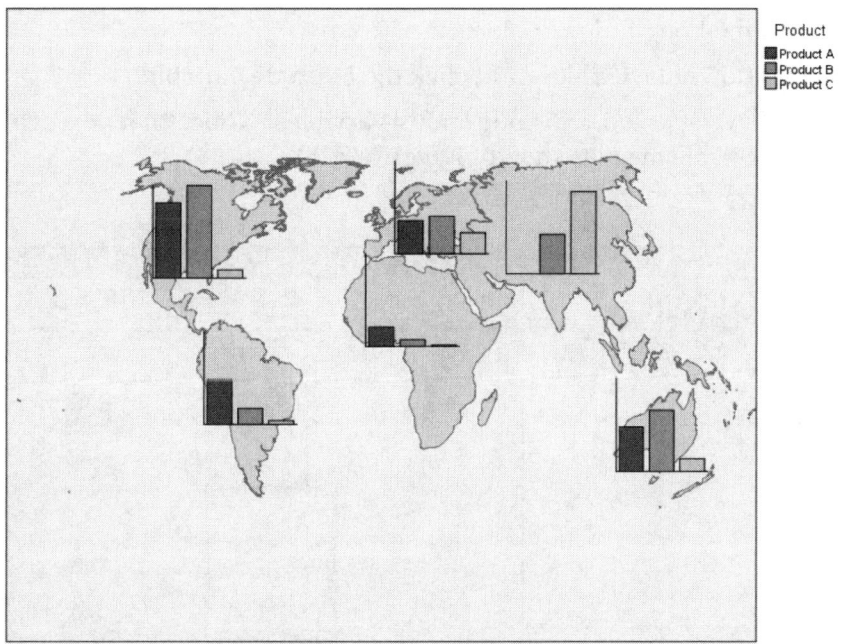

Figure 7-14: Bars on a Map

This type of map can be used to show the number of sales of different products in different areas where you do business or how different types of crimes relate to home values in different neighborhoods. In our example, the map shows total revenue by the Product category breakdown within each Continent. So we see that South America and Africa had the greatest revenue from Product A, Asia had the greatest revenue from Product C, and North America, Europe, and Australia had the greatest revenue from Product B.

Creating Maps Using Geographical Coordinates

In these next examples, we will use the file Coordinates.sav. This file contains latitude and longitude coordinates of customer location. Longitude and latitude coordinates can be created using freeware on the Internet from many different pieces of geographical information including addresses, zip codes, cities, and so on.

Coordinates on a Reference Map

Coordinates on a Reference map uses two continuous variables—one representing longitude, and one representing latitude—and then draws a map that displays points using longitude and latitude coordinates.

First let's create a map using latitude and longitude coordinates:

1. Click Graphs ⇨ Graphboard Template Chooser.

2. Click the Longitude variable.

3. Hold down the Ctrl key and click the Latitude variable.

    You have selected two continuous variables. Notice that you can create one possible map (as shown in Figure 7-15).

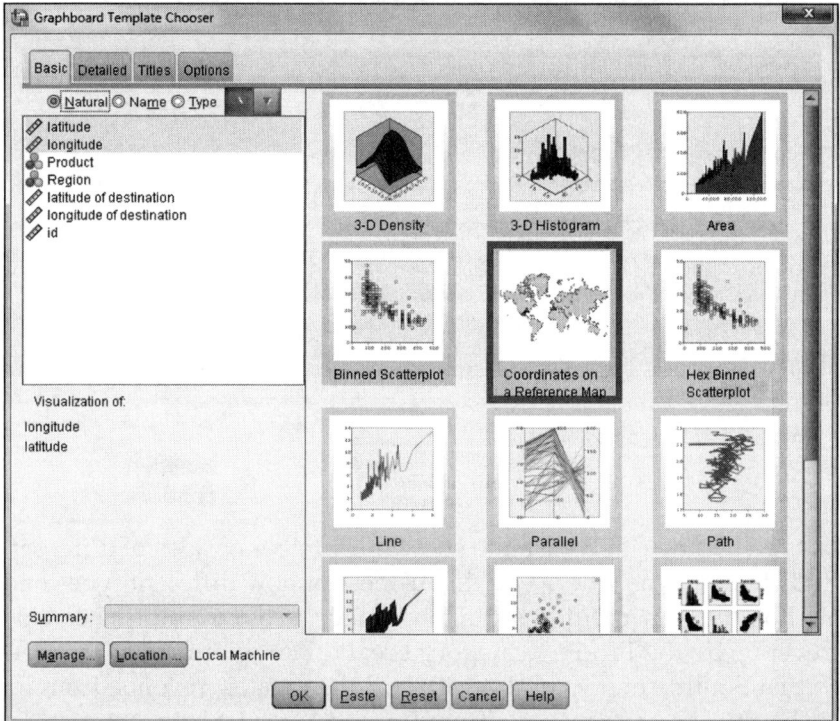

Figure 7-15: Two continuous variables selected

4. Click the Coordinates on a Reference Map icon.

    Make sure that you are using the Continents map and that the latitude and longitude variables point to the correct location.

5. Click OK. You should see the map shown in Figure 7-16.

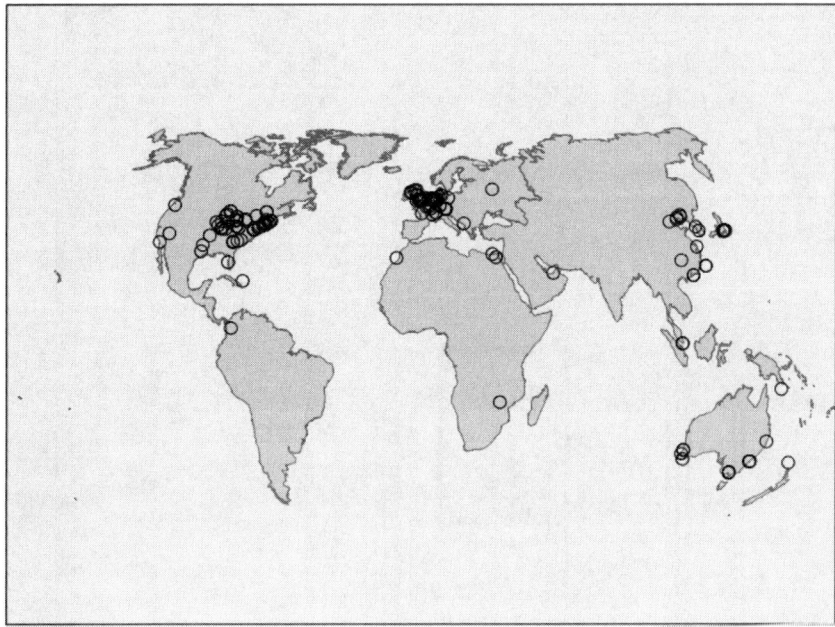

Figure 7-16: Coordinates on a Reference map

This type of map can be used to show where different crimes are committed, or the spread of disease, or where customers are located, or to modify school bus routes where children live. In this example we can see that most of our customers are located in the Eastern United States and Western Europe.

Coordinates on a Choropleth of Counts

The Coordinates on a Choropleth of Counts map uses two continuous variables that represent longitude and latitude coordinates and one categorical variable that represents the color depicted on the map.

Now let's create a Coordinates on a Choropleth of Counts map:

1. Click Graphs ⇨ Graphboard Template Chooser.
2. Click the Longitude variable.
3. Hold down the Ctrl key and click the Latitude variable.
4. Hold down the Ctrl key and click the Region variable.

   You have selected two continuous variables and one categorical variable. Notice that you can create two possible maps (as shown in Figure 7-17).

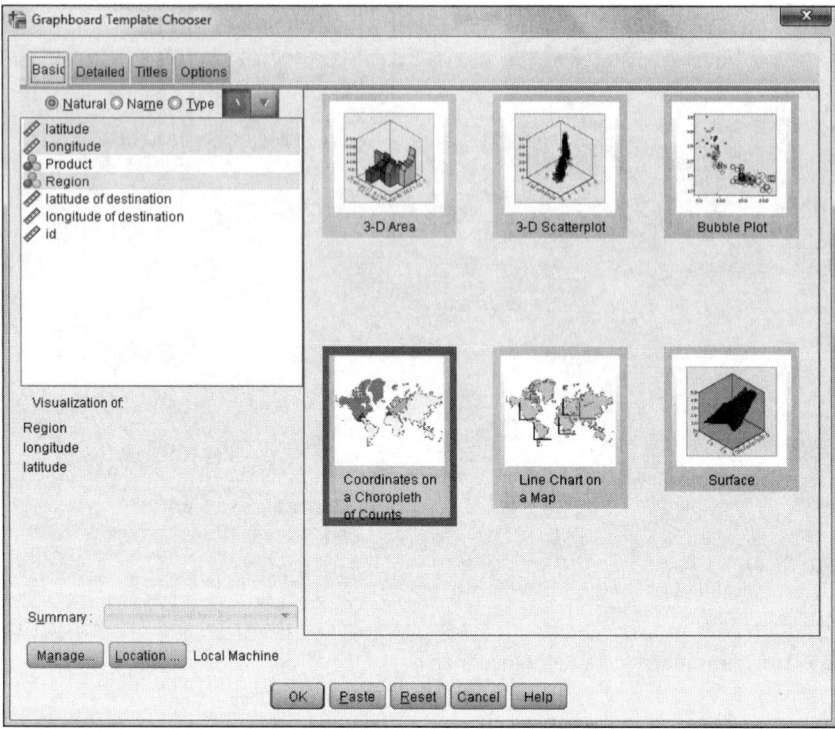

Figure 7-17: Two continuous variables and one categorical variable selected

5. Click the Coordinates on a Choropleth of Counts icon.

    Make sure when using the Detailed tab that you are using the Continents map file and that the latitude and longitude variables point to the correct location.

6. Click OK to display the map shown in Figure 7-18.

The longitude and latitude coordinates are used to identify points on a map, and color saturation (here, darker values represent higher values) is used to represent the number of cases that correspond to the variables depicted on a map. We can see that we have the least number of customers in Africa and South America because they have the lightest color, and North America and Europe are the continents where we have the most customers because they have the darkest color.

Arrows on a Reference Map

The Arrows on a Reference map uses four continuous variables for starting and ending coordinates. These variables represent the starting longitude and latitude coordinates and the ending longitude and latitude coordinates. These types of maps are ideal for displaying the spread of disease, or movement, or distance traveled.

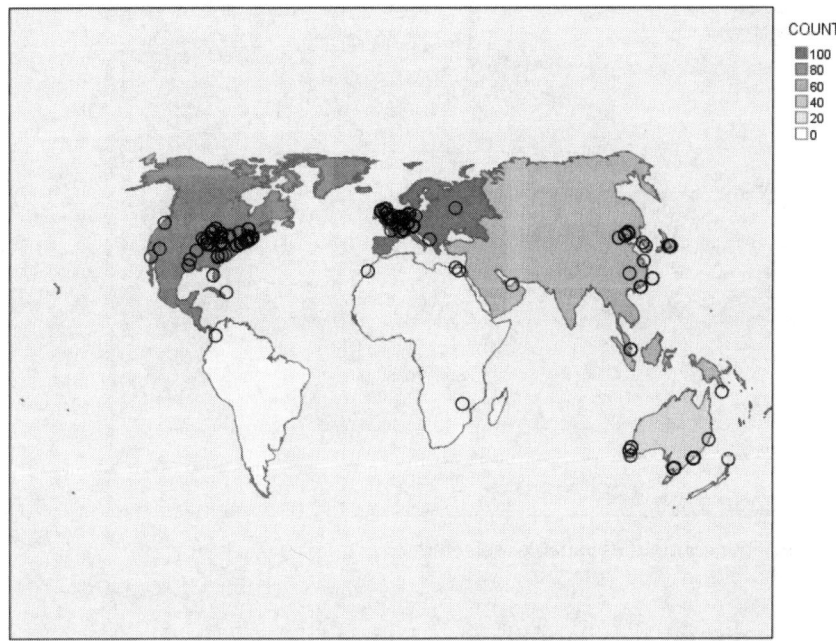

Figure 7-18: Coordinates on a Choropleth of Counts map

Now let's create one final map:

1. Click Graphs ➪ Graphboard Template Chooser.
2. Click the Longitude variable.
3. Hold down the Ctrl key and click the Latitude variable.
4. Hold down the Ctrl key and click the Longitude of destination variable.
5. Hold down the Ctrl key and click the Latitude of destination variable.

   You have selected four continuous variables. Notice that there is one possible map you can create (as shown in Figure 7-19). Note that depending on your preference settings, variable names or labels appear on the variable list.

6. Click the Arrows on a Reference Map icon.

   In the Detailed tab make sure that you are using the Continents map file and that the latitude and longitude variables are in the correct location.

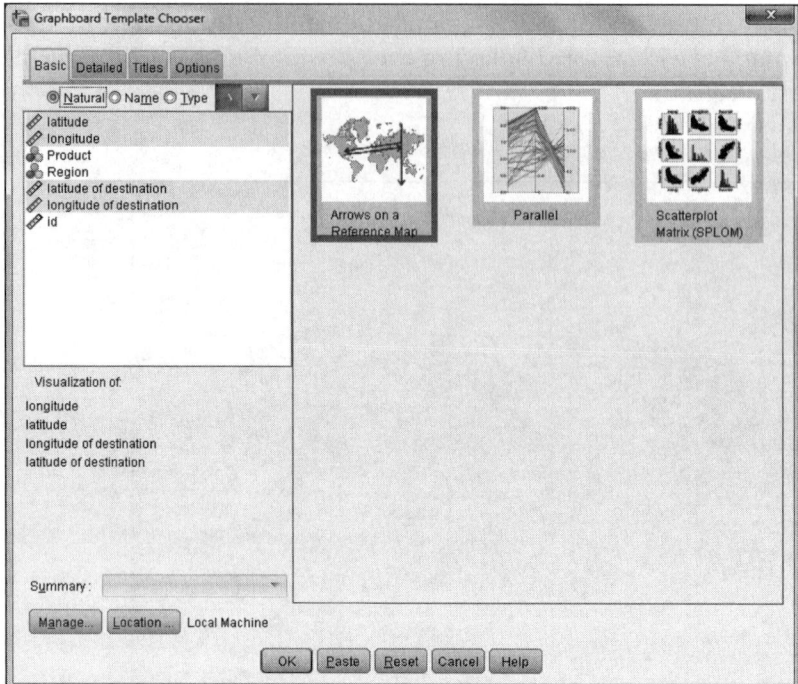

Figure 7-19: Four continuous variables selected

7. Click OK to display the map shown in Figure 7-20.

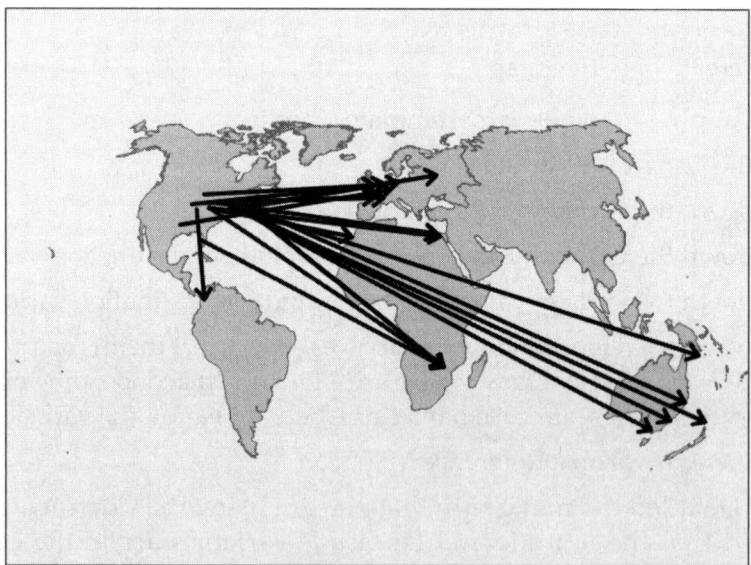

Figure 7-20: Arrows on a Reference map

The Options tab of the Graphboard Template Chooser controls how missing data is handled. As a default, listwise deletion is used. Notice that in our dataset we only have ending coordinates for people that originated in North America, so we can easily see where each person in North America traveled.

In SPSS Statistics V23, three new mapping procedures are introduced: Geospatial Association Rules, Spatial Mapspec, and Spatial Temporal Prediction. These are covered in Chapter 8, and they are the natural evolution from the simple mapping approach illustrated here.

Geospatial Analytics

The majority of data that businesses deal with is associated with a particular location. For many problems, incorporating where events occur can improve predictions and help you better understand the data. Almost all spatial data exhibits some type of spatial dependence, and exploiting that dependence is what spatial analysis is all about.

Two new spatial analytic techniques have been added to SPSS Statistics Version 23: Geospatial Association Rules and Spatio-Temporal Prediction. Both techniques are available to all users. Both techniques can take a set of data that has an associated set of X and Y coordinates, or has a field that associates it with a particular map file (for example, a ZIP code) and then generate predictions for an area given a set of map locations and additional variables associated with those areas.

This chapter provides a walkthrough of each technique applied to different case studies of crime analysis. Crime tends to be highly clustered in certain areas, and so many police departments conduct geographic analysis to identify these hot spots of crime. Police departments then frequently deploy more resources at these hot spots, such as conducting more patrols, writing more traffic tickets, or having community police officers meet with community members to discuss local problems and potential remedies. Each of the new geospatial analytic techniques in SPSS can facilitate the types of analyses many police departments or other businesses undertake.

Geospatial Association Rules

The association rules technique finds the items that occur the most frequently together, often among a set of very many different items. The most common examples are in basket analysis, in which association rules identify the most common items people purchase together. One surprising example of this type of analysis is that males tend to purchase diapers and beer together.

We can think of the overlap in terms of a crosstabs table, where each cell defines whether a shopper buys neither beer nor diapers, buys one or the other product, or buys both. When you are only examining two items it is simple to see the overlap, but the task becomes more complicated when you have many different items, and the associations may be between more than two items. Geospatial Association Rules is an automated procedure to find those categories that have a large degree of overlap. The Association Rules algorithm can search over many different crosstabulations and return sets of items that meet user-specified criteria.

With SPSS's Geospatial Association Rules, instead of the unit of analysis being an individual shopper, the unit of analysis is a particular place. To continue the example of basket analysis, say the analyst has different sales figures for stores by ZIP code. Do ZIP codes that tend to sell more beer also tend to sell more diapers? Even if the individual-level association between beer and diapers exists, that does not guarantee that the relationship will also exist at the ZIP code level. (The reverse is true as well, that a relationship at the aggregate level will not necessarily exist at the individual level; this is known as the *ecological fallacy*.) For the basket analysis example, differences between ZIP codes may suggest different marketing strategies in different ZIP codes.

Case Study: Crime and 311 Calls

This section provides an example of geospatial association rules between reported crime and 311 calls-for-service in Washington, D.C., in 2013 at a set of 500 meter by 500 meter grid cells. The types of crime that will be examined are thefts from auto, burglary, robbery, and aggravated assault with a weapon. 311 calls-for-service are non-emergency complaints directed toward city agencies. A 311 hotline is not available in all places in the United States (unlike 911), but many large cities have a 311 system. 311 complaints encompass quite a large number of categories, but some examples in D.C. are loose garbage on the street, a broken parking meter, or a sidewalk that needs to be repaired. The original data is publicly available at `http://data.octo.dc.gov/`, and this book provides a set of files to reproduce the analysis.

The theory of the relationship between crime and 311 calls is the *broken-windows theory* of crime. The theory states where there is one broken window, more are likely to follow. The reasoning behind this relationship is that when an individual sees one broken window, it shows that no one cares, and if that individual breaks another window there is unlikely to be repercussions. The analogy of broken windows can be extended to other visible signs of disorder, such as throwing garbage on the street, spray painting graffiti, or pan handling.

A popular technique conducted by police departments to combat disorder problems in communities is called *problem-oriented policing*. This entails looking at the particular problems faced by a community, and even if they aren't directly crime related to try to help the community solve them. Even in high crime areas people complain more often about visible signs of disorder, like vacant lots and pan handling, than they do about more serious crime. Problem-oriented policing strategies frequently involve reducing such disorder.

Geospatial Association Rules can help crime analysts to identify areas that have high levels of particular 311 calls and different types of crimes. This can aid problem-oriented policing, and part of the reason the 311 number was originally reserved in the U.S. was to aid the police in measuring disorder problems. If one believes the broken-windows theory of crime, reducing such physical disorder problems will result in crime reductions. Another potential avenue for crime reduction is that if police spend more time in a particular area, no matter what they do, they are likely to deter more crime. So identifying areas with both high disorder problems and particular crime problems for community police officers to focus on can facilitate a *two birds with one stone* type crime and disorder targeting strategy.

To start the example, open the SPSS data file `DC_Crime_2013.sav`, which contains the crime data with geographic coordinates, and `Agg311_Data.sav`, which contains a set of 311 complaints aggregated to grid cells in D.C., and then follow these steps:

1. To start the example, open the SPSS data files `DC_Crime_2013.sav` and `Agg311_Data.sav`. The `DC_Crime_2013.sav` data file contains the crime data with geographic coordinates, and the `Agg311_Data.sav` data file contains a set of 311 complaints aggregated to grid cells in D.C.

2. Open up the Geospatial Modeling Wizard from the Analyze menu and select Spatial and Temporal Modeling ➪ Spatial Modeling. It does not matter which dataset is the active one when starting the wizard. Unlike most SPSS dialogs, the Geospatial Modeling Wizard will have access to all opened datasets.

   Figure 8-1 shows the Geospatial Modeling Wizard.

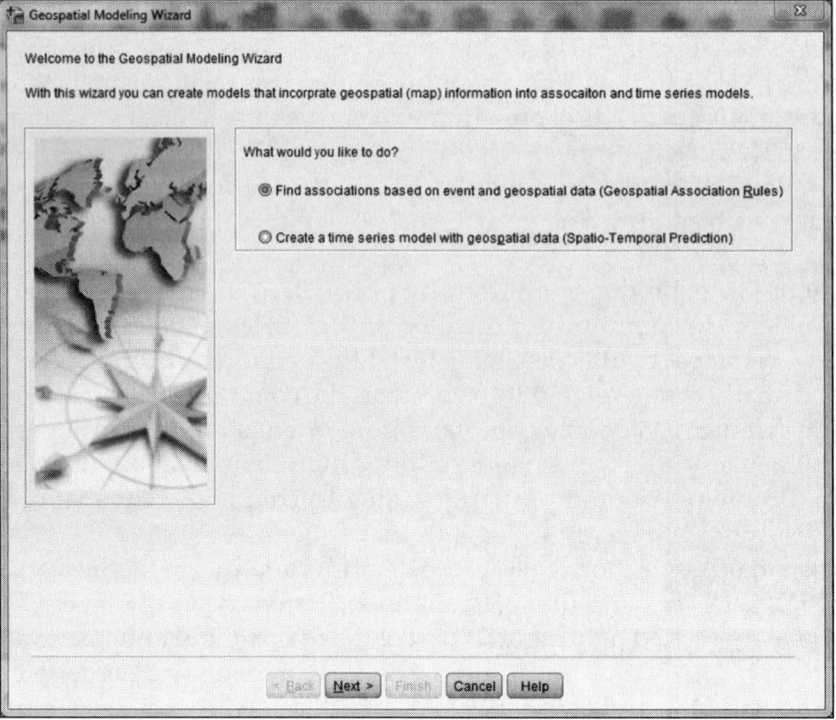

Figure 8-1: Opening the Geospatial Modeling Wizard

3. For this analysis, select the "Find associations based on event and geospatial data (Geospatial Association Rules)" option.

4. Click Next. The dialog that opens will then set up the map data.

5. Click the Add Map File button, and then navigate to the DC_Fishnet.shp shapefile to import the regular grid.

   For both Geospatial Association Rules and Spatio-Temporal Prediction you need to associate a map file, and these define the areas for which predictions are generated. Figure 8-2 shows the expected output. For this example, we have a set of polygon data, and so each crime will be (by default) associated with the polygon that it falls within. You can use other types of spatial data for Geospatial Association Rules, such as points, and have individual events associated with those points. An example might be if you have point locations of stores, and you want to associate home locations to the nearest store. You can set these types of associations via the Relationship button.

   You can also add supplemental information as background layers into the map. For example, for reference data you could add in areas of bodies of water, or a road network. Separate layers can help provide references to locations in the map.

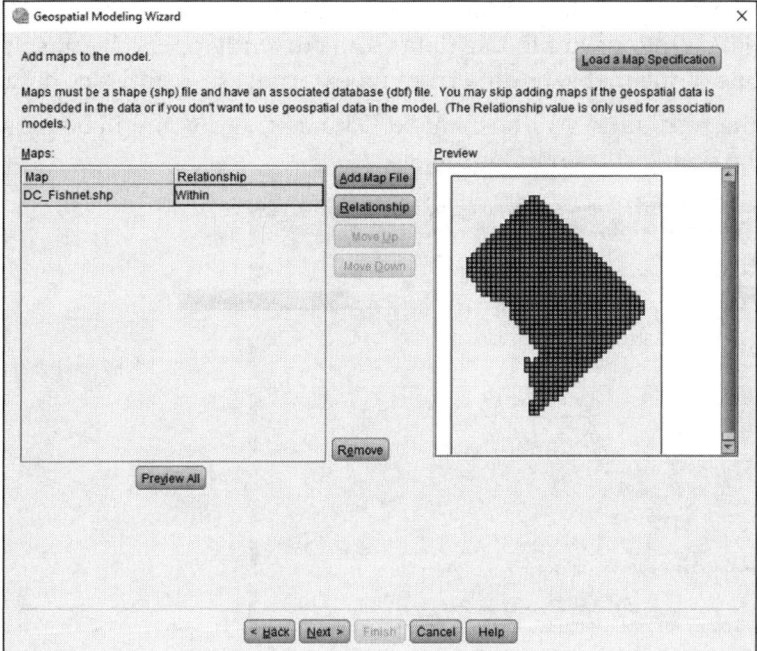

Figure 8-2: Adding map data

6. After the map is set up, as shown in Figure 8-2, click the Next button, and you will be prompted by a dialog to set data to be *context* and the *event* data (the data to be predicted), shown in Figure 8-3.

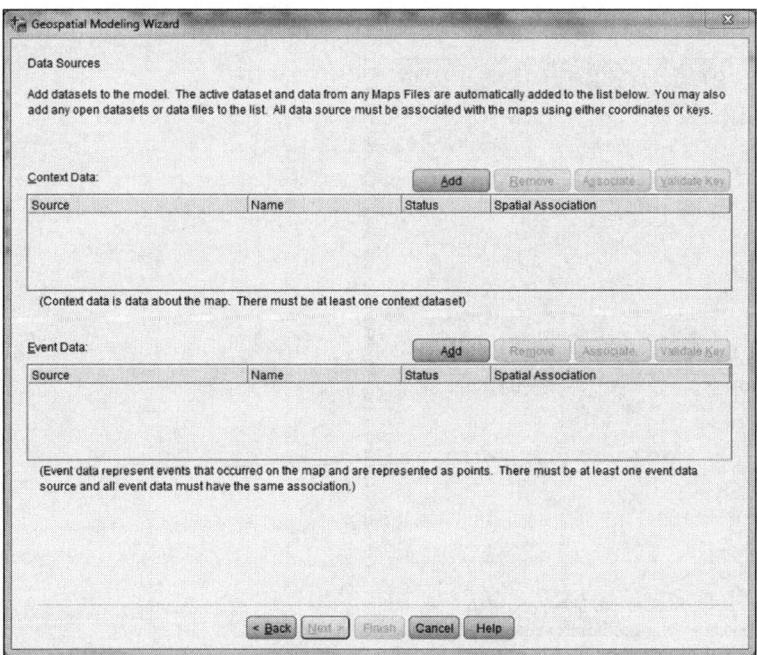

Figure 8-3: Assigning context and prediction data

Here you assign different data sources to either the *context* data or the *event* data. Options are to use data from currently opened datasets, data from one of the maps, or data from an external SPSS statistics data file.

7. Click the Add button in the Context Data box, and you will be presented with the dialog shown in Figure 8-4.

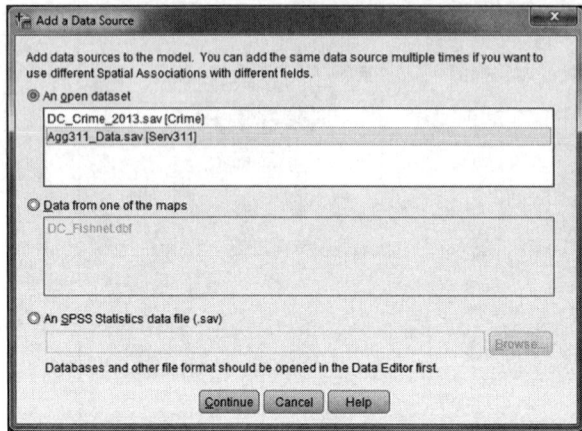

Figure 8-4: Associating map data

8. Select Agg311_Data.sav and click Continue.

You will then be prompted with the dialog shown in Figure 8-5 that associates the SPSS data to the geographic units in the shapefile. Here the FishId variable is the key that matches the records in Agg311_Data to their associated polygon in the DC_Fishnet shapefile.

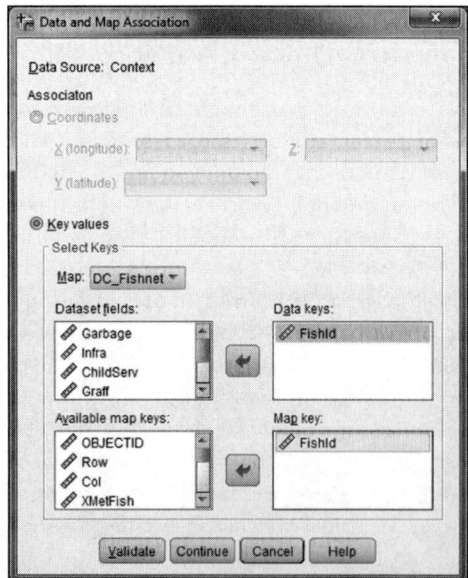

Figure 8-5: Associating fields from data to the map

9. For both the Dataset fields and the map keys select the FishID variable and place it to the right in the Data keys and Map key boxes.

   You can click Validate to see whether your keys were correctly matched between the two different data sources, and see a summary of fields that were not matched.

10. Click Continue, and you will be back at Figure 8-3. Click the Add button in the Event Data field, and select the DC_Crime_2013.sav dataset.

11. Click Continue.

    When following these prompts for the Event dataset, you will have to associate the X and Y coordinates of the data, as opposed to identifying a field to match the prediction data to the map polygons.

12. Using the DC_Crime_2013 data for the predictions, assign the fields BLOCKXCOORD and BLOCKYCOORD to the X (longitude) and Y (latitude) fields, respectively, as shown in Figure 8-6.

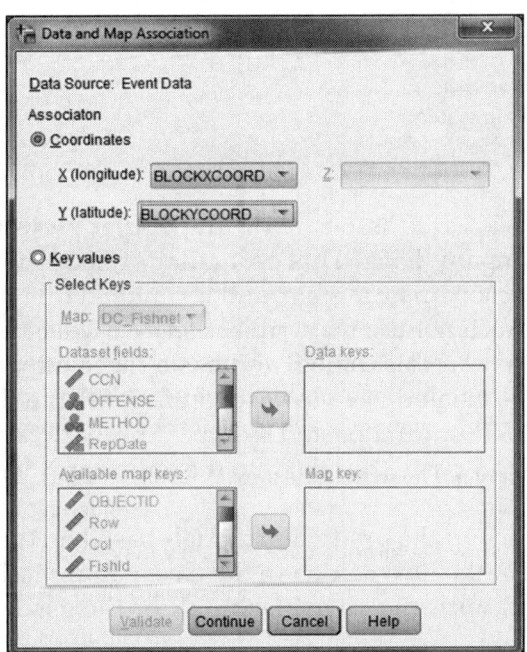

Figure 8-6: Assigned geospatial coordinates

13. Click Continue.

    A dialog will then appear on the screen that asks you to identify the projection of the coordinates. Geographic data can come in the form of spherical longitude and latitude coordinates, or it can be projected into some other coordinate system. Most maps that examine a small area (as is the case for most police departments) use some type of local projection.

14. Here the well-known ID (WKID) of the projection is 26985, so select that option and input the value, as shown in Figure 8-7.

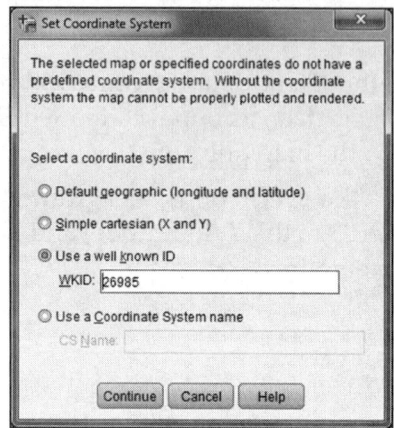

Figure 8-7: Setting the coordinate system

The WKID is simply a numeric value associated with popular projections, originated by the mapping company ESRI. This particular projection is one associated with the state plane coordinate system, and is centered directly on D.C. One way to find out the WKID of the map projection is to select simple Cartesian (X and Y) as the option in this dialog, and paste the syntax at the end. If your shapefile has an associated `.prj` (projection file), SPSS will recognize this and supply the WKID in the pasted syntax. Another way is to upload your `.prj` file (or copy-and-paste the text) into the online app `http://prj2epsg.org/search`.

Now we can move onto setting up the prediction models based on the context and prediction datasets. On the next screen in the Geospatial Modeling Wizard you will be presented with the variables in all of the associated data sources:

1. Click the Event Data in the Data Sources box to see the variables shown in Figure 8-8. Place the OFFENSE categorical field in the Prediction only box.

2. Now click the Context data in the Data Sources box, and then move the variables Garbage, Infra, Graff, and Parking into the Condition only box, as shown in Figure 8-9.

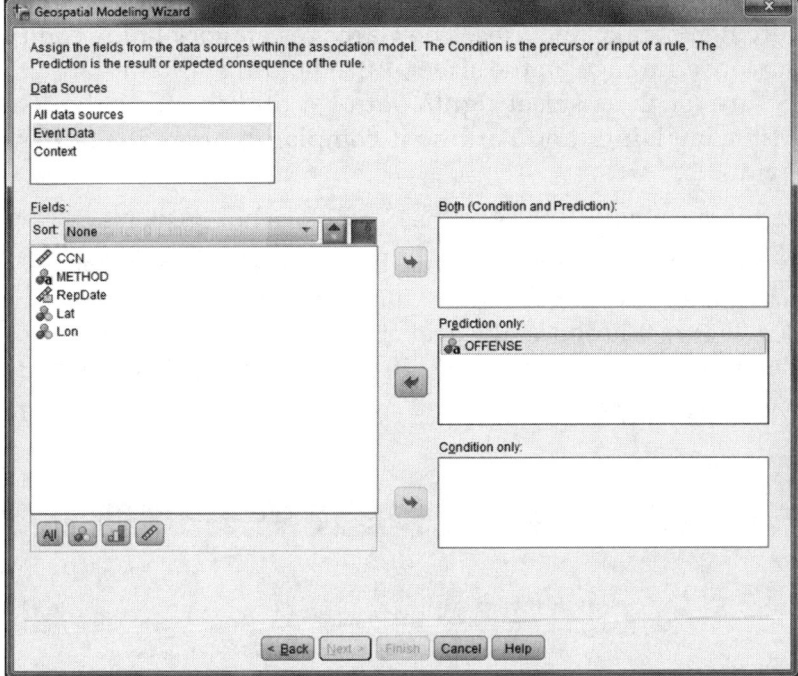

Figure 8-8: Setting the prediction variables

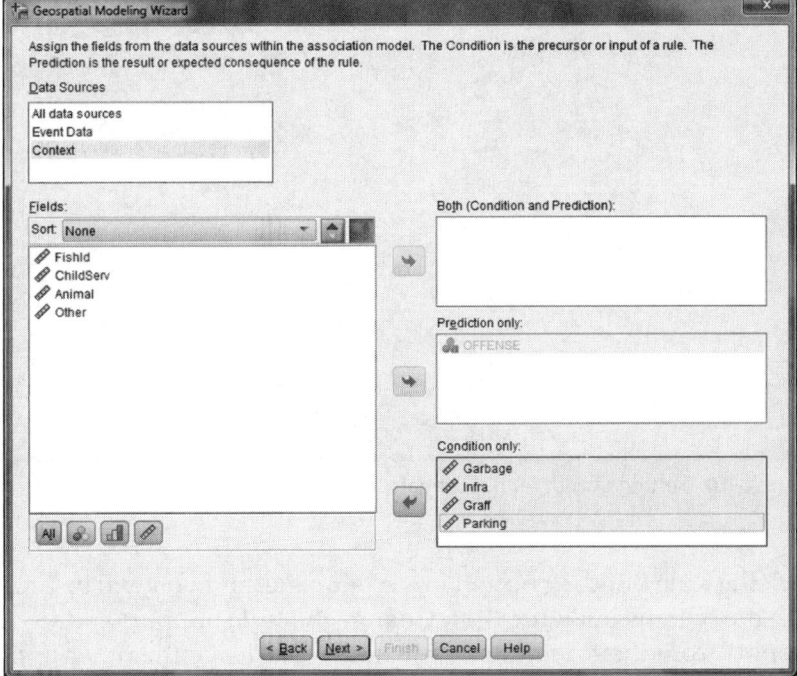

Figure 8-9: Setting the condition variables

These particular fields are counts of 311 complaints classified into different general categories. The Garbage category holds complaints about loose garbage on the street, Infra holds complaints about infra-structure (such as street lights out or a broken sidewalk), Graff is graffiti complaints, and Parking is complaints about illegally parked individuals.

3. After those variables are set in the Conditions box, click Next.

   Now you will be presented with the dialog for setting the output, deciding the criteria for selecting rules, and running or pasting the syntax from the dialog. Figure 8-10 shows the available options for the output. Keep the default settings, except check the Lift tab for both the Rules Tables section and the Map section.

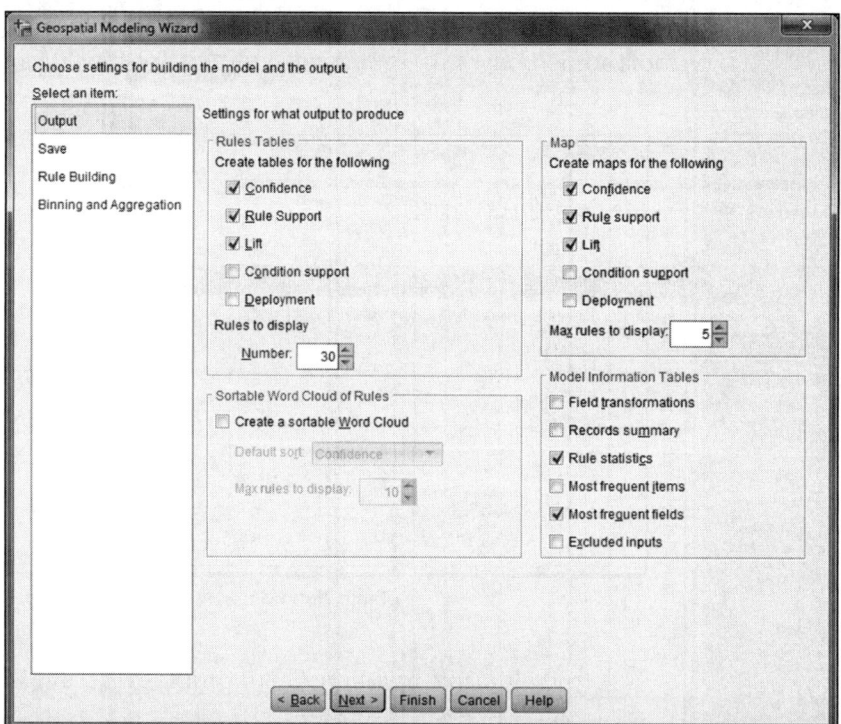

Figure 8-10: Setting output for geospatial association rules

4. Click the Rule Building option in the left pane, and you will be presented with the options in Figure 8-11. Change the Rule Support and Condition Support from their defaults of 5% to 1%, but leave the other options at their default values.

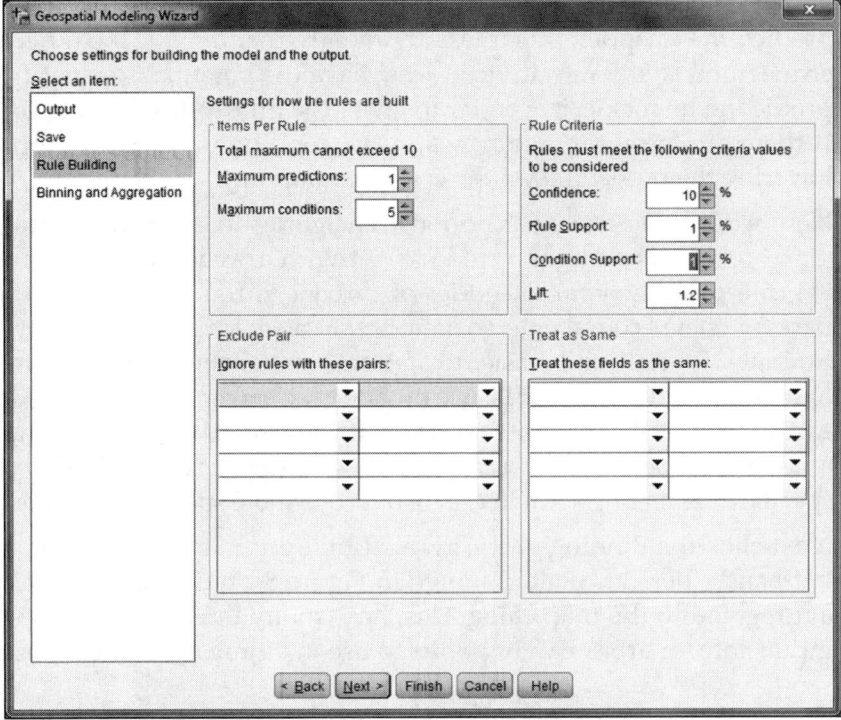

Figure 8-11: Setting the rules

The criteria specified in these options limits what associations the procedure will identify. These criteria are based on marginal and conditional properties for each of the categories.

Rule Support is the proportion of the data values that meet both the predicted category and the condition. For example, if a rule is X & Y (with X the condition and Y the predicted category), the rule support is the percentage of cases that meet both X & Y in the sample. Written in probability terms, rule support is then P(X = True And Y = True). Confidence is the value of rule support divided by the base probability of the condition, X, in the sample. So Confidence is equal to P(X = True AND Y = True)/P(X = True). The Lift field has the same numerator, the rule support, but the denominator is the base probability of the predicted category in the sample, P(X = True AND Y = True)/P(Y = True). Condition support is simply the probability of the condition, P(X = True).

When setting conditions for particular rules to display, you need to keep in mind the baseline probabilities for the categories, in particular potential small numbers problems. If there is either a very small probability for either the condition or the predicted category, rule support will always be very small, and so the algorithm will always exclude that particular combination. For instance, if we included the offense of homicides to predict, they happen much less frequently than any of the other listed crimes, and so if you want to at least have the potential to identify rules predicting homicide, it is better to lower the probability for rule support. If there are fairly rare outcomes in the conditions, the same applies to lowering the probability of the condition support.

Here we have restricted the offense categories to thefts from auto, burglary, robbery, and aggravated assault with a weapon, and aggregated 311 calls to the general categories of garbage, infrastructure, graffiti, and parking related complaints, so none of the categories are very small in this example. Typically, it is easier to approach association rules with a broad to specific workflow. That is, use broader and fewer categories to identify easily interpretable rules at first. Then, if warranted upon identifying rules among the broader set, you can drill down to see if you can identify more specific rules among a smaller set of data or a more specific set of categories.

5. Next click the Binning and Aggregation option in the item box on the left-hand side. This dialog, shown in Figure 8-12, defines how fields are aggregated to the map categories, how many bins to split continuous inputs into, or arbitrary cut points to use in binning the categories.

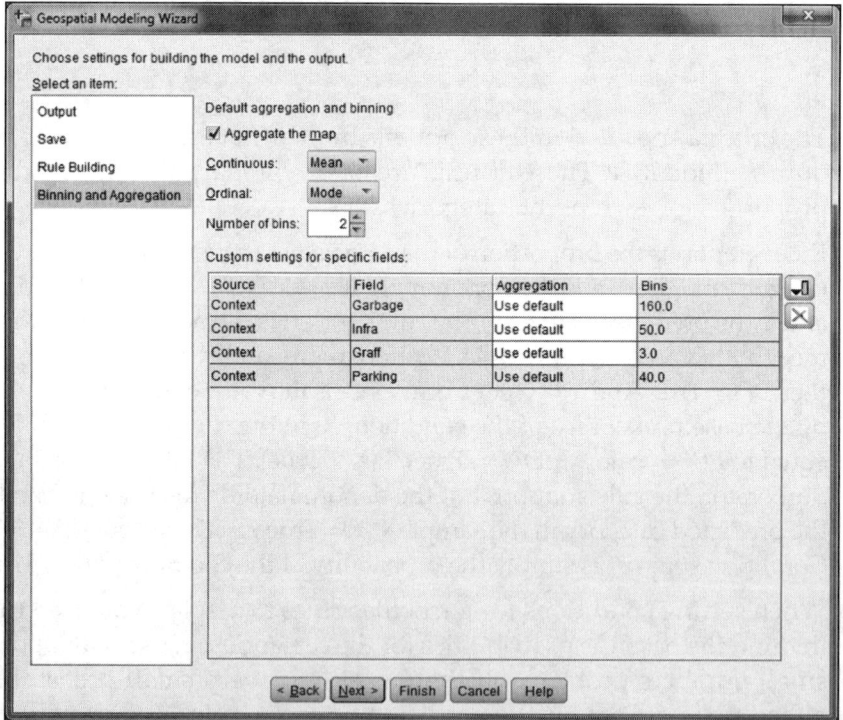

Figure 8-12: Defining bins

The Aggregate the map option is checked by default, but for this example it does not matter, because each of the records in `Agg311_Data.sav` are only associated with one polygon in the map. If it was the case that we had different types of relationships between the context data and the map data (for example, associating stores to the nearest ZIP code), we can choose different types of aggregation schemes (such as the mean or the sum) when aggregating to the spatial units of analysis used in the map.

Here I will be changing the cut points for each of the 311 fields. I inspected the data previously, and define cut points for each of the 311 variables based on approximately the 75th quantile of the data. So above the cut point are locations that have relatively high amounts of that particular type of 311 call-for-service. Again this is motivated by identifying broader and more interpretable rules at first. If you made more bins besides high and low categories, the rules will end up being more difficult to interpret.

6. To set custom settings for specific fields, click the scale icon on the right-hand side of the GUI, and then select the four fields.

7. Once the four fields are placed in the Custom settings table, click within the Bins column for each variable to set its cut point. Here I use 160 for garbage complaints, 50 for infrastructure, 3 for graffiti, and 40 for parking.

8. Once you finish inputting the cut points, you are ready to click Next and go on to the final screen.

NOTE If you want to save a map plan for the future, you can select the Save option before navigating to the final screen.

9. On the final screen, you will be presented with a preview map, and an option to either run the command or paste the syntax for future use. Go ahead and keep the default, Run Model.

10. Click the Finish button. For this example dataset, the association rules algorithm takes about 2 to 3 minutes before returning results.

In the output you are then presented with a series of tables and maps. The maps are interactive, and show both of the predicted offense points, with blue colored points being ones that are associated with the rule, and salmon colored points being ones that are not associated with the rule. Polygons that meet the rule are highlighted as a brighter shade of green, although these examples are covered by so many points they are harder to identify. You can toggle different rules in the bar chart on the left-hand side and update the map. By double-clicking on the map, you can also pan and zoom in the map to see locations up close.

Figure 8-13 shows an example rule and map. There are high concentrations of areas with Theft F/Auto and over three Graffiti complaints in several areas of the city. These include both the central part of the city that has more bars and other nightlife attractions, as well as more northwestern parts of the city that encompass American University and are more residential.

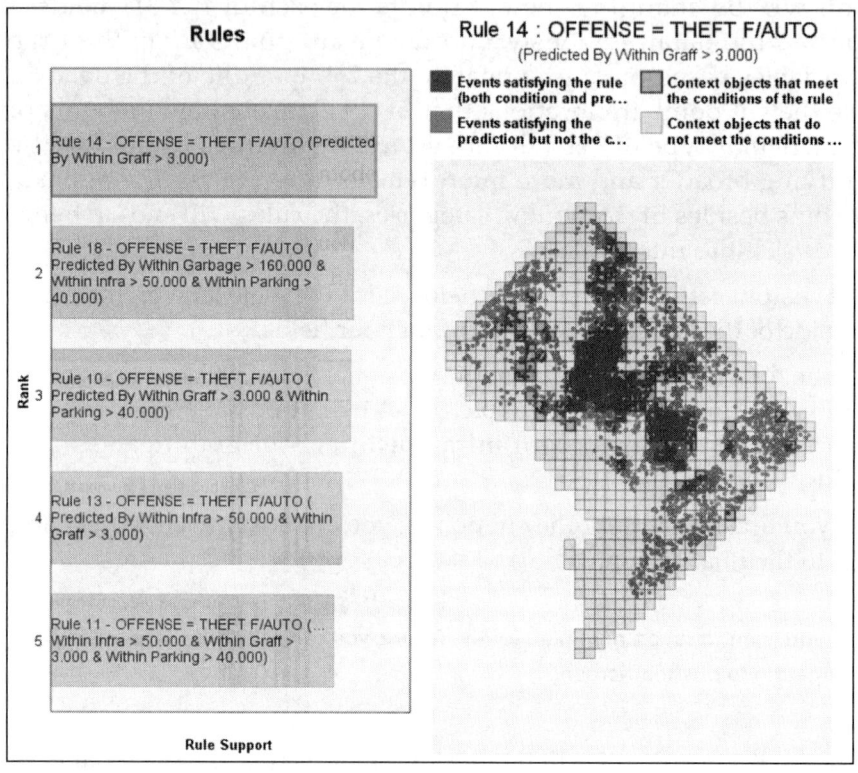

Figure 8-13: Rule 14: Theft F/Auto and Graffiti > 3

Figure 8-14, and its example rule for Assault w/Dangerous Weapon, shows quite a different spatial pattern. The majority of the blue points that meet the condition are in the southeastern part of the city, what happen to be more residential neighborhoods south and east of the Anacostia River. Notice the rule is associated with high levels of garbage complaints, but otherwise low levels of infrastructure, graffiti, and parking complaints. Thus these much smaller areas are places where community police officers may consider focusing on garbage complaints as opposed to other types of less frequently reported problems.

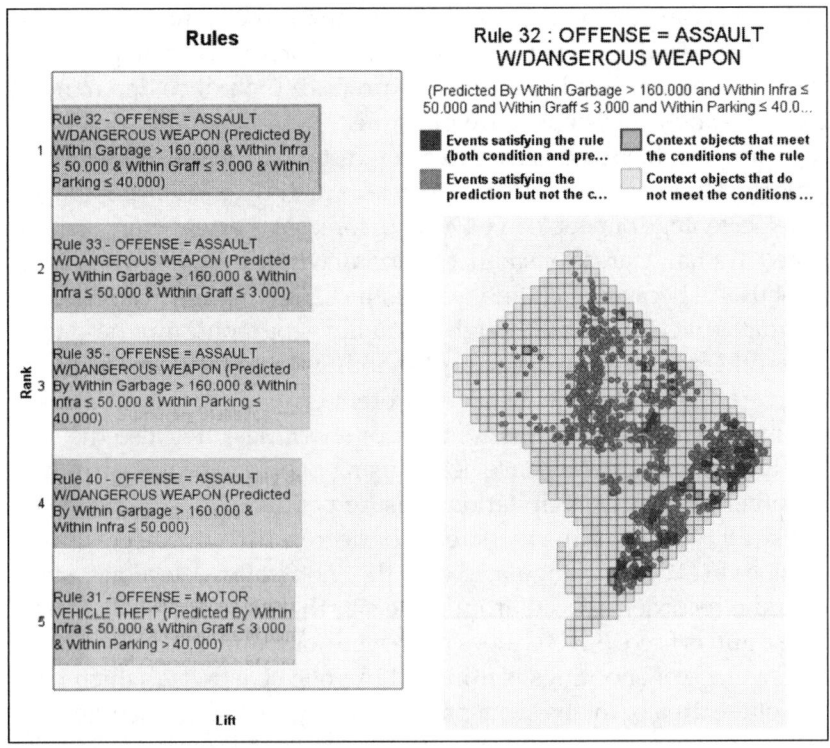

Figure 8-14: Rule 32: Assault w/Dangerous Weapon

Spatio-Temporal Prediction

The second geospatial statistical procedure introduced in SPSS Statistics V23 is Spatio-Temporal Prediction. In this module you can take a set of point data, or data associated with particular areas, and predict future counts for geographic areas given temporal measures of other variables. It subsequently provides helpful interpretation at the geographic level, to see in what areas what time series are more correlated with one another, and it also provides a tool to predict future values. It also provides similar mapping capabilities as those shown in Geospatial Association Rules to explore your data after the models are fit.

Case Study: Predicting Weekly Shootings

This case study will be predicting weekly shooting locations from prior shootings as well as other reported crime in Washington D.C., an example of *predictive policing*. Unlike the Tom Cruise movie *Minority Report*, this simply means forecasting the number of crimes that will occur in the future at some location given historical numbers and other pertinent data. It does not mean predicting who will commit a crime before it happens!

Police departments forecast future counts of crime for the same reasons any business forecasts future values of variables of interest. Forecasts can help allocate resources to where they are needed most, and prepare the police department to try to take the best possible steps to deter crime.

If a police department is interested in long-term forecasts for an entire city, they may use demographic predictors, such as expected increases in the residential population or changes of the percentage of people in poverty to forecast future crime counts. If they are interested in smaller areas or smaller temporal windows, the demographic measures are not useful because such fine-grained measures are not available.

One source of data that is available though at smaller geographic units and temporal windows is other crimes. The majority of shootings are retaliatory in nature, and so shootings are sometimes precipitated by other crimes, such as an assault, robbery, or a burglary (besides in response to prior shootings). It is also the case that other external factors, such as intense heat causing people to be more irritable, or very cold weather or heavy precipitation causing people to stay indoors, can respectively cause all types of crime to increase or decrease from week to week.

Shooting locations in D.C. are triangulated with the ShotSpotter detection system. This is a set of audio recorders placed around the city that can specifically detect when and where a gun is fired. But D.C. does not have ShotSpotter sensors covering the entire city. Coverage of shootings is minimal in police District 2, which happens to be most of the area of the western part of the city, including Georgetown and Rock Creek Park. Crime locations are the same ones that were used in the prior Geospatial Association Rules, but aggregated to the grid cells at the weekly level from 2011 through 2012, and other reported crimes are also included. Only locations that have an average of over 0.1 shootings per week are included in these datasets (that is, at least one shooting every two and a half months on average).

> **NOTE** See this Washington Post article for a description of the sensors: `http://www.washingtonpost.com/wp-srv/special/local/dc-shot-spotter/`.

These steps show how to use the Spatio-Temporal Prediction procedure to forecast shootings.

1. Open the SPSS data files `ShootingsWeekly.sav` and `ForwardCrime_toScore.sav`.

2. Then, just like in Geospatial Association Rules, open up the Geospatial Modeling Wizard by clicking the Analyze menu and selecting Spatial and Temporal Modeling ⇨ Spatial Modeling.

3. Select the option "Create a time series model with geo-spatial data."

4. Click Next.

   You will then be prompted with the same map dialog screen as in the Geospatial Association Rules (refer to Figure 8-2).

5. Follow those same steps (refer to Figures 8-2 to 8-5) to choose the DC_Fishnet.shp shapefile as the resulting map, and set up the ShootingsWeekly.sav file as the context data.

6. Then set the association between the map key and the data key to FishID. This file contains both the explanatory crime variables and the weekly shooting data, so there is no need to set up a separate prediction file.

Although the wizard can take the shooting data directly as X and Y coordinates (similar to Geospatial Association Rules) and predict the density of shootings within grid cells, it still expects some context data to be provided. That is, you cannot simply base the prediction of the future data on the prior values, and it is expected that you will provide other information to inform future predictions. It is also the case when using X and Y coordinates as input that there needs to be a non-zero density for each of the space-time units. In this dataset (as there will be with most crimes police departments would be interested in predicting) there will be locations in which crimes are sparse, and there will be weeks with zero shootings for many locations. So it is necessary to include zero values for particular week/grid-cell combinations in this example.

After setting up the map and the context data on the next screen you will be presented with the familiar regression type dialog, shown in Figure 8-15.

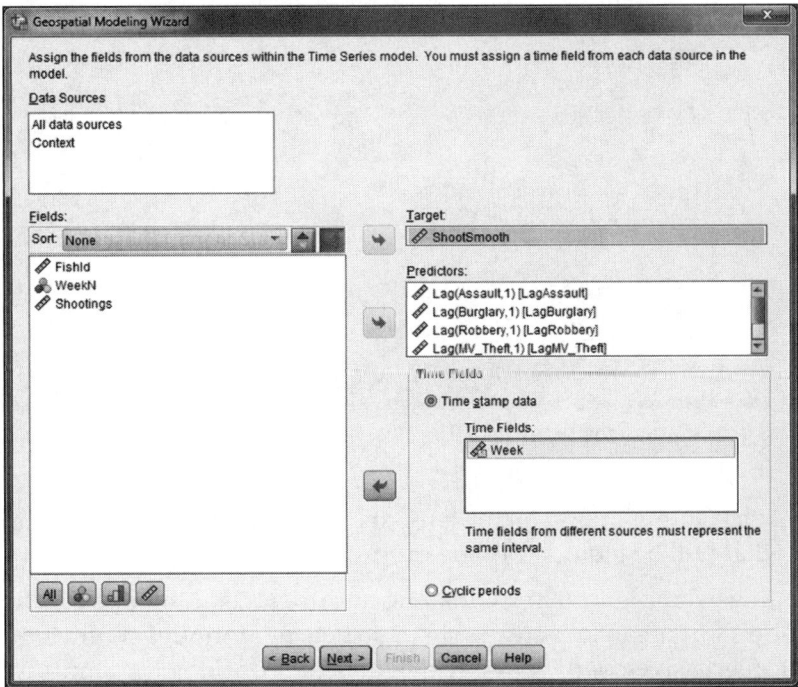

Figure 8-15: Setting target and predictor fields for spatio-temporal modeling

7. Here we place ShootSmooth in the target field, and place all of the Lag variables (crimes in the lagged week) in the Predictors box.

8. We then place Week in the time stamp data field. For the sensor shooting data there are anomalous high values near the New Year and around the Fourth of July, which are attributed to false-positive shootings based on fireworks. (Being somewhat high is expected, as some individuals actually do shoot guns in celebration.) The variable ShootSmooth corrected these values by interpolating weeks before and after those particular dates (where the variable Shootings are the original counts).

9. After clicking Next, SPSS will then open to the screen shown in Figure 8-16. Here SPSS auto-recognizes that the time intervals are weeks.

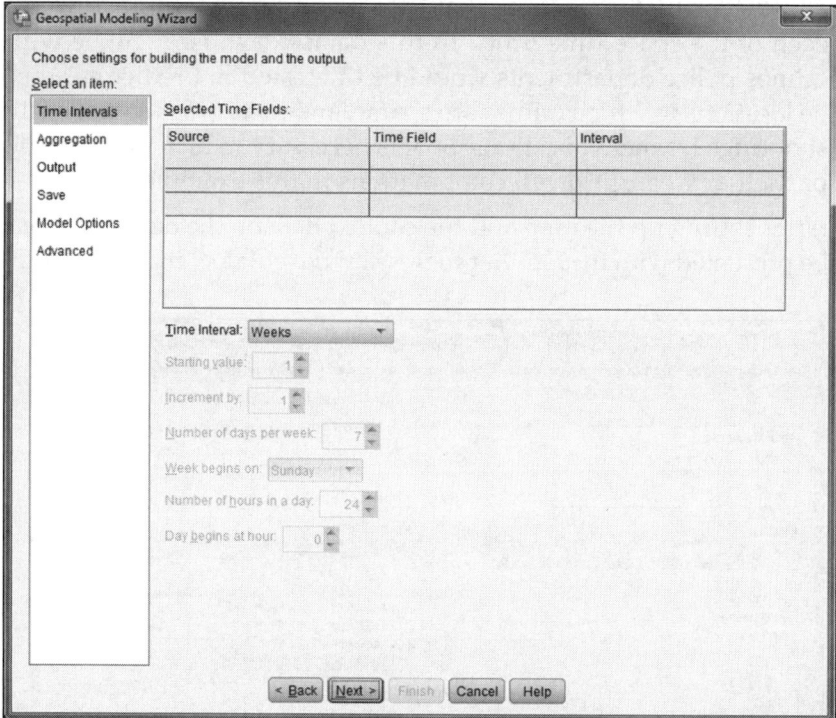

Figure 8-16: Setting the time intervals

10. Click the Output option on the left-hand side to bring up a series of options for what will be included in the output.

11. For this example, unclick Clusters, and then click the options for Test of effects in mean structure, Mean structure of model coefficients, and Autoregressive coefficients. Leave all other options the same, and the dialog will appear like Figure 8-17.

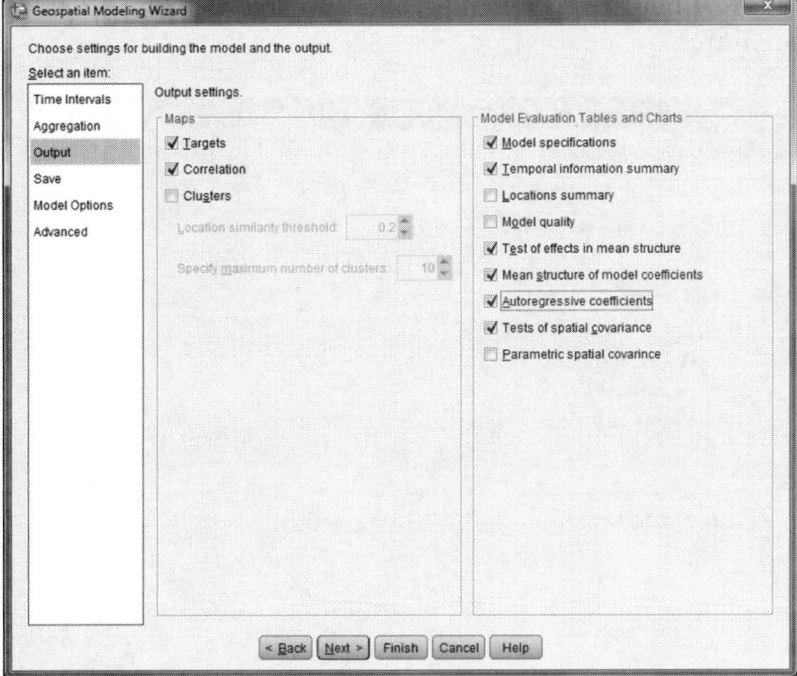

Figure 8-17: Setting the output

12. Next, click the Save option in the tab on the left-hand side.

    On the Save dialog shown in Figure 8-18, you will then be presented with options to save the map and context data as a map specification (to prevent going through all of the same steps in the future) as well as an interface to score either an open dataset or another SPSS data file. Scoring is how SPSS provides predictions for future data.

13. Select "Score an open dataset" and then select the open table `ForwardCrime_toScore.sav`. This file contains the same lagged values that are used as predictors, which SPSS will use (along with prior values of ShootSmooth) to predict future shootings for the grid cell areas.

14. Leave all other options as their default, and then click the Finish button. You will be presented with a preview map, and then be given the option to either run the model or paste the syntax.

15. Click Finish again to run the model. The model takes around a minute to finish, after which you will be presented with a series of tables and maps. You can set further options about how the spatial covariance is estimated in the Model Options tab, but in this case SPSS automatically determines that the default model parameters are not appropriate, and

so estimates the spatial covariance parameters using a non-parametric procedure.

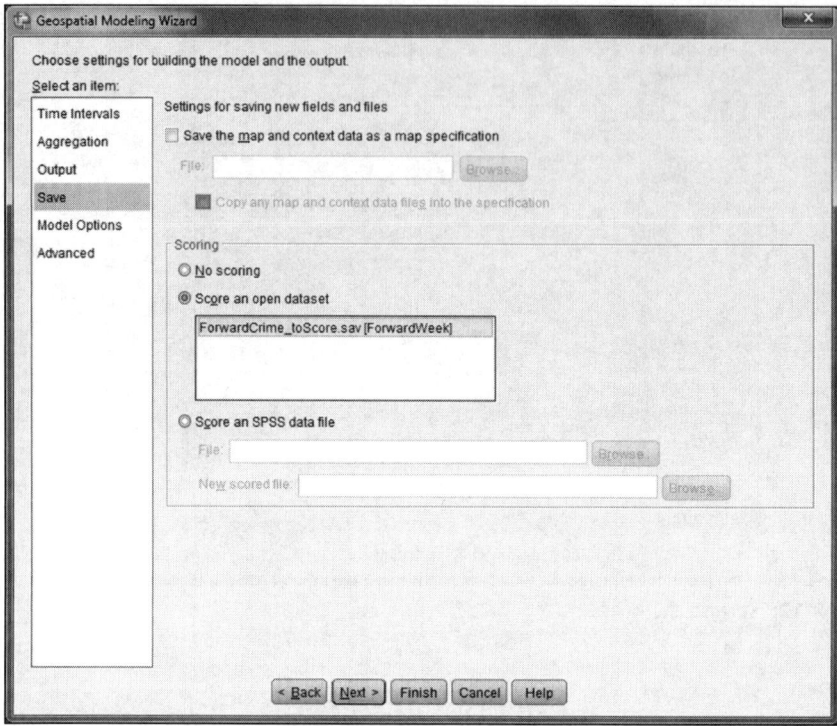

Figure 8-18: Scoring a separate file

Figure 8-19 displays two of the regression coefficient tables. You can see that the effects of all of the lagged crime counts are statistically significant predictors of shootings, but all have relatively small coefficients. The lagged counts of assaults, burglaries, and mv theft have a positive effect on shootings, while thefts from auto and other thefts have a negative coefficient.

For interpretation of the lagged assault coefficient, an increase in one assault in the prior week increases the expected number of shootings by 0.05. So if there were 20 more assaults than usual in the prior week, you would expect 1 more shooting than usual in the current week. Burglaries and motor vehicle thefts have a similar interpretation.

While the effect of the prior week's robberies is statistically significant, the coefficient is very small and is still zero when rounded to two decimal points. Thefts from auto and other thefts have a negative effect, which is somewhat counterintuitive but not altogether unsurprising. It may be the case that areas with more property crimes have more people interacting (for example, a shopping mall), and due to there being many people around these areas are less likely to be locations where shootings occur.

Interpretation

Mean Structure of Model Coefficients Table

Model Term	Coefficient	Std. Error	t	Sig.	95% Confidence Interval	
					Lower Bound	Upper Bound
Intercept	.28	.00	968.45	.00	.28	.28
Lag(Assault,1)	.05	.00	303.53	.00	.05	.05
Lag(Burglary,1)	.04	.00	302.06	.00	.04	.04
Lag(Robbery,1)	.01	.00	54.47	.00	.01	.01
Lag(MV_Theft,1)	.03	.00	166.85	.00	.03	.03
Lag(Theft_fr_Auto, 1)	-.03	7.94E-5	-411.31	.00	-.03	-.03
Lag(Theft_Other, 1)	-.01	7.63E-5	-137.49	.00	-.01	-.01

Autoregressive Coefficients Table

Lag	Coefficient	Std. Error	t	Sig.	95% Confidence Interval	
					Lower Bound	Upper Bound
1	.16	.00	97.21	.00	.16	.17
2	.15	.00	123.98	.00	.14	.15
3	.05	.00	58.39	.00	.05	.06
4	.07	.00	80.13	.00	.07	.07
5	.06	.00	89.78	.00	.06	.06

Autoregressive coefficients are estimated based on the residuals from the mean structure model accounting for spatial dependence.

Figure 8-19: Regression coefficient tables

The second table displays the autoregressive coefficients, and you can see that SPSS automatically chooses the first five lags for the AR model. These autoregressive coefficients are all quite large compared to the lagged counts of crime, so this would suggest that prior shootings are a better predictor of future shootings, compared to other crimes.

In the output there will be a series of additional maps that allow you to explore different summary statistics, as well as to interactively choose several locations and explore the time series values among them or their spatial autocorrelation. Also, because we chose to score the ForwardCrime_toScore dataset, we are given predictions for the week of 12/30/12.

Figure 8-20 shows a screen shot of the variables that SPSS added to the dataset, which included the predicted number of shootings, the standard error, and the upper and lower prediction intervals. These predictions can subsequently be mapped using SPSS's other map making facilities, as shown in Chapter 7.

You can see in Figure 8-20 that the intervals for the predictions frequently go into negative values, and often have a range of around 2 to 3 shootings. The point forecasts, though, are positive in the majority of cases. It is of course the case that counts of shootings cannot be below zero, and so you could logically only consider ranges in predictions from zero to the upper forecast interval. It is also the case that SPSS will not provide a forecast interval in the case that the standard error is too large, as can be seen in the last visible row in Figure 8-20.

LagTheft_Other	ShootSmooth_Predicted	ShootSmooth_StdErr	ShootSmooth_Lower	ShootSmooth_Upper	var
2	.107	.172	-.229	.444	
1	.242	.360	-.463	.947	
0	.850	.548	-.224	1.923	
3	.081	.380	-.664	.826	
0	.540	.557	-.552	1.632	
1	.225	.802	-1.346	1.796	
0	.178	.951	-1.686	2.041	
0	.338	.836	-1.301	1.977	
0	.197	.327	-.445	.839	
0	.138	.284	-.419	.695	
0	.203	.282	-.351	.756	
0	.158	.867	-1.541	1.857	
1	.111	.765	-1.388	1.610	
0	.679	2.849	-4.906	6.264	
0	.230	1.589	-2.884	3.343	
2	.277	.298	-.307	.862	
0	.379	.645	-.885	1.642	
0	.096	.857	-1.584	1.777	
0	.445	.391	-.322	1.211	
0	.370	.959	-1.511	2.251	
0	.358	1.465	-2.514	3.230	
1	.198	.424	-.634	1.029	
0	-1.659	.266	-2.181	-1.138	
0	.307	.586	-.841	1.455	
0	10.509				

Figure 8-20: Predictions of future shootings

In this particular example, while providing interesting evidence for the relationship between prior crime and future shootings, whether the predictions provided by the model will be informative enough to shape policing practice is an open question. Even if the forecasts are overall accurate, it may be the case that the prediction intervals are too wide to be of much use.

Potential modeling strategies to improve the forecasts may be to estimate generalized Poisson or negative binomial time series models predicting the counts (and potentially zero-inflated or hurdle variants intended for outcomes with many zero events). Because such models restrict the range of forecasts to positive values, they may provide more accurate forecast intervals, although potentially the linear time series model provides better point forecasts. Also, there may be other information that can be incorporated into the model to better predict future shootings. Such new variables may be other crimes, weather forecasts, the number of parolees in an area, and interactions between any of these variables.

Another strategy would be to predict shootings over longer time periods. It is often the case that shorter time periods show a larger amount of variance, and so aggregating to monthly or quarterly periods may produce more accurate predictions. Typically for an analyst there is a give-and-take between the needs of the agency for particular forecasts to inform certain actions and the feasibility to produce accurate forecasts. Analysts in general may describe basing certain decisions on inaccurate forecasts as *chasing the noise,* but a synonymous colloquial phrase often used among crime analysts is *chasing dots on a map.*

For an example, a police agency may develop a specific team of officers intended to reduce violence. Initial plans may be to have this team focus on a new area every week that is at a high risk of violence based on forecasts. If the predictions from the weekly shooting data are deemed too erratic to justify changing locations every week, an analyst may incorporate other crimes into the prediction. For example, predicting shootings and aggravated assaults is likely to be more accurate, because aggravated assaults occur with a much greater frequency. Or an analyst may decide that weekly forecasts for any crime are too variable to justify changing locations on a weekly basis, and so may suggest only setting new target areas for the team on a quarterly basis.

Many predictive policing initiatives currently focus only on what can be accurately forecast, but what the agency plans on doing with that information should equally factor into what forecasts are generated and the temporal time period that is being predicted. For the hypothetical example, it may be reasonable for the agency to produce forecasts over a longer period of time, but it wouldn't be reasonable to change the forecasts to burglaries instead of shootings simply because burglaries are easier to forecast.

Perceptual Mapping with Correspondence Analysis, GPL, and OMS

This chapter is a bit different from the others in that while it introduces two new topics, Correspondence Analysis and Multiple Correspondence Analysis (MCA), it presents a case study that also incorporates techniques from Chapters 6 and 17. Note that both techniques require the Categories module. Graphics Production Language (GPL) and Output Management System (OMS) play a sufficiently important role in the solution that two new techniques will be discussed (but in somewhat less depth here than they would be in a chapter that was dedicated solely to them). Correspondence Analysis and MCA actually differ to a greater degree than their names would suggest. Brigitte LeRoux and Henry Rouanet wrote a well-received book, *Multiple Correspondence Analysis* (SAGE Publications, Inc., 2009), that treats MCA as a "method in its own right" and neither discusses nor assumes knowledge of Correspondence Analysis. Implied in their decision, certainly, and consistent with other chapters in this book, is that these two techniques could each be worthy of their own chapters, or even their own books. While the final result of these techniques, a perceptual map, is the focus of this chapter; we won't explore the theory behind these techniques in detail.

The focus on the combined use of statistical analysis, powerful graphics, and OMS is done without apology because combining tools within SPSS Statistics is such an important theme of the book. SPSS Statistics users may sometimes be tempted to look elsewhere for their graphics solutions, feeling that other, perhaps more familiar, graphical solutions are readily available. Excel is a favorite of many. What is forgotten is how some powerful "number crunching" can be combined with fairly straightforward graphics, and a little bit of automation—all of which SPSS provides. The combination of all three is the key. This gives you a complete solution that is completely SPSS Statistics, and is uniquely in the spirit of this book. OMS is drawn upon, but not discussed as a general set of techniques in the same way that it is presented in Chapter 17. Ideally, Chapter 17 is seen as a companion to this chapter, and in the same way, Chapter 6 treats GPL "from scratch" in a way that is not possible in this chapter.

The best way to become familiar with this approach is to jump in at the end, with the final result, an effective perceptual map. In their government report for the UK's Department for Culture Media and Sport, "Understanding the relationship between taste and value in culture and sport" (`https://www.gov` `.uk/government/uploads/system/uploads/attachment_data/file/77966/` `DCMS_taste_and_value_document.pdf`), Andrew Miles and Alice Sullivan produce a powerful visualization revealing complex interactions between numerous demographics and activities, all in a single, very digestible "map." Their use of the word "taste" in the title is no accident. They are referencing the work of the pioneer of this approach—the sociologist Pierre Bourdieu. (See the "A Taste for Correspondence Analysis" sidebar later in this chapter for more about the history of this technique.)

Take a moment to reflect on Figure 9-1, which appears in their report. Like many other types of effective complex visualizations, it rewards careful study. Like a well-designed roadmap or subway map, a good perceptual map can take several minutes of attention before it reveals its multiple patterns. We notice that map locations for younger respondents seem to be found toward the top, with older toward the bottom. As the authors of the study note, non-participation tends to be found toward the middle "reflecting the fact that non-participation is the norm." Gender seems to reveal that females are more closely related to "no computer games," and males more closely to "no arts and crafts." Like factor analysis, cluster analysis, and other exploratory techniques, there is no formal definition of Axis 1 and Axis 2. Their meaning has to be deciphered, is subject to debate, and is somewhat subjective. The basic notion, as we will see, is that proximity on the map implies a relationship. (If you want to jump ahead, our first perceptual map made in SPSS with OMS and GP is shown in Figure 9-17.)

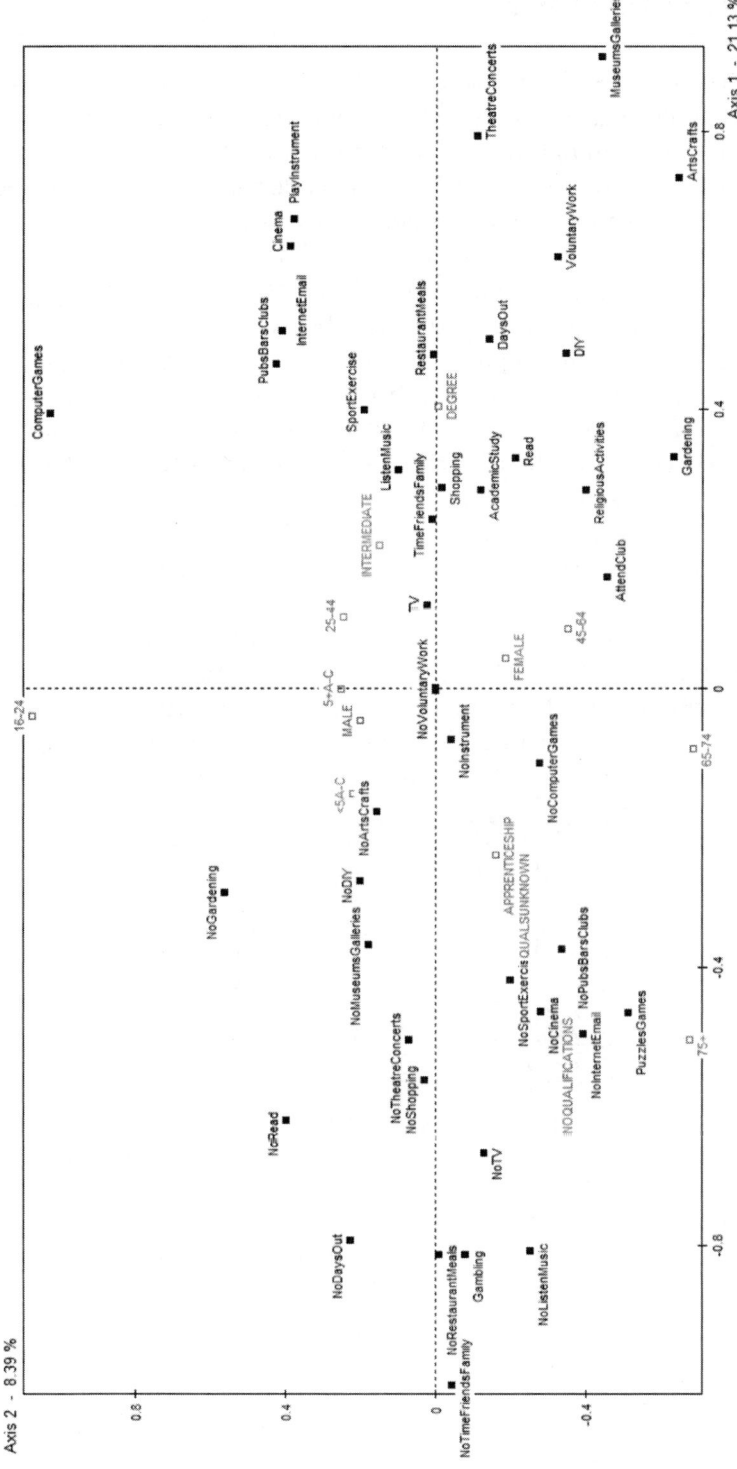

Figure 9-1: Culture and sport perceptual map

Contains public sector information licensed under the Open Government Licence v3.0. (https://www.nationalarchives.gov.uk/doc/open-government-licence/version/3/)

Starting with Crosstabs

Now let's get to work in SPSS Statistics. We will be using a modified version of the LeRoux and Rouanet dataset. Our version is different in two ways from other versions you may find: The Multiple Imputation feature of SPSS Statistics has been used to replace the missing Income values, and AutoRecode has been used to replace the string values with numeric values and labels. The version of the data that we will be using is called `Taste_Imputed.sav`, which is available on the book's website.

We will begin with Correspondence Analysis. The trick in selecting appropriate variables for this technique is to remember a couple of key points. First, Correspondence Analysis allows just two variables: a row variable and a column variable. Second, the whole point of the technique is to display on two dimensions information that otherwise would be difficult to display on two dimensions. So, if you only have a 2x2 crosstabulation matrix you don't need it. Also, if you have strong linear associations between two ordinal variables you can probably visualize that with less effort. The variables most appropriate will be a pair of nominal variables with several categories. While there is no rule that we must pair a demographic variable with a behavioral variable, it is an approach that is quite common. For instance, if you are a film studio, you might want to know which demographic patterns are associated with film attendance. While it might also be quite interesting to relate film preference with concert attendance, it might not be as immediately actionable as the demographics. With this in mind, we will set up the Crosstabs menu with TV, Film, Art, and Eat in rows, and Income and Age in Columns (Figure 9-2).

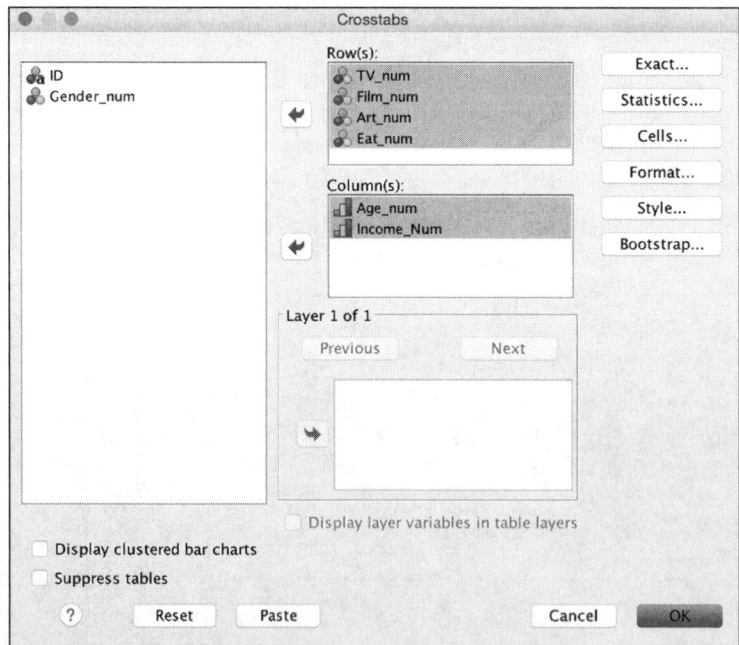

Figure 9-2: Crosstabs main menu

The choice of row and column is arbitrary. Also, Gender will be left out because with only two categories, we don't really need the power of Correspondence Analysis to decipher the pattern. A simple table would be just as useful. We are beginning with Crosstab because we can use some of its features to ferret out which variable pair has the strongest relationship. Several measures of association are supported in the Statistics submenu. Our choice is not especially critical. We will use Phi and Cramer's V (Figure 9-3). This way we can find the variable pair with the strongest association with which to try Correspondence Analysis.

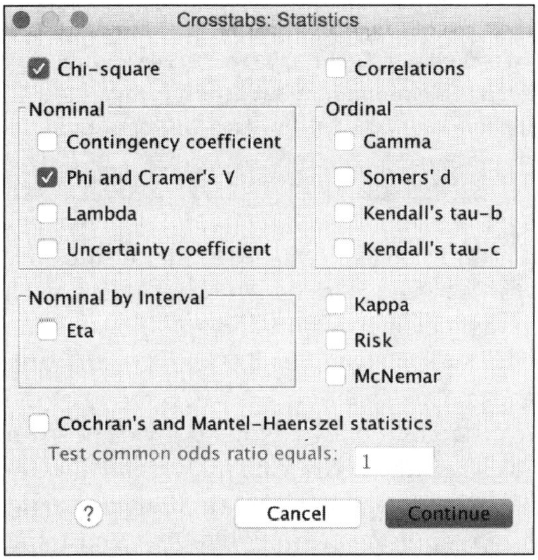

Figure 9-3: Crosstabs: Statistics submenu

A TASTE FOR CORRESPONDENCE ANALYSIS

Virtually all discussions of Correspondence Analysis and Multiple Correspondence Analysis pay homage to Pierre Bourdieu, the innovator of the technique. Perhaps it is because the technique is fairly young compared to some other statistical techniques, dating only to the 1970s with the publication of Bourdieu's *Distinction* (1984, Harvard University Press) in French and its translation into English in the '80s, that it is still closely tied to a single individual. So complete is his influence that not only is the technique associated with him, but also the kind of study he reports in *Distinction*.

The subtitle of the book is *A Social Critique of the Judgement of Taste*, and many practitioners of the technique have imitated his data as well as his approach. Both the book and the report cited earlier do this. Here, "taste" is referencing cultural taste. Which movie actors are the favorites of opera fans? Which magazines are read by the working class? Such patterns emerge casually around the dinner table, but Bourdieu attempted to quantify and describe them. If one tried to capture the basic idea in a single word, one might choose the same word that Jon Elster of the London Review of Books chose to title his review of Bourdieu when the French edition was first released: "Snobs." In other words, opera goers tend not to like pop culture, and vice versa.

Continues

(continued)

In the preface to the English edition, Bourdieu himself speculates "Is Brigitte Bardot like Marilyn Monroe? Is Jean Gabin the French John Wayne, or Humphrey Bogart or Spencer Tracy?" If this all seems a little too academic, imagine that you are trying to define a brand. One can quickly see why this has been embraced by marketing research. While snobbery is not particularly flattering, some brands embrace it, and other brands avoid it. It is powerful indeed to be able to examine several demographic factors along with numerous cultural preferences all in one visualization.

While we will not make further reference to the Miles and Sullivan report, it is worth seeking out because they have several figures as complex as the one shown in Figure 9-1. The "Taste" dataset compiled by LeRoux and Rouanet many years after Bourdieu's own study has become popular in the R community, and constitutes a classic example of the type of data that Bourdieu collected. We will use this dataset for our first exploration of the technique.

While the output shows the association measure results for all eight of the variable pairs (not shown), the results for Age and Film has the largest Cramer's V with a value of .216. The pair also has a clearly significant p value for the Pearson Chi-Square (Figure 9-4). The Chi-Square would be a poor choice to rank the results, however, as it is not a measure of association, and all but one of the pairs produced a p value of zero to three decimal places. Note that we chose an association measure for nominal variables because we ran an analysis for several pairs of variables. There are other additional association measures that you might chose with pairs that include one nominal and one ordinal, like Age and Film. We will stick with Cramer's V, but the other choices can be seen in Figure 9-3.

Chi-Square Tests

	Value	df	Asymptotic Significance (2-sided)
Pearson Chi-Square	293.62[a]	35	.000
Likelihood Ratio	282.183	35	.000
Linear-by-Linear Association	3.126	1	.077
N of Valid Cases	1253		

a. 0 cells (0.0%) have expected count less than 5. The minimum expected count is 5.21.

Symmetric Measures

		Value	Approximate Significance
Nominal by Nominal	Phi	.484	.000
	Cramer's V	.216	.000
N of Valid Cases		1253	

Figure 9-4: Crosstabs results

Now that we know our most promising pair, let's take a closer look at the crosstab's residuals. To request the residuals we will select Standardized in the Cell Display submenu, shown in Figure 9-5.

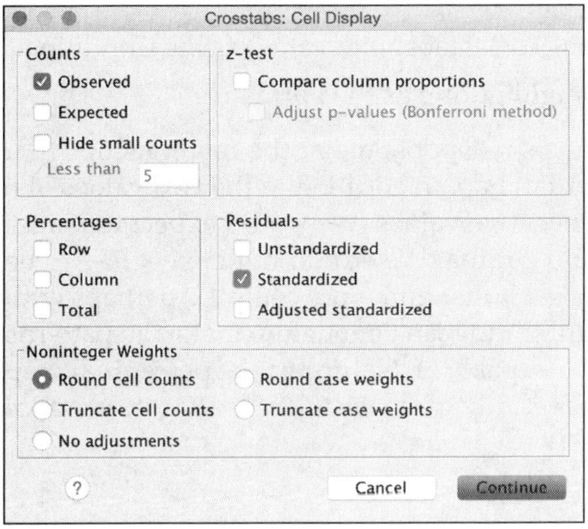

Figure 9-5: Crosstabs Cell Display submenu

The interpretation, in terms of its magnitude, would be similar to interpreting z scores. Scores with absolute values greater than 3 would be especially noteworthy. What patterns can we anticipate in our perceptual map? The two largest values (not shown) are positive residuals of 6 or greater for Musical and older respondents, and Horror and younger respondents. Let's take advantage of the Style submenu (available since version 22) and make this especially easy to see (Figure 9-6).

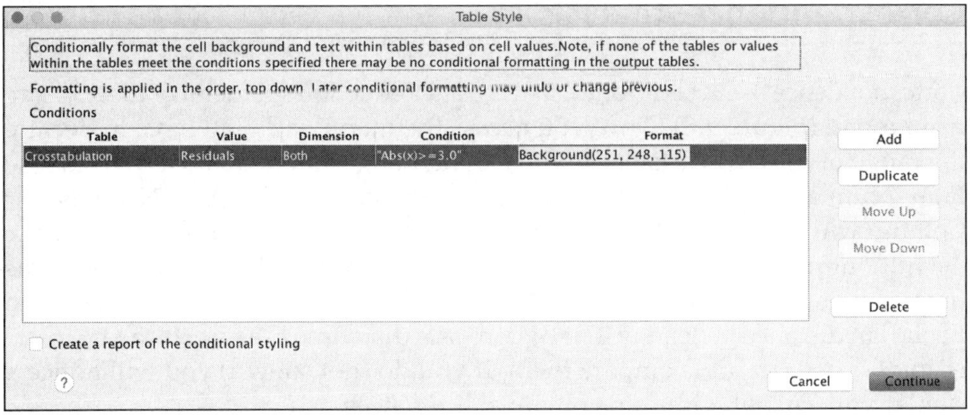

Figure 9-6: Crosstabs Style submenu

Within the submenu, make the following changes:

1. Choose Crosstabulation as the Table type.

2. Choose Residuals as the Value.

3. Choose Both as the Dimension.

4. Choose Greater Than or Equal To 3.0 (absolute value) as the Condition.

5. Choose yellow Background highlighting as the Format.

The highlighting (Figure 9-7) helps us spot some of the relationships that we can expect to see in the perceptual map. In addition to the two values of 6 or higher, we also see some large negative values. We would expect that ages 25–34 will not be close to Costume Drama. We would not expect 65+ to be close to Comedy. As tables like this get larger and more complex, perhaps with many dozens of cells, even the highlighting isn't enough to make the patterns as clear as what a perceptual map is capable of. Naturally, the perceptual map is also visually more compelling, especially when we take the effort to produce a good and easy-to-read map.

Film_num * Age_num Crosstabulation

Standardized Residual

		Age_num					
		1 18–24	2 25–34	3 35–44	4 45–54	5 55–64	6 65+
Film_num	1 Action	−.9	1.5	1.3	.7	−.3	−2.7
	2 Comedy	3.8	1.7	.5	.5	−1.7	−3.7
	3 CostumeDrama	−2.8	−4.1	−3.0	.0	4.7	5.1
	4 Documentary	−2.5	−2.8	.8	−.7	.9	3.5
	5 Horror	6.0	.8	.6	−1.9	−2.1	−1.8
	6 Musical	−2.3	−2.6	−2.2	−1.5	1.5	6.6
	7 Romance	−.5	.5	1.4	1.2	−1.3	−1.6
	8 SciFi	−.5	3.3	−.5	.1	−1.4	−1.4

Figure 9-7: Crosstabs results (with highlighting style)

Correspondence Analysis

Correspondence Analysis is found in the Data Reduction submenu of the Analyze main menu (Figure 9-8). Once you access the menu, you will have to declare the range of the two variables in the Define Range submenus. We will choose Film_Num as our Row, with a range of 1 through 8, and Age_Num as our Column with a range of 1 through 6 (Figure 9-9). We will simply allow for the default output—we will make no modifications in the other submenus at this time. However, it is worth noting that in the Model submenu you can choose Euclidian distance instead of Chi-Square as a distance measure. It can be interesting to run both and compare them. If you do (not shown) you will notice a similar pattern, but with some obvious differences.

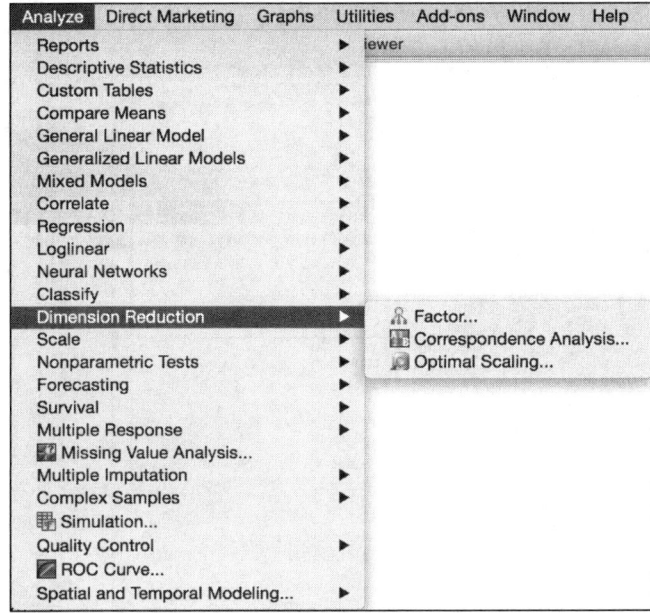

Figure 9-8: Dimension Reduction menu

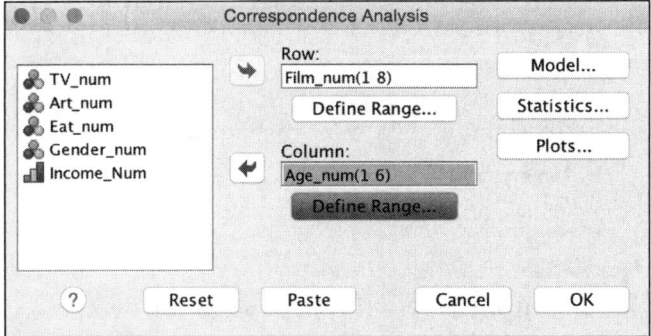

Figure 9-9: Correspondence Analysis

Scroll all the way down to the bottom of the resulting output, and you will find our perceptual map (Figure 9-10). It has a distinctive "horseshoe" pattern, which is not unusual with Correspondence Analysis. There is a clear pattern of decreasing age moving up and to the right, and then down around the horseshoe. However, it is less clear what the up and down direction on Dimension 2 could represent. It appears as if there is really just one dimension that has been bent, with Musical and 65+ at one end, and 18–24 and Horror at the other end.

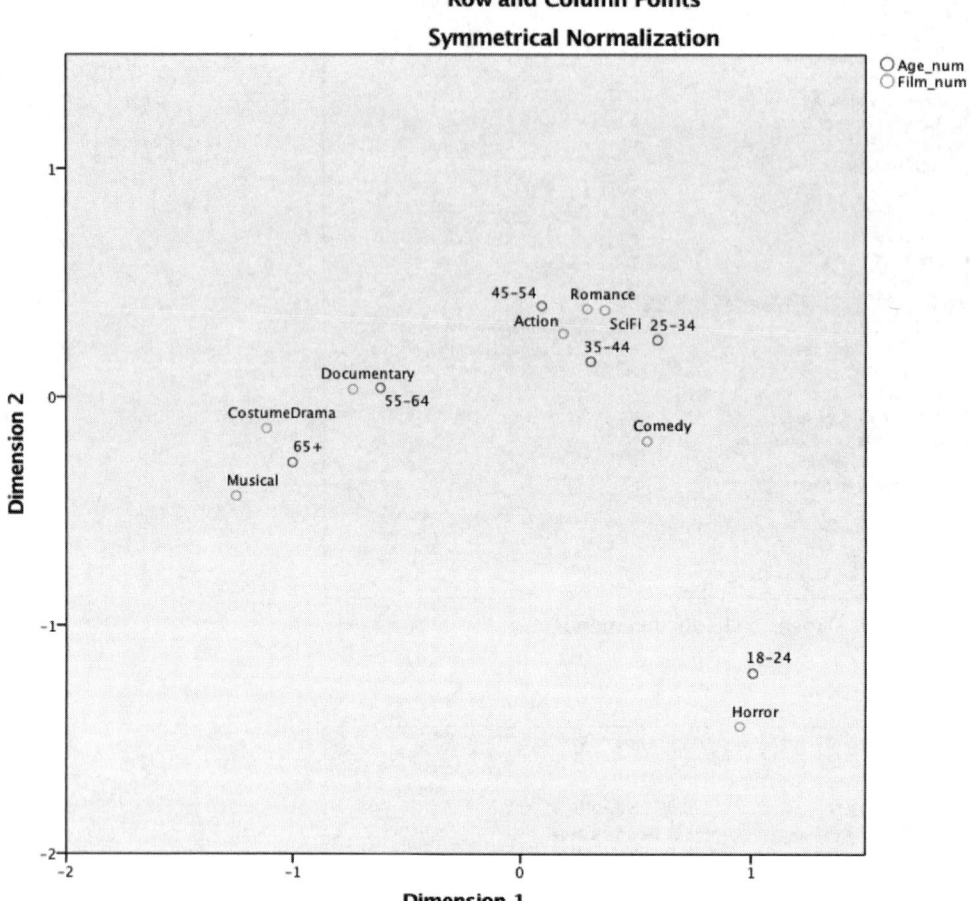

Figure 9-10: Initial attempt of the perceptual map

An examination of the tabular output makes this interpretation even more clear. Specifically, in the Summary table, shown in Figure 9-11, we see that the "Proportion of Inertia" in the first dimension is quite high at .782. Inertia, a measure of variance, reveals here that an attempt to explain the variance with just one dimension would explain the majority of the variance. The second dimension doesn't add very much in comparison. In addition to the concern that our map is not entirely successful, there is an added problem. We would have to coach any readers of the map to pay attention more to Dimension 1 than to Dimension 2 because of its greater importance. This is difficult to do in practice. Despite our best efforts, anyone examining the map will almost certainly attend to diagonal distance, which would be a distortion of the pattern.

We wouldn't consider more than two dimensions as the technique is generally used to create a flat, two-dimensional visualization. It is conceivable that one could attempt a third dimension, and to display it with a three-dimensional plot, but as anyone who has attempted a three-dimensional scatter plot can attest, they can be tricky to get right, and tricky to interpret. Not only that, since the cumulative intertia for dimensions 1 and 2 is 91.7%, there would be little value in attempting to add a third dimension to a plot.

Summary

Dimension	Singular Value	Inertia	Chi Square	Sig.	Proportion of Inertia		Confidence Singular Value	
					Account ed for	Cumula tive	Standard Deviatio n	Correlat ion 2
1	.428	.183			.782	.782	.025	.199
2	.178	.032			.136	.917	.036	
3	.098	.010			.041	.958		
4	.093	.009			.037	.996		
5	.032	.001			.004	1.000		
Total		.234	293.615	.000[a]	1.000	1.000		

a. 35 degrees of freedom

Figure 9-11: Correspondence Analysis Dimension Summary

There is plenty more about the menus we could explore, and numerous ways in which we could polish our visualization aesthetically. We won't pursue either of those avenues just yet because there is an easy trick to incorporate Gender into the mix that might improve our perceptual map. While Correspondence Analysis allows for only two variables, we can recode Age and Gender into a combined variable. The Syntax that we used is provided for your reference:

```
DO IF  (Gender_num = 1).
RECODE Age_num (1 thru 6=Copy) INTO Age_Gender.
ELSE IF  (Gender_num = 2).
RECODE Age_num (1=7) (2=8) (3=9) (4=10)(5=11) (6=12) INTO Age_Gender.
END IF.

VALUE LABELS Age_Gender
  1.00 'M 18-24'
  2.00 'M 25-34'
  3.00 'M 35-44'
  4.00 'M 45-54'
  5.00 'M 55-64'
  6.00 'M 65+'
  7.00 'F 18-24'
  8.00 'F 25-34'
  9.00 'F 35-44'
  10.00 'F 45-54'
  11.00 'F 55-64'
  12.00 'F 65+'.
```

For the preceding code, we could also simply leverage multiplication, and the following would achieve the same result as the DO IF and RECODE commands.

```
Compute Age_Gender =
(Gender_num = 1) * Age_num + (Gender_num = 2) * Age_num * 2.
```

If you are new to Syntax, Chapter 16 provides an introduction.

Let's rerun the Correspondence Analysis, using default settings, and with our new variable. Remember to declare the range, which is 1 through 12. The resulting perceptual map is quite different, and more interesting (Figure 9-12). An examination of the Proportion of Inertia (not shown) also indicates that Dimension 2 gets a larger share of the variance than it did in the last example making us less concerned about the diagonal distance issue that we raised about Figure 9-10.

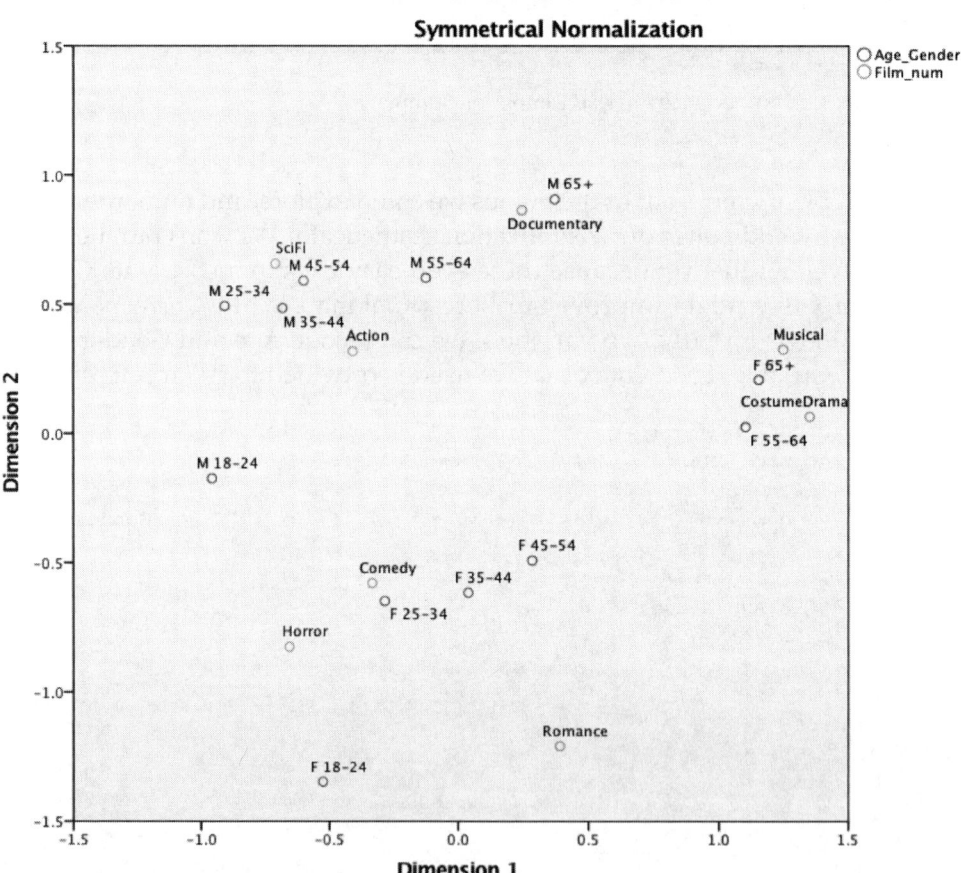

Figure 9-12: Improved perceptual map

We see a handful of natural groupings, the horseshoe is gone, and there is more complexity to the pattern. Males are found in the upper left. Interestingly, older males, 65+, seem to be more interested in Documentaries than older females, who prefer Costume Dramas and Musicals. Horror seems to appeal to both males and females of young age (18–24) equally, but the females of that age prefer Comedy more. Slightly older males like SciFi and Action movies.

Because this perceptual map is more interesting, let's consider some aesthetic changes that we can make to it. The labeling is fine for an analyst, but since the axes are standardized the values are essentially arbitrary. Depending on our audience, they might not be very useful or interesting. Also, the aesthetics of the labeling and points could be improved. Most decision makers won't want to explain Symmetrical Normalization (or have it explained to them). Once the salient features have been explained, and trust in the chart is built, that is probably a detail that we won't want labeled on the perceptual map. If we removed some of the unnecessary information, we could make everything a bit larger and more easily read. For instance, the point labels seem to make the legend redundant.

All of the following would probably help:

- Remove/replace the existing titles and labels.
- Remove the legend and reallocate the space.
- Improve the legibility of the points and point labels.

Editing a graphic in SPSS Statistics directly is often not the ideal solution. We could do it, but it would only improve this particular graphic. Much better would be if we came up with an "assembly line" type approach so that we can rerun this on updated data with minimal effort. In short, we should be using a more syntax-friendly approach. Keep in mind that while we covered GPL in Chapter 6, Syntax and the Output Management System are covered in Chapters 16 and 17. If you are brand new to either, you might want to skim those chapters. However, you won't need all of the detail that is presented in those chapters, and as long as you are prepared for a couple of new concepts you can safely proceed right here with this chapter. Before we can begin in earnest we need to solve a problem—the relevant data we need is in the output window and not in the data window. Let's address that issue first.

In the Output Management System Control Panel, shown in Figure 9-13, we make the following selections:

- Output Type = Table.
- Command Identifier = Correspondence.

- Table Subtypes for Selected Commands is *both* Overview Column Points and Overview Row Points.

- New dataset = "Points" although you can choose your own name as long as you keep track of where you are sending the data.

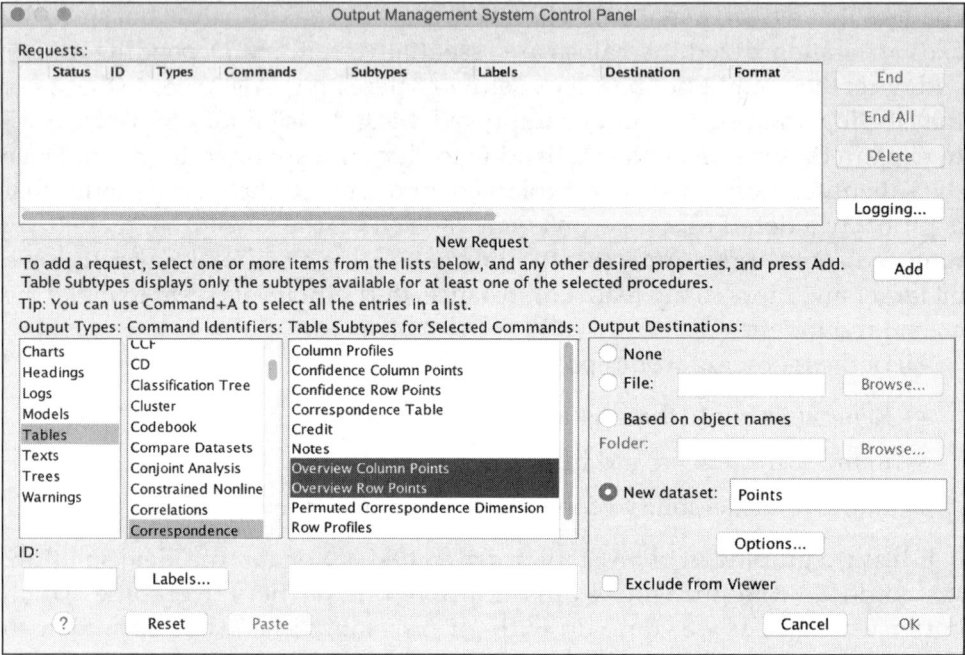

Figure 9-13: OMS Control Panel

Click the Add button to generate the request.

Chapter 17, which is dedicated to OMS, explains all of this in more detail, but in order to get this to work you will have to generate the relevant output by returning to the Correspondence Analysis menu and rerunning the analysis. Finally—and if you are unfamiliar with OMS, this might be the most likely step to miss—you must return to the OMS menu and "End" the request. This lets SPSS know that you want to convert the stored information to data now. It might seem like a strange step, but in certain cases you want the data to continue to accumulate over multiple executions.

You should generate data that looks like Figure 9-14. Note that the Variable View and not the Data View is shown.

	Name	Type	Width	Decimals	Label
1	TableNumber_	Numeric	8	0	Table Number
2	Command_	String	14	0	
3	Subtype_	String	22	0	
4	Label_	String	22	0	
5	Var1	String	64	0	
6	Mass	Numeric	5	3	Mass
7	@1	Numeric	5	3	Score in Dimension 1
8	@2	Numeric	6	3	Score in Dimension 2
9	Inertia	Numeric	4	3	Inertia
10	@1_A	Numeric	5	3	Contribution Of Point to Inertia of Dimension 1
11	@2_A	Numeric	5	3	Contribution Of Point to Inertia of Dimension 2
12	@1_B	Numeric	4	3	Contribution Of Dimension to Inertia of Point 1
13	@2_B	Numeric	4	3	Contribution Of Dimension to Inertia of Point 2
14	Total	Numeric	4	3	Contribution Of Dimension to Inertia of Point Total

Figure 9-14: Variable View of OMS results

After several manual modifications the data looks like Figure 9-15. Note that while these modifications were manual and not discussed in this chapter, all of these modifications could be accomplished with Syntax. The commands would be fairly straightforward for the most part and would include simple-to-use commands like DELETE VARIABLES and RENAME VARIABLES.

	TableNumber_	Label	Row	Column
1	1	Action	−.409	.318
2	1	Comedy	−.331	−.579
3	1	CostumeDrama	1.351	.065
4	1	Documentary	.245	.864
5	1	Horror	−.655	−.826
6	1	Musical	1.248	.326
7	1	Romance	.392	−1.209
8	1	SciFi	−.712	.656
9	2	M 18–24	−.958	−.174
10	2	M 25–34	−.910	.493
11	2	M 35–44	−.683	.485
12	2	M 45–54	−.600	.591
13	2	M 55–64	−.124	.601
14	2	M 65+	.371	.906
15	2	F 18–24	−.525	−1.348
16	2	F 25–34	−.282	−.648
17	2	F 35–44	.040	−.016
18	2	F 45–54	.286	−.491
19	2	F 55–64	1.103	.025
20	2	F 65+	1.154	.207

Figure 9-15: Modified Data View of OMS results

The GPL required is no more complex than the code explored in Chapter 6. While we will not walk through it command by command, it is provided for your reference. The initial GPL was generated using the Chart Builder menu (Figure 9-16) and then a handful of commands were modified manually.

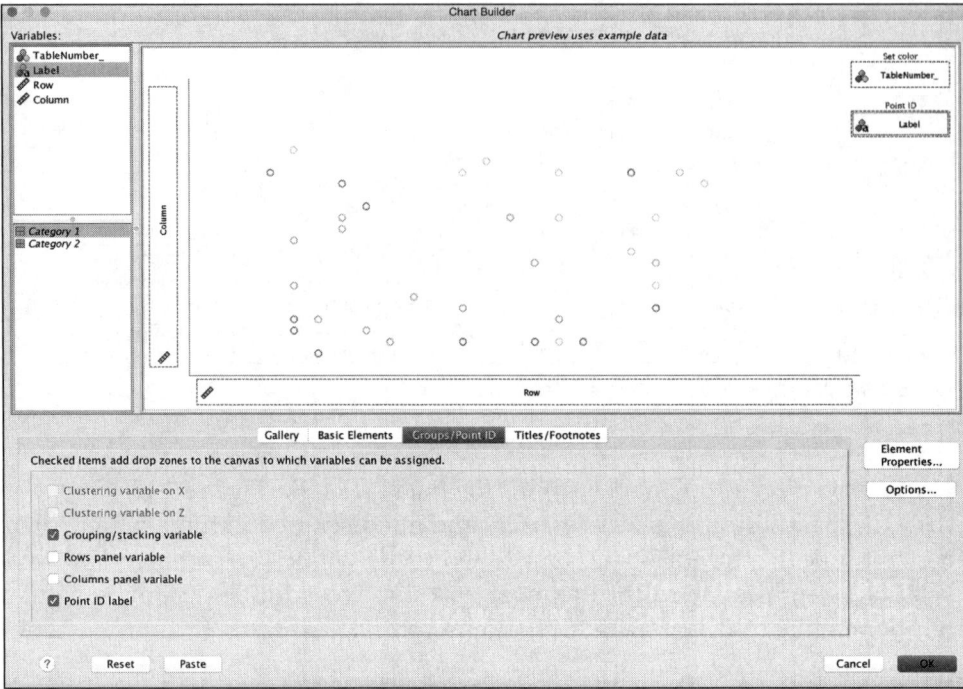

Figure 9-16: Correspondence Analysis dimension summary

Keep in mind that the names have been changed from what was originally produced by OMS. The row variable is Row, the column variable is Column, the color is set by TableNumber_, and the Point ID is Label.

The resulting pasted syntax and GPL is modified to the following:

```
* Chart Builder.
GGRAPH
  /GRAPHDATASET NAME="graphdataset" VARIABLES=Row Column
TableNumber_ Label MISSING=LISTWISE
    REPORTMISSING=NO
  /GRAPHSPEC SOURCE=INLINE.
BEGIN GPL
  PAGE: begin(scale(6in,6in))
  SOURCE: s=userSource(id("graphdataset"))
  DATA: Row=col(source(s), name("Row"))
  DATA: Column=col(source(s), name("Column"))
  DATA: TableNumber_=col(source(s), name("TableNumber_"),
unit.category())
  DATA: Label=col(source(s), name("Label"), unit.category())
  GUIDE: axis(dim(1), null() )
```

```
  GUIDE: axis(dim(2), null() )
  GUIDE: legend(aesthetic(aesthetic.color.exterior), null() )
  GUIDE: legend(aesthetic(aesthetic.color.interior), null() )
  GUIDE: text.title(label("Perceptual Map of Film and Age-Gender"))
  ELEMENT: point(position(Row*Column), color.exterior(TableNumber_),
color.interior(TableNumber_), label(Label), size(size.small))
  PAGE: end()
END GPL.
```

The result, shown in Figure 9-17, certainly represents progress although each analyst might differ somewhat on what modifications they would prefer. Once you become more comfortable with all of the incorporated elements you can completely automate the process. There are no steps that have been demonstrated from opening the file to the final result that could not be produced using a Syntax program.

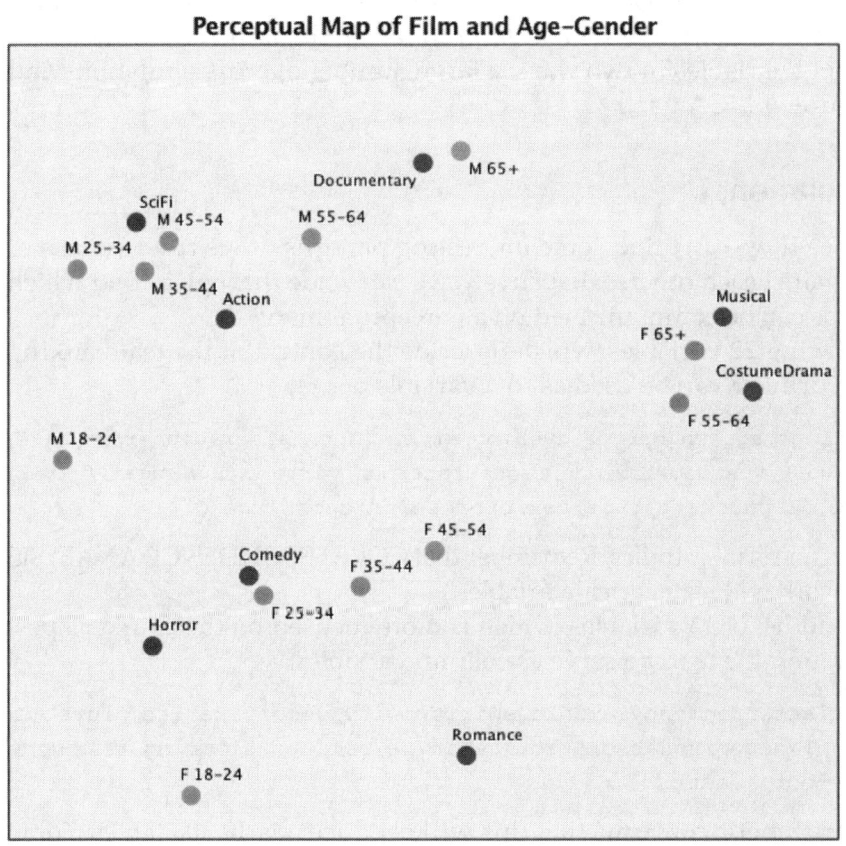

Figure 9-17: Perceptual map with GPL modifications

Multiple Correspondence Analysis

Multiple Correspondence Analysis (MCA) will allow us to use more than one row and one column variable. As in the last example, our focus is on producing a perceptual map, and rehearsing some of the logistics in SPSS Statistics. We address the theory behind the technique only in the most limited way necessary to support this single example. The dataset that we will use, Tea.sav, is a modified version of a popular dataset and is available on the book's website. It has dozens of variables that represent traits and behaviors of tea drinkers exploring the when, where, and how of their tea drinking. In theory, we could simply send all three dozen variables to the menu, and try to sort it out by staring at the resulting perceptual map. In practice, this would not be very efficient. The map can get so cluttered that it is unreadable. However, simply choosing a handful of the variables at random isn't a great strategy either because what makes a perceptual map compelling is being able to see relationships that are strong enough that the map is able to reveal them visually. We will attempt to tackle the issue of paring down the number of variables in two ways: a large number of crosstabulations and then a feature of MCA itself.

Crosstabulations

First, let's see if we can't find some interesting patterns. If we run two lists of variables against each other, exhaustively, we can wade through to find which relationships can be communicated on a perceptual map.

The following 22 variables, which describe the context of the tea drinking and the tea drinker, can be used as row variables:

> breakfast, afternoon.tea, evening, after.lunch, after.dinner, anytime, home, work, tearoom, friends, restaurant, pub, variety, how, sugar, format, place.of.purchase, type, sex, profession, sport, age_Q

(Note that age is in quintiles. Remember that CORRESPONDENCE ANALYSIS and MCA work with categorical variables.)

The second list of 13 variables, which is more focused on the drinker's perceptions around the tea, can serve as column variables:

> stimulant, frequency, exotic, spirituality, goodforhealth, diuretic, friendliness, ironabsorption, feminine, refined, slimming, relaxant, no.effect.health

Simple arithmetic confirms that this will produce nearly 300 tables. Some of the variable pairings are statistically significant, reveal strong relationships, and make intuitive sense, like the one in Figure 9-18, but many of the tables are none of those things. In Figure 9-18, we learn that those who drink more than 2 cups of tea a day disproportionately drink a cup at breakfast. The table shows a standardized residual of 3.2 for the combination of breakfast and "more than 2 per day." While that seems obvious, it seems especially true that the tea drinking of the loyal drinkers includes this meal. The pattern seems stronger than some of the other meals and times of day (not shown).

breakfast * frequency

Crosstab

			frequency				
			1 to 2/week	1/day	3 to 6/week	more than 2/day	Total
breakfast	breakfast	Count	4	47	7	86	144
		Std. Residual	-3.7	.2	-2.3	3.2	
	not. breakfast	Count	40	48	27	41	156
		Std. Residual	3.6	-.2	2.2	-3.1	
Total		Count	44	95	34	127	300

Chi-Square Tests

	Value	df	Asymp. Sig. (2–sided)
Pearson Chi-Square	56.786[a]	3	.000
Likelihood Ratio	62.575	3	.000
N of Valid Cases	300		

a. 0 cells (.0%) have expected count less than 5. The minimum expected count is 16.32.

Figure 9-18: Correspondence Analysis dimension summary

A good example of a weak relationship is the pairing of "friends" with "exotic" as shown in Figure 9-19. The pattern is so consistent with the null hypothesis (no relationship) that the standardized residual is zero. Our perceptual map will be extremely difficult to read if the strong relationships are sharing space with the weak relationships. There will simply be so many dots and labels on top of each other that we won't be able to see the pattern.

Although there are ways to do this systematically and with some automation, reviewing manually is quite labor intensive. We used this technique briefly in preparing the chapter simply to confirm that there were relationships worth exploring, but we did not rely upon this approach only nor did we do an exhaustive search of all of the tables. (One can use "scripts" in SPSS Statistics to automatically hide non-significant results to allow for a less labor-intensive search of the results.) In this case, we will use a feature within MCA itself to try to figure out which variables to use in the perceptual map.

friends * exotic

Crosstab

			exotic		
			exotic	not. exotic	Total
friends	friends	Count	93	103	196
		Std. Residual	.0	.0	
	not.friends	Count	49	55	104
		Std. Residual	.0	.0	
Total		Count	142	158	300

Chi-Square Tests

	Value	df	Asymp. Sig. (2–sided)	Exact Sig. (2–sided)	Exact Sig. (1–sided)
Pearson Chi-Square	.003[a]	1	.956		
Continuity Correction[b]	.000	1	1.000		
Likelihood Ratio	.003	1	.956		
Fisher's Exact Test				1.000	.527
N of Valid Cases	300				

a. 0 cells (.0%) have expected count less than 5. The minimum expected count is 49.23.

b. Computed only for a 2x2 table

Figure 9-19: Correspondence Analysis dimension summary

We will now run the MCA analysis using all of the variables, with one special request, but otherwise on default settings. First, to find MCA go to the Analyze menu and then the Dimension Reduction submenu, and then select Optimal Scaling. You will find the submenu shown in Figure 9-20. Notice that, depending on your selection, you may get routed to a menu other than MCA. We will keep the default settings.

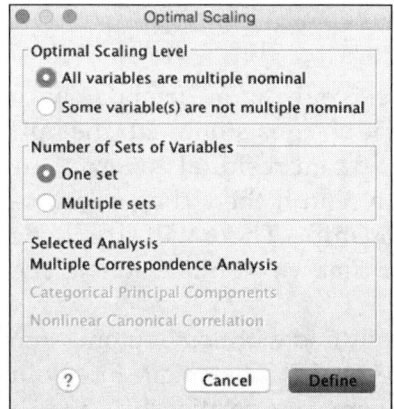

Figure 9-20: Optimal Scaling submenu

We will be using all of the variables with the prefix "num_." (The original file had string values, which crosstabs was content to run, but MCA requires numeric values with labels.) There are many of them—more than you can see in Figure 9-21.

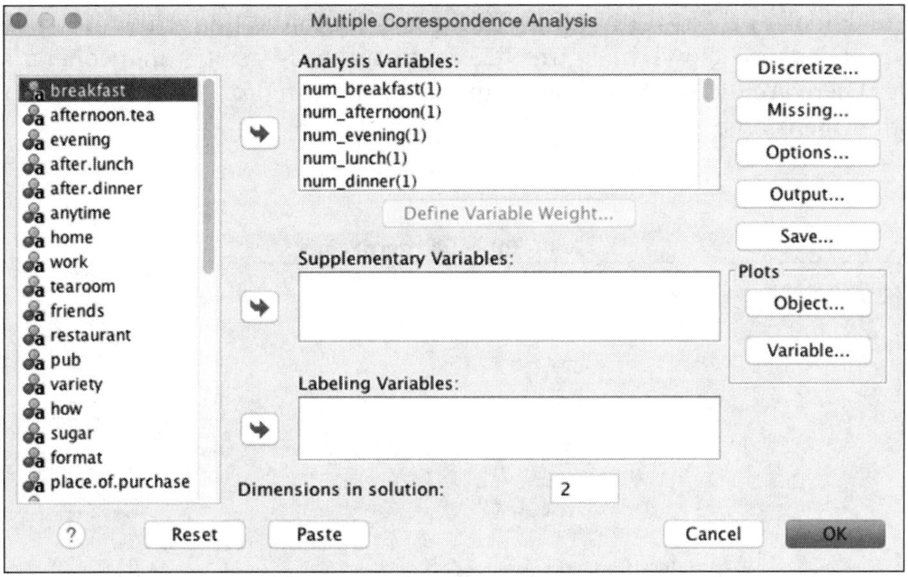

Figure 9-21: Multiple Correspondence Analysis main menu

The one special request that we will make is to request a Joint Category Plot in the Variable Plots submenu using all of the variables as shown in Figure 9-22. (Not all the variables names are visible in the figure.)

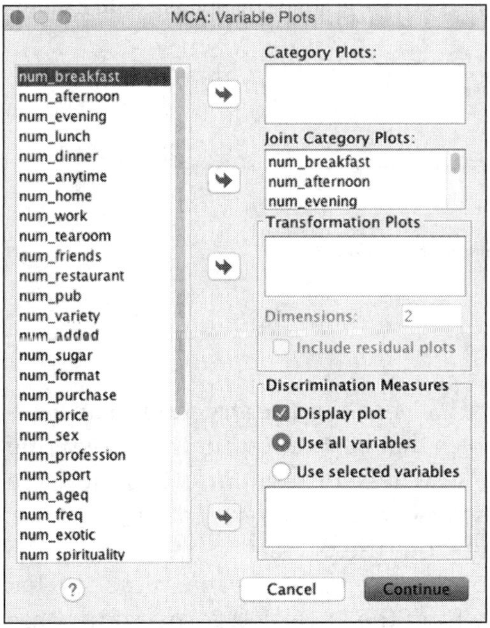

Figure 9-22: Variable Plots submenu

A quick look at the resulting Joint Category Plot found near the middle of the output and also shown in Figure 9-23 confirms our fears. It is an incoherent jumble. There are too many variables and labels fighting for the space at zero on both dimensions.

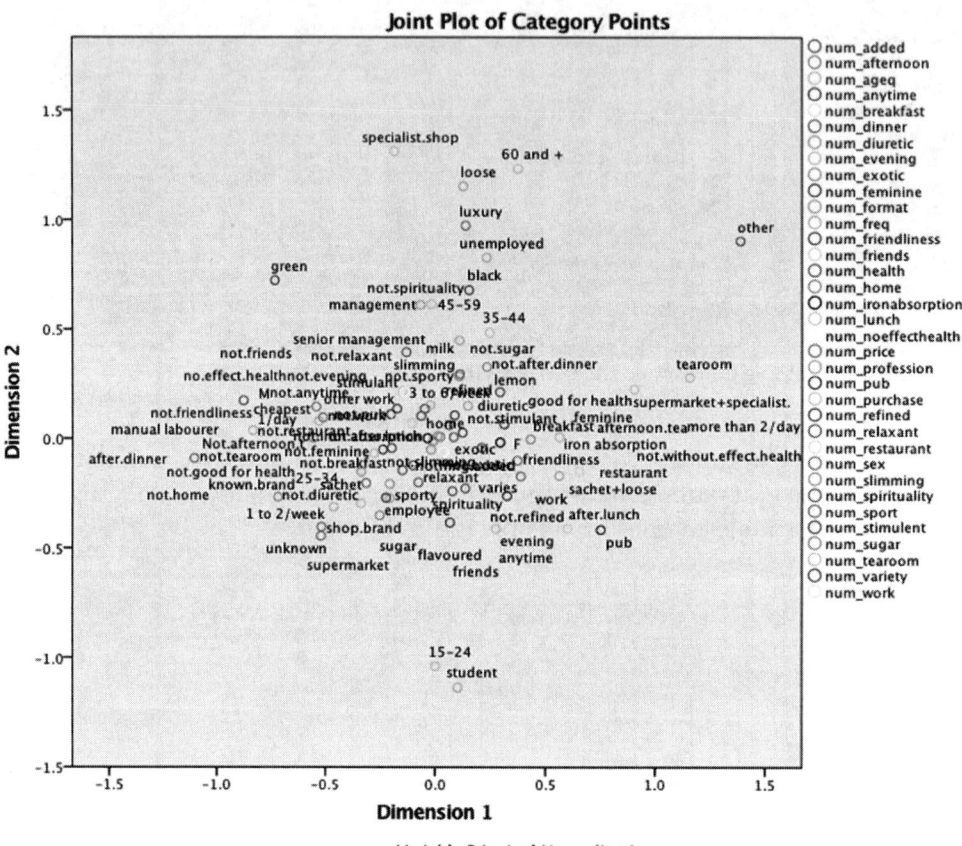

Figure 9-23: Very crowded Joint Category Plot

Mere cosmetic changes won't be enough. We need to make structural changes—namely we need to identify those variables that best represent the underlying pattern. The Discrimination Measures Plot will be of assistance. It is shown in Figure 9-24. Some variables, notably num_ageq, numprofession, num_purchase, and num_afternoon are breaking away from the pack, and are showing an influence on either Dimension 2 or Dimension 1 or both. The magnitude of that impact can be measured by the distance from the lower-left corner. If they are high, they influence Dimension 2, and if they are far to the right, they influence

Dimension 1. If they are neither, they are going to make the center of any Joint Category Plot (our perceptual map) very noisy. Those variables in the lower-left corner need to be removed to avoid this.

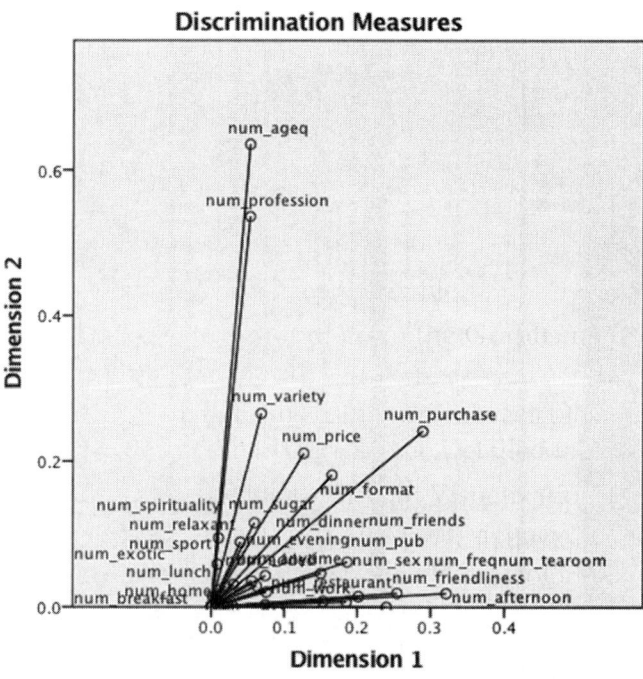

Figure 9-24: Discrimination Measures Plot

One can also review the tabular version of this result (Figure 9-25). There are a lot of variables, but we can see the Dimension 1 and 2 values, and also a mean value.

A review of these results (and admittedly a bit of experimentation) led me to choose the following variables as being a promising list for our perceptual map:

num_afternoon, num_tearoom, num_restaurant, num_pub, num_variety, num_format, num_purchase, num_price, num_sex, num_profession, num_ageq

An interesting trick can be applied to Figure 9-25 if you choose. When in editing mode, you can use the context menu (accessed by right clicking) to sort rows in a pivot table (shown in Figure 9-26).

Discrimination Measures

	Dimension		Mean
	1	2	
num_breakfast	.031	.000	.015
num_afternoon	.240	.000	.120
num_evening	.040	.089	.064
num_lunch	.062	.029	.045
num_dinner	.092	.001	.046
num_anytime	.056	.036	.046
num_home	.016	.002	.009
num_work	.075	.020	.048
num_tearoom	.321	.019	.170
num_friends	.186	.062	.124
num_restaurant	.153	.008	.081
num_pub	.150	.046	.098
num_variety	.068	.266	.167
num_added	.074	.043	.059
num_sugar	.059	.115	.087
num_format	.165	.181	.173
num_purchase	.289	.241	.265
num_price	.127	.211	.169
num_sex	.202	.014	.108
num_profession	.053	.536	.294
num_sport	.008	.059	.034
num_ageq	.052	.635	.344
num_freq	.254	.019	.137
num_exotic	.000	.000	.000
num_spirituality	.008	.023	.016
num_health	.009	.009	.009
num_diuretic	.030	.031	.031
num_friendliness	.185	.007	.096
num_ironabsorption	.010	.000	.005
num_feminine	.074	.003	.039
num_refined	.019	.029	.024
num_slimming	.002	.014	.008
num_stimulent	.024	.001	.013
num_relaxant	.010	.095	.052
num_noeffecthealth	.005	.013	.009
Active Total	3.152	2.858	3.005
% of Variance	9.007	8.165	8.586

Figure 9-25: Discrimination Measures table

Figure 9-27 shows the results of an experiment using just these variables. (The shading has been added manually.) This is more like what we hope to see. The shaded area in the upper right-hand corner shows an interesting clustering of traits and circumstances. Having tea out at a tearoom, pub, or restaurant seems to be more a social activity for the younger crowd: ages 15–24 (college age?) more so than other ages, and more female than male.

Discrimination Measures			
	Dimension		Mean
	1	2	
% of Variance	9.007	8.165	8.586
Active Total	3.152	2.858	3.00
num_ageq	.052	.635	.34
num_profession	.053	.536	.29
num_purchase	.289	.241	.26
num_format	.165	.181	.17
num_tearoom	.321	.019	.17
num_price	.127	.211	.16
num_variety	.068	.266	.16
num_freq	.254	.019	.13
num_friends	.186	.062	.12
num_afternoon	.240	.000	.12
num_sex	.202	.014	.10
num_pub	.150	.046	.09
num_friendliness	.185	.007	.09
num_sugar	.059	.115	.08
num_restaurant	.153	.008	.08
num_evening	.040	.089	.06
num_added	.074	.043	.05

Menu overlay:

Cut   ⌘X
Copy   ⌘C
Paste   ⌘V
Delete   ⌧

Select Table
Select cells with similar significance

Sort Rows ▶   Ascending
              Descending
Create Graph ▶

Table Properties...
Cell Properties...
TableLooks...
Insert Footnote
Delete Footnotes
Hide Footnotes

Pivoting Trays
✓ Toolbar

Figure 9-26: Sorting the mean discrimination measures

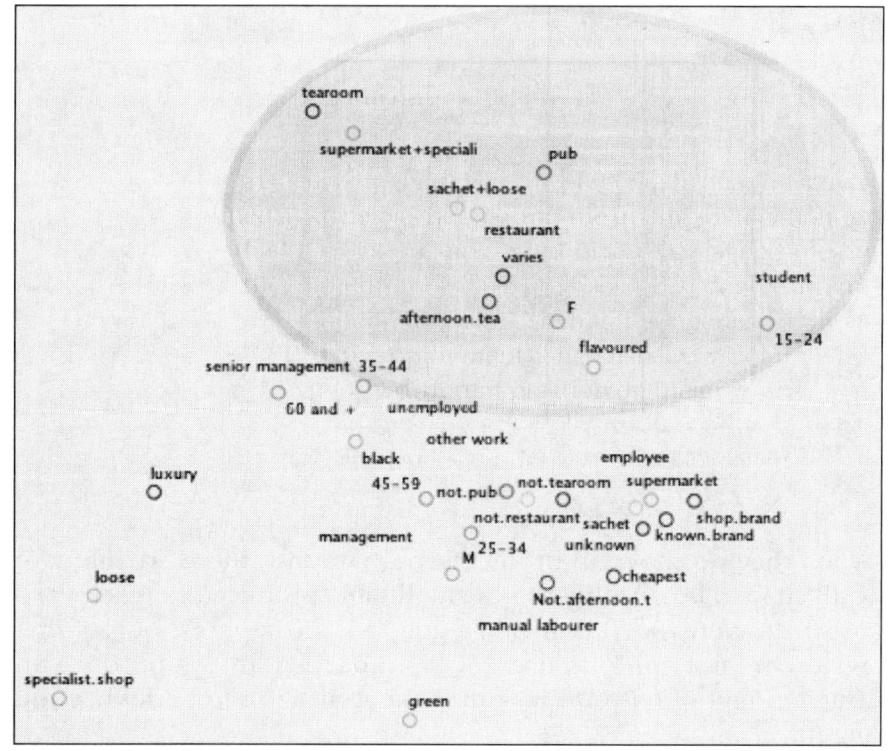

Figure 9-27: Draft map with few variables

The lower left (not shaded) has a possible pattern involving specialist shop, loose tea, and luxury brands.

Let's revisit the techniques that we used earlier in the chapter with Correspondence Analysis to improve this perceptual map.

Applying OMS and GPL to the MCA Perceptual Map

The MCA menus have a few more moving parts, so it will take a bit of care to produce the dataset that we need for our perceptual map. Unlike Correspondence Analysis, MCA does not send the coordinates to the output window by default. We will have to request them using the Output submenu as shown in Figure 9-28.

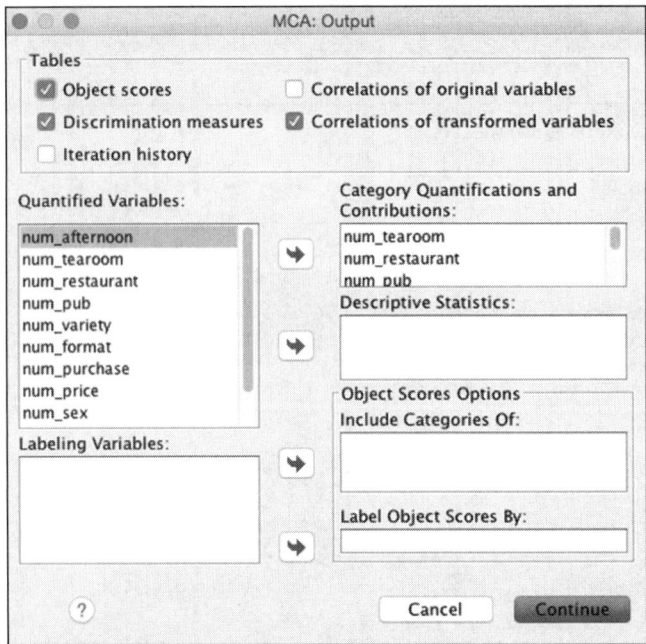

Figure 9-28: MCA Output submenu

Also, when they do show up in the Output window, there are many of them (not all shown) because there is a small table produced for each variable (Figure 9-29). Note that it is always a good idea to suppress output that you know you are not going to use. MCA, in particular, can produce an intimidating amount of output that can make it difficult to find what you are looking for.

Quantifications

Table

num_tearoom

Points: Coordinates

Category	Frequency	Centroid Coordinates	
		Dimension	
		1	2
not.tearoom	242	.179	-.262
tearoom	58	-.746	1.092

Variable Principal Normalization.

num_restaurant

Points: Coordinates

Category	Frequency	Centroid Coordinates	
		Dimension	
		1	2
not.restaurant	221	.049	-.262
restaurant	79	-.138	.734

Variable Principal Normalization.

num_pub

Points: Coordinates

Category	Frequency	Centroid Coordinates	
		Dimension	
		1	2
not.pub	237	-.028	-.234
pub	63	.105	.879

Variable Principal Normalization.

Figure 9-29: Coordinates (partial)

Frankly, the formatting in a single table or multiple tables will have no effect on our plan because we will be using OMS, not the output window. In OMS (Figure 9-30) we want to select the following:

- Tables for Output Type
- Multiple Correspondence Analysis for Command Identifiers
- Quantifications for Table Subtypes for Selected Commands
- New Data with name "Points"

Then click Add.

The resulting dataset seems particularly complex because it contains a number of data points that we don't need (Figure 9-31). The details of this dataset are not important because we will be discarding much of this information.

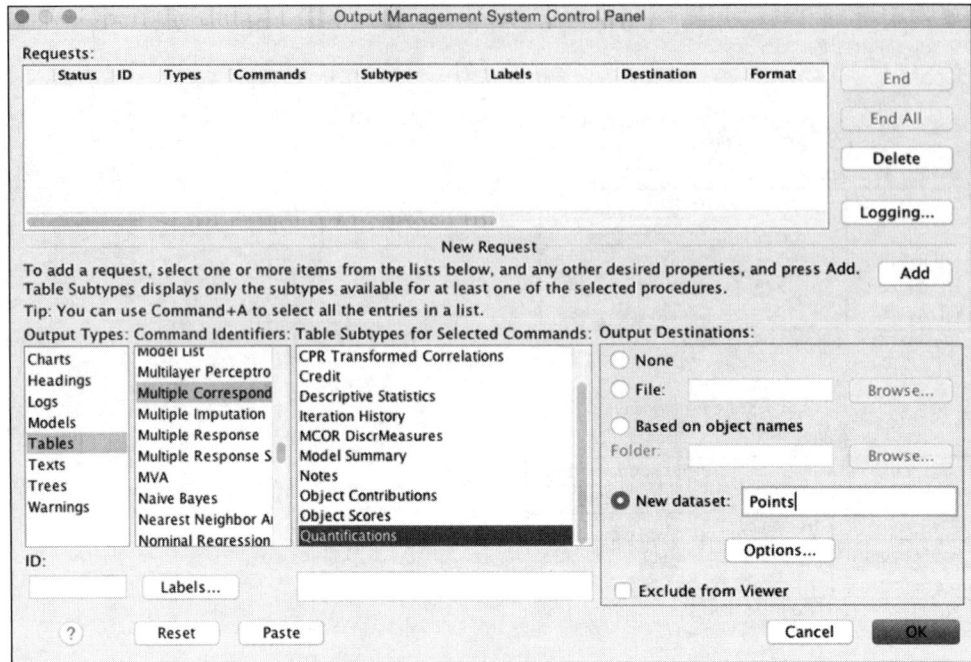

Figure 9-30: OMS Control Panel

	TableNumber_	Command_	Subtype_	Label_	Var1	Var2	Frequency	@1	@2	Mass	Inertia	@1_A	@2_A	@1_B	@2_B	Total
1	1	Multiple Correspondence	Quantifications	num_tearoom	not.tearoom	Coordinates	242	.179	-.262							
2	1	Multiple Correspondence	Quantifications	num_tearoom	not.tearoom	Contributions	242			.073	.018	.010	.024	.134	.286	.419
3	1	Multiple Correspondence	Quantifications	num_tearoom	tearoom	Coordinates	58	-.746	1.092							
4	1	Multiple Correspondence	Quantifications	num_tearoom	tearoom	Contributions	58			.018	.073	.042	.101	.134	.286	.419
5	1	Multiple Correspondence	Quantifications	num_tearoom	Active Total	Contributions				.091	.091	.052	.125			
6	2	Multiple Correspondence	Quantifications	num_restaurant	not.restaurant	Coordinates	221	.049	-.262							
7	2	Multiple Correspondence	Quantifications	num_restaurant	not.restaurant	Contributions	221			.067	.024	.001	.022	.007	.192	.199
8	2	Multiple Correspondence	Quantifications	num_restaurant	restaurant	Coordinates	79	-.138	.734							
9	2	Multiple Correspondence	Quantifications	num_restaurant	restaurant	Contributions	79			.024	.067	.002	.062	.007	.192	.199
10	2	Multiple Correspondence	Quantifications	num_restaurant	Active Total	Contributions				.091	.091	.003	.084			
11	3	Multiple Correspondence	Quantifications	num_pub	not.pub	Coordinates	237	-.028	-.234							
12	3	Multiple Correspondence	Quantifications	num_pub	not.pub	Contributions	237			.072	.019	.000	.019	.003	.205	.208
13	3	Multiple Correspondence	Quantifications	num_pub	pub	Coordinates	63	.105	.879							
14	3	Multiple Correspondence	Quantifications	num_pub	pub	Contributions	63			.019	.072	.001	.071	.003	.205	.208
15	3	Multiple Correspondence	Quantifications	num_pub	Active Total	Contributions				.091	.091	.001	.090			
16	4	Multiple Correspondence	Quantifications	num_variety	black	Coordinates	74	-.585	-.061							
17	4	Multiple Correspondence	Quantifications	num_variety	black	Contributions	74			.022	.068	.033	.000	.112	.001	.113
18	4	Multiple Correspondence	Quantifications	num_variety	flavoured	Coordinates	193	.289	.200							
19	4	Multiple Correspondence	Quantifications	num_variety	flavoured	Contributions	193			.058	.032	.021	.011	.151	.072	.223
20	4	Multiple Correspondence	Quantifications	num_variety	green	Coordinates	33	-.382	-1.035							
21	4	Multiple Correspondence	Quantifications	num_variety	green	Contributions	33			.010	.081	.006	.052	.018	.132	.150

Figure 9-31: Dataset produced by OMS

It is a simple matter to clean it up to get only what we need. This is helpful to see what we are doing in Figure 9-32, but when you are fully automating this you should use the names that OMS produces, and there is no need to drop variables. All we need are the Coordinates and Label_, and Var1 will be useful for labeling. You might also be tempted to rename the variables, but we are simply passing the information to GPL, so it is best to keep everything just as it was produced by OMS.

🔗 Label_	🔗 Var1	🔗 Var2	📏 Frequency	🖊 @1	🖊 @2
num_tearoom	not.tearoom	Coordinates	242	.179	-.262
num_tearoom	tearoom	Coordinates	58	-.746	1.092
num_restaurant	not.restaurant	Coordinates	221	.049	-.262
num_restaurant	restaurant	Coordinates	79	-.138	.734
num_pub	not.pub	Coordinates	237	-.028	-.234
num_pub	pub	Coordinates	63	.105	.879
num_variety	black	Coordinates	74	-.585	-.061
num_variety	flavoured	Coordinates	193	.289	.200
num_variety	green	Coordinates	33	-.382	-1.035
num_format	loose	Coordinates	36	-1.553	-.600
num_format	sachet	Coordinates	170	.447	-.290
num_format	sachet+loose	Coordinates	94	-.214	.754

Figure 9-32: OMS Control Panel

The GPL that we will be using is very similar indeed to the CORRESPONDENCE ANALYSIS example. To create it, we first pasted it from the menus, and then made modifications that are nearly exact to the earlier example. The GPL is here for your reference:

```
GGRAPH
  /GRAPHDATASET NAME="graphdataset" VARIABLES=@1[name="_1"]
@2[name="_2"] Label_ Var1
    MISSING=LISTWISE REPORTMISSING=NO
  /GRAPHSPEC SOURCE=INLINE.
BEGIN GPL
  PAGE: begin(scale(7in,7in))
  SOURCE: s=userSource(id("graphdataset"))
  DATA: var=col(source(s), name("_1"))
  DATA: var3=col(source(s), name("_2"))
  DATA: Label_=col(source(s), name("Label_"), unit.category())
  DATA: Var1=col(source(s), name("Var1"), unit.category())
  GUIDE: axis(dim(1), null() )
  GUIDE: axis(dim(2), null() )
  GUIDE: legend(aesthetic(aesthetic.color.exterior), null() )
  GUIDE: legend(aesthetic(aesthetic.color.interior), null() )
  GUIDE: legend(aesthetic(aesthetic.color.exterior), label("Label_"))
  ELEMENT: point(position(var*var3), color.exterior(Label_),
color.interior(Label_), label(Var1), size(size.small))
  PAGE: end()
END GPL.
```

The resulting map is shown in Figure 9-33. It is much more readable, and some patterns are salient. In addition to the ones already mentioned, there seems to be a pattern—not surprising—of buying cheaper brands at the supermarket to consume at home (not restaurant and not tea room). The professions associated with this pattern are "employees" and manual laborers in their mid-20s to mid-30s.

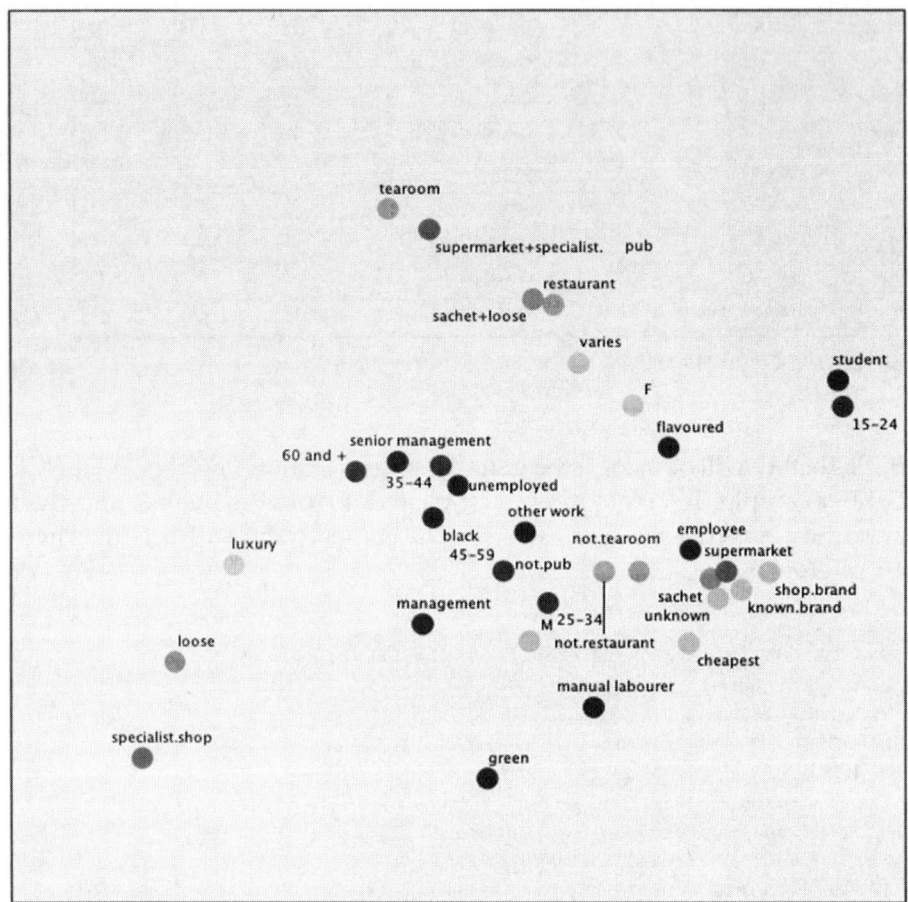

Figure 9-33: MCA perceptual map using OMS and GPL

With the large number of variables, and the complex set of settings available in MCA, we certainly could have explored alternative maps, but the map succeeds in a way that a table (even a highlighted one) might not. Also, the basic skills of using calculations, OMS, and GPL in combination that we explored can apply to a number of areas.

As a brief coda, let's revisit the perceptual map that we produced much earlier in the chapter, Figure 9-12. Now that we've used the MCA menus, we can show the three-variable perceptual map without recoding to create age_gender. Neither the perceptual map nor approach is necessarily superior, but it is interesting to see the alternative, shown in Figure 9-34.

Plot

Category Points

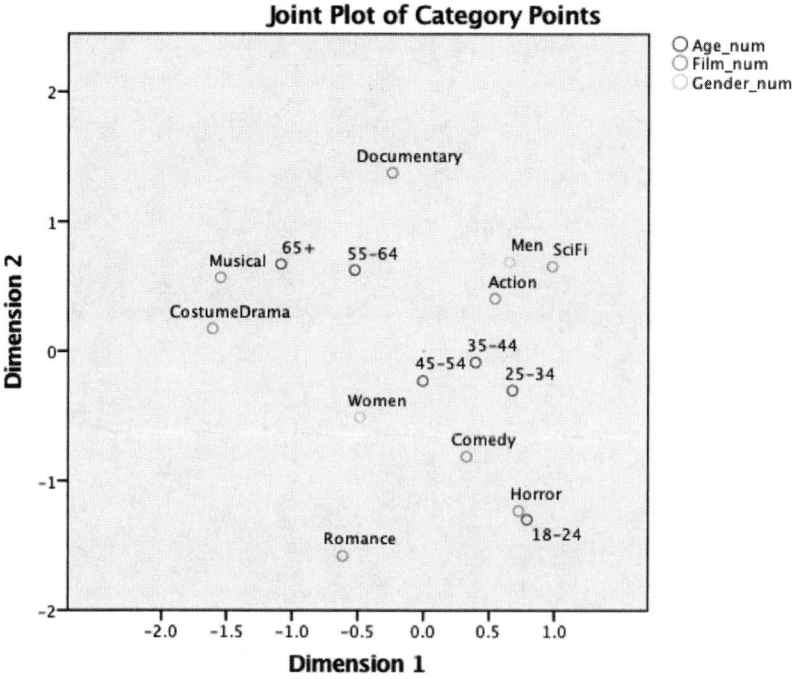

Figure 9-34: MCA version of Figure 9-12

Display Complex Relationships with Multidimensional Scaling

Multidimensional scaling (MDS) is an exploratory statistical technique that positions objects (products, services, and so on) in a graph based on how similar or dissimilar the objects are to each other so as to determine which features are most important in people's perceptions of object relatedness. Multidimensional scaling mathematically transforms the perceived relatedness among objects into a visual display of distance that helps determine which characteristics are most important in detecting the structure or dimensions of similarity judgments. Dimensions are then interpreted by using both subjective and statistical techniques.

As an example, in the area of market research, multidimensional scaling can be used to identify brand positions and the dimensions along which customers view brands. In its most basic form, respondents indicate how similar or dissimilar different pairs of objects (often brands) are from one another. Using ice cream as an example, we can ask respondents, how similar are vanilla and chocolate? Chocolate and strawberry? Vanilla and strawberry? Lemon and raspberry? Multidimensional scaling then attempts to fit these proximity measures by placing the objects in a low-dimensional space so that the distances between the objects in the space reproduce the observed proximities.

Figure 10-1 shows a two dimensional display of the relationships among ice cream flavors. Notice that the first dimension places water-based flavors on one end of the spectrum and milk-based flavors on the other end. We would have to do a little more work to figure out the meaning of the second dimension.

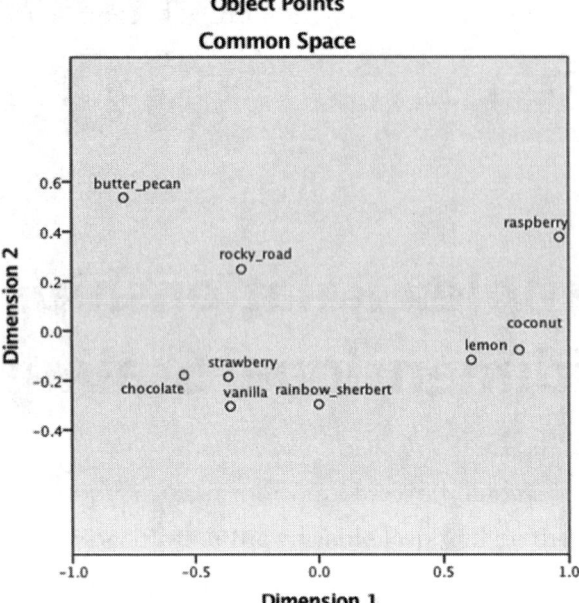

Figure 10-1: Object points plot

Multidimensional scaling can, and has, been used in a number of ways. For example, MDS can be used to position products, political candidates, organizations, or services in a space based on similarity ratings. As an example, one of the book's authors used MDS to study how outpatients used different medical services (for example, dentists, chiropractors, optometrists, and so on) to understand usage patterns.

It is important to note that respondents in these studies need not be asked to indicate how similar objects are along specific attributes. Rather, the expectation is that the dimensions through which respondents view the objects will be understood by viewing how the objects are positioned in the low-dimensional space. In this way, the analyst tries to understand the major dimensions on which respondents differentiate objects without obtaining explicit attribute ratings. However, in some marketing studies involving multidimensional scaling, respondents do rate products on a set of attributes and the scaling is based on product similarities (or dissimilarities) derived from the attribute ratings.

Many forms of multidimensional scaling exist, varying in the assumptions made about the scale of measurement, allowable transformations, means of accommodating individual differences, the method of estimation, and measure of fit, among other factors.

In this chapter you learn about the different kinds of MDS that are available. We use a practice dataset so that you can get a feel for the technique as well as the options that are available in the dialogs associated with MDS. Finally, we cover how to interpret the results.

Metric and Nonmetric Multidimensional Scaling

The basic multidimensional scaling model begins with data containing measures of similarity or dissimilarity for pairs of objects. The model assumes that each object is represented by a point in a space. Objects are positioned in this space so that distances between the objects closely approximate the original proximities. Solutions with different numbers of dimensions can be applied and several measures of fit are available. Two-dimension solutions are popular, because it is easy to interpret two-dimensional plots.

Metric multidimensional scaling assumes that a parametric model relates the proximities to the object distances; that is, it is assumed that distances between objects are either ratio or interval level in nature. Nonmetric multidimensional scaling makes weaker assumptions about this relationship, so that it only assumes that distances between objects are based on rank order or ordinal-level data.

Nonmetric Scaling of Psychology Sub-Disciplines

In this example, we perform a nonmetric multidimensional scaling analysis on data for six psychology sub-disciplines. The goal of this study is to describe how psychology's sub-disciplines relate to each other. The data is in the form of a dissimilarity matrix, where each value represents the distance between a pair of sub-disciplines (lower values indicate that the sub-disciplines are more similar to each other).

To access this data, open the dataset `Psychology.sav`, shown in Figure 10-2.

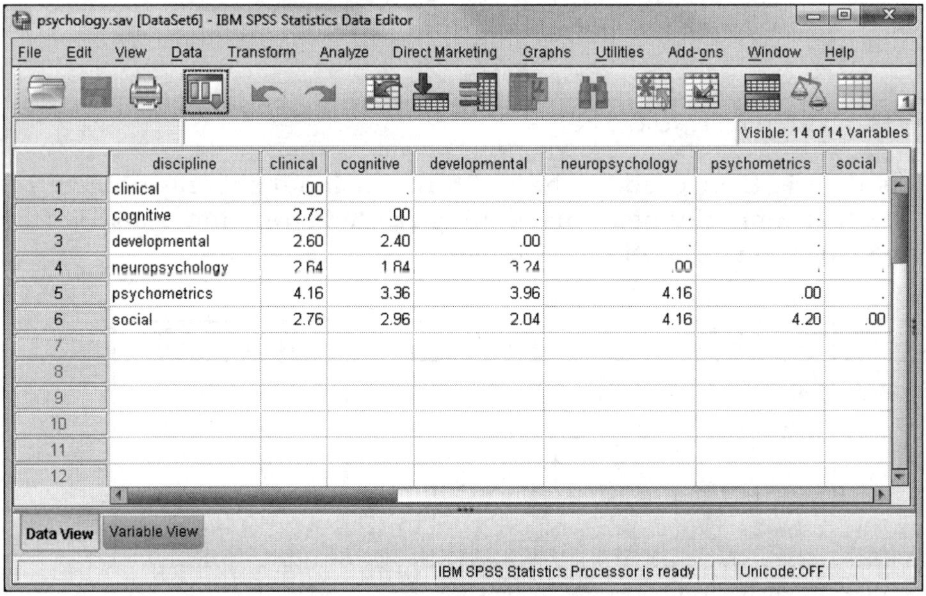

	discipline	clinical	cognitive	developmental	neuropsychology	psychometrics	social
1	clinical	.00	.	.	.	.	.
2	cognitive	2.72	.00	.	.	.	.
3	developmental	2.60	2.40	.00	.	.	.
4	neuropsychology	2.64	1.84	3.24	.00	.	.
5	psychometrics	4.16	3.36	3.96	4.16	.00	.
6	social	2.76	2.96	2.04	4.16	4.20	.00
7							
8							
9							
10							
11							
12							

Figure 10-2: Dissimilarity matrix of psychology data

The data in Figure 10-2 is in the form of a proximity matrix (specifically, dissimilarities, where larger values indicate greater distances) and a single group is involved. We can see, for example, that psychometrics and social psychology are very different from each other (because they have the largest distance value, 4.20), while cognitive and neuropsychology are the most similar (because they have the smallest distance value, 1.84).

Although the dataset we will use in this chapter was specifically collected for multidimensional scaling, I want to point out that you do not need to have your data in the form of a proximity matrix. In fact, it is very easy to perform multidimensional scaling on Likert type rating scales (the most widely used response scales in survey research) or on any type of data. For example, Figure 10-3 shows data on ice cream preferences. Here respondents were simply asked to specify whether they liked (a value of 1) or disliked (a value of 0) different ice cream flavors.

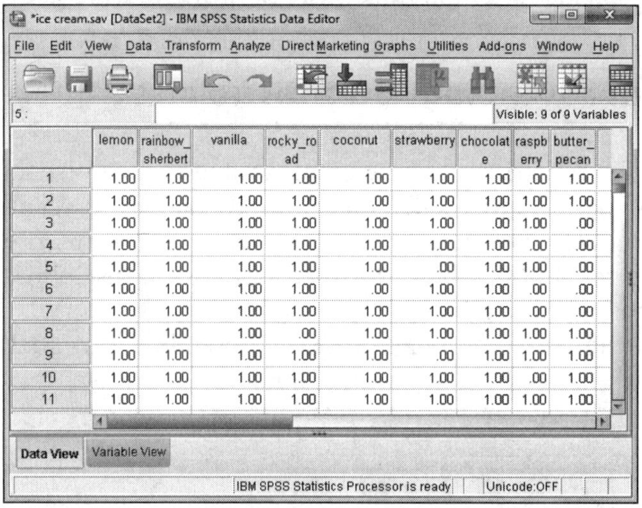

	lemon	rainbow_sherbert	vanilla	rocky_road	coconut	strawberry	chocolate	raspberry	butter_pecan
1	1.00	1.00	1.00	1.00	1.00	1.00	1.00	.00	1.00
2	1.00	1.00	1.00	1.00	.00	1.00	1.00	1.00	1.00
3	1.00	1.00	1.00	1.00	1.00	1.00	.00	1.00	.00
4	1.00	1.00	1.00	1.00	1.00	1.00	1.00	.00	.00
5	1.00	1.00	1.00	1.00	1.00	.00	1.00	1.00	.00
6	1.00	1.00	1.00	1.00	.00	1.00	1.00	.00	.00
7	1.00	1.00	1.00	1.00	1.00	1.00	1.00	.00	.00
8	1.00	1.00	1.00	.00	1.00	1.00	1.00	1.00	1.00
9	1.00	1.00	1.00	1.00	1.00	.00	1.00	1.00	1.00
10	1.00	1.00	1.00	1.00	1.00	1.00	1.00	.00	1.00
11	1.00	1.00	1.00	1.00	1.00	1.00	1.00	1.00	1.00

Figure 10-3: Ice cream preference data

This data is then used in the multidimensional scaling procedure, and internally, multidimensional scaling created a proximity matrix (see Figure 10-4) to run this statistical routine.

Proximities

	lemon	rainbow_sherbert	vanilla	rocky_road	coconut	strawberry	chocolate	raspberry	butter_pecan
lemon	.								
rainbow_sherbert	9.381	.							
vanilla	11.269	8.307	.						
rocky_road	11.619	10.247	9.055	.					
coconut	8.124	10.296	12.288	12.530	.				
strawberry	11.576	9.055	8.185	9.327	12.247	.			
chocolate	11.916	9.274	7.937	9.539	12.649	8.832	.		
raspberry	9.381	12.247	13.964	13.077	9.055	13.491	13.856	.	
butter_pecan	13.928	11.832	10.440	10.247	14.000	10.296	10.100	14.283	.

Figure 10-4: Proximities matrix ice cream preference data

This is why I mentioned in the opening paragraph of this chapter that "this technique could be applied in so many ways if analysts just took the time to dig a little deeper into their data." Essentially MDS takes any type of data and internally transforms the data into a proximity matrix that MDS uses for the analyses.

Multidimenional Scaling Dialog Options

Now that we have data, to perform multidimensional scaling select the Analyze menu and then choose Scale to display the options shown in Figure 10-5. There are two options to perform multidimensional scaling: ALSCAL, which is part of the SPSS Statistics Base system, and PROXSCAL, which is part of the SPSS Categories module. Both support a wide range of multidimensional scaling options; however, PROXSCAL has some additional advanced features. In our case we could use either procedure to run the analysis; we will use PROXSCAL because it offers additional options.

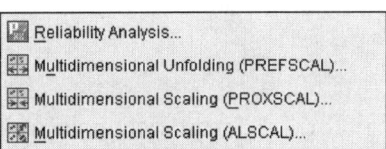

Figure 10-5: Analyze ⇨Scale menu options

Within the multidimensional scaling procedure, we need to indicate whether the data source contains proximities or the actual data values. If you do have proximities, then the format of the proximities must be specified. If the data source does not contain proximities, they will be calculated from the data (as shown in Figures 10-3 and 10-4). The Number of Sources section (see Figure 10-6) concerns whether we will be forming a single-group analysis (One matrix source) versus an individual-differences or multiple-group analysis (Multiple matrix sources).

> **NOTE** Multidimensional scaling also includes models that allow for group and individual differences. Individual differences or *weighted multidimensional scaling* (INDSCAL), as it is often called, assumes that sources (or individuals) differ on the characteristics they use to define or construct a configuration and/or on the importance they place on each dimension within a given configuration. Aside from this important distinction, weighted MDS operates in a similar manner as unweighted MDS.

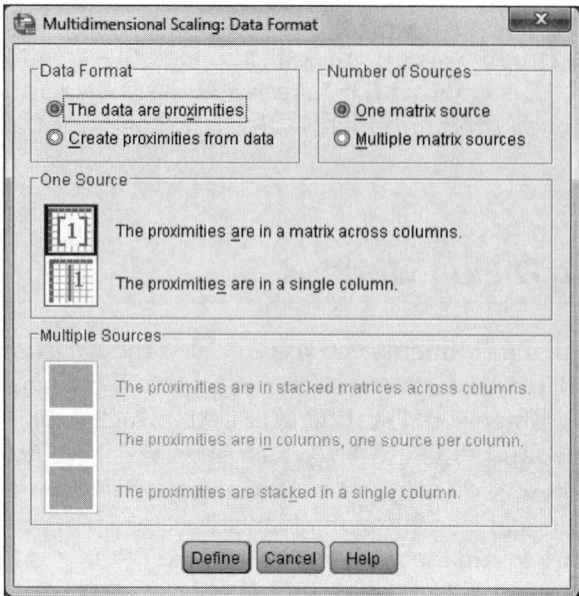

Figure 10-6: Multidimensional Scaling: Data Format dialog

A matrix of proximities can be read in a matrix format across data columns (our situation) or as one data element per line with row and column identifiers. In our case the data are proximities so:

1. Click the Data are proximities option button in the Data Format group shown in Figure 10-6.

2. Click the Define button. This will open the dialog shown in Figure 10-7.

3. As shown in Figure 10-7, place the six psychology sub-disciplines into the Proximities list box. The Sources list box is inactive because we are running a single source (group) analysis.

   Weights can be assigned to each proximity variable (here representing an object), but are not needed in our analysis.

4. Move the variables from clinical to social into the Proximities list box.

5. Click Model at the top of the right-hand group of buttons to open the Multidimensional Scaling: Model dialog shown in Figure 10-8.

   Because we are working with a single data source, options pertaining to the type of individual-difference (group) model are inactive. We also need to specify the form of the proximity matrix, and as we saw in Figure 10-2, we have a lower-triangular matrix (which is the default).

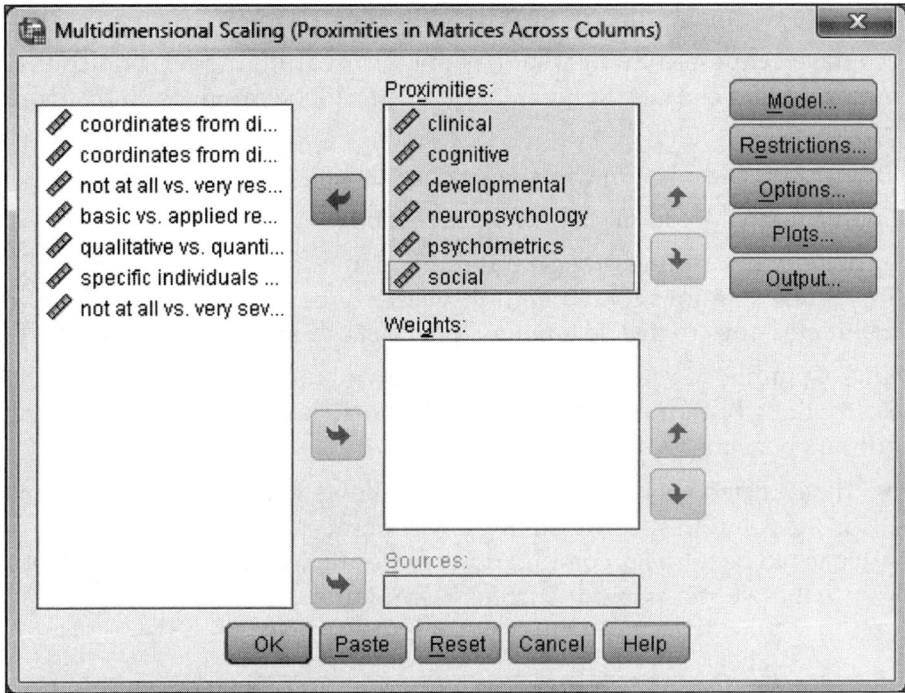

Figure 10-7: Multidimensional Scaling: (Proximities in Matrices Across Columns) dialog

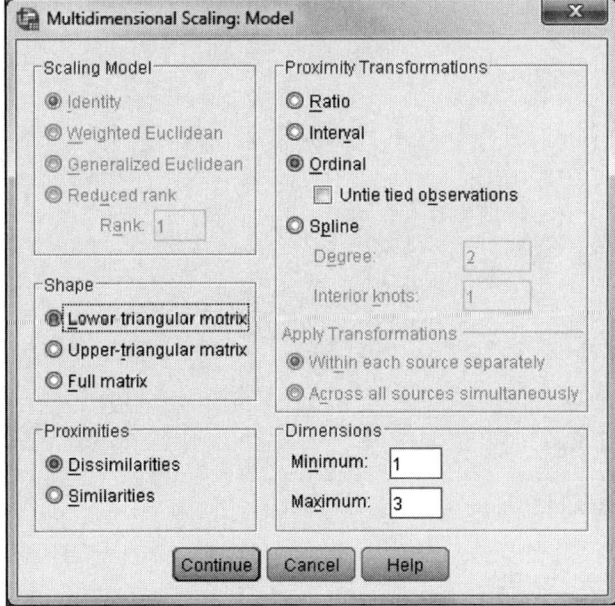

Figure 10-8: Multidimensional Scaling: Model dialog

6. Click the Ordinal button in the Proximity Transformations area.

   We have requested an ordinal (nonmetric) scaling model. Notice that metric scaling choices (Ratio, Interval) are available, along with the more general spline.

7. Enter **1** in the Minimum Dimensions text box.

8. Enter **3** in the Maximum Dimensions text box.

   By default, a two-dimensional multidimensional scaling solution will be fit. We request solutions containing 1 through 3 dimensions and will examine the fit measures to decide among the models, as shown in Figure 10-8.

9. Click Continue to return to the dialog shown in Figure 10-7. Clicking the Restrictions button opens the Restrictions dialog; clicking the Options button opens the Options dialog.

   ■ The Restrictions dialog (Figure 10-9) allows you to enter restrictions on the solution space (by fixing object points or requiring the solution space to be a linear combination of specified variables—we will not use these options in our current example).

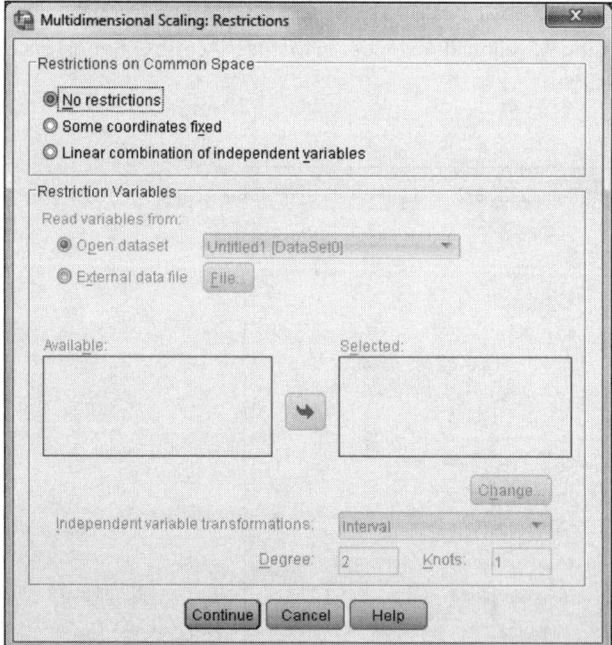

Figure 10-9: Multidimensional Scaling: Restrictions dialog

   ■ The Options dialog (Figure 10-10) controls technical options for the estimation process.

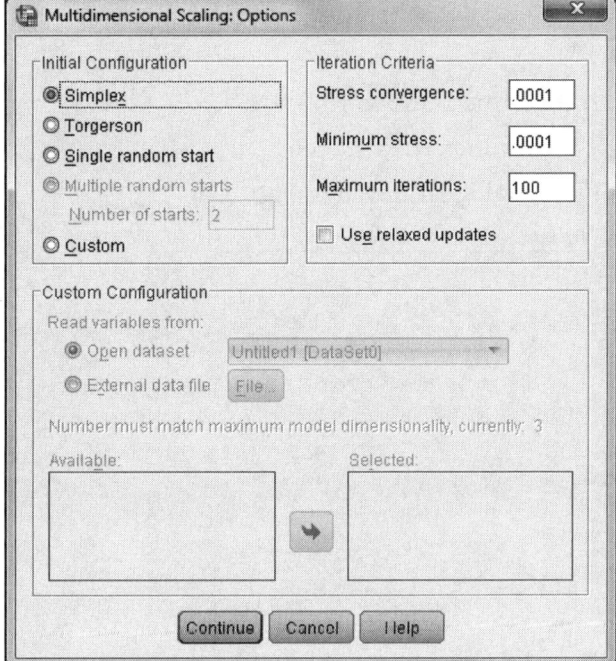

Figure 10-10: Multidimensional Scaling: Options dialog

We will not use any features in the two prior dialogs. Click Continue or Cancel to return to the main Multidimensional Scaling dialog.

10. Click Plots in the Multidimensional Scaling: (Proximities in Matrices Across Columns) dialog (shown in Figure 10-7).

The Plots dialog generates various types of graphs that allow users to determine the adequacy of their solutions. By default, the common space (objects placed in the solution space) will be plotted. The Stress option will produce a plot of stress values (defined a bit later) against the number of dimensions—the scree plot. This choice will only be active when a range of dimensional solutions is requested (as is our current situation). The Original vs. transformed proximities plot choice will graph the original proximities and the transformed (here by an ordinal function, because we chose ordinal in the Model dialog) proximities. This graph provides insight into the nature and effectiveness (when the model is ordinal) of the transformation. The Transformed proximities vs. distances plot provides a visual sense of how well the model reproduces the proximities and identifies exceptions. When multiple data sources (individuals or groups) are analyzed, you can opt to view some of the plots (individual plots and the proximity plots) for only specified data sources.

11. Click the following checkboxes:

    ▪ Stress

    ▪ Original vs. transformed proximities

    ▪ Transformed proximities vs. distances

    The completed Plots dialog is shown in Figure 10-11.

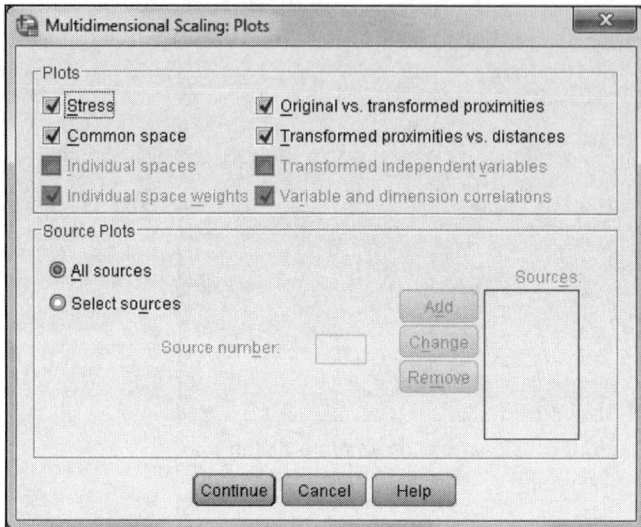

Figure 10-11: Multidimensional Scaling: Plots dialog

12. Click Continue to return to the main Multidimensional Scaling dialog.

13. Click the Output button.

    Additional summaries can be requested in the Output dialog and some of these can be written to an SPSS Statistics data file. If you did not have proximities, you could display the input data, so you can view the calculated proximities on which multidimensional scaling will be run. The Stress decomposition option produces a table that breaks down the stress (lack of fit) into components attributable to each object and group. Here it will provide information about which objects (psychology sub-disciplines), if any, contribute disproportionately to the stress measure (that is, which proximities were not fit as well by the solution). This is useful in identifying sources for a poor fit. The Save to New File box allows you to save important information to different files. For instance, you may want to save the Common space coordinates to later use these to help you statistically interpret the dimensions of the solution (we will do this later).

14. Click the Stress decomposition check box.

    The completed Output dialog is shown in Figure 10-12.

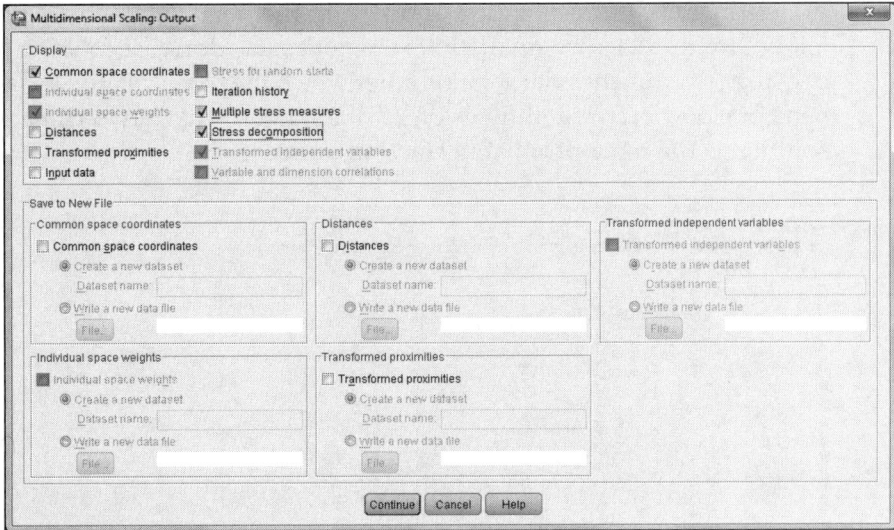

Figure 10-12: Multidimensional Scaling: Output dialog

15. Click Continue to return to the main Multidimensional Scaling dialog.
16. Click OK to run the analysis.

Multidimensional Scaling Output Interpretation

Now let's take a look at the results of the analysis and interpret the results.

1. Scroll down to the Scree Plot.

   The error or lack of fit of a multidimensional scaling model is evaluated by comparing the estimated distances between points in the model space to the transformed proximities. Several variations exist, involving different functions and normalizations, under the general label of stress. They are scaled so that a perfect fit would have a stress value of 0 and the upper bound cannot exceed 1. While smaller values are better, there isn't an agreed-upon cutoff value below which the model fit is regarded as good. Because the stress values typically decrease with increasing dimensionality of the object space, analysts can plot the stress values as a function of the number of dimensions and look for an "elbow" or "bend," representing a point beyond which increasing the dimensionality of the solution results in little improvement of fit. This "scree" plot is also used in factor analysis to investigate the number of factors required to fit a correlation matrix.

   As shown in Figure 10-13, the vertical axis of the scree plot contains the normalized stress values (values closer to 0 indicate better fit), while the dimensionality of the solution appears on the horizontal axis. Although all the stress values are small, there is a noticeable decrease moving from a one- to a two-dimensional solution, after which the plot is relatively flat—the bend or elbow occurs at dimension 2. This suggests that a two-dimensional solution is the most promising starting point.

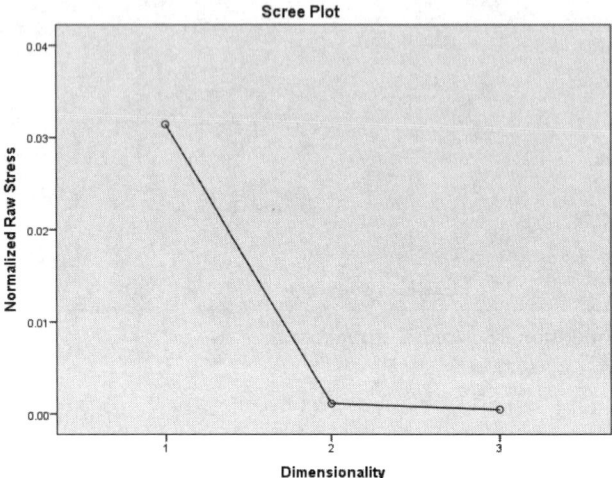

Figure 10-13: Scree plot of normalized raw stress

2. Scroll up to the Stress and Fit Measures pivot table.

Figure 10-14 displays the Stress and Fit Measures pivot table of various measures of model fit. The layer label indicates that these results are for the one-dimensional solution. This is because the solution dimensionality appears in the layer dimension of the pivot table.

Stress and Fit Measures

Dimensionality: 1

Normalized Raw Stress	.03141
Stress-I	.17723[e]
Stress-II	.31120[e]
S-Stress	.05572[f]
Dispersion Accounted For (D.A.F.)	.96859
Tucker's Coefficient of Congruence	.98417

PROXSCAL minimizes Normalized Raw Stress.

e. Optimal scaling factor = 1.032.

f. Optimal scaling factor = .996.

Figure 10-14: Stress and Fit Measures table displaying results for a one-dimensional solution

To examine stress and fit measures for the other solutions, we can either change the layer displayed or move the layer into the column dimension of the pivot table. Either can be easily done within the Pivot Table editor; we will take the latter path.

3. To edit the pivot table, double-click the Stress and Fit Measures pivot table (to invoke the Pivot Table editor).

   If the window of the pivoting trays is not shown, click Pivot ⇨ Pivoting Trays in the Pivoting Trays window.

4. Drag and drop the Dimensionality icon from the Layer below Statistics in the column.

5. Close the Pivot Table editor.

   Figure 10-15 shows the Stress and Fit Measures pivot table of all three solutions. Not surprisingly, because more parameters are fit by the models as the dimensionality of the multidimensional scaling solution increases, the stress measures tend to decrease and the fit measures increase. The greatest changes occur moving from the one- to the two-dimensional solution, which we also saw in the scree plot. When estimating model coefficients, PROXSCAL seeks to minimize the normalized raw stress measure. In any column, each representing a different model, there is considerable variation in values for the different stress measures. This is because they differ in technical aspects (what is used as the norming factor; are differences in distances or in squared distances used; and so on).

Stress and Fit Measures

	Dimensionality		
	1	2	3
Normalized Raw Stress	.03141	.00112	.00046
Stress-I	.17723[e]	.03343[c]	.02153[a]
Stress-II	.31120[e]	.08081[c]	.06600[a]
S-Stress	.05572[f]	.00288[d]	.00095[b]
Dispersion Accounted For (D.A.F.)	.96859	.99888	.99954
Tucker's Coefficient of Congruence	.98417	.99944	.99977

PROXSCAL minimizes Normalized Raw Stress.

 a. Optimal scaling factor = 1.000.

 b. Optimal scaling factor = 1.000.

 c. Optimal scaling factor = 1.001.

 d. Optimal scaling factor = .999.

 e. Optimal scaling factor = 1.032.

 f. Optimal scaling factor = .996.

Figure 10-15: Stress and Fit Measures for three multidimensional scaling solutions

Based on the scree plot and the Stress and Fit Measures table, in the remaining summaries and plots we will focus on the two-dimensional solution. This will involve examining only the two-dimensional solution layer of pivot tables and one of three plots.

So far we have discussed technical measures of fit. Because the purpose of multidimensional scaling is to better understand how the objects (products, brands, companies, and so on) are viewed by the respondents, consideration should be given to how interpretable a solution is. For example, moving from a two-dimensional to a three-dimensional solution may not be justified if the third dimension cannot be meaningfully interpreted. This consideration is also present in factor analysis.

6. Scroll down to the Decomposition of Normalized Raw Stress pivot table shown in Figure 10-16.

Decomposition of Normalized Raw Stress

Dimensionality: 2

		Source	
		SRC_1	Mean
Object	clinical	.0016	.0016
	cognitive	.0015	.0015
	developmental	.0002	.0002
	neuropsychology	.0016	.0016
	psychometrics	.0016	.0016
	social	.0001	.0001
Mean		.0011	.0011

Figure 10-16: Stress decomposition table

Figure 10-16 shows that the objects (here psychology sub-disciplines) are listed in the rows and the different data sources (groups or individuals; here there is a single source) constitute the columns. The mean value across the objects is the normalized raw stress value (.0011) reported in the Stress and Fit Summary table. Examining the stress values for the different sub-disciplines, we find that Developmental and Social psychology have values considerably smaller than the other sub-disciplines. Proximities involving the other sub-disciplines are not modeled as well, and they contribute disproportionately to the normalized raw stress. In practice, knowing which objects or groups are not modeled well can provide some insight into the problem (although in this case the stress values are very low across all objects).

NOTE   If there are many objects, sorting the rows makes it easier to digest this table. Sorting is available in the pivot table editor in recent versions of Statistics by selecting the column, right clicking, and choosing Sort Rows.

7. Scroll down to the Final Coordinates pivot table in the Common Space section.

8. Double-click the Final Coordinates pivot table.

9. Select 2 from the Dimensionality drop-down list (in the Layer area, just above the pivot table).

10. Close the Pivot Table editor.

The Final Coordinates table (Figure 10-17) represents the positioning of the objects (psychology sub-disciplines) in the two-dimensional solution space.

Final Coordinates

Dimensionality: 2

	Dimension	
	1	2
clinical	-.232	-.327
cognitive	.084	-.072
developmental	-.344	.137
neuropsychology	.148	-.595
psychometrics	1.003	.379
social	-.659	.478

Figure 10-17: Coordinates for a two-dimensional solution

Although you can work from this table, most analysts would move to the plot containing these points, shown in Figure 10-18.

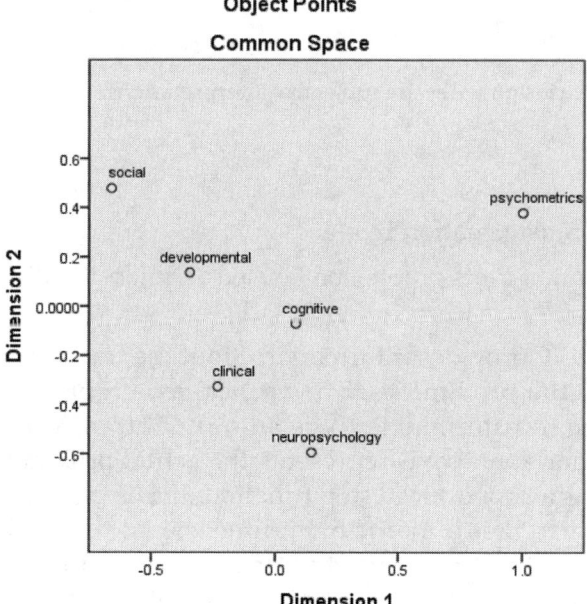

Figure 10-18: Object points plot

11. Click the Objects Points graph icon labeled "Dimensionality 2" in the Outline pane.

Subjective Approach to Dimension Interpretation

The subjective approach to dimension interpretation examines the graphical representation of objects to discover underlying patterns that are based on what one knows about the objects. So basically we have to ask ourselves (based on what we know about the objects) how do these objects differ along each dimension? In this two-dimensional solution, the horizontal axis seems to be a type of data dimension with quantitative sub-disciplines on the right and qualitative sub-disciplines on the left. With regards to the vertical dimension, it might represent either the illness severity typically encountered by psychologists in these different sub-disciplines or alternatively, the generality or specificity of ramifications regarding research in these sub-disciplines. Using the illness severity interpretation, the sub-discipline of social psychology would be viewed as dealing with non-severe illnesses, whereas the sub-discipline of neuropsychology might be thought of as dealing with severely ill populations. Using the ramifications interpretation, the sub-discipline of social psychology would be viewed as having ramifications for society at large, whereas the sub-discipline of neuropsychology might be thought of as having ramifications for specific individuals (we will return to the idea of dimension interpretation in the next section).

NOTE While these can give insight, they are subjective interpretations, not statistical proofs.

1. Scroll down to the Transformation Plot.
2. Click the Transformation Plots graph icon labeled "Dimensionality 2" in the Outline pane.

   The plot in Figure 10-19 provides information about the transformation function applied to the proximities. The vertical axis represents the proximities after the transformation (here an ordinal transformation) is applied, and the horizontal axis represents the actual proximities in the data. The plot has a pronounced step function. If this plot had been smooth and near linear, then a metric multidimensional scaling model could have been used to fit the data. In our case using a nonmetric model for this data was a good choice because this plot is clearly neither smooth nor linear.

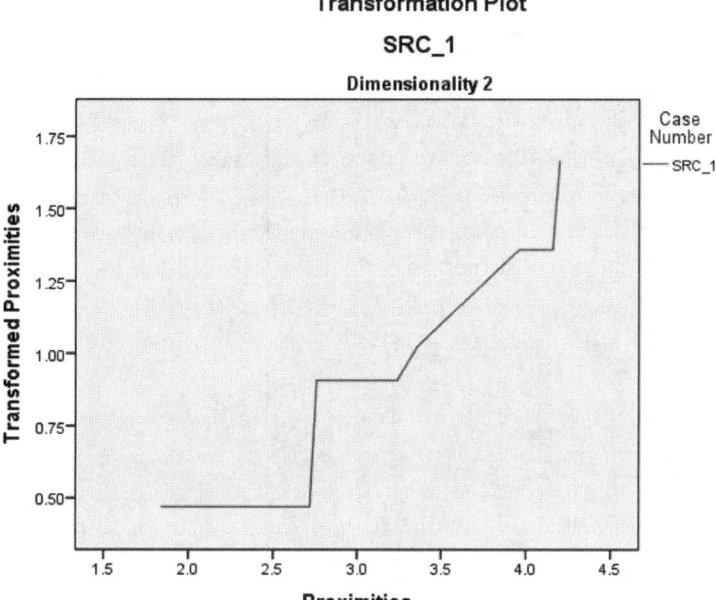

Transformation: matrix conditional, ordinal (ties kept tied).

Figure 10-19: Plot of the actual and transformed proximities (two-dimensional solution)

3. Click the Residuals Plots graph icon labeled "Dimensionality 2" in the Outline pane.

Figure 10-20 displays the model-estimated distances as they relate to the actual proximities (transformed). The points (representing a pairing of sub-disciplines) are tightly clustered around an imaginary 45-degree line. The fact that the points are clustered around this imaginary 45-degree line is consistent with the low stress and high fit measures. Points off the line represent errors by the model (residuals), and points far off the line might be examined in greater detail (that is, what is it about a specific object pairing that might have led to the model failing), just as you would in regression analysis.

> **NOTE**   There is an interesting connection between MDS and TURF analysis. TURF finds bundles of items/objects that maximize the probability that a bundle contains at least one item that consumers like. If you do both TURF and MDS, you would get more insight into the properties of the optimal bundle. With the ice cream data and a three-flavor bundle, TURF picks coconut, rocky road, and vanilla, or butter pecan, coconut, and vanilla (tie), although the top combinations are all very close. With MDS, using the same options as in this example, you see that these flavors are widely separated, which is a major factor in the reach calculation (along with individual popularity).

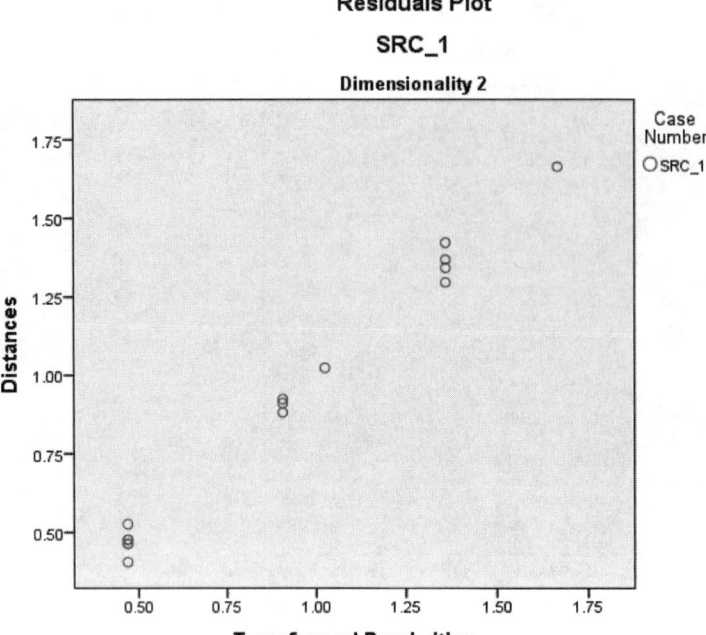

Figure 10-20: Residuals plot of distances

Statistical Approach to Dimension Interpretation

In the previous section we used the subjective approach to dimension interpretation, where we examined the graphical representation of the objects to try to discover underlying patterns. Linear regression or correlations can also be used for dimension interpretation. With this method, data is collected on additional variables that one believes will be related to the position of objects in the configuration (this data can be collected when dissimilarity data was collected or at a later time point). The mean ratings of these additional variables are then used as dependent variables in regression equations, while the coordinates obtained from the configuration are used as predictor variables. Because the coordinates capture the pattern of perceived relatedness among objects, the correlations are measures of how well the coordinates of a dimension fit a possible interpretation, and thus can help confirm or negate interpretations found using the subjective dimension interpretation method.

NOTE The dimension coordinates were obtained by choosing Common Space Coordinates in the Multidimensional Scaling: Output dialog (see Figure 10-12).

NOTE Another approach in some cases would be to do a multigroup MDS.

In our dataset (`psychology.sav`, shown in Figure 10-21) we have the coordinates for each psychology sub-discipline on each dimension, as well as the aggregated means on the following variables: research orientation (that is, not at all research oriented vs. very research oriented), type of research (basic research vs. applied research), type of data collected (qualitative vs. quantitative), ramifications for research (specific individuals vs. society at large), and severity of illnesses ordinarily encountered (not at all severe vs. very severe).

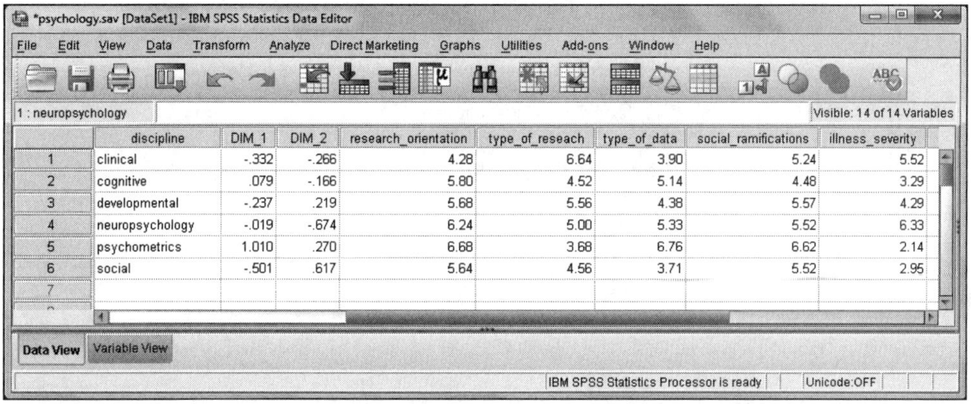

	discipline	DIM_1	DIM_2	research_orientation	type_of_reseach	type_of_data	social_ramifications	illness_severity
1	clinical	-.332	-.266	4.28	6.64	3.90	5.24	5.52
2	cognitive	.079	-.166	5.80	4.52	5.14	4.48	3.29
3	developmental	-.237	.219	5.68	5.56	4.38	5.57	4.29
4	neuropsychology	-.019	-.674	6.24	5.00	5.33	5.52	6.33
5	psychometrics	1.010	.270	6.68	3.68	6.76	6.62	2.14
6	social	-.501	.617	5.64	4.56	3.71	5.52	2.95
7								

Figure 10-21: Dimension coordinates and aggregated mean rating on additional scales

NOTE **I had previously hypothesized what the dimensions might represent; therefore, I collected additional data to try to describe the dimensions.**

To assess the relationship between the dimensions and rating scales, we will perform correlations:

1. Click Analyze ➪ Correlate ➪ Bivariate.
2. Move research_orientation, type_of_research, type_of_data, social_ramifications, illness_severity, dim_1, and dim_2 into the Variables box.

NOTE **To get this view the reader needs to go into the Edit menu, then choose Options ➪ General ➪ Display Names.**

   Because we only care about the correlations between the dimension variables and the rating scale variables, we will use syntax.

3. Click Paste.

   The Paste button opens up the syntax editor, and now we have more options than those available through menus and windows.

4. Type the word **with** between the variables `illness severity` and `dim_1`.

In this situation, as shown in Figure 10-22, the keyword `with` tells SPSS that we should correlate all of the variables to the left (the rating scale variables) of the keyword with all of the variables to the right (the dimension variables) of the keyword.

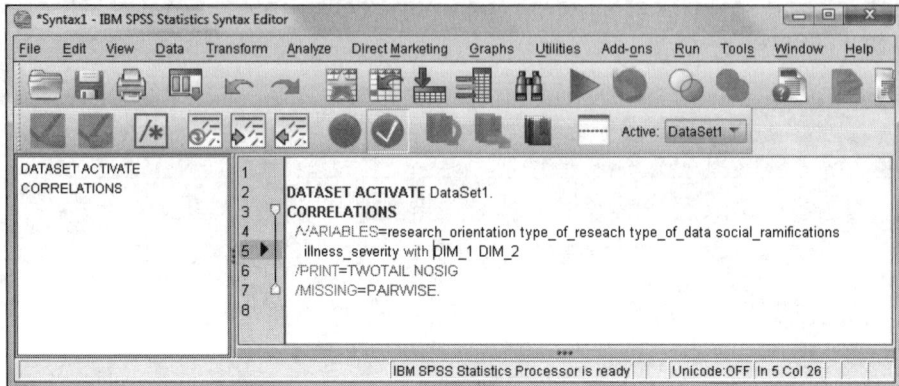

Figure 10-22: Modified correlation procedure syntax

5. Click Run.

6. Scroll down to the Correlations table, shown in Figure 10-23.

Correlations

		coordinates from dimension 1	coordinates from dimension 2
not at all vs. very research oriented	Pearson Correlation	.686	.118
	Sig. (2-tailed)	.132	.823
	N	6	6
basic vs. applied research	Pearson Correlation	-.669	-.369
	Sig. (2-tailed)	.146	.471
	N	6	6
qualitative vs. quantitative	Pearson Correlation	.969**	-.158
	Sig. (2-tailed)	.001	.765
	N	6	6
specific individuals vs. society at large	Pearson Correlation	.600	.352
	Sig. (2-tailed)	.208	.494
	N	6	6
not at all vs. very severe	Pearson Correlation	-.471	-.800
	Sig. (2-tailed)	.346	.056
	N	6	6

**. Correlation is significant at the 0.01 level (2-tailed).

Figure 10-23: Correlations between dimensions and aggregated mean rating scales

The results suggest that for the first dimension, the variable type of data ($r = .969$) better explained this dimension than any of the other variables. For the second dimension, the variable illness severity ($r = -.800$) better accounted for the variation. This statistical technique confirmed the results obtained through the subjective interpretation approach, as well as eliminated possible additional interpretations.

Predictive Analytics

Predictive analytics is a big topic, but a timely one. Virtually all of us who are statistically inclined need some techniques borrowed from our Computer Science, Knowledge Discovery, and Machine Learning colleagues in our predictive analytics toolkit. But that doesn't mean that we need a dedicated tool to do predictive analytics. Dedicated data mining tools like SPSS Modeler are extremely powerful, and they have their place and advantages, but there is much that can be done right in SPSS Statistics. This five-chapter part advances one of the motivating themes of the entire book: *What features of SPSS Statistics constitute untapped resources that can potentially transform the way we use SPSS Statistics?* Specifically, in this part of the book you learn how SPSS Statistics can be used to do data mining. While not absolutely everyone needs the techniques in Part III, an increasingly large proportion of analysts do. Machine learning is mainstream in a way that it wasn't even 10 years ago. Familiarity is wise even if one's day to day statistics work is more traditional.

We don't always have the benefit of a hypothesis. What are we to do when we have a research question, but we don't have a hypothesis? For instance, what if we simply want to know who among our customers are most likely to respond to a particular marketing campaign? They are *our* customers, after all. So we have more information about them than anyone else does. We certainly have some basis for answering the question, but we might be without hypotheses. There is no literature to tap into. We are likely lacking any resources outside of our organization for hypotheses. More importantly, it would be irresponsible to let hunches, even when we have them, influence our behavior when a surprising result is often the most powerful result we can get. Why would we narrow our independent variables down to those based purely on a hunch, *a priori*? We might not guess which are the best variables? It would seem we are in a bit of a bind. It would be inappropriate to throw *out* variables *a priori* with no basis for doing so, yet isn't it also inappropriate to throw all of our potential variables available *in*?

The job of Chapter 11 is to make this argument more thoroughly. Another goal for Chapter 11 is to explore data mining, and to begin the process of explaining the core skills that are necessary to do it well. Toward that end we will demonstrate some features of SPSS Modeler that are used to perform data mining tasks. It is a bit of fun to see them in action in Modeler, and it is an interesting way to explore the concepts because Modeler is specifically designed to specialize in these tasks. The contrast between the approach in Modeler and the approach we will have to use in SPSS Statistics will sharpen the contrast between data mining and statistics. That will, in turn, assist us in our quest of making the leap to a new way of structuring our analysis, albeit without necessarily switching tools.

In the chapter that follows our discussion of data mining tasks, Chapter 12, we will see two of the four key features of the SPSS Statistics Data Preparation module. The other data mining skills will be spread out among three Modeling chapters—Chapters 13, 14, and 15. Therefore, unless you are quite familiar with data mining already, it will be important to start with Chapter 11. We will explore and demonstrate three of the most popular data mining modeling techniques: neural nets, Decision Trees, and K Nearest Neighbors. The remaining chapters in Part III are dedicated to SPSS Statistics. Along the way, as needed, the data mining skills will be introduced. For example, how to create a hold-out partition is shown in the neural net chapter (13), but that same partition is reused in the chapters on Decision Trees and K Nearest Neighbors (14 and 15).

Naturally, the ideal chapter in which to compare the success of the three techniques is the final one. Therefore, it is in the K Nearest Neighbors chapter that we compare the performance of all of the techniques. In statistics, one chooses a technique in advance, *a priori*, based upon theoretical criterion. In data mining, the empirical, the *a posteriori*, is always the proper route. So it is natural, if not required, that we use multiple approaches and then choose the one that is empirically proven to be the better performer on an unseen dataset. There will be more on this approach in Chapter 11.

The goal of the chapters is consistent with the goals of the book: to expand your horizons a bit. Neither the conclusion that SPSS Modeler is unnecessary, nor the conclusion that it is essential, can be drawn from the chapters that follow. The goal is to:

- Sharpen the contrast between traditional statistics and data mining.
- Explore some of the key concepts in data mining.

- Learn which of the most important data mining tasks are easily done in SPSS Statistics and how to do them.

In This Part

SPSS Statistics versus SPSS Modeler: Can I Be a Data Miner Using SPSS Statistics?

In this chapter, I will attempt to answer three questions:

- What is "data mining," and how is it different from statistics?
- What is the SPSS Modeler data mining workbench?
- Is it possible to perform data mining tasks effectively in SPSS Statistics?

Our discussion focuses on two case studies, which will help us address these questions. One case study has a continuous dependent variable ("target" as Modeler users would call it), and the other has a binary dependent variable. Along the way, we will learn a number of tricks and tips. As you may have guessed, it is indeed possible to do data mining effectively in SPSS Statistics, but it is not always obvious how to perform all of the tasks, or even what the required tasks are.

What Is Data Mining?

My own definition of data mining has evolved slightly over the years, but this one has served me well:

Data mining uses historical data, accumulated during the normal course of doing business, and involves selecting, preparing, and analyzing the data, finding (and confirming) previously unknown patterns, building predictive models, and deploying the models on current data.

Each element of the definition is worth elaborating:

- **Historical data:** Data mining needs data for which the outcome of interest has been achieved. The resulting model is then applied to newer data for which the outcome is currently unknown, but can be predicted.

- **Normal course of business:** In statistics, one often has a hypothesis and then creates an experimental design to capture data capable of testing the hypothesis. Data mining data was captured to run the business, not to perform experiments.

- **Selecting and preparing:** It is often believed that data mining is conducted on all of the data that you have, and that the algorithms automatically search for patterns. This is not true. Data mining is almost always conducted on a much smaller portion of the data. It is not random sampling in the same sense as in a political poll, but it is selecting that portion of the data that is relevant to the business problem.

- **Previously unknown patterns:** Data mining is not about having a hunch, and exploring the data to confirm that hunch. It is also quite different from hypothesis testing, and the contrast between the two gets an entire section in this chapter. It is a systematic search for patterns that can provide value to the business. A search without some valuable surprises would be a disappointment, but it is actually very rare.

- **Models:** A model, usually in the form of a formula like a regression formula, or a set of rules like a Decision Tree, is a systematic way of recoding the patterns so that they can be applied to new data. The ability to apply to new data is the goal, not up or down conclusions about the importance of each variable. Most data mining techniques will give you limited information, or perhaps no information, on overall model significance or the significance of each predictor.

- **Deployment:** We believe that a project that is not deployed is incomplete. The model only provides value if it is inserted into the business process, driving better decisions, and shown to provide a measurable benefit to the business.

What Is IBM SPSS Modeler?

SPSS Modeler, formerly called Clementine, is explicitly described as a "data mining" workbench. What is it, and how is it different from SPSS Statistics? Modeler uses an approach called "visual programming." You essentially draw a flowchart, and the flowchart represents a process that is easily repeated on new data. In Modeler, the flowchart (shown in Figure 11-1) is called a "stream." In this sense, Modeler is much more like working in SPSS syntax than it is like using the menus in SPSS Statistics. The symbols in Modeler are called "nodes," and in the following simple example we explore just three of the many available nodes in Modeler. You learn more about Modeler as the chapter progresses.

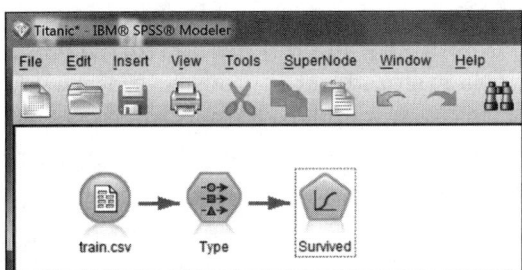

Figure 11-1: An SPSS Modeler "stream"

In this simple Modeler stream you get the idea of how a process would be set up. Files are not opened, per se. Rather, the stream points to the location of the data. The data stays right where it is, and if the file is very large, we can select portions of it and have the large file stay on the server or wherever the file is located. In short, SPSS Modeler is potentially more scalable than SPSS Statistics, but SPSS Statistics can handle a lot itself. How large is large? Most would consider 10s or 100s of millions large, whereas 10,000 or 100,000 or even a million should pose no problem in either package. This is a complex issue, and large scale is a moving target with hardware improving every year. Another advantage of having a "source node" pointing to a file is that there is virtually no tendency to create multiple versions of a data file. Most of us are guilty, in SPSS Statistics, of having filenames like Survey_original, Survey_clean, Survey_Final, Survey_with_new_vars, and so on. The reason we all tend to do this, at least to a degree, is that in SPSS Statistics we save our work by saving our data file. In Modeler, we save the stream. Saving a stream is similar to saving a syntax file, but it is not like saving a data file.

The Type node is much like the variable view. In the Type node we declare the level of measurement, and missing values, for instance. Declaring a role is a bit of an obscure feature in SPSS Statistics, but in Modeler it is terribly important. By declaring our target, which in the Titanic dataset is "survived," our dependent variable and all of our independent variables are set for all appropriate modeling methods. Train.csv and Test.csv are available on the book's website, and have been adopted from the data mining competition on the kaggle.com website. Aside from a different design, there are other reasons why we don't approach it this way in SPSS Statistics. It would be strange to be testing hypotheses and to use multiple algorithms. One uses the correct algorithm given the hypothesis and the data. In data mining, it is natural to use many algorithms and to try multiple settings, and to even consider using the models in combination. We will see combinations of models, usually called "ensembles," later in this chapter in the section "Creating Ensembles."

The Logistic node has the caption Survived because that is the variable that we have declared as our target. We can often run the node without making any further declarations. When we do, a diamond-shaped node appears. That is our model—that is, the resulting formula is stored in this node so that we can very efficiently score new data. Figure 11-2 shows both a diamond shaped gold "nugget" as well as a second source node.

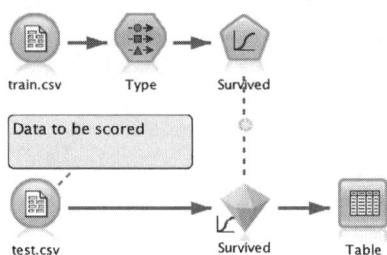

Figure 11-2: Stream with model

Can Data Mining Be Done in SPSS Statistics?

If you have access to the appropriate modules, you can use SPSS Statistics to perform a number of the very same data mining algorithms that are in SPSS Modeler. They aren't all possible, but some of the most important ones are available, including:

- Decision Trees
- Neural nets
- Nearest Neighbor

Decision Trees, neural nets, and Nearest Neighbor each get a dedicated chapter in Part III of this book.

You may already be familiar with Stepwise techniques. Stepwise is available for Linear Regression, Logistic Regression, and Discriminant Analysis. No doubt about it—these are data mining techniques. We will get a sense as to why these are data mining techniques, and how to validate these kinds of models later in this chapter.

In addition to these algorithms, which can help you use predictive analytics to classify future cases, supporting routines help you prepare and explore your data. Both Optimal Binning and Identify Unusual Cases are nearly identical to similar procedures in SPSS Modeler. Chapter 12 explores some of the features of the SPSS Data Preparation module, which is really more focused on data preparation for data mining in many ways than it is focused on data preparation for statistics. As much as we might dread data preparation for statistical analysis, the modest number of independent variables restricts the amount of effort to something manageable. When the number of predictors multiplies, the effort to perform proper data preparation often requires some automation.

HISTORY OF MODELER

Modeler had a completely different corporate and development history before SPSS, Inc. bought the company that created Modeler, then called by its original name, Clementine. In the early '90s a British company, ISL, offered some data mining algorithm software, starting with neural nets and the ID3 Decision Tree algorithm, and suddenly found itself in the consulting business. Colin Shearer headed up the new data mining practice for ISL, and eventually created Clementine to meet an emerging need: "We were finding that data mining projects involved a lot of hard work, and that most of that work was boring. Unearthing significant patterns and delivering accurate predictions...that part was fun. But most of our effort went on mundane tasks such as manipulating data into the formats required by the various modules and algorithms we applied." (From Colin Shearer's forward to the *IBM SPSS Modeler Cookbook*, Packt Publishing, 2013)

Tom Khabaza, a colleague of Colin's at ISL, would eventually coauthor the "Cross Industry Standard Process for Data Mining" (CRISP-DM Consortium, 1999) with Colin and a consortium drawn from a number of major European companies. In his "The Story of Clementine," he explained the inspiration for Clementine's design: "As these projects succeeded one another, it became clear that we were performing the same coding tasks repeatedly; ISL had also been involved in some R&D projects involving visual programming, and it was from these two threads that Clementine was born. Colin Shearer's design for Clementine combined re-useable versions of the modules we had developed for specific projects with a visual programming interface which made it extremely easy to 'plug together' these modules to form a data mining process." (https://www.cs.bham.ac.uk/research/projects/poplog/isl-docs/1999-AISBQ-TheStoryofClementine.pdf)

A critical feature of Modeler is also, perhaps, its sharpest contrast with SPSS Statistics. Shearer: "We made an important design decision that predictive models should have the same status within the visual workflow as other 'tools,' and that their outputs should be treated as first-order data. This sounds like a simple point, but the repercussions are enormous. Want more than the basic analysis of your model's performance? No problem—run its output through any of the tools in the workbench. Curious to know what might be going on inside your neural network? Use rule induction to tell you how combinations of inputs map onto output values. Want to have

Continues

(continued)

multiple models 'vote'? Easy. Want to combine them in more complex ways? Just feed their inputs, along with any data you like, into a 'supermodel' that can decide how best to combine their predictions."

Why is Clementine the success that it is? There are many different answers to this question, but here I give the answer closest to the concerns of the AI researcher. Clementine is a success not because of any particular technical innovation, but because it fits the data mining task better than any previous tool.

Tom Khabaza, The Story of Clementine.

Predictive analytics is not just about the latest algorithms, however. There is a quite different way of thinking through a project when you are data mining. The "Cross Industry Standard Process for Data Mining (CRISP-DM)" is a free, software-neutral, and industry non-specific approach to data mining. We will explore Modeler's approach and SPSS Statistics' approach in parallel. This way we can learn some of the key steps in data mining, get a peek at SPSS Modeler, and see what options SPSS has for some of the same steps.

Hypothesis Testing, Type I Error, and Hold-Out Validation

Classical hypothesis testing is the cornerstone of virtually all statistical analyses. Its role in data mining is quite different, and when statisticians stumble during their first data mining project, difficulty surrounding this topic is often the reason. Table 11-1 provides a quick reminder of how it works, but the Internet is overflowing with videos and discussions of this topic if you need a more thorough review. The motivation of the "review" here is really to contrast it with alternatives. Keep in mind, however, that we won't be doing it this way when we are using data mining techniques; we will be pursuing the alternatives, so you won't need to review this now unless you are haunted by the absence of hypothesis testing while data mining.

Table 11-1: Classical Hypothesis Testing

		IN THE POPULATION	
		NULL HYPOTHESIS IS TRUE	NULL HYPOTHESIS IS FALSE
Conclusion from Hypothesis Test Results	Reject Null Hypothesis (usually significance below .05)	False Positive Type I Error	True Negative
	Accept Null Hypothesis	True Positive	False Negative

The definitions of hypothesis testing that we generally use when we are speaking with other statisticians include phrasing like "rejecting the null hypothesis" or "probability that the null hypothesis is true," but in data mining we have no null hypothesis, and the reliance on probability is highly problematic. We need another way, and we need a broader definition. We need to describe the problem behind the Type I error broadly enough so that it applies to both statistics and data mining. Thankfully, this is easy to do.

In both statistics and data mining, we want to screen out patterns in our sample data that will fail to generalize—that is, patterns that will fail to be found in other datasets in the future. That's really all a Type I error is: a failure to generalize. In statistics we avoid the problem through the combination of parsimony, determining hypotheses prior to performing hypotheses tests, distributional assumptions, and probability. In data mining, we use random selection, and validating our model against one or more additional datasets.

Let's explore an example. Data from the famous Titanic disaster will assist us. Note that the data file in support of this chapter, `Titanic.sav`, represents about one half of the passengers on the ship. If you ever decide to attempt the competition on kaggle.com using this dataset, they have retained the second half of the passenger list as a "Test" dataset. Let's test the hypothesis that the three boarding locations—England, France, and Ireland—each had a different mix of passengers that paid a different fare, and were thus in a different class. If we are right, then survival rates might differ for the three embarkation points. We won't let the speculation get too complex; we just have a hypothesis that fare differs for these three groups so we run an Analysis of Variance (ANOVA) in SPSS, much like the ANOVA example you saw in the previous chapter. And sure enough, the probability calculation indicates that our null hypothesis (that they are the same) is likely false, so we conclude that they are different. Voila. Referring to the ANOVA results, shown in Figure 11-3, the key number of the overall significance (labeled Sig.) is zero to three decimal places, well below .05, indicating statistical significance.

ANOVA

Fare

	Sum of Squares	df	Mean Square	F	Sig.
Between Groups	173858	2	86929	38.140	.000
Within Groups	2.0E+6	886	2279.2		
Total	2.2E+6	888			

Figure 11-3: ANOVA results showing a significant difference

What is the probability that we are wrong about that? What is the probability that we have committed a Type I error? Forgive the review, but this is leading up to an important distinction between statistics and data mining. Either by force of habit or by conscious choice, we usually decide that alpha is .05, so therefore we say that we have a 5% chance of committing a Type I error if the null is true. Is it always true? Let's take it a step further.

To compare Ireland and England, Ireland and France, and finally England and France, we request Post-Hoc tests. That's a lot of tests—and we are just warming up if we are going to mine the whole dataset. Two different methods, Least Square Difference (LSD) and Bonferroni, give us slightly different results. Cherbourg in Normandy, France (C), Queensland in Cork, Ireland (Q), and Southampton in the UK (S) produce six significance tests, although a closer inspection reveals that there is redundancy, and there are really only three different tests for each method. All are shown in Figure 11-4. So what was our risk of Type I? "Experimentwise" our chance of avoiding Type I on three tests was .95 cubed, so our risk of committing Type I was 14.26%. That is our answer for the LSD method. For the Bonferroni method, an adjustment has been made forcing our risk to stay at 5%. We do pay a price, however, because our risk of Type II (false negatives) has gone up. The adjustment is also why we easily come in below .05 with LSD, but nearly miss it on identical data, with the Bonferroni. In short, there is no free lunch. This simple little example is more complicated than it seems.

Post Hoc Tests

Multiple Comparisons

Dependent Variable: Fare

	(I) Embarked_C ode	(J) Embarked_C ode	Mean Differen ce (I–J)	Std. Error	Sig.	95% Confidence Interval Lower Bound	Upper Bound
LSD	C	Q	46.678*	6.5701	.000	33.783	59.573
		S	32.874*	4.1359	.000	24.757	40.992
	Q	C	−46.68*	6.5701	.000	−59.573	−33.783
		S	−13.80*	5.7566	.017	−25.102	−2.5055
	S	C	−32.87*	4.1359	.000	−40.992	−24.757
		Q	13.804*	5.7566	.017	2.5055	25.102
Bonferroni	C	Q	46.678*	6.5701	.000	30.919	62.437
		S	32.874*	4.1359	.000	22.954	42.794
	Q	C	−46.68*	6.5701	.000	−62.437	−30.919
		S	−13.804	5.7566	.050	−27.611	.003735
	S	C	−32.87*	4.1359	.000	−42.794	−22.954
		Q	13.804	5.7566	.050	−.00373	27.611

*. The mean difference is significant at the 0.05 level.

Figure 11-4: Post hoc results table showing a variety of test results

The real problem is that the number of variables and the number of categories across the collection of categorical variables will almost always be greater than these kinds of adjustments can handle. Note the Decision Tree, which we study in greater detail in Chapter 14, and shown in Figure 11-5. Seven variables were considered of which four were chosen, but each has subcategories or "bins." This approach also uses a Bonferonni adjustment, but it is still a struggle to find the right balance between Type I and Type II concerns. Many approaches, including many of the best ones, have abandoned probability-based tests altogether.

Their better performance is not a coincidence. The use of legacy techniques that have been redesigned to do something very different is a burden to these more traditional techniques. Hypothesis testing was never designed to handle a large volume of concurrent tests.

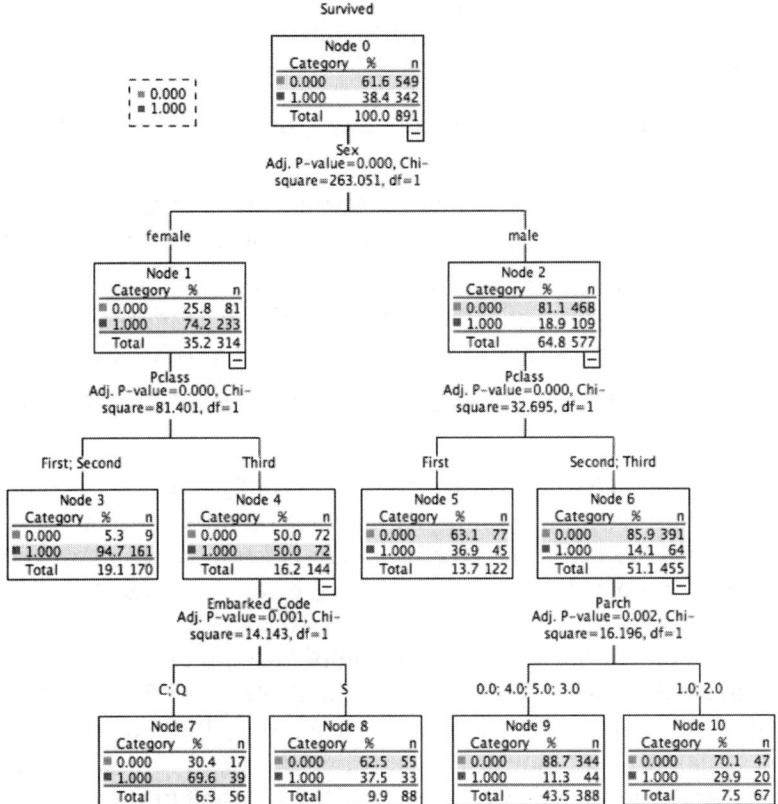

Figure 11-5: A Decision Tree

Further, the large sample sizes we often see in data mining make Type I a near certainty. Why? As sample size goes up, a smaller and smaller effect size will still allow the tests of significance to come in below .05. Fisherian-style hypothesis testing simply cannot be trusted under these circumstances. Its misuse will guarantee what we are trying to avoid—a failure to generalize. While some techniques use aspects of this approach (like Stepwise and CHAID), you absolutely must have an alternative method of avoiding Type I. The data miner's solution, which we discuss in the "Classic and Important Data Mining Tasks" section later in this chapter, is a hold-out sample. Modeler automates this process and makes it very simple using a Partition node.

Significance of the Model and Importance of Each Independent Variable

Those of us who are classically trained look for a number of things in a technique, and when they are absent it can be, at first, a little disappointing. One could differ slightly on the details, but I usually identify four things that statisticians expect to find in a modeling technique:

- **Omnibus test:** A test of the entire model that reports whether the model is significant

- **Goodness of fit:** Some measure that helps determine that the model fits the data well or poorly. R Squared is a famous one, but there are many others.

- **Effect size:** Determined for each and every variable, including interactions when they are tested. For example, the standardized beta in regression can be used to compare the importance of each variable to the other variables.

- **Significance test:** Performed for each and every variable, including interactions

I found that the adjustment to data mining took a substantial amount of time and reflection. A common reaction, but a potentially dangerous one, is to seek out those techniques that are most like what we already know, that have all of the features just listed. The problem with this is that it is too limiting. Stepwise Binary Logistic Regression looks and feels like a statistical technique, but that doesn't make it the right tool for every data mining project. Stepwise is potentially an issue, which we discuss in the "A Caution About 'Stepwise' Techniques" sidebar later in this chapter. I would caution against avoiding those techniques that do not resemble classical techniques. Data mining requires a diverse toolkit because you never know a priori what you are up against. Don't limit yourself. One doesn't need 100 algorithms, but don't limit yourself only to algorithms that report p values, and the other features. Many data mining techniques will be missing some or even all of these four features.

The Importance of Finding and Modeling Interactions

Interactions will be an important theme for us, which will get the most attention in the neural net case study. The way that a data miner deals with interactions is quite different from the way that a statistician deals with interactions. For the statistician, interactions must be formally tested. If they are not formally tested, and this is where even the experienced often err by failing to take steps to include them, they are assumed to be absent. More accurately, they are *forced* to be absent.

Consider the example shown in Figure 11-6. The male employees (the diamonds) and the female employees (the stars) have quite different patterns.

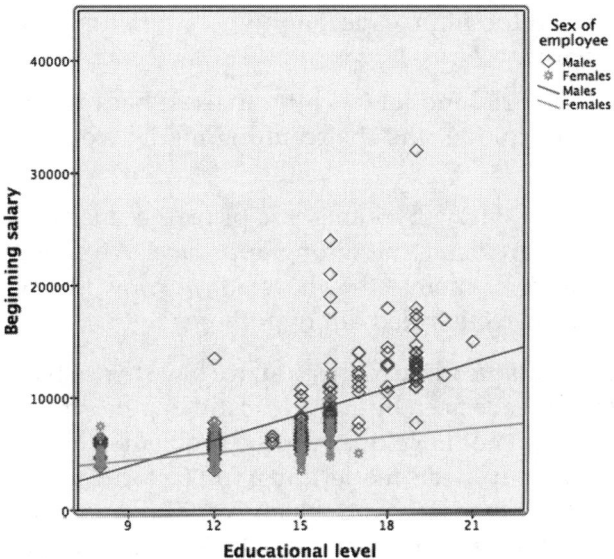

Figure 11-6: Two very different slopes

Obviously, it is striking that the males uniformly earn more. The males with higher education earn more than males without higher education. Females with the highest levels of education seem to be almost entirely absent. Striking, also, is the difference in slopes. There is little difference between the salaries of females at 16 years of education as opposed to those with less than 12. (This dataset, Bank.sav, which is provided on the book website, shows a salary bias that, although from many years ago, clearly shows a very distinct interaction.)

Consider the following regression formula:

$$Y = B0 + B1(\text{Education}) + B2(\text{Sex}) + \text{Error}$$

Unless an interaction term is formally added, the slopes will be forced to be equal, and the resulting lines would be forced to be parallel. The only way to avoid this is to test the interaction by adding an additional coefficient, which requires the creation of a new variable:

$$Y = B0 + B1(\text{Education}) + B2(\text{Sex}) + B3(\text{Education} * \text{Sex}) + \text{Error}$$

So, what is the big deal? This seems to be Regression 101. Perhaps. The issue is that in data mining we are at an impasse. This seemingly trivial issue turns out not to be trivial at all. If we don't have a hypothesis, and in data mining we do not, and should not, and cannot, we can't explicitly test all possible interactions because we could easily find ourselves testing thousands of possible interactions. A hundred variables, which is a modest number, would have

100 * 99/2 two-way interactions, and higher-order interactions might also occur. So the impasse takes the following form:

1. We cannot rely on a main effects model (no interactions) because the risk of some interactions is much too high, especially when the number of independent variables is large.

2. We cannot rely on a full factorial model (all interactions) because the number of variables would explode, and the resulting model would be highly flawed and unstable.

3. We have no option of formally stating hypotheses, a priori, because if we are in a position to do so we are using the wrong approach. We should not be data mining. If we were to attempt this, how do we know that we have correctly ruled in and correctly ruled out hypotheses?

So even if we use traditional techniques, like regression, we have to use them in a different way. Techniques that have been built specifically to perform this kind of analysis, like neural nets, do not have this specific problem—they do not require this choice between a main effects model and a full factorial model. As we shall see, there simply is no way of making the choice. The model will converge on a solution that takes the data into account, whether the variables interact or not, or are linear or not. Neural nets are not without shortcomings, however. What we lose, and some may consider this a high price, is an explicit significance value for the interactions. Some techniques will reveal the patterns more explicitly than others, but we will generally lose something as specific as the significance of B3—the coefficient associated with the Education * Sex Interaction.

A CAUTION ABOUT "STEPWISE" TECHNIQUES

Few technical topics provoke the ire that Stepwise does in discussion groups on the Internet. One might think that the topics were politics or religion. It is not our purpose in this section to fuel the debate, but weigh the logic at your leisure, and you will probably conclude that the critics have the stronger hand. These approaches are common enough that we will not outline their logic, nor the debate around them in this chapter. They are still in common use, and we, the authors, use them ourselves, although we usually do not use the results in the final deployed model directly, and they are usually more useful for exploration. What is not, or should not, be in debate is that Stepwise Regression, Stepwise Logistic Regression, and Stepwise Discriminant Analysis are data mining techniques. As such, they are mentioned in this chapter to ensure that if you do use them, you take advantage of the appropriate procedures, as outlined in the next section. In particular, all Stepwise models should be validated

Continues

(continued)

with a hold-out sample. In fairness, it can be argued that it is a bit of a false dichotomy because there are newer techniques that are superior to stepwise, including L1 and L2 shrinkage methods. Our goal at the moment, however, is to continue to contrast statistics with data mining.

Setting aside the quality of the stepwise approach and the resulting quality of the models, it is simply fact that these are not confirmatory techniques. Type I error risk is elevated by the very nature of these techniques, so partitioning and validation when using these techniques are a requirement. The Selection Variable approach, which will be demonstrated, will go a long way toward combating the elevated Type I risk. Also, like all data mining techniques, you will assess their appropriateness to the data empirically, not theoretically, so it will be natural to try them right along with other techniques. Comparing models, even something more elaborate like an ensemble, and all of the other procedures in the next section, apply to Stepwise as much as techniques like neural nets. Without getting carried away too much with procedural speculation, one could imagine using a Decision Tree to pare down the number of independents, and then follow up with a logistic regression using only the utilized variables. The need for stepwise selection goes away, but one still gets to deploy a logistic regression solution. There are as many ways to combine techniques like this as there are data mining projects.

Classic and Important Data Mining Tasks

In this section we discuss some features that are unique to data mining, and quite different from statistics. All of them are easily done in Modeler with features specifically designed for that purpose. In SPSS Statistics, they are always more hidden, and sometimes absent. Generally, though, you can do a pretty thorough job. You will just need the coaching from this chapter, a little persistence, a willingness to live without some shortcuts, and a willingness to consider forgoing with some niceties altogether. As Table 11-2 shows, this chapter explains the concepts and shows short demonstrations in Modeler. In the following four chapters we learn how to perform several equivalent (or near equivalent) operations in SPSS Statistics. The goal is to use the SPSS Modeler demonstrations to clarify the concepts, delaying our procedural walkthrough in SPSS Statistics until after we have gotten the big picture. It will also be a great opportunity to satisfy, briefly, the curiosity that any SPSS Statistics user would have about the sibling product and how it differs.

Table 11-2: Common Data Mining Procedures in SPSS Statistics and SPSS Modeler

PROCEDURE	PROCESS IN SPSS MODELER	PROCESS IN SPSS STATISTICS	DEMONSTRATED IN SPSS MODELER?	DEMONSTRATED IN SPSS STATISTICS?
Anomaly Detection	Anomaly Node	Data Prep Module	No	Chapter 12
Optimal Binning	Binning Node	Data Prep Module	No	Chapter 12
Partitioning	Partition Node	Selection Variable	Current Chapter	Chapter 13
Selecting Inputs	Feature Selection Node	Data Prep Module	Current Chapter	No
Balancing	Balance Node	Would be difficult	Current Chapter	No
Comparing Results	Analysis Node	Requires Syntax	Current Chapter	Chapter 15
Creating Ensembles	Ensemble Node	Requires Syntax	Current Chapter	Chapter 15
Scoring New Records	Model "Nugget"	Scoring Wizard	Current Chapter	Chapter 14

Partitioning and Validating

When we build a model, how can we be sure that it will generalize to new datasets? In data mining, we take what I believe to be the most obvious possible action—we use a second dataset. To accomplish this we divide our original data into two portions. In the first portion, called the Train dataset, we allow our modeling algorithms to explore patterns. In the second portion, called our Test dataset, we verify that our model generalizes. It really couldn't be simpler.

This actually raises the question, prompting us to remind ourselves, what action are we taking when we try to prevent the same problem while doing statistics? It is not a simple process at all. As routine users of statistical techniques, we've learned it, but usually don't have to compare it side by side with hold-out validation. We've explored this already in our discussion of Type I error, but essentially what we are doing is comparing our results to a probabilistic proxy of additional datasets—really a kind of fictional collection of datasets—using distributional assumptions. This is why meeting distributional assumptions is so important while using this approach. The material in Chapter 2 will also help in exploring this because those techniques represent a third way of addressing this issue. One can summarize the three approaches in the following way:

1. Hold-Out Validation uses random assignment to produce an actual second "Test" dataset.

2. Traditional Hypothesis Testing uses distributional assumptions as a proxy for a second Test dataset, in a more accurate sense a proxy for a whole collection of datasets.

3. Bootstrapping and Monte Carlo Simulation use random numbers to generate numerous datasets for comparison using the same data from the original dataset. The collection of datasets allows for distributions of virtually any statistic to be created.

SPSS Modeler makes Hold-Out Validation very simple indeed. Let's consider the first case study dataset, the famous Titanic dataset. Recall that our sample size is smaller than the number of passengers on the fateful night.

We've already learned a little bit about SPSS Modeler in the very beginning of the chapter. Now, let's zoom back, literally, and see a small little stream, Figure 11-7, sitting in the "canvas" of the entire interface. Modeler is composed of that full Tcanvas area, shown in Figure 11-8, dominating the image in size: a toolbar and menus, a set of "palettes" down at the bottom filled with collections of "nodes," and some areas to the right where we organize our work product. The details are not going to be important to us because our goal is to review the key tasks, while making note that SPSS Modeler has dedicated menus, specifically designed to perform these tasks. Once we better understand the tasks, we will learn how to mimic them in SPSS Statistics.

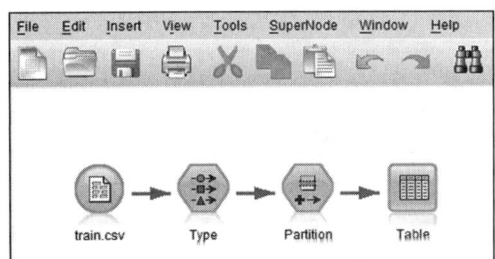

Figure 11-7: A closer look at the stream

Let's take a closer look at the stream. We've seen a node like the circular source node, labeled "train.csv," before. It indicates where our data is, but it does not open the data in the sense that we open it in SPSS Statistics, so the table that we will examine shortly is essentially a print screen of our data allowing us to see it. The Partition node is our focus at the moment, and we see an interface in Figure 11-9 dedicated to this one task. In fact, just click OK and you will get a reasonable result.

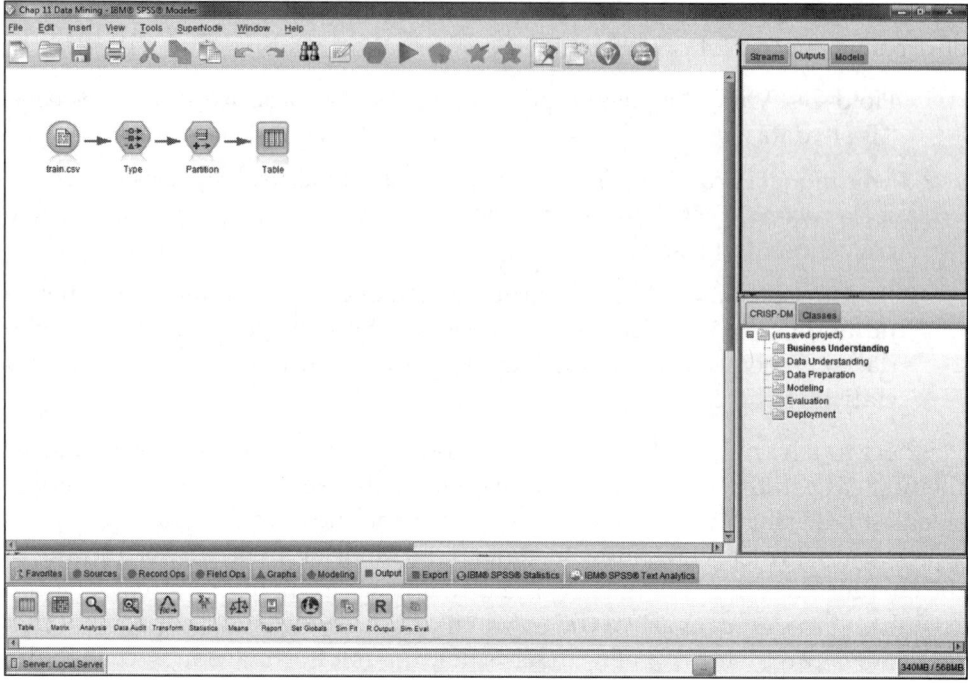

Figure 11-8: A stream shown on the full canvas area

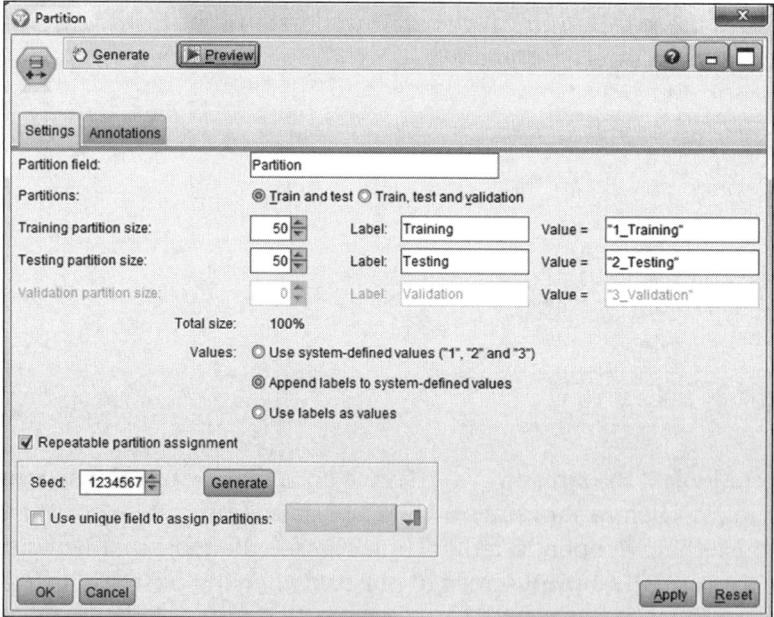

Figure 11-9: Partition node settings

Most Modeler nodes are dedicated to very specific tasks with reasonable defaults, so connecting them in their proper place is sometimes all you have to do. This case uses the widely adopted strategy of assigning half of our data to the "train" dataset to build our model, and half of our "test" dataset is used to verify that our model generalizes effectively to unseen data. What is impressive is not just that we don't have to give this node any instruction, but that we don't have to give the Modeling nodes or the evaluation nodes any instruction either. In most situations all of the "downstream" nodes will behave quite appropriately on defaults, and we don't have to take any action to make explicit what we want done with the partitions.

Creating two random halves of our data is an easy matter in SPSS Statistics, but the complete process takes more work in SPSS Statistics because the rest of the interface does not automatically recognize what we want done with the partitions. Briefly, what we need is to have the modeling algorithms ignore the test data, but the evaluation nodes to use both datasets, and report them separately. It will all be automatic. If we look at the data, we see that for now it has flagged each case as belonging to one group or the other. As shown in Figure 11-10, the data, which shows just 10 passengers and just a portion of the variables, shows that 7 out of the first 10 have been assigned the Training partition. This new variable, created by the data passing through the Partition node, will communicate that status to other nodes that will eventually be added to the stream.

Survived	Pclass	Name	Sex	Age	Partition
0	3	Braund, Mr. Owen Harris	male	22	1_Training
1	1	Cumings, Mrs. John Bradley (Florence Briggs Thayer)	female	38	1_Training
1	3	Heikkinen, Miss. Laina	female	26	2_Testing
1	1	Futrelle, Mrs. Jacques Heath (Lily May Peel)	female	35	2_Testing
0	3	Allen, Mr. William Henry	male	35	1_Training
0	3	Moran, Mr. James	male	$null$	1_Training
0	1	McCarthy, Mr. Timothy J	male	54	2_Testing
0	3	Palsson, Master. Gosta Leonard	male	2	1_Training
1	3	Johnson, Mrs. Oscar W (Elisabeth Vilhelmina Berg)	female	27	1_Training
1	2	Nasser, Mrs. Nicholas (Adele Achem)	female	14	1_Training

Figure 11-10: Result set

Feature Selection

In statistics, the issue of feature selection, the section of input variables (independent variables) takes on a completely different form. Because we would typically be testing hypotheses when doing statistics, the choice of which variables to include among our independent variables is based upon our theory, our literature review, and our research design. While most analysts, when pressed, will admit that they have added or dropped variables in their models during the modeling process after having examined the data, we all recognize it to be a dangerous practice. It, deservedly, would be described as a kind of fishing. Taken to the extreme, some researchers, behind closed doors, will manually perform a kind of "best subsets" approach, trying the combination of independent variables every which way until they optimize the model. This is dangerous, and does not resemble the correct approach.

When data mining, the trick is to try all of the reasonable variables systematically, and verify the model against the test partition. The catch is that "all of the variables" might be hundreds, or even more. For some algorithms we need to narrow it down, but cannot do so on a hunch, and cannot do it based on hypotheses. So we must narrow it down, but empirically, based on strength of the relationship with the target and with data quality. SPSS Modeler provides a way to do just this, the Feature Selection node, shown incorporated into the stream in Figure 11-11. It should be used with caution for the following two reasons. One, strength is measured using bivariate pairs, which runs the risk of missing interactions. Two, data quality does not assess which variables can be repaired and which variables should be dropped. Which algorithms need this preprocessing step more than others is a big topic, and beyond the scope of this discussion. One can summarize, however, by simply stating that some algorithms are quite content to accept hundreds of variables and choose which variables it needs. Keep in mind, however, that data quality affects virtually all techniques, although some techniques are more sensitive to this than others. Simple examples include when all the data is null or blank. Another is when a categorical variable has only one value. We will limit the discussion to what, and how, the Feature Selection node does.

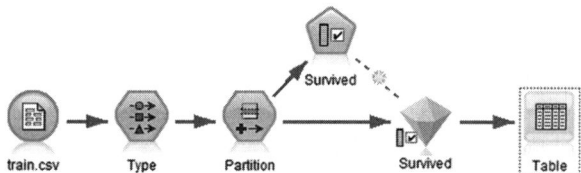

Figure 11-11: Feature Selection node and model added to stream

A pentagon-shaped node with the caption Survived is visible in the stream as well as a diamond-shaped node with the same caption. The pentagon node is the modeling node, with settings and menus inside, and its operation created the gold colored diamond (sometimes called a "nugget" as in gold mining). Inside the diamond (seen by editing the node) we get some insight into what it is trying to do. The results, Figure 11-12, show that none of the variables had enough data quality issues to be screened: "0 Screened fields." The mistake that some rookies make is to give up on these variables too quickly. Better data cleaning might allow such screened fields to be rescued. For example, in many instances a null value is known to really be a zero value. This is very common when converting transactional data to customer-level data. One might think that if you have hundreds there is no urgency in fixing fields with problems. This would be a mistake. Every variable deserves the possibility of inclusion until you have actual evidence that it should be left out. In general, you can summarize the difference between choosing variables in statistics and choosing variables in data mining in the following way: In statistics we include only when we have evidence to include, and in data mining we include until we have evidence to exclude.

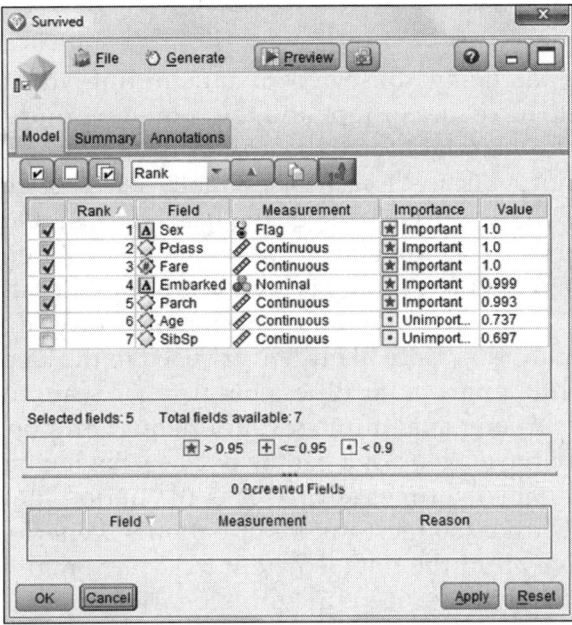

Figure 11-12: 0 screened fields

We also discover that Sex is the best predictor, and that seems in keeping with what we know about this famous accident, but normally we would treat this ranking with some skepticism because it is based on bivariate relationships. The real magic happens when we model the multivariate relationships. We start with bivariate because it is scalable, less complicated, and expedient. It is not without risks. We know that interactions are critical in this kind of modeling. Finally, Age and SibSp, which is the number of siblings and spouses traveling with the passenger, are deemed "unimportant," so Modeler automatically dropped them. With a large dataset—certainly larger than 7 inputs—this feature must be necessary to produce good modeling performance downstream. Unfortunately, how much of this is necessary is so algorithm specific that it is very difficult indeed to provide good guidelines. One can say that one or two dozen inputs is rarely a problem for any technique that is useful in data mining. Some can handle one hundred well, but above one hundred I would certainly consider the possibility of feature selection. Techniques like Factor Analysis potentially play a role. It is a challenging phase of the data mining process. SPSS Statistics Base is capable of all of the discrete functions that this node performs, but doing it using Base would be labor intensive. The Data Preparation module has features that would be very similar. Chapter 12 looks into two features of the module, but does not include a discussion of the equivalent operations of this particular node.

Balancing

Sometimes, when encountering balancing, those new to data mining find it somewhat artificial. The idea is to force rare groups and the common groups to be equally sized. For instance, one might force the group that gets heart disease and the group that does not get heart disease to be equally sized before using an algorithm to try to find the key drivers of getting heart disease. On reflection, however, this is something we constantly do in statistics. When doing this in preparation of data collection, we call it "oversampling." Recall that equally sized groups are desirable in ANOVA because it makes meeting the homogeneity of variance assumption more likely. We are used to the idea of recruiting a lot of patients with a particular illness because we want to understand them, and then recruit an equal number (but unequal proportion of the general population) of those who don't get the disease. Balancing isn't that different. The aspect that sometimes surprises is the notion that some data is being discarded. Unlike the recruitment of patients scenario, in data mining, we usually have all of the data, so we would have many more patients without the disease than we need. In both scenarios we do it because it works—the algorithms do a better job if we prepare the data in this way. And we will know if it does a better job because we will verify its efficacy on the test dataset, which will not be balanced.

SPSS Modeler has a dedicated node just for this purpose. A Distribution of the target variable Survived shows that of this sample of the passengers (just half of the ship) about 1/3 survived. A Distribution is much like a Frequencies report combined with a bar chart. By using the Generate menu, Modeler automatically calculates the proportion of the larger group (those that died) to retain at random. By discarding some, and creating roughly equally sized groups, virtually all algorithms have the possibility of performing better. It is difficult to predict in advance, so like most all data mining decisions, it should be determined empirically. However, few data miners would balance this dataset because it is not sufficiently out of balance. How extreme an out-of-balance condition would cause a problem? A ratio of 70/30 or 80/20 might prompt action. Few would ignore a situation at 90/10. Again, it is best to try it both ways. The Distribution node results shown in Figure 11-13 indicated 61.62% and 38.38%. An additional logistical challenge is the requirement that a valid test of our model requires that the test be performed on unbalanced data. Modeler does this downstream automatically, and makes it easy.

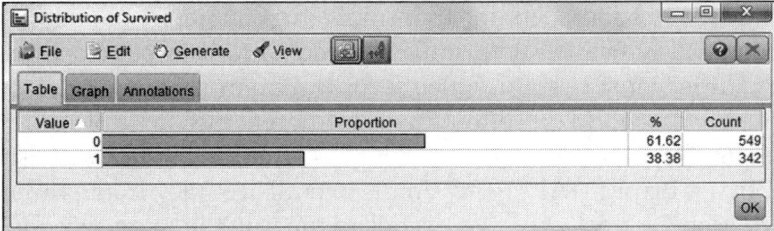

Figure 11-13: Distribution node results

In this case, if balancing were required, SPSS Modeler would give each survivor a 62.3% chance of being retained. What would make this very challenging in SPSS Statistics would not be the random sampling. The challenge would be balancing the train dataset, but not balancing the test dataset: having the modeling algorithms use balanced data, and having the evaluation nodes automatically know to ignore any balancing. SPSS Modeler makes it comparatively easy. If you use the Generate menu, it does the math for you, resulting in the Balance node shown in Figure 11-14.

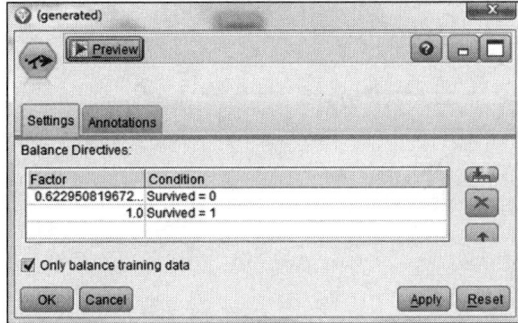

Figure 11-14: Generated Balance node calculation

Comparing Results from Multiple Models

Comparing model results is possible in SPSS Statistics, but it is largely accomplished by comparing the results, by eye, in the output window. Frankly, I've never seen it as a shortcoming because I typically use only one technique when doing statistics, the recommended one for the situation at hand. In fact, if we are really playing by the rules, we should use just a selection of settings, and one set of independent variables. Data mining is very different, however. I'm so accustomed to the Analysis node in Modeler, that I might find comparing neural net results to Decision Tree results in the output window a little clumsy and frustrating. However, there is no reason that it can't be done.

The approach that I have adopted for the three modeling chapters (Chapters 13, 14, and 15) is to come out with an easy formula that can allow easy comparison. Two analysts could differ considerably on their favorite measure of model performance, and in the statistics world one often chooses different measures of model fit for each technique. We will be focused on comparison, however, so I will use Mean Absolute Percent Error (MAPE) and simple overall accuracy in the three modeling chapters. Modeler primarily uses overall accuracy in the Analysis node. I'm not trying to argue that MAPE is ideal, but rather that it is possible to compare models in SPSS Statistics. You may choose to use a different formula.

At this point in our discussion, we will want to explore how SPSS Modeler compares models. The Analysis node is easily demonstrated as we shall see. Although the Feature Selection node is not really necessary—with only 7 original inputs—it has been kept in place to show how a stream grows over the course of an analysis. The current stream, with some additions, is shown in Figure 11-15. It actually prevents the two weakest variables from being considered: the two that were deemed "unimportant" by the Feature Selection algorithm.

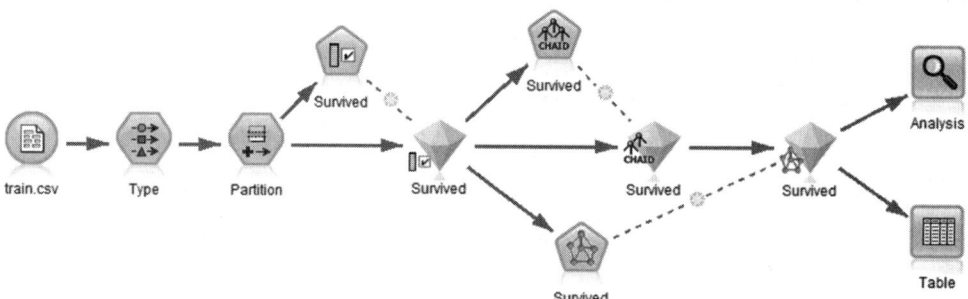

Figure 11-15: Stream with two models added

The CHAID nugget and the neural net nugget (second and third from left after the feature selection nugget, which is the first nugget from left to right) are essentially in competition with each other. The second one in no way benefits from the prediction of the first one. They simply both make predictions, which are processed downstream. In this case, the Analysis node is the key. It is the job of this node to automatically take into account information passed to it down the stream from the Partition node, the CHAID nugget, and the neural net nugget.

What is perhaps most impressive about the Analysis node's report (shown in Figure 11-16) is that it was run purely on defaults. No instruction had to be given except to drag it into place downstream of the other nodes. Modeler automatically knows how to process the two partitions. The phrase "Comparing $R-Survived with Survived" means comparing the first model's prediction with the actual outcome. The phrase "Comparing $N-Survived with Survived" is referring to the second model. The prefixes can be confusing, but $R is always associated with CHAID, and $N is always associated with neural net.

Results for output field Survived
  Individual Models
    Comparing $R-Survived with Survived

'Partition'	1_Training		2_Testing	
Correct	357	81.51%	359	79.25%
Wrong	81	18.49%	94	20.75%
Total	438		453	

    Comparing $N-Survived with Survived

'Partition'	1_Training		2_Testing	
Correct	346	79%	353	77.92%
Wrong	92	21%	100	22.08%
Total	438		453	

  Agreement between $R-Survived $N-Survived

'Partition'	1_Training		2_Testing	
Agree	379	86.53%	393	86.75%
Disagree	59	13.47%	60	13.25%
Total	438		453	

    Comparing Agreement with Survived

'Partition'	1_Training		2_Testing	
Correct	322	84.96%	326	82.95%
Wrong	57	15.04%	67	17.05%
Total	379		393	

Figure 11-16: Analysis node results

We are interested in two things in the top half of the report: accuracy and generality. We see that in both cases, $R-Survived and $N-Survived, the Training performance and Testing performance are fairly close. By "close" most analysts use a rule of thumb of 5%. As applied to this example that means that the Test performance is within 5% less of the Training performance that the models generalize reasonably well. Remember that failure to generalize is essentially what a Type I error is. Both meet the rule of thumb requirement here. In terms of accuracy, the Training accuracy is not paramount. What we are really interested in is Test performance. CHAID's prediction, with the $R prefix, appears to be the stronger performer. Keep in mind that this is just a first attempt and was run on default settings. It would not be unusual to try dozens of models during a project. At the moment, CHAID seems like it is the leader by a small margin. We will learn that this kind of analysis is possible in SPSS Statistics, but it will require a bit of effort and will require SPSS syntax. We will review the steps carefully in Chapter 15.

Let's briefly examine the rest of the Analysis node report. We learn that $R-Survived and $N-Survived generally agree, about 86% agreement in both samples. When they agree, the combined accuracy is almost 83%. At first, this news seems pretty exciting: 83% is much better, but it comes with a cost, that 83% is only measured on the cases where they agree. Combining models can be powerful, but this report tips the scales a little too much in favor of pursuing a combined model. Such models, called ensembles, can be created with the dedicated Ensemble node and are the subject of the next section.

Creating Ensembles

The concept of model ensembles is more subtle than what we saw implied in the Analysis node. The Analysis node gave us some clues as to whether an ensemble might be fruitful. In order to produce an ensemble, however, there has to be some way of resolving conflict among the models. It simply is not acceptable to ignore those cases where the models do not have a consensus prediction. In fact, that is really what "agreement" in the Analysis node implies—complete consensus. Cases where consensus is not reached are simply not used in the calculation in the Analysis node so it really just hints as to whether an ensemble might possibly be useful. The goal is to produce a new model that uses predictions from all of the input models.

Clearly, the input models will not always agree, and that is the interesting and compelling aspect of building an ensemble. When they all agree, they are very often all right. The "secret sauce" is doing a clever of job of figuring out what the prediction should be when they do not all agree, and there are numerous ways of doing so. Unfortunately, the fact that there are numerous ways would make creating ensembles in SPSS Statistics labor intensive. Labor intensive makes experimentation difficult, which is a problem in data mining.

It can certainly be done, but would be done by using formulas in SPSS syntax. Something like:

```
IF (PredA = 'true' and PredB = 'true') PredEnsemble = 'true'
```

All possible combinations would have to be taken into account, and typically you would want the formulas to involve confidence scores, which would complicate things considerably. Would I rule out ensembles if I was working in SPSS Statistics? Each situation is different, but I would have to be convinced that the ensemble was worth it, and I would want to be collaborating with a team that was comfortable with SPSS syntax.

SPSS Modeler makes it so easy that there might be a tendency to do ensembles a little too often. They are incredibly enticing, and when there is no barrier in the form of complicated implementation the temptation can be hard to resist. Why so tempting? Well, quite simply, ensembles almost always look like a good idea when you examine the Analysis node. We have already discussed why this is the case, but even when the models don't agree often, accuracy tends to go up, just on a smaller and smaller proportion of the cases. So, it looks better than it would be in practice. Ensembles are most powerful when models with different strengths and weaknesses are combined to make a more effective team. For instance, on one major project I once paired a neural net, which was my most accurate model but which was sensitive to missing data, with a C&RT Tree, which was a bit less accurate but more resilient to missing data. The combination was stronger on the entire dataset than either was alone. Let's take a look at an example (see Figure 11-17).

Modeler makes it easy. We simply place an Ensemble node downstream of the two models. Inside the Ensemble node we see an impressive array of choice on how to resolve conflict between the models. Also note that it filters out the earlier models by default. However, that can be turned off, and

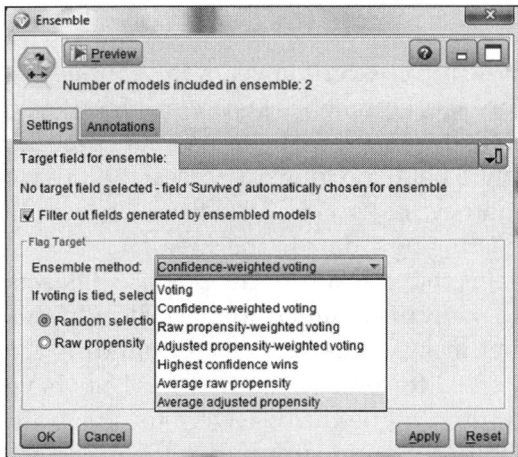

Figure 11-17: Ensemble methods

we can examine the Analysis node again. I've chosen Confidence-weighted voting as the tie breaker.

We will look at just the top half of the new Analysis node, and we actually learn that the ensemble, with the prefix $XF, is the weakest of the three (see Figure 11-18). Ensembles are a powerful technique, but they are challenging to do in SPSS Statistics, not because of the IF statements and the syntax, but rather because trying multiple variations would be labor intensive, and the evaluation of all of those variations on the theme would also be labor intensive. While possible, I would focus my attention on the other tasks, and probably consider living without the ensemble strategy when using SPSS Statistics. Many successful models, including several members of the top 10 of the famous million-dollar Netflix prize, were ensembles. However, no ensemble will succeed unless the component models are the best that they can be, so focus on improving your individual models first.

⊟ Results for output field Survived
　⊟ Individual Models
　　⊟ Comparing $R-Survived with Survived

'Partition'	1_Training		2_Testing	
Correct	357	81.51%	359	79.25%
Wrong	81	18.49%	94	20.75%
Total	438		453	

　　⊟ Comparing $N-Survived with Survived

'Partition'	1_Training		2_Testing	
Correct	346	79%	353	77.92%
Wrong	92	21%	100	22.08%
Total	438		453	

　　⊟ Comparing $XF-Survived with Survived

'Partition'	1_Training		2_Testing	
Correct	349	79.68%	349	77.04%
Wrong	89	20.32%	104	22.96%
Total	438		453	

Figure 11-18 Comparing models to ensemble results

Scoring New Records

SPSS Statistics has added a number of features over the years to facilitate the scoring of new data. Not that many years ago, I might have written SPSS syntax, using the coefficients found in the output. It would have been a manual process, but fairly easily done, if you know how. That is no longer necessary. Now we have a wizard to help us do it. Scoring new records in Modeler is especially easy—it essentially just involves connecting new data to the stream.

An interesting fact about our dataset is that it is one of the practice datasets on the kaggle.com data mining crowd sourcing competition website. On this site data miners compete and are sometimes awarded money for building the best model. The Titanic dataset is provided for practice on the site. They have divided the data into two, and they only provide the "answer" for the Train half. If we wanted to score the Test half we would simply run the new data through the best model, which for us was the CHAID model. I've made a copy of the CHAID nugget (through a simple copy-and-paste operation) and simply allowed the test.csv data to flow through it to the Table node (see Figure 11-19). Two new variables have been appended to the far right of the data. Data for the first 10 passengers in test.csv are shown revealing that only 2 are predicted to survive. The values with the $RC prefix are the confidence scores of that prediction and are shown in Figure 11-20.

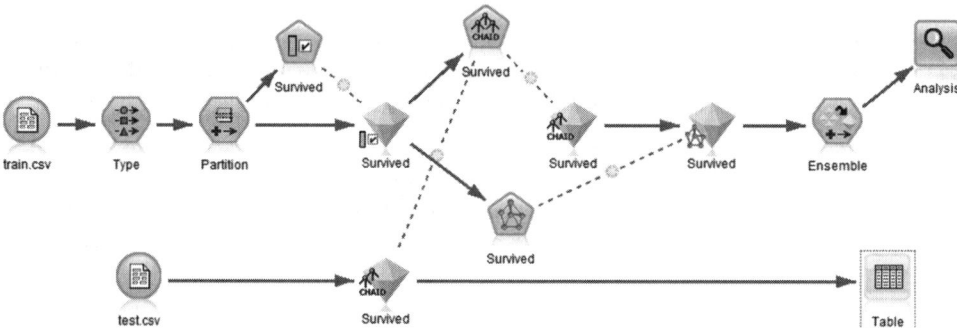

Figure 11-19: Stream with scoring of test.csv added

$R-Survived	$RC-Survived
0	0.880
0	0.609
0	0.880
0	0.880
0	0.609
0	0.880
1	0.690
0	0.754
1	0.690
0	0.754

Figure 11-20: Scoring results for 10 passengers

In the final table of the chapter (Table 11-3), a substantial list of dozens of algorithms shows that with access to some of the modules an SPSS Statistics user can do a very large chunk of what an SPSS Modeler user can do. Keep in mind that access to Modeling algorithms is only half the battle. We've seen that on the tasks there are some real differences, and more differences kick in when you consider either huge datasets or automated deployment. Nonetheless, the SPSS user has access to considerable resources right in SPSS Statistics.

Table 11-3: Data Mining Algorithms

CATEGORY	TECHNIQUE	MODELER	STATISTICS MODULE OR COMMAND EXTENSION
Decision Tree	CHAID	Yes	Trees
	C&RT	Yes	Trees
	C5.0	Yes	STATS C5.0 extension command
	QUEST	Yes	Trees
Association	A Priori	Yes	SPSSINC APRIORI extension
	CARMA	Yes	
	Sequence Detection	Yes	
	Association Rules Node	Yes	
Classification (Statistical)	Discriminant	Yes	Base
	Logistic	Yes	
	Loglinear	No	
Numeric Prediction	Linear Regression	Yes	Base
	Automatic Linear Modeling	Yes	Base
	CHAID	Yes	Trees
	C&RT	Yes	Trees
	Neural Net	Yes	Neural
Classification	Neural Net	Yes	Neural
	SVM	Yes	STATS SVM Extension
	Bayes Net	Yes	Statistics Server Only

Continues

Table 11-3 (*continued*)

CATEGORY	TECHNIQUE	MODELER	STATISTICS MODULE OR COMMAND EXTENSION
	Decision List	Yes	
	Nearest Neighbors	Yes	
Clustering	Hierarchical	No	
	K-Means	Yes	Base
	Two Step	Yes	
	Kohonen	Yes	

IBM SPSS Data Preparation

IBM SPSS Statistics is comprised of a base system, which has many options for data preparation, graphing, and data analysis. Users can also add modules that provide additional functionality. Personally, I would recommend some of these modules, like the Custom Tables module, to just about every user. Other modules, like the Forecasting module, are very specialized, and I would only recommend it to users that truly require these techniques. One module that SPSS Statistics users may not be aware of but which can be very useful is the Data Preparation module.

The Data Preparation module consists of four techniques: two (Validation and Identify Unusual Cases) are located under the Data menu; and two (Optimal Binning and Data Preparation for Modeling) are positioned under the Transform menu. These four techniques can be used to improve the quality of your data before performing data analysis.

Unfortunately, to provide a complete example of each of the techniques would result in an incredibly long chapter, therefore I will only cover two of these techniques (Identify Unusual Cases and Optimal Binning). I have chosen these two procedures because I wanted to show at least one technique from each menu (Data and Transform), but also because I find Identify Unusual Cases and Optimal Binning to be the most useful of the four components of the Data Preparation module.

NOTE Because this chapter does not have space to cover two of the components of the Data Preparation module, here is a brief description of those two components. These components are designed to improve the data analyst's efficiency in what is often the most time consuming part of a project.

■ **Validation:** Data validation functions by defining rules, either based on a single variable or across variables. These rules check for several types of errors and problems in your data, such as incorrect labels, values, or missing value codes, out-of-range values, odd distributions, outliers, skip instructions being followed incorrectly, logical inconsistencies, and acquiescence bias. The output includes both reports that can help the analyst assess the quality of the data and reports that can be used by the data providers to make corrections in the data. Rule violations can be recorded as variables in the data and used for further analysis of error patterns.

■ **Data Preparation for Modeling:** Data preparation analyzes data and screens out fields that are problematic or not likely to be useful, derives new attributes when appropriate, and improves performance through various screening techniques. It can make substitutions for missing data as part of its data preparation, and can even adjust the measurement level of variables automatically. It can also extract information from date and time fields. You can use this technique in a fully automatic fashion, allowing it to choose and apply changes, or you can use it in an interactive fashion, previewing the changes before they are made.

Identify Unusual Cases

Unusual data is not always a cause for concern. Sometimes unusual cases can be errors in the data. For example, a school teacher's recorded salary of $1,000,000 is most likely due to an extra zero that was added during data entry. Sometimes unusual cases can be extreme scores; for example, a customer that purchased 5,000 speakers in the last month, where typically monthly orders range from 100 to 1,000 speakers per month. Sometimes unusual cases can be interesting cases; for example, a patient with cystic fibrosis who is 52 years old, where life expectancy for this disease is in the mid-30s.

In addition, sometimes unusual cases can be valuable. For example, there might a small group of customers that use their cell phones a lot and so this group is valuable as customers, but we might want to analyze their data separately so they do not distort the findings of typical customers. Or sometimes unusual cases can be a real cause for concern, such as when investigating insurance fraud.

Whatever you call them, outliers, unusual cases, or anomalies can be problematic for statistical techniques. By definition, an outlier is a data value unlike other data values. Someone can be an outlier on a single variable or they can be an outlier on a combination of variables. Outlier detection can be as simple as running a series of graphs or frequencies to detect outliers on a single variable. It is also relatively simple to identify outliers on a combination of two or maybe three variables—many times a graph, like a scatterplot, can detect these situations. However, detecting unusual cases on a combination of many variables is almost impossible to do manually, and even low-dimensional error detection can be time consuming.

IBM SPSS Statistics includes the ability to Identify Unusual Cases on a combination of many variables in an automatic manner. This technique is an exploratory method designed for the quick detection of unusual cases that should be candidates for further analysis. This procedure is based on the TwoStep clustering algorithm, and is designed for generic anomaly detection, not specific to any particular application. The basic idea is that cluster analysis is used to create groups of similar cases. Cases are then compared to the group norms and the cases are assigned an anomaly score. Larger anomaly scores indicate that a case is more deviant (anomalous) than the cluster or group. Cases with anomaly scores or index values greater than two could be good anomaly candidates because the deviation is at least twice the average. In addition, this technique not only identifies which cases are most unusual, but it also specifies which variables are most unusual.

Identify Unusual Cases Dialogs

In this example we will use the file Electronics.sav. The Electronics.sav file has several variables and we will use the Identify Unusual Cases procedure to look for unusual cases on the combination of all the variables:

1. Select the Data menu, and then choose Identify Unusual Cases, as shown in Figure 12-1.

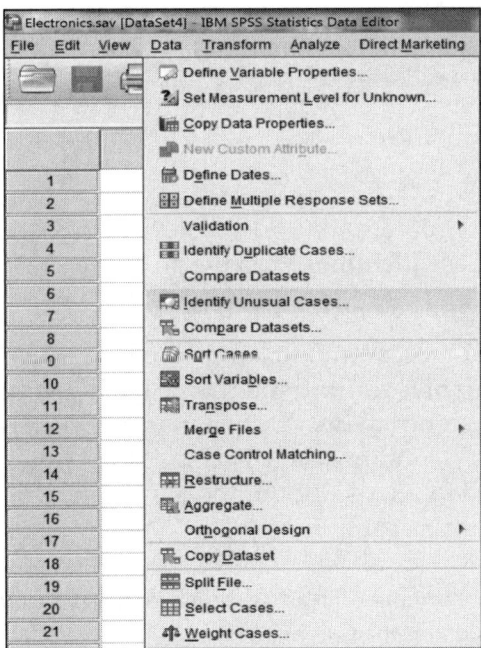

Figure 12-1: Data menu

The Identify Unusual Cases: Variables dialog allows you to specify the variables to use in the analysis. You can optionally place a case identification variable in the Case Identifier Variable box to use in labeling output, and you must place at least one variable in the Analysis Variables box. Typically you would place all the variables that you would use in your models in the Analysis Variables box, as shown in Figure 12-2.

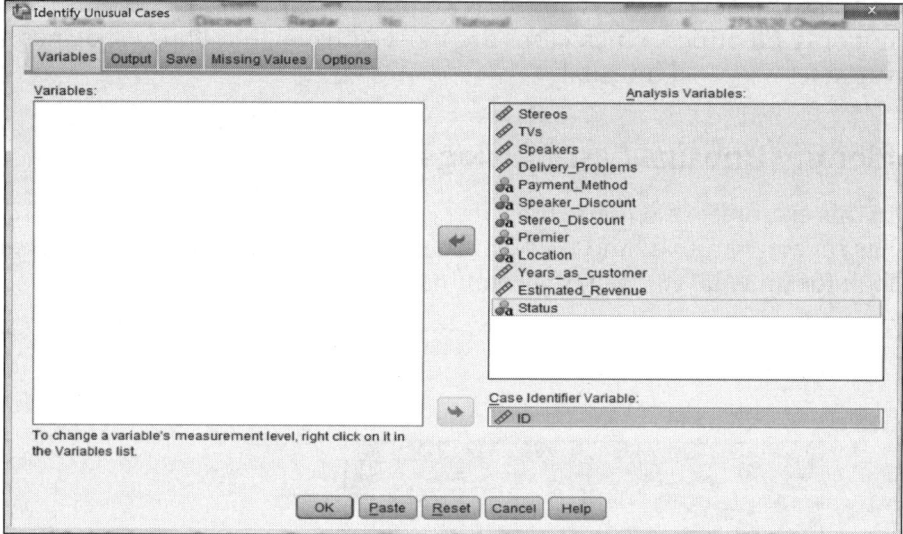

Figure 12-2: Identify Unusual Cases: Variables dialog

2. Place the variable ID in the Case Identifier Variable box.

3. Place all the other variables in the Analysis Variables box.

   This procedure works with both continuous and categorical variables and it assumes that all variables are independent. Each continuous variable is assumed to have a normal distribution, and each categorical variable is assumed to have a multinomial distribution, although this technique is fairly robust to violations of both the assumption of independence and the distributional assumptions.

NOTE Measurement level affects the computation of the results for this procedure, so all variables must have a correctly defined measurement level.

4. Click the Outputs tab.

   The Identify Unusual Cases: Output dialog (see Figure 12-3) allows you to specify what output you would like to view.

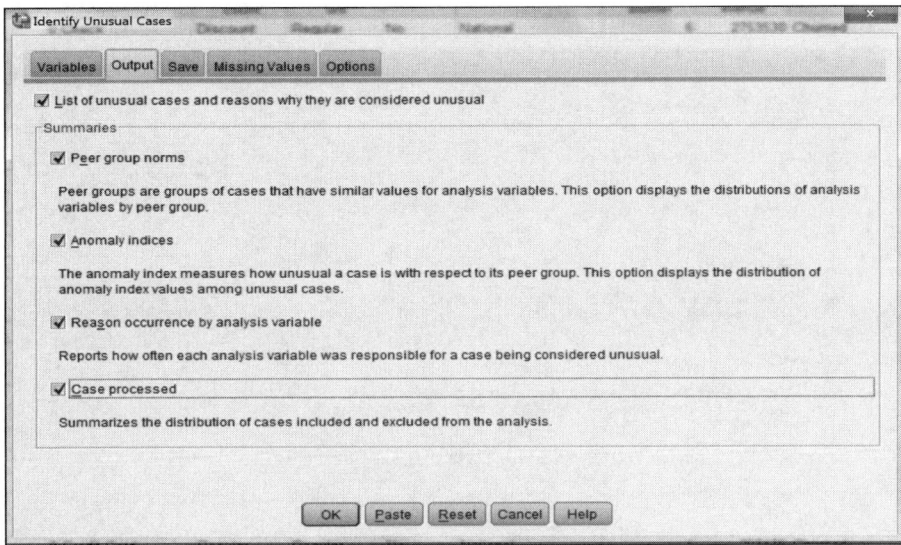

Figure 12-3: Identify Unusual Cases: Output dialog

   ■ The List of unusual cases and reasons why they are considered unusual option produces three tables that display the unusual cases and information concerning their corresponding peer groups. Anomaly index values are also displayed for cases identified as unusual and the reason (variable) why a case is an anomaly is also displayed.

   ■ The Peer group norms option produces peer group norms for continuous and categorical variables.

   ■ The Anomaly indices option produces anomaly index scores based on deviations from peer group norms for cases that are identified as unusual.

   ■ The Reason occurrence by analysis variable option produces variable impact values for variables that contribute most to a case considered unusual.

   ■ The Cases processed option produces counts and percentages for each peer group.

5. Choose all of these options, as shown in Figure 12-3, so that we can discuss these.

6. Click the Save tab.

The Identify Unusual Cases: Save dialog (shown in Figure 12-4) allows you to save model variables to the active dataset. You can also choose to replace existing variables whose names conflict with the variables to be saved.

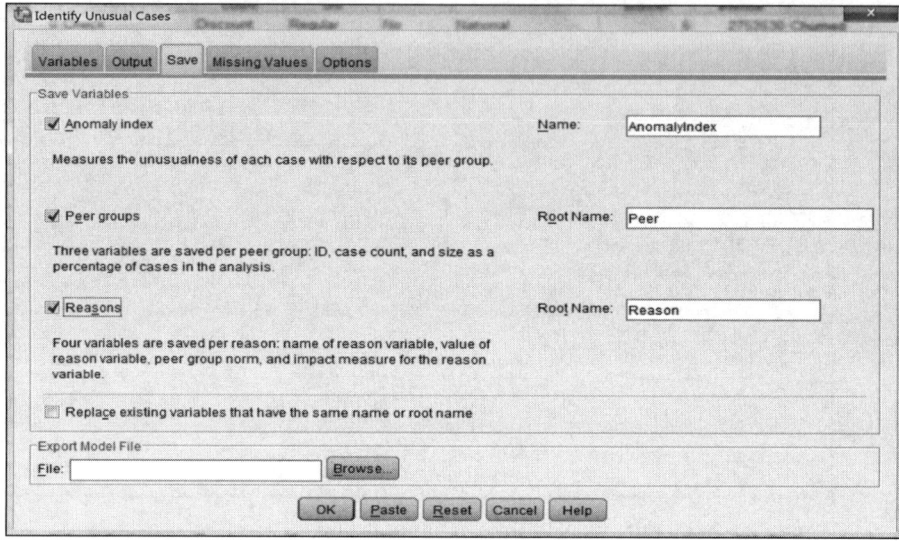

Figure 12-4: Identify Unusual Cases: Save dialog

- The Anomaly index option saves the anomaly index value for each case.
- The Peer groups option saves the peer group ID, case count, and size as a percentage for each case to variables.
- The Reasons option saves sets of reasoning variables. A set of reasoning variables consists of the name of the variable as the reason, its variable impact measure, its own value, and the norm value. The number of sets depends on the number of reasons requested on the Options tab.
- The Replace existing variables checkbox is used when repeating this procedure.
- The Export Model File option allows you to save the model in XML format.

As shown in Figure 12-4, again choose all of these options, so that we can discuss these.

7. Click the Missing Values tab.

The Identify Unusual Cases: Missing Values dialog (see Figure 12-5) is used to control how to handle user-missing and system-missing values.

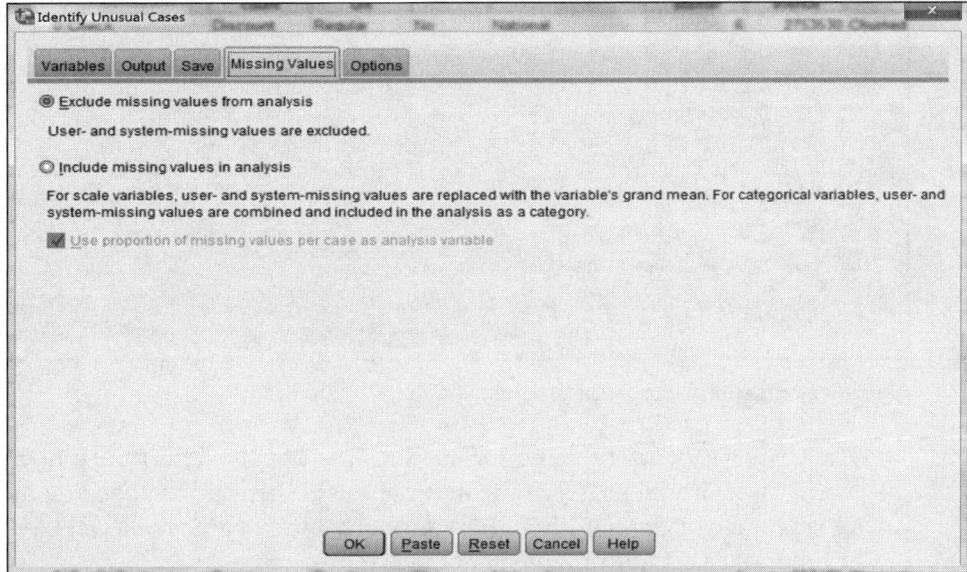

Figure 12-5: Identify Unusual Cases: Missing Values dialog

- The Exclude missing values from analysis option excludes cases with missing values from the analysis.

- The Include missing values in analysis option substitutes missing values of continuous variables with means, and groups missing values of categorical variables together so they are treated as a valid category. Optionally, you can request the creation of an additional variable that represents the proportion of missing variables in each case and use that variable in the analysis.

Single or multiple imputation missing value analysis is available in separate procedures.

In our dataset we have no missing data, so in our case either option will produce the same result (see Figure 12-5).

8. Click the Options tab.

   The Identify Unusual Cases: Options dialog (shown in Figure 12-6) allows you to specify the criteria for identifying unusual cases and to determine how many peer groups (clusters) will be created.

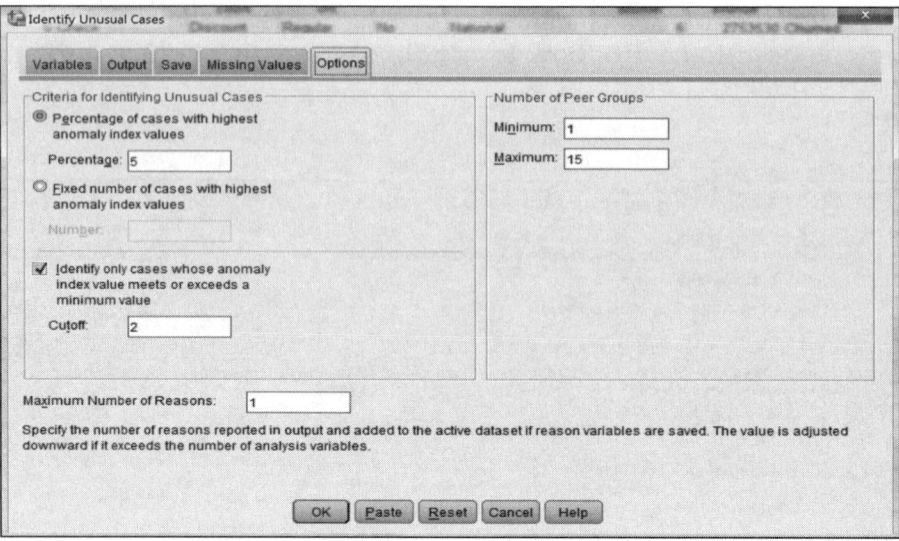

Figure 12-6: Identify Unusual Cases: Options dialog

- The Criteria for Identifying Unusual Cases option determines how many cases are included in the anomaly list. This can be specified as a Percentage of cases with highest anomaly index values or as a Fixed number of cases with highest anomaly index values.

- The Identify only cases whose anomaly index value meets or exceeds a minimum value option identifies a case as anomalous if its anomaly index value is larger than or equal to the specified cutoff point. This option is used together with the Percentage of cases and Fixed number of cases options.

- The Number of Peer Groups option searches for the best number of peer groups between the specified minimum and maximum values.

NOTE   The results of the cluster solution may depend on the order of cases. To minimize order effects, randomly order the cases. To verify the stability of a given solution, you may want to obtain several different solutions with cases sorted in different random orders.

- The Maximum Number of Reasons option controls the number of sets of reasoning variables in the Save tab. A set of reasoning variables consists of the variable impact measure, the variable name for this reason, the value of the case on the variable, and the value of the corresponding peer group.

We will just go with the default options as shown in Figure 12-6.

9. Click OK.

Identify Unusual Cases Output

The Case Processing Summary table (Figure 12-7) displays the counts and percentages for each peer group (cluster). In our data three clusters were found and the largest cluster was Peer ID 1 with a total of 1,659 cases or almost 50% of the sample.

Case Processing Summary

		N	% of Combined	% of Total
Peer ID	1	1659	49.7%	49.7%
	2	691	20.7%	20.7%
	3	988	29.6%	29.6%
Combined		3338	100.0%	100.0%
Total		3338		100.0%

Figure 12-7: Case Processing Summary table

The Anomaly Case Index List table (Figure 12-8) displays cases that are identified as unusual and displays their corresponding anomaly index values. This table lets us know who the unusual cases are, so now we can further investigate. In our data cases 714 and 1835 had the largest anomaly index values (3.925). This means that these cases had a deviation that is almost four times the average.

NOTE All tables are sorted by anomaly index values in descending order. Also note that the IDs of the cases are displayed if the case identifier variable is specified on the Variables tab.

Anomaly Case Index List

Case	ID	Anomaly Index
714	714	3.925
1835	1835	3.925
1381	1381	3.263
2191	2191	3.263
2913	2913	3.263
3313	3313	3.263
279	279	3.019
1622	1622	3.019
3031	3031	3.019
744	744	2.723
2609	2609	2.723
262	262	2.578
2378	2378	2.578
593	593	2.430
522	522	2.302
1731	1731	2.302
3080	3080	2.302
1109	1109	2.061
909	909	2.003

Figure 12-8: Anomaly Case Index List table

The Anomaly Case Peer ID List table (Figure 12-9) displays unusual cases and information concerning their corresponding peer groups. For example, we can see that Case ID 714 is in Peer ID group 1 and that this peer group has 1659 cases, which account for about 50% of the data file.

Anomaly Case Peer ID List

Case	ID	Peer ID	Peer Size	Peer Size Percent
714	714	1	1659	49.7%
1835	1835	1	1659	49.7%
1381	1381	3	988	29.6%
2191	2191	3	988	29.6%
2913	2913	3	988	29.6%
3313	3313	3	988	29.6%
279	279	2	691	20.7%
1622	1622	2	691	20.7%
3031	3031	2	691	20.7%
744	744	1	1659	49.7%
2609	2609	1	1659	49.7%
262	262	1	1659	49.7%
2378	2378	1	1659	49.7%
593	593	1	1659	49.7%
522	522	1	1659	49.7%
1731	1731	1	1659	49.7%
3080	3080	1	1659	49.7%
1109	1109	3	988	29.6%
909	909	1	1659	49.7%

Figure 12-9: Anomaly Case Peer ID List table

The Anomaly Case Reason List table (Figure 12-10) displays the case number, the reason variable, the variable impact value (percentage of anomaly score due to that variable), the value of the case on the variable, and the norm (typical value) of the variable for each reason. As an example, Case ID 714 as we have seen has a high anomaly index score, 3.925 (see Figure 12-8). This case was most unusual on the variable Speakers. The contribution of this variable to Case ID 714's anomaly index score was .678. Case ID 714 had a score of 411 on the Speakers variable while the mean score for peer group 1 on this variable was only 54.64. Note that if the variable impact value is low, it suggests that the case was classified as an outlier because of unusual values on more than one variable.

Anomaly Case Reason List

Reason: 1

Case	ID	Reason Variable	Variable Impact	Variable Value	Variable Norm
714	714	Speakers	.678	411	54.64
1835	1835	Speakers	.678	411	54.64
1381	1381	Speakers	.774	404	42.28
2191	2191	Speakers	.774	404	42.28
2913	2913	Speakers	.774	404	42.28
3313	3313	Speakers	.774	404	42.28
279	279	Speakers	.685	451	56.21
1622	1622	Speakers	.685	451	56.21
3031	3031	Speakers	.685	451	56.21
744	744	Speakers	.525	312	54.64
2609	2609	Speakers	.525	312	54.64
262	262	Speakers	.666	338	54.64
2378	2378	Speakers	.666	338	54.64
593	593	Speakers	.678	332	54.64
522	522	Speakers	.616	311	54.64
1731	1731	Speakers	.616	311	54.64
3080	3080	Speakers	.616	311	54.64
1109	1109	Speakers	.608	292	42.28
909	909	Speakers	.628	295	54.64

Figure 12-10: Anomaly Case Reason List table

So now not only do we know which cases are unusual, we also now know on what variables these cases are most unusual.

NOTE We chose to display only one reason, but we could have chosen more than one reason, and that may have given us more information. Additionally, notice that the main reason for all of these outliers is the variable Speakers. At this point you might want to further investigate this variable to try to better understand what might be happening here. It may be that the problem is not with cases, but with the variable. For example, the variable may have been coded incorrectly or if this was a survey question, the question may have been misunderstood. In this situation the Validate Data procedure for such variables could be a useful tool to use on the reason variables.

The Scale Variable peer group Norms table (Figure 12-11) displays the mean and standard deviation of each continuous variable for each peer group. The mean of a continuous variable is used as the norm value to compare to individual values.

Scale Variable Norms

		Peer ID			
		1	2	3	Combined
Stereos	Mean	15.19	14.00	11.00	13.71
	Std. Deviation	8.596	9.201	10.269	9.417
TVs	Mean	.02	3.81	.09	.83
	Std. Deviation	.168	3.542	.362	2.228
Speakers	Mean	54.64	56.21	42.28	51.30
	Std. Deviation	52.956	53.851	55.151	54.104
Delivery_Problems	Mean	.00	.62	.00	.13
	Std. Deviation	.000	.779	.000	.434
Years_as_customer	Mean	6.27	6.36	6.59	6.38
	Std. Deviation	2.584	2.615	2.485	2.565
Estimated_Revenue	Mean	5149357.04	5393846.93	4590350.15	5034510.94
	Std. Deviation	2769371.357	2768829.427	2915790.150	2828800.406

Figure 12-11: Scale Variable Norms table

The Categorical Variable Norms table (Figure 12-12) displays the mode, frequency, and frequency percentage of each categorical variable for each peer group. The mode of a categorical variable is used as the norm value to compare to individual values.

Categorical Variable Norms

		Peer ID			
		1	2	3	Combined
Payment_Method	Most Popular Category	Credit Card	Credit Card	Credit Card	Credit Card
	Frequency	952	392	582	1926
	Percent	57.4%	56.7%	58.9%	57.7%
Speaker_Discount	Most Popular Category	Regular	Regular	Discount	Regular
	Frequency	838	363	496	1693
	Percent	50.5%	52.5%	50.2%	50.7%
Stereo_Discount	Most Popular Category	Regular	Regular	Regular	Regular
	Frequency	1147	483	686	2316
	Percent	69.1%	69.9%	69.4%	69.4%
Premier	Most Popular Category	Yes	No	No	No
	Frequency	1165	366	833	1693
	Percent	70.2%	53.0%	84.3%	50.7%
Location	Most Popular Category	National	National	National	National
	Frequency	993	410	571	1974
	Percent	59.9%	59.3%	57.8%	59.1%
Status	Most Popular Category	Current	Churned	Churned	Current
	Frequency	1659	461	988	1889
	Percent	100.0%	66.7%	100.0%	56.6%

Figure 12-12: Categorical Variable Norms table

The Anomaly Index Summary table (Figure 12-13) displays an overall summary of the descriptive statistics for the anomaly index of the cases that were identified as the most unusual. You can see that for our data, 19 cases were identified as unusual and you can see the minimum, maximum, and mean values.

Anomaly Index Summary

	N in the Anomaly List	Minimum	Maximum	Mean	Std. Deviation
Anomaly Index	19	2.003	3.925	2.840	.562

N in the Anomaly List is determined by the specification: anomaly percentage is 5% and anomaly index cutpoint is at least 2

Figure 12-13: Anomaly Index Summary table

The Reason Occurrence by Analysis Variable table (Figure 12-14) displays the frequency and percentage of each variable's occurrence as a reason. The table also reports the overall descriptive statistics of the impact of each variable. As was mentioned previously, only one variable appeared as the main reason for all of these outliers, and you can see the minimum, maximum, and mean values.

Reason Summary

Reason 1

	Occurrence as Reason		Variable Impact Statistics			
	Frequency	Percent	Minimum	Maximum	Mean	Std. Deviation
Payment_Method	0	0.0%	.	.	.	.
Speaker_Discount	0	0.0%	.	.	.	.
Stereo_Discount	0	0.0%	.	.	.	.
Premier	0	0.0%	.	.	.	.
Location	0	0.0%	.	.	.	.
Status	0	0.0%	.	.	.	.
Stereos	0	0.0%	.	.	.	.
TVs	0	0.0%	.	.	.	.
Speakers	19	100.0%	.525	.774	.666	.075
Delivery_Problems	0	0.0%	.	.	.	.
Years_as_customer	0	0.0%	.	.	.	.
Estimated_Revenue	0	0.0%	.	.	.	.
Overall	19	100.0%	.525	.774	.666	.075

Figure 12-14: Reason 1 table

Now let's take a look at the Identify Unusual Cases procedure created in the data editor.

1. Switch to the Data Editor.

2. Right-click the AnomalyIndex variable and choose Sort Descending, as shown in Figure 12-15.

AnomalyIn...	PeerId	PeerSize
	Cut	
	Copy	
	Paste	
	Clear	
	Insert Variable	
	Sort Ascending	
	Sort Descending	
	Descriptives Statistics	
	Spelling...	

Figure 12-15: Sorting data

Figure 12-16 shows the new variables that were saved to the data file. As you can see, the data has now been sorted on the anomaly index value so it is easy to identify the unusual cases and begin further investigations. Now the researcher will need to determine if the unusual cases should be kept, removed, or modified.

AnomalyIn...	PeerId	PeerSize	PeerPctSize	ReasonVar_1	ReasonMeasure_1	ReasonValue_1	ReasonNorm_1
3.93	1	1659	49.70	Speakers	.68	411	54.64
3.93	1	1659	49.70	Speakers	.68	411	54.64
3.26	3	988	29.60	Speakers	.77	404	42.28
3.26	3	988	29.60	Speakers	.77	404	42.28
3.26	3	988	29.60	Speakers	.77	404	42.28
3.26	3	988	29.60	Speakers	.77	404	42.28
3.02	2	691	20.70	Speakers	.69	451	56.21
3.02	2	691	20.70	Speakers	.69	451	56.21
3.02	2	691	20.70	Speakers	.69	451	56.21
2.72	1	1659	49.70	Speakers	.53	312	54.64

Figure 12-16: New variables sorted

Optimal Binning

After exploring a data file, you often need to modify some variables. One common type of modification is to transform a continuous variable into a categorical variable; this is often referred to as *binning*. Note that since binning necessarily results in a loss of information, it should only be done where necessary. You might do this for several reasons:

- Some algorithms may perform better if a predictor has fewer categories.

- Some algorithms handle a continuous field by grouping it; however, you may wish to control the grouping beforehand.

- The effect of outliers can be reduced by binning.

- Binning solves problems of the shape of a distribution because the continuous variables are turned into an ordered set. Note that binning followed by treating a variable as a factor allows for nonlinear effects of predictors in a regression context.

- Binning can allow for data privacy by reporting such things as salaries or bonuses in ranges rather than the actual values.

SPSS Statistics has several procedures that allow users to bin continuous variables. For example, you can use the Visual Binning technique to create fixed-width bins (a new variable with groups of equal width, or ranges, such as age in groups of 20–29, 30–39, and so on). You can also use Visual Binning to divide a field into groups based on percentiles so that you create groups of equal numbers of cases. You can also use Visual Binning to create a field based on a z-score, with the groups defined as the number of standard deviations below and above the mean. Lastly, you can use Visual Binning to create customized bins.

Optimal Binning Dialogs

Optimal binning is another technique that bins a continuous field. Here, however, the transformation is based on the help of a separate categorical field that is used to guide or "supervise" the binning process. The transformation is done so that there is maximum separation between groups in the binned field's relationship with the supervising field. The supervising field should be at least moderately related to the field to be binned. Note that this technique is only for continuous variables; however, the STATS OPTBINEX extension command (Data ⇨ Extended Optimal Binning) extends this technique to allow binning of categorical variables by using the CHAID algorithm from the TREES procedure.

NOTE Before binning, it is a good idea to examine the relationship between the continuous and categorical variables to see whether the categorical variable might successfully supervise binning.

1. To use Optimal Binning, select the Transform menu, and then choose Optimal Binning, as shown in Figure 12-17.

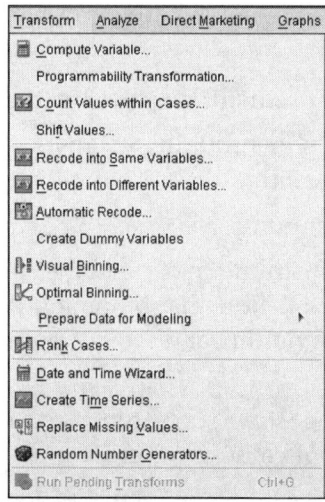

Figure 12-17: Transform menu

The Optimal Binning: Variables dialog allows you to specify the variables to use in the analysis. You will need to place your categorical supervisor variable in the Optimize Bins with Respect to box and you must place at least one continuous variable in the Variables to Bin box. By optimally binning a predictor variable with the outcome variable, we create the ideal cutpoints to best separate—predict—the outcome's values. Because the supervising variable must be categorical, this procedure can only be used with categorical outcome variables. However, you can always use another categorical variable in your data to bin a continuous predictor variable.

2. Place the variable Status in the Optimize Bins with Respect to box.

3. Place Stereos, TVs, and Speakers in the Variables to Bin box, as shown in Figure 12-18.

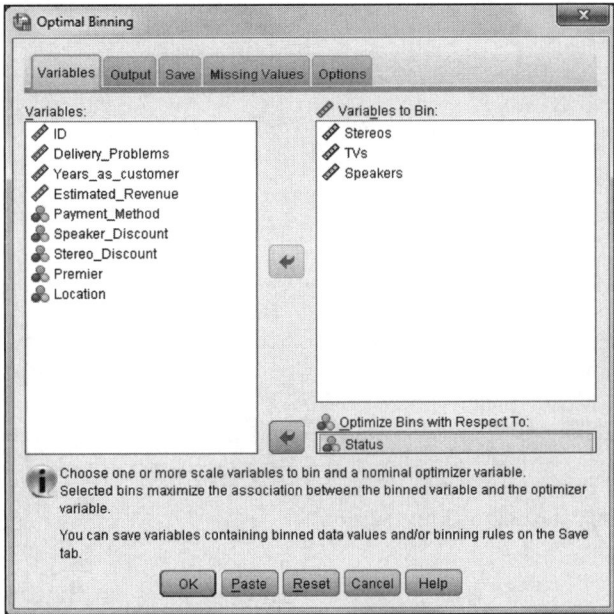

Figure 12-18: Optimal Binning: Variables dialog

4. Click the Output tab.

The Optimal Binning: Output dialog (Figure 12-19) allows you to specify what output you would like to view.

- The Endpoints for bins option creates a table for each binned variable that displays the cutoff values for each bin.

- The Descriptive statistics for variables that are binned option produces a table that shows the minimum and maximum values for each original field, as well as the number of unique original values and the number of bins that were created for each new binned field.

- The Model entropy for variables that are binned option produces the entropy scores for each binned field. The transformation is done so that there is maximum separation between groups in the binned field's relationship with the supervising field. If there is only one value of the categorical variable in a bin of the continuous variable, then the entropy is a minimum (equal to 0). That is the ideal, but the entropy will always be greater than 0 in practice.

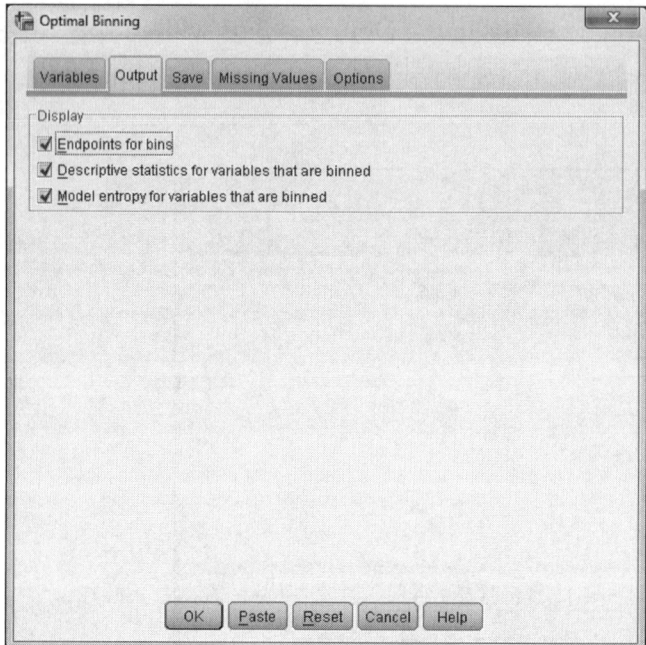

Figure 12-19: Optimal Binning: Output dialog

Choose all of these options, as shown in Figure 12-19, so that we can discuss these.

5. Click the Save tab.

   The Optimal Binning: Save dialog, shown in Figure 12-20, allows you to save binned variables to the active dataset. You can also choose to replace existing variables whose names conflict with the variables to be saved.

6. Select Create variables that contain binned data values.

7. Click the Missing Values tab.

   The Optimal Binning: Missing Values dialog, shown in Figure 12-21, is used to control how to handle missing values. Listwise deletion only uses cases that have complete data across all the variables that will be used in the analysis (this ensures that you have a consistent case base across all of the newly created variables). Pairwise deletion, on the other hand, focuses on each binned variable separately; therefore, it uses as much data as possible.

However, this results in not having a consistent case base across all of the newly created variables. As mentioned previously, in our dataset we have no missing data, so in our case either option will produce the same result.

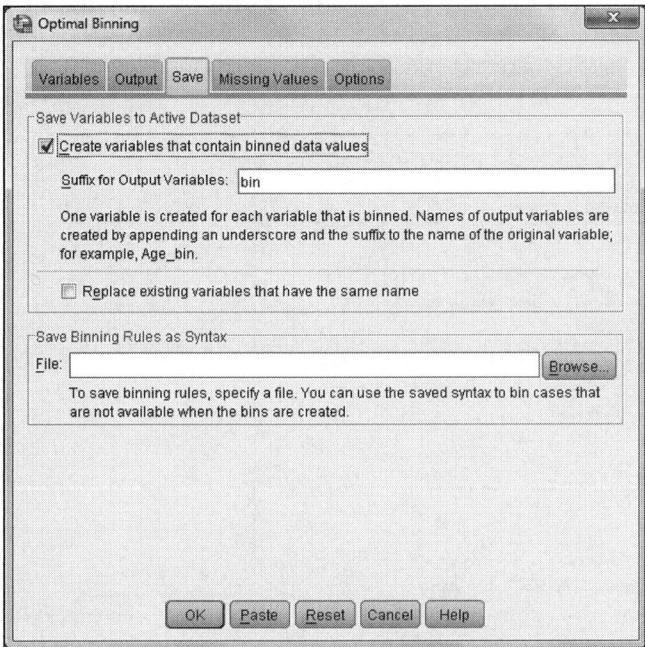

Figure 12-20: Optimal Binning: Save dialog

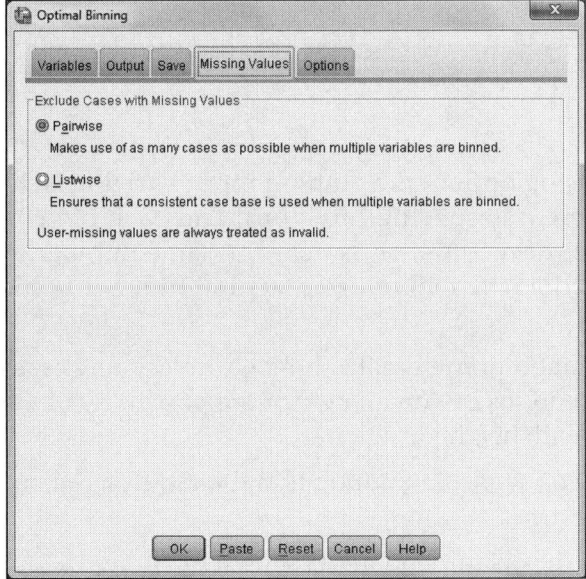

Figure 12-21: Optimal Binning: Missing Values dialog

8. Click the Options tab.

The Optimal Binning: Options dialog (see Figure 12-22) allows you to specify the maximum number of possible bins to create, identify criteria for bin endpoints, and define how to handle bins with a small number of cases.

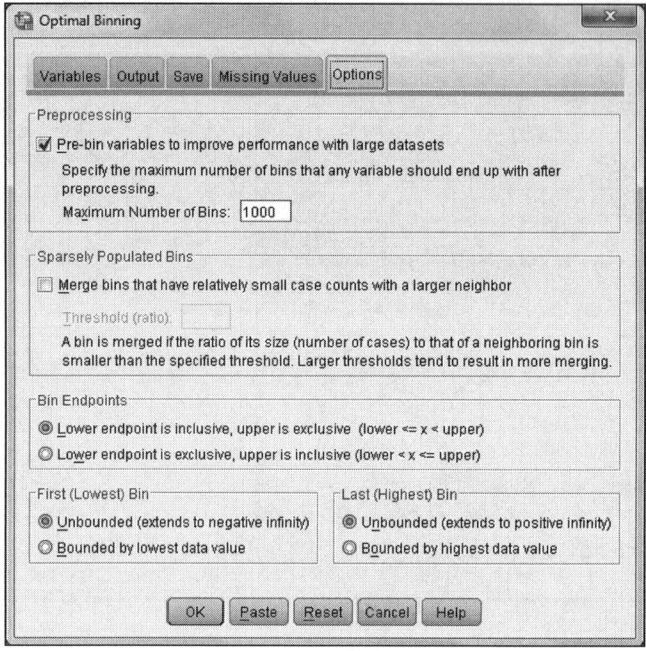

Figure 12-22: Optimal Binning: Options dialog

- In the Preprocessing option, the binning input variable is divided into n bins (where n is specified by you), and each bin contains the same number of records, or as near the same number as possible. This is used as the maximum potential number of bins, by default 1,000.

- Sometimes optimal binning creates bins with very few cases. The Sparsely Populated Bins option allows for the possibility of merging small-sized bins with neighboring bins.

- The last couple of options, Bin Endpoints and First/Last Bin, focus on bin criteria preferences.

We will just go with the default options as shown in Figure 12-22.

9. Click OK.

Optimal Binning Output

The Descriptive Statistics table (Figure 12-23) displays the number of cases, and the minimum and maximum values for each original field, as well as the number of unique original values and the number of bins that were created for each new binned field. In our data we can see that two bins were created for the variables Stereos and Speakers, while three bins were created for the variable TVs.

Descriptive Statistics

	N	Minimum	Maximum	Number of Distinct Values	Number of Bins
Stereos	3338	0	30	31	2
TVs	3338	0	10	11	3
Speakers	3338	0	451	209	2

Figure 12-23: Descriptive Statistics table

The Model Entropy table (Figure 12-24) shows the entropy values for each new binned variable. As mentioned in the table, lower entropy scores are associated with a stronger relationship between the binned and supervisor variables. In our case, all the entropy scores are similar; however, the new binned version of the variable, Stereos, has a slightly stronger relationship with the supervisor variable than the other binned variables.

Model Entropy

	Model Entropy
Stereos	.908
TVs	.921
Speakers	.910

Smaller model entropy indicates higher predictive accuracy of the binned variable on guide variable Status.

Figure 12-24: Model Entropy table

The binning summary tables (Figure 12-25) display the number of bins for each newly created variable, as well as the endpoints. Furthermore, we can see how the newly created binned variables relate to the supervisor variable. In our data, for example, we can see that two bins were created for the variable Stereos and that the first bin captures all the values from negative infinity to one, while the second bin captures all the values from two to positive infinity (the presentation of these endpoints is controlled in the Optimal Binning Options dialog). We can also see that the first bin is associated with churned customers, since of the 422 cases in this bin, 361 (86%) are churned customers. Meanwhile, the second bin is associated with current customers, since of the 2916 cases in this bin, 1828 (63%) are current customers.

Stereos

| Bin | End Point | | Number of Cases by Level of Status | | |
	Lower	Upper	Churned	Current	Total
1	a	1	361	61	422
2	1	a	1088	1828	2916
Total			1449	1889	3338

Each bin is computed as Lower <= Stereos < Upper.

a. Unbounded

TVs

| Bin | End Point | | Number of Cases by Level of Status | | |
	Lower	Upper	Churned	Current	Total
1	a	2	1093	1796	2889
2	2	4	98	4	102
3	4	a	258	89	347
Total			1449	1889	3338

Each bin is computed as Lower <= TVs < Upper.

a. Unbounded

Speakers

| Bin | End Point | | Number of Cases by Level of Status | | |
	Lower	Upper	Churned	Current	Total
1	a	5	309	37	346
2	5	a	1140	1852	2992
Total			1449	1889	3338

Each bin is computed as Lower <= Speakers < Upper.

a. Unbounded

Figure 12-25: Binning summary table

We have now created binned versions of the variables: Stereos, TVs, and Speakers. As a simple test, we can do a quick analysis to determine if these binned versions of these variables are indeed more strongly related to the outcome variable, Status, than the original variables. To do this, we will run a stepwise logistic regression.

To use logistic regression:

1. Select the Analyze menu, choose Regression, and then choose Binary Logistic.

2. As shown in Figure 12-26:

   a. Place the variable Status in the Dependent box.

   b. Place the variables Stereos, TVs, Speakers, Stereos_bin, TVs_bin, and Speakers_bin in the Covariates box.

   c. Choose Forward:LR in the Method box.

   Now we have specified our outcome variable as well as the predictors. The Forward:LR method is a form of stepwise logistic regression that selects the predictor variable that has the strongest relationship with the outcome variable. It will choose the predictor variable that has the second strongest relationship with the outcome variable second (after controlling for any previously selected variables), and so forth. The Forward:LR method will stop once it can no longer incorporate additional significant predictors.

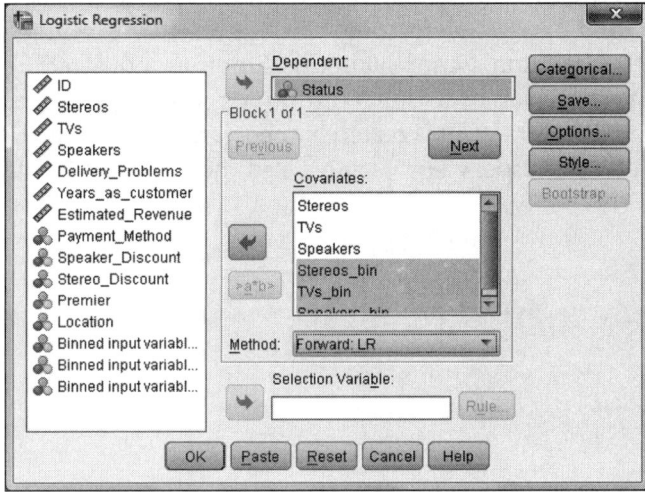

Figure 12-26: Logistic Regression dialog

3. Click OK.

Because the purpose of this logistic regression is just to show that the binned versions of the Speakers, TVs, and Stereos variables are more strongly related to the outcome variable, Status, than the original variables, scroll through the output until you find the output shown in Figure 12-27.

Variables in the Equation

		B	S.E.	Wald	df	Sig.	Exp(B)
Step 1[a]	Stereos_bin	2.297	.144	255.733	1	.000	9.943
	Constant	-4.075	.280	212.553	1	.000	.017
Step 2[b]	Stereos_bin	2.591	.145	318.802	1	.000	13.348
	TVs_bin	-1.102	.068	261.610	1	.000	.332
	Constant	-3.260	.285	130.914	1	.000	.038
Step 3[c]	Stereos_bin	1.544	.252	37.504	1	.000	4.684
	TVs_bin	-1.103	.068	262.263	1	.000	.332
	Speakers_bin	1.399	.303	21.283	1	.000	4.052
	Constant	-3.963	.354	125.153	1	.000	.019

a. Variable(s) entered on step 1: Stereos_bin.

b. Variable(s) entered on step 2: TVs_bin.

c. Variable(s) entered on step 3: Speakers_bin.

Figure 12-27: Variables in the Equation table

The Variables in the Equation table (Figure 12-27) shows that the first variable in the equation was Stereos_bin, and this is the variable with the strongest relationship to the outcome field status (incidentally, this is also the variable that had the lowest entropy score). The second variable admitted into the model was TVs_bin, and this is the variable with the second strongest relationship to the outcome variable after controlling for the previous variables in the equation. The third variable in the model was Speakers_bin, and this is the variable with the third strongest relationship to the outcome variable after controlling for the previous variables in the equation. Note that in this simple demonstration, all of the binned variables were chosen over their continuous counterparts; thus, the Optimal Binning procedure successfully created binned variables that maximized the relationship between the supervisor variable and the variables of interest.

Model Complex Interactions with IBM SPSS Neural Networks

In this chapter, we are going to use a demonstration and two different case studies to explore artificial neural networks, as a technique available in the IBM SPSS Statistics Neural Networks module. Along the way, we are also going to pick up on some general data mining skills. In particular, we will learn how to create and use a partition variable in SPSS Statistics even though there is no dedicated menu for creating partitions. We will also discuss some theory, but focus on what is necessary to know regarding the why and how of the technique. A key strategy for that will be to use linear regression as a point of comparison.

We could explore a number of other related topics, but we choose not to pursue them here, with the goal of achieving sufficient depth in the topics that we do explore. We will discuss only multilayer perceptrons. We will not discuss the theory or the practice of radial basis functions, which is another kind of artificial neural network (ANN). Both are available types of neural nets in SPSS Statistics. We make the choice we do because it is the more commonly used and because it is more closely tied to the earliest incarnations of the technique. It will make it easier to make the transition between the history of the technique and the examples we will run in SPSS. Also, we will spend minimal time on the "tuning" of models. Changing settings in order to boost performance is of value, but it can be very time consuming to both explore our choices and to actually walk through the process in the text. For this reason, we will discuss the important aspect of tuning data mining models only in Chapter 14, via decision trees, but neither in this chapter nor in the KNN chapter (Chapter 15). Finally, comparing all the three techniques in the output window will wait for Chapter 15.

We noted in our discussion in Chapter 11 the importance of interactions. In this chapter, the last section compares the neural net and linear regression models to demonstrate this. We need a way to compare them—R Squared is the classic measure of regression model fit, but it doesn't really suit our desire for a simple calculation that we can use to compare both techniques side by side. One could reasonably suggest other choices, but the demonstration in this chapter uses Mean Absolute Percent Error (MAPE). It is an easy formula, and it is just as easily calculated for both approaches.

Our goal, clearly, is to make the case for neural net, but not at the cost of suggesting that linear regression is not a fantastic technique. It is. Most of us will need linear regression more often than we will need neural nets. However, at the risk of spoiling some of the potential suspense, the case study in this chapter will show off some of neutral net's strengths. As for potential weaknesses, the most famous limitation is the issue of how it is a so-called "black box" technique. The demonstration in this chapter, and specifically the output, will show this, but we will stay focused on the strengths, especially in regards to addressing variance that linear regression seems to miss.

By comparing neural nets to linear regression we are not trying to make a straw man argument. It may seem at times that regression is competing with one arm tied behind its back. There are many forms of regression that overcome some of the limitations that we will discuss. We will limit the discussion to fairly basic regression options, however, to keep the comparison easy to follow. We will stay focused on what neural nets are and why they are sometimes useful.

Why "Neural" Nets?

The history of artificial neural nets dates back more than half a century. The history is a tale told many times, and more completely than it is appropriate to do here. *Data Mining Techniques: For Marketing, Sales, and Customer Relationship Management* by Gordon S. Linoff and Michael J. A. Berry (Wiley, 2011) provides a practical, yet detailed, review of all of this. Nonetheless, the history is arguably the best way to explain the theory because the approach has evolved substantially over the years. The first important event was the proposal by F. Rosenblatt in the late '50s of the concept of the perceptron in his paper "The Perceptron: A Probabilistic Model for Information Storage and Organization in the Brain" (Psychological Review, 1958). It was the first attempt to use computers to imitate a biological neuron in a way that we would recognize today. It had major limitations, and in 1969 there was a very influential book, *Perceptrons* by

Marvin Minsky and Seymour A. Pappert (MIT Press, 1987) that pretty much convinced everyone that neural nets were not going to work out. This critique inspired the demonstration comparing neural networks and regression covered in the next section of this chapter. The relevance to us is the following: The artificial neural net approach that we currently use, and that we will be demonstrating in this chapter, was a response to the limitations of the earliest attempts. In the '80s some improvements came together that gave neural nets new life, and they took on a form much like what we use today. We will explore those earlier limitations next, but we won't worry about the perceptron beyond our brief discussion here. Instead we will be comparing the more sophisticated multilayer perceptron to linear regression. Figure 13-1 offers a visual depiction of a perceptron.

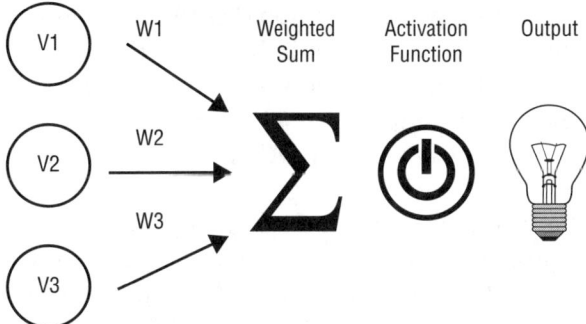

Figure 13-1: An illustration of a perceptron

Many discussions of neural nets discuss their similarity with biological neurons. The salient characteristic is that each biological neuron receives input signals from many other neurons via the receiving neuron's dendrites. The whole process is fascinating, and numerous books on machine learning discuss the process. Those numerous inputs are *weighted*, and their *combined* signal strength causes the neuron to fire or not (it is binary in nature), if the weighted input exceeds a threshold, thereby sending its signal to other neurons. An artificial "perceptron" like the illustration in Figure 13-1 also has multiple inputs, generally one for each of the input variables, and they are also weighted and combined. In the case of a binary classification problem, the act of firing or not signals which of two outcomes are predicted. The power switch is a metaphor for this firing (or not), causing the light bulb to light (or not).

If the notion of combing the product of inputs and weights sounds like regression, it's because the resemblance is quite strong. The weights are like beta coefficients. In regression, the weights are combined via the regression formula. In a perceptron, the weights are combined with an "activation function." In Rosenbaltt's original description the activation function was a step function that produced either a 0 or a 1, thus the similarity to a light switch. More detailed discussions of this topic often describe several different activation functions—not always step functions. We will revisit this topic when we perform an example in SPSS.

In the next section, we will see why neither regression nor perceptrons can solve an important class of problems. So important, in fact, that it will almost always create problems for the data miner. We will learn how the multilayer perceptron addressed the issue. In the sections that follow, we will get some exposure to the fact that the neural net menus in SPSS allow you to choose from different multiple choices for activation function, but we will not demonstrate multiple activation functions in the chapter.

The Famous Case of Exclusive OR and the Perceptron

Most discussions of neural nets that go into enough detail to mention the perceptron and the development of the multilayer perception (MLP) also mention this example. It can be easily found on the Internet, or in books on the subject. Berry and Linoff cover this ground in their discussion of the history, but we aren't concerned with repeating the history here. Our goal is to use this famous example to illustrate an instance where an MLP would succeed, but linear regression would fail.

Exclusive OR is a relationship between two facts in Boolean algebra. It can be simply stated as "either, but not both." A truth table (see Table 13-1) is another way of making clear what Exclusive OR (XOR) is all about. When both inputs are the same, XOR is false. When "either, but not both" are true, XOR is true.

Table 13-1: XOR Truth Table

INPUT 1	INPUT 2	OUTPUT
0 (False)	0 (False)	0 (False)
1 (True)	0 (False)	1 (True)
0 (False)	1 (True)	1 (True)
1 (True)	1 (True)	0 (False)

We are not concerned with Boolean algebra, so how does this help us? It can be shown that a perceptron cannot address this pattern, but an MLP can. The XOR pattern is not "linearly separable," meaning that a single straight line cannot be drawn that separates the two outcome categories. More important for us, we will show that regression is much like a perceptron and also cannot handle this situation. In short, if you have interactions or non-linearity you are in trouble with regression unless you intervene in some way and fix the problem by including interaction terms. An MLP, on the other hand, can address the problem, and without intervention. Of course, in a real-world situation, the pattern might not be deterministic in this way. It might be true that a value of 1 on both inputs was paired with a value of 0 on the output only most of the time. There is no doubt, however, that real-world patterns exist that cannot be addressed with a single straight line, and we will see one in the next section.

Most discussions of this use diagrams and logic to make their case. We will do some of that, but we will mostly use an actual dataset exhibiting the XOR relationships, and run the data through SPSS and then examine the SPSS output. We will let regression take a shot at it, but we will easily confirm that one equation doesn't work. As we shall see, you need two equations.

First, we take the XOR.sav dataset (available from this book's web page). (See the "Creating the XOR Dataset" sidebar for how the dataset was created.) Linear regression does not attempt to identify a line that separates the two output categories. We know that it is attempting to minimize the error in predicting the relationship between the inputs and the output. Nonetheless, the scatterplot of Input 1, Input 2, and the Output makes the problem very clear. Regression is struggling, and to use a football analogy, it punts. It simply cannot produce a regression line that accomplishes our goal of predicting when Output will be 1, and when Output will be 0. The slight variation in the coefficients is just noise resulting from the fact that not all four groups are exactly equal in sample size. A flat regression line, as shown in Figure 13-2, means that we have no variance explained.

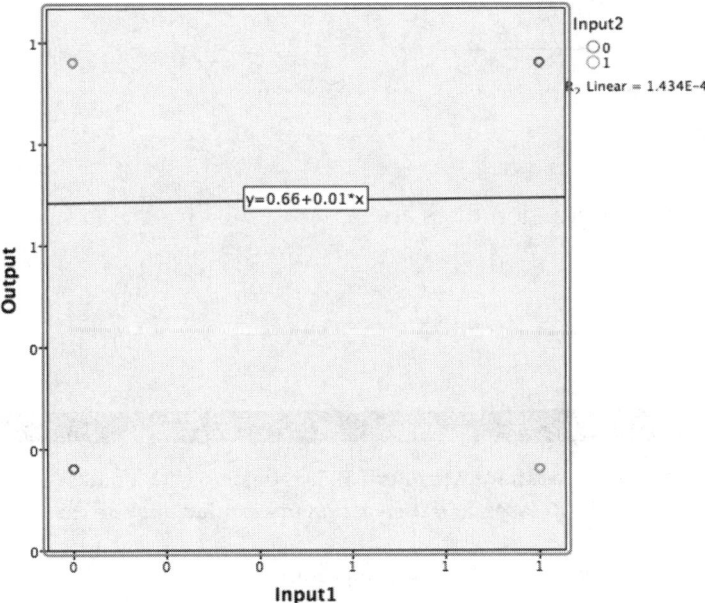

Figure 13-2: A flat regression line

Admittedly, we have been using regression to predict a binary dependent which might seem strange, but the next figure will show the second line (Figure 13-3). Here we have used the "Fit Line at Subgroups" feature of SPSS's scatterplots. Two regression lines are fit, and they are fit perfectly. R2 shows 100% of variance explained. One regression line intersects the upper left (Input1 = 0, Input 2 = 1), and the lower right (Input1 = 1 and Input2 = 1). The second regression line intersects with the opposite corners.

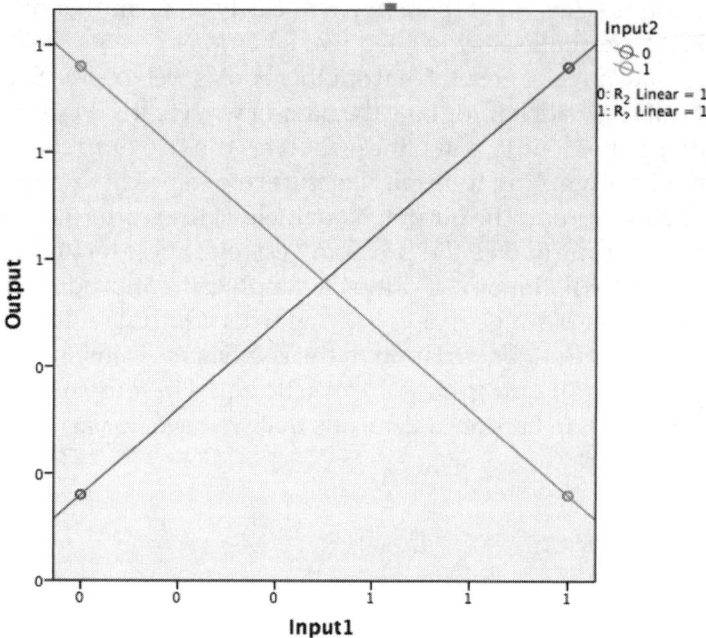

Figure 13-3: Two regression lines

The formulas for the two regression lines are:

$$Y = 0 - 1 * X$$

$$Y = 0 + 1 * X$$

CREATING THE XOR DATASET

Regression and neural net will give us strange results if SPSS is dealing with a dataset that only has 4 cases. I generated 100 cases, and then assigned a random number to the new variable X.

The random variable is easily done with the following command:

```
COMPUTE x=RND(RV.UNIFORM(0.5,4.5)).
```

RND **simply ensures that we will get integers, and using a uniform distribution will give us approximately the same number of each. The rest simply applies the relationships for XOR that we saw in the truth table.**

XOR Example Syntax

```
DO IF (x=1).
COMPUTE Input1 = 0.
COMPUTE Input2 = 0.
COMPUTE Output = 0.
ELSE IF (x=2).
COMPUTE Input1 = 1.
COMPUTE Input2 = 0.
COMPUTE Output = 1.
ELSE IF (x=3).
COMPUTE Input1 = 0.
COMPUTE Input2 = 1.
COMPUTE Output = 1.
ELSE IF (x=4).
COMPUTE Input1 = 1.
COMPUTE Input2 = 1.
COMPUTE Output = 0.
END IF.
```

How will we know when a single regression relationship is insufficient? When data mining, we won't because we won't have any *a priori* sense of the relationships. This is clearly a problem. Regression does offer a partial solution, but it won't be using more than one regression formula. We need to explicitly create interaction terms and fit more coefficients to those terms. We will demonstrate this, later, using the ANN_Bank_Results.sav dataset (available on the website). The same bank data provides an example of needing an interaction term. See Figure 13-4. The regression line for males at the bank is the steeper of the two lines indicating that as education goes up, beginning salary goes up. This is also true for females, but the slope of the line is much more modest. They are not parallel lines. The gender gap for pay is not uniform. The rate of change is different for males and females. There is an interaction between gender and education in predicting beginning salary.

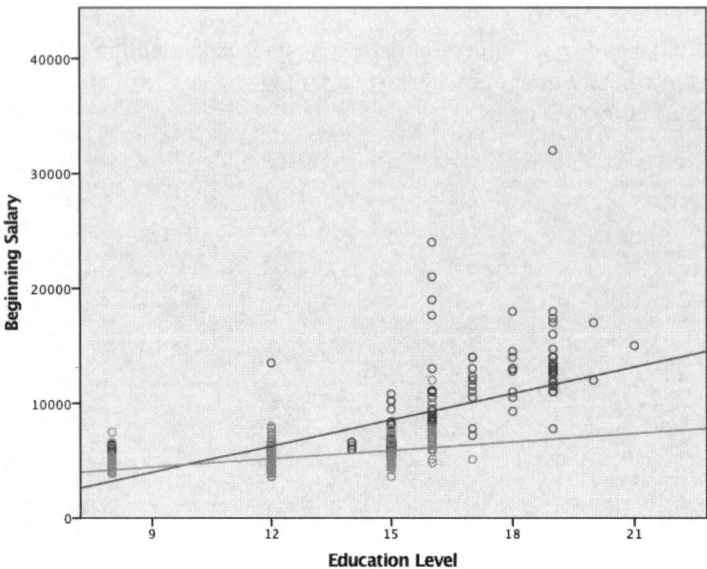

Figure 13-4: Displaying interaction

The reason that the possibility of adding interaction terms is only a partial solution is that we generally won't know what those interactions are *a priori.* That is the real problem. If we knew in advance what the relationships were, we wouldn't be in a data mining situation. As the number of predictors increases our ability to discover these relationships is reduced as well. (The observation that we are always in ignorance of specific relationships *a priori* has been dubbed No Free Lunch for the Data Miner by author and thought leader Tom Khabaza in his *Nine Laws of Data Mining,* http://khabaza.codimension.net/ index_files/9laws.htm.) Now let's briefly consider neural net's ability to tackle this same XOR problem.

What Is a Hidden Layer and Why Is It Needed?

Just as the regression failed with a single straight line, the neural net will need a way to allow the inputs to relate to the output in at least two ways. The solution to this problem was the multilayer perceptron. Instead of fitting weights from the inputs to the activation function of output directly, the inputs are first fed to an activation "hidden layer." In this section we will focus on the hidden layer, and in a following section on Error Backpropagation, we will explain how the weights are calculated. Each input has a weight assigned to each "node" in the hidden layer. The job of the hidden layer is to allow a more complex relationship to emerge. The hidden layer, via its own set of weights, gets fed to the activation function of the output. So, in Figure 13-5 both inputs are used in the activation function of both hidden layers. One way of thinking about the two nodes in the hidden layer is that each is a perceptron—two perceptrons working together, combined at the output layer. Two nodes in the hidden layer allow for two different patterns, not at all unlike the two lines, but which is which is arbitrary. In a neural net applied to a real world problem, this arbitrariness makes interpretation nearly impossible.

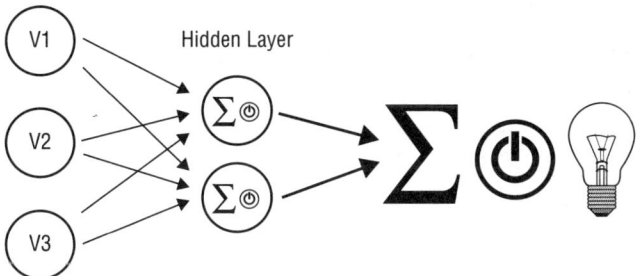

Figure 13-5: An illustration of a multilayer perceptron

Neural Net Results with the XOR Variables

For years, I've had a certain stubborn fascination with neural network weights. The more I was told that "they aren't very interesting," the more intrigued I became. In addition to showing how the neural network addresses the problem we are exploring—the same problem that regression and the perceptron failed to address—I want to resolve what the weights are up to. We will explore them in some detail, with the expectation that you will probably be quite content to ignore them in the future, focusing your attention on more important aspects of your neural net models.

The result shown in Figure 13-6 from the SPSS Statistics output window reflects a default neural network run on the XOR dataset. No instructions were given regarding the architecture, called the *topology*. In other words, SPSS figured out, on its own, that two nodes in the hidden layer were sufficient to fit this data, and as it turns out, it fits the data perfectly. Consistent with the regression example, the target was declared as a scale variable. It is also possible to define this as a binary classification problem, and we will actually try that approach as well. This solution resembles the two-line regression solution. Note the parameter estimates in Figure 13-7.

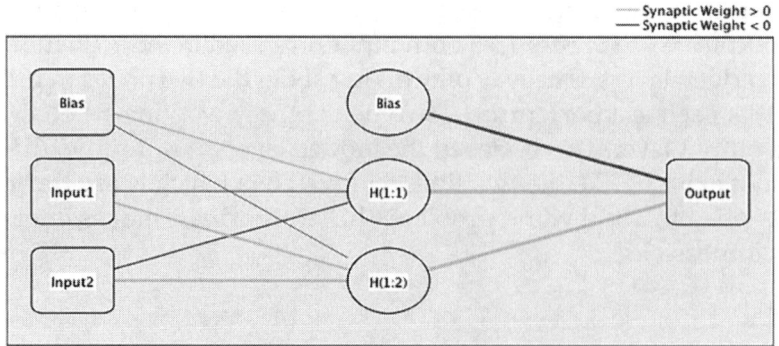

Hidden layer activation function: Hyperbolic tangent

Output layer activation function: Hyperbolic tangent

Figure 13-6: The neural net "topology"

Parameter Estimates

		Predicted		
		Hidden Layer 1		Output Layer
Predictor		H(1:1)	H(1:2)	Output
Input Layer	(Bias)	1.709	-.859	
	Input1	-1.267	2.384	
	Input2	-1.273	2.471	
Hidden Layer 1	(Bias)			-2.563
	H(1:1)			3.297
	H(1:2)			3.232

Figure 13-7: Parameter Estimates for the neural net

The weights and the biases (similar functionally to a Y intercept) are essentially arbitrary. You can try to get your mind wrapped around which is negative and which is positive, but the exact values are also essentially arbitrary. Also, which node in the hidden layer has the job of which aspect of the relationships is arbitrary. If there were dozens of inputs, and several nodes in the hidden layer, trying to figure out the pattern would be difficult, and would ultimately yield little insight. Even the signs are arbitrary, except to show contrast. However, the contrast is the key to the whole problem. The weights from Figure 13-7 as well as some calculations are shown in Table 13-2 to make it easier to examine them.

Table 13-2: Calculating the Output Using the Weights

I 1	I 2	H(1:1)	H(1:2)	PRED. OUTPUT	OUTPUT
0	0	0.937	−0.696	−0.938	0 (False)
1	0	0.415	0.910	0.941	1 (True)
0	1	0.410	0.923	0.944	1 (True)
1	1	−0.681	0.999	−0.918	0 (False)

WEIGHTS	H(1:1)	H(1:2)	OUTPUT LAYER
(Bias)	1.709	−0.859	−2.563
Input 1	−1.267	2.384	3.297
Input 2	−1.273	2.471	3.232

If you compare this to the two regression lines we fit earlier, you can begin to see a certain vague resemblance. Somehow we need to replicate "lines," one having a "positive slope" and another having a "negative slope." The neural net doesn't deal in lines and slopes in the same sense, but the resemblance can still be seen in the interplay between the positive weights and the negative weights. Notice that some of the weights are very similar in size, seemingly canceling each other out. Essentially, there is a node in the hidden layer with positive weights for the inputs, and a node with negative weights for the inputs. For the following Predicted Output values, note that adjusted normalized values fall between −1 and 1. This is the required rescaling method for scale-dependent variables if the output layer uses the hyperbolic tangent activation function, which was the chosen activation function in this case.

$$H(1:1) = TANH(1.709 + (-1.267 \times Input\ 1) + (-1.273 \times Input\ 2))$$

$$H(1:1) = TANH(-0.859 + (-2.384 \times Input\ 1) + (2.471 \times Input\ 2))$$

$$Predicted\ Output = TANH(-2.563 + (3.297 \times Input\ 1) + (3.232 \times Input\ 2))$$

So, in this simple case the weights tell a story of sorts. They force us to rehearse the math behind the TANH Activation Function, making it less mysterious. They clarify what the hidden layer is doing. What they do not do is establish clearly that Input 1 is positively correlated with the Output, or that Input 1 is more important than Input 2. I think this simple example also makes clear that a real example would not be simple at all. An alternate run of the same model, in Figure 13-8, is just as accurate, but all of the weights have completely changed. The reason that everything changes will be further explained in the next section.

Parameter Estimates

Predictor		Predicted		
		Hidden Layer 1		Output Layer
		H(1:1)	H(1:2)	Output
Input Layer	(Bias)	1.320	1.207	
	Input1	−2.918	−1.049	
	Input2	−2.892	−1.027	
Hidden Layer 1	(Bias)			−2.160
	H(1:1)			−3.489
	H(1:2)			4.182

Figure 13-8: Alternative weights from a second neural net

ALTERNATE XOR DEMONSTRATION DEPENDENT DECLARED AS A NOMINAL

Figures 13-9 and 13-10 and Table 13-3 show the results if the Output Variable was declared as a Nominal. The interpretation would be the same except that the adjusted normalization does not apply, so the output values are between 0 and 1 instead of -1 and 1. Both approaches produce perfect classification with no errors.

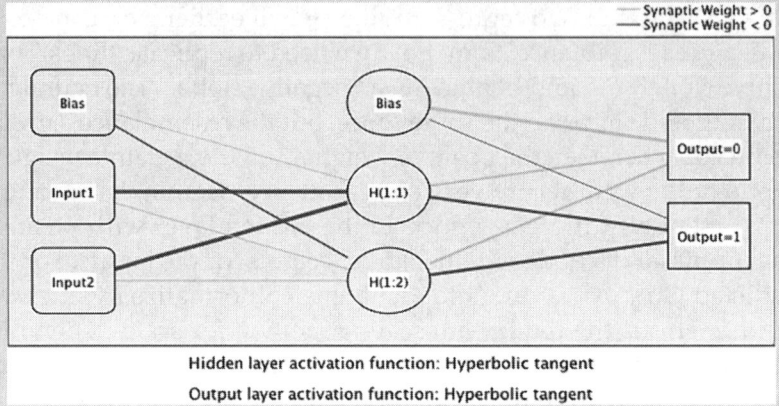

Hidden layer activation function: Hyperbolic tangent

Output layer activation function: Hyperbolic tangent

Figure 13-9: Topology with outcome declared as nominal

Parameter Estimates

		Predicted			
		Hidden Layer 1		Output Layer	
Predictor		H(1:1)	H(1:2)	[Output=0]	[Output=1]
Input Layer	(Bias)	−1.920	1.044		
	Input1	1.363	−2.836		
	Input2	1.330	−2.649		
Hidden Layer 1	(Bias)			2.773	−.583
	H(1:1)			1.962	−2.316
	H(1:2)			1.876	−2.090

Figure 13-10: Parameter Estimates with outcome declared as nominal

Table 13-3: Weights and Calculations for Neural Net with Nominal Outcome

I 1	I 2	H(1:1)	H(1:2)	OUTPUT 0	OUTPUT 1	OUTPUT
0	0	−0.958	0.779	0.982	0.006	0 (False)
1	0	−0.506	−0.946	0.006	0.988	1 (True)
0	1	−0.530	−0.922	0.003	0.988	1 (True)
1	1	0.649	−1.000	0.974	0.004	0 (False)

H(1:1)	H(1:2)		Output 0	Output 1
−1.920	1.044		2.773	−0.583
1.363	−2.836		1.962	−2.316
1.330	−2.649		1.876	−2.090

How the Weights Are Calculated: Error Backpropagation

The *SPSS Algorithms Guide* (available in the SPSS Help system) helps to clarify the exact nature of the implementation of MLP in SPSS. This is necessary because the broader literature will speak of many different flavors and variants:

> *The multilayer perceptron (MLP) is a feed-forward, supervised learning network with up to two hidden layers. The MLP network is a function of one or more predictors (also called inputs or independent variables) that minimizes the prediction error of one or more target variables (also called outputs). Predictors and targets can be a mix of categorical and scale variables.*

In other sections, two further clarifications are given. SPSS uses the common "Error Backpropagation" method with either a "Scaled conjugate gradient" or "Gradient Descent." Gradient Descent is what you will encounter in most introductions to the subject. Although the default setting is Scaled conjugate descent, we will explain the more basic method here. We will not get deep into the theory, but will explore it in enough detail to help you understand two key aspects:

- How the weights are calculated
- Why the weights change when you rerun the neural net

Neural networks are iterative learners. The weights get a little closer to optimal each time a record passes through the learning process. "Optimal" is a better word than "correct" because "correct" would imply the same results each time. Each neural net will make very similar predictions, but the underlying weights may be dramatically different, especially with the necessary presence of the hidden layer. A change in one area of the network can have a ripple effect to other nodes in the network, with all kinds of compensation effects, sign changes, and canceling out being the result. So to be clear: Two networks can make near identical predictions while having extremely different weights and even architectures (topologies).

How does it all work? Dean Abbott, in *Applied Predictive Analytics* (Wiley, 2014), provides a great metaphor for how an ANN learns:

> The learning process is similar to how I learned to catch fly balls as a boy. First, imagine my father hitting a ball to me in the outfield. In the beginning, I had absolutely no idea where the ball was going to land, so I just watched it until it landed, far to my left. Since my goal was to catch the ball, the distance between where the ball landed and where I stood was the error. Then my father hit a second fly ball, and, because of the prior example I had seen, I moved (hesitantly) toward where the ball landed last time, but this time the ball landed to my right. Wrong again.
>
> But then something began to happen. The more fly balls my father hit, the more I was able to associate the speed the ball was hit, the steepness of the hit, and the left/right angle—the initial conditions of the hit—and predict where the ball was going to land.

The process in SPSS for MLPs is as follows:

1. Random weights are assigned.

2. Errors are calculated for each case.

3. Weights are updated for each case.

4. After a minimum of one "epoch," Stopping Rules are checked.

Random weights are assigned. Keep in mind that there are weights associating the inputs to the hidden layer(s) as well as weights associated the hidden layer(s) to the output(s). For each case in the Training partition the output is compared to the actual value, and an error is calculated. All of the weights are updated to reduce the error on the next try. The "learning rate" is used to determine how much of an adjustment to make to all of the weights. For gradient descent, an Initial Learning Rate is set, and with each epoch the learning rate is reduced until the Lower Boundary of the Learning Rate is reached. "Momentum" is also involved in this process by controlling how much weight to give to prior weight changes. In other words, with each adjustment, it gets closer and closer to a solution and makes smaller and smaller changes. A single complete data pass of the Training sample is referred to as an "epoch" in the menus, Figure 13-11.

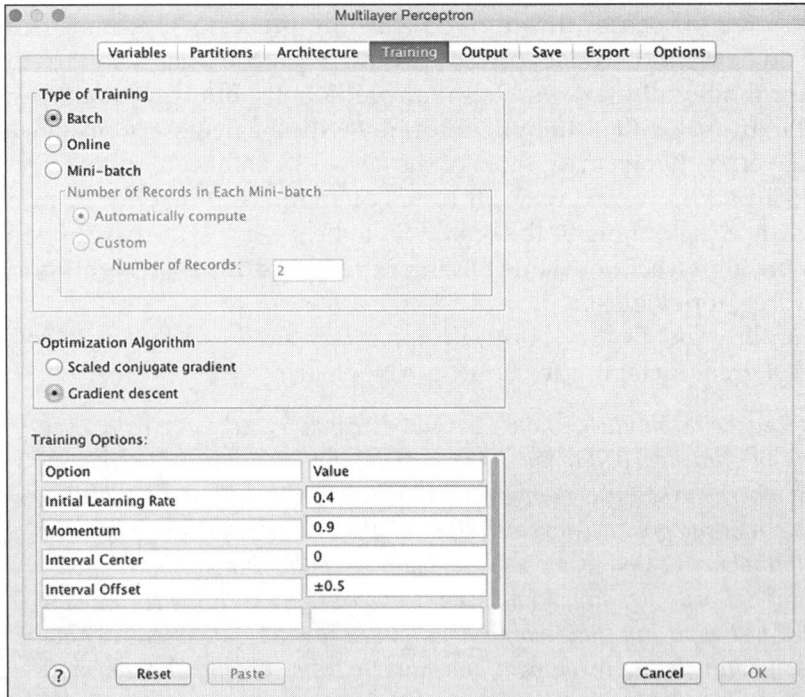

Figure 13-11: Training submenu

The Stopping Rules are checked, and if not met, the training continues. Stopping Rules naturally include failing to make a minimum change to the errors, but also include a time limit since training a neural network can take a very long time. See Figure 13-12.

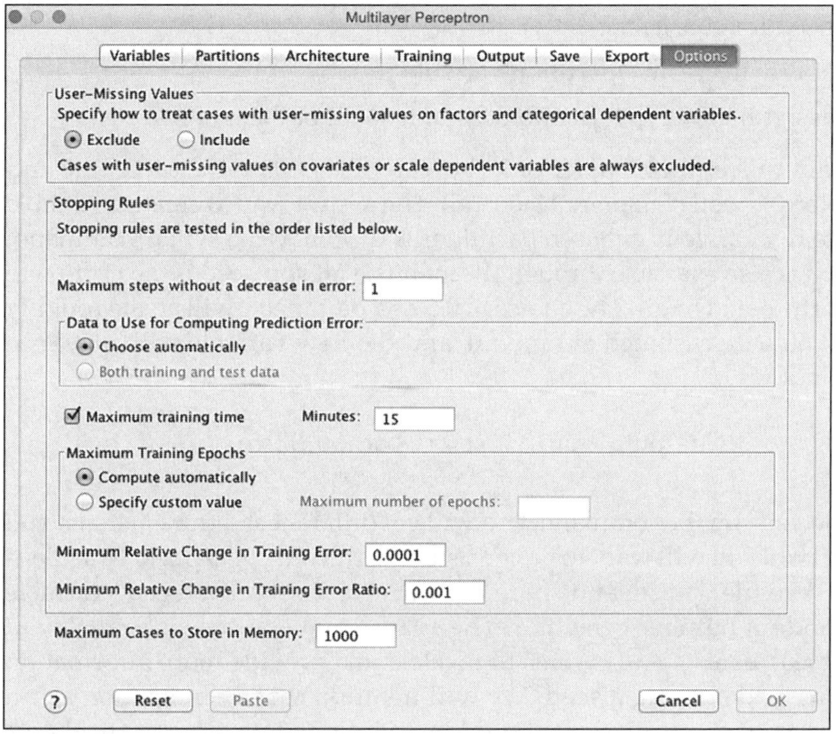

Figure 13-12: Options submenu

Few practitioners will choose to make changes to these settings (and perhaps even fewer should), and the briefing in this section would be incomplete training to do so. Experts will make changes, and it can help if they have the proper training, but even then only a modest proportion of the model's performance depends upon these settings. Even without that expertise, you will now be able to recognize the role played by some of the settings in the creation of the network and the fitting of the weights. The hope is that neural networks are considerably less mysterious. We will draw attention to key features and interpretation during our discussion of the two case studies. First, in the next section, we will learn how to create a reusable partition variable.

Creating a Consistent Partition in SPSS Statistics

In SPSS Statistics, we do not have a dedicated process like the Partition Node in SPSS Modeler. Instead, the necessary features are distributed in a couple of different places. Importantly, all of the necessary features are accounted for:

- The need for consistency
- The ability to create a partition variable
- The assignment of the partition variable to all of the models

We explain this in this chapter only, but it applies to the Decision Tree and KNN chapters as well (Chapters 14 and 15). The easiest way to create a variable divided into two randomly chosen partitions is the following syntax command. The function is also available through the menus—all you need is the portion to the right of the equals sign. The choice of 0.5 as a parameter will create roughly 50% 1s and 50% 0s, assigned at random, and the new variable will appear in the data window:

$$\text{Compute Train}\_\text{Test} = \text{rv.bernoulli}(0.5)$$

Each time you run the command, you will get different assignments, so if you are sharing data you will want to be consistent with your colleagues. To achieve this either save the dataset and share the variable, or share a "seed" variable with the random number generator. The `Train_Test` variable is available in the dataset `ANN_Bank_Results.sav`. SPSS Help can provide more information on assigning and sharing a seed. We will mention this phenomenon again later, but for proper emphasis it should be mentioned now that neural nets will produce a different result each time, so the `ANN_Bank_Results.sav` dataset also has the neural net prediction values. If you were to follow the steps with the original data you could produce variability in two distinct ways: having a different partition or simply producing a different neural net. The steps are straightforward, but they will not produce identical results even when using identical data.

The final step in using the partition variable is assigning it when it comes time to run the model. The "Selection Variable" variable selection box is available in a number of menus including Linear Regression as shown in Figure 13-13.

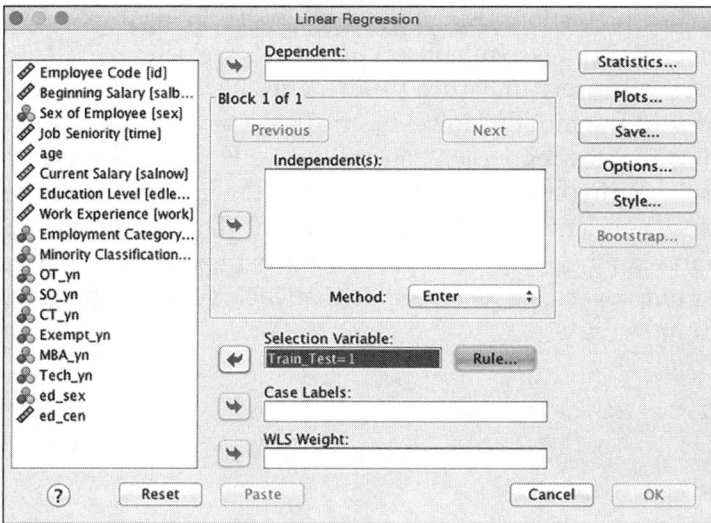

Figure 13-13: The Selection Variable option in Linear Regression

By declaring "1" in the Rule submenu (as shown in Figure 13-14), the 1s will be assigned to the Train partition, and the 0s to the Test partition. The impact of this setting on the output will be discussed in the example in the next section.

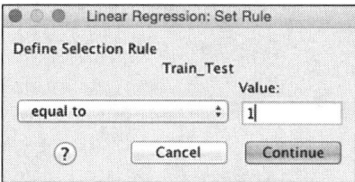

Figure 13-14: Set Rule submenu

Comparing Regression to Neural Net with the Bank Salary Case Study

We are going to begin a series of models and modeling approaches in this section beginning with a regression with two main effects, but no interaction term. Beginning salary is the dependent variable, and Education and Sex are the independent variables, but Education has been transformed. It has been "centered"—that is, zero on the transformed variable represents average education, not zero education. This transformation is not necessary yet, but will be necessary when we explore interactions using regression, so it is being introduced now for consistency. This dataset is available on the book's website.

The output (shown in its entirety in Figure 13-15) makes it clear that only the 1s are being using to build the model. However, the 0s do have a role to play. That data is used to show that the regression generalizes well to other data. Note that the multiple R for the Train data (.664) is very close to the multiple R for the Test data (.695). Both independent variables are significant. The gender gap of $1804 is nontrivial in an era when total annual salary was thousands, not tens of thousands for most employees. Ed_cen reveals that each year of schooling adds about $532 to annual salary.

Regression

Variables Entered/Removed[a,b]

Model	Variables Entered	Variables Removed	Method
1	ed_cen, Sex of Employee[c]	.	Enter

a. Dependent Variable: Beginning Salary

b. Models are based only on cases for which Train_Test = 1.00

c. All requested variables entered.

Model Summary[b,c]

Model	R		R Square	Adjusted R Square	Std. Error of the Estimate
	Train_Test = 1.00 (Selected)	Train_Test ~= 1.00 (Unselected)			
1	.664[a]	.695	.441	.436	2295.128

a. Predictors: (Constant), ed_cen, Sex of Employee

b. Unless noted otherwise, statistics are based only on cases for which Train_Test = 1.00.

c. Dependent Variable: Beginning Salary

ANOVA[a,b]

Model		Sum of Squares	df	Mean Square	F	Sig.
1	Regression	964432517	2	482216258	91.544	.000[c]
	Residual	1.222E+9	232	5267613.80		
	Total	2.187E+9	234			

a. Dependent Variable: Beginning Salary

b. Selecting only cases for which Train_Test = 1.00

c. Predictors: (Constant), ed_cen, Sex of Employee

Coefficients[a,b]

Model		Unstandardized Coefficients		Standardized Coefficients	t	Sig.
		B	Std. Error	Beta		
1	(Constant)	7559.363	204.864		36.899	.000
	Sex of Employee	-1804.007	318.117	-.293	-5.671	.000
	ed_cen	532.433	54.017	.510	9.857	.000

a. Dependent Variable: Beginning Salary

b. Selecting only cases for which Train_Test = 1.00

Figure 13-15: Complete Regression Output

Now we will proceed with an ANN using the same predictors as shown in Figure 13-16. Education has not been transformed as this precaution is unnecessary with ANN. By default, the neural net module does its own partitioning, but we have used the same `Train_Test` variable for consistency as shown in Figure 13-17.

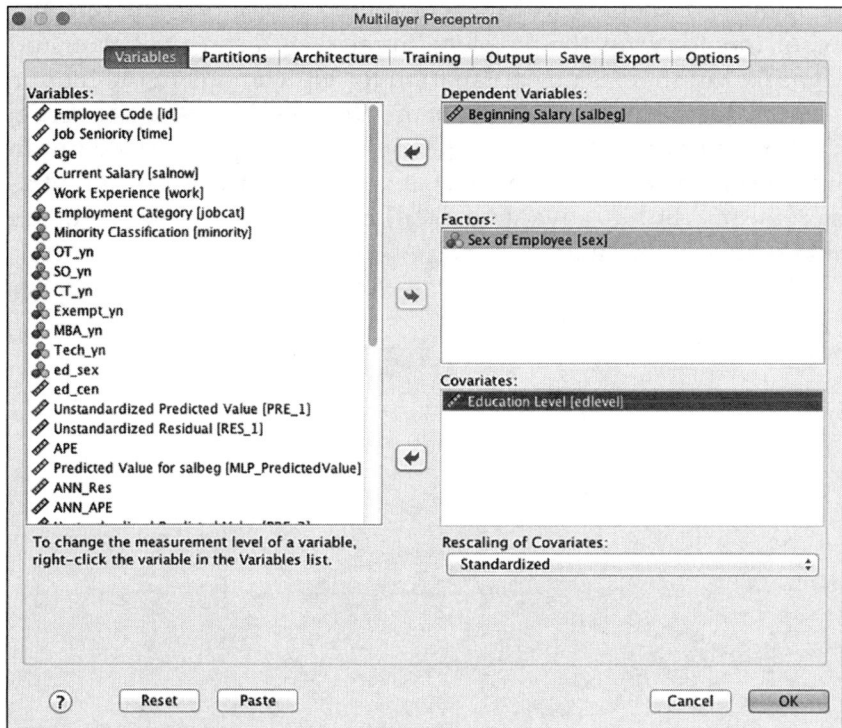

Figure 13-16: Multilayer Perceptron main menu

Figure 13-17: Partitions submenu

Let's examine the results. The network topology diagrams (Figure 13-18) are very visually compelling, but they ultimately don't tell us much about the model, at least not in the same way as our regression output did. We do see that sex and edlevel behave a bit differently. Sex is shown as two inputs because it is a factor, but edlevel is only shown once because it is a covariate. There are four nodes in the hidden layer. We did not choose this, nor influence it. The neural net algorithm determined that it was the optimal architecture, or topology, for the problem. Some weights are positive, and some are negative, but there is no explanation for which node in the hidden layer represents which aspect of the problem. We could request the actual weights, but it would not resolve these questions, and a positive weight in one run could reverse in the next. In short, it is not nearly as transparent as the regression output, but its advantages will become clear as we compare some variants with each method.

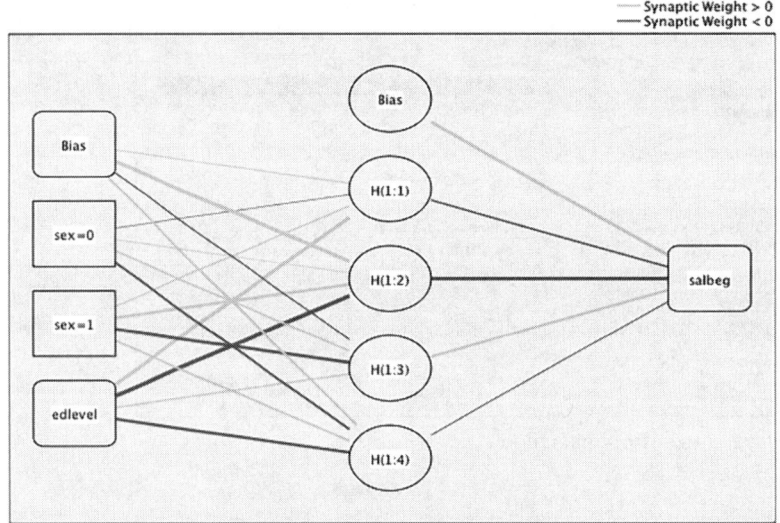

Hidden layer activation function: Hyperbolic tangent

Output layer activation function: Identity

Figure 13-18: Network topology diagram

Calculating Mean Absolute Percent Error for Both Models

Regression provides us with a residual (named RES_1) when we ask for it. In the case of ANN_Res, we are calculating our own:

```
COMPUTE APE=(ABS(RES_1)/salbeg)*100.
COMPUTE ANN_Res=salbeg-MLP_PredictedValue.
COMPUTE ANN_APE=(ABS(ANN_Res)/salbeg)*100.
```

Armed with these calculations, it is a simple matter to compare the two (Figure 13-19). We find that the neural net results, ANN_APE, are much better than the regression results. Lower is better since these are errors. Recall that the .00 results represent our most important Test results as they reflect the ability of the models to perform on unseen data. Comparing the .00 results to the 1.00 results vertically shows good consistency at 13.1% and 13.8% for the ANN. The regression's consistency, 19.2% versus 23%, is not awful, but it is not good either. Looking only at the test results, the 13.1% is much better than the 19.2%. These reflect an accuracy of 86.9% and 80.8% (by subtracting the error from 100%). Why is the ANN so much better? It's not magic, of course. It means that one is missing something that the other one has captured. How? They seemingly have the same ingredients.

Report

Train_Test		ANN_APE	APE
.00	Mean	13.1080	19.156
	N	237	237
	Std. Deviation	11.69311	14.1412
1.00	Mean	13.7685	23.048
	N	235	235
	Std. Deviation	12.79244	15.0937
Total	Mean	13.4368	21.094
	N	472	472
	Std. Deviation	12.24422	14.7369

Figure 13-19: Comparing performance

Regression requires the human analyst to manually create interaction terms, and the neural net does not. So it appears to be an apples-to-apples comparison, but the neural net has an advantage that the regression cannot overcome without help. We will now provide that help by adding an interaction term, and continue with more models and more comparisons (Figure 13-20).

Regression

Model Summary[b,c]

	R				
Model	Train_Test = 1.00 (Selected)	Train_Test ~= 1.00 (Unselected)	R Square	Adjusted R Square	Std. Error of the Estimate
1	.704[a]	.718	.496	.489	2185.172

a. Predictors: (Constant), ed_sex, Sex of Employee, ed_cen

b. Unless noted otherwise, statistics are based only on cases for which Train_Test = 1.00.

c. Dependent Variable: Beginning Salary

Coefficients[a,b]

Model		Unstandardized Coefficients		Standardized Coefficients		
		B	Std. Error	Beta	t	Sig.
1	(Constant)	7395.099	197.804		37.386	.000
	Sex of Employee	-1985.564	305.051	-.323	-6.509	.000
	ed_cen	727.774	64.616	.697	11.263	.000
	ed_sex	-532.966	106.731	-.306	-4.994	.000

a. Dependent Variable: Beginning Salary

b. Selecting only cases for which Train_Test = 1.00

Figure 13-20: Regression results with interaction terms

We can see that the performance is considerably better. An interaction term has been formally created and added to the model. Ed_sex is simply the product of our two other independent variables—simple multiplication and nothing more. However, this is why we centered the variable earlier. If we hadn't, the regression would have suffered from multicollinearity. The R2 has increased from 44.1% to almost 50%. Also, the interaction term, ed_sex, is clearly significant, giving a clue as to why the main effects-only version had trouble competing with the neural net.

We will name this result APE2. The updated Compare Means report (Figure 13-21) shows improvement in both stability (comparing 17.9% to 20.9%) and accuracy on the test partition (17.9% compared to last time, 19.2%). It still hasn't caught up with the neural net:

```
COMPUTE APE2=(ABS(RES_2)/salbeg)*100.
```

Report

Train_Test		ANN_APE	APE	APE2
.00	Mean	13.1080	19.156	17.9344
	N	237	237	237
	Std. Deviation	11.69311	14.1412	15.27827
1.00	Mean	13.7685	23.048	20.8770
	N	235	235	235
	Std. Deviation	12.79244	15.0937	14.72876
Total	Mean	13.4368	21.094	19.3995
	N	472	472	472
	Std. Deviation	12.24422	14.7369	15.06343

Figure 13-21: Updated results with three models compared

We will now consider a more complete, but also more complex Regression approach (Figure 13-22).

Minority classification and a collection of variables representing job classification have been added. Most of the individual variables are significant. Interactions with these new variables could be considered, but the regression is already getting rather complex. Minority status is not significant, but it could be shown to be significant as a main effect if alone in a model (not shown). There is sometimes a temptation to keep some of the occupation variables, and remove the others. This is usually not recommended as they represent a single categorical variable and have simply been transformed. Also, neural net doesn't even present us with that choice as it doesn't require any transformation, accepting the occupation variable as it is. A chapter-length treatment of this case study as a regression would provide the opportunity to explore several improvements to this model, but in shorter form here it is a worthy enough attempt for our purposes. It is not yet optimal, but more than merely a straw man challenger to the neural net. R2 is now 82%.

Model Summary[b,c]

Model	R		R Square	Adjusted R Square	Std. Error of the Estimate
	Train_Test = 1.00 (Selected)	Train_Test ~= 1.00 (Unselected)			
1	.905[a]	.887	.819	.811	1329.568

a. Predictors: (Constant), Tech_yn, MBA_yn, SO_yn, ed_sex, Exempt_yn, Minority Classification, CT_yn, OT_yn, Sex of Employee, ed_cen

b. Unless noted otherwise, statistics are based only on cases for which Train_Test = 1.00.

c. Dependent Variable: Beginning Salary

Coefficients[a,b]

Model		Unstandardized Coefficients		Standardized Coefficients	t	Sig.
		B	Std. Error	Beta		
1	(Constant)	6406.874	180.209		35.553	.000
	Sex of Employee	-1242.112	203.746	-.202	-6.096	.000
	ed_cen	229.563	56.433	.220	4.068	.000
	ed_sex	-138.754	75.550	-.080	-1.837	.068
	Minority Classification	-166.979	226.564	-.023	-.737	.462
	OT_yn	-85.505	217.548	-.013	-.393	.695
	SO_yn	430.518	447.261	.033	.963	.337
	CT_yn	2919.169	358.103	.273	8.152	.000
	Exempt_yn	6159.373	416.479	.509	14.789	.000
	MBA_yn	6489.508	1379.366	.138	4.705	.000
	Tech_yn	10422.874	714.214	.442	14.593	.000

a. Dependent Variable: Beginning Salary

b. Selecting only cases for which Train_Test = 1.00

Figure 13-22: Results for a more complex regression

Let's give the neural net an opportunity to use the same inputs.

Again, the network diagram, shown in Figure 13-23, is very compelling visually, but doesn't reveal much. It does show that only edlevel is being treated as a covariate. All of the factor variables have an input for each category.

Now we are in a position to compare all five versions. As shown in Figure 13-24, the latest regression Absolute Percent Error result is named APE3, and the latest ANN results is called ANN_APE2.

The regression is much better than any earlier regression. The neural net is better as well. In terms of accuracy, the neural net is only a half point better. Both are stable. Perhaps with more work on the regression that gap could be closed even more. So what might we conclude? The neural net is not magic, but to compete with it, the regression needed considerable help from the human analyst. The main effects only model, APE, did not offer much competition to ANN_APE. Only the regression models with interaction terms added produced results that were comparable to the neural net. One lesson learned is that with enough persistence, a skilled analyst should be able to build a pretty good regression model, but when the number of input variables balloons up into the hundreds, the techniques that were used here to improve the regression become unrealistic. While the "black box" nature of neural nets sometimes makes them an imperfect choice, the approach definitely has its merits.

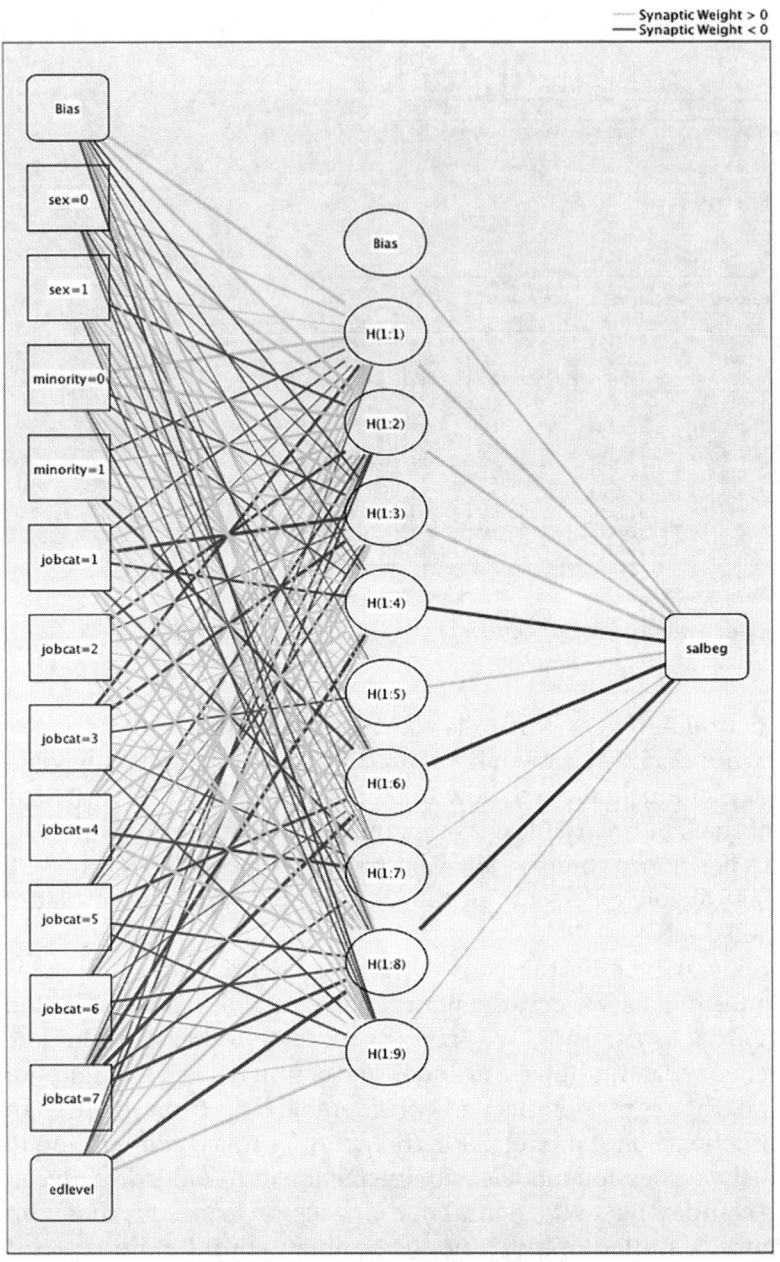

— Synaptic Weight > 0
— Synaptic Weight < 0

Hidden layer activation function: Hyperbolic tangent

Output layer activation function: Identity

Figure 13-23: Topology diagram for the more complex neural net

Report

Train_Test		ANN_APE	APE	APE2	APE3	ANN_APE2
.00	Mean	13.1080	19.156	17.9344	12.0528	11.6798
	N	237	237	237	237	237
	Std. Deviation	11.69311	14.1412	15.27827	9.71809	9.38028
1.00	Mean	13.7685	23.048	20.8770	11.8329	11.5585
	N	235	235	235	235	235
	Std. Deviation	12.79244	15.0937	14.72876	9.63601	9.51421
Total	Mean	13.4368	21.094	19.3995	11.9433	11.6194
	N	472	472	472	472	472
	Std. Deviation	12.24422	14.7369	15.06343	9.66766	9.43736

Figure 13-24: Comparing five models

Classification with Neural Nets Demonstrated with the Titanic Dataset

We will briefly build a neural network for classification in this example so that we can compare to other classifications' attempts in the next two chapters. In order to do that, we will create a partition variable again. The variable is already created in the Titanic_Results.sav dataset.

This time a 70% Train/30% Test partition will be used:

```
COMPUTE Train_Test=rv.bernoulli(0.7).
```

The Dependent variable is Survived, and there will be four predictors. Pclass (passenger class) and Sex are Factors and Age and Parch (which refers to number of parents and children aboard) are covariates. In theory, the neural net could handle the entire dataset, but neural nets tend to become overly complex and we won't have the opportunity in this section to do a proper job of feature selection. One should be a bit cautious about giving neural net variables that have a very weak relationship to the Dependent as it will always use all variables. Weak predictors will be not be given large weights, but they will make the model more complex nonetheless. So to make it simple in this case, the variables chosen are variables known to have an ability to predict Survived (Figure 13-25).

Note that since the output variable is binary there are two nodes in the output layer as shown in Figure 13-26.

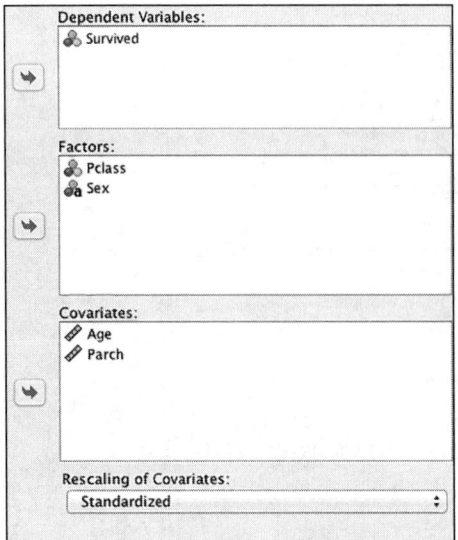

Figure 13-25: Variables selected for the neural net

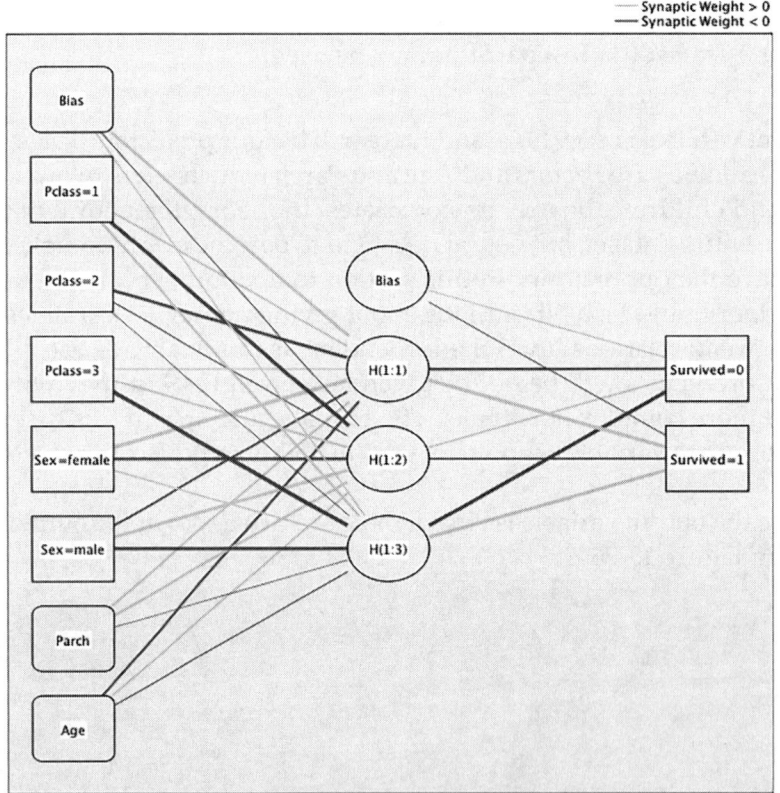

Hidden layer activation function: Hyperbolic tangent

Output layer activation function: Softmax

Figure 13-26: Neural net topology diagram

We have much more to say about the results in Chapter 15. The accuracy is OK, but not stellar (Figure 13-27). Although the accuracy degrades on the Testing partition, the amount that the accuracy has dropped is within acceptable limits, but just barely. It has dropped from 82.0% to 77%. A common rule of thumb is that a drop of greater than 5% would indicate that it is unstable. It does a better join with non-survivors (83.2%) than survivors (70.1%). This might tempt us to balance the data (as discussed in the previous chapter), but balancing in SPSS Statistics would be a bit time consuming and a bit of a challenge. (However, seemingly difficult steps like this can be much easier with a good extension command. We discuss this in Chapter 18.) This result is acceptable enough to represent neural net in the "competition" in Chapter 15. If neural net were to win, we might want to revisit the model and see if we couldn't improve both stability and accuracy a bit. Nonetheless, we will give it one more try.

Classification

Sample	Observed	Predicted 0	Predicted 1	Percent Correct
Training	0	259	31	89.3%
	1	75	125	62.5%
	Overall Percent	68.2%	31.8%	78.4%
Testing	0	122	12	91.0%
	1	24	66	73.3%
	Overall Percent	65.2%	34.8%	83.9%

Dependent Variable: Survived

Figure 13-27: Classification accuracy results

We will now add more variables (Figure 13-28), but the additional variables will make the network diagram more complex (not shown). SibSp is a count of family members traveling with the passenger, siblings and spouse.

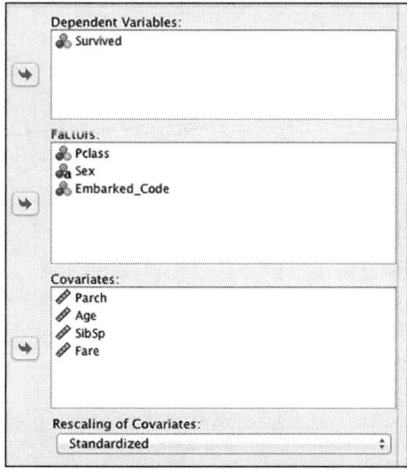

Figure 13-28: Adding additional variables

We will also request some options under the Save tab (Figure 13-29). This will allow us to compare this second neural net to other models in Chapter 15.

Finally, we will take a peek at the accuracy and stability of the second neural net (Figure 13-30). It is slightly less accurate on the Testing sample, but it is more stable. The two accuracies are much closer. A rule of thumb that is often used is that a drop in accuracy of more than five points is a cause for concern. The first model seems unstable. Based on a quick glance, the second model seems the stronger model.

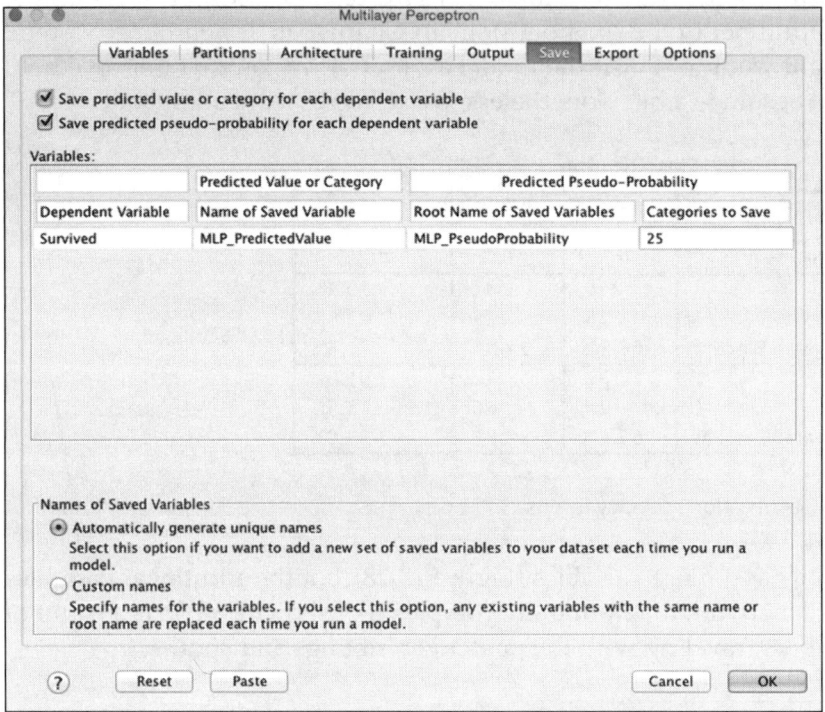

Figure 13-29: The Save submenu

Classification

Sample	Observed	Predicted 0	Predicted 1	Percent Correct
Training	0	271	19	93.4%
	1	68	130	65.7%
	Overall Percent	69.5%	30.5%	82.2%
Testing	0	121	13	90.3%
	1	23	67	74.4%
	Overall Percent	64.3%	35.7%	83.9%

Dependent Variable: Survived

Figure 13-30: Model accuracy for the second attempt

In a real situation, these two models would be compared more closely, and more than two models would likely be considered. Just one example of something that we are not looking into carefully is the relative ability of the two models to find the 1s and the 0s. In most real world situations we care more about finding those at high risk than those at low risk. These models are better at finding 0s than 1s. That is often a consideration. Nonetheless, we have two more algorithms to discuss in Chapters 14 and 15 before we can revisit this issue, so we will conclude this section choosing the second model to represent neural net in the Chapter 15.

Powerful and Intuitive: IBM SPSS Decision Trees

Now that we've seen Artificial Neural Nets, we are going to move on to another technique. Decision trees are more accurately thought of as a class of techniques as they represent multiple algorithms. The chapter that lays the groundwork for what we will see in this chapter, and all of Part III, is Chapter 11. If you are new to data mining, in general, you may want to start there. IBM SPSS Decision Trees offers four "Growing Methods": CHAID, Exhaustive CHAID, CRT, and QUEST. The C5.0 Tree extension command offers a fifth possible option. Extension commands will be discussed in Chapter 18. We will demonstrate just CHAID and CRT, but running more than one iteration of each. CHAID and CRT provide a number of contrasts to each other so those two will give a good understanding of the decision tree approach. By altering the settings of both CHAID and CRT, it will allow the differences to become even more clear. A deeper understanding of two will prove a more satisfying introduction than a brief introduction of all five. (Note that Exhaustive CHAID, as the name implies, is quite similar to CHAID.) Finally, at the close of the chapter we will demonstrate the Scoring Wizard.

Building a Tree with the CHAID Algorithm

We'll use the `Titanic_Results.sav` dataset (available in this chapter's downloads), and the same partition variable, `Train_Test`, that was created near the end of Chapter 13. As shown in Figure 14-1, Pclass, Age, Sex, and Parch (as scale) will be chosen as Independent Variables. Train/Test validation using a partition variable is not the only method, however, and alternatives are covered in the "Alternative Validation Options" section near the end of this chapter.

> **NOTE** We use this same partition variable throughout Part III of this book to allow us to compare the results of Chapters 13, 14, and 15. A side-by-side comparison of three techniques, from three chapters, is shown in the final section of Chapter 15.

Notice that the button for the Validation submenu is selected in Figure 14-1. We move to that submenu next. Note the symbols next to the variables in the figure indicating level of measurement. Different levels of measurement declarations in the Variable View could result in a different tree, as the algorithm will treat nominal, ordinal, and continuous independent variables differently.

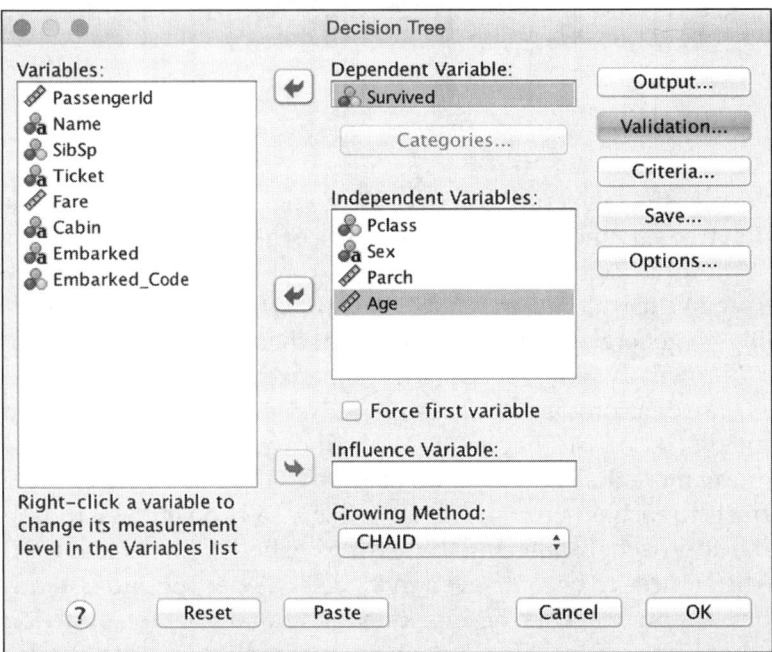

Figure 14-1: Decision tree main menu

Restricting the variables like this is temporary while you get used to this new technique. Once we review the basics, we will be using all of the available variables. Tree algorithms are generally quite good at performing feature selection as part of model building.

As mentioned, we will also perform a couple of iterations to show what it is like to repeat the model a number of times. In statistics, confidence in one's result comes from carefully choosing a single approach that is recommended by theory. When using these predictive modeling techniques rigor comes from systematically attempting all plausible options, carefully documenting what you have tried, and validating all attempts against a hold-out sample (or similar alternative approaches like N-fold validation). The choice of the final model is justified empirically, not on theoretical grounds.

The partition variable is declared in the Validation submenu shown in Figure 14-2. Using an external variable is not the default, but the necessary choice is easily indicated. Select "Use variable" and indicate that we will "Split Sample By" `Train_Test`.

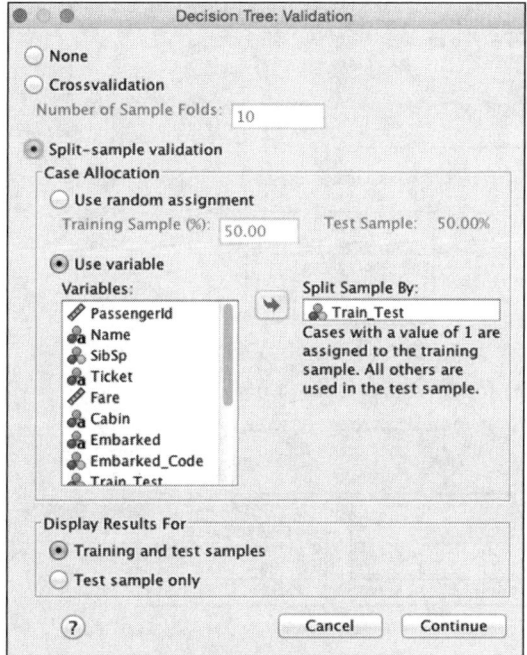

Figure 14-2: Validation submenu

Otherwise, we will let the model run on defaults. The result in the output window shows us the Training Sample tree, shown in Figure 14-3, as well as the Test Sample tree, shown in Figure 14-4. The shape of the two trees will be the same since the shape was built using the Training Sample only. However, the tree can be thought of as a set of rules. For instance, this rule:

If Female and First/Second class then Survive

can be applied to any other data. So the Test Sample tree has the identical shape to correspond to the same rules, but the values are drawn from the Test dataset so the exact values will be somewhat different. However, since the Train and

Test datasets were chosen at random, they are structurally the same—they have the same variables and the same possible categories. Any future dataset for which you used the tree model to make predictions would also have the same variables and categories.

Training Sample

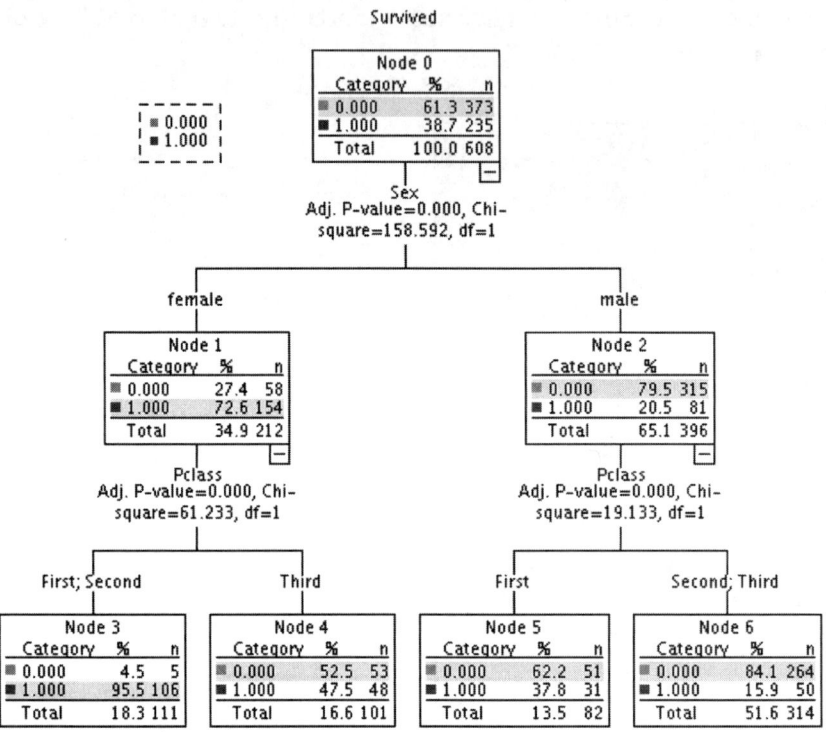

Figure 14-3: Training Sample tree

For example, let's consider the rule involving female passengers in First or Second class, the survival rate in the Training Sample is 95.5%, but a tad lower at 93.2% in the Test Sample. (The relevant information is in Node 3 in both cases.)

While we are at it, let's review some more details of the tree using the Training Sample. Remember that the Training Sample tree is the one shown in Figure 14-3. We observe the following:

- The "Root Node" (Node 0) reveals that we have a total sample size of 608, of which 38.7% survived.

- The most important variables are Gender and Pclass, in that order.

- There are four "leaf nodes" (Nodes 3, 4, 5, and 6). Their sample sizes add up to 608, and they represent a mutually exclusive and exhaustive segmentation of the sample.

- The lowest survival rate is found in Node 6 (15.9%) and the highest (95.5%) in Node 3.

Test Sample

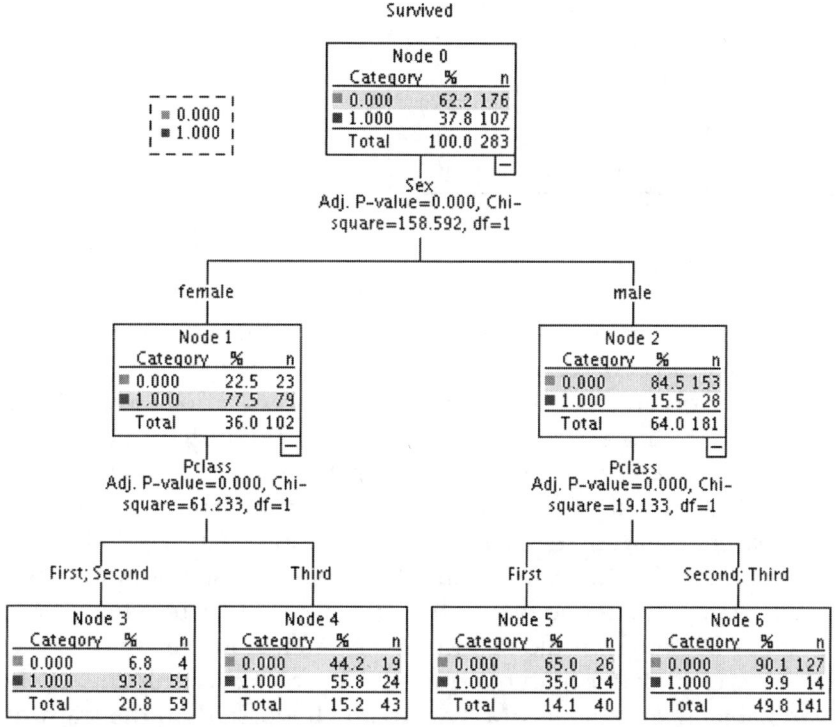

Figure 14-4: Test Sample tree

Finally, if we observe the survival rates for the same nodes, 6 and 3, but this time in the Test Sample tree, Figure 14-4, we find that while they are not identical, they show a similar pattern.

Next we will consider our overall accuracy. Figure 14-5 gives us a report of the performance of the tree as a whole. There are four figures in the table that we will focus on:

- The Training Risk Estimate: .220

- The Test Risk Estimate: .198

- The Overall Percentage Correct for the Training Sample: 78.0%

- The Overall Percentage Correct for the Test Sample: 80.2%

Risk

Sample	Estimate	Std. Error
Training	.220	.017
Test	.198	.024

Growing Method: CHAID
Dependent Variable: Survived

Classification

		Predicted		
Sample	Observed	0	1	Percent Correct
Training	0	368	5	98.7%
	1	129	106	45.1%
	Overall Percentage	81.7%	18.3%	78.0%
Test	0	172	4	97.7%
	1	52	55	51.4%
	Overall Percentage	79.2%	20.8%	80.2%

Growing Method: CHAID
Dependent Variable: Survived

Figure 14-5: Overall accuracy results

The "Risk" is simply a measure of inaccuracy. Why report for the training sample .22 wrong instead of .78 correct? This is because, by reporting that along with a standard error, you can build a confidence interval around it. When reporting to others, the more salient facts will be the stability in the form of comparing the training accuracy to test accuracy (here 78.0% and 80.2%), and the test accuracy. The accuracy for the test sample is especially important since it is based on "unseen" data, but the most conservative approach is reporting the lower accuracy of the two. This result would be considered stable, but a closer level of accuracy between the two would have been desirable. In other words, the test accuracy is OK, but it would be nice to do better. However, the fact that the test accuracy is even better than the training accuracy certainly makes the model appear stable. If the test accuracy were much worse than the training accuracy we would be concerned about stability.

It is noteworthy that the tree didn't grow all that much. We only have four leaf nodes. We will make some changes to our settings and give this another shot. First, however, let's review what CHAID is doing behind the scenes to produce the tree.

Review of the CHAID Algorithm

Note that Sex was the first split variable. It was chosen over Pclass. Let's refer to the Crosstab results, which have been produced using the Crosstab menus, shown in Figures 14-6 and 14-7, to explore why. Although both Sex and Pclass have Asymptotic Significance results (p values) that are very small, and well below .05, the result for Sex is smaller. That is why Sex is the top branch of the tree.

Sex * Survived

Crosstab

| | | | Survived | | |
			0	1	Total
Sex	female	Count	81	233	314
		% within Sex	25.8%	74.2%	100.0%
	male	Count	468	109	577
		% within Sex	81.1%	18.9%	100.0%
Total		Count	549	342	891
		% within Sex	61.6%	38.4%	100.0%

Chi-Square Tests

	Value	df	Asymptotic Significance (2–sided)	Exact Sig. (2–sided)	Exact Sig. (1–sided)
Pearson Chi–Square	263.051[a]	1	3.712E-59		
Continuity Correction[b]	260.717	1	.000		
Likelihood Ratio	268.851	1	.000		
Fisher's Exact Test				.000	.000
N of Valid Cases	891				

a. 0 cells (0.0%) have expected count less than 5. The minimum expected count is 120.53.
b. Computed only for a 2x2 table

Figure 14-6: Crosstab results for Sex variable

NOTE The cell format properties of the Chi-Square test has been adjusted so that the scientific notation can reveal which of the two extremely small values is smaller, and shows that one has a larger exponent of 59 for Sex.

Pclass * Survived

Crosstab

| | | | Survived | | |
			0	1	Total
Pclass	First	Count	80	136	216
		% within Pclass	37.0%	63.0%	100.0%
	Second	Count	97	87	184
		% within Pclass	52.7%	47.3%	100.0%
	Third	Count	372	119	491
		% within Pclass	75.8%	24.2%	100.0%
Total		Count	549	342	891
		% within Pclass	61.6%	38.4%	100.0%

Chi-Square Tests

	Value	df	Asymptotic Significance (2–sided)
Pearson Chi–Square	102.889[a]	2	4.549E-23
Likelihood Ratio	103.547	2	.000
Linear–by–Linear Association	101.967	1	.000
N of Valid Cases	891		

a. 0 cells (0.0%) have expected count less than 5. The minimum expected count is 70.63.

Figure 14-7: Crosstab results for Pclass variable

We've just seen that in CHAID the top branch is awarded to the lowest p value, but in actuality, our Crosstab demonstration is concealing a step. First, we have to determine if our ordinal variable will collapse any categories. Reference to the tree diagrams will show that collapsing has, indeed, occurred. However, the left branch and right branch differ. Why is this occurring? To answer, we need a more descriptive Crosstab result. As shown in Figure 14-8, we need to split on gender to show that the Pclass crosstab, when examining only females, is different when we examine only males. We noticed that the survival rate for First class and Second class females is actually very similar—96.8% and 92.1%—so the CHAID algorithm first collapses them and uses the two-category version of Pclass for a new Chi-Sq p value (not shown). For males, Second class and Third class are very similar (15.7% and 13.5%) so the CHAID algorithm collapses those two categories. Scale variables pose an interesting problem because Chi-Sq is not designed to investigate scale variables. CHAID buckets scale variables into deciles (a default setting which can be changed), and then treats them as ordinal variables. While the results work pretty well, recognize that the boundaries between the deciles are essentially arbitrary. These differences in treatment serve as an important reminder that the independent variables must have their levels of measurement declared properly in the very first step (Figure 14-1). We will see later that CRT finds boundaries with a more granular level of precision using a very different approach.

Pclass * Survived Crosstabulation

Sex					Survived 0	Survived 1	Total
female	Pclass	First	Count		3	91	94
			% within Pclass		3.2%	96.8%	100.0%
		Second	Count		6	70	76
			% within Pclass		7.9%	92.1%	100.0%
		Third	Count		72	72	144
			% within Pclass		50.0%	50.0%	100.0%
	Total		Count		81	233	314
			% within Pclass		25.8%	74.2%	100.0%
male	Pclass	First	Count		77	45	122
			% within Pclass		63.1%	36.9%	100.0%
		Second	Count		91	17	108
			% within Pclass		84.3%	15.7%	100.0%
		Third	Count		300	47	347
			% within Pclass		86.5%	13.5%	100.0%
	Total		Count		468	109	577
			% within Pclass		81.1%	18.9%	100.0%

Figure 14-8: Crosstab showing all three variables

THE TROUBLE WITH P VALUES

We are taught in Statistics 101 that lower p values do not mean greater "importance," but we also recognize that many investigators can't help themselves in the prose that they write about their findings. While a lower p value does provide stronger evidence for rejecting the null, we are coached to use other tests to get at issues like the strength of a relationship. Or we are cautioned that the p value simply reflects a threshold that is met or not. Yet, we award a triple asterisk to findings at 99.9%

confidence, and only one asterisk for 95% confidence in some academic papers. The podiums of different heights in the Olympics come to mind. Although this is somewhat out of fashion—so much so that it has become very controversial—its influence is still felt. It is actually the very basis of variable ranking in CHAID. While CHAID has stood the test of time, and is still popular, the fact that this p value ranking is done after so many decimal places should give us pause. Certainly, it should not give us any special comfort that CHAID uses "significance testing" while CRT does not. Some new to predictive analytics actually refuse to use modeling techniques that don't utilize p values, at first. Their presence should not give the technique any particular status as they are not being used in the traditional way. The value of our models will be demonstrated in their ability to generalize to new data in the form of the Test dataset, not in the incorporation of a few traditional ingredients in their algorithms.

Adjusting the CHAID Settings

In order to let the tree grow more aggressively, we will allow for a depth of 5 and smaller Parent/Child sizes, as shown in Figure 14-9. One could also describe the result as being more flexible, or even more "liberal" as the word is used in statistics. In short, the tree will become a larger tree with more branches and leaf nodes, as shown in Figure 14-10. We will also allow all of the available independent variables to be used (not shown). There is nothing magic about these adjustments. Given our sample size the default settings of 100 and 50 are a bit high. Is a maximum tree depth of 5 too aggressive? It is more aggressive than 3, but we are simply responding to the fact that we got a fairly parsimonious tree on the first attempt, so we are attempting to get a more "bush like" tree with more branches. If the more aggressive settings produce an unstable tree, we have a failed experiment. If it is more accurate (bush-like trees are always more accurate on the training sample), but also stable (accurate on both training and test samples), then we have a successful experiment.

Figure 14-9: Decision tree criteria

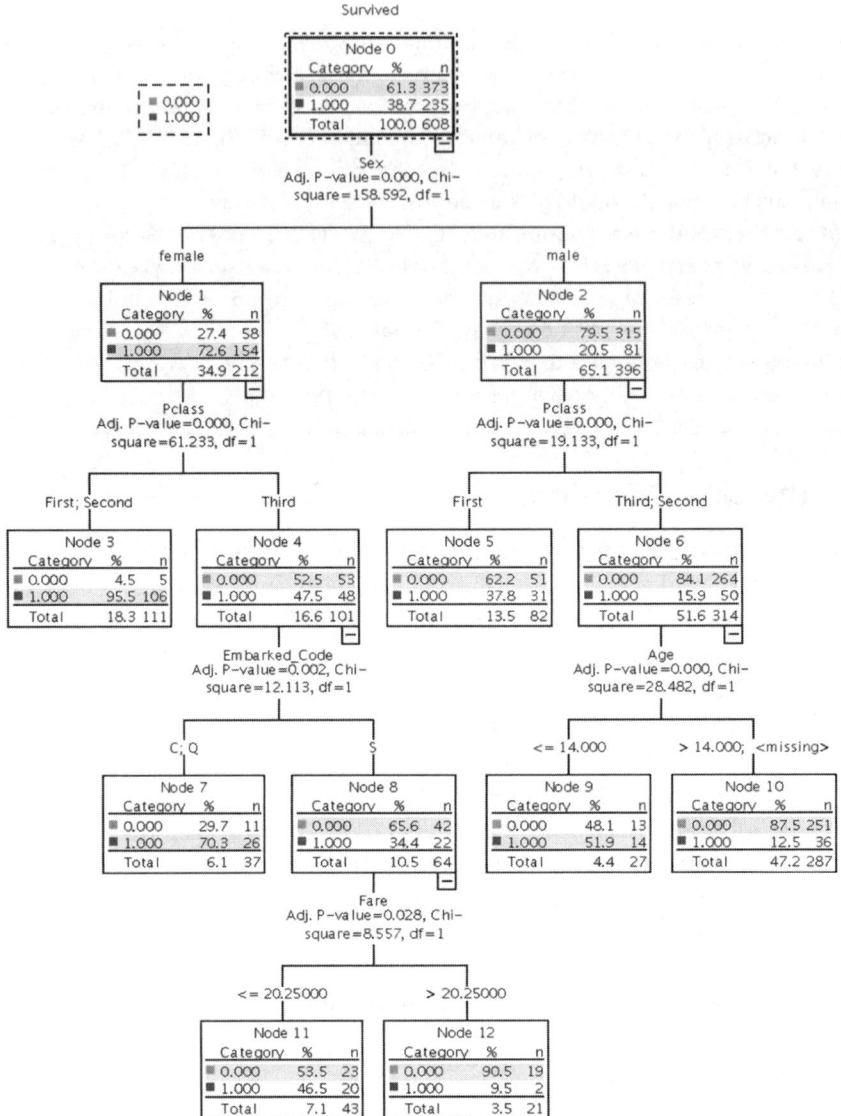

Figure 14-10: Training tree after changing settings

The tree is much expanded. The top half of the tree (Train Sample) is the same. Three new variables have joined Sex and Pclass: Embarked Code, Age, and Fare. Embarked Code represents where the passenger boarded the Titanic. It made three stops in Europe before entering the North Atlantic. The new variables create a more granular tree, and we now have a segment with a lower survival rate than we saw in our Training Sample tree before. Node 12 has a survival rate of 9.5%. Note that Age has been split (or rather its deciles have been collapsed down to two categories). Those missing Age have a survival rate somewhat like the passengers over 14 years of age so CHAID has combined them with this group. We will see that CRT has a very different approach. Fare has also been collapsed down to two groups even though it too would have started with deciles.

Let's examine the accuracy and stability of this example using the results shown in Figure 14-11. It won't always be the case, but we achieved considerably better results on the second try. Sometimes you might need a compromise between the conservative and aggressive settings. You may also choose to change the settings shown in the CHAID tab (not shown). These settings would include changing from 95% confidence levels to something either more or less aggressive like 90% or 99%. Lowering to 90% would allow for an even larger tree. Raising to 99% would make it more conservative, resulting in a potentially smaller tree. A half dozen or even a dozen different versions of settings for just the CHAID algorithm would not be unusual. Because it is more accurate, and quite stable (even better performance on the Test is always nice) this model is now in first place, and we will try another algorithm. It is worth noting that it is more common to have a slight degrading of performance on the test. Having better performance on the test is less common. However, the more important fact is that the numbers are fairly similar, indicating stability.

Risk

Sample	Estimate	Std. Error
Training	.194	.016
Test	.177	.023

Growing Method: CHAID
Dependent Variable: Survived

Classification

Sample	Observed	Predicted		
		0	1	Percent Correct
Training	0	344	29	92.2%
	1	89	146	62.1%
	Overall Percentage	71.2%	28.8%	80.6%
Test	0	161	15	91.5%
	1	35	72	67.3%
	Overall Percentage	69.3%	30.7%	82.3%

Growing Method: CHAID
Dependent Variable: Survived

Figure 14-11: Accuracy results for the larger tree

CRT for Classification

Set the configuration for this example in the dialog shown in Figure 14-12. We will change the Growing Method to CRT, but not make any other changes. All of the possible inputs will be used (which was the case for our second CHAID attempt). The variables as shown are Pclass, Sex, Parch, Age, SibSp, Fare, and Embarked_Code. As we noted with CHAID, remember that the Level of Measurement declaration has an impact on the outcome. Validation remains the same—use the Train_Test variable. For Criteria use the settings we just chose for the second CHAID attempt—depth of 5, 30 for parent minimum, and 15 for child minimum. The result, shown in Figure 14-13 is a much larger tree.

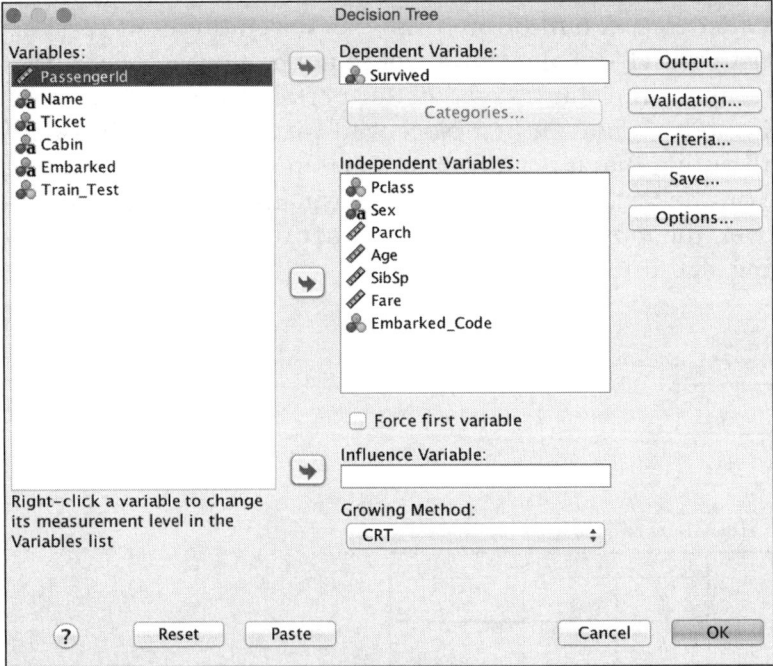

Figure 14-12: Decision tree main menu

CRT has produced a considerably more complex tree. Its performance is about the same as the second CHAID attempt. It is also fairly stable (see Figure 14-14). Note that it uses Age as the second most important variable for males. Also, Fare is used multiple times with subtle and tiny little differences between the cut-off points.

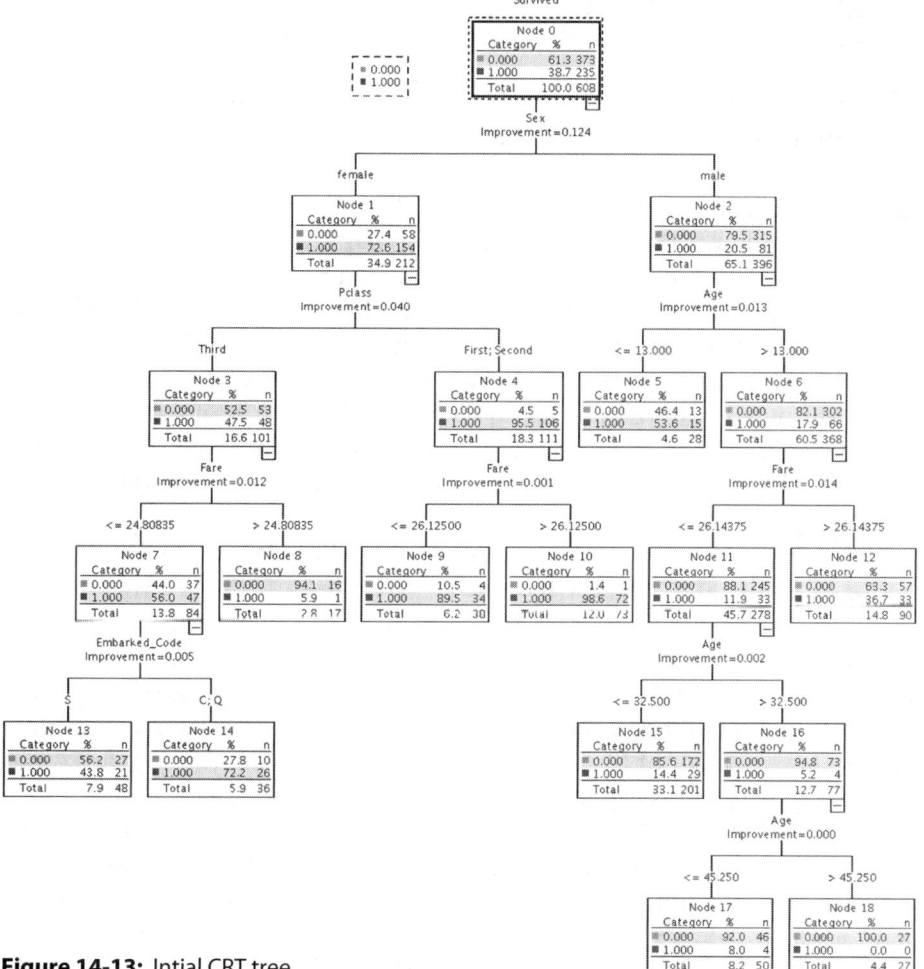

Figure 14-13: Intial CRT tree

Risk

Sample	Estimate	Std. Error
Training	.191	.016
Test	.180	.023

Growing Method: CRT
Dependent Variable: Survived

Classification

		Predicted		
Sample	Observed	0	1	Percent Correct
Training	0	345	28	92.5%
	1	88	147	62.6%
	Overall Percentage	71.2%	28.8%	80.9%
Test	0	158	18	89.8%
	1	33	74	69.2%
	Overall Percentage	67.5%	32.5%	82.0%

Growing Method: CRT
Dependent Variable: Survived

Figure 14-14: Accuracy results for CRT tree

Understanding Why the CRT Algorithm Produces a Different Tree

The CRT algorithm was first described in 1984 by Leo Breiman, Jerome Friedman, Charles J. Stone, and R.A. Olshen in their book *Classification and Regression Trees* (Chapman and Hall/CRC). However, a key component of the approach is to use the Gini Coefficient, which is 75 years older. Sociologist Corrado Gini's Gini Coefficient is used to describe income disparity in countries. A Gini Coefficient of zero would describe a country where everyone has the same income, and a Gini coefficient of 1 means that one person has all the income. The CRT algorithm repurposes this in a clever way. Ultimately the goal of a decision tree is to identify leaf nodes where there is no "disparity" in the target variable. Alternate vocabulary serves us better in the context of a decision tree. In a "pure" leaf node, all values of the target variable would be the same. So, when using CRT or adjusting settings we generally use the words "purity" and "impurity."

So there are two key observations to make about the fact that CRT selected Sex as the first variable. First, CRT *always* produces a binary split. CHAID, as we have seen, does not always do so. So two trees, one CHAID and one CRT, will tend to look quite different, but may be similar, or even identical in their predictions. Second, since reduction in impurity is a goal, Sex must have produced a substantive reduction in impurity. The overall survival rate is about 40%, which is not terribly far away from the percentage that would maximize impurity. A binary target with 50% in each category would achieve that. In contrast, after splitting on Sex, the survival rate for females climbs, moving away from 50% within Node 1, and the opposite occurs for Males. CHAID's search for the lowest p value tends to produce the same effect, but with CRT we move rather directly to the goal of pure leaf nodes. If you reflect carefully on this approach, you should grow concerned. A leaf node with only one case will always be pure. This is disconcerting, but the CRT algorithm addresses this by weighing "balance" equally with the reduction in impurity. While Nodes 1 and 2 are not equal in size, their sizes of 212 and 396 are not terribly out of balance. The Sex variable was the strongest option when weighing both purity and balance, and therefore CRT split on Sex first.

Scale variables are handled elegantly in CRT. It need not transform them as an initial step. As we have seen, CHAID converts scale variables into deciles and then treats them as ordinal variables in later steps. CRT's algorithm considers every possible cut point. Naturally, the first and last cut points would produce a very unbalanced split, but it calculates them all. In the instance of this dataset we see that young boys have a much higher survival rate than male teens and adults. Of all the possible cut points for age, 13 years old was the optimal for purity and balance. And of all the possible variables with which to subdivide Males, Age was the best.

Missing Data

Surrogates are a fascinating solution to the problem of missing data. In contrast to CHAID, CRT does not treat missing data as a separate category. A substantial number of passengers are missing a value for age in the Titanic data, for instance. CHAID's behavior in this regard makes its treatment of missing data rather transparent because you can easily see where the cases with a missing value are in the tree. Instead, when CRT encounters a missing value, it attempts to determine whether that case should join the left branch or the right branch. What is brilliant about the solution of using surrogates is that it does not require a very precise estimate of age. Imputation, a well-known technique, would involve trying to estimate the passenger's age, producing an estimate such as 5 years old, or 48 years old. With surrogates, we simply need to identify if the passenger is more likely to be younger or older than 13 since that was the threshold that we just discussed. CRT identifies five variables from among the variables specified for the tree that allow us to make this determination. If they are traveling with a spouse or their own children, for instance, they are certainly unlikely to be under 13 years old. Each node has up to five surrogates, and obviously they will be different depending on what is missing. The five variables will be those five that the complete data reveals to be the most correlated with the missing information.

Changing the CRT Settings

We can change a number of settings with CRT to produce a larger or smaller tree. We could change the maximum depth or the parent/child settings. We could also change the "minimum change in impurity" found on the CRT tab, which has a line of coaching on the effect of increasing or decreasing this setting: "Large values tend to produce larger trees." Try adding or dropping a zero (or two) at first so that you have more or fewer decimal places. That should serve as a guideline for how much of a change will have a noticeable effect. We will only be attempting one additional CRT tree in this chapter, and will choose Pruning as the criterion to change. This is a terribly important setting, is how CRT is designed to work, and frankly should be on by default. It can be interesting to examine an unpruned tree as an exploratory step, but generally this setting should be turned on. The Pruning submenu is shown in Figure 14-15.

Decision Tree: Criteria

Growth Limits | CRT | Pruning | Surrogates

☑ Prune tree to avoid overfitting

Maximum Difference in Risk (in Standard Errors): [1]

After the tree is grown to its full depth, pruning trims the tree down to the smallest subtree that has an acceptable risk value.

Enter the maximum acceptable difference in risk between the pruned tree and the subtree with the smallest risk.

To produce a simpler tree, increase the maximum difference. To select the subtree with the smallest risk, enter 0.

Cancel | Continue

Figure 14-15: Pruning criteria submenu

The resulting tree is very different, and much smaller (the Training Sample tree is shown in Figure 14-16).

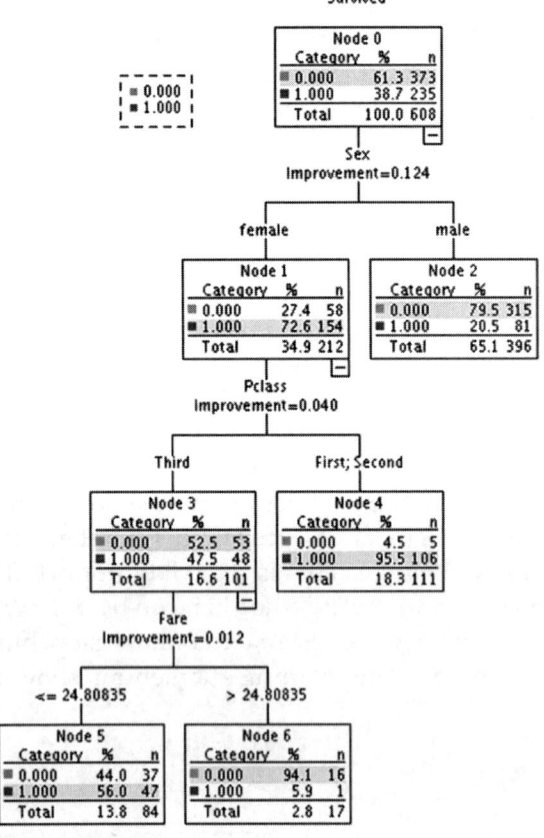

Figure 14-16: Second CRT tree

The original developers of the CRT algorithm approach (Breiman et al.) experimented with a number of variations on the algorithm and discovered that the best results were found when they grew a tree aggressively and pruned it back. This was better, for instance, than constraining the growth of the tree without pruning. What "cost complexity" pruning attempts to do is remove those branches that have more complexity than they are "worth." Branches that increase accuracy enough are worth it, but branches that fail to increase accuracy enough are not. It is this ratio between complexity and the increase in accuracy that is being weighed.

The stability is quite good—the Overall Percentage accuracy is similar in both the Training and Test samples. The accuracy is also good, at 83.4% for the Test data. It actually appears to be the best so far, as shown in Figure 14-17.

Risk

Sample	Estimate	Std. Error
Training	.204	.016
Test	.166	.022

Growing Method: CRT
Dependent Variable: Survived

Classification

		Predicted		
Sample	Observed	0	1	Percent Correct
Training	0	331	42	88.7%
	1	82	153	65.1%
	Overall Percentage	67.9%	32.1%	79.6%
Test	0	158	18	89.8%
	1	29	78	72.9%
	Overall Percentage	66.1%	33.9%	83.4%

Growing Method: CRT
Dependent Variable: Survived

Figure 14-17: Second CRT tree accuracy results

Comparing the Results of All Four Models

Let's compare the results of the four models. We can apply many criteria in comparing and contrasting these results. Table 14-1 shows just one possible way to examine the results in a table. In data mining consulting work, it is not unusual to consider more than 100 models using many algorithms and dozens of settings.

Table 14-1: Comparing our four tree attempts

	FIRST CHAID	SECOND CHAID	FIRST CRT	SECOND CRT
Number of Variables Used in Tree	Two	Five	Five	Three
Number of Leaf Nodes	Four	Seven	Ten	Four
Highest Survival Rate (Train)	95.5%		98.6%	95.5%
Lowest Survival Rate (Train)	15.9%		0%	5.9%
Settings	Default	Increased depth, and reduced Parent/Child	Reduced Parent/ Child	Reduced Parent/Child and Pruning
Train Accuracy	78.0%	80.6%	80.9%	79.6%
Test Accuracy	80.2%	82.3%	82.0%	83.4%

KHABAZA'S VALUE LAW

The most accurate model should not be assumed to be the "winner." In Tom Khabaza's 9 Laws of Data Mining, the 8th Law of Data Mining is The Value Law: "The value of data mining results is not determined by the accuracy or stability of predictive models." This is not to say that accuracy and stability play no role, but rather to say that they are not the whole story. As Khabaza puts it, "A high degree of accuracy does not enhance the value of these models when they have a poor fit to the business problem."

In a real world modeling exercise, the input variables might have different costs to acquire or to measure, creating a trade-off between accuracy and cost. One's IT colleagues might explain that fare is not recorded until the tickets are paid for, and if a travel agent books the trip that information might be delayed.

We might need to use only models that use variables that were reliably available at the time of departure because at that time we might still have an opportunity to do something about risk. Understanding the risk of an individual passenger might cause us to move the cabin of someone who was at high risk before the ship leaves port. The final selection would be made by considering many factors, all focused on how well the model solves the business problem. The 9 Laws are easily found on the Internet, and are worth seeking out.

Given the results here, we would probably be inclined to go with the Second CRT. We've been lucky in that all four are stable. None have a dramatic gap drop in accuracy moving from Train to Test. In fact, all did better in the Test, so all are viable in that sense. The last one has somewhat better Test accuracy, and once we establish stability we don't care that much about Train accuracy.

Finally, the fourth model is even somewhat parsimonious. It is not an overly complex tree. With that in mind, we will save the predicted values as a new variable in the dataset to be used in the next chapter. We will close the chapter with a discussion of the Scoring Wizard, using our best model for the example. But first, we will discuss alternative validation options.

Alternative Validation Options

Let's consider an alternative setting for our validation. We have been using the same variable, `Train_Test`, in order to compare multiple algorithms. It is possible, and quite easy, to have SPSS generate partition variables as shown in Figure 14-18. Note that we've chosen 70% for the Training Sample because the sample size is a bit small in the Titanic dataset. When faced with that challenge it is usually recommended to increase the Training Sample somewhat, just as we did with the `Train_Test` variable.

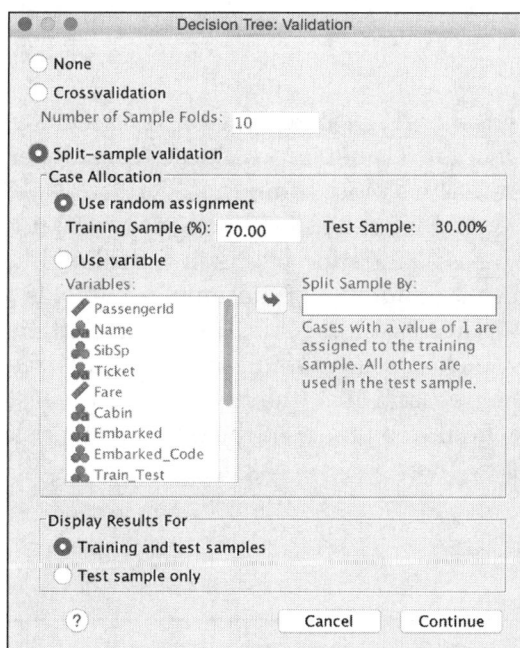

Figure 14-18: Using a random assignment

The results when rerunning with the same settings as the second CRT tree indicate a lower value for Test accuracy, 80.8%, than for Training accuracy, 81.1%. The steps in creating the tree are not reshown, but the Risk results are in Figure 14-19.

Risk

Sample	Estimate	Std. Error
Training	.189	.016
Test	.192	.024

Growing Method: CRT
Dependent Variable: Survived

Classification

Sample	Observed	Predicted 0	Predicted 1	Percent Correct
Training	0	343	35	90.7%
	1	82	160	66.1%
	Overall Percentage	68.5%	31.5%	81.1%
Test	0	149	22	87.1%
	1	30	70	70.0%
	Overall Percentage	66.1%	33.9%	80.8%

Growing Method: CRT
Dependent Variable: Survived

Figure 14-19: Results using the random assignment

This pattern, of higher Train accuracy, is more typical than higher Test accuracy. As we have seen several times in this chapter, it is not impossible to have higher Test accuracy, but the pattern in Figure 14-19 is more common.

You may have noticed another option in Figure 14-18. Although we will not repeat our analysis using this option, cross-validation works in the following way. Crossvalidation divides the sample into a number of subsamples, or "folds." The default is 10, but you can specify up to 25 sample folds. Each time a different fold is withheld. For example, if you choose the default of 10, the first tree would use 90% of the data to build the tree, and 10% (the first 10%) as the test data. Crossvalidation reveals a single, final tree model in the output. The risk in the output is the average risk of all the trees.

The Scoring Wizard

In order to show the Scoring Wizard, we are going to save our model as an XML file as shown in Figure 14-20. While we are going to demonstrate only one scoring method, there are actually numerous options. For example, the TREES procedure (the SPSS Syntax command for producing decision trees) offers a number of other formats for saving the rules that may be useful in other scoring contexts. The

RULES subcommand of the TREE procedure allows you to generate SQL statements. If you are new to SPSS Syntax, you will want to read the chapters in Part IV of this book, starting with the introduction to SPSS Syntax in Chapter 16. It is not uncommon to find features—like the SQL rules option—that are available in SPSS Syntax, but are not found in the menus.

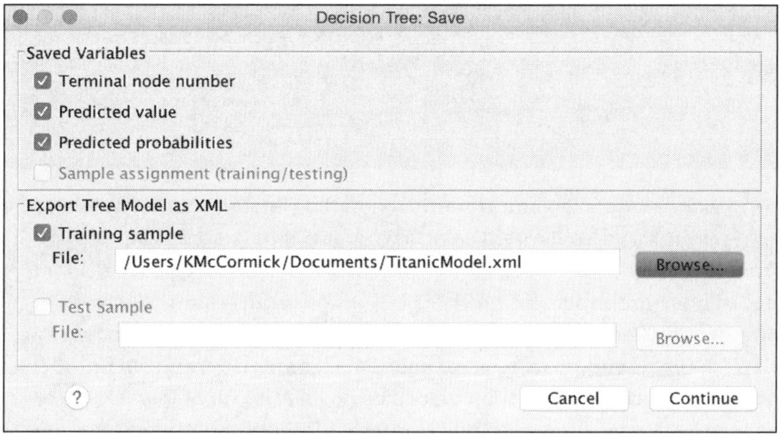

Figure 14-20: Scoring Wizard first menu

To be consistent with the figures, be certain to use the settings of the second CRT model that we've decided was our best option.

Now load a different data file. We will use the Titanic_Test.sav file. This file contains the same variables except that it is lacking the Survived variable. A willing suspension of disbelief is required here. We all know that the Titanic sank a hundred years ago, so naturally we know the outcome of all of the passengers, but we are going to pretend to *not* know the outcome for the Test data. We are going to use our Train dataset's model, but use it to score the Test dataset. This is a bit different in SPSS Modeler, as we have seen with its unique partition node, and so on, but SPSS Statistics is quite capable of doing a hold-out sample validation as well, and it does it quite elegantly as we are about to rehearse. Please ensure that Titanic_Test.sav is not only open, but is the active file.

The Scoring Wizard is found in the Utilities menu. It will list any .xml files that can be used. Note that it may also display .zip files that you might have on your machine. We are only interested in the file that we just made: TitanicModel .xml. The opening screen is shown in Figure 14-21.

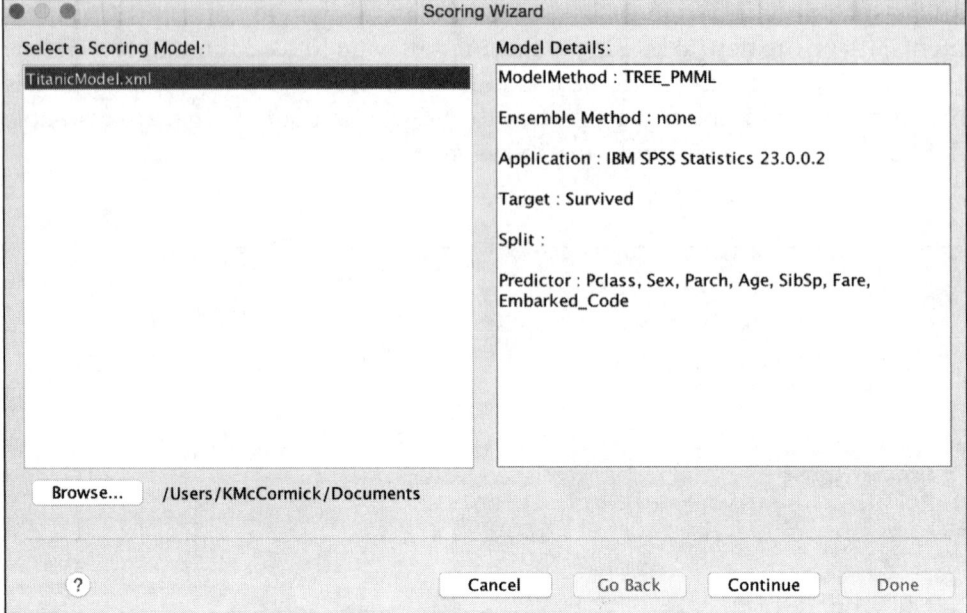

Figure 14-21: Scoring Wizard second menu

SPSS wants to verify that the variables referred to in the model are also found in the Test dataset, shown in Figure 14-22. They should indeed align, which allows us to continue.

Dataset Fields	Model Fields	Role	Measure	Type
Pclass	Pclass	Predictor	Nominal	Numeric
Sex	Sex	Predictor	Nominal	String
Parch	Parch	Predictor	Nominal	Numeric
Age	Age	Predictor	Continuous	Numeric
SibSp	SibSp	Predictor	Continuous	Numeric
Fare	Fare	Predictor	Continuous	Numeric
Embarked_Code	Embarked_Code	Predictor	Nominal	Numeric

Figure 14-22: Scoring Wizard third menu

Finally, we have to decide which new scored variables are to be created by the Scoring Wizard. These differ by model type, and are affected by what we requested when we built the .xml file. We will request the latter three choices: Node Number, Predicted Value, and Confidence as shown in Figure 14-23.

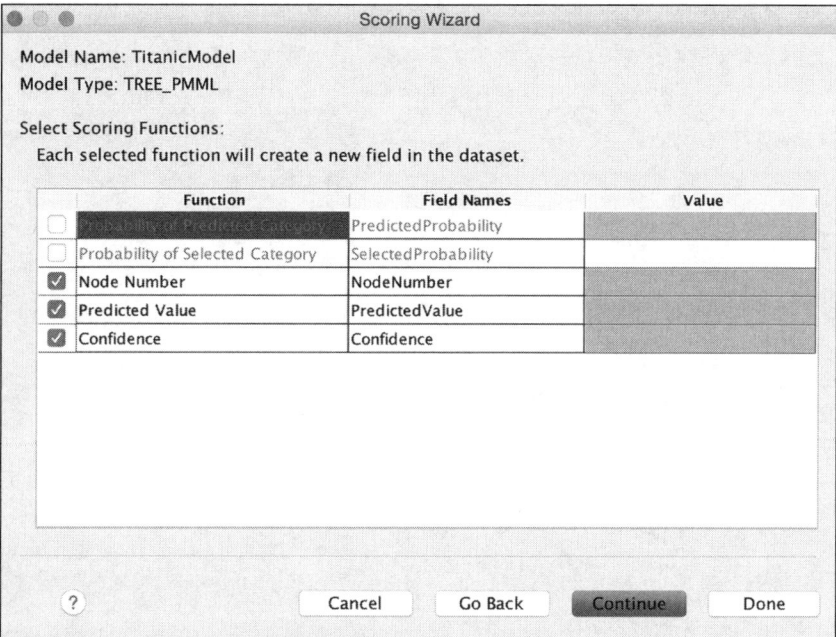

Figure 14-23: Scoring Wizard fourth menu

The predictions for the Test passengers should now be visible in the data window, Figure 14-24. (The Name variable has been moved to make it easy to view the predictions.)

Name	NodeNumber	PredictedValue	Confidence
Kelly, Mr. James	2.00	.00	.79
Wilkes, Mrs. James (Ellen Needs)	5.00	1.00	.56
Myles, Mr. Thomas Francis	2.00	.00	.79
Wirz, Mr. Albert	2.00	.00	.79
Hirvonen, Mrs. Alexander (Helga E Li...	5.00	1.00	.56
Svensson, Mr. Johan Cervin	2.00	.00	.79
Connolly, Miss. Kate	5.00	1.00	.56
Caldwell, Mr. Albert Francis	2.00	.00	.79
Abrahim, Mrs. Joseph (Sophie Halaut...	5.00	1.00	.56
Davies, Mr. John Samuel	2.00	.00	.79

Figure 14-24: Predictive scores for some passengers in the Test dataset

We covered the Scoring Wizard in some detail, showing each screen, but as you can see it is really quite straightforward. It is one of many SPSS Statistics features that fewer people know about than those that can benefit from it. For instance, many SPSS Statistics users use linear regression, but few also know that they can score new records with their regression model using this same menu.

Find Patterns and Make Predictions with K Nearest Neighbors

K Nearest Neighbors (KNN) provides an interesting contrast to the other two algorithms that we have seen in this section of the book, neural networks and decision trees. It also offers the sharpest contrast with traditional techniques. The basic concept is simple: When a new case is presented to the algorithm, it simply finds a small number of training cases that are most like the new case, and classifies the new case on the assumption that it will fall into the same category as the majority of the closest cases. If you are trying to predict the salary of an employee, and k = 5, the predicted salary will be the average of the 5 employees in the training dataset most like the new case. So, although we will start by predicting survival with the Titanic dataset, you could also use this technique for predicting salary with the Bank dataset used in the neural net chapter (13). After we've discussed finding "neighbors" and using KNN as a classifier, we will end the chapter with a comparison of the performance of the three classifiers we've seen in Part III.

There is no generalization in the form of a model made from the training set. There are no coefficients. There is no significance testing, and no goodness of fit like R2. The phrase that computer scientists specializing in machine learning often use to describe this is that KNN is a "lazy learner"—that is, it does not create a model in the traditional sense. The "model" is really just all of the locations of the training data, and for that reason it is often described as a "memory based" or "instance based" technique. Related to these features, it can be rather slow because it is "memorizing" the entire training dataset. Data miners, as we have seen, do not pass judgment on an algorithm because they are impressed (or not) with a technique's sophistication. There is almost no theory here. There are no distributional assumptions. The concept is simple, so the effectiveness of the algorithm will have to be proven with its practical use. Does it predict well on new data? Since KNN is the last of our three algorithms using the Titanic dataset we will perform a side by side comparison of the ability of each to predict values in new data using the same train and test partition. As mentioned at the end of the previous paragraph, we'll also briefly explore what it could be like to use them in conjunction with each other, a so-called ensemble.

Using KNN to Find "Neighbors"

KNN need not be used only to classify (which is discussed in the next section). It is sometimes used solely to find distances—usually with the goal of finding which data points are closest. We could simply run the technique without a target variable to find passengers that are similar to other passengers on the input variables. This aspect of the technique could also apply in a case like the eHarmony dating website service. In the case of a dating website like eHarmony, it is not predicting in the traditional sense. It is simply identifying those records (men, for instance) that are proximate (literally in terms of Euclidean distance or some other distance measure) from other records (women whose minimal distance implies similar answers on the survey questions). The theory behind the approach in the case of a dating website is that a "connection" with someone is made more likely through "compatibility" as measured by similar answers on a large set of questions. The notion of a dating website also helps us imagine what deployment of a model like this would be like. The algorithm would "memorize" the locations of the men, and then could be deployed on a single woman. The reverse could be done if we were trying to find the closest women for a single man.

In the *IBM SPSS Modeler Cookbook* (McCormick et al., Packt Publishing, 2013)—Modeler also supports this technique—there is another example. This one involves matching sales personnel in a fictional call center to inbound calling customers that have similar profiles: the sales reps in terms of sales they had handled and the customers in terms of purchases that they had made. Table 15-1 shows ratios of rep sales and customer spend, and reveals an identical pattern across the ratios for a certain Customer/Rep pair. The pairs that are closest have similar dollar ratios in these categories. In the Figure, both the Customer and the Rep have zero in all categories except for Video Games. Not all pairs would be identical, but if they are "nearest neighbors" the pattern on the ratios would be very similar.

Table 15-1: "Neighboring" Customer and Sales Rep Pair

CUSTOMER_ ID	ENTERTAIN- MENT	GAME CONSOLES	HARD- WARE	MOVIES	SOFT- WARE	STREAM- ING	VIDEO GAMES
100004832	0.000	0.000	0.000	0.000	0.000	0.000	1.000

REPID	ENTERTAIN- MENT	GAME CONSOLES	HARD- WARE	MOVIES	SOFT- WARE	STREAM- ING	VIDEO GAMES
32	0.000	0.000	0.000	0.000	0.000	0.000	1.000

Rep #32 is the closest "neighbor" for this customer, so one can imagine an automated system that routes the best matching rep to each inbound customer. As long as it didn't create a delay in the queue for any customers, routing to a better match might be a better system than simply routing to first available. If they were being paired permanently—perhaps an investor and a broker—then it might be especially useful. Their similarity should prove valuable because it implies similar interests and experiences.

The Titanic Dataset and KNN Used as a Classifier

KNN as used for classification is a little different than when used to find the proximity of data points. First we find the nearest "neighbors," then we determine which category on the target variable was the most common for the neighbors. That category becomes our predicted category for any scored record. Of course, one of the interesting things about using the Titanic dataset with this technique is that we will see the names of the "focal point" and the "neighbors" in the output. Sometimes the name itself will reveal something intriguing about the person, like a child named "Master" Eugene Rice.

For this example we will be using the `Titanic_Results.sav` file, which is available on the book's website. This file has variables that represent the predictions of a tree model and a neural net model, both of which were created using steps explained in Chapters 13 and 14.

We will begin with only minor adjustments to the settings, and with four predictors. Specifically, as shown, we will predict Survived with Pclass, Age, Sex, and Parch (Figure 15-1). We could add SibSp and Embarked as well, but we know from Chapters 13 and 14 (using trees and neural nets) that these are the most important four. The KNN output will be a little easier to digest with fewer inputs. (Note that the variable order makes a difference because part of the output we will examine will only show the first three.) Include Name as the Case Label, as shown.

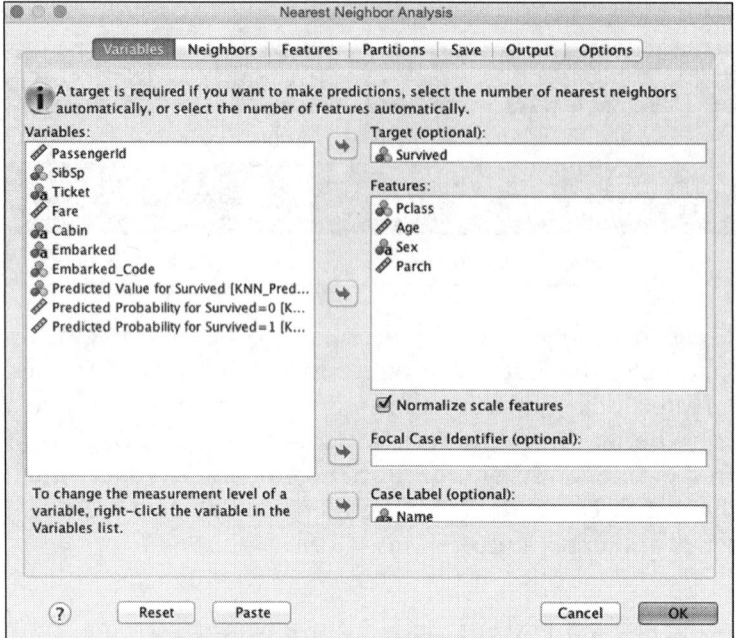

Figure 15-1: Nearest Neighbor Analysis main menu

The final predictor, Parch, is the number of parents and children traveling with the passenger. Including this predictor will help you determine, for example, whether having a dependent to worry about makes movement on the ship more difficult. Or, alternatively, whether having dependents increases the likelihood that an adult male might survive because he might stay with the rest of his family. Note that Parch has been declared as a scale variable. When a scale variable has a small number of integer-level categories, SPSS will often default to treating it as a nominal. We will use Name as a Case Label. This will add the passenger's name to the output. In order to compare neural net, decision trees, and KNN easily, we will ensure that KNN is using the same Partition Variable (Figure 15-2) that we created for the other algorithms. (Make sure that you are using the file `Titanic_Results.sav`, which has the results of a tree model and a neural net from Chapters 13 and 14.)

To see the results you must double-click the Model Viewer in the output window. In our results, we can click a particular "Focal Point." The circle will turn red (Figure 15-3). When you do so a second diagram will appear on the right. From the image alone, it might be difficult to pinpoint the individual who is the "focal record." As further examination will reveal, he is Mr. Johan Svensson.

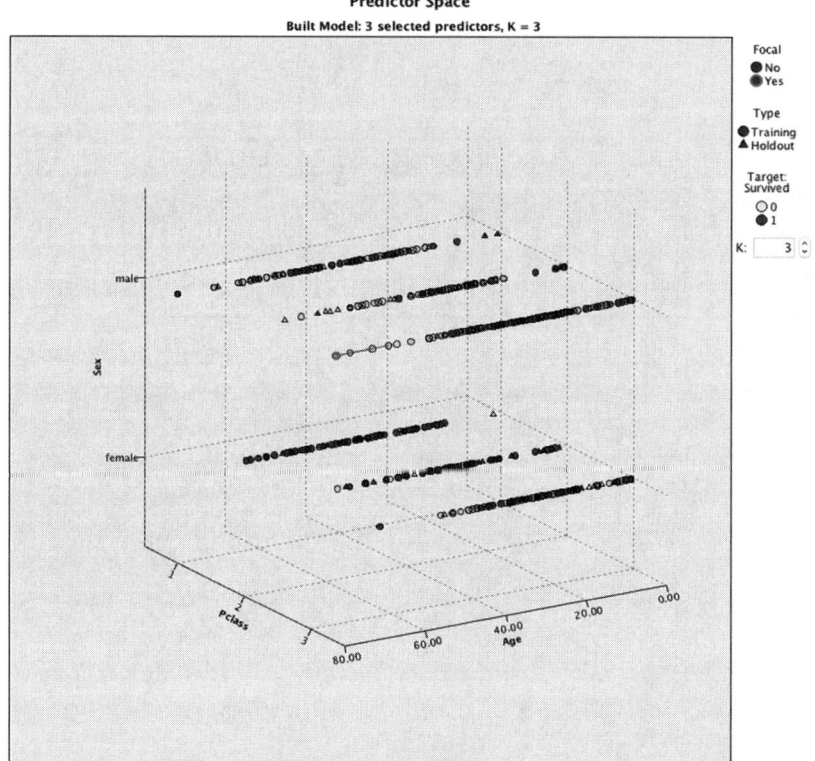

Figure 15-2: Partitions submenu

Predictor Space

Built Model: 3 selected predictors, K = 3

Select points to use as focal records

This chart is a lower-dimensional projection of the predictor space, which contains a total of 4 predictors.

Figure 15-3: Mr. Svensson as focal record

There are a few choices for which diagram to show on the right. One choice is the "Neighbors and Distances" chart displayed in Figure 15-4. It shows up to three full names, in order, from closest to furthest, since we went with the default of k=3. As you can see, Mr. Svensson's nearest "neighbors" are Mr. Patrick Connors, Mr. Frank Duane, and Mr. Johan Hansen Nysveen.

k Nearest Neighbors and Distances

Displayed for Initial Focal Records

Focal Record	Nearest Neighbors			Nearest Distances		
	1	**2**	**3**	**1**	**2**	**3**
Svensson, Mr. Johan	Connors, Mr. Patrick	Duane, Mr. Frank	Nysveen, Mr. Johan Hansen	0.088	0.226	0.327

Figure 15-4: Mr. Svensson's neighbors

There is also the Peers chart, shown in Figure 15-5, which takes a closer look at the closest passengers on the variables we've chosen. Mr. Svensson was a victory for the technique as shown in the "Peers Chart" since all of his neighbors shared the same fate, confirming, in this case, its effectiveness as a classifier. As we would anticipate, adult males often died in the accident, as did all three of Mr. Svensson's nearest neighbors. All were male, 3rd class, and in their 60s or early 70s. Mr. Svensson was the oldest at 73. None had dependents on board. Note that when there are too many predictors to display, you can use the Select Predictors option to show fewer.

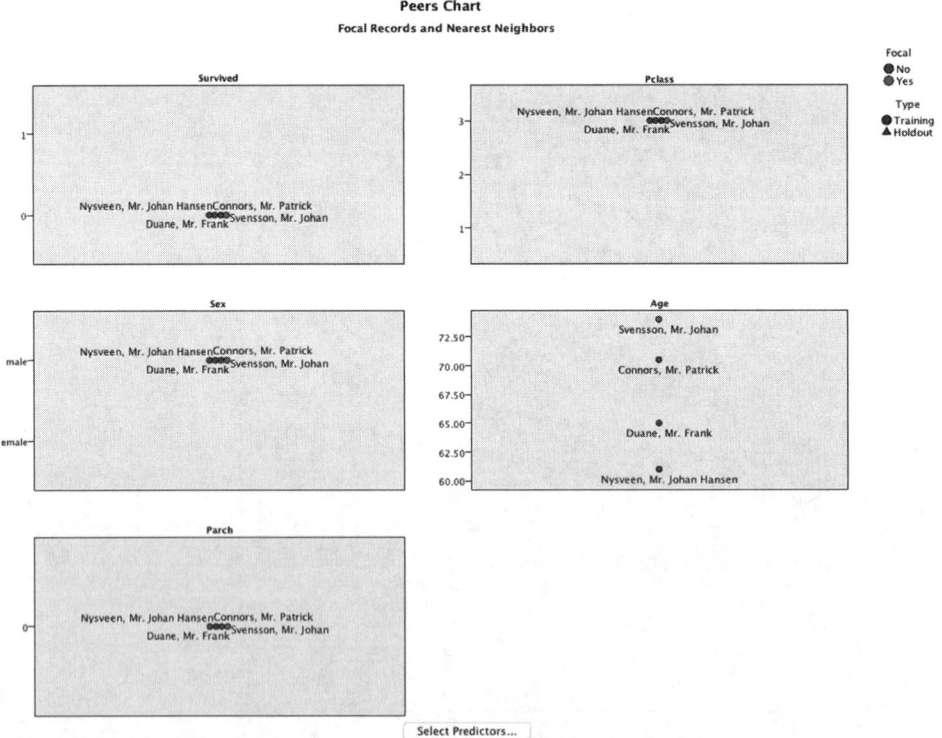

Figure 15-5: Mr. Svensson's Peers Chart

One of the features of nearest neighbors that I've always found fascinating is the individual detail it provides. As you might imagine, it can be revealing in the case of something like insurance fraud. The nearest cases might be investigated to see if they had the same *modus operandi*. In fact, wouldn't it be fascinating if two fraud cases turned out to have the same culprit working under two different names? However, despite our efforts to consider every variable during a *manual* examination of a case file, this sort of discovery simply isn't possible in practice. If Mr. Svensson had been a perpetrator of fraud as opposed to the victim of a famous accident, one might read the entire case files of Mr. Duane, Mr. Connors, and Mr. Nysveen. In practice, this might be prompted by a high fraud risk score for Mr. Svensson, thus warrenting extra attention. There might be some information that had never been made available in electronic form, or that simply wasn't used in the model. You might notice something interesting in the unstructured data like the case notes or a police report. Knowing which individual cases to examine more closely would be enough of a hint that it would be worth reading those case files in detail. If a major discovery was made you might iterate back to the modeling phase and add some new input variables to the models.

Finally, we will take a quick look at the accuracy of the model when used as a classifier. The results, shown in Figure 15-6, reveal pretty good accuracy on our Holdout (Test) data. This is comparable to the results we were able to achieve with the decision tree and the neural net. We are doing a somewhat better job predicting those that died, at about 85% as opposed to those that survived. But the accuracy for the 1s in the training dataset and test dataset are not as stable as we would like. It would be nice to get better performance for our test dataset (labled "Holdout" in the figure), but a difference this large does make one doubt the stability of the model, and question what performance might look like on future data. While we won't engage in extensive experiments in this chapter, we will explore ways to improve our model in the next section.

Classification Table

Partition	Observed	Predicted 0	Predicted 1	Percent Correct
Training	0	244	46	84.1%
	1	67	133	66.5%
	Overall Percent	63.5%	36.5%	76.9%
Holdout	0	114	20	85.1%
	1	22	68	75.6%
	Missing	0	0	
	Overall Percent	60.7%	39.3%	81.2%

Figure 15-6: Model accuracy

The Trade-Offs between Bias and Variance

In trying to fine-tune our models, we obviously want accuracy, but we also want generality beyond the training dataset. If we make our model more complex, the accuracy on the training dataset will almost certainly improve, but the ability to generalize to other datasets, including the test dataset, might suffer. This is often described as a trade-off between bias and variance:

- *Bias* is the measured difference between our predictions and the actual values. High bias is low accuracy, and is associated with underfitting.

- *Variance* is the magnitude of the variability of our predictions. High variance is associated with overfitting and allowing noise to mix in with the signal.

We've discussed these kinds of issues before in the "Partitioning and Validating" section of Chapter 11, but KNN offers a direct way to examine this trade-off. Increasing k decreases variance and increases bias. Decreasing k increases variance and decreases bias—with the risk of overfitting. We can see it for ourselves with an experiment. In the Neighbors submenu we can request "Automatically select k" and provide a range. We've chosen a range between 1 and 15 as shown in Figure 15-7.

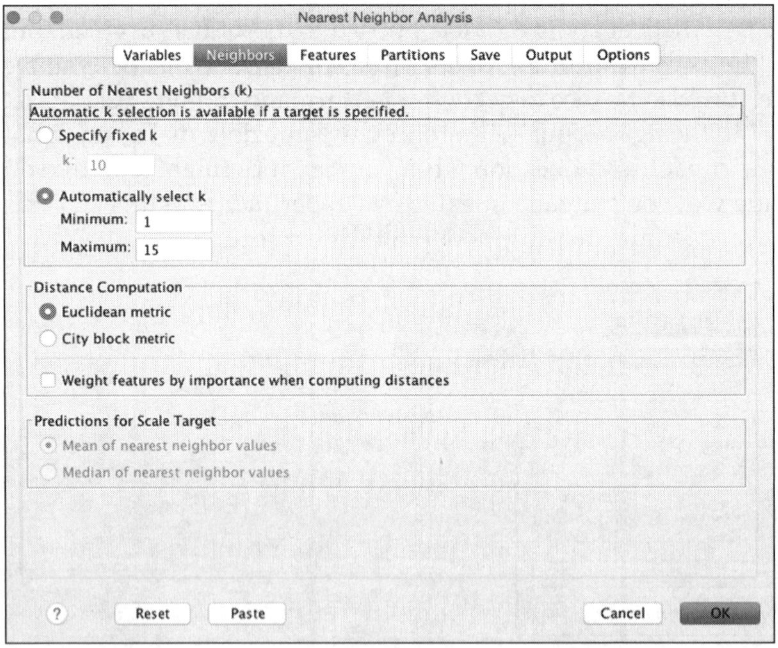

Figure 15-7: Neighbors submenu

The result shows us that the lowest error rate is a compromise between a low and high value for k (Figure 15-8). Error is on the y axis, so lower is better. And the "winner" seems to be k=6. However, the k=4 option is in second place and fairly close. It is not a bad idea to try both.

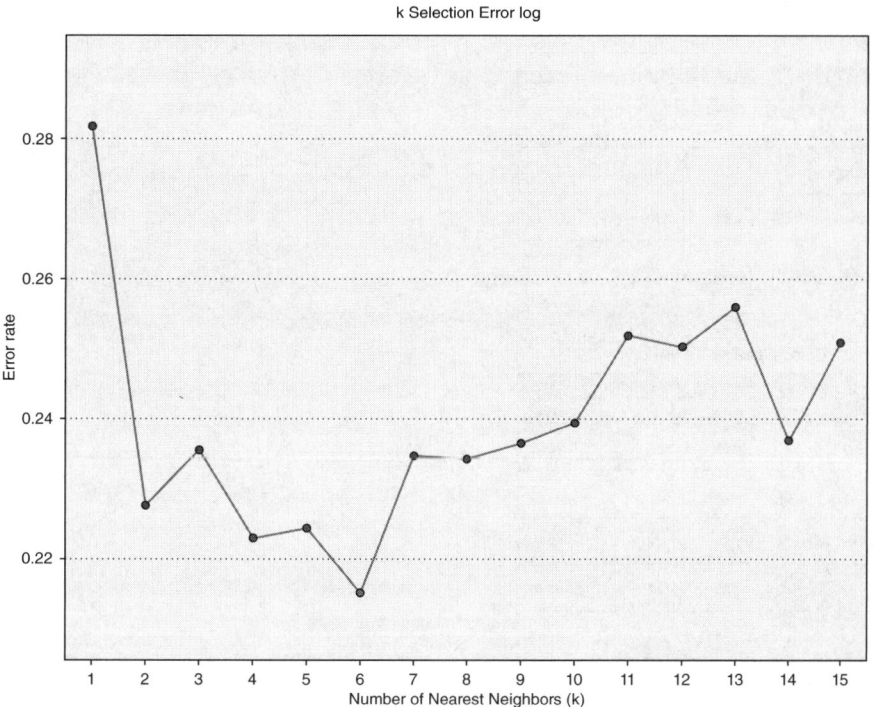

Figure 15-8: Optimal value for k

Note that in the Partitions submenu we learn that "V-fold cross-validation is performed if you choose automatic k selection but do not choose feature selection." Because the V-folds are chosen at random, the results will vary somewhat. With that in mind, we will explicitly request k=4 and k=6 to get our results. If you refer to the k=6 solution when k was automatically chosen your results will be similar, but not identical to the results in this book because the Train_Test partition will not be used.

First we will look at the k=6 option, shown in Figure 15-9. The results are not dissimilar to the run with k=3, but the comparison of train and test seems more stable, which is also true of the k=4 option, shown in Figure 15-10. The best hold-out accuracy, which is the more important, does seem to be k=6. Also, the k=6 option seems to be better for both predicting survivors as well as those who died. So we have determined our representative for the KNN approach for the next section. We will go with k=6.

Classification Table

Partition	Observed	Predicted 0	Predicted 1	Percent Correct
Training	0	264	26	91.0%
	1	73	127	63.5%
	Overall Percent	68.8%	31.2%	79.8%
Holdout	0	124	10	92.5%
	1	30	60	66.7%
	Missing	0	0	
	Overall Percent	68.8%	31.2%	82.1%

Figure 15-9: Results for k=6

Classification Table

Partition	Observed	Predicted 0	Predicted 1	Percent Correct
Training	0	263	27	90.7%
	1	78	122	61.0%
	Overall Percent	69.6%	30.4%	78.6%
Holdout	0	122	12	91.0%
	1	31	59	65.6%
	Missing	0	0	
	Overall Percent	68.3%	31.7%	80.8%

Figure 15-10: Results for k=4

Comparing Our Models: Decision Trees, Neural Nets, and KNN

In this section, we will use the two model predictions that are already in our dataset from the work in Chapters 13 and 14, add the predictions from our KNN model, and then compare all three. In order to save the predictions, check that k=6, and that you are not doing a range of values for k. Then, in the Save submenu select the following two options (Figure 15-11):

▪ Predicted Value or category
▪ Predicted probability (categorical target)

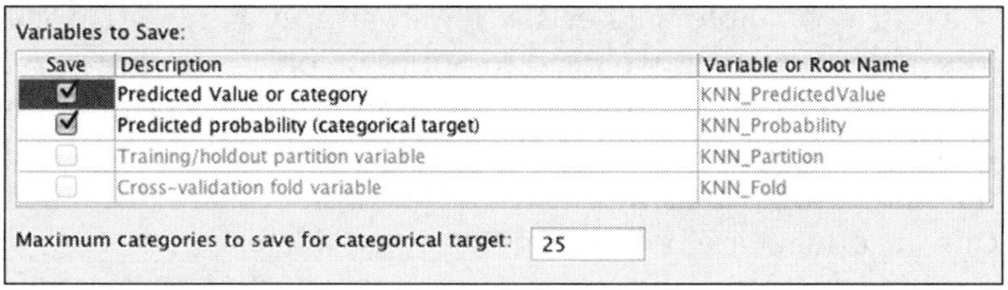

Save	Description	Variable or Root Name
☑	Predicted Value or category	KNN_PredictedValue
☑	Predicted probability (categorical target)	KNN_Probability
☐	Training/holdout partition variable	KNN_Partition
☐	Cross-validation fold variable	KNN_Fold

Variables to Save:

Maximum categories to save for categorical target: 25

Figure 15-11: Output submenu

We will have to come up with our own process for comparing the models. There is no central location for generating an accuracy table—each technique does so individually in the output window. Of course, we saw this throughout Part III including the previous section of this chapter. Also, it would be an interesting project to come up with a way of doing this using the programmability features that are discussed in Chapter 18. For now, we will adopt a manual approach, but it won't be difficult or time consuming. As a first step, we have to calculate a variable to help us display overall accuracy. If we attempted to use a simple crosstabulation, we would run into a problem (Figure 15-12). Note that I have "split" on Train_Test. This is demonstrated in the next example.

Survived * Predicted Value for Survived Crosstabulation

Train_Test				Predicted Value for Survived		Total
				0	1	
Test	Survived	0	Count	124	10	134
			% within Survived	92.5%	7.5%	100.0%
		1	Count	30	60	90
			% within Survived	33.3%	66.7%	100.0%
	Total		Count	154	70	224
			% within Survived	68.8%	31.3%	100.0%
Train	Survived	0	Count	264	26	290
			% within Survived	91.0%	9.0%	100.0%
		1	Count	73	127	200
			% within Survived	36.5%	63.5%	100.0%
	Total		Count	337	153	490
			% within Survived	68.8%	31.2%	100.0%

Figure 15-12: Output submenu

We can see that with the Test group, the accuracy for the survived passengers is 92.5%, and for those that died it is 66.7% accurate. However, we don't see overall accuracy. We can use numerous options to add overall accuracy, but one of the easiest is to simply calculate a new variable. The following syntax will give us what we need:

```
COMPUTE Tree_Correct_YN = (Survived = PredictedValue).
COMPUTE NN_Correct_YN = (Survived = MLP_PredictedValu).
COMPUTE KNN_Correct_YN = (Survived = KNN_PredictedValue).
```

Now that we have the variable we need, we will simply run a stripped down Descriptives table. However, we need to Split File on `Train_Test` first (Figure 15-13). The Split option is found near the bottom of the Data main pull-down menu. The impact of this, as we have just seen, is to give us two (or more) sets of tabular results in a single pivot table. (Split is useful for much more than just this. Its effects are not limited to pivot tables.)

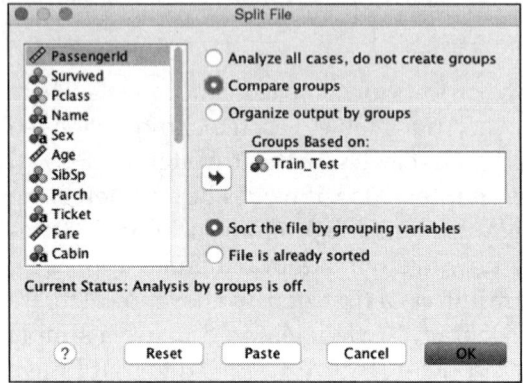

Figure 15-13: Output submenu

Now that Split File is in effect, we will run a Descriptive Statistics report using the three variables that we just created with syntax. The results are shown in Figure 15-14. The results are not as extensive as the Classification Table produced by KNN, or the accuracy results from the other algorithms, but it meets our bare minimum need. Because the Test performance is the more important of the two, and because all three appear to be stable, it seems that the neural net model currently looks like our strongest performer.

Descriptive Statistics

Train_Test		N	Mean
Test	Tree_Correct_YN	283	.8339
	NN_Correct_YN	224	.8393
	KNN_Correct_YN	224	.8214
	Valid N (listwise)	224	
Train	Tree_Correct_YN	608	.7961
	NN_Correct_YN	488	.8217
	KNN_Correct_YN	490	.7980
	Valid N (listwise)	488	

Figure 15-14: Comparing the models with Descriptives

We don't want to miss an opportunity to apply something that we learned in Chapter 2. Bootstrapping is quite appropriate here to build confidence intervals around these accuracies—and it is easy to do. The results are shown in Figure 15-15. Given the sample size of the test data (only the test data is shown), it is not terribly surprising that the widths of the intervals are wider than the differences between the algorithms. The decision tree, in particular, has very close to the same performance, so you should factor in the entirety of the business problem when choosing which model you will deploy. Overall accuracy is just one of those considerations. The relative transparency of the decision tree may weigh more heavily in many cases.

Descriptive Statistics

Train_Test: Test

		Statistic	Bias	Std. Error	95% Confidence Interval Lower	Upper
			Bootstrap[a]			
					95% Confidence Interval	
		Statistic	Bias	Std. Error	Lower	Upper
Tree_Correct_YN	N	224	0	0	224	224
	Mean	.8348	.0007	.0251	.7902	.8839
NN_Correct_YN	N	224	0	0	224	224
	Mean	.8393	-.0003	.0251	.7902	.8839
KNN_Correct_YN	N	224	0	0	224	224
	Mean	.8214	.0005	.0261	.7723	.8750
Valid N (listwise)	N	224	0	0	224	224

a. Unless otherwise noted, bootstrap results are based on 1000 bootstrap samples

Figure 15-15: Descriptives with Bootstrapping

Building an Ensemble

Now we are ready to consider a fourth option. We will allow the three models to vote, thereby creating an "ensemble." There are many ways of building an ensemble. It is simply multiple models working together to make the prediction. Some ensemble methods are quite complex, and it can be thought of as a modeling approach in its own right. Our demonstration will be quite straightforward, however. We will simply use "two out of three wins" as our voting method. Recall that in section "Creating Ensembles" in Chapter 11, we saw the Ensemble Node in SPSS Modeler. Revisiting that section will give you just a few ideas of how we could calculate the vote differently. We could envision a number of ways to calculate this, but among the easiest is to calculate an average of the three predicted value variables. Because they are coded 0 or 1, an average of the three can only yield four results: 0, 1/3, 2/3, or 1. Any vote with a mean greater than .66 will indicate a 1, and all other values will be 0. The following three lines of syntax will give us the new information that we need. The first calculates the mean. The second creates Boolean variables indicating if the vote is for 1 or 0, and the third adds a fourth variable to our collection of "Correct_YN" variables:

```
COMPUTE Vote=Mean(PredictedValue,MLP_PredictedValue,
KNN_PredictedValue).

COMPUTE Vote_PredictedValue = (Vote >= .66).

COMPUTE Vote_Correct_YN = Survived = Vote_PredictedValue.
```

All we have to do is run another Descriptives report with all four variables. We will continue to request bootstrapping, but in Figure 15-16 I've requested 90% confidence. There is certainly no rule that we must always use 95%, and with the lower sample size, 90% may be the better choice. In fact, there is no rule that 80% could not be considered in a context like this.

Descriptive Statistics

Train_Test: Test

		Statistic	Bootstrap[a]			
			Bias	Std. Error	95% Confidence Interval	
					Lower	Upper
Tree_Correct_YN	N	224	0	0	224	224
	Mean	.8348	.0005	.0245	.7857	.8839
NN_Correct_YN	N	224	0	0	224	224
	Mean	.8393	.0001	.0243	.7902	.8839
KNN_Correct_YN	N	224	0	0	224	224
	Mean	.8214	-.0004	.0251	.7723	.8661
Vote_Correct_YN	N	224	0	0	224	224
	Mean	.8438	-.0001	.0241	.7946	.8884
Valid N (listwise)	N	224	0	0	224	224

a. Unless otherwise noted, bootstrap results are based on 1000 bootstrap samples

Figure 15-16: All four models compared

We find that the ensemble does quite well. On the test data, its overall accuracy is just over 84% (only test data is shown). However, ensembles will tend to favor accuracy as they are more complex. (This is true for the reasons discussed in the previous section on bias and variance.) In this case, it does seem to test well, so there is no immediate concern that it is overfit, but this solution requires all three models and a final calculation on top of that. This does not rule it out, but that should be considered. Ensembles become a bit of a black box even if they are composed of relatively transparent models because the combination of models itself becomes complex. In this case, we have the neural net involved, which lends its own complexity. Ensembles should not be ruled out, though. In recent years virtually all data mining competitions, like those conducted on Kaggle.com and the KDD Cup, are won by teams employing ensembles. They are not a magic bullet, but they can be a very powerful technique.

Syntax, Data Management, and Programmability

The general introduction mentioned that we wanted to encourage greater sophistication with the "mechanics" of SPSS Statistics. We consider programming and data management to be among the most important examples of this in the book. Among the scores of available books on SPSS Statistics, very few invest pages on this topic, and we think that is a mistake. A likely reason is that most readers naturally want to focus on analysis and interpretation because that is why we all use SPSS. However, virtually all SPSS users will employ some aspect of SPSS Syntax in their work at some point. Many embrace it, but a large group avoids it, turning to it only when they must. Both groups will benefit from these three chapters, but may target different chapters.

We collect data to test theories and explore the conceptual, but while our final reports might discuss these theories and concepts, when we sit down in front of SPSS we are confronted by data. Our datasets are numbers and symbols. In our effort to test our theories we have to manipulate that data. Whether or not programming is something that we enjoy, it is often the path of least resistance to get our data in the form that we need. Finally, when it is done effectively, it is the easiest way to do it. That is precisely why we recommended upgrading your skills in this area. We don't suggest SPSS programming for its own sake. Use it only when it is your best option. Often weaker ways of tackling certain problems prevail simply out of ignorance that SPSS has an easy way to do it.

The first chapter in this part, Chapter 16, written by Keith, introduces best practices. If you are new to syntax you should absolutely start there. Chapter 16 is mentioned in some earlier sections of the book that use syntax, so you might have jumped to it at that time and then returned to those earlier chapters. Chapter 16 is written with the newer user of SPSS Syntax in mind. If you have considerable experience with SPSS programming you may find substantial parts of this chapter are review. However, the general approach to writing SPSS code will be of some value even if some of the commands are familiar to you.

The second chapter in this part, Chapter 17, is an introduction to the Output Management System (OMS), written by Jesus. If our interaction with colleagues and clients is a good indication, many have not heard about this powerful feature. When it was released, several years ago now, it truly transformed our options in SPSS. If you are not an expert SPSS programmer, but you've always been intrigued with what they can do, you may discover that the menus offer tremendous untapped power. If you know just a little bit more about how SPSS programming is working behind the scenes, SPSS makes it easier than ever before to tap into those resources. Once you've had a chance to learn the material in Chapters 16 and 17, you might want to read (or reread) Chapter 6. It uses Graphics Programming Language (GPL) and OMS as major elements in its case study. You will have a richer understanding of that chapter after reading the chapters in Part IV.

We are very fortunate to be able to offer an introduction to SPSS extension commands in Chapter 18, written by Jon Peck, someone who was instrumental in creating this option in SPSS. Jon has been a key collaborator on the entire book, and agreed to author this chapter. Extension commands create the easiest path to incorporating R and Python into your SPSS programming. They represent another area that absolutely need not be difficult, yet is not widely understood. This topic deserves more attention, and we hope that Chapter 18 ushers in a wider understanding of it. Perhaps the whole notion of learning additional languages might seem intimidating, but as the chapter explains you have numerous ways of taking advantage of these resources without learning R or Python. Some of the new features can be accessed into the SPSS menus. They are powerful, and everyone can and should take advantage of them.

In This Part

Write More Efficient and Elegant Code with SPSS Syntax Techniques

Many SPSS users rarely (or never) use SPSS Syntax. Others remember when Syntax was the only way to interact with SPSS. Back in the '90s, not everyone embraced the graphical user interface (GUI) at the same time or to the same extent. The GUI definitely leapt forward around the time of Windows 95. It is easy to forget that SPSS was already in its fourth decade at that time, first written in 1968! Now, few SPSS users ignore the GUI completely. However, the reverse, predictably, has occurred—many SPSS users don't learn about Syntax. If you are among them, why learn now? If you are rusty, what is the latest news regarding Syntax? If you are expert, are there any commands that you might be missing out on?

When I (Keith) was first faced with SPSS in college (late '80s), my project advisor dropped a very big and very heavy tome on the desk. It was the programming manual for SPSS-X, an older version of SPSS that would have forced me to learn SPSS Syntax in earnest. I was studying computer science so I wasn't particularly reluctant about using code, but having to worry about statistics theory, the specifics of the project, deadlines, and learning a new programming grammar all at the same time was daunting. Fortunately, I had just won a research grant. It was a small grant, but it allowed me to purchase my own copy of the much newer version of SPSS with a graphical user interface. It reduced the amount left over to pay me for the research considerably. My advisor thought that quite a prodigal move given my age and resources, but I somehow knew that it would pay off in the long run. My coauthor, Jesus, had a similar initial frustration with Syntax, which he describes in the next chapter.

Why did I avoid Syntax at the time, and why do I embrace it to such an extent now? Frankly, Syntax has a bit of a learning curve, which I feared would slow me down. I was more enthusiastic about the results, and wanted to jump right in. Also, I was at the stage in the project during which I was exploring data. I've always felt that the menus make that easier and faster. However, when the analysis becomes routinized and repetitive, switching to Syntax can increase efficiency by an order of magnitude. I can say without exaggeration that some analyses are simply not possible (or at least not practical) without some coding. Quite simply, you can't be a power user of SPSS without it.

The goals of this chapter are to move you along to your next milestone in your journey of using Syntax, and to prepare you for some of the topics in this section of the book. Many SPSS users are a bit intimidated by Python and R, for instance. One can actually make the argument that as a programming language Python is easier to learn than Syntax. However, you have to get used to using code, and not clicks, to control SPSS. What if you are already using Syntax? Your next milestone is learning about commands that cannot be pasted from the menus, which means learning of their existence, adopting strategies that use them, and writing better and more readable code as a result. Even if you are doing all of that, this chapter reviews those topics in a way that prepares you for the chapter on programmability and extension commands, Chapter 18.

The themes of this chapter are efficiency, elegance, and readability/maintainability. Efficiency is simply working smart, and ultimately working briskly. Computers are generally pretty quick, so efficiency means working on the slower half of the human/computer interface. It means getting past performing tasks like pointing and clicking the same steps repeatedly, or needless copying and pasting. Elegance is about writing code that is easy to read (by our colleagues and ourselves), correct, and easy to maintain. Code that is easy to read and easy to maintain is relatively short and easier to validate. Code that is hundreds of pages long is a challenge on both counts. Easy to read implies well-documented code. Easy to maintain involves concepts like parameters and loops, which we will explore. These techniques allow us to keep our code reasonable in length.

We are going to take precautions and assume that you haven't used Syntax at all before. We show how to "paste" commands and review the grammar. This is a brief transition before the real nuts and bolts of the chapter: using Syntax well and being brilliant in the basics of Syntax.

A Syntax Primer for the Uninitiated

If you've never used Syntax before, the best place to start your journey is not with typing in a blank syntax window, but rather with using the Paste button. This is not the same as "cut and paste," as we will see. Consider the Frequencies dialog shown in Figure 16-1. The Paste button is shown at the bottom of the dialog on the left. (Its position on a windows version will be somewhat different.)

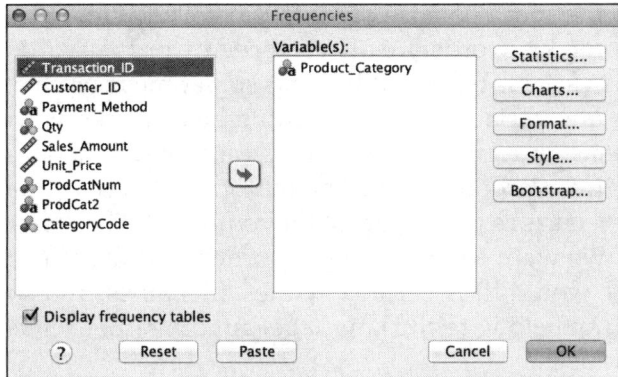

Figure 16-1: Frequencies main dialog

Let's examine the results as they appear in the Syntax window, shown in Figure 16-2.

Figure 16-2: Resulting Syntax in the Syntax Editor

Note that the SPSS Syntax window is not merely a text editor. It has features specifically designed to help you write Syntax. On the left is a list of commands. At the moment, we have just two. On the right we have line numbers and the complete Syntax code. The color coding is important; you can see it when working in the Syntax window. Commands are blue, and appear right up against the left margin. Back in the day, when punch cards were still used, starting commands in the first column was a requirement but that is no longer the case. The use of capitals is not required, but it is conventional to use uppercase for commands. In contrast, variable names, like Product_Category, are conventionally typed in mixed case or lowercase.

Our first command is DATASET ACTIVATE. This can be valuable when using multiple data windows, but we will set aside our discussion of this command until later. The second command, FREQUENCIES, is the command we were expecting because it is the dialog that we are working in. Subcommands appear in green. We have one subcommand, /ORDER. The subcommands allow you to take advantage of the potentially numerous features of the commands. In the Syntax Reference Guide, available in the Help menu, you will find many pages dedicated to some of the more complex commands. They can have numerous subcommands. Some keywords are also reserved words—words are not available to be used as variable names. While it is sometimes possible, it is rarely a good idea to use any variable name that could be confused with commands or keywords. When Syntax users speak of *keywords* they generally mean the words appearing in a maroon color in the editor. In this case, the ANALYSIS portion of /ORDER = ANALYSIS is this part of the command. The ORDER subcommand indicates that we want to designate the order, and ANALYSIS makes explicit what order we would like. Variable names, filenames, and so on appear in black. They do not belong to the language, but are rather referring to the specifics of our dataset.

NOTE You may not be able to detect the colors in this book (because the images are printed in black and white), but if you experiment in the editor, you will be able to see how the commands' structure is revealed in color.

Note well that both commands—not all three lines—end in periods. This is critical. If we violate this rule, the color coding will change, and we run a considerable risk of an unexpected result or no result at all. Note as well that the subcommand is indented and has a slash. The indentation is not as critical as it was in the punch card days. The slash punctuation, however, remains very important.

Two important buttons are visible in Figure 16-2. The Run Selection button, which looks like a "play" button, is indicated with a green arrow and can be used to run selected code. Four icons to its right is the symbol showing a page and question mark. It is the Syntax Help button. An example of Syntax Help is shown in Figure 16-3.

The results of requesting Syntax Help might be a bit different than you were expecting. It is essentially a grammar chart. There is hypertext in the document that takes you to examples and explanations of the command, but the primary purpose of this button is to show you the available subcommands, and available choices for each subcommand. Notice, for instance, that in lieu of /ORDER = ANALYSIS we could have chosen /ORDER = VARIABLE. Brackets ([ ]) indicate that the entire subcommand or a portion of it is optional, and braces ({ }) indicate our choices on the subcommand.

Note that virtually everything is optional. We could actually type the following, and it would run just fine:

```
FREQ Product_Category.
```

```
Reference > Command Syntax Reference

FREQUENCIES

FREQUENCIES is available in the Statistics Base option.

FREQUENCIES VARIABLES=varlist [varlist...]

[/FORMAT= [{NOTABLE }] [{AVALUE**}]
          {LIMIT(n)}  {DVALUE  }
                      {AFREQ   }
                      {DFREQ   }

[/MISSING=INCLUDE]

[/BARCHART=[MINIMUM(n)] [MAXIMUM(n)] [{FREQ(n)    }]]
                                     {PERCENT(n)}

[/PIECHART=[MINIMUM(n)] [MAXIMUM(n)] [{FREQ   }] [{MISSING  }]]
                                     {PERCENT}  {NOMISSING}

[/HISTOGRAM=[MINIMUM(n)] [MAXIMUM(n)] [{FREQ(n)  }] [{NONORMAL}] ]
                                                    {NORMAL  }

[/GROUPED=varlist [{(width)      }]]
                  {(boundary list)}

[/NTILES=n]

[/PERCENTILES=value list]

[/STATISTICS=[DEFAULT] [MEAN] [STDDEV] [MINIMUM] [MAXIMUM]
             [SEMEAN] [VARIANCE] [SKEWNESS] [SESKEW] [RANGE]
             [MODE] [KURTOSIS] [SEKURT] [MEDIAN] [SUM] [ALL]
                [NONE]]

[/ORDER=[{ANALYSIS}] [{VARIABLE}]]

** Default if subcommand is omitted or specified without keyword.
```

Figure 16-3: Syntax Help

In contrast, the full command, as SPSS pastes it into the Syntax Window, appears in Figure 16-4. Note that the code has been highlighted which is required is you are going to use the Run Selection button (green arrow icon) which we discussed earlier. The menus also offer you the option to Run All (not shown) which would not require this step.

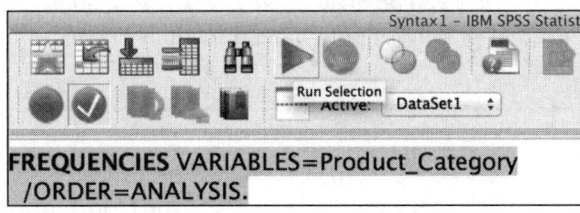

Figure 16-4: Frequencies command in the Syntax editor

You won't want to get bogged down in the details. The key point is that pasting easily produces accurate Syntax that we can save and rerun when we need the same result in the future. However, that doesn't mean that you will never want to modify the result. In particular, pasting on default settings will produce an EXECUTE command. See the side bar on this subject.

THE EVIL EXECUTE COMMAND

EXECUTE is the most misunderstood and misused command in Statistics. It forces a data pass, which causes any pending transformations to be executed immediately. While this refreshes the Data Editor contents, it is almost always a waste of time. For efficiency, transformations such as COMPUTE or SELECT IF are carried out by "lazy evaluation," which means that they are piggy-backed on the next required data pass, which would be a procedure such as FREQUENCIES. This saves data passes, which can be expensive. So a set of transformations followed by a procedure would all happen on one pass automatically unless an EXECUTE intervenes, in which case two or more passes would occur.

There are only two situations when EXECUTE is needed, apart from immediately updating the Data Editor:

■ There are transformation commands in the transformation block that would be executed out of order and change the result of a previously read but not yet executed command.

■ The LAG function is used and sample selection follows in the same transformation block.

Out-of-order commands include commands like MISSING VALUES, which take effect as soon as they are read and before, say, a COMPUTE command that actually precedes them in the block. An intervening procedure prevents this. Out-of-order execution is noted in the Command Syntax Reference descriptions.

There is a preference setting in Edit ⇨ Options ⇨ Data that controls whether the Transform ⇨ Compute Variable and other transformation dialogs generate EXECUTE after every command. The default value is to generate it so that the Data Editor shows the results of transformations immediately, but changing the setting can save a lot of time. This default setting plus, perhaps, the somewhat similar but necessary RUN command in SAS leads to much overuse. And if you do need to see the transformation results immediately, you can use Transform ⇨ Run Pending Transformations to run that EXECUTE.

This rapid-fire review is enough to get you through the chapter, but if it is a brand new topic to you, you should read the following chapters of the Command Syntax Reference:

▪ Introduction
▪ Universals

You can find this extensive (and huge) document in the Help menu, as shown in Figure 16-5. Note that the Help menu in version 24 is abbreviated and doesn't have as many options listed, but the Command Syntax Reference is still available in the menu. Don't get dissuaded by the size of the document—the two recommended chapters are manageable.

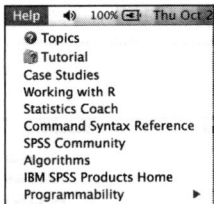

Figure 16-5: Help menu showing the Command Syntax Reference

Making the Connection: Menus and the Grammar of Syntax

Understanding commands, subcommands, and keywords is very easy if you compare some pasted Syntax to the dialogs. The name of the dialog corresponds, sometimes exactly, with the command. The subcommands are generally modified via subdialogs and the keywords are modified with check boxes. This is not always followed in the design of the dialogs, but using two commands as examples we will explore how the dialogs and the resulting Syntax relate to each other. We will take a closer look at the familiar Frequencies and Crosstab commands.

The first example of the command (Figure 16-6) was done with default settings (Lines 1–2). "Old school" syntax practitioners who mastered syntax without the menus sometimes find the "extra words" distracting, but it is harmlessly making the defaults explicit. Line 4 provides an example stripped of the defaults.

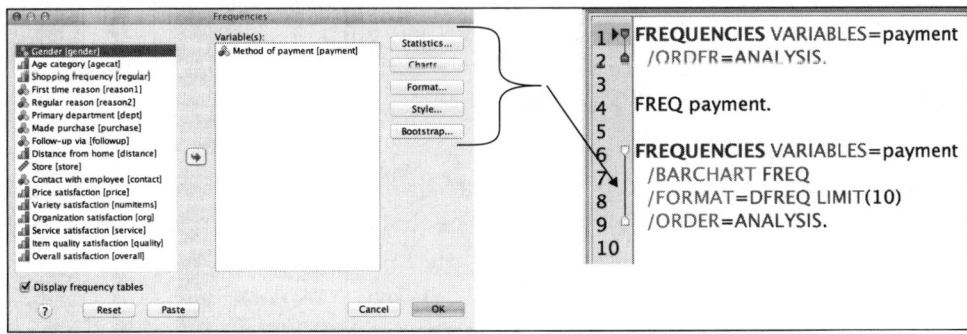

Figure 16-6: Frequencies dialog and Frequencies commands

Noteworthy is the near one-to-one correspondence between the rectangular buttons in the upper right-hand portion of the menus, and the three pasted commands (Lines 6–9). /BARCHART, inserted with the Chart button, and /FORMAT, inserted with the Format button, are two examples. The Charts subdialog, accessible by pressing the Charts button, is shown in Figure 16-7.

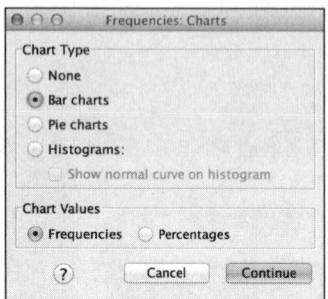

Figure 16-7: Charts subdialog

Figure 16-7 shows the check boxes within the menus. In this case, Bar Charts have been requested and that is visible in the syntax as the /BARCHART subcommand with the keyword FREQ. Figure 16-8 shows the Crosstabs main dialog and the Cell Display subdialog.

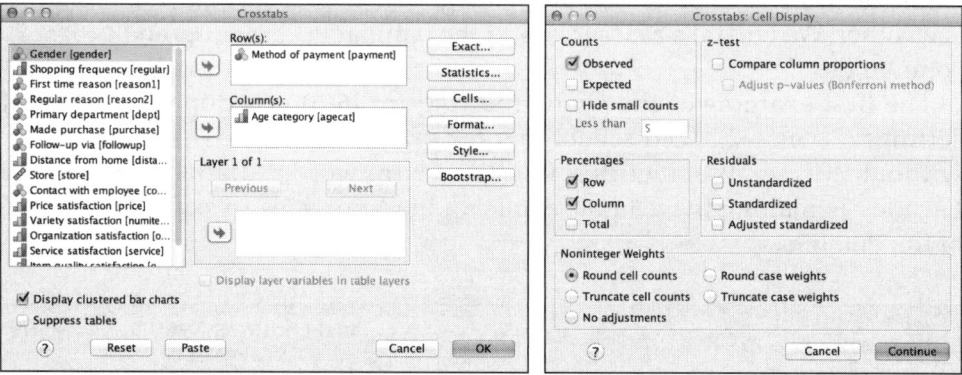

Figure 16-8: Main dialog and Cell Display subdialog

The CROSSTABS command provides an additional example of the relationship between the dialogs and the commands. The first pasted bit of code (Lines 11–15) imitates our last example in that it was pasted with default settings. Line 17 in Figure 16-9 shows an example that has been typed with abbreviations. Though this is an old style, it is not just nostalgia. Because you will find collections of code written like this lurking about in organizations that have been using SPSS Syntax for decades, seeing it might help you understand why it looks that way.

```
11  CROSSTABS
12    /TABLES=payment BY agecat
13    /FORMAT=AVALUE TABLES
14    /CELLS=COUNT
15    /COUNT ROUND CELL.
16
17  CROSS payment BY agecat.
18
19  CROSSTABS
20    /TABLES=payment BY agecat
21    /FORMAT=DVALUE TABLES
22    /STATISTICS=CHISQ
23    /CELLS=COUNT ROW COLUMN
24    /COUNT ROUND CELL
25    /BARCHART.
26
```

Figure 16-9: Three CROSSTABS examples

NOTE Autocomplete in the editor makes typing complete commands easy so there is no need for abbreviations. Avoid them.

Let's examine some of the specifics of this example. In the third example of the CROSSTABS command (Lines 19–25) you can see the keywords that have been chosen. The format has been changed—Line 21. The choice of the Chi-Square statistic (check box not shown) adds a new subcommand with keyword CHISQ. The additional, non-default check boxes Row and Column are visible on Line 23. The choice to Display cluster bar charts is visible on Line 25.

What Is "Inefficient" Code?

Obviously for a series of pasted syntax commands to be useful, they have to work, and they have to reproduce the correct result consistently. However, we want to set the bar higher than merely "working." They should also be easy to read and easy to modify.

Many organizations get trapped in a situation where a single Syntax user produces some code, often running dozens or hundreds of pages, and colleagues struggle to read it, making it impossible to modify or maintain. Even if it is well documented, it is very difficult to maintain a large program. There are ways of shortening the code, and this is not a trivial improvement as it eases readability and modification. Code that "works" but ties the organization to something that no one can adapt to current processes can do considerable harm in the long run. Many an SPSS expert has been asked to visit an organization to address a problem like this that has been accumulating over many years.

Another big problem area is copying and pasting that produces many very similar jobs that all have to be maintained separately. This can grow into thousands or tens of thousands of jobs, which paralyzes the organization. Attention should be paid to ways to generalize the code to minimize the number of jobs.

Most discussions of SPSS command syntax are organized around a series of commands with one or more examples per command. In the case of the massive (albeit necessary) Command Syntax Reference the commands are arranged alphabetically, all 2000+ pages of it. The majority of shorter introductions follow the same basic approach. We will use a different approach. We will take a single extended case study, and introduce only those commands that support the case study.

The Case Study

In the case study, we begin with two datasets from a fictional media distribution firm. It sells media services to hotels, bars, college dorms, and so on. It specializes in one time fee-for-service sales like in room hotel pay per view, but it offers some monthly plans and bundles as well. Along the way, we are going to make some simple formatting changes, merge and label the datasets, restructure the resulting dataset, and make some calculations. If we assume that these files are pulled off routine systems like Point of Sale or CRM systems, these are tasks that we might have to perform monthly or even daily. Therefore, automating them seems appropriate if not critical. Doing so in a way that enables multiple members of the team to understand, modify, and execute the code is important. If this supports a routine reporting function and is mission-critical data, then the vacation, or illness, or departure of the code author cannot jeopardize the data. If the code is opaque to all but the author, this is exactly what can (and often does) happen.

The first dataset is called `Media Sales Transactions Start.sav`. We notice two issues that can be easily resolved in the menus. The currency column, `Sales_Amount`, needs its formatting corrected because we cannot see decimal places that we know are expected. Also, a nominal variable, `Category_Code`, needs labeling. We could use the Variable View tab (Figure 16-10), but it is not recommended in this instance.

	Customer_ID	Sales_Amount	Category_Code
1	100000111	7	103
2	100000111	30	103
3	100000111	7	202
4	100000111	98	203
5	100000111	6	204
6	100000111	9	204
7	100000111	18	204
8	100000111	360	205
9	100000199	150	205
10	100000199	150	402

	Name	Type	Width	Decimals	Label	Values	Missing	Columns	Align	Measure	Role
1	Customer_ID	Numeric	9	0		None	None	9	Right	Scale	Input
2	Sales_Amount	Numeric	4	0		None	None	14	Right	Scale	Input
3	Category_Code	Numeric	3	0		None	None	22	Right	Scale	Input

Figure 16-10: Data View (above) and Variable View (below)

Using the Define Variable Properties window (accessed from the Data menu) is a better choice because we can paste from it (Figure 16-11). We only have three variables so we will scan all three.

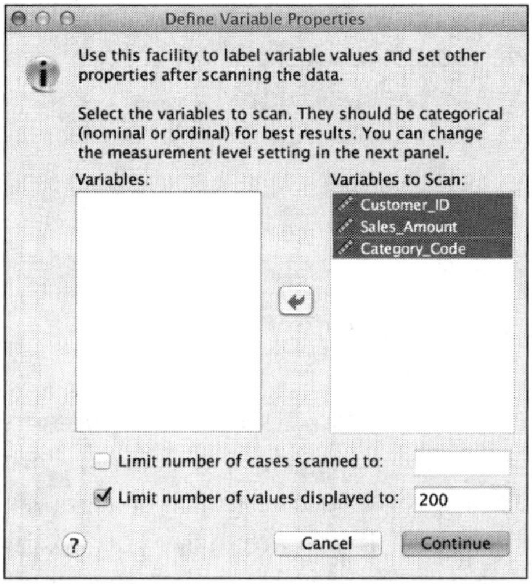

Figure 16-11: Define Variable Properties dialog

As shown in Figure 16-12, to correct `Sales_Amount`, we will simply choose Currency, and adjust the width. The width refers to the total width, so when displaying two decimals, this allows for the amount to display tens of thousandths, which is sufficient.

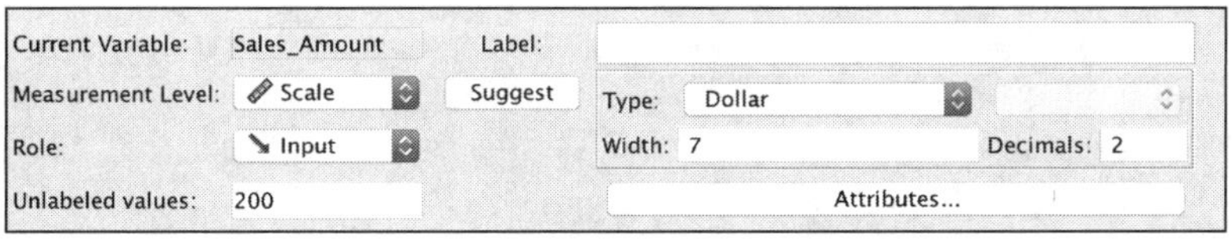

Figure 16-12: Declaring the Sales_Amount variable

To correct our nominal variable's value labels, we are going to employ a little trick. First we are going to label just one category in the menus (Figure 16-13). Add the label "Special Event" to the code 101, and then click the Paste button.

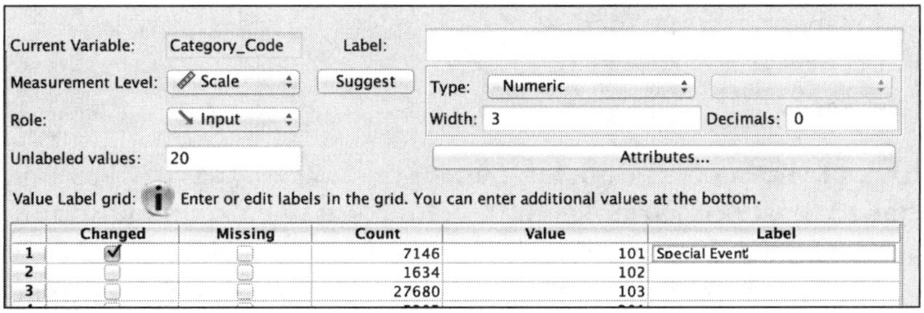

Figure 16-13: Adding a Value Label to Category_Code

The resulting syntax is quite easy to read (Figure 16-14). The FORMATS line declares Sales_Amount as Dollar, just as we indicated in the dialog. Now, we will turn our attention to completing the VALUE LABELS command.

```
1 * Define Variable Properties.
2 *Sales_Amount.
3 FORMATS Sales_Amount(DOLLAR7.2).
4 *Category_Code.
5 VALUE LABELS Category_Code
6   101 'Special Event'.
7 EXECUTE.
```

Figure 16-14: Pasted code from the Define Variable Properties dialog

The "trick" used here is that we only pasted one of twenty one categories in the menus. The structure of the command is easily grasped, so we can imitate the structure using just that one example, supplying the relevant codes (see Figure 16-15). We simply add additional value labels. If you are lucky you might have a Word doc with these code and label pairs lying about that has been maintained by others in the organization, which would allow you to copy and paste them into the Syntax window. There is no assumption that this is another SPSS user. These product category codes tie the products with their descriptive labels so they can probably be found somewhere in electronic form. You will almost certainly have to alter the list to meet the grammatical requirements, but it will still save time.

```
10 Value Labels Category_Code
11   101 'Special Event'
12   102 'Individual Episode'
13   103 'TV Season'
14   201 'Movie'
15   202 'HD Movie'
16   203 'Still in Theatres'
17   204 'HD Movie Upgrade'
18   205 'Special Promotion Movie'
19   301 'Internet on TV'
```

Figure 16-15: Value Labels with additional category codes

With only twenty one codes, we wouldn't worry about this too much, but if there were a thousand, we would ask everyone we could if the values were available in a spreadsheet somewhere before we resorted to typing. This might seem trivial, but this is just about the easiest command to learn, and there is little reason to do labeling in the menus.

Customer Dataset

Let's take a look at the second dataset, Customer Financial Start.sav. This dataset has a variety of variables that include credit card and shipping information (all completely faked data). This represents the most recently available personal financial information for each customer, and is pulled from the most recent transaction. Much of it is unnecessary to the analysis and can be deleted, but some of the information will be important to us (Figure 16-16). In particular, we are going to rehearse three examples of formatting steps:

- Fixing the four-digit ZIP codes in Massachusetts and elsewhere
- Addressing the fact that some cities' names are in caps, and others are not
- Parsing the e-mail addresses to place the domain name in a new variable

	StreetAddress	City	State	ZipCode	Country	EmailAddress
27	1953 Hilltop Street	HUNTINGTON	MA	1050	US	Jack.L.Serpa@trashymail.com
28	4104 Kinney Street	NORTHAMPTON	MA	1060	US	Darin.M.Hightower@trashymail.com
29	1107 Kinney Street	NORTHAMPTON	MA	1060	US	Renee.W.Morse@dodgit.com
30	2296 Hilltop Street	NORTHAMPTON	MA	1060	US	Clara.J.Evans@dodgit.com
31	3822 Kinney Street	NORTHAMPTON	MA	1060	US	Cindy.B.Cluck@dodgit.com
32	4462 Lyon Avenue	OAKHAM	MA	1068	US	Christopher.S.Levron@spambob.com
33	2238 Leverton Cove Road	PALMER	MA	1069	US	Donald.A.Ritenour@mailinator.com
34	3678 Leverton Cove Road	WARE	MA	1082	US	Caroline.J.Ferguson@pookmail.com
35	4241 Leverton Cove Road	WARE	MA	1082	US	Brian.C.Foote@trashymail.com
36	1528 Leverton Cove Road	WARREN	MA	1083	US	Mark.H.Durham@trashymail.com
37	2029 Leverton Cove Road	WARREN	MA	1083	US	Donna.R.Casavant@spambob.com

Figure 16-16: A few rows of address information in the customer data

Fixing the ZIP Codes

Our first task, fixing the ZIP codes, is straightforward enough, but will require using some conversion functions and string functions. The actual solution is a bit more involved than you might guess because SPSS doesn't allow you to do this kind of conversion in one step. Also, the conversion is only part of the problem. We have to add (or "pad") the zeros that are missing. We can do the first step in the windows. If you are really savvy with functions in SPSS or even Excel, you might question the creation of ZipCode2. Note the use of the Type and Label subdialog in Figure 16-17. I'm approaching it this way to make a point—a point that will become clear by the end of the example. If we paste this, we get the code shown in Lines 1–2 (Figure 16-18). We've already discussed that you won't always need the DATASET ACTIVATE line that is pasted. Also, as we've seen, we don't need an EXECUTE after every transformation. All of that has been removed. Note that the sidebar in the Syntax Primer section of this chapter discusses EXECUTE in some detail.

For ZipCode3, Lines 4–5, we introduce two functions, and notice that they've been nested. The LTRIM portion gets rid of the leading space that has filled the vacuum. We must remove that space before CHAR.LPAD can do its job of making sure that all of the ZIP codes have five characters.

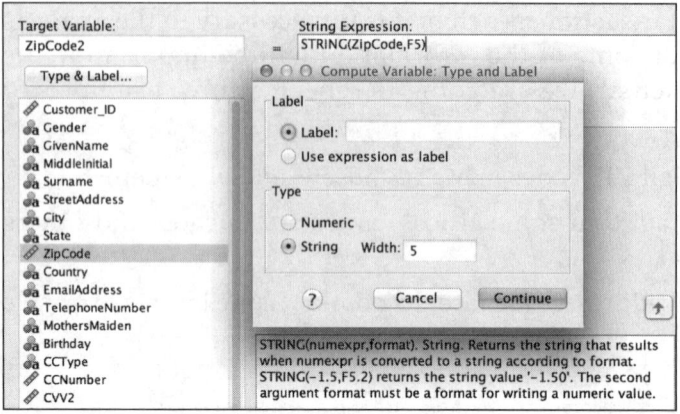

Figure 16-17: Type and Label subdialog

```
1    STRING  ZipCode2 (A5).
2    COMPUTE ZipCode2=STRING(ZipCode,F5).
3
4    STRING  ZipCode3 (A5).
5    COMPUTE ZipCode3=CHAR.LPAD(LTRIM(ZipCode2),5,'0').
```

Figure 16-18: The STRING command

NOTE　Some U.S. ZIP codes actually start with a double zero. They are not common, so we don't address that here, but being a good programmer includes expecting the unexpected.

Now, let's take a look at some ways to improve what was pasted. We don't really need to keep ZipCode2. It is an intermediate step. Nesting is one way to try to address this, but in this case a very easy way is to make ZipCode2 a "scratch variable" by adding a # symbol. As a result it will never appear in the data window. It will have meaning only in the Syntax Window, and only until SPSS encounters a procedure command.

Because you can't put string values in a numeric value, it is easier to just create a new variable and give it a meaningful name. We might have 9-digit ZIP codes for some addresses, so Zip5 seems like a good name. We no longer need the original, so we apply DELETE VARIABLES to it (Figure 16-19). We could try using RENAME VARIABLES to go back to the original if we wanted (not shown). A little documentation would be wise as well. Also, note that DELETE VARIABLES won't execute (yet) until it is followed by a procedure command. (The difference between procedure and transformation commands is discussed in the sidebar "The Evil Execute Command" earlier in this chapter.)

```
8
9     STRING  #ZipCode2 (A5).
10    COMPUTE #ZipCode2=STRING(ZipCode,F5).
11    STRING Zip5(A5).
12    COMPUTE Zip5= CHAR.LPAD(LTRIM(#ZipCode2),5,'0').
13    DELETE VARIABLES ZipCode.
```

Figure 16-19: Code examples using scratch variables

Addressing Case Sensitivity of City Names with UPPER() and LOWER()

Some cities are mixed case and some are all uppercase. Why should we be concerned? A number of operations are case sensitive, including merging (it is the variable key that causes the problem) and reporting. For instance, consider the frequencies output shown in Figure 16-20. Boca Raton has 51 sales and Boise has 91, but we have to get out our scratchpad to confirm that because both cities have variation in the use of upper and lower case. Of course, there are misspellings and other issues, but we will address just the mixed case for now. It will be sufficient to accomplish our goal—identify the Top 10 cities.

City

	Frequency	Percent	Valid Percent	Cumulative Percent
Boardman	11	.0	.0	9.4
BOARDMAN	2	.0	.0	9.4
BOAZ	2	.0	.0	9.4
BOBTOWN	3	.0	.0	9.4
Boca Raton	43	.1	.1	9.5
BOCA RATON	8	.0	.0	9.5
BODCAW	1	.0	.0	9.5
BODEGA BAY	1	.0	.0	9.5
Boerne	1	.0	.0	9.5
BOERNE	2	.0	.0	9.5
Bogalusa	2	.0	.0	9.5
BOGART	1	.0	.0	9.5
Bohemia	15	.0	.0	9.6
Boise	90	.2	.2	9.7
BOISE	1	.0	.0	9.7

Figure 16-20: City names in mixed case

We could simply make everything all uppercase:

```
COMPUTE City = UPCASE(City).
```

But we will try a command that is a little more interesting:

```
COMPUTE City =
CONCAT( CHAR.SUBSTR(City,1,1) , LOWER(CHAR.SUBSTR(City,2)) ).
```

In theory you could work exclusively with the mouse to perform these functions, but when you are writing functions inside of functions it is easier to work in the Syntax window, and it is much easier to save your work. The new frequencies with the descending cases output shown in Figure 16-21 shows that we have made progress.

City

		Frequency	Percent	Valid Percent	Cumulative Percent
Valid	New york	984	1.7	1.7	1.7
	Los angeles	853	1.4	1.4	3.1
	Houston	748	1.3	1.3	4.3
	Chicago	682	1.1	1.1	5.5
	Philadelphia	597	1.0	1.0	6.5
	Dallas	553	.9	.9	7.4
	Atlanta	466	.8	.8	8.2
	San francisco	399	.7	.7	8.9
	Seattle	397	.7	.7	9.5
	Washington	395	.7	.7	10.2

Figure 16-21: City names in descending case

We could be considerably more ambitious. For instance, "New york" has a space in its name, and we have not addressed that. It leaves the second word in its name lowercase. For this, and similar complications, we will delay a richer solution until we get to Chapter 18.

Parsing Strings and the Index Function

For this example, we are going to extract the e-mail domain information from the client's e-mail addresses. Domains sometimes have slightly different rules on what e-mail attachments are allowed. This information might help our marketing materials successfully reach our clients. In our fake data, the e-mails are unnaturally uniform, and some of the domain names are odd, but there are plenty of formatting issues to contend with. We are only interested in the string between the @ symbol and the period that follows the @ symbol.

First we have to find the locations and the length of the domain name:

```
COMPUTE At_Loc=CHAR.INDEX(EmailAddress,'@').

COMPUTE Period_Loc=CHAR.RINDEX(EmailAddress,'.').

COMPUTE Domain_Length = (Period_Loc-At_Loc)-1.
```

Run these and examine the results. We get the locations, as an integer, of the symbols. Note that the RINDEX looks for the last instance of the period. Now, we will use the STRING and SUBSTRING functions again while converting our new variables into scratch variables:

```
COMPUTE #At_Loc=CHAR.INDEX(EmailAddress,'@').
COMPUTE #Period_Loc=CHAR.RINDEX(EmailAddress,'.').
COMPUTE #Domain_Length = (#Period_Loc-#At_Loc)-1.

STRING Domain(A16).
COMPUTE Domain=CHAR.SUBSTR(EmailAddress,#At_Loc+1,#Domain_Length).
EXECUTE.
```

This dataset is ready to merge, so we are going to switch back to the other dataset and finalize it for merging.

Aggregate and Restructure

We are almost ready to combine the datasets so we are going to switch back to the transactional dataset. We will use the Restructure Data Wizard, but for that we have to aggregate first. In a sense, this is the most sophisticated data manipulation thus far, but the menus do all the work. Take a closer look at the first customer, as shown in Figure 16-22.

	Customer_ID	Sales_Amount	Category_Code
1	100000111	$6.90	TV Season
2	100000111	$29.90	TV Season
3	100000111	$6.90	HD Movie
4	100000111	$98.00	Still in Theatres
5	100000111	$5.90	HD Movie Upgrade
6	100000111	$8.90	HD Movie Upgrade
7	100000111	$17.90	HD Movie Upgrade
8	100000111	$359.90	Special Promotion Movie

Figure 16-22: A few rows of the transactional dataset

Currently there are two lines for TV Season; restructuring forces us to have just one line. The same problem exists for HD Movie Upgrade. Aggregating easily solves the problem. We will choose both `Customer_ID` and `Category_Code` as break variables and sum customer spending within the categories. Importantly, we are using the `DATASET` commands for the first time. `DATASET DECLARE` will give our new dataset a name. This is not at all the same as saving it to a drive. If we were to exit SPSS without saving it, we would lose the new data file. When we restructure we will reference this data window by name using `DATASET ACTIVATE`:

```
DATASET DECLARE Media_Trans_AGGR.
AGGREGATE
  /OUTFILE='Media_Trans_AGGR'
  /BREAK=Customer_ID Category_Code
  /Sales_Amount_sum=SUM(Sales_Amount).
```

The restructure menu (see Figure 16-23) presents three choices. We want the middle choice because we want to convert a "tall dataset" into a "wide dataset." Specifically, a transactional dataset needs to become a customer-level dataset. When you've made the selection, click Continue.

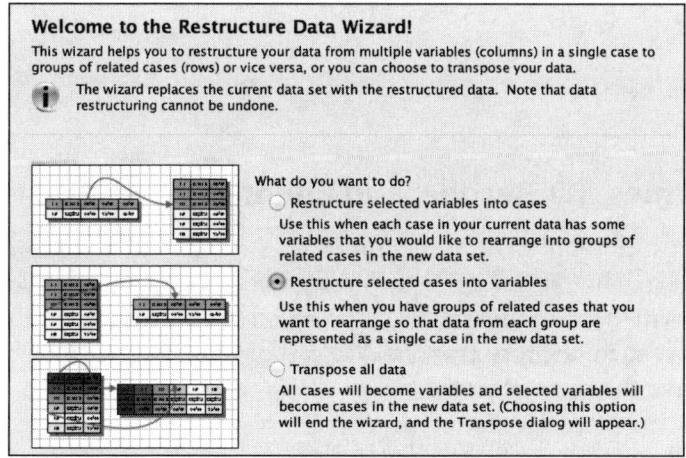

Figure 16-23: First screen of the Restructure Wizard

We want `Customer_ID` to define the height, or number of rows, of the dataset. `Category_Code` is in the important Index Variable Role and will define the columns of the dataset. The only variable that should be remaining, `Sales_Amount_Sum` will populate the body of the resulting table. See Figure 16-24. Press continue and paste the syntax.

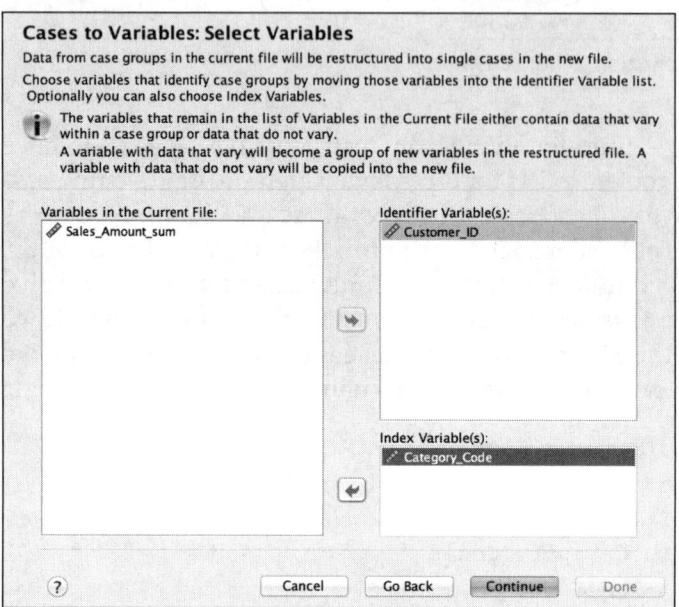

Figure 16-24: Second screen of the Restructure Wizard

The resulting Syntax follows:

```
DATASET ACTIVATE Media_Trans_AGGR.
SORT CASES BY Customer_ID Category_Code.
CASESTOVARS
  /ID=Customer_ID
  /INDEX=Category_Code
  /GROUPBY=INDEX.
```

Pasting Variable Names, TO, Recode, and Count

Next we have to create a sum of all of our customers' spending so that we can use it as our denominator. The menus offer up many ways to save time. We could go into the Transform ⇨ Compute menu, and drag all of the variables into place, but there is also a way to be more creative. We can use just two variables to make sure that we have the proper grammar:

```
Compute Total_Spend = SUM( Sales_Amount_sum.101,
Sales_Amount_sum.102).
```

Then use the following trick. From the Utilities menu click Variables (Figure 16-25). Choose all of the variables you need, and then click Paste. The variables will appear in the Syntax window. All you have to do now is add some commas and writing the command is quite quick. You still have to understand the command, and how to write it, but you've saved yourself considerably on the typing.

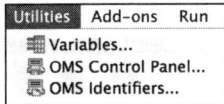

Figure 16-25: The Utilities Menu

```
Compute Total_Spend = SUM( Sales_Amount_sum.101,
Sales_Amount_sum.102, Sales_Amount_sum.103,
Sales_Amount_sum.201, Sales_Amount_sum.202,
Sales_Amount_sum.203, Sales_Amount_sum.204,
Sales_Amount_sum.205, Sales_Amount_sum.301,
Sales_Amount_sum.401, Sales_Amount_sum.402,
Sales_Amount_sum.403, Sales_Amount_sum.501,
Sales_Amount_sum.502, Sales_Amount_sum.503,
Sales_Amount_sum.601, Sales_Amount_sum.701,
Sales_Amount_sum.702, Sales_Amount_sum.703,
Sales_Amount_sum.704, Sales_Amount_sum.705).
```

There is an even better trick we can use when we don't have to worry about the commas. Let's use the Count Values within Cases menu option (Figure 16-26). Located in the Transform menu, this is going to be the easiest way to determine how many null values (more accurately called "system missing" and identified with the dot in the cell) there are in our sales ratios for each customer. This will allow us to figure out how many departments they have made purchases in. Customers who shop in only one department might need a different marketing approach than those who shop in many departments. When we load the variables and Define Values as being system missing, SPSS lists all of the variables. That is OK, but our code will be easier to read if we place the TO keyword between the first and last Sales_Amount_sum variable. As an added twist, we will try a scratch variable again.

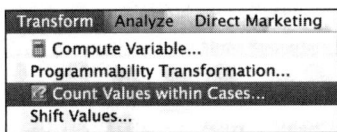

Figure 16-26: Count Values within Cases menu option

```
COUNT
#NumMiss=Sales_Amount_sum.101 TO Sales_Amount_sum705(SYSMIS).
```

Because we want to know how many departments they've shopped in, and not how many that they have failed to shop in, we will perform the following calculation. Now the new variable NumCats will tell us in how many sales categories they have a non-SYSMIS value:

```
COMPUTE NumCats = 21 - #NumMiss.
```

The same TO keyword can be used with the RECODE command. Note that this is the equivalent of RECODE into SAME VARIABLES in the menus because no new variable name is given. RECODE into DIFFERENT VARIABLES would require the optional INTO keyword, as shown in Figure 16-27.

RECODE

For numeric variables:
```
RECODE varlist (value list=newvalue)...(value list=newvalue) [INTO varlist]
     [/varlist...]
```

Figure 16-27: RECODE command in Syntax Help

Our RECODE command will be the following:

```
RECODE Sales_Amount_sum.101 TO Sales_Amount_sum.705 (SYSMIS=0).
```

DO REPEAT Spend Ratios

We now need to create 21 ratios. We could use 21 COMPUTE statements, but we are going to use a kind of loop. The DO REPEAT command may not be familiar to you or your colleagues, but it is easily explained with just a sentence or two of documentation. It will take up less space, which makes the total code easier to read and easier to test. When a section of code is longer than a page (or a screen) it invites mistakes. We have to take 21 Numerators (one for each sales category) and divide all of them by our sum. That's it. DO REPEAT makes it easy.

First we declare what the Command Syntax Reference calls a *stand-in variable*. Ours is called numerator. Using the TO keyword we can refer to all of them as long as they are contiguous—which they are. In the case of our new variables, we are going to list them all explicitly. We must because they don't exist yet, and because the names are not a simple increment. Note that if they had names like ratio1, ratio2, and so on, we could use a code fragment like this:

```
ratio = ratio1 to ratio21
```

Because we can't do that, we write them out explicitly, being careful to place a period at the end of this section of code. The grammar requires that we separate the declarations of the stand-ins with a slash, and terminate the section with a period.

Next we have a COMPUTE statement embedded in the middle of the command:

```
COMPUTE ratio = numerator / Total_Spend.
```

The formula uses our two stand-ins as well as our variable Total_Spend. The entire command successfully creates 21 new variables. The optional PRINT keywords display the 21 COMPUTE statements as they are actually performed by SPSS:

```
DO REPEAT numerator = Sales_Amount_sum.101 TO Sales_Amount_sum.705
    / ratio = Sales_Ratio.101, Sales_Ratio.102, Sales_Ratio.103,
    Sales_Ratio.201, Sales_Ratio.202, Sales_Ratio.203,
    Sales_Ratio.204, Sales_Ratio.205, Sales_Ratio.301,
    Sales_Ratio.401, Sales_Ratio.402, Sales_Ratio.403,
    Sales_Ratio.501, Sales_Ratio.502, Sales_Ratio.503,
    Sales_Ratio.601, Sales_Ratio.701, Sales_Ratio.702,
    Sales_Ratio.703, Sales_Ratio.704, Sales_Ratio.705.
COMPUTE ratio = numerator / Total_Spend.
END REPEAT PRINT.
```

Merge

You are likely familiar with the MERGE commands in the menus. If you have been using SPSS for a while, you might be a bit surprised by the pasted command. When you paste from the Merge menus you get the STAR JOIN command. Let's begin in the menus. We are going to write the code to be in the Customer Financial Start dataset at the time of the merge, so we want to indicate to SPSS that we want to merge with the [Media_Trans_AGGR] dataset. Untitled9 (shown in Figure 16-28) may or may not be the filename. It is an indication of how busy a session you have had. It is not important here. What is important is the "window name"—the one that we reference with DATASET ACTIVATE and DATASET NAME.

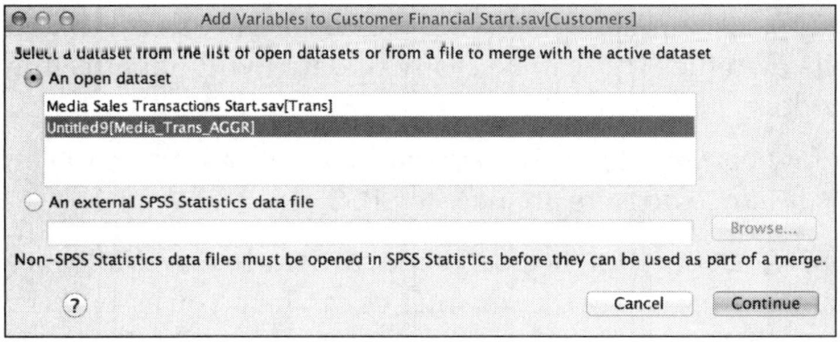

Figure 16-28: First screen of Add Variables

In the next step, we will have an opportunity to remove some variables that we do not need. We choose Match cases on key variables, and choose Customer_ID as our key. We simply exclude Zip Code (because we've made a new version) and the private variables Mother's Maiden name, CCNumber, CVV2, and NationalID (Figure 16-29).

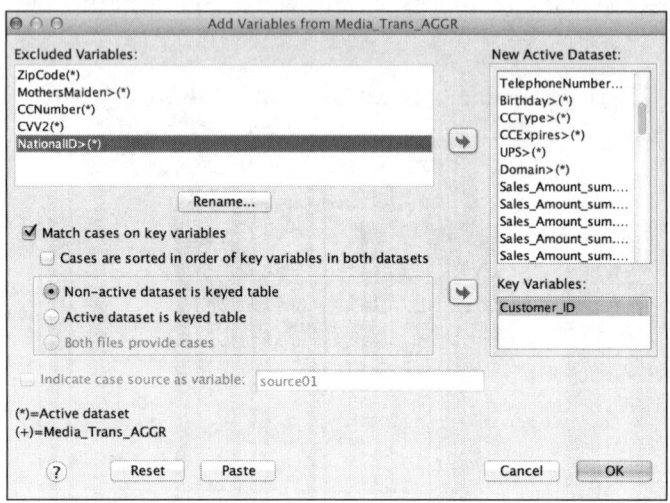

Figure 16-29: Second screen of Add Variables

We will also paste a SAVE command into our Syntax.

Let's briefly review some little improvements that are found in the final version. (You can find the complete program in the final section of this chapter.) Consider reviewing the final syntax file in the Syntax window where the color coding may ease your review.

- We've consolidated everything into one file including the GET FILE commands. These can be easily generated from the menus.

- We've added the FILE HANDLE command and declared both file handles at the top of the file where they can be easily changed.

- We've used the INSERT command, allowing the VALUE LABELS command to be stored in its own file. This can be easily updated without affecting the rest of the code.

- We've added a few comments for documentation. We could add even more, especially if our coworkers are new to SPSS.

There is always more to be done, but the goal of the case study was to advance your knowledge of Syntax by showing that the menus can help you assemble a single cohesive program that can perform potentially complex tasks. There are hundreds of commands to learn, but any commands that were learned were a side benefit of the primary goal: Syntax programs do not have to be stolen little bits of code. Syntax programs can be solutions to routine problems that can be documented and shared, saving you and your colleagues much time in the process.

Final Syntax File

Here is the final code in its entirety. Use this code carefully. Download the code from the book's website. Do not attempt to type it or copy and paste it. There are three complications that make it useful for reference only, but prone to error if you are not careful.

■ Embedded carraige returns can impact SPSS even when they are not visible. This is primarily a problem when there is a carraige return within quotes. Consider the first three lines of code:

```
FILE HANDLE Trans /NAME = '/Users/KMcCormick/Documents/Wiley SPSS
Stats/Syntax Chapter/Media Sales Transactions '+
    'Start.sav'.
```

The + symbol gets around this problem, but with a lengthy section of code it is easy to miss. So, again, be careful.

■ Publishing has different limits for the width of code than the SPSS Syntax editor does. What fits on the line can change the appearance in a way that if imitated in the editor could cause problems. Effort has been made to minimize the effect, but in the age of electonic books and devices, it would be easy to have an error introduced by changing display column widths or font sizes.

■ In a related problem, indenting code is often quite useful when writing code in the SPSS Syntax editor, but it takes up columns in print potentially exacerbating the issues listed already. In the following section (abreviated), an indent would be encouraged (as shown):

```
DO REPEAT numerator = Sales_Amount_sum.101 TO Sales_Amount_sum.705
    / ratio = Sales_Ratio.101, Sales_Ratio.102,
  Sales_Ratio.103, Sales_Ratio.201,
  Sales_Ratio.705.
  COMPUTE ratio = numerator / Total_Spend.
END REPEAT PRINT.
```

There is enough value in being able to see the "big picture," however, that the code is listed dispite the risks. It should be able to give you a better feel for the flow of the code, especially if you are reading a traditional print book, during some stolen moments away from your laptop.

```
FILE HANDLE Trans /NAME = '/Users/KMcCormick/Documents/Wiley SPSS Stats/
Syntax Chapter/Media Sales Transactions '+
    'Start.sav'.

FILE HANDLE Customers /NAME='/Users/KMcCormick/Documents/
Wiley SPSS Stats/Syntax Chapter/Customer Financial Start.sav'.

FILE HANDLE Categories /NAME = '/Users/KMcCormick/Documents/
Wiley SPSS Stats/Syntax Chapter/Category Code Labels.sps'.

GET FILE = Trans.
DATASET NAME Trans WINDOW=FRONT.

* Define Variable Properties.
*Sales_Amount.
FORMATS  Sales_Amount(DOLLAR7.2).
*Category_Code.
VARIABLE LEVEL  Category_Code(NOMINAL).

* The following INSERT applies labels found in an external file.

INSERT File = Categories.

DATASET DECLARE Media_Trans_AGGR.
AGGREGATE
  /OUTFILE='Media_Trans_AGGR'
  /BREAK=Customer_ID Category_Code
  /Sales_Amount_sum=SUM(Sales_Amount).

DATASET ACTIVATE Media_Trans_AGGR.
SORT CASES BY Customer_ID Category_Code.
CASESTOVARS
  /ID=Customer_ID
  /INDEX=Category_Code
  /GROUPBY=INDEX.

Compute Total_Spend = SUM( Sales_Amount_sum.101,
Sales_Amount_sum.102, Sales_Amount_sum.103,
Sales_Amount_sum.201, Sales_Amount_sum.202,
Sales_Amount_sum.203, Sales_Amount_sum.204,
Sales_Amount_sum.205, Sales_Amount_sum.301,
Sales_Amount_sum.401, Sales_Amount_sum.402,
Sales_Amount_sum.403, Sales_Amount_sum.501,
```

```
Sales_Amount_sum.502, Sales_Amount_sum.503,
Sales_Amount_sum.601, Sales_Amount_sum.701,
Sales_Amount_sum.702, Sales_Amount_sum.703,
Sales_Amount_sum.704, Sales_Amount_sum.705).

COUNT #NumMiss=Sales_Amount_sum.101 TO Sales_Amount_sum.705(SYSMIS).

COMPUTE NumCats = 21 - #NumMiss.

RECODE Sales_Amount_sum.101 TO Sales_Amount_sum.705 (SYSMIS=0).

* ratio = ratio1 to ratio21.

DO REPEAT numerator = Sales_Amount_sum.101 TO Sales_Amount_sum.705
 / ratio = Sales_Ratio.101, Sales_Ratio.102,
 Sales_Ratio.103, Sales_Ratio.201,
 Sales_Ratio.202, Sales_Ratio.203,
 Sales_Ratio.204, Sales_Ratio.205,
 Sales_Ratio.301, Sales_Ratio.401,
 Sales_Ratio.402, Sales_Ratio.403,
 Sales_Ratio.501, Sales_Ratio.502,
 Sales_Ratio.503, Sales_Ratio.601,
 Sales_Ratio.701, Sales_Ratio.702,
 Sales_Ratio.703, Sales_Ratio.704,
 Sales_Ratio.705.
 COMPUTE ratio = numerator / Total_Spend.
END REPEAT PRINT.

Get File = Customers.

DATASET NAME Customers WINDOW=FRONT.

* Mixed Case.

COMPUTE City = CONCAT( CHAR.SUBSTR(City,1,1) ,
LOWER(CHAR.SUBSTR(City,2)) ).

* Domain Name.

COMPUTE #At_Loc=CHAR.INDEX(EmailAddress,'@').
COMPUTE #Period_Loc=CHAR.RINDEX(EmailAddress,'.').
COMPUTE #Domain_Length = (#Period_Loc-#At_Loc)-1.

STRING Domain(A16).
COMPUTE Domain=CHAR.SUBSTR(EmailAddress,#At_Loc+1,#Domain_Length).
EXECUTE.
```

```
* Zip Code.

STRING  #ZipCode2 (A5).
COMPUTE #ZipCode2=STRING(ZipCode,F5).
STRING Zip5(A5).
COMPUTE Zip5= CHAR.LPAD(LTRIM(#ZipCode2),5,'0').

STAR JOIN
  /SELECT t0.Gender, t0.GivenName, t0.MiddleInitial, t0.Surname,
t0.StreetAddress, t0.City,
t0.State, t0.Country, t0.EmailAddress, t0.TelephoneNumber, t0.Birthday,
t0.CCType, t0.CCExpires,
t0.UPS, t0.Domain, t1.Sales_Amount_sum.101,
t1.Sales_Amount_sum.102, t1.Sales_Amount_sum.103,
t1.Sales_Amount_sum.201, t1.Sales_Amount_sum.202,
t1.Sales_Amount_sum.203, t1.Sales_Amount_sum.204,
t1.Sales_Amount_sum.205, t1.Sales_Amount_sum.301,
t1.Sales_Amount_sum.401, t1.Sales_Amount_sum.402,
t1.Sales_Amount_sum.403, t1.Sales_Amount_sum.501,
t1.Sales_Amount_sum.502, t1.Sales_Amount_sum.503,
t1.Sales_Amount_sum.601, t1.Sales_Amount_sum.701,
t1.Sales_Amount_sum.702, t1.Sales_Amount_sum.703,
t1.Sales_Amount_sum.704, t1.Sales_Amount_sum.705,
t1.Total_Spend, t1.NumCats, t1.Sales_Ratio.101,
t1.Sales_Ratio.102, t1.Sales_Ratio.103,
t1.Sales_Ratio.201, t1.Sales_Ratio.202,
t1.Sales_Ratio.203, t1.Sales_Ratio.204,
t1.Sales_Ratio.205, t1.Sales_Ratio.301,
t1.Sales_Ratio.401, t1.Sales_Ratio.402,
 t1.Sales_Ratio.403, t1.Sales_Ratio.501,
t1.Sales_Ratio.502, t1.Sales_Ratio.503,
t1.Sales_Ratio.601, t1.Sales_Ratio.701,
t1.Sales_Ratio.702, t1.Sales_Ratio.703,
t1.Sales_Ratio.704, t1.Sales_Ratio.705,
    t0.Zip5
  /FROM * AS t0
  /JOIN 'Media_Trans_AGGR' AS t1
    ON t0.Customer_ID=t1.Customer_ID
  /OUTFILE FILE=*.

SAVE OUTFILE='/Users/KMcCormick/Documents/Wiley SPSS Stats
/Syntax Chapter/Syntax Chapter Complete.sav'
  /COMPRESSED.
```

Automate Your Analyses with SPSS Syntax and the Output Management System

When I first started using SPSS Statistics, the version of the software that my university supported only consisted of a blank screen where we had to enter in our data and type command syntax to run any routine. Needless to say, I did not like using SPSS.

Some years later, still as an undergraduate student, I was working on a consulting project for which, among other things, we had to use The Sixteen Personality Factors Questionnaire (16 PF) to predict career interest scores on both the Strong Interest Inventory (SII) and the Campbell Interest and Skill Survey (CISS). At first this seemed like an easy enough task; I had to build a linear regression model, using all 16 personality factors, to predict interest in each career (of which several hundred careers exist between the two tests).

Using a newer version of SPSS Statistics (that had menus and windows), I ran my first regression, I looked over the results, and everything seemed okay. I ran a second regression, I looked over the results, and everything seemed okay. I did this a few more times and then I realized that this project was going to take a lot longer than I originally thought, unless I resorted to my old "friend" syntax.

So I rebuilt my first regression using menus and windows, clicked the Paste button to open the Syntax Editor, and then I copied my syntax and pasted it several hundred times within the Syntax Editor. Then I changed the name of the dependent variable for each equation, ran the syntax, saved the syntax and output files, and I was done in less than an hour; or so I thought.

The final piece of this project was that I needed to take the regression co-efficients and do some additional analyses. Put in simple terms, I needed to take SPSS output and convert it into SPSS input (data). I did not know how to do this; nor did anyone I asked. It should have been easy to simply move data from one screen over to another, and yet there was no way to do this. So, did I enter all of these coefficients back into SPSS by hand? No, I managed to copy and paste them into SPSS Statistics, but first I had to copy the coefficients table into Notepad to make the table editable (back then the output was not as editable like it is now). Then I had to copy the editable table into Excel so I could remove all the other output that I did not need, and this way I only kept the regression coefficients. From there I was able to bring the data back into SPSS so that I could do my additional analyses.

I never forgot this experience. Some years later, I was working on my dissertation, trying to validate a creativity measure I had developed. In this case I had to obtain the correlation between my measure and each of the other creativity measures that had been administered. That is, I simply used the Bivariate Correlations procedure. I also wanted to determine the average correlation between my measure and all of the other creativity measures. This is not as easy to do, because again, I had to take SPSS output (in this case the actual correlation coefficients) and convert it into SPSS input (data), so that I could obtain a mean correlation. By this time, however, SPSS Statistics version 12 included a technique called the Output Management System (OMS), which among several other things, allows users to take SPSS output and convert it into data.

In this chapter we discuss the basics of the output management system and go over an example of how to use this technique.

Overview of the Output Management System

The Output Management System enables users to automatically write selected types of output to different formats. The supported formats include SPSS Statistics data, Viewer files, and Web Reports files, as well as Word, Excel, XML, text, PDF, and HTML files. This means that the OMS provides a way to automatically write pivot table output from a procedure (for example, Correlations or Regression) to files in one of these formats. This enables SPSS Statistics users to use the OMS as a way to export output or just use the output as input in subsequent analyses (you can even do bootstrapping this way if you'd like).

Additionally, the OMS facility can also automatically exclude selected types of output from the Output Viewer, so that you do not need to see logs, or notes, or case processing summary tables, for example. This option to exclude certain types of output can be useful if you want to save only selected types of tables in your SPSS Statistics Viewer. For example, if you only want to save the coefficients table from the regression procedure, you can use the OMS to exclude all other types of output from regression.

Although you can use the OMS facility to automatically send output to different destinations, it is not designed to be a replacement for the SPSS Statistics Export facility. The main purpose of the OMS is to turn tabular output automatically into an SPSS data file, an option that is unavailable in the Export facility. Then after saving pivot table output into SPSS Statistics data files, you can use that output as input in subsequent commands or sessions. It can also save output into the XML workspace where it can be accessed through Python, R, or Java programmability.

The Output Management System can be run through either menus or SPSS syntax. Let's go through an example of how to use the OMS. In this example we will use the file `satisf.sav`, which you can find in the following location: `C:\Program Files\IBM\SPSS\Statistics\22\Samples\English`.

Running OMS from Menus

The `satisfy.sav` file has several satisfaction variables. We will use SPSS Statistics to run correlations among these satisfaction variables and then we will use the OMS to capture these correlations and send them back into SPSS Statistics as a data file. After we have the correlation coefficients as data, we will be able to determine the average correlation among the variables. That is, we will get the average correlation between one measure and all the other measures.

1. To begin, open the OMS control panel by selecting the OMS Control Panel option from the Utilities menu, as shown in Figure 17-1.

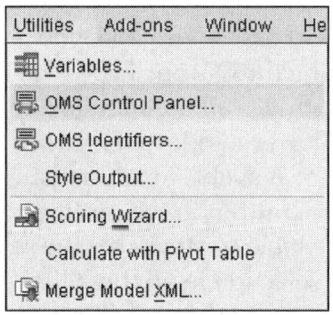

Figure 17-1: Utilities menu options

You can use OMS control panel, shown in Figure 17-2, to both start and stop the routing of output or to exclude types of output from the Viewer. The OMS accomplishes these tasks by specifying the output types. These output types are associated with SPSS Statistics commands to explicitly identify any output that has been generated.

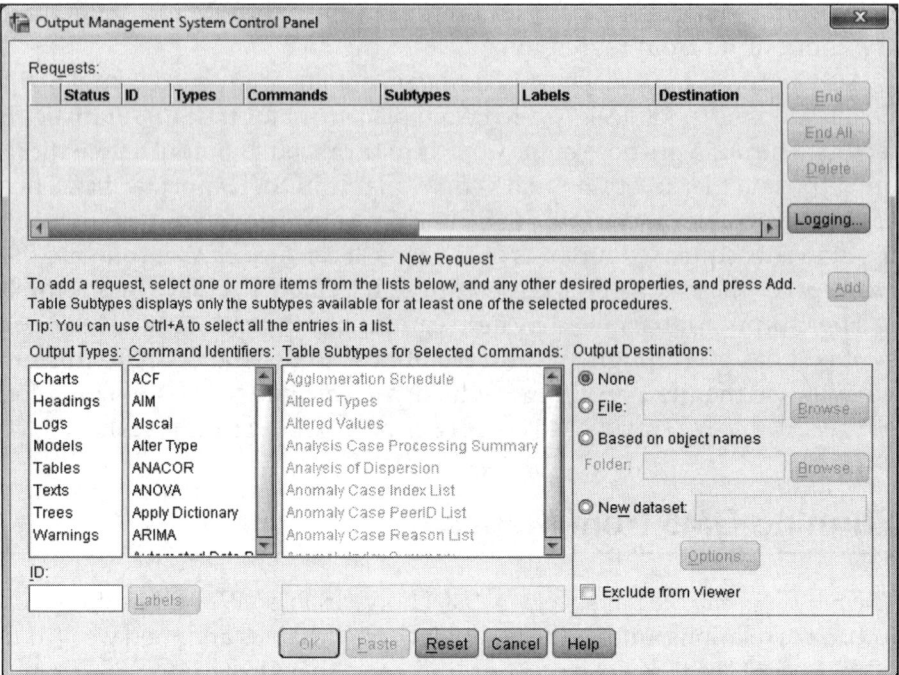

Figure 17-2: Output Management System Control Panel dialog

After the output to be manipulated has been identified, the user specifies what actions should be taken. These are specified as OMS Requests from the OMS Control Panel. When the specific output is generated, the requested action is taken.

2. Now add an OMS request. To do so, you must first specify the type or types of output you want to work with by selecting the Output Type. The listing in the Control Panel dialog (Figure 17-2) includes all the standard types of output that SPSS Statistics creates in the Viewer window. Then you select one or more Command Identifiers, which are available for all statistical and graphing procedures that produce blocks of output in the outline pane of the Viewer. Finally, you select one or more table subtypes for the selected commands. You can make more than one selection in all three lists.

Automatically Writing Selected Categories of Output to Different Formats

Because in this example we are focusing on correlations:

▪ Select Tables in the Output Types box.

- Select Correlations in the Command Identifiers box.
- Select Correlations in the Tables Subtype for Selected Commands box.

The completed Output Management System Control Panel is shown in Figure 17-3.

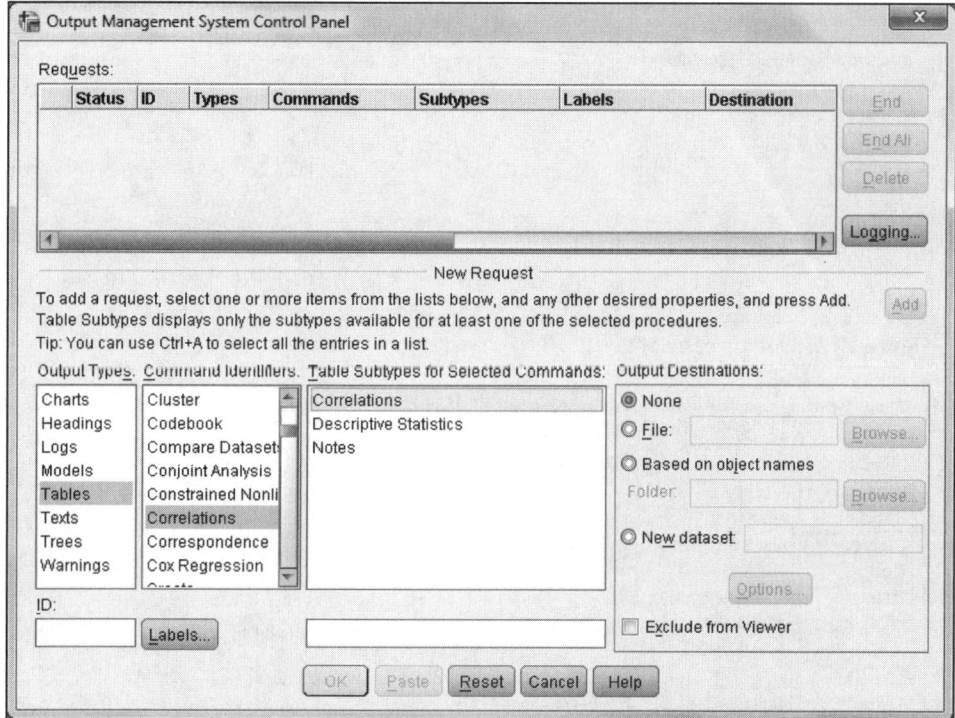

Figure 17-3: Completed Output Management System Control Panel dialog

---

OMS LABELS

Occasionally you might not know all the information (or it may not be available) to specify an Output Type and/or Command Identifiers and/or Table Subtypes for the Selected Commands option. In these cases you can identify output by using its OMS Label.

You can copy OMS labels by right-clicking any output item from the Outline pane of the Viewer (see Figure 17-4) and then choosing Copy OMS Label.

After you have copied the OMS label, you can paste it into the OMS Control Panel directly by clicking the Labels radio button and placing the label there (see Figure 17-5). Now the object is identified and you can manipulate it.

Continues

(continued)

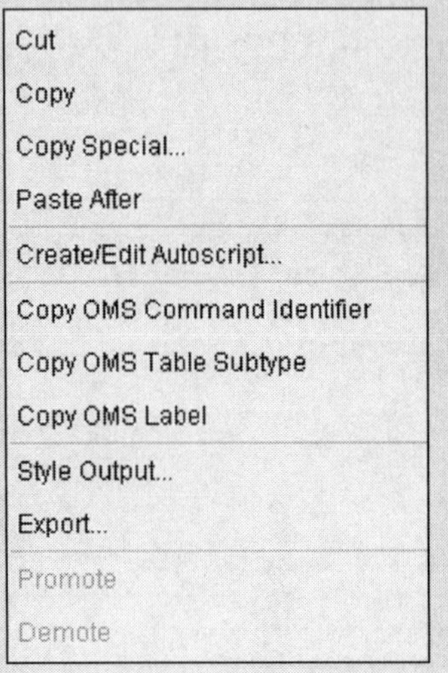

Cut
Copy
Copy Special...
Paste After
Create/Edit Autoscript...
Copy OMS Command Identifier
Copy OMS Table Subtype
Copy OMS Label
Style Output...
Export...
Promote
Demote

Figure 17-4: Outline pane options

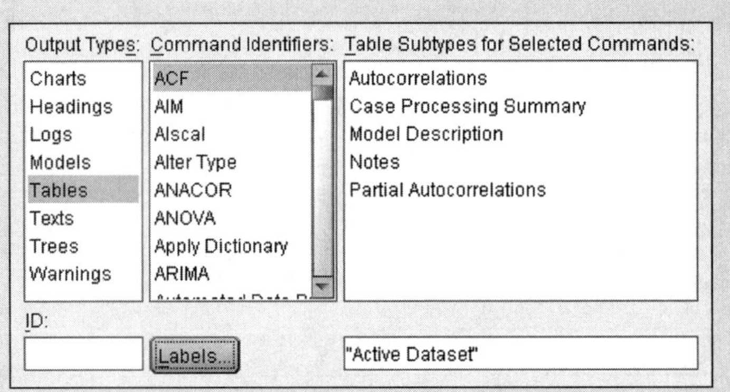

Output Types:	Command Identifiers:	Table Subtypes for Selected Commands:
Charts	ACF	Autocorrelations
Headings	AIM	Case Processing Summary
Logs	Alscal	Model Description
Models	Alter Type	Notes
Tables	ANACOR	Partial Autocorrelations
Texts	ANOVA	
Trees	Apply Dictionary	
Warnings	ARIMA	

ID:

[ ] [Labels...] "Active Dataset"

Figure 17-5: OMS label added

Now that we have specified the type of output we are interested in (correlations), we need to specify the destination of the output.

Once output has been identified, the user then needs to decide what action should be taken once the output is generated. Two actions can be specified (see the Output Destinations section in Figure 17-3):

- ■ Suppressing output
- ■ Automatically writing selected categories of output to different formats

Suppressing output is useful if a minimal amount of output is required. For example, maybe only regression coefficient tables are required from the Regression procedure as opposed to the many tables of output that are normally generated.

This option can be very useful when planning to export output. If a lot of output is generated, rather than going through the generated output and removing what is not needed before exporting, you can do this more efficiently by suppressing what is not needed as the output is created.

Writing selected categories of output to different formats can be very useful if tabular output requires further manipulation or if output needs to be sent to an alternative format. When exporting pivot tables they can be handled in several ways. For example, if exporting a frequency table back to an SPSS Statistics data file, the table columns become the variables and the table rows become the cases in the newly created file. This is the default operation but this structure can be changed.

Next, calculate an average correlation:

1. We need to get the correlations into a data file and then use an appropriate set of commands for the calculation:

    a. Select File in the Output Destination box.

    b. Click the Options button.

    c. Select SPSS Statistics Data File from the Format drop-down list (see Figure 17-6).

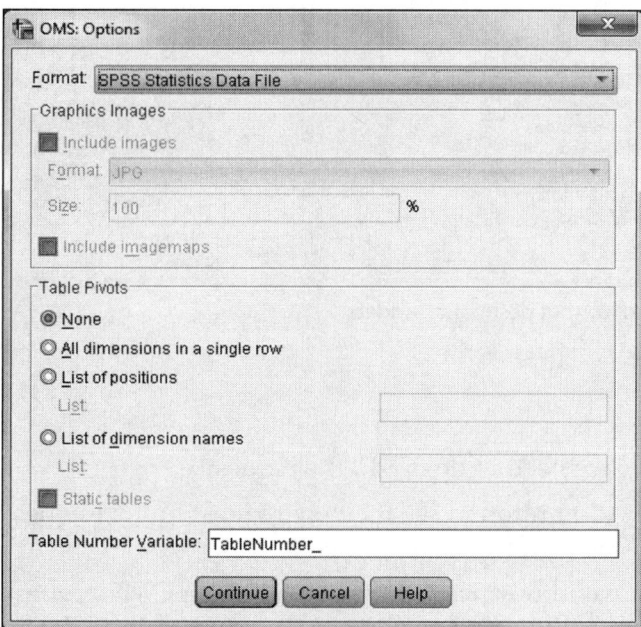

Figure 17-6: OMS: Options dialog

At this point we have specified that any correlations we run will be sent to an SPSS Statistics data file. Note that we could have sent the output to various other file types.

2. Now we need to name the new file with the correlations:

   a. Click Continue to open the Output Management System Control Panel.

   b. Click the Browse button next to the File option (see Figure 17-7).

   c. Name the new file Correlations.

   d. Click Save.

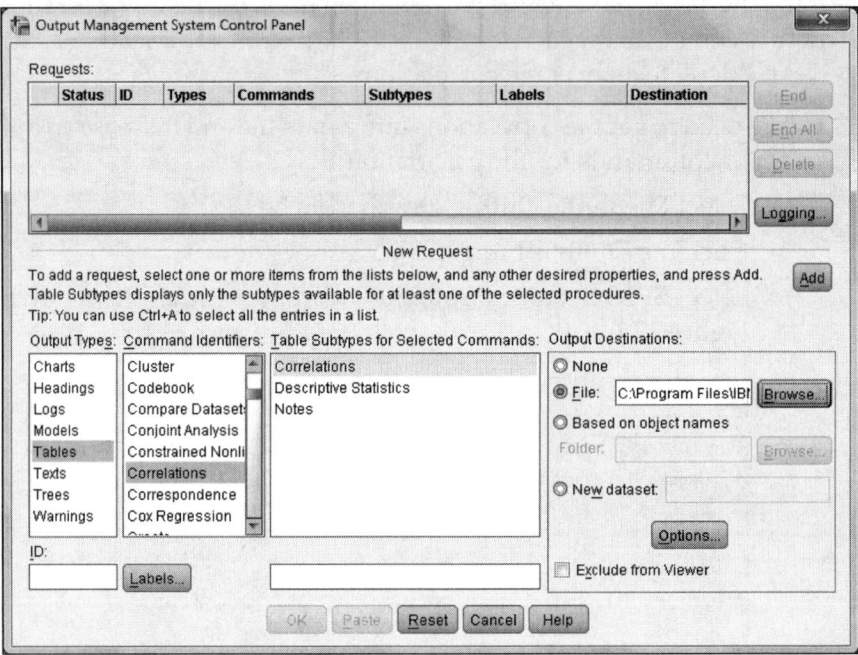

Figure 17-7: Output destination added

3. The last thing we need to do is add the request:

   ▪ Click the Add button to see the new request in the Requests list (see Figure 17-8).

We have now created our first OMS request. Each OMS request remains active until it is explicitly ended or when the session ends. A destination file that is specified as an OMS request is unavailable to other procedures and other applications until the OMS request is ended.

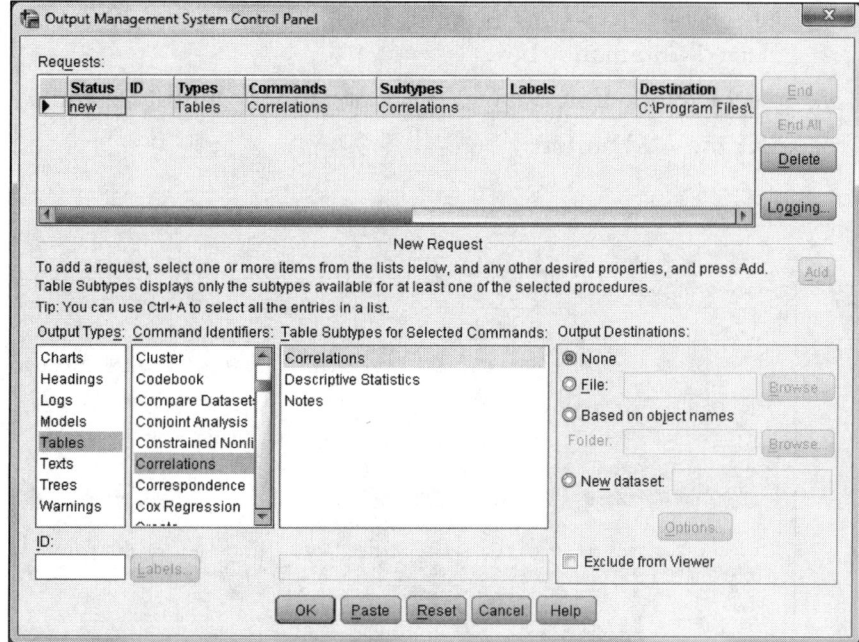

Figure 17-8: New OMS request added

NOTE It is important to remember that while an OMS request is active, the specified destination files are stored in memory (RAM), so active OMS requests that write a large amount of output to external files may consume a large amount of memory. However text format files are streamed to disk rather than being kept in memory.

Suppressing Output

Let's create a second OMS request (see Figure 17-9). In this request we show how to suppress output. The Case Processing Summary table and the Notes table are not essential to the output from any SPSS Statistics procedure, although the Case Processing Summary does show the number of valid and missing cases for an analysis. We will suppress these two tables for all commands with the following steps:

1. Select Tables in the Output Types box.
2. Select all commands in the Command Identifiers box (you can use Ctrl+A since there is no button that automatically selects all the commands).

3. Select Case Processing Summary and Notes in the Table Subtypes for Selected Commands box.

4. Select Exclude from Viewer check box in the Output Destinations box.

5. Click the Add button.

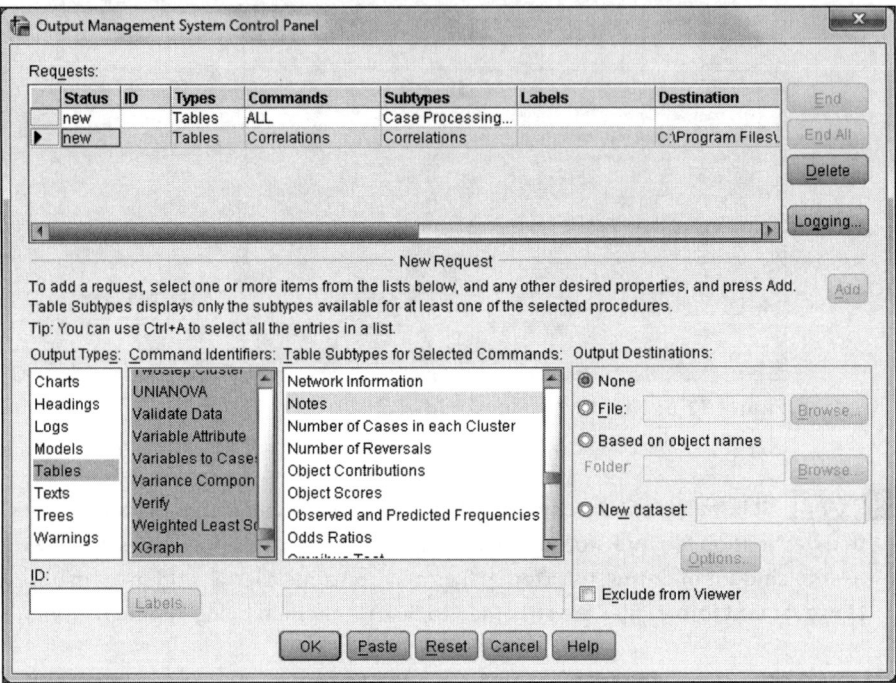

Figure 17-9: Second OMS request added

We now have multiple OMS requests that will be active once we click OK, and the requests are independent of each other. So it is possible that the same output can be routed to different locations in different formats.

To create and run the requests, follow these steps:

1. Click OK.

   Once OK is selected in the OMS Control Panel, the request will be created.

   The Summary alert window (Figure 17-10) informs us that the request will be created and active until we end it or end the session. Now that the OMS is activated, the next time the appropriate output is generated the specific action will take place.

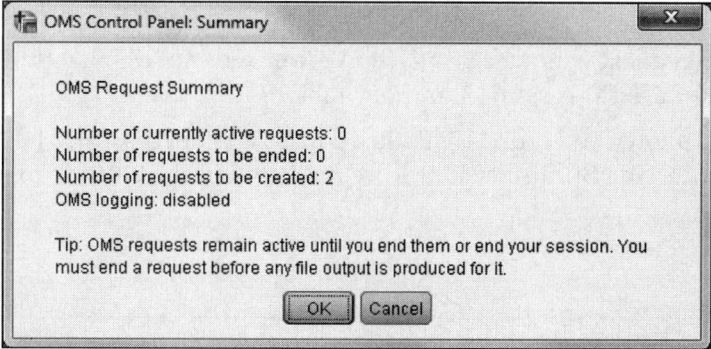

Figure 17-10: OMS Control Panel: Summary dialog

2. Click OK.

   There is no Viewer output from the OMS Facility. To determine whether the requested actions are working properly, we'll run a Crosstabs and a Bivariate procedure, as shown in Figure 17-11.

3. Click Analyze ➪ Descriptive Statistics ➪ Crosstabs.

4. Place Age Category in the Row(s) box.

5. Place Gender in the Column(s) box.

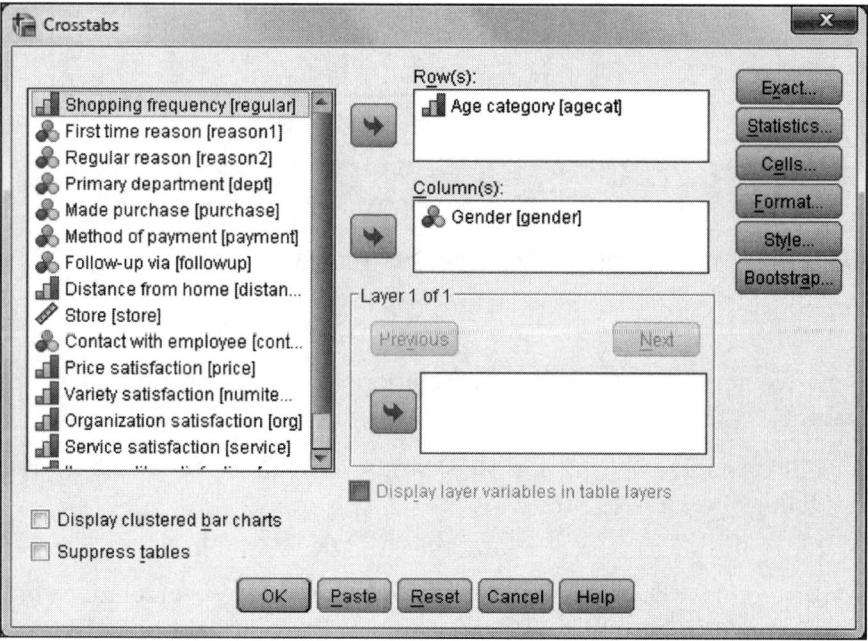

Figure 17-11: Crosstabs dialog

6. Click OK.

If the OMS request was successful, the Viewer will not display the Notes table or the Case Processing Summary table.

Notice that, as shown in Figure 17-12, the request was successful. The Notes and the Case Processing Summary tables are not listed in the Outline pane nor displayed.

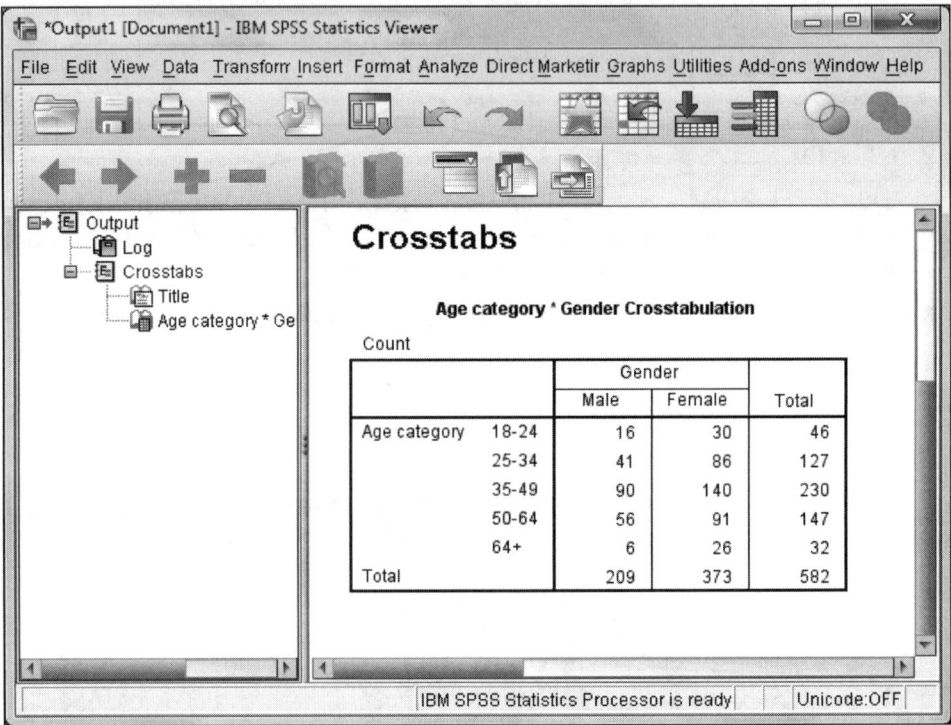

Figure 17-12: Output without Case Processing Summary table

Now we need to request the Correlations procedure with the appropriate variables:

1. Click Analyze ⇨ Correlate ⇨ Bivariate to open the Bivariate Correlations dialog shown in Figure 17-13.

2. Move the six satisfaction variables into the Variables box.

At this point we could click OK, and we would create a correlations table like the one shown in Figure 17-14, where we see the correlations between all the bivariate combinations.

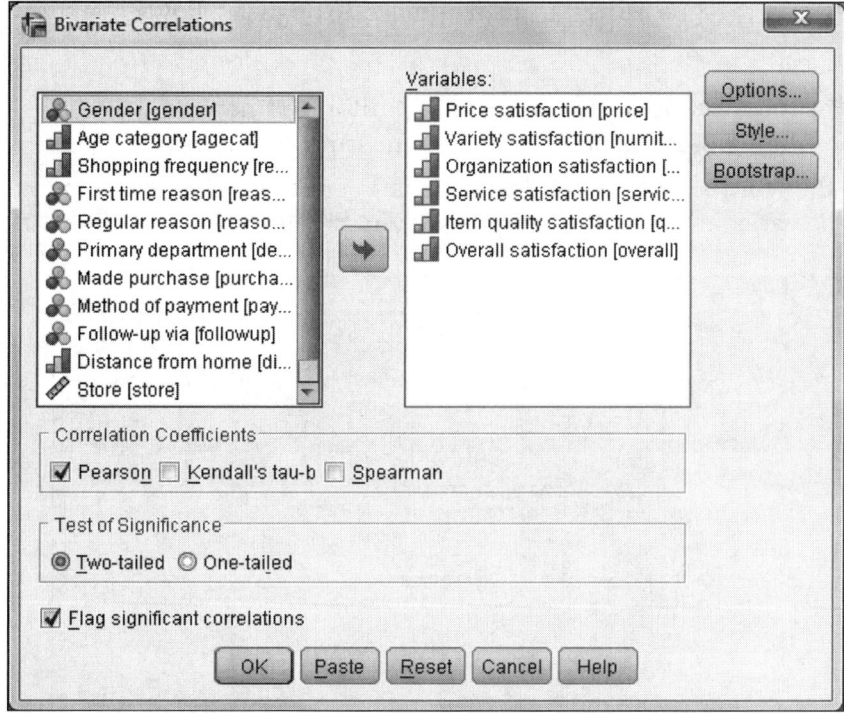

Figure 17-13: Bivariate Correlations dialog

Correlations

		Price satisfaction	Variety satisfaction	Organization satisfaction	Service satisfaction	Item quality satisfaction	Overall satisfaction
Price satisfaction	Pearson Correlation	1	.694**	.306**	.585**	.505**	.585**
	Sig. (2-tailed)		.000	.000	.000	.000	.000
	N	582	582	582	582	582	582
Variety satisfaction	Pearson Correlation	.694**	1	.182**	.604**	.529**	.572**
	Sig. (2-tailed)	.000		.000	.000	.000	.000
	N	582	582	582	582	582	582
Organization satisfaction	Pearson Correlation	.306**	.182**	1	.279**	.210**	.233**
	Sig. (2-tailed)	.000	.000		.000	.000	.000
	N	582	582	582	582	582	582
Service satisfaction	Pearson Correlation	.585**	.604**	.279**	1	.424**	.602**
	Sig. (2-tailed)	.000	.000	.000		.000	.000
	N	582	582	582	582	582	582
Item quality satisfaction	Pearson Correlation	.505**	.529**	.210**	.424**	1	.457**
	Sig. (2-tailed)	.000	.000	.000	.000		.000
	N	582	582	582	582	582	582
Overall satisfaction	Pearson Correlation	.585**	.572**	.233**	.602**	.457**	1
	Sig. (2-tailed)	.000	.000	.000	.000	.000	
	N	582	582	582	582	582	582

**. Correlation is significant at the 0.01 level (2-tailed).

Figure 17-14: Traditional correlations output

This table is certainly useful, but what if we only wanted to see the correlations between the Overall Satisfaction variable and the other variables; that is, we only want to see the last column on the table?

The easiest way to request this is by using syntax. To do that, follow these steps:

1. Click Paste.

   The Paste button opens up the Syntax Editor and now we have more options than those available through menus and windows.

2. Type the word **with** between the variables `quality` and `overall`, make sure the variables are in the order as shown in Figure 17-15.

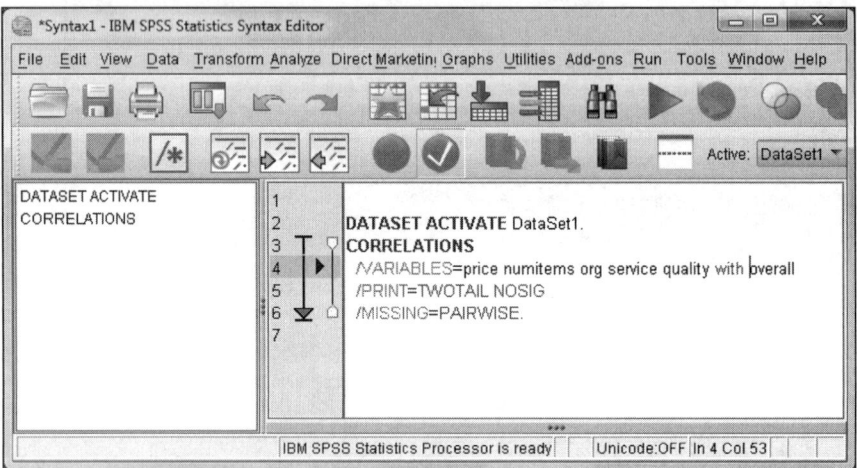

Figure 17-15: Manipulated correlations syntax

In this situation, the keyword `with` tells SPSS that it should correlate all of the variables to the left of the keyword with all of the variables to the right of the keyword.

3. Click Run to display the Correlations output shown in Figure 17-16.

Correlations

		Overall satisfaction
Price satisfaction	Pearson Correlation	.585[**]
	Sig. (2-tailed)	.000
	N	582
Variety satisfaction	Pearson Correlation	.572[**]
	Sig. (2-tailed)	.000
	N	582
Organization satisfaction	Pearson Correlation	.233[**]
	Sig. (2-tailed)	.000
	N	582
Service satisfaction	Pearson Correlation	.602[**]
	Sig. (2-tailed)	.000
	N	582
Item quality satisfaction	Pearson Correlation	.457[**]
	Sig. (2-tailed)	.000
	N	582

[**]. Correlation is significant at the 0.01 level (2-tailed).

Figure 17-16: Manipulated correlations output

Now that we have the correlations we want, we must end the OMS request to close the newly created dataset so that we can open it in a Data Editor window:

1. Select OMS Control Panel from the Utilities menu to display the screen shown in Figure 17-17.

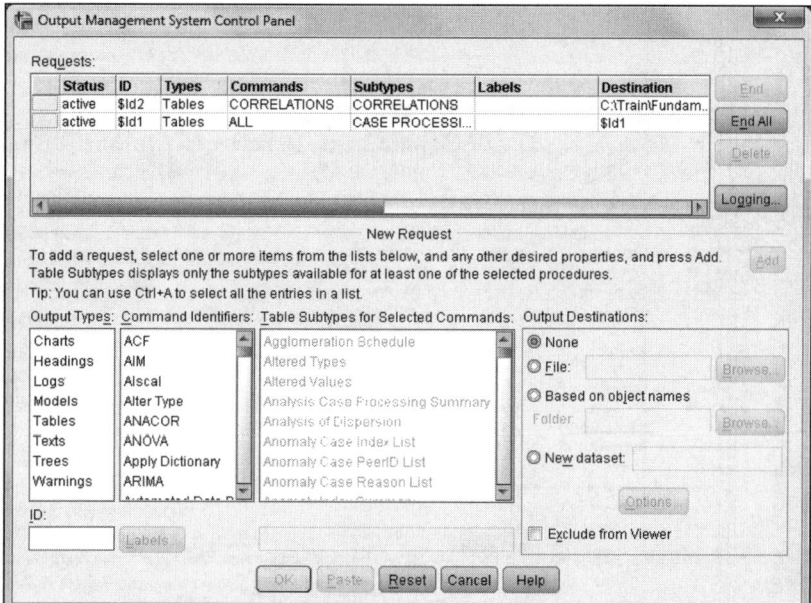

Figure 17-17: Ending OMS requests

The requests that we made are still available.

2. To end the requests, click End All.

3. Click OK.

We have now ended the two OMS requests (see Figure 17-18).

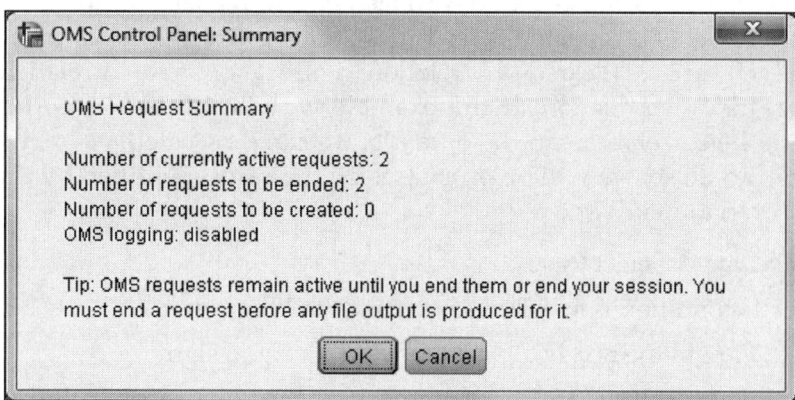

Figure 17-18: OMS Control Panel: Summary dialog

4. Click OK.

Working with OMS data

Now we need to open the new Correlations dataset, shown in Figure 17-19. Navigate to where you saved the `Correlations.sav` dataset and open it.

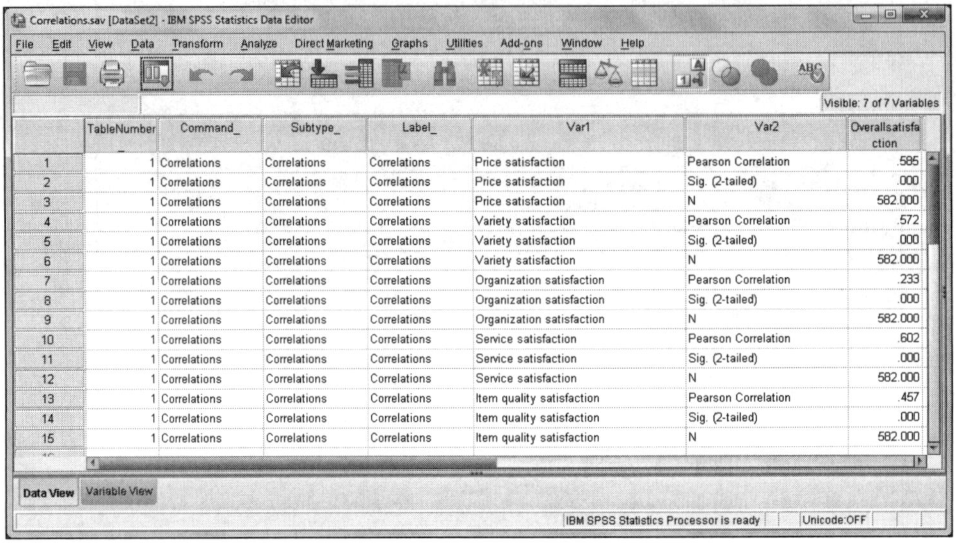

Figure 17-19: Correlations dataset

There are identifiers in the first few columns for the Table, the Command, the Subtype, and the Label (the selections we made in the OMS Control Panel). This is followed by variables that record elements of the table itself.

The variable label is repeated three times because three statistics are associated with each variable (Pearson Correlation, significance of the correlation, and sample size for the correlation). In this example, we will only use the correlation itself. With the correlations in the data file, we can now calculate an average correlation. To do so, we will only use (select) the cases identified by the text Pearson Correlation in Var2:

1. Click Data ⇨ Select Cases.

2. Click If condition is satisfied, then click the If button.

3. Place Var2 in the text box, and then add an equal sign.

4. Add the text "Pearson Correlation" after the equal sign, including the quotes, as shown in Figure 17-20.

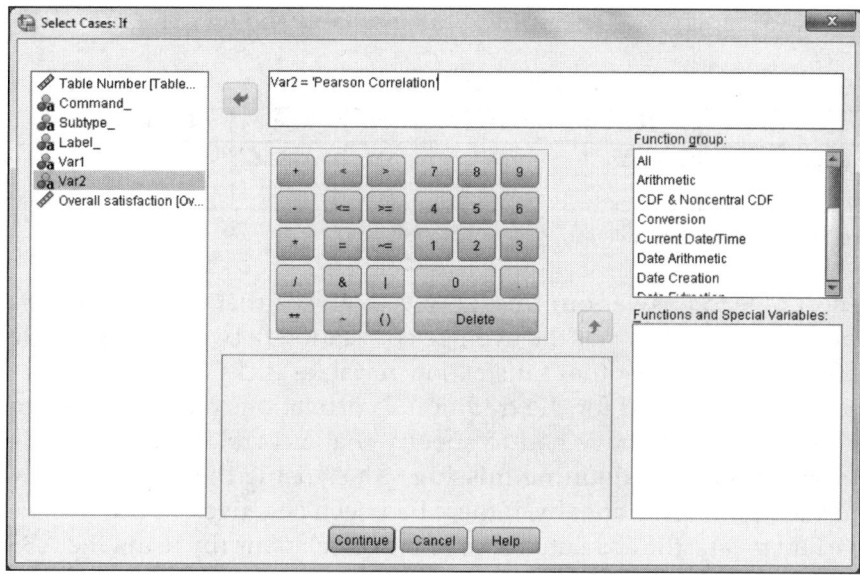

Figure 17-20: Select Cases: If dialog

5. Click Continue.

6. Click OK.

We are now ready to calculate the average correlation between the variable Overall Satisfaction and all the other satisfaction variables. We will use the Descriptives procedure to report on the average for the correlations variables:

1. Click Analyze ➪ Descriptive Statistics ➪ Descriptives.

2. Place the variable Overall Satisfaction in the Variables box as shown in Figure 17-21.

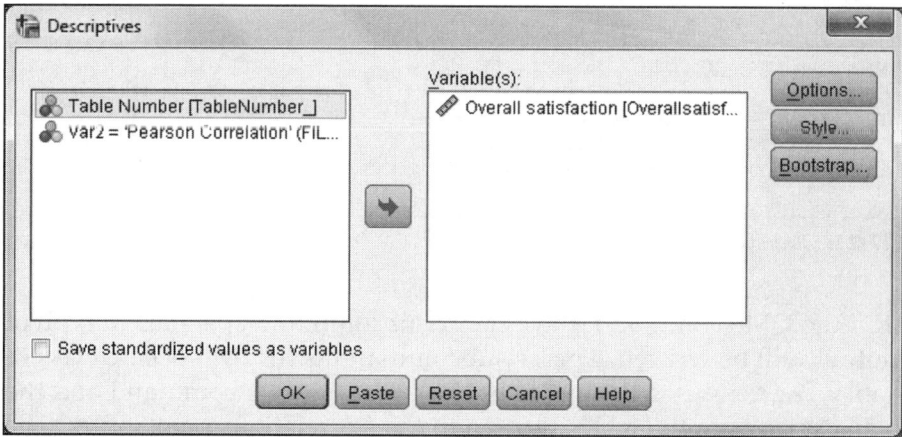

Figure 17-21: Descriptives dialog

3. Click OK to display the Descriptive Statistics table shown in Figure 17-22.

Descriptive Statistics

	N	Minimum	Maximum	Mean	Std. Deviation
Overall satisfaction	5	.233	.602	.48996	.154486
Valid N (listwise)	5				

Figure 17-22: Average correlation

We are now able to answer our question. We can see that the correlations range from .233 to .602 and that the average correlation between the variable Overall Satisfaction and the other satisfaction variables is .49.

Note that if we had asked for the traditional correlations output as shown in Figure 17-14, we would have had to specify that a correlation of one (the diagonal) was missing (by defining missing values using the Variable View tab of the Data Editor). Additionally, if there had been negative correlations we would have had to take the absolute value of the correlations (by using the ABS function in the Compute Variable dialog).

Running OMS from Syntax

If you want to automate the OMS facility, you can run it from syntax. The syntax can be pasted from the OMS Control Panel. For example, the OMS command shown in Figure 17-23 was pasted from the previous example.

```
1
2   * OMS.
3   OMS
4     /SELECT TABLES
5     /IF SUBTYPES=['Case Processing Summary' ' Notes']
6     /DESTINATION VIEWER=NO.
7   * OMS.
8   OMS
9     /SELECT TABLES
10    /IF COMMANDS=['Correlations'] SUBTYPES=['Correlations']
11    /DESTINATION FORMAT=SAV NUMBERED=TableNumber_
12      OUTFILE='C:\Program Files\IBM\SPSS\Statistics\22\Samples\English\Correlations.sav'.
13
```

Figure 17-23: OMS syntax

Within the OMS command, the SELECT subcommand specifies that pivot table output will be written. The IF subcommand gives the specific class of pivot table. The COMMANDS list indicates the Correlations command and the SUBTYPES list restricts the tables written to the Correlations pivot tables. The DESTINATION subcommand is used to specify the output file format (here SAV, or an SPSS data file), with the file destination listed in the OUTFILE subcommand (here the open dataset "Correlations").

If you choose to build the OMS command directly, an OMS Identifiers dialog is available to aid you in specifying just which output types and subtypes from which commands should be written.

To help build your OMS command syntax, the OMS Identifiers dialog, shown in Figure 17-24, can paste the command and subtype identifiers into a Syntax window.

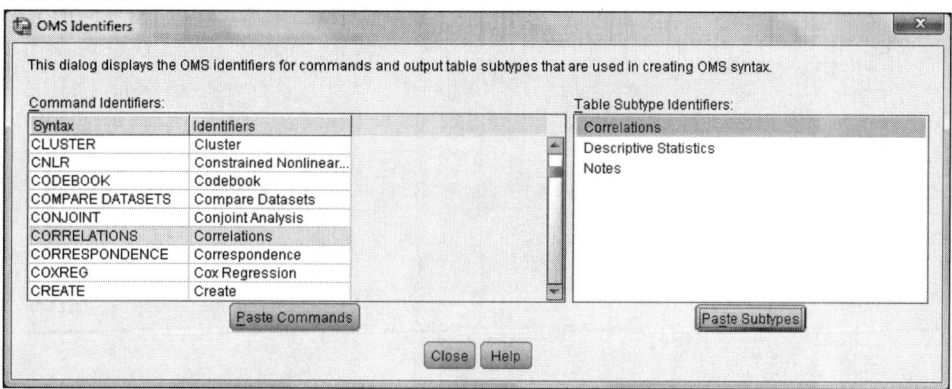

Figure 17-24: OMS Identifiers dialog

1. Click Utilities ➪ OMS Identifiers.
2. Select Correlations in the Command Identifiers list.

The OMS Identifiers dialog allows users to receive some help if you want to build an OMS request directly within syntax.

The following are some additional points to bear in mind regarding OMS requests directly within syntax:

- Syntax users should not assume that the name of a command is also the OMS command identifier. In most cases it is, but this is a common source of error.

- Extension commands do not appear in the Control Panel or OMS Identifiers tables, but their output is subject to OMS just like built-in commands. Users should right click in the outline on an instance of the output to select and pick the command and table identifiers, as appropriate. In fact, this can be more convenient than using the OMS Identifiers table.

- If the target output is empty, it is often because one of the identifiers was incorrect.

- If the OMS requests will need to operate independently of the current output language setting, users should avoid using the labels choice. The OMS Command and Subtype identifiers are independent of the output language.

CHAPTER 18

Statistical Extension Commands

SPSS Statistics has a large number of statistical procedures and other commands built in, but there is always a need for more. Starting with version 14 in 2006, SPSS Statistics, then just called SPSS, added the ability for users to use standard programming languages within the product to extend its capabilities. First Python, then R, and then Java were added in subsequent releases. This is referred to as programmability.

Programmers can write and run code in these languages directly, but programmability also provides a way to create new commands that look to the user like built-in commands. Called *extension commands*, they can have a dialog box interface, traditional syntax, and produce traditional pivot table and graphical output in the Viewer. They can greatly expand the built-in capabilities of SPSS Statistics.

This chapter explains what an extension command is and then illustrates the use of three extension commands available for statistical analysis and one for computation on pivot tables. The first three do not require any knowledge of Python or R to use them; the fourth one uses a snippet of Python with the extension command.

What Is an Extension Command?

Python, R, and Java programmers can run their programs directly within the regular syntax stream by enclosing the code in a BEGIN PROGRAM ... END PROGRAM block. The code can use any of the facilities of these languages and uses libraries of IBM application programming interfaces (APIs) provided via a plug-in for the language. A *plug-in* is a module that is installed in the main product. The APIs are important to the programmers but do not need to be learned by those using programs written by others. Programs can access and modify the variable dictionary and data, build and run regular Statistics commands, manipulate the output, and do other tasks. *Programming and Data Management* (SPSS Inc., 2016), available from the SPSS Community website, contains many examples of solving SPSS Statistics tasks with programmability.

These programs add great power to do things that are difficult or impossible to do with standard syntax, but they require some knowledge of those programming languages. The extension command mechanism makes it possible to create commands that can be used by general users without any such knowledge because they behave like the built-in commands.

For people who want to create extensions, all the necessary information is available from the Help menu. The Custom Dialog Builder, which is included in Statistics Base, provides an easy, no-programming way to create a dialog box interface. A number of utility modules are provided to facilitate processing the command specifications. Extension bundles, which are the main way to package and distribute extensions, are created using Statistics Base.

People who just want to use already developed extensions can download and install them using the Statistics menus or update them directly from the website if they are not included in the many that are installed with Statistics. Extensions written in R require also that R and the R Essentials be installed separately from Statistics. At the time of this writing, over 100 extension commands, including those discussed in this chapter, have been created and made available by IBM and other authors. Forums and Q&A pages are available on the community site for discussing extensions.

> **NOTE** In Statistics 22 and 23, use Utilities ⇨ Extension Bundles. Starting with version 24, use Extensions ⇨ Extension Hub. The IBM SPSS Predictive Analytics website is at https://developer.ibm.com/predictiveanalytics. The R Essentials can be obtained from that site. R can be obtained from the CRAN site. Users can also install extensions not available from the website using these menus.

The three extension procedures discussed in this chapter are SPSSINC TURF (Analyze ⇨ Descriptive Statistics ⇨ TURF Analysis), SPSSINC QUANTREG (Analyze ⇨ Regression ⇨ Quantile Regression), and STATS SVM (Analyze ⇨ Classify ⇨ Support Vector Machines). SPSSINC TURF is implemented in Python and is included in the standard Statistics installation, while the other two are implemented in R and are included in the installation of the R Essentials as of version 23, but must be installed from the website for earlier versions. After TURF is installed, you would see Figure 18-1 on the Analyze menu.

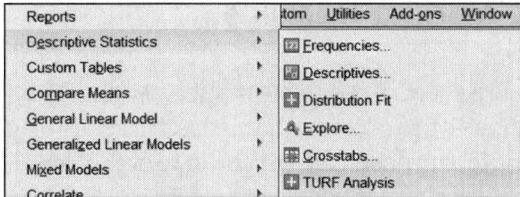

Figure 18-1: The menus show the installed extensions. Extension commands have a white "+" icon.

The IBM SPSS Predictive Analytics website downloads section allows you to filter and search the available extensions and install or update the ones you want. For example, you might see Figure 18-2 in the downloads section of the site.

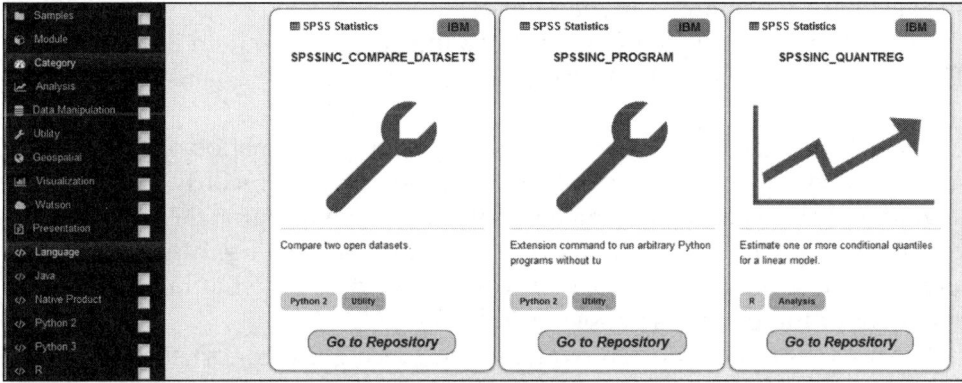

Figure 18-2: Available extensions are listed on the website.

The command names for extensions created by IBM always start with SPSSINC or STATS except for a few very early extensions that have one-word names such as FUZZY and GATHERMD, so you can usually tell that a command is an IBM extension by the first word of the name. Extensions are not documented in the *IBM SPSS Statistics Command Syntax Reference*, but browser-based help is available by pressing F1 on the command in the Syntax Editor in version 23 or later. In earlier versions run *COMMAND NAME/HELP*.

Unlike the built-in commands in Statistics, extensions are delivered in source code form, so users with the requisite skills can read the extension source code to understand nuances not covered in the documentation and can make corrections or enhancements on their own.

Extension commands from IBM are free, and new ones appear often. Look for them on the Predictive Analytics Community website or from the extension command menus within Statistics.

TURF Analysis—Designing Product Bundles

TURF (Total Unduplicated Reach and Frequency) Analysis is a technique developed in market research to solve a class of problems that arise in designing bundles of product offerings. For example, suppose you are going to set up small shops or carts such as often seen in airports that sell frozen yogurt. You can offer only a limited number of flavors. How do you pick a small set of flavors in such a way that the most customers possible who come into the shop will like at least one flavor and will make a purchase?

In another application, suppose you are offering a conference in several locations, and you want to maximize the probability that potential attendees will attend one of the locations. A third application is media advertising. Suppose you want to advertise in a set of magazines or on websites in such a way as to maximize the probability that a potential buyer will see at least one ad. Problems such as these are common in marketing.

Reach is the percentage of buyers who like at least one item in the bundle. The *frequency* is the total number of likes for a bundle. The goal is to maximize the reach.

The data on which to base the bundle selection is information on preferences from a survey or other source such as historical purchase records. For example, you might have a survey in which people rate various yogurt flavors, or a survey indicating whether they would or would not attend a seminar in various locations. In a media example, you would have data on what magazines, TV channels, or Internet sites people visit.

The obvious bundle design strategy, considering the yogurt shop example, would be to pick the most popular flavor, then the next most popular flavor, and so on. In the media example, you might pick the most watched TV station, the next most watched station, and so on. This will generally not produce the optimal combination, however, because of overlapping preferences.

Consider the preference sets represented in Figure 18-3.

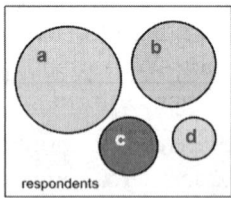 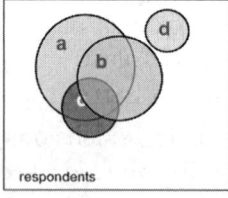

Figure 18-3: Two preference sets

The circles represent the sets of survey respondents who like options a, b, c, and d. The sizes represent the number in the set who like the item. In the left figure, the sets of respondents are disjoint. In other words, no one likes more than one item. Therefore, one would maximize the reach by first choosing the largest circle, which is item a, then item b, and so on. The naïve strategy works.

In the more realistic figure on the right, respondents' preferences overlap. Many people who like item a also like item b, and some like a, b, and c, while d has a disjoint set of respondents. Even though the size of the group that likes item d is the smallest, it might be a better choice than group c likers because of the overlap.

The reach is the set union of liking respondents for the combined options. The union of the a and b likes would be a set containing all the respondents who like either item a or item b or both. If there are 100 a likers and 50 b likers, the union will have between 100 and 150 respondents. If all b likers also like a, the size will be 100, and if there is no overlap, the size is 150. The computational problem in calculating the best reach bundle is, given a set of respondent preferences and the number of items to go into a bundle, to find the combination of items that maximizes the reach; that is, the combination with the largest union of liking respondents. In this four-item example, if the bundle size is three, the possibilities are (a, b, c), (a, b, d), (a, c, d), and (b, c, d). It is computationally easy to calculate the union of respondents in each group. Although Statistics does not have a set data type, we could use the OR operator in COMPUTE. For example, the likes for the bundle (a,b,c) could be computed as shown in Figure 18-4, assuming that the variables are coded as 0 and 1.

```
COMPUTE abc = a OR b OR c.
DESCRIPTIVES abc /STATISTICS=SUM
```

Figure 18-4: Computing reach manually

Even if we want to know the reach for sets of size 1, 2, and 3, there are only 14 set unions to calculate (including the trivial unions of size 1).

Suppose, however, that we have more items. With 20 items, we have to calculate 1,350 set unions, and the problem size grows rapidly as the number of items increases. The SPSSINC TURF extension command (Analyze ⇨ Descriptive Statistics ⇨ TURF Analysis), which is implemented in Python, does these calculations efficiently. The input data for TURF is one variable for each item. In the simplest case these variables are like/dislike dichotomies represented as 0 or 1 values. If we had ratings, we would specify the rating values that constitute a like. For this example, we have 20 variables, x1 to x20, and 280 respondents who evaluated each flavor. (The data for this example is proprietary and not publicly available.) Looking at the "like" frequencies as produced by TURF, we see that item x12 is the most liked at 51.8%, and item x8 is the least liked at only 2.9%. The naïve strategy for picking the best items would add x18 for the best two, x11 for the best three, and x14 for the best four. Figure 18-5 shows the single-variable frequencies in order of reach.

Maximum Group Size: 1. Reach and Frequency.

Variables	Statistics			
	Reach	Pct of Cases	Frequency	Pct of Responses
x12	145	51.8	145	10.4
x18	122	43.6	122	8.7
x11	109	38.9	109	7.8
x14	99	35.4	99	7.1
x17	98	35.0	98	7.0

Variables: x1, x10, x11, x12, x13, x14, x15, x16, x17, x18, x19, x2, x20, x3, x4, x5, x6, x7, x8, x9

Figure 18-5: Maximum Group Size: 1. Reach and Frequency

Figure 18-6 shows the SPSSINC TURF dialog.

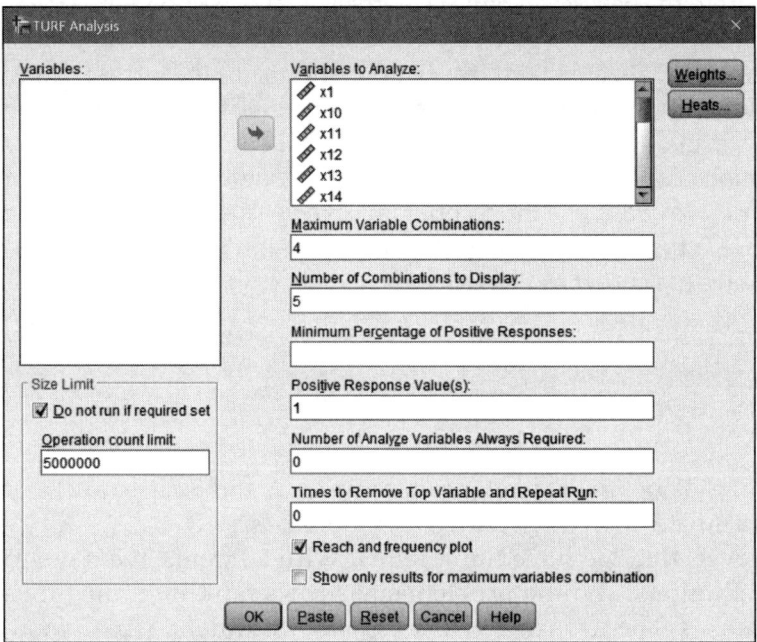

Figure 18-6: The TURF dialog box

All twenty variables are selected; we ask for the best four combinations but ask for the best five for each best-n output. This is useful for seeing how close the top contenders are to each other, because there may be other considerations in choosing the bundle. The variables are coded as 0/1, so the positive response value of 1 is appropriate. If variables were coded, say on a 1 to 5 scale, we might list 4 and 5 here to count the top two ratings. We can also specify a minimum threshold to discard variables that have virtually no chance of making it into a best combination. We discuss heats later: They are not used for this example.

The Times to Remove Top Variable and Repeat Run control allows you to explore subgroups. It removes the single best variable from the collection and runs TURF again using only those cases where the best variable did not have a positive response. For example, if the best flavor is vanilla, it would run TURF excluding vanilla as a flavor on the cases that do not like vanilla. This can be repeated, each time removing the then-best variables cumulatively. The results are generally very similar to the normal TURF results. By default, no removal cycles are performed.

The output displays the best n combinations for sizes one through four. For size two, we get the results shown Figure 18-7.

Maximum Group Size: 2. Reach and Frequency.

Variables	Reach	Pct of Cases	Frequency	Pct of Responses
x11, x12	220	78.6	254	18.2
x12, x18	218	77.9	267	19.1
x12, x17	207	73.9	243	17.4
x12, x19	200	71.4	231	16.6
x14, x18	191	68.2	221	15.8

Variables: x1, x10, x11, x12, x13, x14, x15, x16, x17, x18, x19, x2, x20, x3, x4, x5, x6, x7, x8, x9

Figure 18-7: Maximum Group Size: 2. Reach and Frequency

Variables x11 and x12 are selected even though x11 was not the second-best variable. It has noticeably fewer positive responses than x18. x11 and x12 were selected because of the overlapping preferences. Of those who like x12, 40% also like x18 while only 30% like x11. The difference in reach, however, for x11 and x12 versus x12 and x18 is small. Skipping to the best-four table shown in Figure 18-8, we see a reach of 99.6% using x11, x12, x17, x2, although x2 was eighth in the individual variable order.

Maximum Group Size: 4. Reach and Frequency.

Variables	Reach	Pct of Cases	Frequency	Pct of Responses
x11, x12, x17, x2	279	99.6	425	30.5
x11, x12, x17, x18	273	97.5	474	34.0
x11, x12, x10, x20	271	90.8	440	31.5
x11, x12, x17, x19	271	96.8	438	31.4
x11, x12, x18, x19	270	96.4	462	33.1

Variables: x1, x10, x11, x12, x13, x14, x15, x16, x17, x18, x19, x2, x20, x3, x4, x5, x6, x7, x8, x9

Figure 18-8: Maximum Group Size: 4. Reach and Frequency

Although it did not happen here, it can happen that a lower ranked variable can actually drive out a higher one as the size of the variable combination increases. This means that another naïve search strategy is also not optimal in general. That is, start with the best variable; then add the variable that increases the reach the most given the first variable; then add the variable that increases the reach the most given the first two, and so on. Because lower ranked variables can drive out higher ones and give a better reach, this naïve search strategy can also fail to produce the optimal result. To get the optimal result, it is necessary to allow variables to be removed as the bundle size increases.

This analysis presumes that the bundle size is fixed; however, TURF shows the effect of varying the size, which can help determine the optimal size. Figure 18-6 shows how the reach and frequency change as the group size increases. The reach and frequency increase with the group size, but diminishing returns set in. Figure 18-9 is the reach and frequency plot for bundle sizes of one to ten. Although the frequency continues to increase, the reach has essentially reached its maximum at size 4, so the return to increasing the number of items beyond that point is negligible unless having a higher frequency (number of likes) given the reach is important.

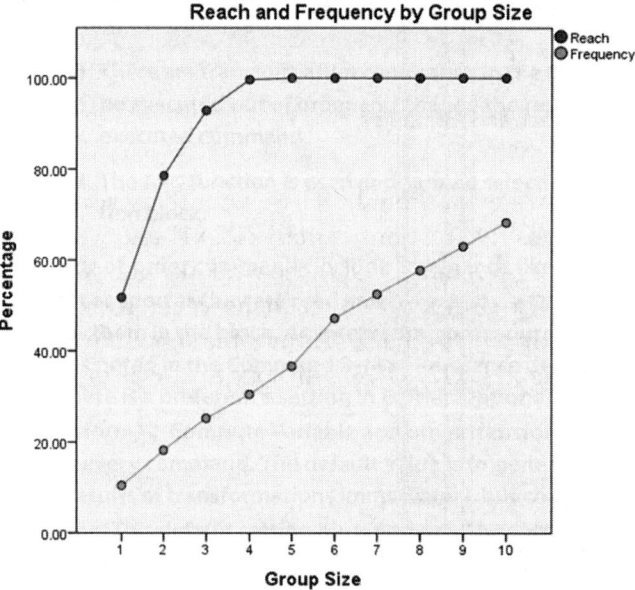

Figure 18-9: Effect of group size

It may happen that data is available on the value to the business of respondents. For example, if purchase history is available, you may want to weight respondents by their purchase frequency or purchase value. (RFM analysis, which is available in the Direct Marketing option, can help define the best customers.) You can do this by assigning the value as the case weight. Another type of weighting is of the variables. Some items might be more profitable than others, for example. TURF allows variable weights to be assigned using the Weights subdialog or the equivalent IMPORTANCE subcommand. When importance weights are assigned, the mean and total importance for each combination is displayed, but the weight is not used in the optimization. By displaying a number of combinations for each bundle size, the impact of the importance can be seen.

Sometimes certain variables are required in the selected bundle regardless of their effect on the reach. This might happen if an incremental change is to be made to an existing offering. By listing the required variables first in the dialog box and specifying the number of these in the Number of Analyze Variables Always Required field, only bundles containing those variables will be considered. (Older versions of this procedure do not offer this option, but the installed version can be updated if necessary as described above.)

It will often happen that the top contender combinations will be very close in reach, so other considerations may be used to make the final choice. In using the TURF results, it is important to realize that TURF may overfit the survey data, so the results with new respondents may not perform as well as the results on the sample used for fitting. It may be wise to construct a random holdout sample to test the TURF results on, if enough survey data is available. At this writing, TURF does not do this for you, but you could do it by first partitioning the dataset, holding out, say, 30% of the data (Data ⇨ Select Cases ⇨ Random Sample of Cases); then running TURF; then switch to the holdout sample; and finally, use code like the preceding example for the (a, b, c) bundle. Doing this for the top few selected bundles would be a sufficient reality check. This functionality may be incorporated into TURF at a future time.

Large Problems

As described earlier, the computational burden of enumerating all possible bundles grows rapidly as the number of variables increases and makes TURF impractical. In addition, the degree of overfitting is likely to grow with the number of variables. The Heats mechanism in TURF overcomes the computational burden problem while producing answers that are only approximately optimal. In practical experience, the Heats approach is usually very close to the optimal solution.

Heats work the way you would expect in a tournament. First, the variables are assigned randomly to one of a number of heats. The number of heats is chosen so that the size of the heats is small enough that the TURF calculation can be carried out quickly. Then the TURF analysis is carried out for each heat, and the winning combination or the first few combinations of variables are collected from each heat, and the second round TURF analysis takes place with those inputs. In principle there could be further rounds, but problems large enough to need more rounds are unlikely to be encountered in practice. The Heats subdialog or the corresponding HEATS subcommand allows you to change the default size, 18, and the default number of winning combinations, 2, from each heat or to not use heats at all. The defaults avoid the computational explosion, keep the size of the final round manageable, and capture most of the power of the best variable combinations.

Using heats, the computation time for large problems is dramatically reduced. In one large test, the run time was reduced from three days to thirty minutes. Just as with sports tournaments, the heat structure does not guarantee that the global best winners will be found, but in various tests with real and simulated data, the results have been very close. Because the initial assignment of variables to heats is random, running TURF more than once can be useful in assessing the results. This is practical because of the large reduction in run time.

Quantile Regression—Predicting Airline Delays

Ordinary regression estimates the mean of a continuous dependent variable conditional on a set of explanatory variables:

$$Y = X\beta + \epsilon$$

where Y is an Nx1 vector of the dependent variable values, X is an Nxk matrix of explanatory variables, and ϵ is an Nx1 vector of independent, identically distributed unobserved random errors that is independent of the explanatory variables and has variance σ^2. Given a set of X values, the distribution of Y has conditional mean $X\beta$. If, as conventional, we assume that ϵ has a Normal distribution, then Y, conditional on X, does also. The parameters are typically estimated by Ordinary Least Square (OLS) using a procedure such as REGRESSION in Statistics.

This model works well in a wide variety of real applications, but sometimes we are interested in aspects of the conditional distribution of Y other than the mean but do not want to depend on the normality assumption for the error term or to assume that the X variables have the same effect throughout the distribution of Y. For example, suppose you are an airport manager, an airline planner, or a traveler who needs to make a connection at a particular airport. You want to know how much time should be left between flights so as to give travelers a high probability of making the connection. In addition to the known time required to get from arrival to departure gate, arrival delays may occur.

Arrival time delays depend on a number of factors such as the time of day, the day of the week, the specific airline, air traffic, weather, and the arrival and destination airports. We can model the average arrival delay of an inbound flight as a function of such variables using ordinary regression, but the question of interest here is how often the arrival delay will be great enough that the traveler will miss his or her connection. Quantile regression can help us to answer that question. Instead of being interested in the mean arrival delay of the inbound flight, we would like to estimate more of the delay distribution, say, the 90th percentile conditional on our explanatory variables. We may want to estimate many quantiles of the arrival delay distribution. If the ordinary regression assumptions are satisfied, we could apply OLS and add the appropriate quantile of the error distribution, but we may not want to make those assumptions. We might also consider logistic regression, cutting the distribution at various amounts of delay, but quantile regression gives us the most comprehensive picture of the delay distribution, and it allows us to test whether the effect of the explanatory variables differs across quantiles.

As a practical matter, there are other complications beyond the scope of this example such as correlation between arrival and departure delays at the connection airport, but the example focuses on the difference between the traditional regression approach and the quantile regression approach.

The data for this example comes from the United States Department of Transportation Bureau of Transportation Statistics. The dataset records arrival and departure information for all commercial flights in the U.S. A convenient source is available here: http://stat-computing.org/dataexpo/2009/. The entire dataset is very large. Table 18-1 contains a description of some of the variables as modified for this example. CRS stands for Computerized Reservation Systems, that is, scheduled times. You can find detailed definitions of the original variables here: http://aspmhelp.faa.gov/index.php/Types_of_Delay. We will use data for one year and focus on the two very busy Chicago airports, O'Hare (ORD) and Midway (MDW), where many transfers take place.

Table 18-1: Variable Definitions

VARIABLE	DESCRIPTION
Month	1–12
DayofMonth	1–31
DayOfWeek	1 (Monday)–7 (Sunday)
DepTime	Actual departure time (local, hhmm)
CRSDepTime	Scheduled departure time (local, hhmm)
ArrTime	Actual arrival time (local, hhmm)
CRSArrTime /CRSArrTimeHr	Scheduled arrival time (local, hhmm)/hh
UniqueCarrier/ UniqueCarrierCollapsed	Unique carrier code
ActualElapsedTime	In minutes
CRSElapsedTime	In minutes
AirTime	In minutes
ArrDelay	Arrival delay, in minutes

Continues

Table 18-1 (*continued*)

VARIABLE	DESCRIPTION
DepDelay	Departure delay, in minutes
Origin	Origin IATA airport code
Dest	Destination IATA airport code
Distance	In miles
CarrierDelay	In minutes. Delay within control of the carrier
WeatherDelay	In minutes. Extreme or hazardous forecasted or actual
NASDelay	In minutes. Nonextreme weather, airport operations, traffic
LateAircraftDelay	In minutes. Late arrival at a previous airport

The dataset includes delay variables CarrierDelay, WeatherDelay, NASdelay, SecurityDelay, and LateAircraftDelay, but they are not reported—that is, are missing—unless the arrival delay is at least 15 minutes. These variables are, of course, not known when planning a trip, and they partition the dependent variable, so we will not use them here. Modeling cancellations and diversions might be useful for travelers, but you would miss the flight anyway, and these are a very small percentage of the data. Small carriers, representing less than 2% of flight volume, have been collapsed into an OTHER category, leaving eight categories, and a small number of cases with missing data and cases for cancelled or diverted flights have been discarded.

Running DESCRIPTIVES on our one-year dataset, we see that it records 7,000,728 flights. Selecting out only arrivals at Chicago airports (Dest = ORD or MDW), we have 419,322 flights. Plotting a population pyramid of arrival delays at both airports, we see that the distribution is quite asymmetrical as shown in Figure 18-10.

TIP Data is traditionally saved in an SPSS .sav file, which compresses the data to some degree depending on the nature of the variables, but the newer .zsav format generally gives much better compression. A .sav file holding all of this data for one year is 854MB, while the same data in .zsav format is 275MB—about 1/3 the size. However, processing time for a .zsav file may be greater.

Calculating some statistics with SUMMARIZE, we have the results shown in Figure 18-11.

This confirms the skewness we see in the graph in Figure 18-10. Notice also that the mean delay is much greater at ORD, but the median delay is almost the same. These statistics suggest nonnormality of the delays, but we have not yet controlled for any variables, and it is normality of the error terms, not the distribution of the Y variable that matters for regression.

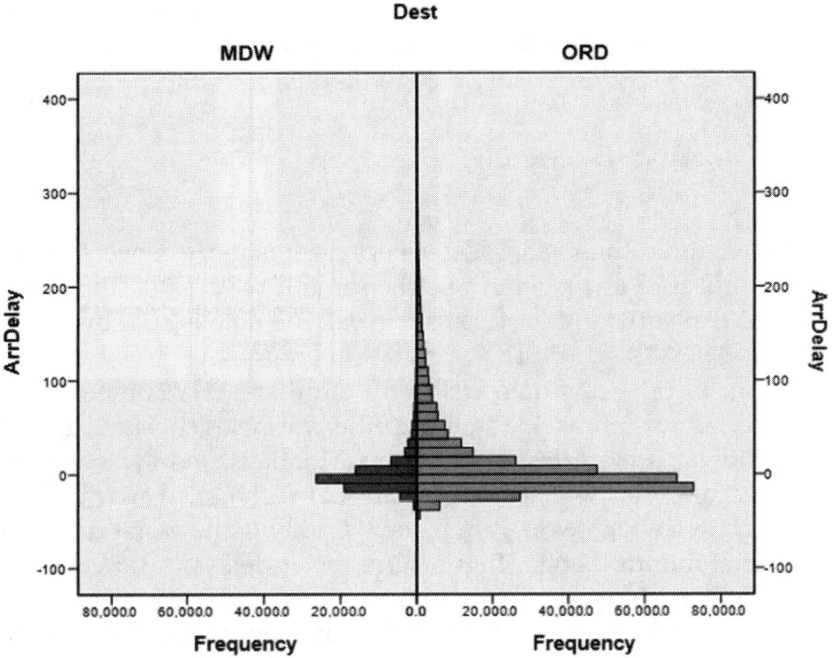

Figure 18-10: Arrival delays by airport

Case Summaries

ArrDelay

Dest	N	Mean	Median	Skewness
MDW	85,991	4.78	-3.00	4.486
ORD	333,331	15.15	-2.00	3.776
Total	419,322	13.03	-2.00	3.968

Figure 18-11: Arrival Delays by Airport

For airport management study of delays, we are more concerned about causes than forecasting, while for traveler decision making, we are more interested in forecasting, which requires estimating the independent variable values at the time of a particular trip. If we were using the delay variables, and not knowing some of these in advance, we might use averages for the destination airport. For our regression model, we will use Month, DayOfWeek, uniqueCarrierCollapsed, and CRSArrTimeHr as factors, and CRSElapsedTime as a covariate. We will save the predicted values for comparison with the quantile regression results.

The syntax generated from the Analyze ➪ General Linear Model ➪ Univariate dialog is shown in the following code snippet:

```
SORT CASES  BY DEST.
SPLIT FILE BY DEST.
UNIANOVA ArrDelay BY Month DayOfWeek CRSArrTimeHr uniqueCarrierCollapsed
WITH CRSElapsedTime
 /SAVE=PRED(RegPred)
 /PRINT=PARAMETER
 /DESIGN=Month DayOfWeek CRSArrTimeHr uniqueCarrierCollapsed
CRSElapsedTime.
```

We use UNIANOVA rather than REGRESSION, because it is more convenient for handling factors, but the results would be the same if we created the factor variable dummies explicitly and used REGRESSION. The data is split by DEST, which has values "MDW" and "ORD."

All of the factors and the covariate are highly significant. We do not show all the results here, but to summarize, holding other variables constant, arrival time delays for Midway are greatest at 6am–8am, Mondays, and in December. Longer flights have fewer delays. For O'Hare, 2am–3am scheduled arrival times have large delays, after which 6am–7am is next. Friday is the worst day, and December the worst month. Longer flights have lower delays, –.3.96 minutes per hour versus –.974 at Midway.

We turn next to quantile regression. The following code snippet shows the syntax for the same model generated by Analyze ➪ Regression ➪ Quantile Regression:

```
SPSSINC QUANTREG DEPENDENT=ArrDelay
  ENTER= Month DayOfWeek CRSArrTimeHr uniqueCarrierCollapsed
CRSElapsedTime
    QUANTILES = .5 .7 .9
 /OPTIONS METHOD = BR STDERR = IID MISSING=LISTWISE.
```

This estimates the 50%, 70%, and 90% quantiles of the arrival delay. With split files on, we get separate estimation results for the two airports. We are using the default estimation method, which is Barrodale-Roberts (BR), but we are using a nondefault method for the coefficient standard errors for reasons that will be discussed later. In order to save residuals and predicted values, we would add:

```
/SAVE PREDDATASET=qrpred RESIDUALSDATASET=qrresids id = id.
```

We can also test whether the regression coefficients differ for the selected quantiles by specifying ANOVA=JOINT or ANOVA=SEPARATE on OPTIONS for a joint equality test of all the coefficients or separate tests for each coefficient. If the coefficients, apart from the intercept, do not differ, that is, all the quantile lines are parallel, the simpler regression model may be adequate.

Comparing Ordinary Least Squares with Quantile Regression Results

We will focus on just the ORD results in this section.

As a first step, we can look at the OLS residual histogram for evidence on whether the error distribution satisfies the usual assumption about that distribution. Figure 18-12 shows the residual histogram with a normal curve superimposed for regression. Clearly the residuals are not normally distributed.

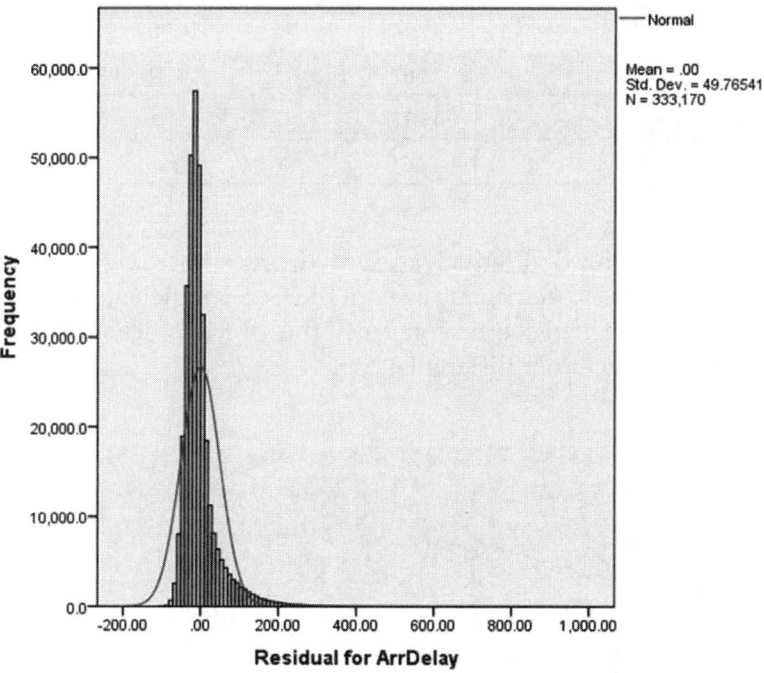

Figure 18-12: Regression residuals histogram

One obvious way to compare the results is to inspect the coefficients. For prediction purposes, the QR coefficients have the same meaning as from OLS. The coefficients for the month factor are displayed in Table 18-2.

Table 18-2: Month Regression Coefficients

MONTH	OLS	QUANTREG(.5)	QUANTREG(.9)
1	3.62	0	0
2	4.12	3.28	-6.17

Continues

Table 18-2 (*continued*)

MONTH	OLS	QUANTREG(.5)	QUANTREG(.9)
3	-9.488	-6.84	-29.54
4	-14.73	-8.45	-48.67
5	-16.83	-9.27	-49.33
6	-.211	-.361	-20.96
7	-13.81	-8.60	-45.65
8	-21.29	-12.47	-60.30
9	-20.32	-11.97	-54.36
10	-26.87	-13.61	-66.27
11	-26.86	-15.31	-65.41
12	0	-1.66	-4.26

The coefficients are normalized differently by the two procedures. Figure 18-13 shows a graph of the QUANTREG coefficients against the OLS coefficients for two quantiles. While the .5 QUANTREG coefficients track the OLS coefficients fairly closely, the .9 coefficients are rather different.

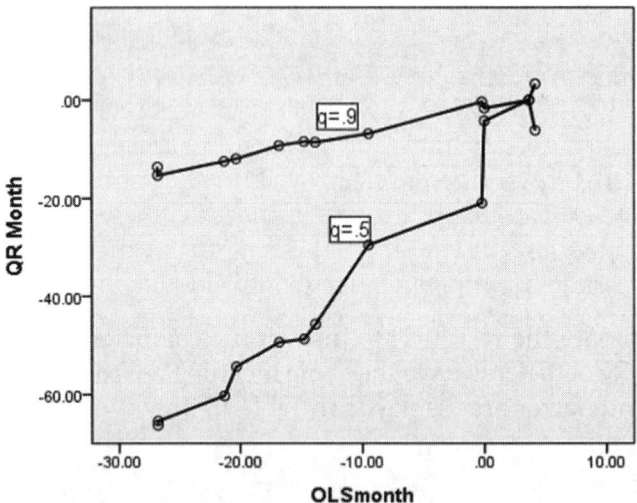

Figure 18-13: OLS vs. QR coefficients for month

The CRSElapsedTime coefficient is −.066 for OLS, −.003 for QUANTREG(.5), and −.061 for QUANTREG(.9) with QUANTREG standard errors of .001 to .005 suggesting that the constant effect from OLS is an oversimplification.

To compare residuals and fitted values between the two techniques, we need to merge the quantile regression residual and predicted value datasets with the input dataset containing the regression residuals. They can be combined by a simple MATCH FILES command using the QUANTREG-generated datasets as table matches. Before doing that, we need to change the ID variable to numeric, since the QUANTREG ID values are always strings. ALTER TYPE makes that easy.

The residuals for regression, which is the first variable, are highly correlated with the quantile regression equivalents, but the correlations are lower for the quantile of most interest, .9, as shown in Figure 18-14.

Correlations

		Residual for ArrDelay	tau = 0.5	tau = 0.9
Residual for ArrDelay	Pearson Correlation	1	.986**	.915**
	Sig. (2-tailed)		.000	.000
tau = 0.5	Pearson Correlation	.986**	1	.842**
	Sig. (2-tailed)	.000		.000
tau = 0.9	Pearson Correlation	.915**	.842**	1
	Sig. (2-tailed)	.000	.000	

**. Correlation is significant at the 0.01 level (2-tailed).

Figure 18-14: Residual correlations

The tails of the distribution are of interest here. One way to compare the distributions is to do a Q-Q plot of the OLS and QUANTREG residuals. The standard Statistics Q-Q plot compares a variable with a specific theoretical distribution, so instead we use the SPSSINC QQPLOT2 extension command (Analyze ⇨ Descriptives ⇨ Two-Variable or Group Q-Q Plot), which allows us to easily compare the distributions of two variables. Figure 18-15 shows the plot for the .9 quantile. As an aside, notice that the QUANTREG residuals have a higher mean: the regression residuals must have mean zero (as long as a constant term is included), but the QUANTREG residuals have a mean of –51.9. Conversely, the regression residuals have a median value of –11.25 while the .5 QUANTREG residuals have a median of 0. The .9 residual median is –55.9. The QUANTREG .9 residuals have a larger range, reflecting the lower sensitivity to outliers, but the difference is small in this case (1083 vs. 1192). As shown in Figure 18-15, the QUANTREG residual distribution has fatter tails and, in fact appears more normally distributed.

The correlation output shown in Figure 18-14 shows different results for the two quantiles. This suggests that the quantile functions are different, and indeed a joint test for equality in the two quantiles rejects equality with an $F_{(46, 666,294)}$ of 513.127.

It may be useful to study how the coefficients change with the quantile. Using PLOT on the OPTIONS subcommand produces a plot of the coefficient value against the quantile including, if possible, a confidence band. The plots are too small to be useful if there are many coefficients, but Figure 18-16 shows an example with a simplified equation estimated for six quantiles. The X axis is the quantile, and the Y axis is the coefficient. The CRSElapsedTime plot, for example, shows a positive effect at the .7 quantile but negative effects at the .2 and .9 quantiles.

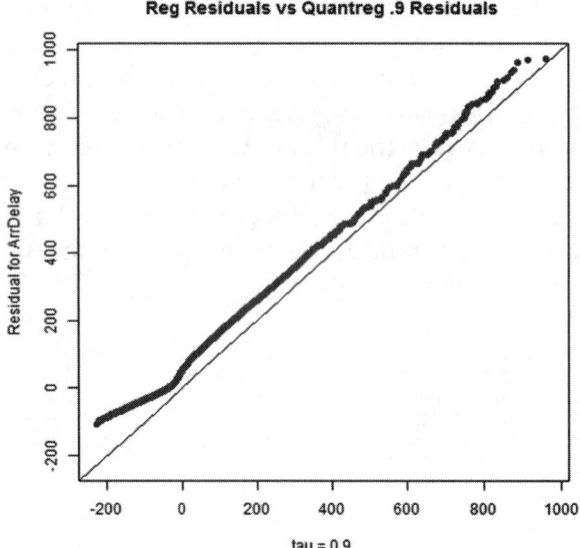

Figure 18-15: Q-Q plot of OLS against QUANTREG residuals

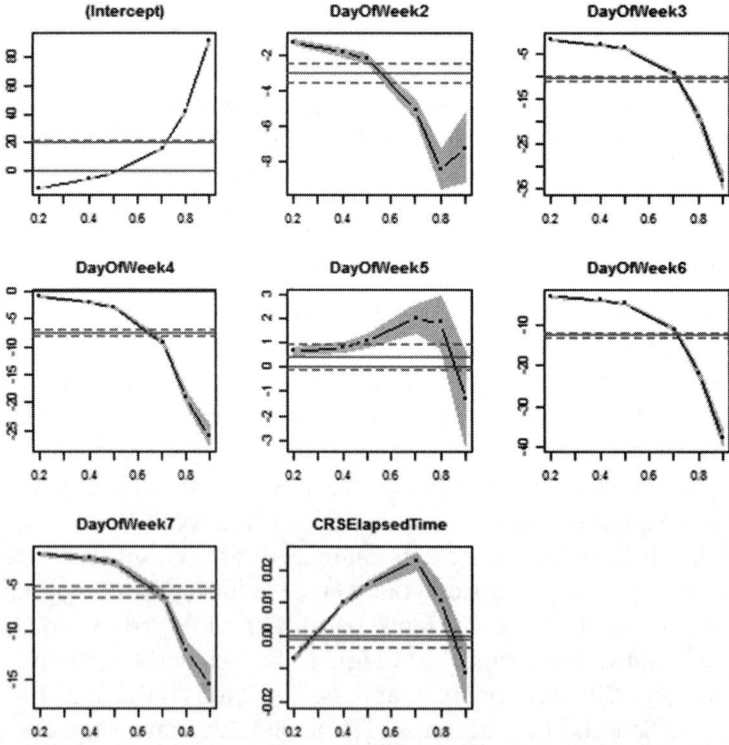

Figure 18-16: QR coefficients by quantile

DIGGING DEEPER

In ordinary least squares, the parameter estimates are chosen to minimize the residual sum of squares $(y - X\hat{\beta})'(y - X\hat{\beta})$, which can be done by solving a set of linear equations. Quantile regression estimation is more complicated. For each quantile estimated, there is a different set of estimates. One common choice is the 50th quantile, that is, the median. Since the estimate of the median of the distribution of y is the value of m that minimizes $\sum |(y - m)|$, the median quantile regression estimate is found by minimizing $\sum |(y - X\hat{\beta})|$. Generalizing this to any quantile, α, we minimize

$$\sum \alpha |(y - X\hat{\beta})| I(y > X\hat{\beta}) + (1 - \alpha) |(y - X\hat{\beta})| I(y \le X\hat{\beta})$$

with respect to $\hat{\beta}$ where I(·) is the indicator function whose value is 1 if the condition is true and 0 otherwise. If $\alpha = .5$, this reduces to the equation for the median. If $\alpha = .75$, for example, we find estimates such that 75% of the residuals are negative and 25% are positive. Actually performing this minimization is more difficult and time consuming than performing the minimization required for OLS, but that's what computers are for. Quantile regression estimates can be calculated by solving a linear programming problem. We won't discuss the computation further here except to note that the QUANTREG procedure provides three choices for solving the linear programming problem that differ in their run times for various problems. They should all give the same result if they complete, but it may be necessary to try more than one in case of failure.

One immediate difference from OLS is that since the minimization criterion is absolute value instead of quadratic error, quantile regression is less influenced by large outliers. More importantly for our airline example, though, is that by estimating multiple quantiles, the entire distribution of the errors, and, hence, the entire conditional distribution of y can be characterized. Furthermore, while inference with the OLS model relies on the normality of the errors for certain results, although that may not matter with large samples, that assumption is not required here.

Operational Considerations

Two technical issues need to be considered when using SPSSINC QUANTREG: the estimation method and how to compute the standard errors. There are three choices of estimation methods: Barrodale-Roberts (BR), Frisch-Newton (FN), and Frisch-Newton with preprocessing (PFN). The first is efficient for problems up to a few thousand cases; the third is better for very large problems, and the second is appropriate in between. The actual estimates are the same, but the time required for estimation varies. On a small problem, PFN may take twice as long as BR, but both complete quite quickly. On a very large problem, BR is slower than PFN. It can happen that FN and PFN fail reporting singularity when BR succeeds. If this happens, a slight perturbation of the quantile values may succeed. In this example, the .5 quantile failed for PFN, but .501 succeeded. The author of the R package said in a personal communication that .5 is particularly problematic for technical reasons when the independent variables include a lot of factors.

> **NOTE** There are five ways to compute the standard errors necessary for judging the precision of the estimates. RANK, which is the default, produces confidence intervals. The others produce standard errors and t statistics. The different methods make different assumptions, particularly concerning whether the errors are i.i.d, and can give substantially different results (Buchinsky, Moshe [1998] "Recent Advances in Quantile Regression Models: A Practical Guideline for Empirical Research." *Journal of Human Resources*, Vol 33, No 1, pp 88–126).
>
> There is no definitive choice, but the bootstrap method (STDERR=BOOT) makes the fewest assumptions. However, it requires the most computing time. As with the estimation method, some choices for the standard error method may fail or may take an excessively long time to compute. In the airline example, it was necessary to use the IID method in order to obtain results.

The regular output from SPSSINC QUANTREG provides confidence intervals or T-Tests for the coefficient estimates for each quantile, but if all the slope coefficients were equal, the model would be much simpler to present and understand, and this hypothesis may be of considerable interest. The SPSSINC QUANTREG command can test the joint hypothesis of equality for all slope coefficients across quantiles, and it can test equality for individual coefficients. To obtain the former test, specify ANOVA=JOINT on the OPTIONS subcommand. ANOVA=SEPARATE tests the individual coefficients. See the Koenker vignette, which you can access as described later in this section, for details of the testing methods. Plots of the coefficients across quantiles are obtained by specifying PLOT on the OPTIONS subcommand. These plots include confidence intervals when available.

A final issue is the treatment of categorical (nominal or ordinal) independent variables. Such variables are automatically treated as factors by the procedure. The levels of the factors are the values taken by these variables, and the output is labeled accordingly.

The SPSSINC QUANTREG command is based on the R quantreg package written by Roger Koenker. Detailed information about the package is available in the R documentation for quantreg. R packages, including this one, sometimes include a vignette, which is an explanatory article with examples. You can access the vignette for quantreg by running this code from a syntax window:

```
begin program r.
library(quantreg)
vignette("rq")
end program.
```

> **NOTE** For more information, see *Quantile Regression* by R. W. Koenker (Cambridge U.P., 2005) and "Regression quantiles" by R. W. Koenker and G. W. Bassett in *Econometrica*, Vol 46, pp 33–50.

Support Vector Machines—Predicting Loan Default

Support vector machines (SVM) and random forests are mainstays in machine learning. While they are not much to look at, because they don't provide a crisp, comprehensible model, they can be very effective for mean prediction of continuous variables and classification of categorical ones. SVM is provided in Statistics by the STATS SVM extension command; random forests are available in the SPSSINC RANFOR for estimation and SPSSINC RANPRED for prediction extension commands but will not be discussed further here. SVM is implemented using the R e1071 package by David Meyer and others. You can access details beyond the introductory material in this chapter via the R vignettes for these packages. For the SVM vignette, run this code from a syntax window:

```
begin program r.
library(e1071)
vignette("svmdoc")
end program.
```

NOTE For an extensive mathematical treatment of SVM, see *The Elements of Statistical Learning, Second Edition* by T. Hastie, R. Tibshirani, and J. Friedman (Springer, 2009).

Background

SVMs (and random forests) can be used both for regression problems, where there is a continuous dependent variable, and for classification problems where the dependent variable is categorical with two or more values. We first discuss the classification problem and then the regression problem.

Suppose we have data on a dichotomous variable y representing two groups and a set of explanatory variables $X_1, \ldots, X_n$. We might model y using discriminant analysis (DISCRIMINANT), or logistic regression (LOGISTIC REGRESSION or NOMREG; these can handle more than two groups as well). These methods, as well as SVM, find the equation of a separating hyperplane—with two variables that is just a line. That is, they find a linear combination of the X variables that partitions the n-dimensional space of the X variables so as to best predict the group (the y variable). A perfect classifier would draw a line or hyperplane that perfectly divides the cases into groups if such a line exists; that is, the groups are separable. In the real world, of course, the groups are probably not separable, and the hyperplane will leave some points on the wrong side, but the SVM goal is to find the best possible division subject to considerations discussed later in this chapter.

The details of the SVM algorithm are beyond the scope of this chapter, but two points are noteworthy. First, the SVM differs from discriminant analysis or logistic regression in that extreme points (points that are far from the separating hyperplane) do not matter. The only points that matter are those that are misclassified by the hyperplane or that lie in the margin of the hyperplane—that is, are close to it—these are called the support vectors. The other points do not contribute to the definition of the hyperplane. In contrast, discriminant analysis is based on the means and variance-covariance matrix of all the data. Logistic regression is more similar to SVM, but all points contribute, although it is less sensitive to extreme values than is discriminant analysis. Thus SVM is more robust than discriminant analysis or logistic regression.

Second, the number of support vectors will increase as the margin is widened, which is related to the cost parameter. This tuning parameter controls the tradeoff between bias and variance. A narrow margin means a tighter fit to the estimation data and low variance compared with a wider margin and more support vectors and more bias. More support vectors means potentially less robustness.

If y has more than two values, we can construct the hyperplane for each pair of values. If the values are a, b, and c, for example, we construct the SVM for (a,b), (a,c), and (b,c), or in general with k values, we construct $k(k-1)/2$ SVMs. For prediction, each case is classified using each SVM, and the prediction outcome is chosen by voting. The category that was assigned most often wins.

With a continuous y, ordinary regression would minimize the sum of squared errors. For SVM, instead, small residuals in absolute value don't count, and the minimization is of the sum of squared errors greater in absolute value than some constant.

A simple hyperplane separation boundary based on the X variables will not always exist. In the other models, one might introduce nonlinear functions of the Xs to account for interactions or polynomial effects, although with many predictors, this can introduce a large number of parameters to be estimated. In SVM, in contrast, nonlinear effects are accommodated by using a nonlinear kernel. The SVM estimation is based on the distances between all pairs of points. For a linear kernel, the distance between two cases is calculated simply as the inner product of the (standardized) explanatory variables, that is, Euclidean distance. By choosing different distance measures, nonlinear effects can be introduced. The hyperplane becomes a "hyperwiggle" allowing the boundary to be more flexible. The distance measure is referred to as the kernel, and the SVM procedure provides three parameterized alternatives to the linear kernel. The authors of the package underlying the R code recommend the Radial Basis Function (RBF) as the first choice as it subsumes the linear kernel and is similar to the sigmoid kernel in some cases (G. James, T. Hastie, and R. Tibshirani, *An Introduction to Statistical Learning with Applications in R*, Springer, 2013). However, if the number of variables is very large, the linear kernel may be preferable (Chih-Wei Hsu,

C. Chang, and C. Lin, *A Practical Guide to Support Vector Classification,* `http://ntucsu.csie.ntu.edu.tw/~cjlin/papers/guide/guide.pdf`).

NOTE You can find detailed technical information about kernels and SVM types as implemented in this package in *LIBSVM: A Library for Support Vector Machines* by **Chih-Chung Chang, and C. Lin** at `http://ntucsu.csie.ntu.edu.tw/~cjlin/papers/libsvm.pdf`.

The challenge with the kernels other than the linear one is how to choose the parameter values. For the polynomial kernel, you must specify the degree and the weight for the inner product; for most of the others, you must specify the rate of decay, and so on. The procedure provides default values, but these are not optimal for any particular problem, and experimentation is required for best results. The procedure provides a mechanism for a grid search over the parameter space, which allows you to explore the space and choose good values. Starting with a coarse grid and refining this for promising regions can keep the computation time reasonable.

The gamma parameter applies to all but the linear kernel. Gamma determines the rate of decay of the effect of one X vector on another. Large values mean rapid decay and hence little smoothing and small values meaning slow decay, or a lot of smoothing. The default is 1/(number of variables).

The cost parameter, which defaults to 1, is the misclassification cost. A large value means a high penalty for misclassification, which is associated with low bias but high variance and may overfit the training set, while a small value has the opposite effect.

Whatever kernel is used, it is sensitive to the scale of the independent variables. To avoid having the distances arbitrarily dominated by variables with large values, the variables should be placed on the same scale. By default, the procedure scales all variables to have zero mean and unit variance. If the data is already scaled or you want to customize the scaling, you can turn off the default scaling and perform the appropriate transformations prior to running the procedure.

The generalizability of the estimated model on the training data input to the estimation process can be assessed by cross validation, in which the training data is randomly partitioned into an estimation set and a testing set. This process is repeated a specified number of times and the accuracy or error rate is reported. Cross validation can mitigate the overfitting problem, which may make a seemingly good performing SVM generalize poorly.

If the sizes of the categories of the dependent variable vary considerably, that is, the data is unbalanced, it may help to assign category weights. All categories start with a weight of 1, but increasing the weight for an important but rare category may improve the result. For example, modeling loan defaults, where the default rate is low, might result in simply choosing nondefault as the best prediction for all cases. Assigning a larger weight to the default cases addresses this issue.

An Example

We use the `bankloan.sav` dataset shipped with Statistics as an example. To facilitate comparison of the methods, we standardize the X variables using `DESCRIPTIVES`. (`STATS SVM` can do the standardization itself.) The variables are age in years; level of education from 1 = less than high school to 5 = post-graduate degree; income in thousands; and total debt, which is computed as the sum of credit card and other debt. The dependent variable is occurrence of default, which is 0 or 1. Cases with no loan history are screened out. The preparation syntax is:

```
SELECT IF MISSING(default) = 0.
COMPUTE totalDebt = CREDDEBT + OTHDEBT.
DESCRIPTIVES VARIABLES=age(zAge) ed(zEd) income(zIncome) TotalDebt
(zTotalDebt).
```

There are 700 cases, of which 26% defaulted.

Starting with `DISCRIMINANT` (Analyze ⇨ Classify ⇨ Discriminant), we obtain these classification results (shown in Figure 18-17) using the option of taking prior probabilities from the estimation group sizes. Seventy-six percent of the cases are correctly classified.

Classification Results[a]

			Predicted Group Membership		
		Previously defaulted	No	Yes	Total
Original	Count	No	497	20	517
		Yes	148	35	183
	%	No	96.1	3.9	100.0
		Yes	80.9	19.1	100.0

a. 76.0% of original grouped cases correctly classified.

Figure 18-17: Discriminant classification

With `LOGISTIC REGRESSION` (Analyze ⇨ Regression ⇨ Binary Logistic), this error rate is very similar, as shown in Figure 18-18. Here the cut point for the classification table is set to 0.739, the same percentages of "No" values in the dataset.

Classification Table[a]

			Predicted		
			Previously defaulted		Percentage Correct
	Observed		No	Yes	
Step 1	Previously defaulted	No	512	5	99.0
		Yes	169	14	7.7
	Overall Percentage				75.1

a. The cut value is .739

Figure 18-18: Logistic regression classification

Focusing on STATS SVM (Analyze ➭ Classify ➭ Support Vector Machines), we first estimate with all the default settings, which means that the kernel is RBF, gamma = .25, and the cost is 1. Figure 18-19 shows the classification table (referred to as the Confusion Table in the procedure).

Confusion

Confusion

Actual	Fitted			
	0	1	Total	% Correct
0	513.000	4.000	517.000	99.230
1	158.000	25.000	183.000	13.660
Total	671.000	29.000	700.000	76.860
% Correct	76.450	86.210	NA	NA

Percent Correct: 76.857

Figure 18-19: SVM classification

The syntax to produce this result omitting some irrelevant parameters, generated by the dialog, is:

```
STATS SVM CMDMODE=ESTIMATE DEPENDENT=default
INDEP=zAge zEd zIncome zTotalDebt SVMTYPE=AUTOMATIC
KERNEL=RADIAL
/OPTIONS GAMMA=.25 COST=1
NUMCROSSFOLDS=0 PROBPRED=NO MISSING=OMIT
/SAVE WORKSPACE=CLEAR
/OUTPUT FEATUREWEIGHTS=YES.
```

If we employ a grid search, the output includes a table showing the error rate. Figure 18-20 shows an example. In this case, the default gamma is the best within the granularity tested. The table includes all the possible parameters even for other kernels, so in this instance, only the gamma column is of interest, because the others are not varied or do not apply to the RBF kernel. In order to specify a grid search, enter the values as shown in Figure 18-21.

Tuning Performance

Parameter Tuning Performance

	degree	gamma	coef0	epsilon	cost	nu	Error	Dispersion
1	3.000	.100	.000	.100	1.000	.500	.251	.040
2	3.000	.250	.000	.100	1.000	.500	.249	.041
3	3.000	.500	.000	.100	1.000	.500	.256	.037
4	3.000	.750	.000	.100	1.000	.500	.257	.032

Error is classification error or mean squared error depending on dependent variable type.
Parameters actually used depend on kernel choice and svm type.

Figure 18-20: SVM parameter tuning

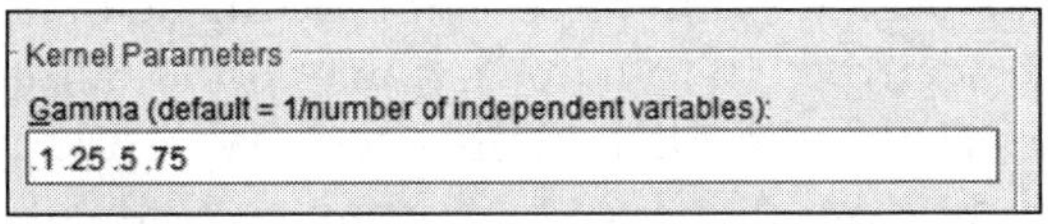

Kernel Parameters

Gamma (default = 1/number of independent variables):

.1 .25 .5 .75

Figure 18-21: Entering grid search parameters

The grid search can be over multiple parameters. Searching on both gamma and cost produces the table shown in Figure 18-22, where the minimum error occurs for gamma=.75 and cost=2, although gamma = .75 and cost=10 is very close. Note that there is some randomization in the tuning, so your results might be slightly different from these.

Tuning Performance

Parameter Tuning Performance

	degree	gamma	coef0	epsilon	cost	nu	Error	Dispersion
1	3.000	.100	.000	.100	1.000	.500	.247	.040
2	3.000	.250	.000	.100	1.000	.500	.253	.046
3	3.000	.500	.000	.100	1.000	.500	.250	.048
4	3.000	.750	.000	.100	1.000	.500	.247	.050
5	3.000	.100	.000	.100	2.000	.500	.247	.050
6	3.000	.250	.000	.100	2.000	.500	.243	.055
7	3.000	.500	.000	.100	2.000	.500	.241	.050
8	3.000	.750	.000	.100	2.000	.500	.231	.039
9	3.000	.100	.000	.100	5.000	.500	.239	.058
10	3.000	.250	.000	.100	5.000	.500	.244	.054
11	3.000	.500	.000	.100	5.000	.500	.236	.035
12	3.000	.750	.000	.100	5.000	.500	.237	.027
13	3.000	.100	.000	.100	10.000	.500	.240	.054
14	3.000	.250	.000	.100	10.000	.500	.240	.049
15	3.000	.500	.000	.100	10.000	.500	.239	.033
16	3.000	.750	.000	.100	10.000	.500	.233	.039

Error is classification error or mean squared error depending on dependent variable type.
Parameters actually used depend on kernel choice and svm type.

Figure 18-22: SVM Parameter tuning with two parameters

The confusion matrix in Figure 18-23 using the best tuning parameters shows that we have increased the percentage of correct predictions of default to 38.25% from the original 13.66%. The number of support vectors has increased from 377 to 390, which is 56% of the sample. If we perform crossfold validation, the overall accuracy is somewhat lower as we would expect.

Confusion

Confusion

	Fitted			
Actual	0	1	Total	% Correct
0	503.000	14.000	517.000	97.290
1	113.000	70.000	183.000	38.250
Total	616.000	84.000	700.000	81.860
% Correct	81.660	83.330	NA	NA

Percent Correct: 81.857

Figure 18-23: SVM classification result with tuning

It is reasonable to think that a lender's principal interest is in guarding against default and would want to trade some accuracy in the prediction of nondefault for a more accurate prediction of default when it will actually occur. Weighting the default category more heavily than nondefault can emphasize that category. We can do this by assigning a weight to the category of default with the CLASSWEIGHTS keyword, which accepts a list of category values and weight pairs. Using CLASSWEIGHTS = 1 5 specifies that the loan default category, 1, has a weight five times as large as loan nondefault. If no weights are specified, all categories have a weight of 1. It is only necessary to specify weights where a category should have a nondefault weight. Using the default RBF settings with this weight produces the confusion table shown in Figure 18-24.

Confusion

	Confusion			
	Fitted			
Actual	**0**	**1**	**Total**	**% Correct**
0	263.000	254.000	517.000	50.870
1	17.000	166.000	183.000	90.710
Total	280.000	420.000	700.000	61.290
% Correct	93.930	39.520	NA	NA

Percent Correct: 61.286

Figure 18-24: SVM classification results with weighting

Comparing this with the confusion table shown in Figure 18-19, we see that the accuracy of the default prediction increases from 13% to 90% while the nondefault percent correct falls from 99% to 51%.

Operational Issues

The STATS SVM command and dialog operate in two modes. Figure 18-25 shows the dialog.

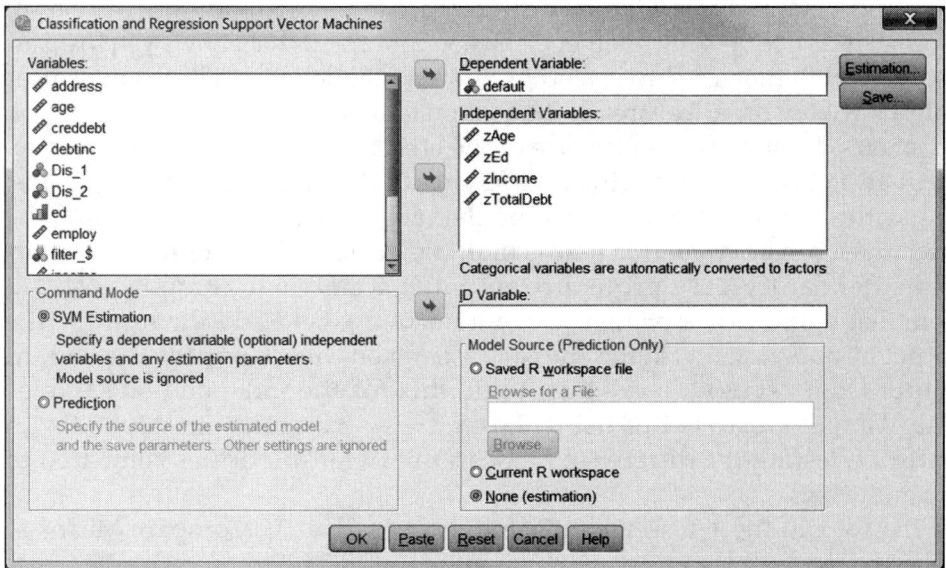

Figure 18-25: The SVM dialog

In the first mode, SVM Estimation, the model is estimated and estimation results displayed. Predictions can be made for the estimation data at the same time. The model can be saved to disk as an R workspace file. It can also be retained in memory for immediate use in making predictions with new data.

In the second mode, Prediction, you specify the model source as a file or the current R workspace and apply it to new data. The X variables in the new dataset must have the same names and measurement levels and, for factors, the same category values as in the estimation dataset. The Viewer output displays a summary of the specifications from the estimated mode.

In both modes, the predicted values, which are categories or in the regression case, values, are written to a new dataset, which can be merged with the input data using MATCH FILES. It is a good idea to include an ID variable when making predictions to facilitate a correct match.

Discriminant analysis, logistic regression, and SVM all make different assumptions and are sensitive to different aspects of the data. SVM handles large numbers of variables and nonlinearities in the relationship better than the other techniques, and is more robust. It has more tuning options and ways of handling nonlinearities than the other methods and is among the most popular techniques in machine learning.

Computing Cohen's d Measure of Effect Size for a T-Test

The extension commands we have discussed so far do not require any knowledge of programming in Python or R in order to use them. In this section we show an example of using another extension command that allows you to insert a snippet of Python code to extend its built-in functionality. The example uses only a few very basic features of the Python language.

Cohen's d statistics is a measure of the effect size of a treatment or group. In a T-Test, it is the standardized difference of the means in the two groups. Unlike the T-Test, it is not affected by the sample size. By standardizing the measure, it can be compared across multiple datasets. Although it is not part of the standard T-TEST procedure output, it is simple to compute by hand from that output. However, we can automate this and add the result to the output by applying one of the Statistics extension commands to the standard output from T-TEST. Here's how to do this for the independent samples case. We will illustrate this using the `employee data.sav` file shipped with Statistics, testing the difference in mean salary for minorities compared to nonminorities.

First we run the T-Test, which is found at Analyze ⇨ Compare Means ⇨ Independent-Samples T Test as shown in Figure 18-26.

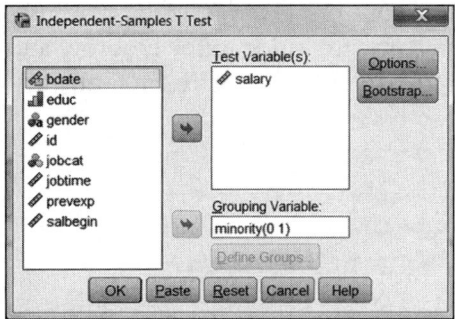

Figure 18-26: The T-Test dialog

Figure 18-27 shows the output (it has a different custom tableLook applied from the earlier output examples).

T-Test

Group Statistics

	Minority Classification	N	Mean	Std. Deviation	Std. Error Mean
Current Salary	No	370	$36,023.31	$18,044.096	$938.068
	Yes	104	$28,713.94	$11,421.638	$1,119.984

Independent Samples Test

		Levene's Test for Equality of Variances		t-test for Equality of Means					95% Confidence Interval of the Difference	
		F	Sig.	t	df	Sig. (2-tailed)	Mean Difference	Std. Error Difference	Lower	Upper
Current Salary	Equal variances assumed	28.487	.000	3.915	472	.000	$7,309.369	$1,867.111	$3,640.491	$10,978.246
	Equal variances not assumed			5.003	262.188	.000	$7,309.369	$1,460.936	$4,432.707	$10,186.030

Figure 18-27: The T-TEST output

The numbers we need are all in the first table, so we could just use a calculator to calculate d, but we would like to automate this and have the d statistic as part of the output. To do this we will use the STATS TABLE CALC extension command (Utilities ⇨ Calculate with Pivot Tables). This command does calculations on cells in pivot tables and adds those results to the table. In this case we want to add a column to the Group Statistics table showing d in the first row. TABLE CALC can apply a formula to each row or column of a table based on values in that row or column, but here we need values from multiple rows. To do that we create a small custom function in Python and apply it with the TABLE CALC command. The function, named d, is stored in a module we call cohen.py. It could be created directly in a BEGIN PROGRAM block, but it is tidier to put this in a separate file for reuse. The file must be saved in a location where Python can find it. (One way to find a suitable location is to run SHOW EXTPATH and save it to one of the locations listed under EXTPATHS EXTENSIONS.)

Figure 18-28 shows the function. Even if you do not know Python, you can easily read this code and see the formula. The calls to GetUnformattedValueAt extract values from the pivot table cells, which are numbered counting from 0. So, for example, `datacells.GetUnformattedValueAt(0, 2)` returns the value in the first row and third column of the table, which here is the standard deviation of the first category.

```python
import math
def d(datacells, roworcol):
    """Compute Cohen's d statistic from the Group Statistics table

    datacells is the data in the Group Statistics pivot table
    roworcol is the current row or column being processed"""

    if roworcol > 0:  # Only display in first row
        return ""
    sd1 = float(datacells.GetUnformattedValueAt(0, 2))
    sd2 = float(datacells.GetUnformattedValueAt(1,2))
    mean1 = float(datacells.GetUnformattedValueAt(0,1))
    mean2 = float(datacells.GetUnformattedValueAt(1,1))
    n1 = float(datacells.GetUnformattedValueAt(0,0))
    n2 = float(datacells.GetUnformattedValueAt(1,0))

    pooledsd = math.sqrt(((n1-1) * sd1**2 + (n2-1) * sd2**2) / (n1+n2))
    return (mean1 - mean2) / pooledsd
```

Figure 18-28: The Python plugin code for Cohen's d

Now we apply this function using TABLE CALC, which we run right after the T-Test command. Figure 18-29 shows the Calculate with Pivot Tables dialog. We select the table to process using the OMS table subtype, and we call our d function using the TABLE CALC formula field. datacells passes the entire data portion of the table to the function, and rowsorcols passes the current row number each time the function is called.

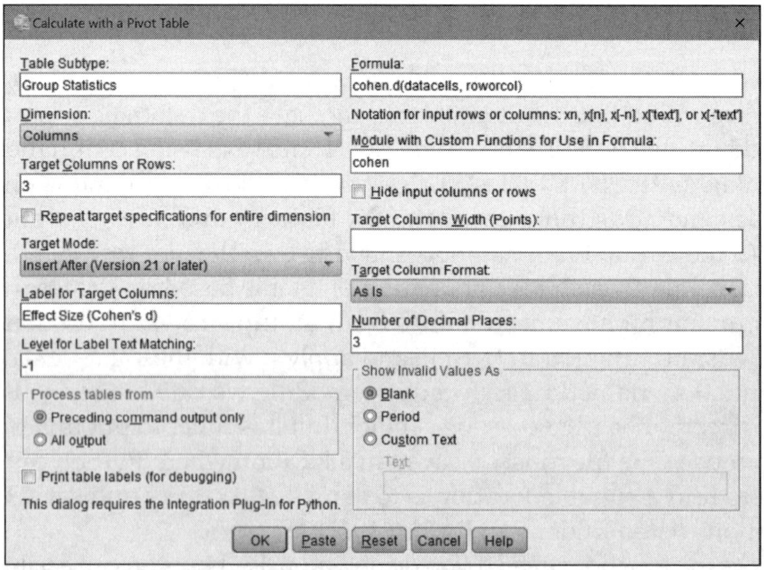

Figure 18-29: The Calculate with a Pivot Table dialog

The equivalent syntax is shown in Figure 18-30.

```
STATS TABLE CALC SUBTYPE="Group Statistics" PROCESS=PRECEDING
/TARGET FORMULA="cohen.d(datacells, roworcol)" DIMENSION=COLUMNS LEVEL = -1  LOCATION=3
  REPEATLOC=NO LABEL="Effect Size (Cohen's d)" MODE=REPLACE CUSTOMMODULE="cohen" HIDEINPUTS=NO
/FORMAT CELLFORMAT="asis" DECIMALS=3  INVALID="".
```

Figure 18-30: The TABLE CALC syntax

The result is added as a new column to the table. We show only the first table, which now has a new column with Cohen's d in the first cell, as shown in Figure 18-31.

T-Test

			Group Statistics			
	Minority Classification	N	Mean	Std. Deviation	Std. Error Mean	Effect Size (Cohen's d)
Current Salary	No	370	$36,023.31	$18,044.096	$938.068	0.435
	Yes	104	$28,713.94	$11,421.638	$1,119.984	

Figure 18-31: The modified T-TEST output

STATS TABLE CALC can be used with most table types and allows you to customize or augment the standard output however you need.

Index